BUSINESS PROCESS MANAGEMENT

Business Process Management, a huge bestseller, has helped thousands of leaders and BPM practitioners successfully implement BPM projects, enabling them to add measurable value to their organizations.

The book's runaway success can be attributed partly to its overview of all major useful frameworks (such as LEAN and Six Sigma) without over-investment in one over another, and a unique emphasis on BPM's interrelationship with organizational management, culture and leadership—**BPM is about people as much as processes**. Its common-sense approach teaches how BPM must be well-integrated across an entire business if it's to be successful: augmented and aligned with other management disciplines.

This highly anticipated third edition brings Jeston and Nelis' practicable frameworks and solutions up-to-date with the latest developments in BPM, including the application of the frameworks to **value-driven BPM**.

This thoroughly revised and updated new edition includes:

- Enhanced pedagogy to help students learn and tutors use the book for their classes: now includes learning outcomes, chapter topics, learning objectives, highlighted key points, chapter summaries, critical discussion points and self-test questions

- New and revised case studies throughout

- New chapters on questions that have become more crucial since the second edition's publication: How should you start—top-down or bottom-up? Should we be customercentric?

- How does BPM link to today's most pertinent management and technology issues? What are the critical success factors?

- Due to popular demand, a new and expanded section on IT in BPM

- Brand new companion website including slides and assignment answers!

John Jeston has over 40 years' experience in senior executive and consulting positions. He runs an international consultancy, Management By Process Pty Ltd.

Johan Nelis works for Oakton, an Australian consulting and technology firm as Business Improvement Practice Manager. He was co-founder and Vice Chairman of the Dutch BPM Forum and Chairman of the Sydney Forum.

BUSINESS PROCESS MANAGEMENT

Practical guidelines to successful implementations

Third edition

JOHN JESTON AND JOHAN NELIS

Routledge
Taylor & Francis Group

LONDON AND NEW YORK

First published 2006
Second edition 2008
By Butterworth-Heinemann

Third edition published 2014
by Routledge
2 Park Square, Milton Park, Abingdon, Oxon OX14 4RN

and by Routledge
711 Third Avenue, New York, NY 10017

Routledge is an imprint of the Taylor & Francis Group, an informa business

British Library Cataloguing in Publication Data
A catalogue record for this book is available from the British Library

Library of Congress Cataloging in Publication Data
Jeston, John.
  Business process management/John Jeston and Johan Nelis. –
  Third edition.
  pages cm
  Includes bibliographical references and index.
  1. Workflow – Management.   2. Reengineering (Management)
  3. Business planning.   4. Industrial management.   I. Nelis, Johan.
  II. Title.
  HD62.17J47 2013
  658.5'33 – dc23
  2013015403

ISBN: 978-0-415-64175-3 (hbk)
ISBN: 978-0-415-64176-0 (pbk)
ISBN: 978-0-203-08132-7 (ebk)

Typeset in Minion Pro and Futura
by Florence Production Ltd, Stoodleigh, Devon, UK

CONTENTS

CONTENTS

FIGURES

TABLES

CONTRIBUTORS

John Jeston has over 40 years' experience in senior executive and consulting positions. Executing strategy to deliver business benefits is difficult. John has deep experience in working with senior executives in assisting them in business transformation and to set up their strategy for success. He has serious experience in getting things done—the right way. For over 40 years he has covered business transformation, Business Process Management (BPM), business process reengineering, project management, shared services creation, strategic procurement, systems development, outsourcing, and general management. He has held the positions of Divisional Manager; Company Director; HR Director and Chief Information Officer (within GM); and Partner.

John is an internationally recognized thought leader in BPM transformation strategy and implementation. He has provided these services to significant organizations throughout Australia, Europe, Saudi Arabia, Dubai, the United Kingdom, Mexico, Brazil, Portugal, Asia, Russia, Turkey, the USA and southern Africa. John has advised some of the largest organizations in the world on BPM implementations. He has authored a number of books and more than 30 articles on BPM and high performance management, worked with the London Business School and the London Speakers Bureau. He is a regular speaker at conferences, a Master Project Director and is a Chartered Accountant. John can be contacted at: johnjeston@managementbyprocess.com.

Johan Nelis has a proven track record for over 20 years as an international Business Process Management and Transformation Advisor delivering results. He works for Oakton, an Australian consulting and technology firm (www.oakton.com.au) as Business Improvement Practice Manager. He established and managed BPM practices in Europe and Australia. He was co-founder and Vice Chairman of the Dutch BPM Forum and Chairman of the Sydney Forum. Johan started his career as Advisor to the United Nations. He is known for his eagerness to share knowledge and experiences, and is renowned for supporting and coaching executives and professionals. He initiated many BPM training courses, presented at seminars and hosted workshops at BPM conferences around the world.

Johan has successfully completed BPM and Transformation initiatives in a wide variety of sectors, such as Finance, Retail, Property, Education, Telecom and Government. He specializes in aligning processes with strategy, business objectives and IT; Business & Finance Transformation and execution of strategy to achieve the intended benefits. He has established and strengthened Centers of Excellence, performed process audits, identified fundamental problems and provided quick wins as well as innovative and sustainable solutions; improved customer experience, assisted in improving service management and service integration, initiated and managed implementations of BPM; enhanced BPM maturity and achieved significant and sustainable improvement in performance.

Johan is available for international presentations and/or training. He can be reached at: johannelisbpm@gmail.com or http://au.linkedin.com/in/johannelis

CONTRIBUTORS TO THE THIRD EDITION

Tonia de Bruin completed her PhD at Queensland University of Technology, Brisbane, Australia, while researching business process management maturity. Following her acceptance as a CPA in 2001, Tonia obtained an MIT from QUT in 2004. Tonia has an extensive background in the financial sector, where she has worked for more than 20 years as both a manager and consultant. Experience managing process improvement projects has seen Tonia develop a strong interest in the relationship between business processes and IT.

Jerry Dimos is a Singapore-based management consultant with over 15 years' experience helping Fortune 500 firms design and implement business transformation initiatives across Asia Pacific.

A highly experienced Business Process Management (BPM) practitioner, Jerry is a BPM advocate for its practical role in transforming complex firms into more agile and productive businesses. By optimizing the way work is performed (the interplay between people, processes and technology), he has successfully implemented projects to reduce waste, unnecessary complexity and process inefficiencies that lead to margin erosion.

Jerry has used BPM tools and techniques to assist global clients, especially those growing or consolidating their operations in Asia to realign their traditionally fragmented operating models. The end result is a more agile, centrally managed, trade-efficient business model that delivers real and measurable shareholder value.

In 2008, Jerry began research into applying BPM to the areas of Sales and Marketing, particularly in the highly competitive Consumer Markets sector. He has been helping clients leverage new technologies to integrate their end-to-end processes and single view of the customer to maximize the returns from marketing investments. This is an area of particular interest to Jerry and he co-authored a book on marketing ROI in 2010, and has written several articles.

Brad Power is the Principal, Palladium Group and Executive Director, Process Management Research Center at Babson College. With over 20 years of management consulting and research experience across a variety of industries around the world, he addresses the important business opportunities and problems of clients by combining human, technological and business perspectives. From 1981 to 1997, Brad worked for CSC Index, the business reengineering firm. In addition to leading many process-innovation consulting projects, he led CSC Index's research service in business reengineering for three years, working with over 30 senior executives leading major reengineering initiatives, and the founders of business reengineering. Brad has an MBA from UCLA and a BS from Stanford University.

Michael Rosemann is a Professor for Information Systems and Co-Leader of the Business Process Management Group at Queensland University of Technology, Brisbane, Australia. He received his MBA (1992) and his PhD (1995) from the University of Muenster, Germany. His main areas of interest are business process management, business process modeling, enterprise systems and ontologies. In his current research projects he is exploring, among other things, the critical success factors of process modeling, issues related to process modeling in the large, and the actual application of process modeling. Michael has intensive consulting experience, and has provided process management-related advice to organizations from various industries including telecommunications, banking, insurance, utility and logistics. Besides more than 40 journal publications, 70 conference publications and 35 book chapters, he has published two books on logistics management and process modeling, and is editor of three books: *Reference Modelling; Business Process Management* and *Business Systems Analysis with Ontologies*. He is a member of the Editorial Board of six journals, including the *Business Process Management Journal*.

Andrew Spanyi is internationally recognized for his work on Business Process Management. He is the author of four books: *Business Process Management is a Team Sport; More for Less: The Power of Process Management;* and *Operational Leadership*.

He has delivered keynote speeches at conferences in North America, Europe and Australia. He has published over 40 articles with a broad cross-section of print and e-magazines. He is currently on the Board of Advisors with The Association of Business Process Management Professionals. Previously he was an adjunct professor at Babson College; a member of the research team at the Babson Process Management Research Center; and an editorial board member with the BPM Institute.

He has over three decades of management and consulting practice experience. He has managed or consulted on over 140 major improvement projects and led the development and delivery of dozens of sales and management training programs.

Amy Van Looy holds a Ph.D. in applied economics. She is a lecturer and scholar at Ghent University (Belgium). Before entering academia, Amy worked as an IT consultant, mainly as a business and functional analyst, on various large e-government projects.

Her research focuses on business process maturity and capabilities in both public and private organizations. Particularly, she builds a maturity theory based on a large sample of business process maturity models (BPMMs). Furthermore, to orient practitioners to the right BPMM, Amy conducted an international Delphi study with BPM experts, resulting in an online decision tool, called "BPMM Smart-Selector" (http://smart-selector.amyvanlooy.eu/). Other research interests include business process integration and business process modeling (BPMN, UML).

Her research and publications can be accessed at http://www.amyvanlooy.eu/. Amy may be contacted via email (info@amyvanlooy.eu). You can subscribe to her tweets at http://twitter.com/AmyVanLooy.

FOREWORD

Thomas H. Davenport

This book shouldn't be unusual, but it is. It should have been written a long time ago, but it wasn't. All books on business process management should be similar to it, but they aren't. Books that purport to tell people in organizations how to do something should be this clear, but they seldom are. Process management should have already been demystified, but it hasn't been.

What's exceptional about the book is its extraordinary common sense. It suggests seemingly prosaic ideas, such as that multiple different levels of process change are necessary under different circumstances, and that technology alone isn't sufficient to bring about process change. These ideas seem obvious, but they are not often encountered in the world of business process management, or BPM. In fact, in order for you fully to appreciate the virtues of this book, you need to know something about what's wrong with BPM.

A BRIEF HISTORY OF BUSINESS PROCESS MANAGEMENT

The idea that work can be viewed as a process, and then improved, is hardly new. It dates at least to Frederick Taylor at the turn of the last century, and probably before. Taylor and his colleagues developed modern industrial engineering and process improvement, though the techniques were restricted to manual labor and production processes. The Taylorist approaches were widely practiced in the early 1900s, but were largely forgotten by mid-century.

The next great addition to process management was created by the combination of Taylorist process improvement and statistical process control, by Shewhart, Deming, Juran and others. Their version of process management involved measuring and limiting process variation, continuous rather than episodic improvement, and the empowerment of workers to improve their own processes. It turned out that Japanese firms had both the business need—recovering from war and building global markets—and the discipline to put continuous improvement programs in place. Other firms in other societies have adopted continuous improvement and "total quality management" based on statistical principles, but it requires more discipline than most can muster.

Toyota, in particular, took these approaches and turned them into a distinctive advance in process management. The Toyota Production System (TPS) combined statistical process control with continuous learning by decentralized work teams, a "pull" approach to manufacturing that minimized waste and inventory, and treating every small improvement in processes as an experiment to be designed, measured and learned from. But few firms have been able to successfully implement the TPS, and even Toyota has had more success with the approach in Japan than at its foreign plants. A somewhat less stringent approach to the TPS is present in the "lean" techniques that many American firms have recently adopted.

The next major variation on BPM took place in the 1990s, when many Western firms were facing an economic recession and strong competition from global competitors, particularly Japanese firms. Business process reengineering added, to the generic set of process management ideas, several new approaches:

- the radical (rather than incremental) redesign and improvement of work
- attacking broad, cross-functional business processes
- "stretch" goals of order-of-magnitude improvement
- use of information technology as an enabler of new ways of working.

Reengineering was also the first process management movement to focus primarily on non-production, white-collar processes such as order management and customer service. It did not emphasize statistical process control or continuous improvement. Many firms in the United States and Europe undertook reengineering projects, but most proved to be overly ambitious and difficult to implement. Reengineering first degenerated into a more respectable word for headcount reductions, and then largely disappeared (though there are some signs of its return).

The most recent process management enthusiasm has revolved around "Six Sigma," an approach created at Motorola in the 1980s and popularized by General Electric in the 1990s. In some ways Six Sigma represents a return to statistical process control; the term "Six Sigma" means one output defect in six standard deviations of a probability distribution for a particular process output. Six Sigma also typically involves a return to focusing on relatively small work processes, and presumes incremental rather than radical improvement. Most frequently, however, Six Sigma improvement techniques have been employed on an episodic basis, rather than continuously, and while employees are somewhat empowered to improve their own work, they are generally assisted by experts called "Black Belts." Some firms are beginning to combine Six Sigma with more radical reengineering-like approaches to processes, or with the "lean" techniques derived from the Toyota Production System. It is simply too early to tell whether Six Sigma will continue to prosper; I see some signs of its weakening, but it is certainly still popular in many US firms.

The approach to BPM described in this book is a welcome amalgam of all of these previous approaches. It doesn't focus heavily on statistical process control or bottom-up experimentation, but addresses the basics of process improvement and change. It doesn't view IT as being the core of process change, but doesn't ignore it as did TQM and Six Sigma. It considers all of the major vehicles by which organizations understand, measure and change how they work.

LESSONS FROM HISTORY

What can we learn from this history, and how does it relate to the book you have in your hands? First, it's clear that process management has been somewhat faddish in the past.

It has been a bit immature, coming and going in various forms as a management fad. This does not mean that there is no value to the concept—indeed I am a strong believer in it—but rather that managers and firms may have latched onto the more fashionable, short-term elements of the approach instead of the more timeless ones. Some managers have even made comments to me such as the following: "We're doing Six Sigma—we're not really into process management." This inability to see the forest for the individual tree is problematic if (or, more likely, when) the appeal of an individual process management offering begins to fade.

Perhaps the excitement of a "new" approach (or at least a new combination of previous ideas with a new name) is necessary to get people excited, but the problem is that they become less excited after a time with each new variant of process change. Basic business process management—the essence of each of these faddish enthusiasms—may not be sexy, but it is clearly necessary. Perhaps it should be adopted whether it is sexy or not, and then maybe it will persist over the long term at a moderate level of popularity. This book is admirably free of faddish elements, and provides a good guide to the basic principles of process management. The authors refer to the "demystification" of process management, and they are correct that the field has been clouded by faddishness and mystification for far too long.

It's also apparent that process management, as it has changed over time, is an increasingly synthetic discipline. This book, I am happy to note, also takes a synthetic, broad approach to process management. Each new process management approach has built on previous foundations, and added one or more new elements. Ideally, an organization would be able to draw upon all of the elements or tools available to meet the process management needs of any individual project. However, to wrap all of the possible process management tools into one consolidated approach would be a bit unwieldy. They can't all fit into one normal-sized book. Therefore it seems likely that, in the future, firms will assemble the tools they need to address a particular project using a customized or configured methodology. Such a configuration process would require either very experienced process management consultants who could assemble the proper tools or perhaps even software that could help a less experienced user configure a methodology.

Despite these methodological issues, process management all boils down to human change. This is true of all variations on process management. As Jeston and Nelis point out, people are the key to implementing new process designs. If they don't want to work in new ways, it is often very difficult to force them to do so. Hence any successful process management effort requires a strong emphasis on culture, leadership and change management. Several chapters of the book are devoted to these issues.

Process management doesn't replace everything else in organizations, and it's not a panacea. There have been other authors and publications that have strongly suggested that all an organization needs to do to be successful is process improvement. This book does not make that mistake; it simply argues that process management must become one of the abiding approaches to managing organizations. It must augment and align with strategy, human resource management, financial management, information management and the other traditional management disciplines. This and other perspectives within the book may appear to be only common sense. They are indeed sensible, but they are not sufficiently common.

PREFACE

This book began in 2003, when I was engaged in the early stages of a BPM project within a large financial organization. I was struggling with how to help develop the skills of the consultants in our BPM consultancy practice faster than just "on the job training."

I searched the Internet and book shelves for a comprehensive text on "how to successfully implement a BPM project." I did not just want a big picture view but a detailed step-by-step guide that we could give to our consultants and clients, and one that would force me to be less intuitive (although I still think this is the most powerful insight one can have) and more formal in approaching BPM projects. So I started to document my thoughts over the next twelve months.

In mid-2004, we received the resumé of Johan from the Netherlands, where he headed up the BPM practice of Sogeti (part of Cap Gemini). Johan was looking to migrate to Australia; here he joined me in a BPM consultancy practice and soon thereafter we began the journey of completing this book.

The journey has continued spectacularly fast as I have been invited to travel all over the world to deliver conference keynote speeches, talks, training, advice and consulting services to many varied organizations, including some extremely large commercial and government organizations. This has enabled me to gain a unique insight to the critical success factors, what works well and what could have worked better within organizations; and it has continued to provide practical intellectual property for further editions of this book.

John Jeston

I have always found it amazing that in a time of information, the skills and expertise of a BPM consultant are still predominantly based on experience, and grey hair is still an indicator of this. BPM is still more an art than a science. There are very few sources of information for people to rely on when delivering a BPM project: there are very few good books that cover all the relevant aspects; Internet searches are crowded with advertising of vendors; and few seminar or training courses live up to their promises.

I have always been very passionate about exchanging expertise and experience—right from my first job at the United Nations Industrial Development Organization which was not just about achieving results but also knowledge transfer. During my career at Sogeti B.V., The Netherlands, I enjoyed the support and opportunities provided to develop process reference models and guidelines; give BPM training and lectures as well as setting up a BPM expert group and the Dutch BPM Forum. Jeroen Versteeg and Klaas Brongers have been very supportive in this regard.

Writing a book that combines both a holistic view and the necessary details has been a long cherished dream. When I moved to Australia and John told me about his plans for this book and showed me the outline of the Framework, I knew that this dream would be fulfilled.

Johan Nelis

INTRODUCTION

WHO IS THIS BOOK FOR?

Business professionals

- *Senior business executives* seeking an understanding of what BPM is; the critical success factors; and why and how to implement it within their organization.

- *Information systems managers and Chief Financial Officers* also involved in supporting the implementation of BPM and process management.

- *Project managers* on how better to manage a process-focused project or program of work.

- *Process professionals, process analysts and business analysts* to enhance their learning on how to implement BPM and process-focused activities; together with detailed tools and templates.

Students

This book provides students with the ability to gain a practical example and understanding of how to implement Business Process Management from a small BPM activity or project inside an organization through to an enterprise-wide process-focused business transformation program. It will support the following students in their studies:

- *Professionals studying; postgraduate students on specialist Master's degrees; MBA students.* The book provides a comprehensive coverage of business processes, and process management and implementation. It will provide non-business professionals (for example, engineers, scientists) with an understanding of business and process management.

- *Undergraduate students* who select this topic to gain an understanding of how businesses work in practice and how to complete process-based projects improvements and business transformation.

WHAT DOES THIS BOOK OFFER TO LECTURERS TEACHING THESE COURSES?

This book is intended to be a comprehensive guide to all aspects of implementing and managing BPM or process-focused business transformation activities within an organization. It is based upon sound research and wide and deep consulting experience with international BPM programs.

Lecturers will find this book has a wide range of case study examples to support their teaching.

A student assignment has been included that may be used to provide the context and guidance through a practical BPM activity. This assignment will be continually updated and improved with the latest version always available on a secure website specifically for lecturers. A sample answer will also be provided on the secure website. As with any business project, there may be several "correct" answers. We would encourage lecturers to provide the authors with samples of their best student answers and these will be reviewed and posted on the secure website for the benefit of all lecturers, with the lecturer's and student's permission.

The latest tools and templates will be posted on: www.managementbyprocess.com for the benefit of students and lecturers. Again you are welcome to contribute towards the enhancement and further development of these tools and templates by sending suggestions to: tools@managementbyprocess.com.

LEARNING FEATURES

A range of features have been incorporated in the book to help the reader get the most out of it. They have been designed to assist understanding, reinforce learning and assist readers to find information easily. The features are described in the order you will find them.

At the start of each chapter:

- *Overview*: a short introduction to the relevance of the chapter and what you will learn.
- *Overall learning outcome*: a list describing what readers can learn through reading the chapter and completing the self-test.

In each chapter:

- *Key Points*: critical aspect to the topic referred to in the text.
- *BPM Insight:* real-world examples of best practice approaches.
- *Case Studies*: examples of areas where organizations or consultants have executed things well or not so well. Each case study is provided with a "Message" at the end of it—the lesson to learn as a result of the case study.

In Part II of the book, the section explaining the 7FE Framework, each chapter is also structured to include:

- *Why*: is this phase necessary?
- *Results*: that will be expected once this phase has been executed.
- *How*: the detailed steps involve in the execution of the phase.
- *Outputs to other phases*: how this phase contributes towards the success of other phases and feeds back into earlier phases.
- *Phase risks*: the typical risks that are associated with this phase.

At the end of each chapter:

- *Summary*: intended as a revision aid and to summarize the main learning points from the chapter.
- *Self-test questions*: short questions that will test understanding of terms and concepts described in the chapter and help relate them to your organization.
- *Assignment*: further information on the assignment and guiding questions to assist in the completion of the assignment (for chapters 12 to 26).
- *Checklists*: where appropriate checklists have been provided to assist you in the execution of your BPM activities.
- *Extra reading*: supplementary information on the main themes within the chapter.

At the end of the book:

- *Glossary*: a list of definitions of all terms and phrases used within the text.
- *References and bibliography*: a list of books and articles from where some of the information was sourced and suggested additional reading.
- *Index*: all key words and abbreviations referred to in the main text.

INTRODUCTION TO THE THIRD EDITION

The understanding of BPM and process management has not stood still over the last five years since the second edition of this book.

The authors have continued to work with many organizations in the development and implementation of BPM strategies. This has allowed us to encounter many different and varied business challenges. With challenges come solutions, and it is these challenges and solutions that we wish to share with the readers.

The most dramatic evolution in BPM has been the growing acceptance that BPM is not about the improvement of operational processes alone. BPM is a management discipline focused on using business processes as a significant contributor to achieving an organization's strategy and business objectives by significantly and sustainably improving performance.

Business Process Management is more relevant than ever before and will assist in enabling management to achieve a competitive advantage in a turbulent environment. Our current environment is categorized by fundamental shifts in business models; increased internationalization; increased market transparency; a need to support mobile, social and Cloud functionality; and a need to service more informed, vocal and demanding customers. These trends and how to anticipate and leverage them is now a fundamental necessity in business.

You will read in Chapter 1 (What is business process management?) about the BPM House; a metaphor for what is BPM and what are the various components.

Many of the initial ten chapters have either been rewritten or substantially updated.

The original two phases of the 7FE Framework (Organization Strategy and Process Architecture) have been replaced with BPM Foundations and BPM Enablement. These chapters are totally new and have a unique approach to the building of an enterprise-wide approach to the implementation of a process-focused transformation program. This is critical if you wish to create a sustainable competitive advantage within your organization.

You will learn in Chapter 5 (How should we start—bottom-up or top-down?) that the authors have never seen a bottom-up approach to BPM work, enterprise wide; not unless it changes from bottom-up to top-down.

You will learn what you need to do, from a process perspective, to ensure that a sustainable competitive advantage is created within your organization.

Furthermore, the online appendices have been collapsed and where appropriate included for each chapter.

We are very proud of the book because it has become accepted internationally by both business and educational institutions. It is used in many organizations as the preferred method of implementing BPM. It has become used in many universities by professors and lecturers as a textbook and reference book.

A wonderful example of this acceptance is the story of one CEO who was so impressed with it that he had it translated into his language and then made it mandatory reading for his executives and managers; and they are tested on it to ensure they have read and understand it. This international organization employs more than 250,000 people worldwide.

This third edition has a number of new features which you will notice:

- It is in full color
- Enhanced pedagogy: now includes learning outcomes; chapter topics; learning objectives; highlighted key points; chapter summaries; and self-test questions
- Enhanced case studies
- Specific detailed case studies from three continents
- A reader assignment that allows the reader to make the learning concrete
- A link to the publisher's website for an ability to interact with the authors and obtain the latest material on the assignment
- A link to the latest BPM tools at www.managementbyprocess.com.

LAYOUT OF THIS BOOK

The book is divided into three parts with each having a unique focus.

- **Part I** is aimed at executive level questions and takes a holistic view to a process-focused organization. It asks and provides answers to ten questions. While all these questions do not need to be addressed before an organization commences its BPM journey, some do. All questions will however need to be addressed and answered along the journey.
- **Part II** comprises a detailed explanation of the 7FE Framework. It explains the ten phases and three essentials that are required to be successful. This is where the reader assignment is undertaken.
- **Part III** comprises a chapter that includes three detailed case studies from the USA, Asia and Europe. It also includes two chapters on BPM maturity. One of these chapters is new and provides an insight into how an organization should select a BPM maturity model that is appropriate for itself.
- Within the companion website there are two appendices that provide a summary of the 7FE Framework (phases, steps, tools and techniques, deliverables and gates) and the 7FE Framework Quality Assurance Checklist for project/program managers.

ACKNOWLEDGMENTS

It has been a journey as we have researched and developed the tools and techniques in this book. It is an approach to BPM projects and organizational transformation that has been honed over many practical international consulting engagements, case studies and research. The framework, approaches, scenarios, phases, steps, tools and techniques are what we use in our day-to-day BPM consultancy. Without the ability to consult and develop the intellectual property "on the job" within many large organizations this book would not have been possible.

However, no book can be written in isolation, and there are people we would like to thank who have reviewed, contributed to, critically commented and debated with us in the development of this third edition. In particular we would like to thank Dr Adrian Rossi and Gina Craig.

Adrian's knowledge of BPM technology and implementations is outstanding. He has donated his time to reading and commenting upon drafts of the entire book, and contributed in part to Chapter 7, the technology components of a BPM system.

Gina critically read and edited many chapters in the book and greatly added to the clarity of many chapters.

Once a robust draft of the book was completed, several people contributed their time in reviewing, commenting and making suggestions for improvement. This has significantly contributed to the betterment of the final outcome. As always it is the authors' responsibility for the final product. We would like to specifically thank: Professor Jan Recker, Michelle Parker, Adrian Rossi and Dr Ralf Eder.

Finally, we would like to thank our editorial team of Amy Laurens and Rosemary (Rosie) Baron. Thank you for your trust, support, never-ending encouragement and good humor throughout this journey.

TRAINING SERVICES

Management by Process Pty Ltd offers complete advice, training and coaching services in Business Process Management and process-focused business transformation programs.

The training courses cover the content of this book and other BPM-related topics. Please refer to www.managementbyprocess.com for course outlines, testimonials and further information.

NEW DISTRIBUTOR AND PARTNER ENQUIRIES

Distributor and partner opportunities are available for qualified BPM experts and expert organizations for the training material and courses. If you are interested please contact info@managementbyprocess.com.

POSITIONING OUR BOOKS

This book provides a practical guide to the successful and repeatable implementation of BPM activities. Three reprints in the first year, the release of a second edition, a number of translations into other languages and now this third edition highlight the enormous demand for practical common sense guidance on businesses running their organizations via process management.

Many readers have reacted and welcomed our suggestions regarding BPM activities. However, many of you now face the next challenge: how to achieve a process-focused organization. That is, not just to be able to successfully implement BPM activities but move to the next stage of maturity where an organization needs to support performance management by its processes. This is depicted as part of Figure 0.1

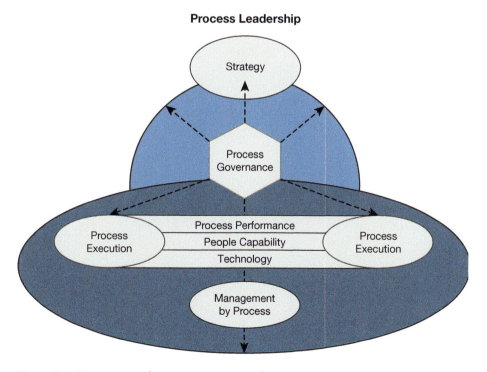

Figure 0.1 Management by Process Framework

Strategy is the foundation and starting point for the formulation of an organization's strategic objectives. However, the strategy is only one part of the journey. Without an outstanding competency in strategy execution, then success will not follow. We believe it is essential to distinguish between two types of execution—project execution and process execution.

Project execution is the topic of this book you are reading now. Process execution is the topic of the our second book which is titled: *Management by Process: A Roadmap to Sustainable Business Process Management*. In our experience with coaching and advising organizations with the implementation of BPM, we have found that the following seven dimensions are critical in the achievement of a truly process-focused and high performance management organization:

1. Process leadership
2. Process governance
3. Process performance
4. Strategic alignment
5. People capability
6. Project execution
7. Technology.

For more information please visit www.managementbyprocess.com

We would be delighted to receive readers' feedback and suggestions. You can provide this by emailing us at: info@managementbyprocess.com

FREQUENTLY ASKED QUESTIONS

Part I is aimed at an executive level of questions and takes a holistic view to a process-focused organization. While all of these questions do not need to be addressed before an organization commences its Business Process Management (BPM) journey, some do; however, somewhere along that journey all will need to be considered. Indeed, the answer to some of the questions will determine how you should start BPM in your organization.

In this third edition of the book we have introduced several new questions to ensure that evolving and contemporary BPM questions are answered. The global financial crisis from 2008 has forced many organizations to take a critical look at their performance, and business process performance, management and control are critical aspects.

We start in Chapters 1 and 2 by providing an explanation of "What is BPM?"; why some people find BPM a little confusing and why it is different from what has come before. This still requires attention, as many people either don't understand or misunderstand these key concepts.

It is critical to know who should be involved in BPM and what the critical success factors are. For an organization and its management, it is critical to have a clear understanding of when you should do BPM and what the main drivers and triggers are. These questions are covered in Chapters 3 and 4.

How to start is always an important consideration. Should it be top-down or bottom-up? This is discussed in Chapter 5.

Our experience of implementing BPM transformations, programs and projects all around the world has led us to believe it is important to improve the processes before, or as part of, automating them. This is addressed in Chapter 6.

Given the importance of BPM technology and the opportunities that it is starting to offer, we outline the nine technology components of a complete BPM technology solution in Chapter 7, together with some thoughts of the future.

The majority of the literature on BPM and Lean will tell you that you must be customer-centric and focus on the customer experience. Is this true? Is it the best approach to achieving customer service and satisfaction? This question is what Chapter 8 is all about.

We then discuss why determining or creating the right foundations for BPM is critical to success in Chapter 9.

In the final chapter of this part, we address why you need a structured approach to implementing BPM if you want to optimize your business benefits and likelihood of success.

CHAPTER 1

WHAT IS BUSINESS PROCESS MANAGEMENT?

OVERVIEW

There are many definitions of BPM and to enable you to gain the most from this book we need to have a common understanding.

OVERALL LEARNING OUTCOME

By the end of this chapter you will be able to:

- Appreciate that BPM is not ALL about technology
- Have a working definition of BPM
- Understand at a high level the BPM House and how the components are essential for BPM success and sustainability.

This is a question that needs to be asked and addressed right at the very beginning to ensure we have a common understanding. There are as many answers to this question as there are vendors, analysts, researchers, academics, commentators, authors and customers.

BPM is just like many other three-letter abbreviations in the recent past, such as CRM (Customer Relationship Management) and ERP (Enterprise Resource Planning), which have been misused and misinterpreted. In time these terms have mostly come to a common interpretation; BPM has still to achieve this status.

Currently, BPM is being used by:

- some vendors who only focus on the technology solution of process improvement. This is still true for some of the world's largest technology companies;
- other vendors who think of BPM as business process modeling or business performance management;

- some consultants who use BPM to continue their message on business process reengineering or improvement;
- other consultants who use BPM to sell their Six Sigma/Lean message to executives;
- some managers who want to jump on the BPM bandwagon, with no idea where it is going;
- some process analysts who use BPM to inflate their process-modeling aspirations.

In our opinion, BPM does *not* equate to a technology tool or initiative for business processes. In our experience, there is significant business process improvement that can be achieved without technology. Can BPM involve technology, and is technology a good thing? Absolutely, in the right circumstances and when it can be justified. Are Business Process Management Systems (BPMS) and process modeling tools useful for achieving process improvements in non-technology circumstances? If the tools referred to are used in the right way, then yes, they can be extremely useful in this process. In fact, it is difficult to complete complex process improvement projects in a time-effective manner without the use of these tools.

BPM INSIGHT

One word of caution: there is a danger of organizations believing that once they have purchased a BPMS or process-modeling tool, it will solve all their problems and the process improvements will just follow. Nothing could be further from the truth. A BPMS or process-modeling tool is just a piece of software, and without a methodology or framework, skilled resources to use it and a genuine commitment from organizational leadership, it is useless: remember the saying "a fool with a tool is still is fool."

Refer to the Extra Reading section at the end of Chapter 27 (Embedding) for how to select a process-modeling tool. If you are going to use a process-modeling toolset in your BPM program or projects then we actively encourage you to use the opportunity to build a process asset. What is a process asset, how it is populated, what are its benefits and use to the business will be discussed in more detail in Chapter 13.

Many of the industry commentators and vendors provide definitions that specify technology (automation tools) as an essential component of BPM—in fact they say that BPM is technology. However, if you take a simple and commonsense view of BPM, it is about the *management of business processes* which will be around for a very long time.

KEY POINT

A definition for BPM is:

A management discipline focused on using business processes as a significant contributor to achieving an organization's objectives through the improvement, ongoing performance management and governance of essential business processes.

Table 1.1 Definition of terms used in our definition of BPM

Management discipline	Management need to clearly understand that business processes are a fundamental and critical part of business success. The proactive management of these business processes will significantly assist in the delivery of an organization's strategic objectives. Process management needs to be a fundamental part of how the business is managed and executive commitment is essential.
Processes	What is a process? There are as many definitions of process as there are processes. However perhaps taking a simple view is best, "it is the way things get done around here."
Achievement	Realizing the strategic objectives as outlined in the organization's strategic plan. At a project level, it is about realizing the value or business benefits as outlined in the project business case and at a process level it is about achieving the team's operational targets.
Organization	The organization in this context refers to either the entire organization or parts of it, perhaps a business unit that is discrete in its own right. BPM relates to the end-to-end business processes associated with this part of an organization. This end-to-end focus extends beyond the boundaries of the organization and should include suppliers and customers, which should lead to a minimization of the silo effect within most organizations.
Objectives	The objectives of a BPM implementation range from the strategic goals of the organization through to the individual process goals. It is about achieving business outcomes. BPM is not an objective in itself, but rather a means to achieving a business objective. It is not "a solution looking for a problem."
Improvement	Improvement is about making the business processes more efficient and effective or indeed turning an organization or industry value chain upside down or inside out. An example of this is a business transformation approach to BPM.
Performance management	This refers to process and people performance measurement and management. It is about organizing all the essential components and subcomponents for your processes. By this we mean arranging the people, their skills, motivation, performance measures, rewards, the processes themselves and the structure and systems necessary to support a process.
Governance of processes	BPM is about managing your end-to-end business processes both now and into the future to ensure they are always relevant to the business. An essential component of governance is to have the ability to measure correctly. If you cannot measure something, you cannot continually improve and manage it. Process governance is also essential to ensure that compliance and regulations are adhered to.
Essential	Not every process in an organization contributes towards the achievement of the organization's strategic objectives. Essential processes are the ones that do.
Business	An implementation of BPM must have an impact on the business by delivering benefits. It should focus on the core business processes that are essential to your primary business activity—those processes that contribute towards the achievement of the strategic objectives of the organization.

It is important to have a common understanding of what we mean by each of the significant words in our definition, so each is defined individually in Table 1.1.

Thus, process management is an integrated part of "normal" management. It is important for leadership and management to recognize that there is no finish line for the improvement of business processes; it is a program that must be continually maintained.

As a management discipline BPM requires an end-to-end organizational view and a great deal of common sense throughout the organization.

Now that we have provided a definition of BPM, let's examine what this means in practice within an organization.

There are many ways to commence BPM activities within an organization and the "right" way will depend upon many factors, such as the organization's culture, process maturity, business drivers, to name a few. There are also several types of BPM activities that may be commenced. Chapter 5 will outline four typical types of BPM activities that will be referred to throughout the book. It also addresses the question of whether the BPM activities should start from the bottom-up or the top-down and why.

Figure 1.1 provides a metaphor to describe BPM with all the necessary components of an organization-wide BPM program strategy. It introduces many terms and some of them may be new to you. If this is the case, please refer to the glossary section for a definition or explanation.

A metaphor of a house has been used in this book—the BPM House.

When building a house you need to have solid foundations or it will not be stable as the walls are erected and the roof installed. BPM is no different. The foundations of the BPM program (BPM Foundations and Enablement) need to provide a solid operational focus that has been agreed and is visible across the organization. Senior management is responsible for determining the organization strategy and ensuring that the business processes support, or contribute to, the fulfillment of the strategy. Processes that are aligned with the strategy are most effective in achieving business objectives and are more sustainable in the medium to long term. The purpose of the BPM Foundations and Enablement is to provide the necessary discussion, determination, agreement and documentation of the high level "foundation rules" for the business and BPM team to work within and apply. The Foundation is determined by the senior management team and provide the very high level outline of these "rules"; while Enablement takes these high level "rules" and expands upon them to make them usable for the business and BPM teams in their execution of BPM programs and projects. Chapters 13 and 14 provide the detail.

The walls provide an outline of the program of work, the frameworks for how the work will be achieved, how the business will be operated and, importantly, how it will be aligned with the organization's strategy. This is where BPM activities:

- align with the organization's strategy; ensuring that all the BPM activities contribute towards the strategic objectives (strategic alignment);

- determine the priorities of which business processes to enhance first; and whether working on the Management Processes or Operational Processes first will bring the most benefit to the organization (or perhaps both together). Chapter 13 (Foundations phase) will define and explain the difference between these two types of business processes (management processes and operational processes);

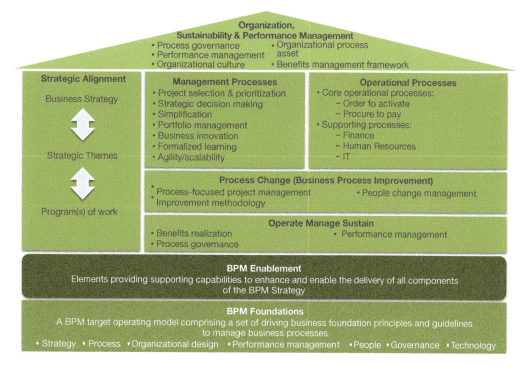

Figure 1.1 BPM House: components of a BPM program strategy

- use the Process Change (business process improvement (BPI) and people change management) methodologies or frameworks. These should be selected and in place first, ensuring the business and BPM team are trained in it (process change);
- Operate, Manage and Sustain aspect refers how BPI projects will be handed over to the business in a sustainable way.

Unless all these components are either in place or in progress within an organization, it will not be able to improve the efficiency and effectiveness of the organization's business processes in a sustainable way.

The BPM roof (Organization Sustainability and Performance Management) holds it all together by providing the organizational-wide process focused culture and governance structures resulting in managing the organization via its business processes. The creation and management of a process asset will greatly assist in meeting these objectives. Without this BPM roof, all the benefits gained from improving the management and operational business processes will dissipate over time; sometimes rapidly.

We will discuss the BPM House in more detail during Chapters 13 and 14 when we discuss the BPM Foundations and Enablement phases of the 7FE Project Framework. The 7FE Framework is the main focus within this book and provides the framework guidelines for successful BPM programs and projects.

Once BPM is viewed as outlined in the BPM House it becomes clear that BPM provides an organization with the ability to commence and sustain a program of work that can

CASE STUDY

A large telecommunications organization had spent a year and many millions of dollars establishing BPM foundations within the organization. It was about to commence several large BPM projects across the organization and they were still having difficulty explaining and gaining agreement on what exactly BPM was for them.

The metaphor of the BPM House, slightly modified to its circumstances, provided the mechanism for agreement within the organization.

transform its business. BPM will provide the mechanisms for changing the business value chain, disrupting industry value chains, substantially altering the way business and decision making is conducted. It will allow customers and employees to be delighted with the services provided by the organization, while simultaneously reducing the organization's costs. When an organization's management processes are addressed, as shown in the BPM House, the organization is provided with an opportunity to create a sustainable competitive advantage; but more of this later.

While the BPM House may appear a little overwhelming to some now, once the 7FE Framework is introduced (from Chapter 11 onwards) it will be explained and expanded upon in far more detail. If you wish to learn more immediately on the BPM House, read Chapters 13 and 14 now.

SUMMARY

BPM is:

- more than just software
- more than just improving or reengineering your processes—it also deals with the managerial issues
- not just hype—it is an integral part of management
- more than just modeling—it is also about the implementation and execution of these processes, and
- the BPM House provides a metaphor for the foundations, walls and roof of an enterprise-wide implementation of BPM.

SELF-TEST

1 Can you implement a BPM project without technology?

2 Name a couple of ways how technology can assist with BPM in your organization.

3 How would you define BPM and explain each of the key words/phrases in your definition?

4 Explain each of the aspects of the BPM House, each of the sub-components and why you think they will be important to an enterprise-wide implementation of BPM?

CHAPTER 2

HOW CAN WE DEMYSTIFY BUSINESS PROCESS MANAGEMENT?

OVERVIEW

Many people find the term BPM a mystery. There is no one definition among the experts and management sometimes wonder if it is yet another three-letter acronym or management fad that will disappear in the next few years. We will explain the history of BPM and then some of the realities of it.

OVERALL LEARNING OUTCOME

By the end of this chapter you will be able to:

- Explain the history of BPM and where it evolved from
- Clarify if it is just the next "big thing" or not
- Explain the BPM hype cycle
- Appreciate what is mystifying about BPM and why
- Explain reality versus perception.

BRIEF HISTORY OF BUSINESS PROCESS MANAGEMENT

The road to Business Process Management (BPM) has been a difficult one that was developed from the successes and failures of various other attempts at achieving process-based organizational efficiency. It has only been in the last several years that BPM has started to gain significant momentum in many organizations around the world.

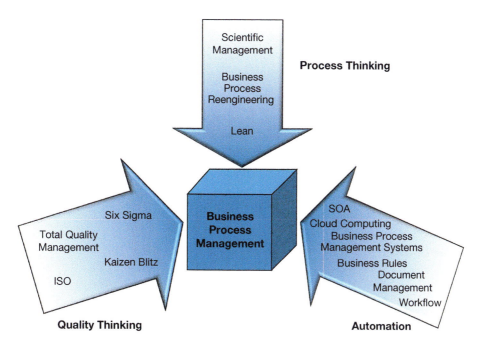

Figure 2.1 How did BPM emerge?

Perhaps it is worthwhile taking a few moments to understand the short history of management's focus on business processes and where BPM had its origins. Figure 2.1 shows these origins.

In the 1980s there was a considerable focus on quality thinking. This was brought to management's attention with the focus on Total Quality Management (TQM), Six Sigma, ISO and then the concepts of Kaizen (Blitz).

The concept of process thinking originated at least as far back as Frederick Taylor in the early last century. It was then supported in the early 1990s by Business Process Reengineering (BPR) as originally written about by Davenport and promoted by Hammer and Champy (1990). BPR had a checkered history, with some excellent successes as well as failures. Lean also gained momentum together with its variants.

In the mid- and late 1990s automation started to come into its own with Enterprise Resource Planning (ERP) systems gaining organizational focus and became the next big thing. These were supposed to deliver improved ways for organizations to operate, and were sold by many vendors as the "solution to all your problems." The ERP systems certainly did not solve an organization's process issues, nor make the processes as efficient and effective as they could have been.

Towards the end of the 1990s and in the early 2000s, many Customer Relationship Management (CRM) systems were rolled out with extensive focus on the customer view and customer experience. While this provided focus on the front office, it did not improve the back-office processes. Automation then grew into the concept of workflow and business rules engines, which then morphed into Business Process Management Systems (BPMS) which we will discuss in detail later in Chapter 7. BPMS incorporated many aspects of technology including integrated document management. Cloud computing has now added a significant and exciting dimension to the possibilities of a process view of the world.

All these components started to merge to bring business processes more to the thinking of management and the term Business Process Management was coined.

At the end of the day, the term is not important. What is important is an organization's focus and ability to manage its business processes and this involves people.

According to Hammer (1993), "Coming up with the ideas is the easy part, but getting things done is the tough part. The place where these reforms die is . . . down in the trenches" and who "owns" the trenches? You and I and all the other people. Change imposed on the "trench people" will not succeed without being part of the evolutionary or revolutionary process:

> **Forceful leadership can accomplish only so much. The shift from machine-age bureaucracy to flexible, self-managed teams requires that lots of ordinary managers and workers be psychologically prepared.**
>
> **(Hammer, 1994)**

THE NEXT BIG THING (OR HOW MYSTIFICATION BEGINS)

While the term BPM has been around since the very late 1990s and early 2000s it is still yet another three-letter acronym!

So why was BPM considered the "next big thing," and why do the "next big things" invariably come and go?

There are usually four steps to the creation of a "next big thing":

1. The concept promoters (vendors/analysts, etc.) hype it up to the market in their advertising, sales pitches, promotional materials, research and successful case studies.

2. These promoters then tend to disparage all the "old big things" that have preceded it, and promote the "new big thing" as simply the best.

3. The next step is to make the "new big thing" very simple so the decision makers can understand it, the message being that it is not complicated and can be easily implemented.

4. Finally, the promoters (vendors in particular) market their existing products and service offerings with this new label (in this case BPM) even if the offerings do not meet the generally accepted definitions of the label. This leads to there being almost as many definitions of the label as there are vendors.

In this case, the new label has been "BPM" and the same problems have emerged. If you examine the historical context of the BPM "next big thing," there is a common thread: it is all about business processes and trying to make them better. Vendors and consultants all latch onto new ideas, which are often extremely good, and hype them up until the idea matures and is able to be used or implemented in a sustainable way.

While it is true that BPM has lasted longer than we expected as a term, we think it has matured over the last decade and there has been a growing acceptance that BPM is really a management philosophy promoting the management of an organization's business processes.

BPM HYPE CYCLE

The BPM hype cycle in Figure 2.2 shows a summarized view of how the process cycle has progressed over the last two decades.

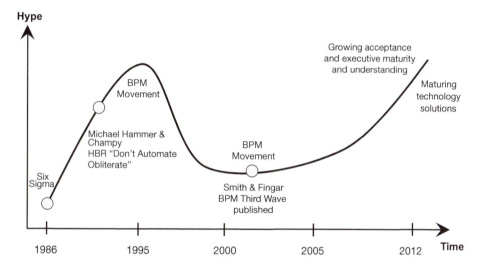

Figure 2.2 BPM hype cycle

Six Sigma was invented in 1986, and created an awareness of "processes." This was followed in July 1990 by Hammer and Champy's (1990) *Harvard Business Review* article "Don't automate, obliterate," and the business process reengineering (BPR) movement started. While BPM has been around for some time, *BPM: The Third Wave* (Smith and Fingar, 2002) created significant interest and discussion; and it could now be argued that BPM is the most important topic on the management agenda.

BPM is now broadly accepted in business and while the level of understanding is good, there is still confusion of what it exactly is and how to go about it, especially at an organization level. Technology has also significantly matured and is getting better by the day.

WHAT IS MYSTIFYING ABOUT BPM?

BPM is advocated by its proponents as being different from and better than what has been available in the past. The major advantages promoted are outlined in Table 2.1, as are our comments supporting or refuting them.

Table 2.1 Promotion v. reality

BPM major "mystifying" points versus reality

1	**BPM is better than the past options for process improvement** BPM has certainly raised the visibility of process improvement for many organizations. BPM has also focused many academics and consultants back onto processes and several organizations have been created solely to focus on process. BPM is also now taught in many universities around the world educating current and future managers in the benefits of managing business processes. This is definitely a good thing, as the discussion on standards and BPM in general continues to raise its profile and maturity in the marketplace. Learning from past experience, such as BPR, has also been taken into consideration. *The key point is that BPM is only as good as the buy-in you get from the organization and senior management and then how well it is implemented.*
2	**BPM uses new and better technology** There is growing evidence that this is true. There are a growing number of fully automated enterprise-wide BPM implementations. In our experience, technology should not be the initial focus of a BPM activity. The initial work should relate to reviewing the current processes with a goal of increased efficiency and effectiveness (the importance of establishing process goals is discussed later in the book). While these new improved processes *could* (if appropriate) contain suggestions for automation, significant process improvements can be achieved without the use of technology. *While technology has improved significantly, the implementers of BPM must ensure it is meeting the needs of the organization.*
3	**There is a robust methodology to support BPM** There are only a very small number of complete and proven methodologies for the implementation of complex BPM programs. *Be careful: a methodology or framework can be a millstone as much as a savior, it is how you use it that matters. While you may think your organization is unique, it is doubtful that you are. Do not start your BPM program by developing your own methodology. It is a waste of time and valuable resources; use an existing methodology, learn and then, if necessary, tailor to your organizational needs over time. Remember, you will be evaluated on the business results and not on the methodology.*
4	**BPM is simple (and, in fact, often oversimplified)** BPM is anything but simple. There are many components and elements to a BPM implementation, and one of the purposes of this book is to explain this in more detail. While each of these components might look simple, it is the way they relate, interact and are implemented that is the challenge. *You do not need to solve all the organization's process problems in one go with BPM. Start small, with one project, learn and get executive buy-in. As the organization matures, BPM can be expanded. We will look at the various ways to start a BPM program of work in Chapter 5.*
5	**External people are needed to implement BPM** This very much depends upon the maturity of the organization and the skill levels and experience within an organization. *Certainly external consultants can assist either in the establishment phases, or acting in a coaching or consulting role if the organizational maturity and/or skill levels are not sufficient. An experienced external BPM program/project manager can provide significant focus that, sometimes, internal project managers are unable to bring to a project.*

> **BPM INSIGHT**
>
> BPM is not a simple concept nor is it simple to implement—it is extremely complex and difficult; and yet, absolutely achievable when approached in the right way.

While the introduction of technology can be a useful contributor for many organizations, BPM does not always need technology to be successful. It is far more important to get your processes right *before* you consider the implementation of technology. However, there is no question, with the correct approach and timing to the implementation of BPM technology, it can be extremely successful and beneficial to an organization.

THE ICEBERG SYNDROME

Icebergs typically only show about 10 percent of their mass above the water. BPM is often like an iceberg; people and organizations only see what is above the water. The interesting observation is that what appears above the surface depends upon the viewer's perception. For example, a vendor sees technology above the surface; a process analyst sees the processes; human resources sees change management and people; IT sees the technology implementation; business management sees short-term gains (quick wins), cost reductions and simple measures of improvement; and the project manager sees short-term completion of project tasks and the deliverables of the project.

People often see the "perception" component as the completion process models, whereas "reality" is addressed in the implementation of these processes and the achievement of business benefits. An excellent strategy is of no use unless it is well executed.

KEY POINT

Execution is important, in fact critical:

You will achieve more from an average strategy that is executed well; than from an excellent strategy that is executed in an average way.

Unfortunately, a BPM implementation is a multifaceted activity, and Figure 2.3 shows that "reality" is what appears below the water line. Unless all the "reality" associated with a BPM implementation is addressed, the risk to the project increases. This needs not only to be addressed, but also made visible to the organization. A ship could cruise very close to an iceberg on one side and not hit anything, and yet do the same on the other side and sink.

We will now briefly explore one of these "realities."

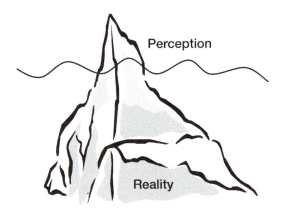

Figure 2.3 Perception, the tip of the iceberg called "reality"

BPM INSIGHT

The visibility of issues and activities is an important part of addressing them, as is the establishment of the foundations necessary to commence a BPM program of work and have the program a success.

EXPLORING "REALITY"

The most important component in any BPM implementation is the management of organizational change and the associated people (staff) impacts. As mentioned earlier, the implementation and its success are owned by the people in the trenches. People and their engagement in the implementation are critical, and a holistic approach in meeting the people and cultural aspects of managing an organization is crucial.

BPM INSIGHT

In fact, in our experience the people change management or organization change management aspects are 60 percent plus of any BPM program effort.

The key to engaging the people in the trenches is leadership. Leadership from the CEO or senior executives of the BPM program and from their line managers for BPM projects. The leaders must be engaged first. The program director, project manager or project team cannot achieve people engagement on their own.

KEY POINT

The level of success of any BPM initiative is limited by the level of commitment and drive from executive management.

It is the people who will determine the success (or otherwise) of your BPM activities. You can have the most effective and efficient new or redesigned processes in the world, but unless you can convince people to use them efficiently, or at all, then you have nothing (refer to Chapter 8). People need to be included as an integral part of the development journey. They need to be consulted, listened to, trained and communicated with on a regular basis. If they do not understand the processes, the reasons for the new processes and why changes to the existing processes are necessary, how do you expect people to take ownership and responsibility for them?

People need to understand clearly what is expected of them and how they fit into the new structure and processes. Their performance measures need to be developed in consultation and agreement with them.

What is the role of management in the transformation? While it may seem obvious that managers need to *manage* the operation of the organization, this is in fact *not* what most managers do in their current positions.

KEY POINT

In our experience, with rare exceptions, today's managers spend most of their time reacting to critical situations and treating the symptoms and not the causes—commonly referred to as "crisis management."

This is not to be critical of managers. In general they are well-meaning and hard-working individuals who generally do a great job with the tools they have to work with. There needs to be a considerable effort in any BPM activity to work with the management and determine what information managers require to *manage the business*. You need to ensure that there is a deep and thorough understanding of how the business operates; what information is required, and how to provide it in a timely manner, to enable managers to move from reactive to proactive management and then to predictive management. It is this journey of management maturity that provides the organization with a long-term continuous and sustainable increase in productivity.

CHANGE MANAGEMENT AND PERFORMANCE MANAGEMENT

The people change management components of programs/projects need to address the organizational culture and modify it towards a new set of management behaviors that will translate into the behaviors of the people they manage.

To support the drive to implement cultural change, management incentives need to be aligned with the management information available, the process goals and organizational strategy. Incentives and targets via performance management need to be well known and realistic. They must also allow the best performers to overachieve, and the rewards need to be worthwhile. This does not always translate as money incentives; human resource departments can be very creative in providing non-monetary options. The challenge is how to measure and manage this change in an effective and acceptable way.

KEY POINT

Most BPM activities just focus on making people able to use the new processes, through training and one-way communication. Change management is about people wanting to use the new processes and requires early, frequent and interactive two-way engagement.

In these first two chapters a definition and metaphor of BPM has been provided, as well as some of the history, mystery and complexities of BPM. Chapter 28 provides three detailed case studies of BPM. The results of one of these case studies (a bank) is outlined here to demonstrate that BPM can not only be implemented, but be extremely successful. A second case study has also been provided.

CASE STUDY

This organization was a large bank, and in the first 3.5 years of its BPM program the results have been nothing short of spectacular. The Consumer division of the Bank:

- reduced their expenses ratio by 50 percent;
- increased the customer facing time within its 300 branches to more than 70 percent. Note: a reputable consultancy completed an industry review that determined that branch staff spent 17 percent of their time with customers. With the removal of the majority of the back-office processing, the bank branch staff are now spending more than 70 percent of their time with customers;
- reduced errors significantly, from 25–30 percent to 3–5 percent, which is considered an acceptable level;
- staff and customer satisfaction increased significantly, as measured by surveys.

A more detailed case study of what can be achieved with BPM and how to achieve it.

Background

This was a small business unit of a much larger bank, insurance and wealth management organization. The business unit had in excess of 100 full-time equivalent (FTE) staff and an annual operating budget of $10m. The business unit develops financial products and sells them via a network of independent intermediaries (financial advisors, banks, building societies and so forth). It develops and markets for the superannuation or pension fund marketplace.

Two business units were joined together following an acquisition. Historically, the main business unit was always client focused. Staff were able to process any request from members or advisors within the one geographic region. The newly acquired business unit was functionally based—that is, a staff member would only process one type of transaction but would do so for every client and advisor regardless of their location.

These two business units were left that way under the one management structure until it was decided to merge them under the one client-focused structure. It was fully understood by management that there would be a significant training exercise required to achieve this new client-focused approach. So customer-focused training was delivered to provide staff with the necessary skills. The business was structured on a geographical regional basis and all work coming into the organization was segregated by region and then processed. Staff had the dual responsibility for processing the transaction and liaising with customers. Management believed that the additional costs associated with this approach would be outweighed by the benefits of increased job satisfaction for staff, greater accountability and better customer satisfaction.

Business challenge

One of the prime goals of this new approach was to improve customer service within six months; this was not achieved, despite extensive on-the-job and formal customer service training. This was further compounded by an unacceptably high expense ratio, work duplication, increasing error rates and service standards not being achieved.

The fact that the two original business units were still being administered on different system application platforms (legacy applications) did not help the situation. It required everyone to be fully familiar with both systems. So a decision had been made to rationalize onto one platform but that was still likely to be several years away.

The customer service in the original business unit, which was originally rated as very good, began to fade. The customer service in the newly acquired business unit, which was rated below average before the amalgamation, failed to improve.

Approach

The overall business unit decided to approach three service providers in the area of business process management to provide proposals of how to remedy the situation. They did not include the incumbent software workflow vendor in the short list as previous experience indicated that the vendor concentrated solely on the workflow software whereas the business unit wanted to review the processes from an end-to-end perspective and then review and understand the business implications.

The management was fully committed to the success of this review project and demonstrated this by the level of management time allocated to the project. The business unit manager and his three client service managers allocated two days a week to the project for the project duration. Other staff, including team leaders and senior fund administrators, were also involved in workshops, reviewing outcomes and revising estimates—a commitment of six staff from the overall business unit of 100+ for about 20 percent of their time over the project.

The selected BPM consultancy recommended a phased approach with several "gates" to allow the business to stop at any stage, ensure it was receiving value for money and that the project was delivering as expected. There were four phases recommended, with the expected duration indicated below:

Approach (phases):

- Discovery (2 weeks)
- Current state analysis (< 5 weeks)
- Future state analysis (~ 6 weeks)
- Final report (2 weeks).

These phases were delivered by the BPM consultancy with a lead consultant and one senior consultant for the duration of the engagement. The consultants:

- met with key stakeholders
- conducted workshops (process execution staff and management)
- ensured that all necessary stakeholders who were external to the main business unit were fully engaged. This included the finance department and IT
- modeled the current processes and the proposed new processes
- completed significant metrics analysis.

At the conclusion of each phase the client received a report that provided an opportunity to evaluate the phase and stop or redirect the project if necessary. The timeframes indicated were met and there was no project overrun from a time or budgetary perspective.

The small project team engaged the staff and management significantly in the project. An early engagement was considered an essential part of the human change management aspects of the project and necessary to achieve the results the business needed.

Project findings

The Discovery and Current state analysis phases revealed a number of significant pieces of information:

- there were 12 quick win opportunities identified and the business commenced implementing six of these immediately
- there were 20 primary business processes, which represented 95 percent plus of the business operational costs, the other processes were considered to be of no great consequence in the context of this project
- the top four processes accounted for 65 percent of the operational costs

CASE STUDY

- a further 23 percent of costs were spent on enquiries and complaints
- checking (to ensure no errors) of the transactions processed was considered necessary because of the exceedingly high error rates and these checking activities accounted for 17.5 percent of staff time.

This provided an indication of where to expend effort in the Future state analysis phase.

Results

At the conclusion of the Future state analysis phase the savings indicated a conservative cost saving of 39 percent, with an 83 percent staff utilization factor.

CONCLUSION

Many people are still confused about what constitutes BPM, which is not surprising when the BPM community itself has not yet agreed on a common definition and approach. BPM is all about the efficient and effective management of business processes—people are at the center of business processes, so make them part of the solution.

KEY POINT

We had improvement programs, but the real difference came when we decided it was no longer a program, it was a business strategy.

(Stephen Schwartz, IBM)

BPM INSIGHT

Without trivializing the work involved in the implementation, the project is the easy part. It is the institutionalization of process improvement and management as a fundamental management practice that is the key, and this cannot be effectively achieved without the ability to manage your processes proactively and predictively.

SUMMARY

While BPM may appear a mystery, there are several ways to unravel it:

- BPM had its origins in the coalescing of quality thinking, process thinking and the evolution of technology.

- We discussed the concept of where the "next big things" come from.
- BPM is now broadly accepted in business and while the level of understanding is good, there is still confusion of what it exactly is and how to go about it, especially at an organization level. Technology has also significantly matured and is getting better by the day.
- The Iceberg Syndrome is a metaphor for the complexity of BPM. What appears above the water is only a small part of any BPM implementation program and will depend upon the viewer's perspective.
- BPM is not a simple concept nor is it simple to implement—it is extremely complex and difficult; and yet, absolutely achievable when approached in the right way.
- The visibility of issues and activities is an important part of addressing them, as is the establishment of the foundations necessary to commence a BPM program of work and have the program be a success.
- The people change management or organization change management aspects of BPM are 60 percent plus of the implementation effort.
- Management focus on "crisis management" needs to be refocused to the causes of issues and not treating the symptoms.

SELF-TEST

1 Where did BPM have its origins?

2 How does mystification begin?

3 List the five mystification factors and their relationship to "reality"?

4 In the Iceberg Syndrome, what are the six different viewers' perspectives that appear above the waterline?

5 Why is people change management important and how much effort should a BPM program expend on it?

CHAPTER 3

WHO SHOULD BE INVOLVED IN BPM AND WHAT ARE THE CRITICAL SUCCESS FACTORS?

OVERVIEW

Once we have a common understanding of what is meant by "involve" and "the type of BPM activity," there are proven answers to the question of who should be involved in BPM. Successful BPM implementations have clearly shown who needs to drive BPM and identified the critical success factors. We will examine these in this chapter.

OVERALL LEARNING OUTCOME

By the end of this chapter you will be able to:

- Have a clear understanding of who should be involved in the various types of BPM activities
- Identify the two aspects of operational management of business processes
- Understand when external BPM experts can add value
- Identify some of the critical success factors
- Have an understanding of a metaphor for BPM.

Before we deal with who should be involved in BPM there are two things we need to define. First, what we mean by "involved"; and second, "what type of BPM activity" are you dealing with.

"Involved," in this instance, includes such diverse aspects as driving BPM, establishing the business activities, detailed process reviews, process modeling, process redesign or

Table 3.1 BPM activities and the type of involvement

Type of BPM activity	Typical leaders	Role
Simple low impact BPM project	Sponsor: business unit leader Manager: Project Manager	• Deliver to the business case • Manage the project effectively
High impact BPM project	Sponsor: Divisional Leader; Senior Executive Manager: Project Director	• Deliver to the business case • Manage the project effectively • Ensure that the organizational change aspects of the project are effectively managed
Large-scale BPM program	Sponsor: CEO or another very senior executive Manager: Program Director	• Personal involvement (not just turning up to steering committee meetings once a month) • Publicly aligning program and individual projects with the organization strategy • Communications—formal and informal to all stakeholders • "Walk the talk"
Enterprise-wide business transformation program	Sponsor: CEO Manager: Transformation Program Director (usually a senior executive)	• Personal involvement (not just turning up to steering committee meetings once a month) • Publicly aligning program and individual projects with the organization strategy, especially to external stakeholders • Communications—formal and informal to all stakeholders • "Walk the talk"

innovation, metrics analysis, BPM implementation, ongoing management and improvement and organizational change management. It could also involve customers, suppliers, suppliers of suppliers, and many other stakeholders.

Second, the "type of BPM activity" could range from a simple small low impact BPM project to improve a process(es); to high impact projects; large-scale BPM programs; and even enterprise-wide business transformation programs being predominantly driven from a process-focus perspective. Table 3.1 outlines these types of activities together with the leaders who would typically drive the activity and an indication of the role they may fulfill.

The first two types of BPM activities shown in Table 3.1 are often initiated or driven from the bottom-up as they are typically projects. Even if a BPM project has a large impact upon a business unit it is often initiated by a knowledgeable and passionate process-focused manager or executive. It most probably will not have significant attention from the Chief Executive Officer (CEO).

Whereas the last two, program and transformation, activities shown in Table 3.1 will typically be top-down driven as they cannot be initiated or successful without the drive and detailed support of the CEO. Even if driven or sponsored by another senior executive, the success will depend upon the continued support of the CEO.

Refer to Chapter 5 for more detail on bottom-up and top-down approaches and why one will never (or rarely) work for an enterprise-wide BPM implementation.

> ## BPM INSIGHT
> It must be remembered that processes are not a goal in themselves. They are simply a means to achieve a business objective.

Processes will not achieve a business objective automatically or by chance; they need continuous and effective management.

KEY POINT

Process management is the management and organization of processes crucial for your business.

Processes need to be as efficient and effective as possible. This can be achieved by periodic projects (step improvements) or larger scale projects to significantly reinvigorate them by introducing innovation. Either way processes can only be sustained by ongoing management and measurement.

MANAGEMENT OF BUSINESS PROCESSES

We would suggest that there are two aspects to operational management of business processes:

1. Management of business processes as an integral part of "management."
2. Management of business process improvement.

Who is involved will vary depending upon which aspect you are addressing.

Management of business processes as an integral part of "management"

This aspect of management is responsible for the realization of the business objectives and ensuring the business processes are linked and contributing to the organization strategy. This management of business processes should be performed by line management (in conjunction with process governance—business process owners/stewards), and cannot be delegated to internal or external BPM consultants, as this role forms an integral part of "management-as-usual." For example, senior managers should be responsible for the end-to-end processes, while middle management should be responsible for the individual process(es) that comprises the end-to-end process or parts of the process. It is crucial for line managers that they take responsibility as the owners of these processes.[1] Typical process ownership related responsibilities include:

- specifying objectives (goals) and measures that relate to the objectives and targets to be achieved—these targets should be broken down into daily or weekly measures to enable continuous monitoring and management;
- communicating the objectives, measures and targets to the people executing the processes and, if necessary, providing rewards and incentives;
- monitoring and managing progress of the targets, and verifying whether the objectives and measures are still accurate and relevant;
- motivating staff to exceed objectives and deal with process disturbances;
- encouraging staff to identify bottlenecks and possible process improvements.

These line managers can be classified according to their main scope of activities:

- Operational managers should be working with clearly defined processes and related objectives. Their main involvement in the processes are to adjust the resourcing of the people aspect of the process(es) (for example, more or less staff) and solve operational problems (for example, errors as a result of the processes).
- Tactical managers will be looking at improvements of the processes.
- Strategic managers will be looking at the business model and the related processes.

Management of business process improvement

This role relates to the identification, development, implementation and roll-out of the benefits of BPM. These managers are responsible for supporting the business/organizational managers in improving their processes, and they should not be responsible for the day-to-day management of the business processes. We call these managers BPM managers, and distinguish between the following types:

- The BPM project manager, whose main responsibility is to ensure that the objectives of the BPM project, as outlined in the business case, are being met.
- The BPM program manager, whose main responsibility is to facilitate multiple BPM projects so they meet the program's objectives and, by sharing best practices and lessons learned, to do it in the most effective and efficient way.
- The manager of the Center of Business Process Excellence, whose main responsibility is to ensure that the business and processes are aligned to ensure that the maximum benefits are obtained from the business processes.
- The chief process officer, whose main responsibility is to ensure that the processes and IT are aligned with the strategy, business and organization, and that this initiative is continuously managed from the executive level of the organization.

In any activity, be it a project, program or business transformation, it is critical that the employees are heavily involved in all aspects.

BPM INSIGHT

In our experience in consulting to and implementing BPM programs/projects all around the world, there is one constant—the people organizational change aspect is 60 percent plus of the effort in all BPM activities. Unless you ensure involvement, transparency and visibility for the people, chances are you will not optimize success and risk outright failure.

Close to the business

All the various types of BPM managers must understand that their role is to assist in the achievement of targets established by the line managers/process owners/process stewards, and not to build a BPM empire. The people working with or reporting to the BPM managers should ideally be sourced from the business units involved with the project, as these people will provide the opportunity for a "closeness" to the business and an understanding of the business processes that cannot be obtained from non-business people. Designing processes on paper is easy, but to be relevant and able to keep on executing them as things change is a challenge and will remain a challenge long after the project is complete.

The most important criterion for success is *not* to have the best "looking" process models or solution, or the most sophisticated process modeling and management tools.

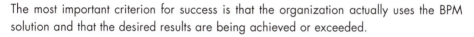

KEY POINT

The most important criterion for success is that the organization actually uses the BPM solution and that the desired results are being achieved or exceeded.

On average, about 80 percent of a business line manager's time should be spent on business-as-usual activities, such as reviewing results, coaching and solving problems, and only about 20 percent on new process development or business initiatives. On the other hand, BPM managers will spend in excess of 80 percent of their time on process improvement activities. (Note: these percentages can of course vary from time to time and situation to situation.)

This difference of focus between the two roles is a reason for tension between the line manager and the BPM manager: the line manager focuses on achieving the short-term target, and any change can affect his or her ability to do this, in the short term. The BPM manager focuses on change necessary to achieve the long-term objectives. Successful managers are those able to agree a win–win solution.

USE OF EXTERNAL BPM EXPERTS

By its very nature—namely, managing people and processes—it is recommended, in the long term, that it is always internal personnel who fulfill the management roles discussed above, to ensure continuity and acceptance. In the initial phases of an organization's BPM maturity and its first few projects, it will be appropriate for the organization to appoint external BPM experts and BPM project managers to assist in bringing BPM experience and knowledge transfer to the internal staff.

After the initial projects, and as the organization process maturity grows, external support for the managers can take on a different set of responsibilities, such as:

- *Setting up a project, program or Center of Business Process Excellence.* External consultants can leverage their experience from multiple organizations and provide guidance. This can be of particular assistance in ensuring that the scope of the activities is not too ambitious or has ambitions that are too small. The activities should start pragmatically. Having no ambition will lead to no fundamental change, while the lack of a pragmatic approach leads to the inability to meet expectations or maintain the initial effort.

- *Monitoring the progress of a project, program or Center of Business Process Excellence.* An external consultant has the ability and independence to ask tough questions. Often internal people become engrossed in the details of process models and the structure of the project, program or Center of Business Process Excellence, and can lose sight of the overall objective.

- *Monitoring the performance of the business and identifying areas for improvement.* The external consultant can periodically review the performance of the business unit and staff. These reviews can then be discussed with the line manager for any necessary corrective action.

- *Conflict resolution and project/program revival.* The external consultant can assist the organization if the original project/program or Center of Business Process Excellence does not deliver the agreed results. The first step is to identify the core problem(s) and determine whether the original objectives can still be met; the necessary steps can then be taken. An external consultant can function as an icebreaker.

- *Support for the manager.* The external consultant can assist the BPM manager if he or she is overburdened with work—which can often occur with large organizational changes. The external consultant becomes an advisor to the BPM manager. The BPM manager should still be responsible for stakeholder management and decision making, and the consultant can assist in analyzing and overseeing the various activities under responsibility of the BPM manager.

- *Evaluating (or quality assuring) project(s) and program(s).* During and at the conclusion of a project or program it is crucial that the results are evaluated; this will assist with formulating lessons learned for the next initiatives and may also assist in evaluating and

BPM INSIGHT

BPM projects/programs can be extremely complex, and there is a growing trend towards providing internal business project managers and BPM managers with a BPM coach.

identifying outstanding key issues that have not yet been addressed within the project. In these situations, an external consultant can ask unpopular questions.

The coaching role is typically filled by a senior BPM consultant (internal or external), who will coach a BPM manager/project manager on a frequent basis about the main challenges and how to deal with them. This can also be appropriate for business line managers who want to introduce process thinking among the employees to achieve sustainable improvements. Most of these coaching engagements commence with a project or workshop, followed by the ongoing coaching sessions.

CRITICAL SUCCESS FACTORS

The *reality* of implementing a BPM solution is far more complex than it first appears to be. A BPM project/program has the potential to (and usually does) cut across departments and, increasingly, organization boundaries, as clients, vendors and partners become more involved. It will involve many varying and complex stakeholder relationships both inside and outside the organization.

While each project will be unique and have its own characteristic success factors there are a small number of *critical* success factors that we believe are common across all organizations and BPM, as shown in Table 3.2.

KEY POINT

If you do not have the first critical success factor, support of the CEO or senior executive team, then you should simply stop. The other critical success factors (2 to 6) will be irrelevant without this dedicated and unambiguous support of the senior leadership team.

To support the view that large-scale BPM programs or enterprise-wide process-focused (BPM) transformation programs need to be driven by the CEO or senior executive team review Table 3.3 and observe at what level within the organization the BPM programs were driven.

There are a number of other considerations and comments to make in support to these success factors. We have created a list below that you should take into account:

- *Leadership*—it has been suggested that unless you have the undivided and total support of the CEO, you should not attempt any BPM projects. The reality is that few CEOs are yet at the point of turning their organizations into totally process-focused businesses. While there is undeniably a growing awareness of the importance of processes to organizations, there is still a long way to go. As we will discuss later, leadership does not always equate to the CEO; there are many leaders within an organization, some of whom are experimenting with BPM projects. Leadership in this context means having the *attention, support, funding, commitment* and *time* of the leader involved in the BPM project. Obviously, the degree of each of these will vary according to the BPM maturity

Table 3.2 BPM critical success factors

	Critical success factor	Description
1	Driven by senior leadership	As shown in Table 3.1, if you are planning to execute a BPM program of work or enterprise-wide business transformation program then you *must* have the demonstrable support of the CEO and senior executives. This is the single most important critical success factor for these types of BPM activities.
2	Clearly understood business drivers	If you do not understand what is driving you to do BPM then stop doing it until you do. You may be solving the wrong problem!
3	Clearly understood project/ program/transformation vision —what will the business look like afterwards?	Vision in this instance is much more than the traditional project "scope" statement. The scope of a BPM project is always difficult to specify early in the project. It does get easier later in a project. BPM program and transformation scopes are near impossible to clearly articulate (in the project scope sense). It is more about agreeing what the business will look like after you have been successful. If you do not "start with the end in mind" (the vision) how do you know you are heading in the right direction? Chapter 13, Foundations phase, will discuss this in more detail.
4	Clearly understood, agreed and measurable business value outcomes—how will the business be better off afterwards?	You need to clearly understand when you have been successful. This requires measures of success. If you can't measure your success, then how do you know you have been successful?
5	Appointed and empowered BPM leader and team	This is especially critical for BPM programs and transformations. Empowered implies having the authority, experience and backing of the CEO and senior executive team.
6	Senior executives, managers and other appropriate people need to be provided with the right incentives and disincentives	People probably will need to be motivated via Key Performance Indicators (KPIs) and rewards. The rewards may be financial, non-financial, promotions, etc. HR departments can be quite creative. There also need to be disincentives for non-performance.

of the organization and leader. *Time* is critical to the project, and does not mean that the leader "turns up" to project steering committee meetings once a month. The time commitment will involve the leader supporting the project amongst colleagues, stakeholders, customers, suppliers and the people within the organization. The leader is the "head sales person" for BPM, and will need to continually "sell" the expected benefits and outcomes and "walk the talk" of BPM.

- *A structured approach to BPM implementation*—without an agreed structured and systematic approach to the implementation of BPM projects/programs that takes into account the organization strategy, how it is to be executed and the significant behavioral aspects of the implementation, a project will be chaotic and have very high risks associated with it.

Table 3.3 Successful BPM organizations and who drove BPM

Organization name	BPM "driver"	Business benefits
Citibank, Germany	Chief Operating Officer (COO) and Board member	• 50+% reduction in operating costs • Increased branch customer facing time: from 17% to 70+% • Error rates down from 25–30% to 3–5% • Increased customer and staff satisfaction
Air Products, global organization	Chief Executive Officer (CEO)	• 32% increased operating return on net assets
Nedbank, South Africa	COO and Chief Information Officer (CIO) (same role)	• Large operational savings • Organizational understanding of time, cost, quality, risk for processes • Increased BPM maturity
Aveant Home Care, The Netherlands	CEO	• 50% reduction in administration staff levels • Significant improvement in operational work rates • Significant reduction in error rates

BPM INSIGHT

BPM projects that are executed using only traditional project management methodologies will yield sub-optimal outcomes. The 7FE Framework described in this book provides the required systematic and structured approach that will significantly increase the likelihood of success and minimize risk.

- *People change management*—processes are executed either by people, or by people supported by technology. It is people who will make or break the implementation of a BPM project, and unless they are "on board" and supporting the project, the chances of failure are high. Human organizational change management on a BPM project/program, in our experience, can take upwards of 60 percent plus of project time, tasks and effort. How often do you hear it said that "people are our greatest assets"? Yet most organizations spend less than 1 percent of project budgets on the people aspects of the project. This is simply not enough in any project, and with the increased impact upon people of processes, this percentage must increase substantially. The project team needs to spend a great deal of time and effort on human change management. The people aspects of every process change and activity need to be assessed and acted upon in an understanding and sympathetic manner.

- *Sustainable performance*—a project has a defined period of life, whereas processes, if maintained, supported, measured and managed, will continue to exist in a business-as-usual environment far beyond the life of the project. It is a project's task to hand over processes in such a way that the business understands how to "look after" them.

The organization must establish a business process structure that maintains the life (efficiency and effectiveness) of its processes.

- *Maintain the "rage"*—there is often a great deal of passion from the BPM zealots within the organization. These are people with "process passion" and they should be encouraged and nurtured. Implementing BPM within an organization is not a six-month event, it can and will take years. While the results can be spectacular, it is important to "maintain the rage" of passion over a longer period of time. BPM is a marathon, not a sprint!

- *Organizational process (BPM) maturity*—the process maturity, or sometimes immaturity, can have a significant impact upon the implementation of BPM. If the organization is new to adopting a process-focused viewpoint, then do not try to become process sophisticated too quickly.

KEY POINT

You must match the speed of your process journey to the process maturity of the organization. If you try to move too quickly and outstrip the process maturity of the organization you will increase the probability of failure.

A METAPHOR FOR BPM INVOLVEMENT

BPM implementation and success is all about balance and cohesion within the organization. Getting this balance correct will allow the BPM project to be finished in a successful way.

A useful metaphor is the Regatta® of Sogeti Nederland, shown in Figure 3.1. The components are:

Objective—relates to the organization's strategy.

Results—are the outcomes from the execution of all the components of the boat (process, people, information and resources). The desire is to execute the *objective* well and win.

Steering—equates to the organization's management team. They provide the direction and focus.

Process and *people*—represent the organization (business or operations) side. Process is on the first oar, and sets the speed for other rowers. In a BPM activity, the business process should be leading and the rest should follow.

Information and *resources*—represent the information and technology side. If a BPM activity and/or organization places too much emphasis on resources and information (the IT aspects), then the project will be pushed onto, and could get stuck on, the organization bank (process and people). Alternatively, if a BPM activity places too much emphasis on the people and process (organization aspects), the project "boat" could get stuck on the IT bank of the project.

The slogan used is:

Speed (effectiveness) and efficiency through balance and cohesion.

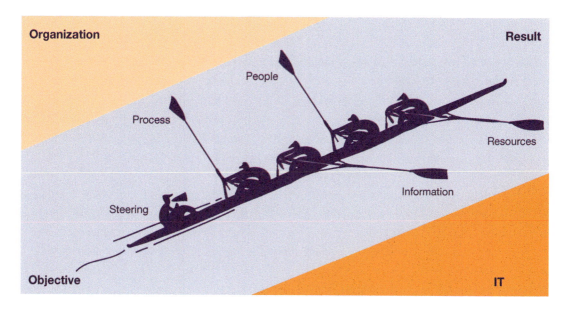

Figure 3.1 Regatta as a metaphor for implementing a BPM activity

Source: Reproduced with kind permission of Sogeti Nederland.

With these components working well, the metaphor goes like this:

Speed (effectiveness) is crucial—the overall aim is to win, and you win by being the first (fastest) across the finish line. In a BPM activity, the aim is to focus on realizing benefits from the business processes; and you win when these benefits have been realized.

Efficiency—relates to ensuring that all the available energy and passion is used optimally to realize the desired result, that is to get the best out of the entire team: "to be the best we can be"; often referred to as organizational culture. In a BPM activity, the aim is to ensure that everyone is contributing effectively to realize the desired results.

Balance—is required to ensure that the boat does not lean sideways or tip over, which will slow its speed and create inefficiency. Balance is achieved by carefully matching the strength, weight and experience of all the participants in the boat, with the parts of the organization in its correct position and making an appropriate contribution. In a BPM activity, the aim is to ensure that all implementation elements (management, process, people, project management, resources and information) are considered and engaged when implementing a solution.

Cohesion—is required to ensure that the team rows as one; all rowers have to follow the same rhythm and technique, which yields optimal speed. In a BPM activity, it is important that all the implementation elements are in alignment and are not treated separately or out of step with each other.

Management—the project manager, chief process officer, project sponsor, steers the boat in a straight line directly to the finish, ensuring that it does not go off course or get stuck on the shore.

SUMMARY

BPM projects are complex business activities that require a defined, structured and organized approach to their implementation.

- They must have the right people involved at the right time, and matched to the type of BPM activity being implemented.
- Operational management of business processes involve both: management of business processes as an integral part of normal management (business-as-usual); and the management of business improvement activities.
- The people working with or reporting to the BPM managers should ideally be sourced from the business units involved in the BPM activities; creating "closeness" to the business.
- External consultants have their place either at the start of BPM activities to assist in the start-up; as coaches for BPM staff or line management; and in a project/program quality assurance capacity.
- When executing large-scale BPM programs or transformation activities if you do not have the support of the CEO or senior executives, then you should simply stop. Other critical success factors will not matter without this dedicated and unambiguous support.
- BPM projects that are executed using only traditional project management methodologies will yield sub-optimal outcomes. The 7FE Framework described in Part II of this book provides the necessary systematic and structured approach that will significantly increase the likelihood of success and minimize risk.
- You must match the speed of your process journey to the process maturity of the organization. If you try to move too quickly and outstrip the process maturity of the organization you will increase the probability of failure.
- Keep the BPM metaphor of the BPM rowing boat in your mind, it is an excellent reminder of who should be involved and how.

SELF-TEST

1 What are the various types of BPM activities?
2 Who is the typical leader of each?
3 Describe the role of the typical BPM leader.
4 What are the two types of operational management of business processes?
5 Describe the high level responsibilities of a process owner/steward.
6 How should an operational manager be involved in the business-as-usual activities of managing business processes?
7 Describe the components of the BPM metaphor of the rowing boat and how do they interact and support each other?

CHAPTER 4

WHEN SHOULD YOU DO BPM—WHAT ARE THE MAIN DRIVERS AND TRIGGERS?

OVERVIEW

While the best time to commence a BPM project or program within an organization will obviously depend upon the individual circumstances within the organization, there are a number of critical questions that need to be asked, answered and understood before you start. This chapter explores those questions and the typical business drivers and triggers for BPM.

OVERALL LEARNING OUTCOME

By the end of this chapter you will be able to:

- Describe the generic business drivers typical to a BPM program
- Describe the generic business events that often trigger the commencement of a BPM project.

When should you start a BPM program or project, and why, are difficult questions to answer in a generic manner. The real answer is, "it depends." It depends upon the circumstances of the organization and the organization's process maturity, and these will vary from organization to organization, and from situation to situation (evaluating an organization's BPM maturity will be discussed in more detail in Chapters 29 and 30).

These are however critical questions to answer before you commence a BPM program or substantial project within your organization. It is also imperative to distinguish between organizational business drivers and any event(s) that trigger the need for process change.

First we should define what is meant by a "driver" and a "trigger."

A *driver* is a business reason or motivator that causes the organization to initiate action to achieve a business objective. For example, an organization wants to expand its international markets, increase its revenue and achieve better economies of scale.

A *trigger* is an event or occurrence that causes the organization to initiate action to overcome or solve an individual issue or problem that is usually of an immediate nature (for example, fraud) or imposed by an external force (for example, legislative changes resulting in compliance changes).

BPM INSIGHT

Unless the business executives and the BPM activity team have a clear understanding of business drivers and/or the business events triggering the need for changes in the way your business processes are executed and managed, then you may be providing an answer to the wrong question.

These drivers and triggers need to be transparent and visible throughout the organization. They need to be clearly documented, communicated and understood. This usually occurs in the Foundations phase of the 7FE Framework and is described in Chapter 13. In the Foundations phase the BPM drivers and triggers will need to be understood as part of step 2 (Understand Organization) and agreed and documented as part of step 4 (Target Operating Model).

CASE STUDY

Don't provide an answer to the wrong question

One of the authors was asked to go to Singapore to work with a large multibillion-dollar organization. The request was to provide a detailed plan of how to implement BPM across the organization. The response was that he was unable to provide it. The client was amazed until he explained that the plan will be significantly influenced by the organizational context and business drivers, and what they expect BPM to deliver. After discussions with the CEO it came to light that they wished to significantly disrupt the industry value chain.

Message: having a clear understanding of the business drivers and organizational context for BPM will significantly influence how it is implemented within an organization.

In Table 4.1 we have categorized some of the likely drivers and triggers that may cause an organization to consider BPM as a possible solution. Looking at, and listing, these drivers and triggers from organizational, management, employee, customer, supplier/partner, product or service, process and IT perspectives. Obviously, there are many occasions where the drivers and triggers overlap with each other.

Table 4.1 Drivers and triggers that may cause an organization to consider BPM

Category	Drivers	Triggers
Organization	• High growth—difficulty coping with high growth or proactively planning for high growth • Mergers and acquisitions—they cause the organization to "acquire" additional complexity or require rationalization of processes. The need to retire acquired legacy systems could also contribute. BPM projects enable a process layer to be "placed" across these legacy systems, providing time to consider appropriate conversion strategies • Reorganization—changing roles and responsibilities • Change in strategy—deciding to change direction to operational excellence, product leadership or customer intimacy • Organization objectives or goals are not being met—introduction of process management, linked to organizational strategy, performance measurement and management of people • The need for business agility to enable the organization to respond to opportunities as they arise • The need to provide the business with more control of its own destiny • Expansion of regions, products and customers	• Compliance or regulation—e.g., many organizations have initiated process projects to meet the Sarbanes Oxley or the recent Dodd-Frank requirements; this has then provided the platform to launch process improvement or BPM activities
Management	• The need for the introduction of a sustainable performance environment • The need to create a culture of high performance • The need to gain the maximum return on investment from the existing legacy systems • The need for the ability to obtain more capacity from existing staff for expansion	• Incorrect decision due to lack of reliable or conflicting management information—process management and performance measurement and management will assist • The need to provide managers with more control over their processes to address detected governance issues • Budget cuts to address poor competiveness
Employees	• The expectation of a substantial increase in the number of employees • The wish to increase employee empowerment	• High turnover of employees, perhaps due to the mundane nature of the work or the degree of pressure and expectations upon people without adequate support, typically if a new start-up in the market attracts (or targets) employees • Training issues with new employees

Table 4.1 *continued*

Category	Drivers	Triggers
		• Low employee satisfaction or engagement out of recent survey • Employees are having difficulty in keeping up with continuous change and the growing complexity

Customers/ suppliers/ partners	• An organizational desire to focus upon customer intimacy
	• Customer segmentation or tiered service requirements
	• The introduction and strict enforcement of service levels
	• Major customers, suppliers and/or partners requiring a unique (different) process
	• The need for a true end-to-end perspective to provide visibility or integration
		• Low satisfaction with service, which could be due to:
		  o high churn rates of staff
		  o staff unable to answer questions adequately within the required timeframes
		• Negative coverage in news or social media on customer service
		• An unexpected increase in the number of customers, suppliers or partners
		• Long lead times to meet requests
		• Losing unique service offerings of key partners to competitors

Products and services	• An unacceptably long lead time to market (lack of business agility) • Each product or service has its own processes, with most of the processes being common or similar • New products or services comprise existing product/service elements • Products or services are complex	• Poor stakeholder service levels
Processes	• The need for provision of visibility of processes from an end-to-end perspective • Lack of process standardization • Lack of communications and understanding of the end-to-end process by the parties performing parts of the process • Service levels not being achieved	• Too many hand-offs or gaps in a process, or no clear process at all • Unclear roles and responsibilities from a process perspective as specified in internal audit • Quality is poor and the volume of rework has reached unacceptable level • Processes change too often or not at all • Lack of clear process goals or objectives

Table 4.1 *continued*

Category	Drivers	Triggers
Information Technology	• The introduction of new systems, for example CRM, ERP, billing systems or finance system, etc. • The purchase of BPM automation tools (workflow, document management, business intelligence), and the organization does not know how to best utilize them in a synergistic manner • Phasing out of old application systems • Existing application system overlaps and is not well understood • Introduction of a new IT architecture • A view that IT is not delivering to business expectations • A view that IT costs are out of control or too expensive • The introduction of Web services or Cloud computing • Leveraging mobile computing/field service computing	

If one or more of the triggers apply it is important to complete a root-cause analysis, as organizations often take the easy way out and fight the symptoms rather than taking fundamental and structural steps to tackle the cause. While completing this root-cause analysis it is important to quantify the impact and consequences the trigger is having upon the organization, for example, any unnecessary costs being incurred or revenue leakage. This quantification will emphasize the importance of the issues and will assist in developing the business case.

Drivers and triggers for the organization to consider an automated solution may include the following:

- a high volume of similar and repetitive transactions;
- a clear flow of high-volume transactions that need to be passed from one person to another, with each adding some value along the way;
- a need for real-time monitoring of transactions (a need to know a transaction status at all times);
- a critical issue with processing time—that is, time is of the essence;
- a need to complete many calculations within the transaction;
- transactions or "files" need to be accessible by many parties at the same time.

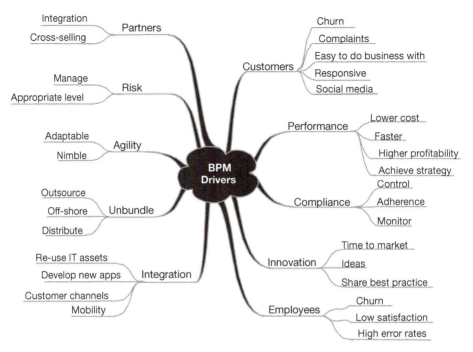

Figure 4.1 Typical BPM drivers

Source: BPMF Analysis of over 100 BPM projects (ammended). Reproduced with permission from BPM Folks (www.bpmfolks.com).

However, never over-automate processes to the extent that the organization loses sight of the need for people involvement. People are best at managing relationships, and their involvement must be engineered into the process in the appropriate way.

As stated at the start of this chapter, when to commence a BPM program/project is a difficult problem. For any given organization, it will be appropriate to start when the right number and combination of the above drivers and triggers occur. This will be different for every organization, and for every situation within the same organization.

Figure 4.1 shows a different perspective to Table 4.1 for typical BPM drivers and triggers. It is a summarized perspective as researched by BPM Focus across 100 BPM projects.

An organization's drivers and triggers indicate the need to commence process improvement and process management activities.

To assist in the communication and acceptance of the drivers and triggers across an organization, it may be useful to condense or summarize them into a list of problems, constraints and opportunities. It is crucial to specify the impact to determine the key metrics (the "so what" factor). This may assist in gaining approval of the need for a BPM activity.

Later we will discuss which type of BPM initiative is appropriate in these varying circumstances.

SUMMARY

When should you do BPM? Only when the business drivers and triggers:

- have been determined and agreed
- have been clearly documented, communicated and understood and
- you are totally confident that they are transparent and visible throughout the organization.

SELF-TEST

1 What is the difference between a business driver and a trigger?
2 Why is it important to clearly understand what your business drivers and triggers are?
3 What other possible factors may influence how you start a BPM activity within your organization?

ACTIVITY

Review the case studies described in Chapters 2 and 28. Create separate lists of both the business drivers and triggers for each case study. These should then be classified as either a problem, constraint or opportunity for the organization.

CHAPTER 5

HOW SHOULD WE START BPM—BOTTOM-UP OR TOP-DOWN?

OVERVIEW

How to start BPM is a very interesting and sometimes difficult question to answer. However there are two approaches—bottom-up and top-down. We have seen both tried many times and have only ever seen one of the approaches work, enterprise wide. In this chapter both approaches will be outlined and their effectiveness discussed.

OVERALL LEARNING OUTCOME

By the end of this chapter you will be able to:

- Outline the two approaches of bottom-up and top-down
- Describe the advantages and disadvantages of each
- Understand some of the complexities of each approach
- Understand which of the two approaches has a much higher probability for success.

We remember sitting in our office one morning and receiving a telephone call from a friend and colleague. He was an extremely well-educated and intelligent person who had presented at several BPM conferences over the years. His boss had just given him the task of implementing BPM within his organization. He called and asked only one question: "How do I start?"

This sounds like a simple question and perhaps if it was a conventional project the first step would be to define the project scope, agree it among the stakeholders, have it signed off, build a business case and have it approved and then start the project.

Table 5.1 BPM activities and BPM approach

Type of BPM activity	Typical BPM initiator	Activity	Drivers/triggers
Bottom-up			
1 Simple low impact BPM project	• BPM passionate person	• Pilot project • Small to medium project	• Specific trigger
2 High impact BPM project	• BPM passionate person • Business manager	• Projects • Small programs	• Specific and/or general trigger(s)
Top-down			
3 Large-scale BPM program	• Senior executive • Divisional manager • CEO	• Medium to large projects/program	• Many triggers—maybe a cumulative effect • Divisional business drivers
4 Enterprise-wide business transform-ation program	• CEO • Board	• Organization transformation program	• Strategic business drivers, heavily linked to strategy

With BPM projects the scope is not always clear at the start—at least compared to a conventional project. With BPM initiatives we need to have a clear understanding and agreement of the business drivers or triggers.

The "how to start" question may be answered in your organization by understanding who is driving the BPM agenda. If it is a passionate person who sees the benefits that BPM can bring to an organization, then he/she will need to "sell" the idea inside the organization to obtain funding and resources. Usually a pilot project will be selected as a means to convince management of the BPM benefits. This we refer to as the bottom-up approach.

On the other hand, if it is the CEO or another senior executive driving BPM, the "BPM sell" is at a different level within the organization and the expectations of the BPM outcomes will be significantly different. This we refer to as the top-down approach.

Table 5.1 takes the four types of BPM activities described in Chapter 3 and relates them to the two approaches, outlining who the typical initiator might be within the organization, the type of activity (project, program or transformation) and what may be driving or triggering it in the organization.

The information within the table is generic and may not apply to every organization.

BOTTOM-UP APPROACH

Typically there is one or more passionate person(s) within the organization who believe that BPM can make a significant difference to the organization. They "sell" the idea to a manager who is able to provide all the resources for a pilot project to prove the concept and the organization's ability to implement it.

This approach is often characterized by an organization with low business and/or process maturity and it is highly unlikely that they will have the attention and backing of the CEO or senior divisional executives.

The thinking behind the bottom-up approach is often that if we start small, implement some pilot projects (probably initially with low potential impact on the organization—in case things go wrong) we will be able to demonstrate the potential benefits of BPM. This will enable management, and the project team members, to learn, gain experience and realize benefits via BPM for the organization. Once the benefits have been demonstrated, management will agree to further projects that will benefit the organization even more. With more projects comes a growing momentum and internal credibility to enable BPM to spread organization wide. Hopefully it will reach a point where the internal credibility, understanding, expertise and support are enough to enable BPM to flip from being bottom-up to top-down driven. The reason this flip is essential is that at some point the CEO (or very senior executive team) must become the BPM advocate and drive and demonstrably support the enterprise-wide BPM implementation.

The components outline in "red" in the BPM House depicted in Figure 5.1 shows the aspects of BPM typically addressed by the bottom-up approach—business process improvement is nearly always directed at the operational aspects of the organization. This approach by its nature cannot address the other aspects of BPM shown in the BPM House.

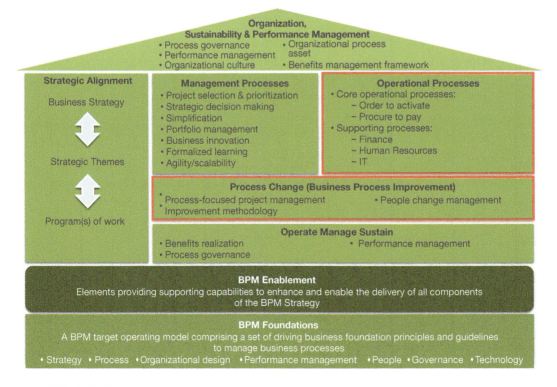

Figure 5.1 BPM House

The advantages of this approach are:

- It will grow internal capability
- Starting with low impact pilots will be low risk to the business
- It will deliver process improvements
- It may be sustainable in pockets of the business
- Enables the people in the organization to grow their process maturity and skills
- Proves BPM within the organization and build internal momentum
- Hopefully it will progressively get management to support BPM.

All this sounds very logical, however, it is not this simple, as we will now discuss.

The disadvantages include:

- It may stay a small divisional initiative
- May be sustainable in pockets of the business, but will dissipate over time
- Will not deliver sustainable process improvement or benefits because the organization does not have a process-focused management structure
- Without the backing of senior executives it may go nowhere or have minimal impact
- The biggest disadvantage in our experience is that we have **never** seen it work well enough to transition to an enterprise-wide BPM initiative.

BPM INSIGHT

While many, perhaps most, BPM initiatives have historically started with the bottom-up approach we have *never* seen it spread to a truly enterprise-wide implementation without flipping from bottom-up to top-down.

TOP-DOWN APPROACH

There is however a growing understanding by senior executives that having a strong process-focused lens on their business is important and they are far more willing to listen to a process-based approach to transforming the organization. This has enabled the top-down approach to grow in credibility.

The approach is often characterized by an organization with senior executives who understand the benefits that a process focus will bring to the organization and therefore BPM maturity is much higher to start with.

BPM INSIGHT

As this is driven by the CEO, the approach is perhaps described as:

Start Small; Think Ahead; Stay Focused.

Start small—while the BPM program may still start with some smaller pilots or projects, the difference is that they have the backing and support of the CEO and senior executive team. The initial projects are usually more about learning and building the implementation teams, not proving the concept.

Thinking ahead—is necessary to plan and build enthusiasm and the necessary foundations for success (refer to Chapter 13). However, do not get too far ahead of yourself. The BPM journey, while needing to be planned, will unfold as you implement it. It is important to be flexible and follow the business benefits trail.

Stay focused—is perhaps the most important aspect. It is why the CEO and the senior management team need to resource and drive the program. Staying focused also means building the future organization to enable BPM to be sustainable in the long run. Usually the top-down approach will also be linked to a future state target operating model.

BPM INSIGHT

The biggest mistake many organizations make in the top-down approach is spending far too much time in planning and building what is perceived as the necessary foundations before BPM starts. Foundations are essential, but there is a balance between doing too much and doing just enough to start to gain the business benefits and BPM momentum in the organization.

We will discuss this balance and how to build BPM foundations in Chapter 13.

The advantages of this approach are:

- It has the backing, resources and drive of the CEO and executive team.
- It has a proven track record of success (refer to Table 3.3 and the case studies described in Chapter 28).
- The benefits are huge, when executed well.
- It works.

Some of the potential disadvantages include:

- If executives are solely driven by a methodology or toolset, for example, Lean or Six Sigma, then while it will provide benefits to the organization, these examples are not enterprise-wide sustainable process-focused approaches to transformation. They are useful tools within a BPM approach, where BPM is defined as the BPM House described in Chapter 1.

- If you do not build the future organization to enable sustainability, then benefits will dissipate quickly.

- It is "hard work."

- It is not a quick fix. It is a multi-year journey.

KEY POINT

You do not "do" BPM. It is a management discipline that requires a sustained focus and often fundamental change in management style.

SUMMARY

How should you start BPM? Top-down or bottom-up?

- Bottom-up is the most common way to start and is usually linked to lower levels of process maturity; executive backing; is often driven by BPM passionate people within the organization; and we have never seen this approach spread organization wide without flipping to a top-down driven approach.

- Top-down is the approach that is required for a successful enterprise-wide BPM transformation. It must have the backing and total support of the CEO and other senior executive management team.

- The top-down approach can perhaps be described as: *Start Small; Think Ahead; Stay Focused.*

- The biggest mistake many organizations make in the top-down approach is spending far too much time in planning and building what is perceived as the necessary foundations before BPM starts. Foundations are essential, but there is a balance between this and the gaining of business benefits and BPM momentum in the organization.

- You do not "do" BPM. It is a management discipline that requires a sustained focus and often fundamental change in management style.

SELF-TEST

1 Who is the typical driver for each type of BPM activity?

2 What are the advantages and disadvantages of the bottom-up approach?

3. What are the advantages and disadvantages of the top-down approach?

4 Which approach has been shown to work in an enterprise-wide BPM implementation and why?

5 What is the biggest mistake many organizations make in the top-down approach?

WHY IS IT IMPORTANT TO IMPROVE BUSINESS PROCESSES BEFORE AUTOMATING THEM?

OVERVIEW

Many organizations automate existing business processes first and then try to improve them. This is not always the best approach. In this chapter we will provide an alternative perspective.

OVERALL LEARNING OUTCOME

By the end of this chapter you will be able to:

- Explain the tendency of people wanting to automate first
- Highlight the problems and root causes arising from this approach
- Explain the need to improve processes first for each of the three process initiatives.

The first rule of any technology is that automation applied to an efficient operation will magnify the efficiency.

The second is that automation applied to an inefficient operation will magnify the inefficiency.

(Bill Gates, Microsoft Corporation)

We have stated before that automation can provide tremendous benefit, however it needs to be applied correctly. Our suggestion in this chapter is to first improve the process prior to automation. The chapter will discuss why the focus should be on improving the processes prior to automation. How to go about this improvement is the main focus of the book and will be addressed in great detail in Part II. The technology components of a BPM system and their benefits are discussed in Chapter 7.

WHAT ARE THE PROBLEMS WITH AUTOMATING FIRST?

Humans are attracted to easy solutions to complex problems. In the business world we learn to solve problems quickly and move on fast. When we can't get our work done quickly enough we've discovered we can automate! In the office environment we've perfected this ability over the past 100 years to the point that we now automate almost everything to get more done faster: first letter-writing, then bookkeeping, reporting, inventory, sales handling, order processing and, more recently, business workflow and document management.

So, when confronted with productivity, efficiency and business control issues today, our first temptation is to buy an automated solution to our problem. This has been reinforced by the benefits communication technology has opened up for processes through new channels, such as the Internet, mobile and Cloud technologies.

Businesses today, especially large organizations with complex service products, are realizing that there's only so much their IT systems can achieve in improving their business operations. Even where core systems are effective and efficient (which is not always the case) it is becoming increasingly difficult to further improve the overall operating efficiency and customer service effectiveness to the extent necessary to meet customer and shareholder expectations at a rate faster than our competitors. Even Bill Gates, the ultimate advocate of technology, notes that automation is only effective when applied to efficient operations.

So, having solved the immediate challenges of automating operational business systems, and having achieved most of the "easy" systems benefits, organizations are now turning to some of the more difficult and systemic operational efficiency areas to achieve their required "step change" business improvement benefits. What is our intuitive solution to these age-old areas of inefficiency? Automate them! After all it worked for systems throughput and productivity and there are now plenty of vendors keen to provide automated workflow, document imaging and business process management system solutions—often "out-of-the-box" for your industry or environment.

WHY IS THIS NOT WORKING?

There are often two different reasons. The first we refer to as the black box syndrome where executives see their processes as a "black box." They don't know the details, but somehow the processes produce outcomes. The executives have a feeling that these processes may not be as efficient, or as effective, as they could be (quality and rework are not measured), but at least the processes work and management are afraid to change anything because change might disrupt these fragile "black box" processes and fixing a problem is tough when you do not understand it. So automating the "black box" is easier because it becomes a project and businesses "do" projects.

The second reason we refer to as the "looking at the edges" syndrome, where the processes and associated people are treated like sacred objects: they cannot, or do not want to, discuss the efficiency and effectiveness or ask the tough questions. Executives keep "looking at the edges" of the problem and not at the heart—solving symptoms rather than the cause. It is far easier for organizations that think this way to bring in a new technology. It sounds so much easier as there is no need to talk about people or processes, just technology. This is because management is focusing on symptoms rather than the root cause, which can explain why so many system replacement projects provide little or no benefits.

If business process inefficiencies could be easily solved by automating them, why are consultants often called in after an organization has purchased an expensive automated solution that has failed to "solve" the problem? Why do automated solutions fail to deliver their expected business benefits? In fact, often organizations experience an increase in paper work or increased rework and diminished quality following automation of key business processes and workflows.

WHY IS THIS SO?

The answer lies in Bill Gates's observation. Automating something doesn't fix its underlying problems—it just helps problems to occur more quickly and in a vastly greater number and frequency. The notion that "we're going to replace what's broken with something much better" is almost never realized in an organization, due to the difficulty in making instant process and cultural change on a broad scale while still running the business. At best, a compromise solution is achieved often following sizable project over-runs in time and cost budgets. At worst, the project fails completely and the status quo is maintained. In both cases, the expected benefits are not realized and employee and customer satisfaction levels may decline dramatically.

So, the obvious question would seem to be: "Why don't organizations fix their processes before they look to automation solutions?"

In most large organizations the basic back-office processes have remained predominantly unchanged for many years—even decades. In the financial services industry, for example, basic banking, insurance and investment processing procedures have been passed down for generations.

Historically, organizations haven't been able to easily fix their operational back office (business processes). Why? Because they are perceived as being:

- *easy*—and all we need to do is automate them to make them faster and take people out of the equation as much as possible; or
- *hard*—and too difficult for management to fix because they do not have the expertise, and the temptation is to purchase a solution which will "solve" the problem (back to the easy option).

NEED TO IMPROVE PROCESSES FIRST

It is important to realize that most system replacements are driven by a technology-centric project approach.

Managers will often say, "first implement technology and we will change processes afterwards." However, during the implementation, too many restrictions are placed in the system which makes it (nearly) impossible to fundamentally change the business processes in an effective and efficient manner. Most people fall for the promises that new systems are agile and can be easily adjusted. However, in most cases it is like concrete—it is fluid initially, but when cast it becomes hard and is difficult to change.

There is however a growing understanding that the most effective application implementations are process-led. Organizations are redesigning and modeling business processes and then "uploading" them into executable work management systems. Even if "out-of-the-box" vendor solutions (for example, insurance claims processing) are used as a starting point and modified to an organization's business requirements, it still needs to be a process-led implementation project.

CASE STUDY

A Telco wanted to introduce a new feature in their billing application. It took a system-centric approach to the solution design and implementation. This enabled the new feature to be introduced within the time allocated. However, they had not analyzed the process needs of the business which required considerable flexibility in its processes. As a result, 50 percent of all future marketing campaigns could not be supported.

Message: Always conduct a process-led analysis of the business and process requirements when making technology changes.

KEY POINT

The role of business analyst is a crucial role. The key word in the title is "business." This means that the "business" requirements must always be the focus and not the IT solution. This is a critical aspect for IT-oriented business analysts to keep in mind all the time.

Organizational business transformations are often aimed at fundamentally changing an organization's business operating model—the way an organization works, which will include its processes, technology and organizational design (people aspects). It is important to remember that technology is an enabler and should never be the first consideration although there is no question that today technology can open up opportunities not perceived in the past. We will address the key aspects of a target operating model in Chapters 13 and 14.

An international organization had planned a global introduction of a single Enterprise Resource Planning (ERP) system. They were purely focused on the system implementation and ignored its business processes and tried to handle the complexity by dividing the work in functional segments. Once they went live it was a "bloodbath" as most orders became lost in the system and the organization had a significant increase in complaints and drop in subsequent orders.

Message: Always adopt an end-to-end business process approach to systems implementations.

KEY CONSIDERATIONS

- BPM activities are aimed at improving a business process(es). If you don't improve the process prior to automation it can result in focusing on either automating the current process (remember Bill Gates's quote) or implementing the default system functionality supplied by the software vendor. The last point is important, because many vendor "out-of-the-box" automated processes will not incorporate the human aspects of a business process. Vendors will inform you that the process has been developed over hundreds of implementations around the world and is considered, by them, to be world's best practice. Ask yourself one critical question: "has the process been optimized for my organization?" In answering the question, ensure you take into account not just your business needs, but the needs of your customers, suppliers, partners, employees, the process maturity of your organization and your organizational culture.

- Continuous improvement is aimed at making changes to the process to ensure it continuously meets business needs. So the process is the focus. Each new continuous improvement BPM activity will require higher benefits than the associated cost. This can typically not be achieved with a pure technical, automation first approach.

- Organizations often state: "we have been doing continuous improvement for years, so we are already in a position to automate." Well, have they? Is continuous improvement the appropriate strategy, and has continuous improvement really dealt with the causes rather than just the symptoms? Is it time to obsolete your process and take a leap forward? Continuous improvement is not the right option in all circumstances.

- Continuous improvement, even if appropriate, is an extremely difficult program to implement "continuously," year after year. It requires managers to be in control of their business, and unfortunately most managers are not in control of their business. They predominantly provide what has been referred to as "band-aid" management, whereby they continually "fix issues and problems" for their staff and the business. The real issue is how much of their time is actually spent on genuinely understanding problems (getting to the root cause) thus preventing problems occurring.

There is a simple measure for this and it is the answer to the question: "how many of your critical business processes or process steps rely on spreadsheets?" This is the Spreadsheet Index. Many organizations would fail to function effectively if spreadsheets were taken away. When they are used to manage processes, the business has the potential to lose control as each person creates their own versions or "control" mechanisms. If used for critical business processes, the information is unable to be easily shared and controlled. Fit for purpose systems should make the use of spreadsheets unnecessary. If an organization is using spreadsheets in its business processes, then it definitely needs to first improve their processes before they are automated.

CASE STUDY

A large property investment and management organization was forced by market investment analysts to implement the financial modules of a large ERP system because the analysts and share market did not trust the financial results being produced. There was a large reliance on spreadsheets as the current financial system had significant short comings.

It was suggested that they should eliminate spreadsheets entirely, perhaps delete the software from the servers! The head of finance thought that was insane. The CIO cheered. It turned out that in a staff of 400 finance people there were 350,000 spreadsheets. Yes that's right, 350,000. Think of the room for errors across the organization.

Message: This is an example of managers not in control of their business. They continually created short-term fixes to problems by implementing yet another spreadsheet and now the spreadsheets were systemic and in control. Getting to the root cause and solving the base systemic problem was the only solution.

CONCLUSION

Management, at the operational level, is predominantly about the improvement and control of the processes essential to your business to achieve the objectives of the organization. Setting the direction and goals for business process improvement is a critical step and one that needs to be addressed by senior management.

While the introduction of technology can be an extremely useful and beneficial contributor for many organizations, business process improvement does not always need technology to be successful. It is far more important to get your processes right before you consider the implementation of technology. Remember that many, perhaps the majority, of process improvements can be achieved without automation at all. However, technology done well and process-led, can yield significant benefits to an organization.

SUMMARY

- Technology can bring significant benefits through speed, accuracy and consistency, provided the process is improved first.

- All types of process activities (transformation, projects and continuous improvement) require that the process is improved prior to automating.

- Most organizations overcome process failures by introducing more spreadsheets and haphazard solutions rather than understanding and solving the root cause.

SELF-TEST

1 What are the common objections to first improving the processes?

2 What counter arguments would you bring in?

3 Describe how a project manager views the process versus automation first question.

4 Describe how a business manager views the process versus automation first question.

5 Describe how an IT manager views the process versus automation first question.

CHAPTER 7

WHAT ARE THE TECHNOLOGY COMPONENTS OF BPM?

OVERVIEW

While technology can and will add significant benefit to a BPM implementation it is important to clearly understand what exactly BPM technology is and the various components. The nine components will be discussed together with how they fit into an implementation.

OVERALL LEARNING OUTCOME

By the end of this chapter you will be able to:

- Describe what components are included within a Business Process Management System (BPMS)
- Understand the three major BPM enablers and their individual components
- Understand which components may be required in your particular BPM implementation
- Articulate potential future technology components and features
- Describe a brief overview of the technology standards applicable to BPM.

It has been stated several times previously that BPM is not all about technology and while this is true there are two critical aspects to consider:

1. The functionality available from technology has grown enormously over the last decade and has huge potential for organizations.

2. The expectations of customers, employees and business partners has also grown and shifted enormously.

> **Technology can transform key business processes out of the old value chain and into new, dynamic, *value networks*.[1] The old value chain started with the purchasing of raw materials and then moved to the production of goods and services, their distribution, marketing, sales and after sales service. The new *value networks* reshuffle the sequence so that customers, distributors and partners are involved more as the business integrates into a flexible, faster moving customer driven extended network of online partners.**
>
> **(Chaffey and Smith, 2008)**

Without the support of technology, meeting these additional expectations and needs of value networks will be impossible.

Technology in the BPM world is often referred to as a BPMS—Business Process Management System.

It is important for management and BPMers to clearly understand the various components of a BPMS and the potential future components. Figure 7.1 shows the nine components that typically comprise a BPMS.

We have grouped them into three categories and called them BPM enablers, namely: modeling and design; execution and tracking; and performance management. Each enabler will now be described as well as their components, how they can assist your organization and where appropriate some thoughts on future features.

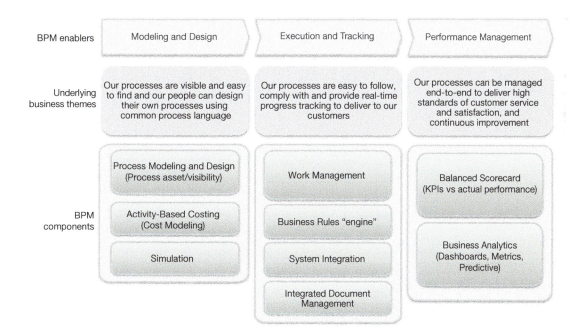

Figure 7.1 BPM technology components

Note: we considered including examples of the vendors and products in each of the nine components, however, decided against it. BPMS offerings are changing rapidly as consolidation continues in the marketplace and vendors introduce new products and product features. If this information is important to you then there are various research organizations that provide the information of vendors, the products offered and rank them according to specific criteria.

MODELING AND DESIGN

This enabler provides the ability to graphically depict business processes and store them in a central repository to provide the business with the ability to create a process asset. For more information on the purpose and benefits of a process asset refer to Chapters 13 and 14. This component will also allow for the determination and capture of the costs associated with the particular process and to simulate various assumption-based current or future process scenarios.

Process modeling and design

This is the component where an organization can model its processes and sub-processes. While this does not require a BPM technology tool, as it could be completed using word processors with simple graphical capabilities (or pencil and paper), it will just take longer, be far less flexible and will not provide you with the opportunity of building a process asset. A technology-based modeling tool will be significantly more efficient and effective. The tools available range from unsophisticated tools that record a process in a simple format, with no or few links to other processes, to tools that are extremely sophisticated, linking processes, sub-processes, an overview of an organization, high-level value chains and the re-use of sub-processes, all on server-based central repository technology. It is this latter toolset that enables the building of your process asset.

The main benefits are:

- the ability for multiple modelers to use and modify models at any one time in any geographical location, resulting in more consistency, less delays and lower costs. Some vendors provide a social media function that allows live chat between process analysts who are working on the same or related processes;
- the ability to manage the process model, e.g., validate its correctness, up-to-date status and effectiveness, resulting in better quality and more results;
- the ability to publish process models (create visibility) so that people can refer to them and the related information (e.g., current templates for letters, web pages, application forms), resulting in more people using the process models, better quality and lower costs;
- as stated multiple times, the ability to build a process asset for the organization.

Figure 7.2 illustrates a flight-booking workflow for an imaginary travel agency in Business Process Modeling Notation (BPMN). As a business-level asset, it should be easily understood by the business, in fact, this is a requirement of any good process model; technical details should be completely absent at this level.

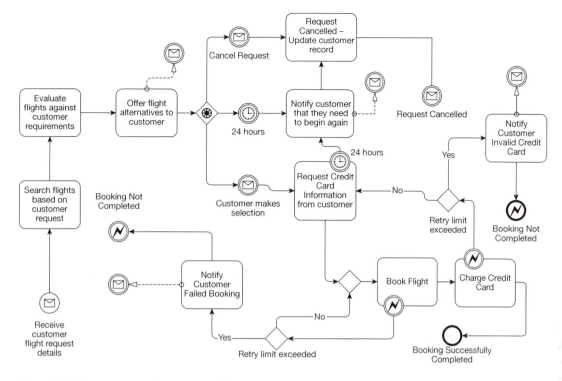

Figure 7.2 Fictitious travel agency workflow

Eventually, this process flow will be translated into a more detailed, executable form for technical analysis and verification by business analysts and architects. Finally, it will evolve into code artifacts that can be deployed to application servers. Some BPMS tools allow an automatic conversion from the process model to execution language. However, care needs to be taken with this expectation, as the process models will often need detailed additional work by skilled resources, and may, in the process, lose their simplicity and usefulness for the business.

This lifecycle management of business processing—from business modeling to code—is what makes BPMN such a powerful technique for communicating what the business needs into what IT systems can deliver to satisfy this need.

Activity-based costing (ABC)

This represents an important add-on tool for existing cost accounting systems. ABC makes the success of BPM projects measurable, and creates transparency in the understanding and, therefore, potential control of process costs. It is the tool to help secure strategic organizational decisions on the cost side and to achieve long-term cost reduction. The ability to generate and utilize competitive advantages requires knowledge of the "right" costs. It can answer questions such as: How much do your critical processes cost? How should you price your products? How many employees do you need to run your business? In which locations do you need them? Which locations are your most efficient?

The recent rise of services-based processes requires that the costs of processes are well understood.

The main benefits are the ability to:

- understand cost components of processes, resulting in prices and costs being more aligned;

- compare various processes and identify areas for improvement, resulting in lower costs.

Simulation

This is where an organization wishes to simulate the viability of its processes to identify process weak points and resource bottlenecks. This is where you determine whether your process can be executed in the way you expect. Based on the simulated process key performance indicators specified (assumptions for the scenario), you can evaluate different alternatives and perform realistic benchmarking prior to making any cost-intensive process changes within the organization.

The main benefits are the ability to:

- determine bottlenecks in the process and dependencies of processes and resources, resulting in better results and lower costs;

- have the right number and skilled staff in the right places;

- compare various processes on the basis of their efficiency and speed and share best practices, resulting in lower costs and better results;

- validate an improved process and test it against various scenarios;

- reduce implementation costs and assist more efficient processes.

EXECUTION AND TRACKING

This BPM enabler provides the ability of executing and tracking your work within the business. Traditionally described as workflow (we have described it as work management), it also provides for the integration with legacy systems and electronic document management.

Work management

The common term used for work management is a workflow system, which describes the automation of internal business operations, tasks and transactions that simplify and streamline current business processes. The work management engine is the software component that executes transactions or events. In order to execute processes, the organization must first model its processes either in the process modeling tool provided by the work management provider, or in a specialized process modeling tool.

The main benefits are the ability:

- to automate work that can be standardized, resulting in decreasing cost and throughput time and increased quality;
- to route work on the basis of dependencies and skills, resulting in reduced throughput time and better quality;
- for staff to focus on more interesting and important work, resulting in more employee satisfaction and better quality.

For the future, identifying the appropriate approach to work management for your organization is very important, especially in challenging economic conditions. Organizations need to be far more agile and work smarter in order to create value for their customers. There are three critical traits of an agile business: rapid decision making and execution; a high-performance culture; and the ability to access the right information at the right time.

BPMS vendors are moving towards providing this agility by the incorporation (some have already achieved this ability) of:

- *Work Sequencing or Guiding*—this provides the ability for a step-by-step guide through the work that must be achieved. It is different from the traditional sequencing associated with workflow. This is particularly useful in organizations that have very large and diverse workforces and complex processes, where training employees in the new or changed processes is logistically difficult. The process "guiding" provides this ability online as the process is executed.
- *Complex Event Processing*—this is relatively new and still needs to be proven. Indeed the concept requires more consensus and clarification.
- *Adaptive/Advanced/Dynamic Case Management*—relates to unstructured processes that require ad-hoc functionality to solve unpredictable events. These processes or way of working defy rigorous definition beforehand because work evolves and unfolds over time, as a worker does their work. Forrester (2011) suggests that "because the need to support change and dynamic work patterns is so critically important to future business success, Dynamic Case Management (DCM) capabilities will become a prerequisite for all BPM vendors within the next five years. BPM suite vendors need to embrace and offer DCM if they want to survive and thrive." Indeed some vendors have already embraced this technology. While some call it the various versions of case management mentioned above, others call it Event Management. Either way, the "processes" are largely, or totally, unable to be process modeled, and therefore improved in the conventional way as they evolve as the management of the work is executed by employees.

Business rules "engine" (BRE)

This provides the kind of agility that the organizations of today need, because it allows an organization to "extract" its business rules from code-based legacy application systems into a business rules engines (BRE). It is part of the drive to give "power" back to the business, rather than relying on the ever present technology bottleneck.

BREs of today provide the ability for a technically competent business analyst, working within the business (not IT), to change business rules very quickly. Rather than the business specifying business rule changes, giving them to the IT department to review and write technical specifications, then quote, schedule, develop and test, a business-based business analyst can complete and test the change, thus providing the business with much increased business agility. This ability to provide instant changes must be kept within the bounds of production promotion policies and management audit needs of the organization, although these policies may require significant review as a result of the new technology ability. The other significant issue that must be addressed is where an end-to-end business process spans multiple business units and a change to a business rule in one business unit may have implications for the other business units. Governance rules will play a significant role in resolving this situation.

The main benefits are the ability:

- to create a business rules repository that allows for your business rules to be visible and reviewed on a periodic basis to ensure their continued applicability for the business;

- to automate more work, resulting in improved quality and reducing costs and throughput time;

- to test and manage the business rules prior to releasing any changes, resulting in better quality and reduced costs;

- for the business to define, monitor and manage the business rules as it doesn't have to rely on IT, resulting in more effective, manageable and agile processes.

As stated above, the process of automating business policies, procedures and business logic is simply too dynamic to manage effectively as application source code. More formally, the Business Rules Group defines a business rule as a statement that "defines or constrains some aspect of the business,"[2] a business rule is intended to assert business structure or to control or influence the business's behavior.

A rules engine evaluates and executes these rules, which are then expressed as if-then statements. A rule is composed of two parts, a condition and an action: When the condition is met, the action is executed. The *if* portion contains conditions (such as payment > \$100), and the *then* portion contains actions (such as "offer discount of 10%"). The power of business rules expressed in this way lies in their ability both to separate business knowledge from its implementation logic and to be altered without modifying the underlying source code.

While the example above is simple (payment > \$100; offer 10 percent discount), where BRE's become very powerful is in the re-sequencing of a business rule, for example the price an insurance company may wish to charge a customer for life insurance may change depending upon the sequence of the questions asked:

From	To
1. Is the customer over 50 years old?	1. Does the customer have a history of heart disease in the family?
2. Does the customer have a history of heart disease in the family?	2. Does the customer skydive?
3. Does the customer skydive?	3. Does the customer scuba dive?
4. Does the customer scuba dive?	4. Is the customer over 50 years of age?

Furthermore, open standards are emerging around the Application Programming Interfaces (APIs) for accessing and executing business rules across vendors. For example, for the Java platform, the specification for the Java Rule Engine API (JSR 94) defines a Java runtime API for rule engines by providing a simple API to access a rule engine. These standards are making it easier to integrate rules engines into other applications.

System integration

This provides the interface layer between the process models within the work management component and the legacy applications of the organization. System integration is a significant component and, unless addressed early within a project, it has the potential to cause a project to fail. We will address this aspect in Chapter 24, when we discuss the potential gates a project must go through.

The main benefits are the ability to:

- implement BPM automation while keeping the existing system, resulting in substantially more benefits with limited costs;

- reduce redundancy and inconsistencies of data, resulting in reduced costs and improved quality;

- make changes more quickly than can be completed via the traditional legacy systems approach, resulting in more agility and substantial lower costs.

Integrated document management

Most processes, certainly in the financial services sector, are accompanied by some form of paper. Hence, if an automated BPM solution is implemented without an accompanying integrated document management system, the organization risks making its processes extremely fast, and then having to wait for the physical paperwork to catch up. Clearly it is much better, from a process perspective, to have scanned images of the paperwork available on an "as required" basis by a process. Such an integrated solution will allow straight through processing thus enabling processing without any manual intervention.

The main benefits are:

- lower costs and better quality in processing documents;
- documents are electronically available, so work can be completed from an electronic version, increasing throughput significantly (no waiting for the paper to arrive);
- retrieval and tracking of documents can be completed more easily, resulting in lower costs and faster throughput times.

PERFORMANCE MANAGEMENT

This is where you manage your organization via your end-to-end business processes. It is where performance targets are established for the processes. Performance management will provide the ability to move from reactive to proactive and, via business analytics, move to a predictive state—this is where huge business benefits can be reaped accompanied by improved decision making. For example, using trends analysis on social media to predict expected revenue for transient products or services, such as souvenirs for one-off events. It also provides, linked with process governance, the ability to deliver continuous process improvement.

Balanced scorecard (BSC)

This provides the ability to establish various measures within the organization—measures such as key performance indicators (KPIs) or other critical measures for the measurement of processes. It can be used not only for the establishment of the quantitative measures, but also for the determination of what parts of the business processes to measure and subsequently report. These can then be linked to the strategic objectives of the organization. BSC will provide the platform for the business analytics component described below. For example, measures can be established for the expected processing costs and timeframes for the execution of processes. These targets can then be compared to the actual costs and timeframes achieved within the business analytics component.

The main benefits are the ability to:

- link processes and their outcome to objectives of the organization, resulting in better results and lower costs;
- monitor the contribution to the organization objectives, resulting in better results and lower costs;
- modify objectives and determine their impact on the processes, resulting in more agility of the processes and the organization as a whole.

Business analytics

Sometimes referred to as business intelligence, it is the collection and examination of performance-related process information and is an essential prerequisite for successfully implementing and evaluating measures for the continuous optimization of business processes.

If you are not measuring it, you are not managing or optimizing it.

Business analytics provides the actual performance measures that can be compared to the targets established within the balanced scorecard component and presents it in the form of dashboards, inquiries, reporting. It automatically identifies performance data from organization processes, especially those that span systems, and thus makes it possible to analyze them. This information can be gathered from the various software application systems within the organization, not just the work management component.

Business analytics provides information that helps to uncover weaknesses in process handling and to optimize processing throughput times. It can provide measures from speed, cost, quality and quantity perspectives. It acts as an early warning system by providing not only historical information but also predictive information for the monitoring of business processes.

The main benefits are the ability to:

- monitor processes in real time (or near real time) and drill down into problem areas, resulting in less problems and lower costs;
- forecast delays and service level agreements (SLAs) that cannot be met, thus allowing for proactive action resulting in better quality;
- benchmark the processes against competitors and industry standards, resulting in better results;
- optimize employee team size and structures by location;
- provide transparency of data across the organization.

There are many products on the market that address business analytics and at their core they all typically provide similar features, including:

- A Web-based interface for data access dashboards; interactive reporting; visualization; analysis; and predictive analytics.
- Reporting capabilities that output to various common formats such as HTML, Excel, PDF and so forth.
- Interactive dashboards that track key performance indicators in a highly graphical, interactive visual interface. These dashboards typically allow drill-down into data, navigation across datasets, data filters, graphical user interface (GUI) customization through drag-and-drop, and integration with external applications such as Google Maps.

For example, a dashboard is shown in Figure 7.3.

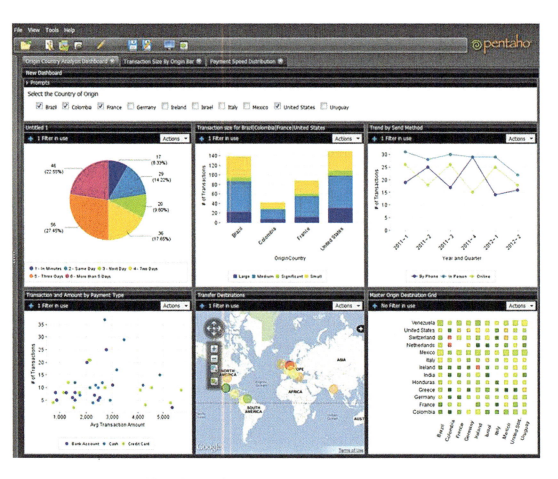

Figure 7.3 Interactive dashboard example

Source: Pentaho® (www.pentaho.com).

BPMS systems are moving towards more sophisticated data mining and analysis which will provide trend analysis, proactive alerts to problems and recommend solutions and/or predictively solve the problems for you before they become an issue.

In looking at the future additional components, or inclusions to the existing components, we would add two additional aspects:

- *Mobile BPM*. While many vendors would claim to have this aspect covered, there are still some issues such as missing standards and security, especially around authentication, that must be addressed in more detail.

- *Social BPM*. Developer ingenuity and business demand will no doubt lead to applications that are Twitter-like and address collaboration and/or enterprise microblogging.

TECHNOLOGY STANDARDS

Modeling and design

Several important open standards are emerging around process modeling, and they are gaining increasing and widespread support amongst the major BPM suite vendors such as IBM and Oracle.

In terms of having a unified visual notation for representing process workflows, Business Process Modeling Notation (BPMN) was developed in 2004 by the Object Management Group (OMG; http://www.bpmn.org/) that manage the specification. The latest version, BPMN2.0 was released in August 2009. BPMN provides businesses with the capability of understanding their internal business processes in a graphical notation and provides organizations with the ability to communicate these processes in a standard way. Concepts such as parallel processing, branching, sub-flows, iteration, roles and activities can all be modeled using this notation, allowing an organization to capture their workflows at the business level, understandable to everyone within the organization and without technical complexity.

Execution and tracking

Work management toolsets that support BPMN typically also provide the ability to transform a sufficiently detailed BPMN diagram into an executable form (usually with the addition of technical settings that are not part of BPMN but represented within the toolset). In order to do this in a vendor-independent way, another standard emerged and was ratified by OASIS[3] around 2003, for executable business process modeling, not surprisingly called Business Process Execution Language or BPEL. This standard actually emerged from efforts to standardize code execution using Web Services and Service Oriented Architecture by vendors such as IBM, Microsoft, SAP and Siebel (to name a few key players). More formally defined as WS-BPEL it creates executable processes using the underlying building block of a Web Service (WS).

A quick diversion is warranted at this point in our discussion to better understand the role of Web Services within system integration. The W3C (the body that manages the Web Services specification) defines a "Web service" as "a software system designed to support interoperable machine-to-machine interaction over a network." It has an interface described in a machine-processable format (specifically Web Services Description Language, known by the acronym WSDL). Other systems interact with the Web service in a manner prescribed by its service contract, typically using SOAP messages and HTTP as the transport protocol, with an XML serialization in conjunction with other Web-related standards.

Web Services essentially standardize how systems talk to each other. They allow any IT system, even legacy systems, to be integrated into a unified communication network, with open standards for message exchange. Using Web Services, a business process is able to invoke IT system functions as a "choreographed" sequence of Web Service calls. In this way, BPEL provides a language for the specification of executable business processes. In effect, it extends the Web Services interaction model and enables it to support business transactions. WS-BPEL defines an interoperable integration model that should help the expansion of automated process integration both within and between organizations.

More advanced modeling tools that support BPMN and BPEL also support simulation. This simulation capability allows organizations to perform "what if" analysis around processes and the human resources they leverage and the physical resources they consume as they execute. Bottlenecks can be identified at an early stage before serious code development begins, potentially with huge savings to the business.

By modeling the "as is" (or current state process) using tools that support the standards above, an organization is able to better understand how they do business today and then decide where they want to go tomorrow through business transformation targeting redesigned or innovated processes. These standards allow portability of design across vendors and support formal documentation of both modeling and design for processes.

Beyond modeling, as previously mentioned, advanced BREs empower non-technical staff with the ability to define, modify and execute business rules without technical intervention. Standardization in this area is still in its infancy; nevertheless the OMG released a specification Semantics of Business Vocabulary and Business Rules (SBVR) in 2008 which has yet to be widely adopted.

Performance management

Most of the major vendors provide performance monitoring tools but few open standards exist yet. However, it is a rapidly growing market. Business Analytics Worldwide business intelligence (BI) platform, analytic applications and performance management (PM) software revenue reached $12.2 billion in 2011, a 16.4 percent increase from 2010 revenue of $10.5 billion, according to Gartner, Inc. The BI, analytics and PM software market was the second-fastest growing sector in the overall worldwide enterprise software market in 2011. Leading vendors in this space include SAP, IBM and Microsoft.

BPM INSIGHT

These nine BPMS components are our suggestions of what automation tools are desirable within an automated BPM solution in a BPM-mature organization. This does not, however, mean that all nine components must be present for a program/project to be successful. An organization may choose the components needed to meet its needs at the time. Clearly, the more components used, the more likely it is that an implementation will achieve higher business benefits. Also, to gain access to all nine components may mean purchasing them from more than one vendor. Very few vendors adequately cover all nine components.

However, "a tool is only a tool"! Unless the tool is used effectively, it will not solve a business problem. It is like purchasing a saxophone—unless the person knows how to play the instrument and then how to play with "heart and soul," the outcome will not be pleasant for anyone!

SUMMARY

A BPMS comprises nine components which we have grouped into three BPM enablers, namely:

- Modeling and design, which includes: process modeling and design; activity-based costing; and process simulation.
- Execution and tracking, which comprises: work management; business rules engine; system integration; and integrated document management.
- Performance management, comprising: balanced scorecard; and business analytics.

Where possible we have included suggestions of future features to be delivered within these components by vendors.

Technical standards also provide useful information that should be considered as part of any toolset purchase and execution.

SELF-TEST

1 Describe each of the BPM enablers and their components.
2 Describe how each enabler would benefit your business and when it is not appropriate to use them.
3 Describe how each component fits together.
4 Provide a brief description of each of the technical standards currently in the marketplace.

CHAPTER 8

SHOULD WE BE CUSTOMER-CENTRIC?

OVERVIEW

The majority of the literature says that we should be customer-centric. Is that true or is there another viewpoint? If there is another viewpoint, then how do we address it and take it into account?

OVERALL LEARNING OUTCOME

By the end of this chapter you will be able to:

• Understand the necessary balance between a customer-centric view and an employee-centric view, from a process perspective

• Articulate the difference between environmental (hygiene) factors and motivational factors and the role they play in employee satisfaction.

Taking a customer-centric approach to process design is considered by many to be sacrosanct. However, should we "really" be customer-centric when we are improving or developing our business processes?

By far the majority, if not all, of the literature we read about BPM promotes the tenet that we *must* be customer-centric. For example, the "outside-in" point of view suggests that we must always place the customer at the center of everything we do. Lean also suggests that the customer must be placed first—"voice of the customer."

Figure 8.1 shows this approach with our clients/customers as the center of the universe. Many organizations will next place an emphasis on the products and services they sell, followed by "Our People" or employees. The figure also shows that the organization's business processes must deliver this service and be supported by the creation or enhancement of an appropriate culture.

Figure 8.1
Customer-centric:
voice of the customer

Even though there is this huge emphasis on customer-centric service, many BPM and business teams do not understand that there is a clear difference between the delivery of customer "service" and an outcome of the customer being "satisfied" (see Figure 8.2).

You can service a customer exceptionally well and yet the customer can still be dissatisfied. We remember personally being "serviced" exceptionally well (at least in its opinion) by a high profile computer company and yet we did not buy one of their laptops again because of the deep dissatisfaction of the way we were serviced.

CASE STUDY

A service organization had five teams providing service to a client. All of the teams were proud that they met all their KPIs and that the dashboards were all green.

However, when interviewed, the client indicated that they were very unhappy with the overall service.

Message: It is critical to think from a customer point of view. The internal employee teams, and their KPIs, must reflect the "real" customer experience.

The general consensus is that it is about 17 times more expensive to gain a new customer than keep an existing one, and yet organizations continually invest significantly in trying to create a "wow" factor, to gain new customers, rather than investing in eliminating the things that annoy the customers (the irritation zone), thus avoiding losing existing customers. The "line of absolute indifference" shown in Figure 8.2 suggests that there is a zone where

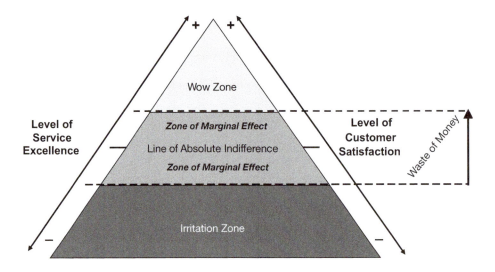

Figure 8.2 Customer levels of service and satisfaction

spending the organization's money on improving service and satisfaction will actually not add any (or little) value to the customer relationship. We will discuss this concept again in more detail in Chapter 16.

If we create business processes that add significantly to the service and satisfaction levels of our customers (let's just call it service from now on), can these services be delivered to a high standard with dissatisfied or unhappy employees? We would suggest not. Operationally average processes will often yield a high level of service to customers if delivered by happy enthusiastic employees; and yet the opposite is not necessarily true.

To deliver both a high level of service and satisfaction, perhaps we should take a different view and place our employees (our people) at the center of our process considerations. After all, operationally average processes plus happy enthusiastic people will most likely equal happy customers. Figure 8.3 shows our people (employees) at the center, with customers next followed by our products and services.

When looking at placing your employees at the center, we are not just speaking about assisting employees to develop their skills and capabilities. It is about engendering the right "attitude" and creating the right environment for them to work in. Employees need to understand and appreciate that their employer and managers care about them. Managers need to empower staff and be servant leaders by supporting, facilitating and coaching. Managers need to be proactive and anticipate potential issues and roadblocks. They should let employees attempt to solve issues themselves and only step in to support and assist when necessary. Remember FAIL stands for First Attempt In Learning.

It is important to note that employees also include partners, such as key suppliers, distributors, contractors or other stakeholders. In the current network economy it is also essential that we adopt a broader view than just the traditional permanent employees of an organization.

Figure 8.3
Employee-centric:
voice of the employee

It is also important to note that the line between customers and employees is blurring, especially with the rise of social media. Customers now have much more access to all the processes of an organization, not just traditional customer care, but also customer data management. For example, customers maintaining their own information online so it is up to date all the time; customer self-service; and for some companies even marketing activities through crowd sourcing, opinion polls and social media.

KEY POINT

Remember, when looking at an organization's culture:

> "Culture is caught, not taught."

If the senior executives and management do not "live" the culture they wish to have, do not be surprised when you do not get the culture you want.

Culture WILL be caught from these senior executives and managers, so behavior and attitude matter, and matter a lot.

So should we be customer-centric or employee-centric?

The reality is we need to be both. Without customers there is no business and therefore no employees. Without employees there is no business and therefore no customers and no employees.

So customers and employees are the Ying and the Yang of business as shown in Figure 8.4. If you get *both* right, supported by a customer- and employee-focused culture and optimized business processes, then your organization will have created a competitive advantage.

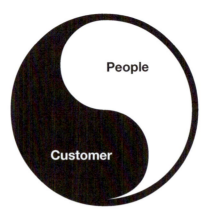

Figure 8.4 To be the best is a balance

How can the organization go about achieving this balance, from a business process perspective?

There are number of suggested strategies that are discussed in more detail in Chapter 17 (Innovate phase). These include: when redesigning business processes always consider them from a customer and employee perspective. Either start the process redesign, at a high level, from the customer perspective; or have several simulations of the proposed new process from both the customer and employee viewpoint. For example:

- *Imagine everyone on the process redesign workshop is a customer.* How efficient and effective is the new process for you? Would you, as the customer, be satisfied that you have received an acceptable level of service and satisfaction from the organization? Maybe ask some customers and/or business partners to attend the process redesign workshop to gain their perspective.

- *Imagine everyone in the process redesign workshop is an employee* (which they probably are). What are the key pain points and frustrations of the existing process and what are the root causes of these? Have these pain points and frustrations been overcome in the new process? How efficient and effective is the new process for you? Ask additional employees to attend who were not involved in the original redesign process.

As the focus of this book is on how to implement BPM, many readers will equate this with the improvement or optimization of business processes. However we have seen that employees, our people, matter. So how do you motivate employees to provide a high level of customer service and satisfaction?

Many organizations speak of "our people are our greatest asset" and yet do not spend anywhere near enough time developing and caring for them.

Let's explore how we should be caring for our greatest asset. Many of the points are going to sound obvious. Unfortunately, while the obvious seems obvious, many of us do not implement it. Managers are often promoted as a result of their ability to solve problems

A process redesign workshop was being conducted for a university enrollment process. The workshop was extremely difficult to facilitate because the participants were arguing with each other and not making any progress.

The facilitator changed the approach and asked all participants to outline the new process, at a high level, from the prospective new student's perspective. The question was asked: "If you were a prospective new student making an application to enroll in a course, what would you want from this process and the university?"

Once this was outlined, at a high level, the workshop became focused and both achieved the design of the new process and satisfied the needs of prospective new students.

Message: Always consider processes from various perspectives: customers, business partners, suppliers, employees, risk, audit, compliance, and so on.

(fighting fires). When managers get really busy fighting these fires the first thing to suffer is the "caring" for their staff. Caring takes time and this is difficult for time-starved managers.

In 1959 Frederick Herzberg proposed the Motivation-Hygiene Theory of job satisfaction. While this was a very long time ago, it is absolutely relevant today. He suggested that people were influenced by two sets of factors:

- motivation factors; and
- hygiene factors.

Figure 8.5 shows the typical components of each factor.

You can see that there are certain factors in the workplace that cause job satisfaction, while a separate set of factors cause job dissatisfaction.

Simply stated:

- If you wish to motivate employees and have them continuously add value to your business and customers, then management needs to create an environment that moves employees towards satisfaction. To enable this you need to focus on the motivation factors outlined in Figure 8.5.
- However, unless the hygiene factors are taken care of, you will cause employee dissatisfaction. No matter how hard management works on the motivation factors, there will never be a movement towards satisfaction, unless the hygiene factors are "neutralized."

Essentially, hygiene factors need to be satisfied to ensure an employee is not dissatisfied. Motivation factors are needed to motivate an employee to deliver a higher level of performance.

Many regard the hygiene factors as maintenance activities that are simply necessary to avoid dissatisfaction, and that is true. Of themselves, they will not move employees towards satisfaction.

Environmental (Hygiene)
- Pay and Benefits
- Organization Policy and Administration
- Relationships with Peers/Boss
- Supervision
- Status
- Job Security
- Working Conditions
- Personal Life

Nature of Work (Motivator)
- Achievement/Challenging Work
- Recognition
- Work Itself
- Responsibility
- Promotion
- Growth

Figure 8.5 Employee motivation and satisfaction

Some years ago one of the authors was a newly appointed number two in the IT area of a large insurance organization. The cultural survey of the entire organization revealed that IT ranked very low on the employee satisfaction index. I was asked by the head of the department (the CIO) to investigate why and what we could do to remedy the situation.

After interviewing many employees and running focus groups (23 percent of all IT staff were involved), it became obvious that the hygiene factors were the first things that needed to be addressed. All the hygiene factors were actually comparatively simple things for management to remedy, it was just that employee care had no current focus and there was no mechanism for employees to voice their issues.

As you would expect, the more difficult aspects to remedy related to the motivation factors. However, once these motivational factors had been identified, work could begin to determine the actions required and then implement them.

Message: The key was the involvement of the employees in this process. Once employees were involved, they felt they had a level of control and ownership. Mechanisms for continual involvement then need to be established.

CASE STUDY

You might also suggest that the same factors are applicable for customers.

Management must work on the hygiene factors to neutralize and avoid employee dissatisfaction. However, it is the motivation factors that require attention to move towards employee satisfaction and a high performance environment.

While Herzberg's theory has its detractors, the basic concepts are valid and make common sense. When you combine this theory with Expectancy Theory of Victor Vroom, it creates a powerful means of providing motivational factors for employees and therefore higher productivity for the organization.

Satisfying and motivating employees is not a one-time event. It requires continuous management attention and a process to ensure it is achieved.

SUMMARY

- It is the balancing of customer-centric and employee-centric views that provide a powerful combination. Customers and people (employees) are the Ying and the Yang of business.

- There is a significant difference between a customer being serviced well by your business processes, and them being satisfied. You need to clearly understand the difference to optimize your process design.

- Culture also provides an essential component to customer and employee satisfaction. Remember—*culture is caught, not taught.*

- It is the combination of hygiene and motivational factors that provide the right environment for employees. You will need to address both.

SELF-TEST

1 Why is customer-centricity alone not enough?

2 Why is employee-centricity alone not enough?

3 Describe the difference between employee satisfaction and service.

4. Describe Herzberg's Motivation-Hygiene Theory.

5 How do the two components of this theory work together?

CHAPTER 9

WHY IS DETERMINING BPM FOUNDATIONS A CRITICAL FIRST STEP?

OVERVIEW

This chapter will define and describe what is meant by BPM Foundations and why it requires BPM Enablement to be effective. When Foundations and Enablement are required will also be discussed, particularly in relation to the various types of BPM activities as well as the benefits of addressing the Foundations before you start or early in the BPM journey.

The purpose of this chapter is to provide a brief overview of the Foundations and Enablement elements of BPM. Chapters 13 and 14 will provide further details of the components; how to build them; which are important to have in place before you start BPM; and examples and case studies.

OVERALL LEARNING OUTCOME

By the end of this chapter you will be able to:
- Define BPM Foundations and BPM Enablement and their components
- Understand how they fit into the BPM House
- Understand which type of BPM activity they relate to
- Understand the benefits of "laying" Foundations early.

In Chapter 1 a definition and explanation of BPM was provided and the concept of the BPM House was introduced, as shown in Figure 9.1. The two base components at the bottom of the figure are the BPM Foundations and BPM Enablement.

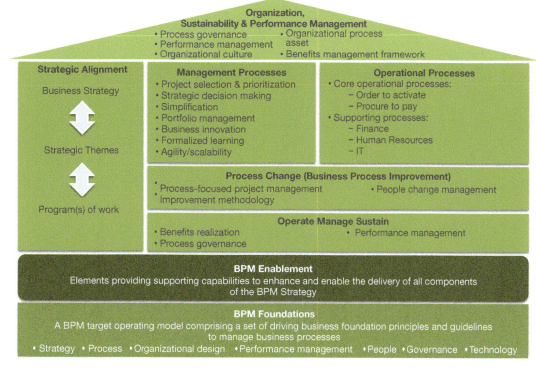
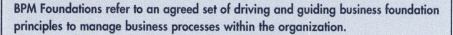

Figure 9.1 BPM House: components of BPM

This set of foundation principles is usually grouped together and referred to as a BPM business operating model or a target operating model if the organization is establishing an aspirational future state. It is referred to generically in this book as a target operating model or TOM. Chapter 13 will examine the BPM Foundations elements in detail and provide a detailed case study.

The BPM Enablement elements will be examined in detail in Chapter 14.

Collectively these are the "foundations" upon which the BPM House is built. As with any house the more solid the foundations the more robust the house is. When foundations are solid and broad they enable substantial future modifications to the house. There is no use in building foundations for a one story dwelling if you think there is even a remote possibility that future extensions to the house may be necessary to accommodate additional levels.

In Chapter 3 the four types of BPM activities were described. If the BPM activity is a simple low impact BPM project or even a high impact BPM project driven from the bottom up (refer to Chapter 5) there may be no or little need for additional effort on BPM Foundations.

BPM INSIGHT

If the BPM activity is a large-scale BPM program or enterprise-wide business transformation program, with a substantial process focus, then the need for Foundations is critical.

For the rest of this chapter only the type of BPM activities referred to as a large-scale BPM program or enterprise-wide business transformation program will be discussed.

How much time, money and effort should be exerted upon these BPM Foundations before "real" BPM activities are commenced? This is a critical challenge for most organizations—getting the balance right is essential.

Many organizations either believe or are led to believe by BPM consultants that the Foundations must be solid and *complete* before *any* BPM activities are commenced. There have been organizations that have spent up to a year and millions of dollars laying these Foundations without delivering any tangible business benefits. Yet other organizations start with no Foundations and wonder why there is no or little agreement or buy-in from senior executives; little consistency once projects have been completed; and no ongoing legacy from which to manage the process performance of the organization.

KEY POINT

The establishment of basic Foundations need not take months or cost a large amount of money if approached in a pragmatic way.

Once basic Foundations have been established and agreed, BPM activities should commence and start yielding value to the business. If the basic Foundations have been established in an appropriate way, each subsequent BPM activity will add more value to the Foundations and they will grow and become more robust over time while delivering business value.

It is this balance that is critical. While there are basic concepts that work in most situations, they need to be tailored for each organization's business and process maturity, ensuring that they are fit-for-purpose.

BPM FOUNDATIONS

As stated earlier, BPM Foundations refer to an agreed set of driving and guiding business foundation principles to manage business processes within the organization. This is usually grouped together and referred to as a BPM business operating model or a target operating model if the organization is establishing an aspirational future state.

BPM Foundations will:

- establish and agree the components and business rules associated with the target operating model;
- ensure there is a clear and transparent linkage between the organization's strategy and the execution of the BPM activities to support it;
- agree the approach—top-down or bottom-up—as discussed in Chapter 5. It would be expected that the Foundations phase is required in the top-down approach, and may be required in the bottom-up approach;
- ensure that significant planning is completed to identify the targeted business areas for BPM activities and sequencing of programs/projects to deliver the desired business benefits.

BPM ENABLEMENT

As stated earlier, BPM Enablement refers to the provision of the key architectures and detailed elements that must be provided to support and enable business capabilities to enhance the successful delivery of all components of the BPM strategy.

BPM Enablement will:

- define and perhaps result in the initial establishment of the organization process architecture. A critical aspect of this will be the creation of a "process asset";
- create and document the benefits management framework;
- complete the agreement and documentation of the target operating model. From a process perspective, the TOM consists of seven core components that synchronously work together to enable BPM. The seven core components will be described in detail in the Enablement phase (Chapter 14) and include:
  - o the organization's strategy and linkage to the current BPM activities
  - o process governance, with clearly defined roles and responsibilities
  - o organization design and governance supporting the strategy, process governance and performance management framework
  - o performance management framework
  - o people and cultural aspects supporting all components of the TOM
  - o process architecture
  - o technology required to support all of the TOM components.

KEY POINT

A target operating model will provide stability to a BPM activity by agreeing a set of "rules" from which to launch programs and projects.

It is important to ensure that the TOM is not totally internally focused and takes into account the appropriate external aspects:

- provide a list of activities and timetable for the establishment and implementation of BPM Enablement;
- provide the BPM program and management maintenance and enhancement framework.

BPM INSIGHT

BPM Foundations and Enablement may seem like an overwhelming activity, however as mentioned previously, if completed in a pragmatic way it need not be overwhelming. There are two things to keep in mind:

- BPM Foundations and Enablement must be fit-for-purpose matching the organization's process and business maturity and not try to address all of the problems within the organization
- Future BPM activities will build on the Enablement components as they are executed, for example, the process asset.

BPM FOUNDATIONS AND ENABLEMENT BENEFITS

BPM Foundations and Enablement are critical if the BPM activity is a large-scale BPM program or enterprise-wide business transformation program, with a substantial process focus.

KEY POINT

If you are experiencing internal challenges gaining agreement that the completion of the BPM Foundations and Enablement is necessary, this only highlights the necessity that they are essential. The executive team must agree on the foundation principles upon which BPM activities will be executed or it will result in even bigger conflicts and frustrations later as the programs and projects are undertaken.

Once it is determined that it is essential to address these aspects up front, then the benefits can include:

- having a clear, transparent and agreed set of foundations, together with the underlying business drivers, will assist in ensuring all aspects of a target operating model are taken into consideration;

- the ability of ensuring that there is a clear and unequivocal link between the organization strategy and the BPM programs/projects being executed;

- the target operating model will provide the aspirational state that the business wishes to operate in. The TOM is the target of what the organization will look and operate like once the business transformation and/or BPM program has been complete. Understanding this is critical because there may be several alternative ways to achieving the TOM. Each alternative approach will need to be evaluated and a best route selected;

- the BPM Foundations will provide guidelines as to how the business manages itself, from a process perspective, in the future. How performance management and measurement, governance, continuous improvement and process enhancements will be managed and achieved;

- BPM is a journey that will take time to deliver. It includes enhancing the organization's business capability and maturity. Creating BPM Foundations up-front will ensure that the organization has clarity as to the business issues that need to be addressed within the BPM program and projects;

- the opportunity of building a "process asset" as projects are completed (the benefits accruing from a process asset are described in Chapter 14). The process asset will be of little use unless it is built in a consistent and structured manner; this is provided by the process architecture and a process asset technology tool;

- one of the biggest areas of weakness in most organizations is the inability to realize business benefits from projects. The benefits management framework will provide the mechanism for tracking and managing the realization of project benefits. Among other things it will establish the roles and responsibilities for benefits realization;

- most BPM-led organization transformations and/or programs evolve over the course of execution. Understanding the Foundations will mean that only the relevant and important aspects are taken into consideration, resulting in maximum organizational flexibility and agility.

SUMMARY

- BPM Foundations refer to an agreed set of driving and guiding business foundation principles to manage business processes within the organization.

- BPM Enablement refers to the provision of the key architectures and detailed elements that must be provided to support and enable business capabilities to enhance the successful delivery of all components of the BPM strategy.

- If the BPM activity is a large-scale BPM program or enterprise-wide business transformation program, with a substantial process focus, then the need for Foundations is a critical activity.

- The establishment of basic Foundations need not take months or cost a large amount of money if approached in a pragmatic way.

- The benefits of creating Foundations, in the right circumstances, are many and varied, and should be clearly understood by the senior management team.

SELF-TEST

1 Define the meaning of BPM Foundations and what it will do.

2 Define the meaning of BPM Enablement and what it will do.

3 Describe how these fit into the BPM House.

4 For what type of BPM activity is the establishment of BPM Foundations and Enablement important?

5 Create a list of benefits of these phases.

CHAPTER 10

WHY DO YOU NEED A STRUCTURED APPROACH TO IMPLEMENTING BPM?

OVERVIEW

Improving business processes seems a very logical thing to do, however, most projects fail to apply a "fit-for-purpose" structured approach, resulting in either outright project failure or suboptimal results. For organizations that do adopt a structured approach, the approach adopted only relates to the improvement of operational processes; often does not provide detailed steps for ongoing performance management; and does not cover all the aspects of BPM as defined in the BPM House (Figure 2.1).

OVERALL LEARNING OUTCOME

By the end of this chapter you will be able to:

- Understand the importance of applying a structured approach to implementing process improvement

- Understand that the approach adopted needs to provide more than just a few high level steps and a bunch of suggested tools

- Have an appreciation of the common pitfalls resulting from applying no approach or the wrong approach.

The Iceberg Syndrome discussed in Chapter 2 showed that an organization's *perception* of a BPM program often only relates to what is above the water line at a project level, but the *reality* is that most of the implementation effort is below the water "out of sight." BPM is not just about projects; it is about the vital contribution that processes make in achieving the objectives of the organization, provided that a process-focus permeates every manager and person in the organization. Certainly an initial BPM pilot project(s) is often the way BPM starts within an organization. Once successful there must be a concerted effort to move beyond this initial project(s) to a blending into the business-as-usual environment.

Historically the way that most organizations approached process improvement projects was using the Deming Cycle (Walton, 1986) of Plan, Do, Check and Act. Over time this evolved into the cycle shown in Figure 10.1, which shows the steps a business improvement project would complete, such as:

1. Conduct a review of the areas to be improved, understand the business objectives (business context), collect stakeholder requirements and select the initial processes to be improved.

2. Complete the "As Is" mapping in sufficient detail to understand the process and learn how to improve it.

3. Agree the timeframe for the delivery of the redesigned processes with the business and complete the "To Be" step to redesign the processes.

4. Develop and implement the redesigned processes.

The first three knowledge areas, shown in Figure 10.2, of the 2009 *Guide to the Business Process Management Common Body of Knowledge (BPM CBOK®)* suggest a very similar approach.

Most organizations have historically stopped at the implementation of the redesigned processes thinking that more efficient processes constitute a successful project. In many cases

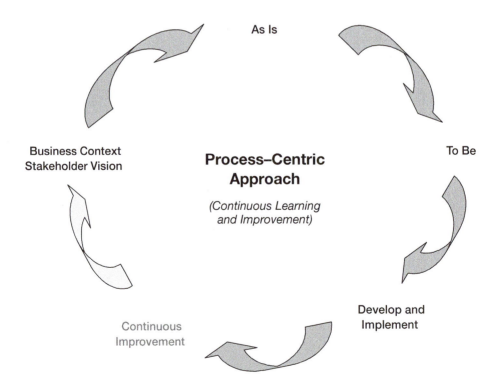

Figure 10.1 Traditional process project approach

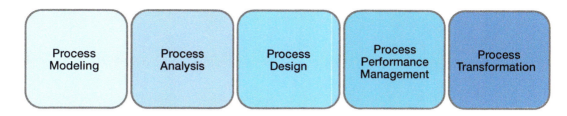

Figure 10.2 ABPMP BPM CBOK®

Source: *2009 Guide to the Business Process Management Common Body of Knowledge (BPM CBOK®).* Developed and published by the Association of Business Process Management Professionals (ABPMP), Version 2.0, Second Release. Reproduced with permission.

this results in another redesign project within the next 18 to 24 months, because the business has changed and the processes have thus become inappropriate.

To overcome this continuous need for new business process improvement projects, organizations establish a continuous process improvement program within the organization to change the processes as the business changes. Process performance management is a critical component of management and a prerequisite to a continuous process improvement program. Many organizations believe that this completes the feedback loop.

One of the key questions in this approach is: "Have you solved the correct problem?" How can you be certain that the way you have redesigned your processes contributes to the organization's strategic vision or intent?

Stace and Dunphy (1996) say that:

strategy is the search for directions which energize the life of an organization; structures provide the social organization needed to facilitate the strategy . . . *Strategy* and *structure* need to be constantly re-examined and realigned to be effective.

The first consideration is therefore to ensure that the organizational strategy and structure support each other. But is that all?

Rummler and Brache (1995), and Harmon (2003) in Figure 10.3 provide an excellent description of an organization's performance levels and performance needs.

Most organizations that wish to improve their business processes start with the middle box, "Process design and implementation." They carry out the "As Is" and "To Be" process modeling, implement the new redesigned process, and wonder why the results do not always meet their expectations, certainly in the medium to long term.

Leo Lewis (1993) stated that "reengineering is not a bed of roses . . . Some statistics say seven out of ten reengineering initiatives fail." McKinsey's found that a majority of companies researched achieved less than 5 percent change due to reengineering (*Newsletter for Organizational Psychologists*, 1995).

How can you redesign processes without knowing what you wish to achieve from the activity—what the new goal(s) of the process will be? Are you trying to improve processing times from five days to two days, or two hours? If it is two hours, the approach to the redesign will be substantially different than with a two-day goal. Are you endeavoring to increase the

Performance Needs

Performance Levels		Goals and Measures	Design and Implementation	Management
	Organization	Organization goals and measures of organizational success	Organization design and implementation	Organization management
	Process	Process goals and measures of process success	Process design and implementation	Process management
	Performance and Measurement	Organizational goals and measures of success	Role design and implementation	People management

Figure 10.3 Performance components

Source: Harmon (2003). Reproduced with permission from Elsevier.

quality of your service offering, even though this could mean an increase in the processing time for some transactions? The approach you take to the redesign process will be totally different depending upon your answer to these questions.

Then you must ask, "How do you know that the process will contribute towards, and add value to, the organization's strategy?" Even if you know the process goals and redesign the processes to meet those goals, will this meet or contribute towards the strategic goals of the organization?

Having linked the organization strategy with the supporting process goals and created the redesigned processes, you must ask, "Who will implement these new processes?" The answer is the people within the organization, perhaps in association with other critical stakeholders, such as business partners. Unless the organization structure, role descriptions, skill sets and reward systems support and are in alignment with the organization direction, you will not be covering all the necessary aspects that an organization needs.

Once all these areas have been addressed, the organization must ensure that there is an ongoing process to "manage" and continuously improve the business processes.

Implementing a BPM project is a multifaceted and complex process that if tackled without a structured approach will either not work or will not meet the expectations of the stakeholders. However, over-applying a methodology or framework will not provide the flexibility required to meet the varying challenges.

What is needed is a practical, comprehensive, structured approach that can be tailored to each organization. The 7FE Project Framework outlined in this book is a proven framework that provides this structured and flexible approach for use in the implementation of BPM projects, programs and process-led organization-wide transformations. The framework has been applied around the world by many organizations for over a decade and covers all of the

Importance of understanding organization strategy

We were asked to review the current processes in the operations area of an organization and to recommend how they should go about an improvement program. There were two options put forward. The first was for incremental process improvement, with no additional automation, and the second was for an automated BPM solution. It was interesting that both options met the designated process goals, which the client had documented. So we asked them to describe their organization strategy for the next three years.

The organization's strategic intent was that it:

will place us substantially ahead of our competition, such that it will be difficult for competitors to match the process and systems service levels able to be consistently achieved. This will form the foundation of our competitive advantage in the near and medium term.

The incremental option would have provided incremental improvement. Only three out of the 25 processes could be redesigned totally, whereas the remaining processes would have only been incrementally improved.

The automated BPM option would have provided substantial innovation and integration with other critical systems, as well as the ability to provide the organization with continuing business agility.

Message: It became obvious for the organization to choose the automated BPM option. Unless the project manager and project business sponsor clearly understand the organization's strategy, and ensure that the project satisfies and adds value to this strategy, then the project runs the risk of "solving the wrong problem."

"reality" of the activities that reside "below the waterline of the iceberg" in a BPM project. The framework consists of ten phases and three *essential* components. Each phase is then broken down into logical steps that, if followed and executed correctly, will ensure the success of your project.

These phases, essentials and steps associated with the framework are common sense. However, as Mark Twain is purported to have once said: "Common sense is most uncommon." In our experience, even though people know these things they rarely execute them well, in a logical sequence or, indeed, at all. The framework groups these various aspects of a BPM project into a logical sequence. However, as stated earlier, a framework or methodology can be as much a millstone as a savior, so it is essential that it is used according to the organization's needs.

Most other BPM methodologies provide all or some of the high level project areas and a number of tools, under each area, that should or could be applied, rather than providing detailed steps and actions (and tools) that should be used as a checklist and guide.

KEY POINT

What makes the 7FE Project Framework different from other BPM methodologies is that it provides a detailed step-by-step guide for organizations, managers and project staff to follow.

The flexibility comes from reviewing each of the suggested steps in detail and determining its appropriateness for the BPM activity, and the organization's culture and level of BPM maturity.

If a step is not appropriate for a particular situation, then it should not be applied. However, each step should be reviewed and non-compliance justified.

TYPICAL COMMON APPROACH PITFALLS

We have listed below a few of the typical commonly experienced pitfalls regarding the use of BPM methodologies:

- **Biggest mistake most large organizations make**

This mistake has been observed time and time again. BPM passionate people inside an organization have been successful in selling the BPM concept to senior management and have been provided with funding and support to commence a large-scale (or not too large-scale) BPM activity. The first thing many of them do is believe that the organization is "special" and "different" from most other organizations. They argue that "existing BPM methodologies or frameworks available in the marketplace [like the 7FE Framework in this book] will not suit 'our' organization and we must spend several months planning and writing/creating a 'fit for purpose' methodology for us." This will significantly delay the delivery of benefits to the business.

KEY POINT

While the creation and writing of a BPM methodology is an intellectually "fun" thing to do (for the BPM "passionates"), it is largely a waste of time and money for the organization. Management want results and, with rare exceptions, organizations are not special and are basically the same.

The BPM team should take a proven BPM framework and start using it. Over time, as the organization and BPM team grow in capability and understanding, the adopted framework, if necessary, can be tailored to the organization's specific needs.

- **Spending too much time on the BPM Foundations before starting to provide business benefits**

The argument here is that, to build a house, you need to lay solid and appropriate foundations. This is difficult to argue against or refute as it makes common sense. However, even though

CASE STUDY

A large global organization established BPM as one of the critical activities it would be implementing over the next several years. BPM had the support of the CEO, Board and executive team.

The BPM team spent many months selecting a BPM System (even though they had no idea what it would be used for yet) and laying what it perceived as the perfect foundations. The business became critical of the senior BPM executive. The response was to change BPM consultants. The new consultant recommended further foundation work particularly the creation of a detailed process architecture. This delayed things even further.

The business became so frustrated that the senior BPM executive was asked to leave the organization and the organization-wide BPM activity became a collection of isolated small projects.

Message: Foundations are necessary, but only in sufficient detail to start the BPM projects. The rest of the foundations and BPM enablement can be developed on the journey.

foundations are essential (we will be discussing this in detail in Chapters 13 and 14), spending too much time on foundations, without delivering any or little benefits to the business, can lose support for the BPM activities.

There is a balance between laying the necessary BPM foundations and enablers required to commence yielding business benefits, and having the "perfect" set of foundations and enablers.

- **Applying a one methodology fits all approach**

When this approach is adopted you are ignoring the fundamental differences between transformation programs, projects and continuous improvement. It's like killing a mosquito with a shotgun (a large system-focused methodology for a small continuous improvement initiative) or keeping an elephant at a distance with a fly-swat (an enterprise-wide transformation program using a Six Sigma approach). The methodology also needs to take into account the process maturity of the organization.

- **Not applying any methodology, only applying common sense**

This "common sense" relies totally upon the experience of the individuals executing the BPM activity. This can often result in forgetting or missing crucial steps, for example, alignment with strategic objectives; benefit identification and realization; and organizational change management. This approach can also result in different team members having different ideas or views to an approach. This ad-hoc approach will therefore require a person to coordinate and reconcile differing viewpoints. The coordinator may become a key bottleneck.

- **Being dogmatic about the methodology**

If this approach is adopted the team will be focused on ensuring that the steps in the methodology are being followed, sometimes blindly, rather than ensuring that the BPM activity will deliver the desired results for the organization.

- **Using only a pure project management methodology, such as PRINCE2 or PMBOK**

This approach can result in project teams being totally focused with meeting the project deadlines and delivering to the defined project scope rather than actually delivering significant and sustainable benefits to the business. Often BPM activities are a journey of discovery and solely following a predefined project scope may limit the success of the project. For example, if additional business benefits/improvements are discovered during the project, these may be ignored and not investigated simply because they are outside "scope" and will impact upon the project delivery timelines.

- **A belief that technology is the first and most important step**

An organization embarks on a BPM activity with the strong belief that an essential first step is to purchase an expensive BPMS from a software vendor. The argument is often that "we can use the process modeling toolset to model our processes, and then it is just a matter of pushing a few buttons to make them executable (operational) in the business"!

It is never a matter of pushing a few buttons to make it executable. The software is often very expensive, complex to configure, operate and requires specialized skills to use; skills that are often new to an organization's employees. Assuming a successful deployment of the BPMS software suite, which can take considerable time and effort, the requirement for skilled administrators and developers immediately emerges. Management at this stage begins to feel pressure to see benefits from the large financial investment in this software. Yet no benefits are able to be extracted since existing staff do not have the skill set needed to leverage these tools, especially once the vendor's consultants have exited the scene.

Management is now forced to react in the only way they can to salvage the situation—they purchase formal training for their staff on the software. Unfortunately, training takes time and is rarely immediately effective. People need time to learn and to put theory into practice. It can take years before they are effective with the new software and the business benefits are delivered. By then, the BPM effort is deemed a failure, the software is abandoned and even the mention of BPM becomes taboo within the organization.

SUMMARY

A rigorous yet flexible framework is essential to facilitate improvements in business processes. The BPM approach adopted needs to recognize that change is ideally driven by people who operate within an organization where:

- the vision and process goals are clear
- organization roles and accountabilities are transparent
- systems, processes and technologies are supportive of the organization's purpose.

The framework must provide a structured approach throughout all types of BPM activities, from project conception and initiation to completion and sustainable business-as-usual.

There must be a thorough understanding of the typical commonly found BPM methodology pitfalls. Avoid them at all costs as they will either waste a lot of an organization's money or be terminal for the BPM activities.

SELF-TEST

1 Why is just adopting a few high level steps and a bunch of suggested tools not enough?

2 What are some of the common pitfalls with regard to BPM methodologies?

3 Why do you need a structured approach for implementing process improvements?

Part 2

BPM—HOW DO YOU DO IT?

The 7FE Framework

This part of the book comprises an explanation of the BPM implementation framework, its various phases and steps, and how to use it in the successful implementation of BPM activities.

Chapter 11 provides a brief overview of the 7FE Framework, the ten phases and three components considered to be *essential* to any BPM project.

Chapter 12 explains how the 7FE Framework can be used, describing two typical ways in which BPM projects are initiated and the resulting four implementation scenarios usually selected by an organization. It also describes the importance of having a clearly understood business operating model and where it is positioned within the business planning, between the organization's strategy and business capabilities.

Chapters 13–22 then explain each of the ten phases in detail, while Chapter 23 introduces the essentials, which are in turn described in Chapters 24–26.

An important aspect in the use of the framework is that although the phases are shown sequentially and typically follow the order indicated, this is not always the case. There may be occasions when a phase is skipped (for example, the Understand phase could be skipped if there were no reason to gain an understanding of the existing processes, such as in the case of a green-field start-up organization). Similarly, the phase steps may also be completed in a different sequence. While skipping a phase is possible, we would strongly recommend that each phase and step is seriously considered and, if the project team determines that it will be skipped, then this should be documented and reported to the project steering committee, justifying the reasons.

It is strongly recommended that the framework section be read in its entirety before an organization commences a BPM activity. One of the reasons for this is explained in the previous paragraph. Another reason is that some phases (such as the Realize value phase) do not have their steps completed within their own separate phase, as they are completed during other phases of the framework.

Each phase is specified as a discrete activity in order to highlight its importance to the project team and organization, ensuring that—in our example of the Realize value phase—the project team focuses on, and brings to fruition, the realization of the benefits shown in the project business case.

In order to utilize the framework correctly it is important to clearly understand and agree what type of BPM activity is being undertaken. As discussed earlier, the BPM activity could be a low impact project or program (group of projects); a large-scale high impact BPM program; or an enterprise-wide BPM-driven business transformation program.

The framework described in Part II of this book is applicable to all these BPM activities. Parts of the framework will however be deployed differently depending upon the type of BPM activity being undertaken. The Sustainable Performance phase (described in Chapter 22) addresses the handover from project status to a business-as-usual activity. Chapter 27 of the book addresses how to embed BPM within an organization to ensure ongoing process management and improvement. However, when an ongoing BPM improvement activity is large enough for the establishment of a "project," the framework will again be applicable.

A unique aspect of this framework is that it can be used in all circumstances:

- from small projects to large transformations;
- projects with or without automation;
- for organizations with low or high process maturity;
- for projects within one business unit to programs expanding across an entire value chain;
- from limited to large-scale cultural and organizational change.

Furthermore the framework builds on the internal capability of the organization while executing BPM activities.

The Six Sigma methodology, while it has excellent tools and techniques, falls short as a methodology to cater for the wide variety of projects as described above, especially in relation to automation and enterprise-wide transformational projects.

7FE is a framework that needs to be adjusted and adopted by experienced BPM practitioners to suit the BPM activity circumstances. It is not a stringent "paint by number" methodology, as this approach may not address the specific needs and circumstances of individual BPM activities.

7FE FRAMEWORK OVERVIEW

OVERVIEW

This chapter provides an overview of the 7FE Project Framework. It explains why strategy requires a business operating model, and then business capabilities to support it. Business capability usually comprises the three aspects of people, process and technology. The ten phases and three essentials of the framework are explained in brief.

OVERALL LEARNING OUTCOME

By the end of this chapter you will be able to explain:

- Why execution is more important than the organization strategy
- How a strategy suggests a business operating model to support it, which in turn requires business capability
- The components of business capability
- What and why the foundations of the BPM success stool are critical
- How the 7FE Project Framework name was selected and why
- A brief overview of each of the ten phases and three essentials.

Business leaders need to establish an appropriate environment and high level guidelines of how the organization's strategy is to be executed. Figure 11.1 shows how alignment can and, indeed, needs to be achieved from the very top of the organization with business strategy being the driver. The devised strategy will *suggest* a number of possible Business Operating Models (BOMs) to management. The BOM selected must be an appropriate model for the organization and is the responsibility of executive management to create.

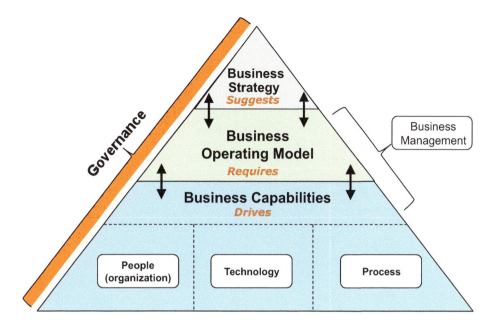

Figure 11.1 Organizational alignment

In order for a business strategy to be implemented the organization's management must establish a set of rules related to how the business will be conducted, and this is the business operating model. Some call this the Business Architecture and it must always remain holistic and pragmatic. The BOM must include, but is not limited to: what the high level business value chain is; what products and services will be sold; via what distribution channels and locations; and the desired degree of business integration and standardization.

KEY POINT

It should be understood that a BOM is not something trivial for an organization to change—it is intrinsic to the way an organization works; hence it retains more of an emergent nature rather than being the object of disruptive change, unless of course the organization is dramatically reinventing itself by a large-scale organization transformation program.

The execution of a BOM will *require* the creation or further development of specific Business Capabilities and it is these required capabilities that drive the creation of the components:

- People (performance management, organizational structure and culture)
- Process (governance and architecture)
- Technology (IT strategy and architecture) within the business.

The *People* component will include: organizational structure; roles and responsibilities; reward structures; and human resource policies. While Technology needs to support the People component, much will need to be known about the Process component in order to design the organizational structure.

The *Process* component requires several capabilities, governance and frameworks (or architectures). These will include: a process asset; process architecture framework; process groups and models; high level value chains; list of end-to-end business processes; and a benefits management framework, to name but a few.

The *Technology* component is constrained and driven by the Business Operating Model. For example, if an organization does not need to share data across business units, then any effort to establish an organization-wide data warehouse will deliver minimal benefits. From this perspective, the effort expended to build business unit specific data marts will deliver the most relevant benefits. IT strategy should reflect these constraints.

It is the combination of the business operating model and the three components of business capability that is often referred to as Business Management.

BPM INSIGHT

Organizations without a business operating model (BOM) often struggle to execute any BPM activity other than just "tweaking" existing processes. The BOM provides guidance to the BPM activities and its participants with regard to:

- what needs to be achieved
- when success is achieved
- where the activity needs to start
- how this will be achieved
- how much change is required
- who needs to be involved.

It is governance that brings all aspects of Figure 11.1 together and provides the alignment between an organization's strategy and its ultimate execution. We will discuss governance in Chapter 14 (Enablement phase).

We have highlighted the three business capability components, and added a fourth, project management, in Figure 11.2, the BPM success stool.

The three components (legs of the stool) are not new; however, the fourth component *is* new, and is the "seat" upon which "success" rests. The foundation upon which the stool sits is also critical to success. The legs to the stool are:

1. *Process.* There must be an appropriate level of business process innovation or redesign linked to the organization's strategy and process goals, and an acceptance of the importance of processes within the organization.

2. *People.* As an organization grows in its maturity of process management, it will understand that people are the key to implementing the proposed new processes.

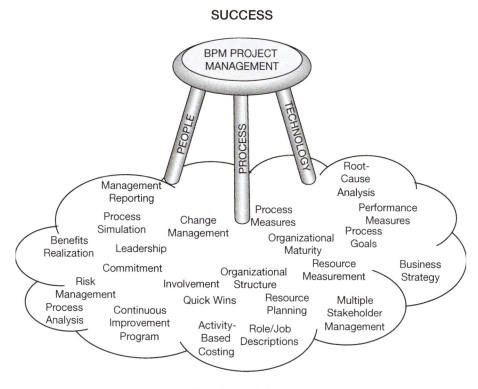

SUCCESS

Firm Foundations

Figure 11.2 BPM success stool

The organization must have the appropriate performance measurement and management structures across key processes. Process management should be proactive and then move towards being predictive, rather than reactive. Amongst other things, this all revolves around the people aspects of a BPM project.

3. *Technology.* This refers to the supporting tools for the processes and people and does not necessarily mean BPM software components or applications (although it could).

KEY POINT

The fourth component, which holds these legs together, is the "seat" of project management, for without a well-run project an implementation is destined to failure.

When we refer to project management in the 7FE Framework, we are describing BPM project management. We will describe the differences with BPM project management and conventional project management in Chapter 24.

If a leg is missing, the stool will fall, and if the seat of project management is missing then all the legs will collapse and the project will fail to meet expectations. BPM projects are complex, and success depends upon all aspects of the project being executed well. These aspects are represented by the "foundations" upon which the stool rests in Figure 11.2. If these foundations are soft (or not executed successfully), then the stool will sink and eventually collapse. If the foundations are firm because they are executed well, the stool will be resting upon a solid foundation and the project will be successful.

BPM INSIGHT

Organizations routinely attempt to execute significant BPM projects without properly addressing all four of these components and the foundations. Just as with the stool, a weak or missing leg will cause the project to collapse.

The BPM activity success stool is not just about aligning strategy and processes, but also people and behaviors. Performance management and measures, change management and communication will also impact a BPM activity. Effective communication across all organizational levels is critical to BPM success.

Different people (or groups of people) within the organization generally execute these components, and the foundations upon which the BPM activity rests. These groups do not always communicate effectively with each other, nor do they coordinate their activities. In fact, it has been suggested that IT, business and customers speak different languages. Project management skills are also often poor within organizations.

Figure 11.3 shows how the perceptions of different stakeholders of BPM can vary across an organization. These varying views need to be acknowledged, reconciled and managed.

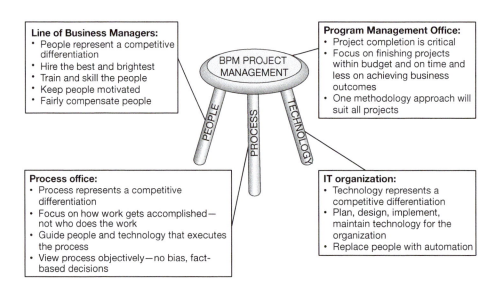

Figure 11.3 Perceptions of BPM vary

Effective execution of all four components and the foundations require different approaches, skills and expertise and these may vary from BPM activity to BPM activity.

Symptoms that indicate an organization is struggling with executing these components are that:

- it doesn't know where to start;
- it is not making the headway that was anticipated or planned;
- it has purchased a technology tool and thinks this is the answer;
- redesigned processes are not implemented;
- insufficient benefits are being realized;
- it is doing process improvement for the wrong reason ("everyone else is doing it, so should we!");
- BPM is making little impact on the organization, perhaps because the scope is too small or too large, or because the organization is endeavoring to be too ambitious;
- the BPM activity is directionless because it is not linked to the organization's strategy or business operating model.

While there are obviously high levels of commonality between organizations, the emphasis required to apply these BPM implementation components and foundations can be different across organizations and within an organization. There are many aspects of an organization that need alignment. Before an organization can improve business processes, there must be an understanding of all the factors that influence it. For example, unless there is full appreciation of the culture and behavior of the people using the processes, you cannot know that the changes will be effective.

KEY POINT

Having alignment within an organization of the strategy, vision and BPM activities will enable the execution of the strategy to be more complete and successful.

To implement successfully, BPM activities must be governed and controlled by a consistent implementation approach, otherwise significant risks will be added to the program.

7FE FRAMEWORK

Creating a BPM implementation framework that is appropriate to all organizations, and that will suit all circumstances, is challenging, especially when organizations are not the same. Even if organizations were the same, the approach to the implementation of BPM varies enormously within an organization.

Experience as BPM consultants and implementation practitioners has provided us with the opportunity of developing such a framework (see Figure 11.4), which has been used and refined in the implementation of BPM activities throughout the world. There are ten phases in the framework, and we will describe them in a little more detail later in this chapter and in much greater detail in subsequent chapters. The phases are the following:

1. Foundations
2. Enablement
3. Launch pad
4. Understand
5. Innovate
6. People
7. Develop
8. Implement
9. Realize value
10. Sustainable performance.

In addition to the ten phases there are three essential components:

1. Leadership
2. BPM project management
3. People change management.

Figure 11.4 shows the phases and essentials of the framework, and this figure should be kept in mind throughout this chapter.

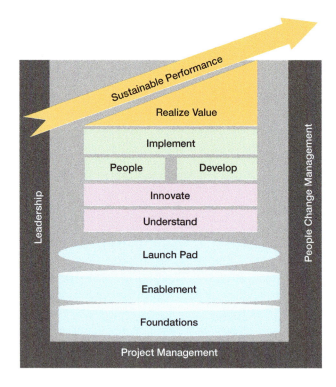

Figure 11.4
BPM Project Framework

Since the publication of the first edition of this book, we have been asked by readers to provide a "name" for the framework. This has been a difficult task (at least we found it to be) because it needs to be relevant and appropriate, and we have decided to call it the **7FE Framework**: where the four "Fs" relate to the grouping of our ten phases (refer to Figure 11.5) and the three "Es" relate to the three Essentials.[1]

As seen in Figure 11.5 the 4Fs relate to Foundations, Findings and solutions, Fulfillment and Future which group the ten phases.

The explanation of these groupings is as follows:

- *Foundations*: The Foundations and Enablement phases establish the solid base for the Launch pad phase from which to launch BPM activities. These three phases form the "foundations" of any BPM activity.

- *Findings and solutions*: This refers to the findings (or analysis) that must take place of the existing processes and is completed in the Understand phase, with suitable solutions being determined and defined in the Innovate phase.

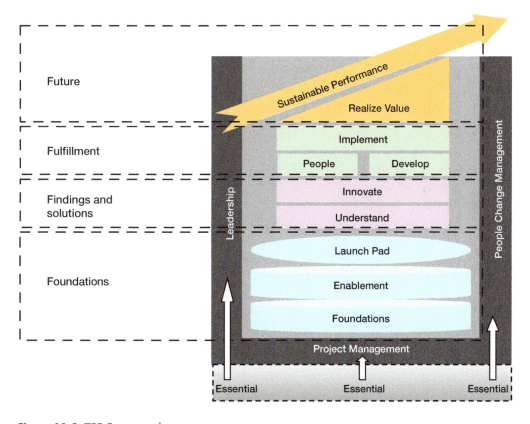

Figure 11.5 7FE Framework

- *Fulfillment:* Fulfillment is the People and Develop, as well the Implement, phases.

- *Future:* Relates to setting the project up for the future and this is achieved by the completion of the Realize Value and Sustainable Performance phases. This moves from the project state to a business-as-usual state, thus ensuring that process improvement projects are repeatable and embedded within the organization.

- *Essentials*—The three essentials—Leadership, BPM Project Management and People Change Management—are simply considered to be mandatory or "essential" throughout the entire BPM activity.

While business process improvement is considered a high priority by most organizations, an organization's attention and approach to BPM varies enormously. The challenge to ensuring that BPM activities are highly successful is to apply a framework or method of implementation that meets all the likely variations. The 7FE Framework is aimed at providing this necessary breadth and flexibility with a set of common phases and steps capable of meeting these various BPM implementation challenges.

BPM INSIGHT

Any framework adopted by an organization needs to be flexible and broad enough in its structure to adapt to each unique project, program and organizational approach.

Figure 11.6 shows that once the Foundations, Enablement and Launch pad phases have been established, there is the opportunity of launching multiple BPM activities simultaneously, providing much needed consistency and synergy.

While some of the phases may initially be skipped, or partially skipped, in certain implementation scenarios, all organizations must eventually come back and complete all phases if BPM or a process-focused organizational view is to be seriously adopted as a critical business strategy.

Each of the phases comprises a series of steps that provide a detailed, structured and yet flexible approach to the implementation of a BPM activity. The framework steps not only show what tasks are to be completed within each phase; they also provide an understanding of how the phases interrelate.

7FE FRAMEWORK PHASES

We will briefly outline each of the phases and essential components here, and then explain them in more detail in the subsequent chapters.

1. *Foundations.* Refers to an agreed set of driving and guiding business foundation principles to manage business processes within the organization. This phase includes ensuring that the organization strategy, vision, strategic goals, business and executive

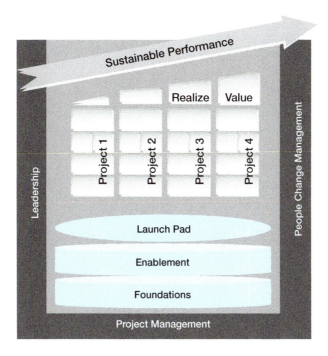

Figure 11.6 BPM Program Framework

drivers are clearly understood by the project team members. Do stakeholders expect short- or long-term gains from this project? Is the value proposition of the organization clear and understood by everyone? It is important to understand that strategy is not a "plan"; strategy "is a purposeful process of engaging people inside and outside the organization in scoping out new paths ahead" (Stace and Dunphy, 1996: 63).

2. *Enablement*. Refers to the creation or provision of the key architectures and detailed elements that must be provided to support and enable business capabilities to enhance the successful delivery of all components of the BPM strategy. This phase is where the key architectures, rules, principles, guidelines and models are specified and agreed to enable the implementation of BPM across the organization.

3. *Launch pad*. This phase has three major outcomes:

   • the selection of where to start the initial (or next) BPM activity within the organization;

   • agreement of the process goals and/or vision, once the processes have been selected;

   • the establishment of the selected activity.

Determining where to start is a difficult exercise in its own right, and the framework will provide you with several ways of determining where and how to start. Process goals and vision need to be aligned with the organization strategy, foundations and the process architecture to ensure that they are enhancing or adding value to the strategy. Once a business unit and processes have been selected and the process goals agreed, the BPM activity must be established to maximize the likelihood of success. Establishing the BPM activity includes deciding the BPM team structure, the scope, the stakeholder management, creation of the initial business case, and expected business benefits. The Launch pad phase ensures that BPM activities benefit from other ongoing or completed BPM activities and increase the success rate of BPM over time.

4. *Understand.* This phase is about understanding enough of the current business process environment to enable the Innovate phase to take place. It is essential that process metrics (including metrics from customers, suppliers and partners) are gathered to allow for the establishment of process baseline costs for future comparative purposes. Other essential steps are root-cause analysis and the identification of possible quick wins. There will be a need to identify, and ideally implement, quick wins along the way, as the business will not (and should not) provide unlimited funding for BPM without benefits being realized. The ideal situation is for the BPM activities to become self-funding because of the gains made by the implementation of these quick wins.

5. *Innovate.* This is the creative phase of any BPM activity, and often the most interesting. It should not only involve the BPM team and the business, but also relevant stakeholders—both internal and external. Once the various new process options have been identified, there may be a need to run simulations, complete activity-based costing, conduct capacity planning and determine implementation feasibility, to enable the finalization of which options are the best. Additional metrics should be completed to allow a comparison with the baseline metrics established during the Understand phase. Additional possible quick wins are identified and prioritized within the business.

6. *People.* This is a critical phase of the framework and it could put the rest of the project at risk if not handled thoroughly and to a high standard. The purpose of this phase is to ensure that the activities, roles and performance measurement match the organization strategy and process goals. At the end of the day, it is people that will make processes function effectively and efficiently, no matter how much automation is involved. The People phase should not be confused with the People Change Management essential (which includes organizational culture) as change management requires attention throughout the project in all the phases.

7. *Develop.* This phase consists of building all the components for the implementation of the new processes. It is important to understand that "build," in this context, does not necessarily mean an IT build. It could involve the building of all infrastructure (desks, PC movements, buildings, etc.) to support the people change management program and changes in the support of the people who execute the processes. It also involves the testing of software and hardware.

8. *Implement.* This phase is where the "rubber hits the road." It is where all aspects of the project (roll-out of the new processes, roll-out of the new role descriptions, performance management and measures, and training) take place. The implementation plans are crucial, as are roll-back and contingency plans. Many organizations believe that the project has been completed after implementation has been successful. However the next two phases are the most important in a BPM project.

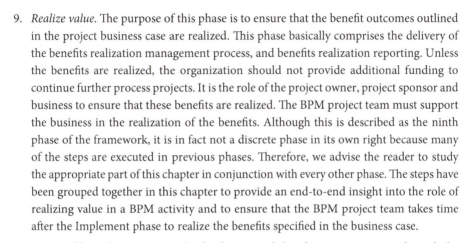

BPM INSIGHT

Common mistakes regarding benefits:

- wait till the very end of the project to start to think about them and as a result miss many opportunities to identify and realize benefits along the way
- consider a project completed as soon as it has been implemented which can result in lack of focus on the actual realization of the benefits.

9. *Realize value.* The purpose of this phase is to ensure that the benefit outcomes outlined in the project business case are realized. This phase basically comprises the delivery of the benefits realization management process, and benefits realization reporting. Unless the benefits are realized, the organization should not provide additional funding to continue further process projects. It is the role of the project owner, project sponsor and business to ensure that these benefits are realized. The BPM project team must support the business in the realization of the benefits. Although this is described as the ninth phase of the framework, it is in fact not a discrete phase in its own right because many of the steps are executed in previous phases. Therefore, we advise the reader to study the appropriate part of this chapter in conjunction with every other phase. The steps have been grouped together in this chapter to provide an end-to-end insight into the role of realizing value in a BPM activity and to ensure that the BPM project team takes time after the Implement phase to realize the benefits specified in the business case.

10. *Sustainable performance.* It is absolutely essential that the project team works with the business to establish a method to ensure that continued process agility and improvements are sustainable. The considerable investment made in process projects must be maintained and enhanced over time. The organization must understand that processes have a lifecycle, and will need continuous improvement after the project's targeted improvements have been realized. If they don't, over time and as the business changes the organization will simply be running its processes in a suboptimal fashion. This phase is about the conversion from a "project" to a "business operational" activity.

KEY POINT

Without Sustainable Performance any process improvement typically reverts back to the original situation. This is often seen in organizations that purely focus on quick wins without a true process management culture.

PROJECT ESSENTIALS

We will now turn our attention to the three BPM project essentials. These are the *essential* components upon which any successful BPM activity rests, and they permeate all phases of the project framework.

1. *Project Management.* The question is often asked, "Can a normal application or business project manager implement a BPM project?" The answer is a qualified "Yes, but nowhere nearly as well as an experienced BPM project manager." The project risks will be significantly higher, and the organization risks missing out on many of the potential benefits that can be achieved from BPM. Can a person without significant project management experience implement a BPM project? This answer is easy—"No." Project management is a fundamental skill or requirement for any project and a BPM project is no different. In fact, the requirement is even higher because of the increased complexity of BPM projects. The reason for these answers is that BPM adds significant complexity to programs and projects and increased skill levels are required. We will discuss these additional skills in Chapter 24.

2. *People Change Management.* The importance of the change management process as it specifically relates to the implementation of the employee aspects of a BPM project/ program will now be briefly discussed as well as the desired performance culture in the organization. There have been many articles written on why process improvement and BPM project failures occur, and we do not propose to mention all the reasons here. However, there is a growing belief that the employee aspects of an improvement project have not always been addressed in sufficient detail. As Michael Hammer stated in 1993, "coming up with the ideas is the easy part, but getting things done is the tough part. The place where these reforms die is . . . down in the trenches"—and who "owns" the trenches? The people in the organization. We would suggest that people change management aspects of any BPM activity is in excess of 60 percent of the effort. Unless this is addressed extremely well throughout every BPM activity the initiative will suffer.

3. *Leadership.* A point acknowledged by all business process change experts is that any change program *must* have the support of senior leadership/management to be successful. According to Keen (1997: 119), "These people's commitment to change matters more than the details of the plan for change." The extent to which executive leaders "delegate" responsibility is crucial to the effectiveness of the outcomes of BPM activities. There have been extremely successful BPM implementations and some poor ones, and the common thread in both types has always been the commitment, attention and process maturity of the executive leaders. The successful BPM activities had excellent executive commitment, attention and understanding, while the poor ones did not.

If the three BPM project essentials are brought together their relationship can be shown diagrammatically in Figure 11.7. This shows that the perception is often that a BPM activity is seen as being above the visibility line (that is, having a high visibility within the organization) whilst the *business operational* activities are seen as not having as high a visibility and hence as being below the visibility line. Project management relates to projects and people change management primarily relates to the business-as-usual activities, because that is where the business people are. Leadership's role is to ensure these two essentials are brought together in a harmonious and seamless manner, because eventually the BPM activity results need to be incorporated into business-as-usual.

More details on how to use the framework are provided in Chapter 12.

BPM INSIGHT

It is important to stress that the 7FE Framework does not need to be followed meticulously; it should be adapted for a specific organization, situation, culture and process maturity.

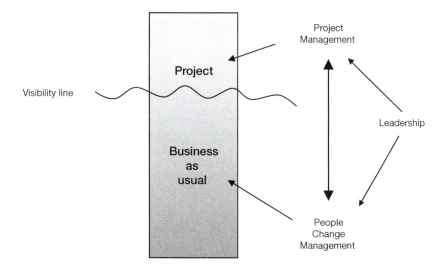

Figure 11.7 Relationship of BPM project essentials

A PROCESS-FOCUSED ORGANIZATION

As the description "process-focused" organization will be referred to throughout the book it is useful to ensure that we have a common understanding of what this means. The easiest way to describe a process-focused organization is to compare it with an organization that is not process-focused (see Table 11.1).

SUMMARY

- While an organization's strategy is important, it is the execution of it that really matters and makes a difference to an organization.
- An organization's strategy will suggest the need and structure for the business operating model (BOM).
- The BOM requires the development or enhancement of business capabilities required to deliver the strategy.

Table 11.1 Process-focused versus non-process-focused organization

Process-focused organization	Non-process-focused organization
Understands that processes add significant value to the organization; understands that processes are a significant contributor to the fulfillment of an organization's strategy	Does not fully appreciate the contribution that processes make to the organization and the realization of the organization's strategy
Incorporates BPM into the management practices of the organization	Management of processes is not a primary focus
Embraces a BPM strategy	Supports no, or a small number of isolated, BPM activities
Senior leadership focuses on processes (especially the CEO, because others will follow the leader)	Understands that processes must be important because of the problems they cause (quality, backlogs, etc.)
Has a clear understanding of their processes	May have a well-defined value chain, and/or isolated lists of processes and sub-processes
Understands the impact of processes on other processes	Perhaps has some processes modeled in unsophisticated tools; process models are not linked or related
Organization structure reflects this process understanding, with either a structure designed around process, or a matrix reporting of process and functional responsibilities	Organizational structure is based upon functional departments that may result in significant friction at hand-off points
Understands that tension can arise between process and functional lines of responsibility and has mechanisms in place to deal with and resolve these tensions—a team understanding approach	Becomes frustrated with inter-departmental process issues; and could have a blame mentality; perhaps wishes to (or already has) inter-departmental service level agreements
Has appointed senior executives as responsible for processes—perhaps a chief process officer and/or process owners	Functionally based with no cross-departmental responsibilities
Rewards and measures linked to process outcomes	Rewards and measures linked to functional departmental outcomes (silo effect)

- Business capabilities comprise three components: people, process and technology.
- While these three components are critical, it is the fourth component of BPM—project management—that holds it together, as shown in the BPM success stool.
- Different parts of the business will have different perceptions of these components and these perceptions need to be recognized and accommodated.
- The 7FE Project Framework comprises ten phases and three essentials.
- It is important to understand the differences between a process-focused organization and one that is not process-focused.

SELF-TEST

1 What are the components of a business operating model?

2 What are the four aspects of the BPM success stool?

3 Why is the fourth aspect important?

4 What are the components of business capability?

5. Briefly describe each of the ten phases of the 7FE Project Framework.

6 Briefly describe each of the three essentials of the framework and why they are important.

ADDENDUM: 7FE FRAMEWORK AND SIX SIGMA, LEAN AND LEAN SIX SIGMA

To ensure there is an understanding or positioning of the 7FE Framework with regard to some other process improvement methodologies, we have outlined below a high level explanation and comparison with Six Sigma, Lean and Lean Six Sigma.

Six Sigma

Six Sigma was developed in 1986 by Motorola to improve the quality of process outputs in manufacturing processes by identifying and removing the causes of defects (errors) and minimizing variability within the processes. The application of Six Sigma was later extended to other non-manufacturing business processes.

The term Six Sigma is associated with statistical modeling in manufacturing processes; and to achieve a *sigma* rating of six, a process is only allowed to have 3.4 defects per million or, put another way, 99.99966 percent of transactions or events through the process will be error free. A defect in Six Sigma terms is described as any process output that does not meet specifications, or could lead to creating an output that does not meet customer specifications.

Achieving an error rate this low in any non-manufacturing environment, such as a bank, insurance or government organization, will never be achievable.

Six Sigma projects follow one of two project methodologies that each comprises five phases.

Perhaps the best known, known as DMAIC, is used for projects aimed at improving an existing business process. DMAIC's five phases are:

- *Define* the problem, the voice of the customer, and the project goals, very specifically;
- *Measure* key aspects of the current process and collect relevant data;
- *Analyze* the data to investigate and verify the cause-and-effect relationships. Perform root-cause analysis of the identified problems ensuring all relationships have been identified;
- *Improve* or optimize the current process based upon data analysis thus creating the future state process. Test the solution, perhaps via pilots, ensuring problems have been eliminated or reduced;
- *Control* the future state process to ensure that any deviations from the desired target state are corrected before they become defects. Ensure that mechanisms are in place to measure and control process execution.

The second Six Sigma methodology is DMADV, sometimes known as DFSS (Design for Six Sigma). Its five phases are:

- *Define*—design goals that are consistent with customer demands and the enterprise strategy;
- *Measure* and identify the characteristics of the process that are Critical To Quality (CTQ), product capabilities, production process capability, and risks;
- *Analysis* to develop and design alternatives, creating high level process designs and evaluate the designs against each other;
- *Design* optimizes the suggested solutions and plans for the verification methods and test runs;
- *Verify* the design by pilot runs or other methods and hand it over to the process owner(s).

Both methodologies use many tools and methods common with the 7FE Framework and other process improvement approaches. These tools and methods include (and are not limited to): 5 Whys; Analysis of Variation; Business Process Mapping; Cause and effects diagram (also known as fishbone or Ishikawa diagram); Cost-benefit analysis; Pareto analysis; Pareto chart; Process capability; SIPOC analysis (**S**uppliers, **I**nputs, **P**rocess, **O**utputs, **C**ustomers).

Most of these tools and methods could, or should, be used within the 7FE Framework.

Comments on Six Sigma

It is important to state that the following comments are about the "pure play" standard Six Sigma methodology. Good practitioners of Six Sigma may well overcome some of the comments made below by using their experience and use of additional methodologies or approaches.

1. DMAIC is narrowly focused on "fixing" an existing process and typically only on the operational processes described in the BPM House in Chapter 1. While there is nothing wrong with this if this is what is needed, it however may:

   - not address a process from an end-to-end perspective
   - miss the opportunity of completely redesigning, or being innovative with, the process
   - limit the opportunities to improve an entire value chain across the borders of organizations
   - ignore the opportunities that automation might provide, as DMAIC focuses more on time-and-motion studies and streamlining.

2. It is a very rigid methodology and has been criticized because of its over-reliance on methods and tools. "In most cases, more attention is paid to reducing variation and less attention is paid to developing robustness (which can altogether eliminate the need for reducing variation)" (Jarrar and Neely, n.d.).

3. Again due to its rigid nature it can have the effect of stifling creativity. For example, a *Business Week* article reported that James McNerney introduced it to 3M and it had this effect. It was removed from the research functional area. Furthermore, the article cites two Wharton School professors who say that Six Sigma leads to incremental innovation at the expense of blue skies research (Hindo, 2007).

4. It has been suggested that "by relying on the Six Sigma criteria, management is lulled into the idea that something is being done about quality" (Jarrar and Neely, n.d.).

5. DMAIC does not relate to the organization's strategy, DMADV mentions it.

6. DMAIC is a sequential method that lacks the 7FE Framework essential components that go across a process improvement activity, for example project management and people change management.

7. Most organizations struggle to embed the improvements as part of business as usual and typically organizations fall back to the situation prior to the improvement.

8. Six Sigma methodology does not create, establish or specifically address all aspects of the BPM House, for example:

   - a process asset
   - a process architecture
   - the target business operating model—relate and build upon it
   - a business rules engine

- sustainability for ongoing process improvement and management. Six Sigma advocates would state that the Control aspect of DMAIC introduces ongoing measurement activities, but as you will learn later in this book, there are many other critical aspects to sustainability of measurement

- a process governance structure, which relates to the point above

- the people change management aspects that are absolutely critical to any successful implementation.

This is not meant to be a definitive list of comments on Six Sigma.

KEY POINT

Six Sigma can be seen as picking low hanging fruit and as such there is a limit to how much can be achieved.

Six Sigma and 7FE Framework

Table 11.2 shows a comparison of DMAIC and DMADV with the 7FE Framework. Understand that the suggestions below relate to the "pure play" Six Sigma methodology and are personal opinions. There is no doubt that advocates will strongly argue against some of the thoughts below. While we understand that good practitioners will cover many of the missing areas below, it could be argued that activities are outside, or in addition to, the Six Sigma methodology.

We defined BPM in Chapter 1 as "a management discipline focused on using business processes as a significant contributor to achieving an organization's objectives through the improvement, ongoing performance management and governance of essential business processes."

If an organization wishes to use process management to gain a sustainable competitive advantage, then this can only be achieved if the foundations and enablement activities are completed enterprise-wide across the organization before process improvement activities commence; and then continually throughout the process improvement activities. Then there is a chance of achieving a sustainable competitive advantage culture.

BPM, if viewed as a management discipline, has the potential of achieving this sustainable competitive advantage. The Six Sigma methodology provides an excellent set of tools and methods to support BPM activities and the 7FE Framework uses many of them.

Lean

Lean is sometimes referred to as lean manufacturing, lean enterprise or lean production. It derived from the Toyota Production System (TPS) management philosophy.

Lean focuses on the creation of value for the end customer and any resources spent that do not add value to the end customer must be eliminated. It is centered on preserving value with less work.

Table 11.2 DMAIC and DMADV comparison with 7FE Framework

7FE Framework	DMAIC	DMADV	Comments on Six Sigma
Foundations		Define	Only partially cover Foundations
Enablement			Methodology does not cover Enablement
Launch Pad	Define	Define	Only partially covers the Launch pad phase activities and typically misses the selection component
Understand	Measure Analyze	Measure	Understand and Innovate cover many more activities and across many processes or areas
Innovate	Improve	Analyze	of the business
People			Methodology does not address this
Develop		Verify	Depending upon the project, may be similar
Implement		Verify	Depending upon the project, may be similar
Realize Value			Not specifically covered by Six Sigma
Sustainable Performance	Control		Control (measurement) is only a part of sustainability
Leadership			It could be argued that if an organization is implementing Six Sigma, it has a commitment from leadership to process improvement
Project Management			Project management is needed for any process improvement activity
People Change Management			Not specifically addressed by the methodology

Lean is a set of tools that assists in the identification and eventual elimination of waste (known as *muda*). The approach assumes that if waste is eliminated quality will improve as will production time and costs will reduce. Value Stream Mapping is a well-known Lean tool.

Waste is described as *muda* and is characterized as: Transportation, Inventory, Motion, Waiting, Overproduction, Over-processing and Defects. While some of these seven aspects can be applied to a non-manufacturing environment, it is obvious that they were originally focused towards a manufacturing situation; as indeed was Lean.

Lean is about getting the right things to the right place at the right time in the right quantity to achieve a perfect flow of work; all while minimizing waste and maximizing flexibility and the ability to change.

These are all good process practices and aspirations.

One of the often heard criticisms of a Lean implementation from employees is that Lean practitioners may focus too much on the tools and methodologies, and fail to focus on the philosophy and culture of Lean. This is a criticism that could be leveled at any methodology or approach.

In an outstanding article in the *Harvard Business Review* (2008) the authors stated that people often ask: "'Tell me the one thing I should learn from Toyota.' That misses the point.

Emulating Toyota isn't about copying any one practice; it's about creating a culture. That takes time. It requires resources. And it isn't easy" (Takeuchi et al., 2008: 104).

The Toyota Production System, from which Lean derived, is often seen as the answer. It isn't. It is simply a component of the answer. It is a subset of the BPM House, and the BPM House is a subset of the answer to business transformation and creating a high performance culture and organization.

Lean Six Sigma

This is the combination of both Lean and Six Sigma and focuses on the elimination of the seven kinds of waste and the provision of goods and services at a rate of 3.4 defects per million opportunities.

- Lean Six Sigma comprises all the Lean and Six Sigma (DMAIC) tools and methods.
- One of the benefits of the Lean and Six Sigma methodologies is that they are well known to management and can be used to gain the attention of management to process management.
- We believe that both Lean and Six Sigma are a subset of what is defined as Business Process Management in Chapter 1.

Readers are encouraged to complete reading the rest of this book and then come back to reread this section again and you will be in a better position to form a view of the suggestions put forward here.

BPM INSIGHT

A review was completed of the work of a Six Sigma team at an insurer. The manager was focused on reducing the mean time to completion from 8.27 to 4.59 days. However, after a brief analysis it became obvious that the insurer had overpaid some of their clients several millions. There is always a need to look holistically at a problem rather than looking at the selective metrics nominated by the Six Sigma methodology.

CHAPTER 12

GUIDELINES ON HOW TO USE THE 7FE FRAMEWORK

OVERVIEW

In previous chapters we have introduced the 7FE Framework and the importance of a structured approach to BPM activities. This chapter discusses how to use the framework as a result of the way an organization initiates BPM activities, and the project implementation scenario selected. This chapter is more oriented towards business readers and users of the 7FE Framework, than for students. Students will find the information in this chapter important if they were to actually conduct a BPM activity within an organization.

OVERALL LEARNING OUTCOME

By the end of this chapter you will be able to:

- Understand that one approach does not suit all organizations
- Distinguish between the three approaches to BPM and how this influences how the 7FE Framework is initiated and used
- Understand the four scenarios in implementing BPM and how to determine which scenario is applicable in various situations
- Understand if it is appropriate to skip a phase or steps within a phase.

WHY A "ONE APPROACH FITS ALL" PHILOSOPHY DOES NOT WORK

The difficulty with any structured approach to business projects, whether a BPM activity or not, is that organizations often adopt a "one approach fits all" philosophy.

Many people suggest that a BPM activity should start by first obtaining the full and complete support of the CEO, and unquestionably this is the ideal method. In reality, though, most CEOs either do not know about the BPM activity or will not be interested because it is considered to be "just another project." If they are aware of the activity and it is one of the first BPM activities within the organization, they might want proof of the benefits that BPM can bring.

Even if the CEO is interested, it is often the case that the BPM initiative does not receive sufficient attention, time and resources from the CEO.

BPM INSIGHT

Business processes are at the heart of an organization and require more than just lip service to monitor, manage and improve them, to achieve high performance. This lack of attention, time and resources can have a significant negative impact on the execution of the BPM initiative.

In addition, most approaches do not cater for the various stages of experience, maturity and embedding of BPM within an organization—from the initial orientation of BPM as an important part of management, through to a business-as-usual activity. There will be a fundamentally different approach depending upon the level of organizational experience and maturity with BPM.

In the ideal situation, the organization will have established and published its strategic vision, objectives and goals. It will have embraced BPM, established the BPM foundations and set about establishing the BPM enablement components and guidelines—these being the pillars upon which individual BPM activities can be launched. The process architecture will also have been aligned with the organization's strategy and the IT and business architectures.

However, most situations are not ideal.

HOW ARE BPM ACTIVITIES INITIATED?

The difficulty with any structured approach to business projects, whether it is a BPM activity or not, is that organizations often state, "but we are different, we have unique requirements, problems and issues and no standard structured approach is applicable for us." This is often the start of failure as the uniqueness is rarely as strong as the benefits of following a proven and consistent structured approach.

KEY POINT

Few organizations are unique. Most organizations face the same or very similar issues. It is important to realize that a proven structured approach will ensure organizations are able to deal with difference issues and situations.

The 7FE Framework (structured approach) must always be tailored to meet the specific requirements of any organization, the specific BPM activity and the organizational process culture and maturity. In fact, we have never implemented it within an organization without the need to provide this flexibility to meet the specific needs of that organization.

At its highest level, it is suggested that there are three approaches and initiators for BPM activities and, in fact, projects in general. How a project is initiated is fundamental in the determination of which approach is to be selected and therefore how the 7FE Framework will be used. Projects are predominantly initiated in one of the three ways:

* *Strategy led*
* *Business issue led*
* *Process led.*

Figure 12.1 shows the three approaches and their interaction with the phases of the framework, together with some of the possible project triggers of each approach. The three approaches will be individually discussed below.

The strategy led approach

The strategy led approach is where the organization's strategy has been determined and documented, and its implementation has resulted in the initiation of one or a number of BPM activities. For example, the strategy could be to transform the organization by taking a

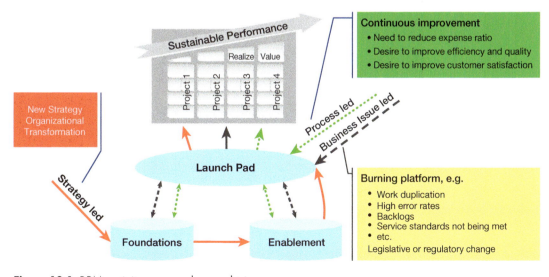

Figure 12.1 BPM activity approaches and triggers

process-focused approach. This is the transition from strategy to a BPM activity implementation, and is "top-down" management of an organization's processes.

Figure 12.1 shows the impact this will have on the use of the 7FE Framework. The sequence is that the foundations will have determined that a BPM activity is necessary and the organization will know, from the process architecture (Enablement phase), which processes, applications and data will be impacted, which will assist in the determination of the BPM activity scope. This will feed into the Launch pad phase—the place where projects are "launched." The process architecture will need to be referenced throughout the project (see Chapter 14 for details). The remaining framework phases will be completed as required.

Figure 12.2 shows how a strategy led project would typically be initiated. The steps would be as follows:

- Organization executives create the strategy that results in a number of organizational objectives.

- A number of objectives would be allocated to sub-managers (say, general managers) to be primarily responsible for the strategy's implementation and realization.

- The general managers, their staff and appropriate stakeholders would devise an Action Plan for each objective—this is the commencement of the Strategy Implementation Plan.

- The Launch pad phase of the 7FE Framework would be used to determine and plan the various options and how these will be turned into projects. This will require the managers to reference the organization's business capabilities, for example, the operational capability of the organization to implement the planned projects, the IT architecture and the process architecture of the organization. It will also determine how the projects will be prioritized and then launched (commenced) in an appropriate, structured and controlled manner.

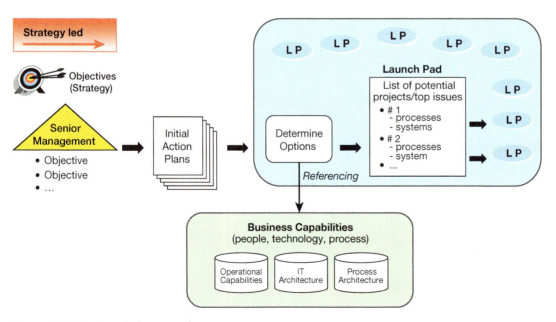

Figure 12.2 Strategy led approach

Business issue led approach

A business issue led initiative will, as the name suggests, be an initiative led or driven by the operational or business issues of an organization, business unit or department. The triggers for this type of BPM activity are likely to originate from a business issue (opportunities, problems or regulatory requirements). Refer to Figure 12.1.

Business issue led initiatives will mean that the determination that a project is required occurs at a lower level in the organization than at the strategy level. The likely starting point for the 7FE Framework will be the Launch pad phase.

A project team will commence several of the Launch pad phase steps, after referring to the Enablement phase outputs to assess and gather sufficient information to know exactly where to start the project and determine its depth. The process architecture will provide the information of which processes, business IT applications and data will be impacted by the required project and the guidelines for the process modeling.

This will mean that the Foundations phase will only be referenced to ensure that the project is in alignment with the organization's strategy and adding value to it. If the project is not in alignment with the organizational strategy then this needs to be acknowledged and accepted as a tactical BPM activity, and a plan and timeframe agreed to bring it back into alignment in the future.

Process led approach

This refers to a project that is initiated by either:

- a process team investigating a part of the business from a process perspective to determine if there are opportunities for business efficiency improvements (this could be part of a continuous improvement program); or
- a business manager recognizing that parts of his/her business are operating suboptimally from a process perspective.

The initial investigation will review the high level processes within the designated business unit/area, establish appropriate high level metrics, and gain some knowledge of where to start the subsequent detailed process investigation (which steps will be necessary and how they will be executed will be discussed in Chapter 15).

During these steps, the Foundations phase will be referenced to ensure that the project will contribute towards the organizational strategy and objectives—for example cost reduction, increased customer service levels. If the project is not in alignment with the organizational objectives (strategy), then it needs to be acknowledged early and accepted as a tactical BPM activity, and then a plan and timeframe agreed to bring it back into alignment in the future (in a similar manner to the business issue led approach).

The Enablement phase guidelines and architectures will need to be referenced and used as required.

All three types of BPM activity, after completion, must always leave a legacy within the business of continuous improvement.

The following simple rules can be applied in determining the type of project:

- if compliance is the reason for commencing a BPM project, it should be considered from a strategic perspective;
- if it has the backing of executive management, then it is a strategic led approach;
- if it does not have the backing of executive management, then it most likely will be considered to be a business issue led approach.

The BPM Foundations and Enablement phase outputs are the foundations of any BPM activity. The more extensive the project, the stronger the foundations must be. This is why, in a strategy led approach project, there must be more effort in the Foundations and Enablement phases than is the case in a business issue or process led approach project.

Typically in less process mature organizations the majority of BPM activities are initiated as business issue or process led. As an organization achieves more and more significant benefits as a result of BPM activities, the organization's process maturity will grow and executive management will push for more strategy led projects.

Table 12.1 Relationship between the type of BPM activity and the various approaches

Type of BPM activity ⟶

BPM activity initiation approach	*Large-scale BPM Program or Enterprise-wide Transformation*			*BPM Program or Portfolio of Projects*			*Isolated BPM Projects*		
Phase	*Foundations*	*Enablement*	*Launch Pad*	*Foundations*	*Enablement*	*Launch Pad*	*Foundations*	*Enablement*	*Launch Pad*
Strategy led	Critical **Start**	Critical	Use	Critical **Start**	Use	Use	Reference	Reference	Use **Start**
Business Issue led	Critical **Start**	Critical	Use	Reference	Use **Start**	Use	Reference	Reference	Use **Start**
Process led	Critical **Start**	Critical	Use	Reference	Use	Use **Start**	Reference	Reference	Use **Start**

Notes
- Refer to Table 5.1 for an explanation of the BPM type of activities.
- **Critical** means that this phase **must** be viewed as an extremely important aspect to the type of BPM activity and approach. The steps or activities completed within this phase will provide critical guidance for the BPM activity. Ignoring the phase will result in either not delivering the results expected or significantly increasing the risk profile of the BPM activity, or both.
- **Reference** means that the components of this phase will need to be referred to and taken into account during the BPM activity. Failure to do so could result in significantly increasing the risk profile of the BPM activity.
- **Use** means that the steps of this phase should be performed during the execution of the BPM activity. Failure to do so could result in significantly increasing the risk profile of the BPM activity or project work may need to be repeated.
- **Start** means this is the phase that will usually initiate the BPM activity.

No matter how the need for a BPM activity is determined, the next decision the organization will need to make is what type of BPM activity should be launched; Table 12.1 outlines the various options and how they interplay with the 7FE Framework.

FOUR SCENARIOS IN IMPLEMENTING BPM

With a generic framework such as 7FE, it is important to realize that there are different scenarios that can be followed. These scenarios drive the scope and engagement within the organization and will ultimately determine the success and benefits from the BPM activity. These four scenarios are heavily linked to the process maturity within an organization. There are four levels of maturity with "Business as usual" being the highest level of maturity and "Under the radar" the lowest.

The following are four BPM project scenarios; which one is selected will be determined by many factors, and these are discussed here.

1. *"Business as usual."* This will be selected by the most BPM-mature organizations. The organization and business managers will be totally committed to a process-focused organization and BPM activities are simply business-as-usual.

2. *"In the driver's seat."* This is the next level of organization BPM maturity, and is where there is a fully informed business manager(s) who is totally committed to the implementation of BPM within the organization or business unit he or she is responsible for and BPM is considered the key driver for any change.

3. *"Pilot project."* This is where there is a fully informed business manager(s) who has yet to be totally convinced of the benefits of BPM and is willing to try it out on a small scale before making a full commitment.

4. *"Under the radar."* This occurs in the least BPM-mature organization, and is where there is a partially informed business manager who is not yet committed and is not paying much (or any) attention to BPM within the organization. This scenario could be a project under the guise of process improvement, and BPM may not be mentioned at all. An interesting observation regarding this type of project scenario is that some organizations may complete many "under the radar" BPM projects and still not obtain the attention of the appropriate business management in order to undertake BPM on a wider scale within the organization.

If an organization has a high level of support for BPM from within and is only completing small-scale BPM activities, then it is potentially being "under ambitious" and should be aiming for higher BPM opportunities.

If an organization has little or no commitment to BPM and the BPM team is attempting large-scale BPM activities, then this is considered "exceeding its mandate" and is high risk. It also has a high potential of pushing the understanding and commitment to BPM further back (negative) from the current situation.

HOW TO DETERMINE WHICH SCENARIO IS APPLICABLE

The appropriate scenario for an organization will depend upon the process maturity of the organization, as evidenced by the level of involvement and commitment of the business manager(s). In this context, the business manager is the person who determines the business strategy—for example the executive general manager or CEO. The more involved and committed this person is, the more impact the project can (and should) have on the organization. This is shown in Figure 12.3, where it is important first to determine the business manager's involvement; only then is it appropriate to review the impact on the organization.

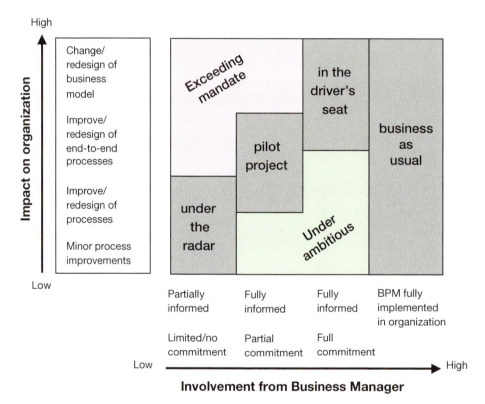

Figure 12.3 Scenarios for process improvement

KEY POINT

Once an organization has fully implemented BPM (is process-focused and BPM mature), all BPM initiatives, whether small or large, will or should be "business-as-usual" projects.

Common characteristics of the various BPM scenarios are listed in Table 12.2.

Once the organization has selected the implementation scenario for the BPM activity and the project team has a clear understanding of how the BPM activity was initiated, it will be able to commence using the 7FE Framework.

Table 12.2 Characteristics of different BPM activity scenarios

	Under the radar	Pilot project	In the driver's seat	Business as usual
Type of BPM initiative	Isolated BPM project	Isolated BPM project BPM program or portfolio of projects	Large-scale BPM program or enterprise wide transformation	Isolated BPM project BPM program or portfolio of projects Large-scale BPM program or enterprise-wide transformation
Experience in BPM	None/limited	None/limited; perhaps one or two successful projects	A number of successful BPM projects or programs	BPM embedded within the organization
BPM maturity of the organization*	Initial (1)	Initial (1) Repeatable (2)	Repeatable (2) Defined (3) Managed (4)	Managed (4) Optimized (5)
Typical Triggers for BPM initiative	Business issue led Process led	Range of wide business issues and process led; strategic issues	Strategic issue led, e.g., mergers, compliance	Process issues Business issues Strategic issues
People impacted	Limited numbers	Medium numbers	Potentially, everyone in the relevant business unit	Depending on size of project, from small numbers to everyone
Organization level	Team Department, projects	Business unit	Organization or business unit	Depends on size of project
Customer involvement	Limited to medium	Medium to large	Large	Limited Medium Large
Partners' involvement	Limited to medium	Medium to large	Large	Limited Medium Large

Note

* The numbers in parentheses refer to the level of BPM maturity described in Chapter 29.

SKIPPING OF A PHASE

It is highly recommended that *all* phases of the framework be considered when executing a BPM project; however, there may be a few situations in which not all the steps must be performed for a particular phase. In a greenfield situation, organizations may skip the Understand phase. However, it is quite rare that an organization or new business line will start from scratch, from a process perspective. In many cases, the organization will have already performed the proposed processes on a small scale and simply want to expand the activities on a larger scale. In this situation, it is important to understand the process experience so far (on the smaller scale) in order to be in a better position to formulate appropriate processes for the future (Innovate phase).

If the organization wishes to skip a phase, or one or more steps within a phase, it is crucial that this is thoroughly reviewed and the impact of this action is determined and understood prior to skipping the phase or step(s). This needs to be documented and subsequently approved by the BPM activity sponsor and/or steering committee.

PARALLELING PHASES

Situations have arisen where the project team has considered it appropriate to complete some phases in parallel. Perhaps the best way of reviewing the applicability of this is by a case study.

In the next chapter, we will commence the description of each phase of the framework.

CASE STUDY

Large ERP implementation

The business and project team believed that they should complete the Understand and Innovate phases concurrently. The rationale was that they were implementing "world's best practice processes" provided by the vendor of the enterprise resource planning (ERP) application being implemented.

The project team believed that the only reason they should be conducting the Understand phase was to ensure that no processes were overlooked or missed being implemented.

The project team did not have a clear understanding of several points:

- ERP application processes are not always (despite their claims) world's best practice and do not take into account the "people" aspects of business processes applicable to an organization.
- ERP applications have multiple versions of each process and the organization needs to determine which version is appropriate for its needs.
- The Understand phase has several benefits over and above identifying all the processes to ensure none are missed. These benefits include: baselining the metrics and people capability required; and providing the first steps in "unfreezing" the organization from the old ways of doing things and understanding the need for change.

Message: If you are thinking of paralleling any of the 7FE Framework phases, the business and project team need to have a clear understanding of the purpose and outputs of each phase of the 7FE Framework to ensure that paralleling is appropriate.

SUMMARY

- One approach to BPM activities does not suit all organizations.

- There are three approaches to BPM: strategy led; business led; and process led. Which approach is selected or initiated will influence how the 7FE Framework is initiated and used.

- There are four scenarios in implementing BPM: under the radar; pilot; in the driver's seat; and business-as-usual. These are related to both the BPM maturity and business manager commitment within an organization.

- It is rarely appropriate to skip a phase in the 7FE Framework. Perhaps in a "greenfields" situation, where the organization is a start-up, the Understand phase may be skipped. However, this needs to be seriously analyzed and there needs to be a thorough understanding that the benefits to be gained from the Understand phase may be missed.

- The 7FE Framework is a process itself and will provide both feedback and feed-forward information to the implementation process.

SELF-TEST

1 Why does a "one approach fits all" approach not work?

2 How are BPM activities initiated?

3 Describe the typical triggers associated with each.

4 Describe how the first three phases of the 7FE Framework (Foundations, Enablement and Launch pad) are used depending on which BPM activity initiative is applicable and the type of BPM activity being conducted.

5 Describe how process maturity of an organization influences the BPM implementation scenarios.

6 When is it acceptable to skip a 7FE Framework phase?

Purpose

The purpose of this assignment is to demonstrate in a practical way the various aspects of a BPM activity using the 7FE Framework. It will enable you to put the framework into action.

From a reader's perspective, the assignment is optional, however completing it will enable you to make concrete some of your learning from reading this book. You should feel free to complete the assignment in a group environment.

The assignment relates to processes that most readers can relate to as they have either completed a university degree or are reading this book as part of a university course.

The authors seek close collaboration with the lecturers and based upon their feedback will periodically update the assignment and publish it, together with a sample answer, on the publisher's dedicated portal for lecturers www.routledge.com/cw/jeston.

We would also encourage lecturers to email student answers that they consider to be outstanding. These will be considered for inclusion on the website.

Please email assignment suggested improvements and student outstanding answers to: assignment@managementbyprocesss.com

Background

The University of BuProMan has recently celebrated its centennial.

It has faculties for Arts, Engineering, Medicine and Management.

The university has ambitious plans to expand overseas and commence offering online double degree postgraduate programs. It believes this will be financially rewarding for the university.

The university has a proud history including a Nobel Prize winner in Medicine. In the last few years the university has dropped in the competitive university ranking from first to fourth place within the State in which it is located. This is mainly due to poor marketing to potential future students, compounded by the fact that many prospective high calibre students do not apply or do not take up their offer at the university, primarily due to the university providing incorrect data.

Its financial situation is becoming worse and the new Chancellor, John Steward, has just commenced a major fundraising drive with large benefactors and alumni and has promised them that the university will regain its number one ranking in the State within the next four years.

Each faculty has its own business processes and administrative systems and the processes are predominantly manual. This has caused some difficulties as recent initiatives have taken a university-wide multi-faculty approach. This has resulted in data entry being required multiple times and resulted in errors and inconsistencies within and between faculties.

ASSIGNMENT

Key metrics

- Full-time students   15,000
- Part-time students   2,000
- Academic staff   600
- Professional staff   900
- Alumni   200,000

Key people

- **John Steward**, the new Chancellor. Has an international strategic consulting background. He is keen to make a difference and has spoken to the Board about making fundamental changes to regain some of the university's former reputation.
- **Beverly Singh**—Personal Assistant of John Steward, has a strong opinion about how the university should be run and is very protective about who should meet with John.
- **Simon Nottingham**—Leading researcher and most vocal opponent to any additional spending on support functions. He believes that all available money should go to research.
- **Peter Ant**—Operations Manager. He has been with the university for over 15 years. He has always been keen to make an improvement, but has lacked executive support to make fundamental changes.
- **Bob the Builder**—Head of Facilities, is keen to replace the aging infrastructure.
- **Kate Redmond**—Board member. Has come from overseas to join the university and is keen to drive international expansion.
- **Kylie Sands**—Vice Chancellor, has been with the university for over 30 years and will retire within 18 months. Kylie is concerned that the initiative will destroy the identity of the university.
- **Daniel Spot**—Deputy Vice Chancellor, and has been focused on reducing costs by negotiating hard with suppliers and cutting corners.
- **Jason Huang**—Six Sigma Master Black Belt. Has demonstrated strong capability in refining existing processes.
- **Mark Spike**—Head of Marketing. Has a background in selling fast moving consumer goods.
- **Julie Morgan**—Editor of the internal newspaper and website, reports to Mark. She is an active blogger which is well read in the university community.
- **Sue Splash**—Chief Financial Officer (CFO) wants to be the first CFO that has managed three consecutive years of profitability.
- **Natalie Network**—newly appointed Chief Information officer (CIO), was previously the network manager. Has a strong technical background.

Assignment task

You are asked to complete the assignment as you read each of the Chapters 13 through 26. There will be questions to guide you during most, but not all, of the chapters. For options

ASSIGNMENT

1 and 2 outlined below, you are *not* required nor expected to answer each of the questions within each chapter. These questions are *only* provided as a guide. You will need to use your initiative and if information is not provided (for example, some metrics) create your own assumptions with regard to the required information. You should not be judged on your assumptions, only your outcomes and approach.

The question(s)

You or your lecturer may select one of three ways of completing the assignment:

- **Option 1: One single presentation**. At the completion of your assignment you, or you and your team, will make a presentation to senior management. You will answer the questions:

  o   Why has this been the most successful BPM activity we have ever conducted?
  o   What did you do and how did you do it?

  The presentation must be no more than 30 minutes and must answer both of these questions.

- **Option 2: One single report.** The same as Option 1 except you will complete a report instead of the presentation. It is suggested that you use the report template in Extra Reading of Chapter 15, Launch pad phase.

- **Option 3: One chapter at a time.** This option is completely different to the first two options. It requires you to specifically answer each of the questions outlined within each chapter, or as instructed by your lecturer.

Assumptions

- The project is to last no longer than three or four months.
- It has no IT system changes as there is no time. Although you may use any existing IT applications used by a faculty for New Student Enrolment.
- The project team comprises two people—you as the team lead and a process analyst, Pia Alwyn.
- You should use all of the phases in the 7FE Framework and all of the steps, or explain why you did not use a particular step.
- If you need to make your own assumptions to complete the assignment, for example process metrics, then please do so and make them clear.

ASSIGNMENT

CHAPTER 13

FOUNDATIONS PHASE

OVERVIEW

Without a robust and adequate set of foundations a house can be started but it just will not stand up or not allow for any additions to it. The BPM House is no different. If you are simply executing various individual BPM projects, then foundations are not nearly as essential as when you are executing a process-focused organizational business transformation via a BPM program of work. In this chapter we will explore the creation and maintenance of these BPM Foundations, always ensuring they are robust enough to last well beyond the immediate needs.

OVERALL LEARNING OUTCOME

By the end of this chapter you will be able to:

- Describe why strategy should be involved in BPM
- Describe why BPM should be involved in strategy
- Describe the strategy execution void
- List the five steps in the Foundations phase
- Differentiate between operational and management processes
- Clearly understand the importance and benefits of optimizing management processes
- Understand the strategy execution void closed loop
- Understand the importance of process design on an organization's: strategic choices; BPM maturity; BPM drivers; width of BPM activities
- Understand the importance of the Red Wine Test
- Understand why determining the BPM approach is critical
- Understand why determining the target operating model components is critical.

> Most of the great cultural shifts—ones that have built great organizations that *sustain* long-term growth, prosperity and contribution to the world—started with the choice of *one* person.
>
> (Covey, 2004: 25)

WHY?

The purpose of this chapter is not to describe how to develop an organization's strategy, as this topic has been covered in many other publications, but to describe how the organization's strategy, process management and the individual processes relate and interact (Figure 13.1) and how the BPM management team can add significant value to the process of executing strategy.

It must always be remembered that processes are not an end in themselves, but rather a means to achieving a business objective. The creation of business objectives or goals and the approach adopted to achieve them can be simply described as the strategy of the organization.

The senior executive team is responsible for determining the organization strategy and ensuring that the business processes support, or contribute to, the fulfillment of the strategy. Processes that are aligned with the strategy are most effective in achieving business objectives and are more sustainable in the medium to long term.

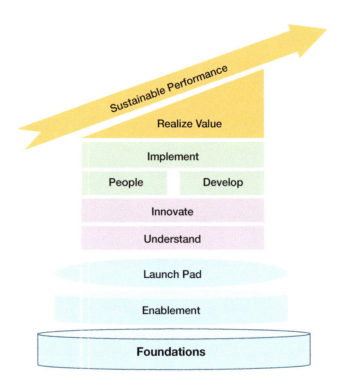

Figure 13.1 Foundations phase

Figure 13.2 Winchester House—why is a plan essential?
Source: http://en.wikipedia.org/wiki/File:Winchester_House_910px.jpg

Having a strategy is critical to an organization's success otherwise the organization and people in it do not have a clear direction and focus. If you look at the photograph in Figure 13.2 you will see a beautiful house known as Winchester House, located in Northern California. It was once the residence of Sarah Winchester, the widow of gun magnate William Wirt Winchester. While it looks beautiful in the photograph, the interesting thing is that the house was under construction around the clock, without interruption, for 38 years and stopped with Mrs. Winchester's death in 1884. It has roughly 160 rooms of which 40 are bedrooms, two ballrooms, six kitchens, two basements and 950 doors (remember only one person lives in it). However it becomes even more interesting because 65 doors open into blank walls, 13 staircases were abandoned and 24 of the skylights go into floors above.

It had 147 builders and no architects and is renowned for its utter lack of any master building plan. There simply were no blueprints or architectural plans. Mrs. Winchester was purported to have provided builders with sketches of individual rooms on pieces of paper or tablecloths over the 38 years it took to complete.

The finished product of Winchester House clearly demonstrates the importance of plans (strategy) and planning ahead so that the "big picture" has clarity and management and employees have an understanding of where they are going and then how to get there.

What are some of the reasons that foundations are needed for BPM activities? Some are outlined below:

- There is a need to clearly understand the current-state position of the organization, particularly with regard to business and process maturity in order to be able to establish realistic targets.

- There is a need to clearly define and communicate the end-state target via a target operating model.

- There is a need to assess various alternatives for achieving the target state and business objectives, and to understand what criteria are to be used in establishing an appropriate approach.

- Business processes are important, however, they are only one strategic element in the creation of a target operating model. It is important to understand how processes will fit into the strategy.

- Automation can play an important role in BPM activities and it is critical to understand the enterprise architecture and IT landscape to ensure alignment.

- Most business transformation programs evolve over time, especially if factors such as strategic redirection, mergers and acquisitions, product innovation and legislative changes are considered. It is important to establish and understand the foundations so that only the relevant aspects need to be addressed or changed as a result of this evolution. Building the foundations and roadmap of the way forward assists in achieving milestones while maintaining momentum.

- Being clear about the foundations and the underlying considerations and drivers will assist in ensuring that all aspects are taken into account, up-front. Many BPM (and other business activities) fail due to people talking about the same thing but having different assumptions or meanings. Having a common language (set of terminology) is critical.

- In a business transformation program business processes (and therefore BPM) will be an important part of the journey. BPM will assist in the building and enhancing of the organizational business capability and maturity. Reviewing and building the necessary foundations up-front ensures that it is also clear what outstanding issues need to be addressed in subsequent activities.

Kaplan and Norton support this view when they stated:

> **Breakdowns in a company's management system, not managers' lack of ability or effort, are what cause a company's underperformance. By *management system* we're referring to the integrated set of processes and tools that a company uses to develop its strategy, translate it into operational actions, and monitor and improve the effectiveness of both. The failure to balance the tensions between strategy and operations is pervasive: Various studies done in the past 25 years indicate that 60% to 80% of companies fall short of the success predicted from their new strategies.**
>
> **(Kaplan and Norton, 2008: 64)**

KEY POINT

There is a growing understanding that establishing a strategy is relatively easy compared to its execution and the success of the execution needs to be reviewed continually to either adjust the strategy or execution approach.

Figure 13.3 shows the gap between strategy and execution and further shows that execution must be segregated into two separate components: operational (process) execution (normal business operations, or business-as-usual); and project execution (the execution or conducting of projects to improve the execution (operations) of the business).

This distinction is necessary because the management of operational execution (the way you run a business; business-as-usual) is substantially different from the management of projects (for example, via PRINCE2™[1] or PMBOK™[2]).

However, there is something missing and the missing component is described as the Strategy Execution Void in Figure 13.3. Kaplan and Norton's comment above and the Harris survey mentioned below remove any doubt that this void exists.

Harris Interactive, the originators of the Harris Poll, surveyed 23,000 U.S. residents employed full-time in key industries in key functional areas with regard to what it called the

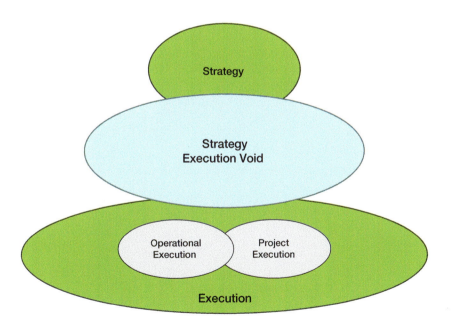

Figure 13.3 Strategy execution void

Source: Jeston (2009), reproduced with permission.

Execution Quotient, that is, the ability of organizations to execute on their highest priorities (strategies). The findings included:

- Only 37% said they have a clear understanding of what their organization is trying to achieve and why;
- Only 1 in 5 was enthusiastic about their team's and organization's goals;
- Only 1 in 5 workers said they have a clear "line of sight" between their tasks and their team's and organization's goals;
- Only 15% felt that their organization fully enables them to execute key goals;
- Only 15% felt they worked in a high-trust environment;
- Only 17% felt their organization fosters open communications that is respectful of differing opinions and that results in new and better ideas;
- Only 10% felt that their organization holds people accountable for results;
- Only 20% fully trusted the organization they work for;
- Only 13% have high trust, highly cooperative working relationships with other groups or departments.

(Covey, 2004: 2, 3)

Now you may read this and find it shocking, or perhaps not surprising at all, and then rationalize it away by saying, "Yeah, that is just what big organizations are like, but they keep working don't they?" It is easy to lose sight of these statistics when an organization employs thousands or tens of thousands of people, so let's take the great example of Stephen Covey to highlight the impact of these findings. Let's imagine that the organization is a football (soccer) team and the same statistics applied:

- Only four of the eleven players on the field would know which goal is theirs;
- Only two of the eleven would care;
- Only two would know what position they play and know exactly what they are supposed to do;
- All but two players would, in some way, be competing against their own team members rather than their opponent.

(Covey, 2004: 3)

KEY POINT

It is of little use for an organization to have a clearly defined and brilliant strategy if they are not able to implement it effectively. Implementation is not just about completing projects to make something better happen inside the organization. It is also about having the right culture and environment to ensure that execution is adaptable and sustainable. True leadership is when the leader formulates the strategy and ensures that it is executed well.

How can a team like that function, let alone win? And yet, this is how leaders and managers are setting up their teams and organizations.

RESULTS

At the completion of the Foundations phase there will be agreement of how the BPM activities within the organization will be approached and supported. There will be documentation for the BPM teams, and organization, of the:

- organization's core value proposition
- BPM maturity of the organization
- BPM drivers
- BPM activities width
- Red Wine Test outcomes
- BPM approach
- components of the target operating model.

HOW?

The BPM approach (top-down or bottom-up) and BPM type of activity (described in Chapter 5) will determine the steps required in the Foundations phase of the framework.

The steps involved in aligning organization strategy and BPM activity are shown in Figure 13.4. While the steps in Figure 13.4 are sequentially numbered, steps 1 to 3 need not be executed in a sequential order; they may be conducted at the same time, if that was appropriate. Similarly step 5, communications could be conducted at the start, end or continually during this phase. Step 4 will normally follow the first 3 steps.

The depth and duration of each of the steps specified in this Foundations phase will vary from organization to organization and depend on the type of BPM activity being executed.

DETAILED STEPS

Step 1: Obtain strategy details

The first thing to note is that it is not the job of any BPM team to create or critique the organization strategy which has been developed by the senior executive team.

Why involve strategy in BPM?

Strategy is very important and is the visionary state that the organization is endeavoring to move towards. Without a strategy the organization will not be moving forward and will ultimately wither and die. All BPM programs of work and projects must add value toward the achievement of the strategy.

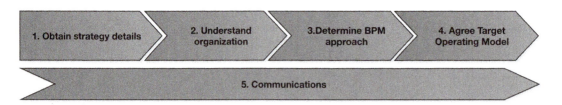

Figure 13.4 Foundations phase steps

BPM INSIGHT

Depending upon the approach and type of BPM activity being undertaken within the organization, the BPM team may need to have either a thorough understanding of the strategy in the case of a process-focused BPM organization transformation or large BPM program or only a basic understanding of the strategy in the case of individual BPM projects and some small programs.

Organizational alignment is an essential part of getting results within an organization, and there are many elements that need to be brought, or kept, in alignment. There has been a great deal of comment and discussion in BPM literature about the need to align BPM activities with an organization's strategy, and rightly so.

Joan Magretta (2011) summarized Michael Porter's ten strategic essentials as:

1. Competitive advantage is not about beating rivals; it's about creating unique value for customers.

2. No strategy is meaningful unless it makes clear what the organization will not do.

3. There is no honor in size or growth if those are profit-less. Competition is about profits, not market share.

4. Don't overestimate or underestimate the importance of good execution. It's unlikely to be a source of a sustainable advantage, but without it even the most brilliant strategy will fail to produce superior performance.

5. Good strategies depend upon many choices, not one, and on the connections among them. A core competency alone will rarely produce a sustainable competitive advantage.

6. Flexibility in the face of uncertainty may sound like a good idea, but it means that your organization will never stand for anything or become good at anything. Too much change can be just as disastrous for strategy as too little.

7. Committing to a strategy does not require heroic predictions about the future. Making that commitment actually improves your ability to innovate and to adapt to turbulence.

8. Vying to be the best is an intuitive but self-destructive approach to competition.

9. A distinctive value proposition is essential for strategy. But strategy is more than marketing. *If your value proposition doesn't require a specifically tailored value chain to deliver it, it will have no strategic relevance.*

BPM INSIGHT

It is important while formulating strategy that the current processes, their strengths, weaknesses, possibilities and constraints are taken into account. A significant percentage of failures in deploying an organization's strategy, and obtaining the anticipated benefits, are caused by ignoring the impact of the strategy on business processes during the strategy formulation steps. It is easy to develop a strategy in isolation, but to ensure that the strategy actually works throughout the organization is far more challenging.

10. Don't feel you have to "delight" every possible customer out there. The sign of a good strategy is that it deliberately makes some customers unhappy.

The Blue Ocean Strategy by Kim and Mauborgne (2005) assists in truly innovating by creating new markets, rather than competing in existing ones:

> Red oceans represent all the industries in existence today—the known market space. In red oceans, industry boundaries are defined and accepted, and the competitive rules of the game are well understood. Here, companies try to outperform their rivals in order to grab a greater share of existing demand. As the space gets more and more crowded, prospects for profits and growth are reduced. Products turn into commodities, and increasing competition turns the water bloody.

> Blue oceans denote all the industries not in existence today—the unknown market space, untainted by competition. In blue oceans, demand is created rather than fought over. There is ample opportunity for growth that is both profitable and rapid. There are two ways to create blue oceans. In a few cases, companies can give rise to completely new industries, as eBay did with the online auction industry. But in most cases, a blue ocean is created from within a red ocean when a company alters the boundaries of an existing industry.

When you read these, think of the process implications for your BPM activities. Read them again and underline the process-related items and think about making a list of what steps you will take to ensure they are addressed appropriately and how these steps will be addressed in the organization's target operating model construct.

Why involve BPM in strategy?

Perhaps the best way of showing how this can be achieved is to take the reader through a case study.

The business was a large multibillion-dollar multinational organization. It caught the attention of the executive team that its major competitor doubled in size over two years as a result of a large BPM transformational program.

A BPM consultant was contacted and asked to supply a detailed project plan for the implementation of BPM over the coming 12 months. The response was that this was not possible. After discussions, the client understood that any large-scale BPM program needs to be created with a thorough understanding of many things before it can commence. As a minimum there needs to be an understanding of the business context, including:

- The business drivers;
- What other business process improvement activities have or are currently being conducted;
- The business and BPM (process) maturity of the key executive stakeholders and employees;
- The culture of the organization (and this client was based across South-East Asia, the USA and Europe, with vastly different cultures);
- Organization structure;
- Executive buy-in and particularly the CEO commitment to BPM.

BPM INSIGHT

Understanding the strategic drivers and the genuine commitment of the CEO are essential preconditions to a top-down organization-wide approach.

Once the client understood that sitting alone in an office in Sydney, Australia, and developing a useful BPM implementation project plan would be of little value without an understanding of the business context, it was agreed that the Management by Process team would meet at one of the client's quarterly worldwide executive sessions in South-East Asia.

The outcome of the six-day meeting was to create the required project plan for a future BPM Roadmap. Figure 13.5 shows the necessary steps to discover and understand the background, commitment and required business outcomes from the BPM activities.

In brief the discovery engagement comprised the following steps.

Days 1 to 3 were about gaining a joint understanding and agreement of the business context for BPM. A presentation of the possibilities of BPM and the likely client approach was created for discussion with the CEO on day 4 and then presented to the Executive Awareness session of the worldwide management team on day 5. The desired outcome of days 4 and 5 was to gain the agreement of the CEO and the executive team (and chairman who was in attendance) to have a half-day workshop at the next executive team meeting in six weeks time. This was achieved.

Over the next six weeks the workshop was developed. The aim of the workshop was to have the senior executives understand which business processes were stopping them from achieving their strategic objectives and group them into strategic themes to enable their improvement.

CASE STUDY

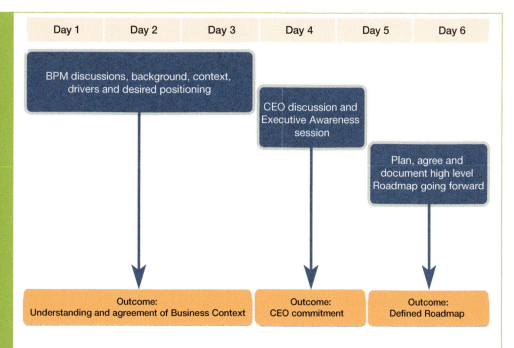

Figure 13.5 Discovery meeting plan

During the workshop delivery there was initial push-back from some senior executives with regard to what was perceived as yet "more process improvement" projects. The reaction was "we have already done Six Sigma. We don't have to do any more process improvement work. We have too many projects going now, we do not need more."

Progressively the executives began to understand that this was *not* more generic process improvement work and began to understand the BPM House concept.

The executive team determined that they did not just wish to significantly improve their own business processes; they wished to implement a process-focused transformation program that would cause a "disruption to the industry value chain." Refer to step 2 (Understand Organization) for the BPM width concept.

To achieve the disruption of the industry value chain it was necessary to first gain a clear and agreed view of the organization's level 1 and level 2 processes.[3]

The template shown in Figure 13.6 was used to develop the level 1 processes. Note that Figure 13.6 was tailored for the organization during the preparation for the workshop.

As the client was a large manufacturing organization it was suggested that what is often referred to as supporting processes should be called "resource management." This name further changed as the workshop evolved.

There is a reason why the customer appears at the start and end of the core processes. The client was unique as its customers came to it with a concept for a product and the customer and the organization then worked together to design the product components to be manufactured. The product is then built and delivered to the customer.

The results of the discussions yielded the level 1 process model shown in Figure 13.7.

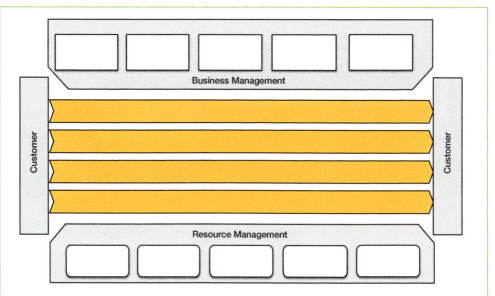

Figure 13.6 Enterprise level 1 process model template

It was agreed that there were four core business processes shown in the middle of Figure 13.7, namely:

- technology development and deployment
- customer engagement and demand creation
- manufacturing/demand fulfillment
- people talent.

People talent, was given prominence as it was a particular area of concern since the international investment company had just purchased two organizations and merged them together. The original organizations had significantly different cultures, were from different parts of the world, and the manufacturing plants in each continent approached research and demand fulfillment significantly differently. One was extremely conservative and the other more progressive. This meant that "People Talent" needed to be addressed separately.

The business management processes, depicted in the top of Figure 13.7 are close to what would be expected within most organizations. The resource management term in the bottom layer of Figure 13.6 evolved to be called "resource lifecycle management" during the workshop.

Once the level 1 processes were agreed, the workshop attendees determined the level 2 processes for each core process, using Figure 13.8 as the template.

Up until this point it had been a typical workshop in which the level 1 and level 2 organization processes were developed and agreed.

The workshop then focused upon the key strategy that the organization needed to double in size (sales) over the next three years and become profitable or it would fail.

In order to achieve this strategic objective the workshop reviewed each of the level 2 processes to determine if it was a hindrance or bottleneck to growth in the next 12 months. If the answer was yes, it was highlighted and marked in red as shown in Figure 13.9.

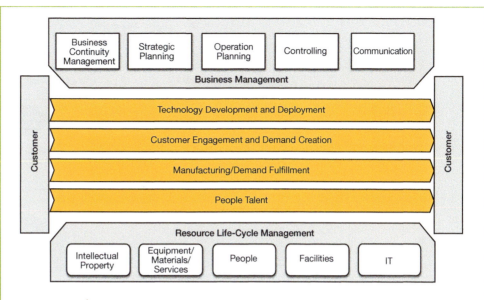

Figure 13.7 Enterprise level 1 process model

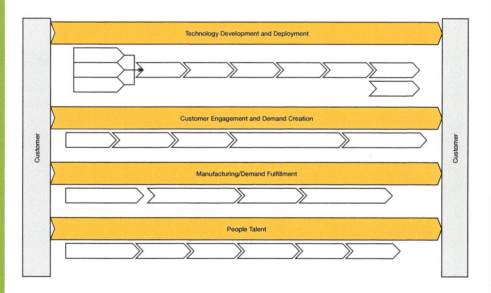

Figure 13.8 Enterprise level 2 process model template

The remaining level 2 processes were reviewed again to determine if they would be a bottleneck after 12 months as the organization grew. These were marked in green as shown in Figure 13.9.

The bottleneck processes (red and green) were then discussed and grouped into strategic themes, once again as shown in Figure 13.9.

CASE STUDY

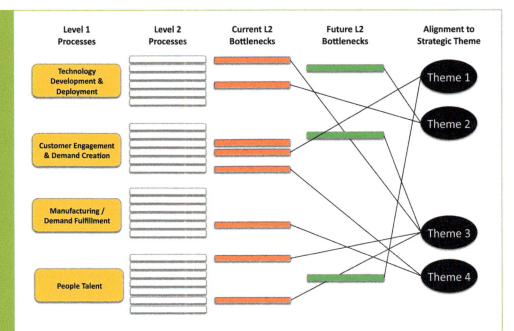

Figure 13.9 Development of strategic themes

	Strategic Theme	Level 2 Processes	
		Current "bottleneck" processes	**Predicted future "bottleneck" processes**
1.	**Theme 1**	• Process 7	• Process 1
2.	**Theme 2**	• Process 2 • Process 3	• Process 4 • Process 8
3.	**Theme 3**	• Process 6 • Process 9	
4.	**Theme 4**	• Process 5 • Process 12	
		7	**3**
	Unallocated Level 2 "bottleneck" processes	• Process 34 • Process 15	

Figure 13.10 Summary of strategic themes

Figure 13.10 shows a summary of the strategic themes and the level 2 bottleneck processes impacting the delivery of the organization strategy. It can be seen that two processes, process 34 and 15, were unable to be allocated to a strategic theme during the workshop, and it was decided that they would be allocated later.

Overall, there were seven level 2 processes that were considered to be a bottleneck over the next 12 months to the delivery of the strategy (double in size), and another three level 2 bottleneck processes after 12 months as the organization grew.

The strategic themes were then agreed and a senior executive was appointed to each theme and would be held accountable for the elimination of the process bottlenecks. The next steps after the workshop were for the strategic theme leaders to complete a series of reviews and report back to the executive group with their recommended plans. This more detailed individual theme review was to include:

- a refinement of which parts of the level 2 processes were causing the bottleneck, and this may require a further dissection down to level 3 processes;
- once there was clarity of the bottlenecks (or perceived bottlenecks) the strategic theme leader would prioritize, scope, plan and cost (including time estimates) the various projects within his/her control to eliminate the bottlenecks;
- once the strategic theme leaders had completed all the investigations and planning, the CEO and appropriate members of the executive team would determine the overall organizational priorities and reprioritize the individual theme plans if necessary;
- once the organization's overall plan was complete the organization began to allocate the necessary funding and commence project execution.

While the above case study concentrated upon the process bottlenecks in the organization, it is not always about process bottlenecks. Many processes provide business opportunities and may require changing to capitalize on that opportunity.

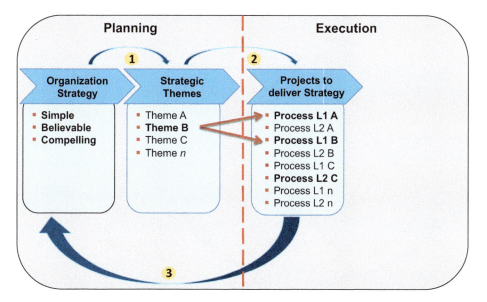

Figure 13.11 Execution plan

However, execution of the overall organizational strategic theme plan is not as simple as just starting. All that has been achieved so far is an alignment of the organization's strategy with the process-related execution plan (a sample of which is shown in Figure 13.11).

The numbers in Figure 13.11 represent:

1. Linking the strategy to the strategic themes to execute.

2. Linking the strategic themes to the level 2 processes that are bottlenecks, or necessary, to the achievement of the strategy.

3. Once the strategic theme projects have been successfully implemented they will aid in the delivery of the organization's strategy.

This simplistic approach ignores the reality that the organization may already be executing a portfolio of programs and projects. Current in-train activities cannot be ignored as they may interfere with or may no longer complement or align with the proposed new projects as determined within the strategic themes. Additionally the current in-train activities will take resources away from these new required projects.

So what is required is a gap analysis of the proposed or planned new projects with the existing projects.

Figure 13.12 acknowledges the existing projects. So, using the number references:

4. The next step is to compare the proposed new projects associated with the strategic themes (projects to deliver strategy) to the current projects (ongoing projects) being executed by the business. If any current project is not delivering to the required strategic themes and strategy, then it should be immediately stopped.

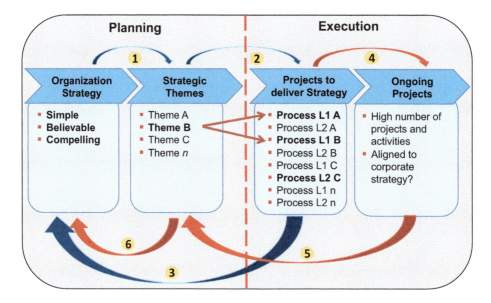

Figure 13.12 Planning to execution accounting for the reality of the organization

5. If current projects are consistent with the strategic themes, are they targeting the right level 1 and 2 processes (to avoid the bottlenecks in this example) and should they continue? A current project may require a level of redirection or may require closing if this is not the case. The fundamental question that must be answered is: "Are we doing the right projects in the right order to deliver our strategy?"

6. Once the projects are successfully delivered and satisfy the strategic themes, then the strategic themes will contribute towards the delivery of the organization's strategy. The fundamental question here is: "If we solve these strategic bottlenecks will we achieve our strategy?"

If we apply this to our case study it shows how the identification and understanding of the level 1 and 2 processes can have a significant impact upon the plans to execute the delivery of the strategy. If the strategy can be delivered via these strategic themes, then it must be clear to the executive team who is accountable and responsible for execution.

If however the analysis of the processes and bottlenecks shows that the strategy cannot be delivered, at all or within the required timeframes, then this information is invaluable and will require the strategy to be modified, or additional resources allocated to the strategy execution.

Strategy execution void

Strategy determination, while difficult, is the easy part. It is the execution of the strategy that is the difficult aspect to achieve.

KEY POINT

One of the authors was in Mexico teaching a number of university professors about BPM and the framework in this book. He met the Dean of Business and IT. The dean stated that most organizations have a similar strategy. The organizations that excel are those that execute exceptionally well.

Execution is everything.

It is of little use for an organization to have a clearly defined and brilliant strategy if they are not able to implement it effectively. Implementation is not just about completing BPM activities (programs/projects) to make something better inside the organization. It is also about having the right culture and environment to ensure that execution is sustainable and adaptable.

It is the failure to execute effectively that is referred to as the strategy execution void shown in Figure 13.13.

KEY POINT

Execution is not just tactics—it is a discipline and a system. It has to be built into a company's strategy, goals, and its culture.

(Bossidy et al., 2002)

Figure 13.13 Management by Process strategy execution void model

The strategy execution void is comprised of two components—management effectiveness and operational efficiency. Both have a significant impact on the operating environment of the organization. From a process perspective, management effectiveness is about the management processes in the organization and operation efficiency is about the operational processes.

When the operating environment functions at an optimal level and is documented and known to all managers and employees, it will allow for the creation of appropriate organizational structures, governance structures, operational business processes, and supporting technology systems and architectures.

In Hamel's "innovation" stack, shown in Figure 13.14, "management innovation" is the equivalent of management effectiveness; while his "operational innovation" is equivalent to operational efficiency.

BPM INSIGHT

The management effectiveness (management processes) creates an effective operating environment for the operational processes. Whenever an organization has suboptimal management processes, it is simply creating a suboptimal environment for the operational processes.

BPM INSIGHT

Competition based upon operational efficiency alone is mutually destructive, leading to wars of attrition that can be arrested only by limiting competition.

(Porter, 1996)

Figure 13.14 The innovation "stack"

Source: Hamel (2008).

Hamel describes each layer as shown in Table 13.1.

As shown in Figure 13.15, management effectiveness will provide the organization with the ability to manage growth effectively.

Operational efficiency has historically been about cutting the slack or fat out of an organization; with the focus on customer service, sometimes.

Management effectiveness and operational efficiency are both required to fill the strategy execution void and provide a sustainable competitive advantage.

Another way to describe management effectiveness processes is shown in Figure 13.16. In Figure 13.16 management processes have been divided into:

- processes that are used to *manage the business*, e.g., budgeting, planning, decision making, culture management, and perhaps a process to bust the bureaucracy within the organization;

- processes that are used to *manage strategy execution*—an example of this process was provided in the detailed case study earlier in this chapter. Some of the horizontal processes shown in Figure 13.16 will form part of the target operation model that will be described in a later step. These include, and are not limited to, risk management; the identification, tracking and realization of business benefits; and, critically, to the governance structure that enables the management of processes within the business.

Table 13.1 Examples of both aspects of the strategy execution void

Stack description	Example	Impact on organization
Management innovation	When focused on big, chunky problems, possesses a unique capacity to create difficult-to-duplicate advantages. For example, managers "would probably find it easier to adjust your fashion preferences than to transpose your religious beliefs" (Hamel, 2008: 34).	Creates a sustainable competitive advantage because it is difficult to duplicate, provided that the management is able to impart this to the entire organization, including business partners.
Strategic innovation	The iPod, iPhone and iPad are not only innovative products, but Apple's iTunes have locked people in to a central repository for music that makes it difficult to change brands in the future.	Can be decoded. Look at low-cost airlines, but it may take time and effort to do so.
Product/Service innovation	Enforceable patent protection, e.g., the pharmaceutical industry.	With the ever increasing pace and variety of technology, patents are more difficult to protect and they eventually expire. Generic drugs then become cheaper and available.
Operational innovation	Belief by organizations that improving the efficiency of the organization will result in a sustainable competitive advantage. Eventually competition will match your efficiencies and there will be nowhere to go but to buy competitors. E.g., low-cost airlines. Toyota and IKEA could be considered exceptions.	Seldom delivers a decisive long-term advantage. One could argue that Toyota and IKEA are exceptions as Operational Innovation is part of their culture or Management Innovation activities. Organizations copying them will always trail as Toyota and IKEA continue to innovate.

If the two aspects of management effectiveness and operational efficiency are now related back to the BPM House they will look like Figure 13.17. The blue box shows the management effectiveness processes; the red box shows the operational efficiency aspects; and the green box shows that both require a structured approach or framework from which to execute and improve the business processes.

BPM INSIGHT

If an organization only addresses the operational efficiency business processes then after completion of the improvement projects you will simply end up with "different sameness."

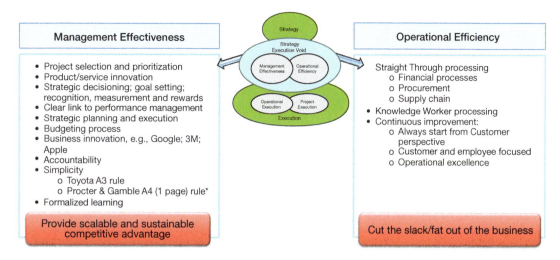

Management Effectiveness

- Project selection and prioritization
- Product/service innovation
- Strategic decisioning; goal setting; recognition, measurement and rewards
- Clear link to performance management
- Strategic planning and execution
- Budgeting process
- Business innovation, e.g., Google; 3M; Apple
- Accountability
- Simplicity
  - o Toyota A3 rule
  - o Procter & Gamble A4 (1 page) rule*
- Formalized learning

Provide scalable and sustainable competitive advantage

Operational Efficiency

Straight Through processing
  - o Financial processes
  - o Procurement
  - o Supply chain
- Knowledge Worker processing
- Continuous improvement:
  - o Always start from Customer perspective
  - o Customer and employee focused
  - o Operational excellence

Cut the slack/fat out of the business

Figure 13.15 Management effectiveness and operational efficiency are used to fill the strategy execution void

Note: * The Toyota A3 rule and the Procter & Gamble A4 rule refer to the fact that both organizations insist that all reports be completed on this size paper. The belief is that people are very busy and do not have the time to read reams of paper in a report. If you cannot write the report succinctly then you do not yet understand the content or problem.

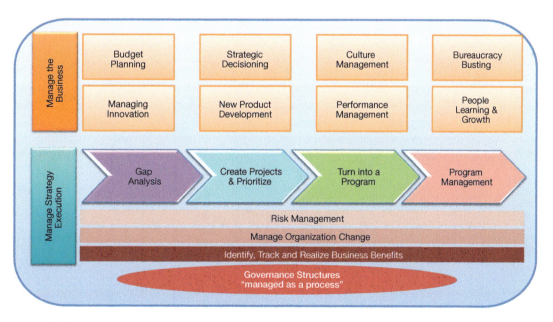

Figure 13.16 Management effectiveness processes

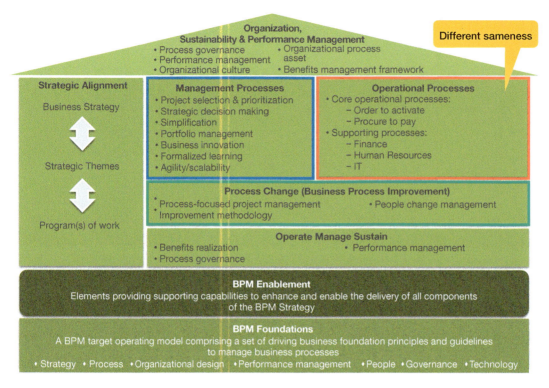

Figure 13.17 BPM House and strategy execution void

The business is really the same as it was before, hopefully a little more efficient, but fundamentally the same with no sustainable competitive advantage created (Different Sameness).

If however both management effectiveness and operational efficiency are addressed, along with the other aspects outlined above, then it will complete or close the loop on the BPM strategy execution model as shown in Figure 13.18 (fill the void).

The numbered steps in Figure 13.18 show how strategy is effectively executed:

1. Once a strategy is created it will be linked to the various strategic themes. Strategy Maps of Kaplan and Norton (2004) provide a useful framework for this.

2. The creation of the strategic themes will provide an understanding of the business processes, especially levels 1 and 2, and the potential bottlenecks and opportunities. These are then grouped into a number of programs/projects to deliver the required management effectiveness and operational efficiency via "project execution." This portfolio management ensures that the programs and projects include management effectiveness processes that will deliver a sustainable competitive advantage.

3. The programs and individual projects are then successfully completed with each program and project building on each other.

4. The handover to the business must be completed to deliver on the program's objectives.

5. This then enables the operational execution (business-as-usual) to deliver the organization's strategy.

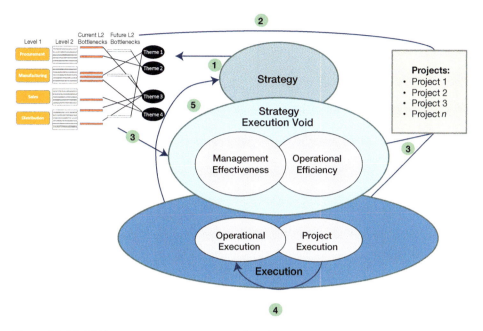

Figure 13.18 BPM strategy execution void closed loop

This is a simple closed loop that appears logical and uncomplicated, and yet most organizations have great difficulty in completing it successfully, as described in Kaplan and Norton's quote earlier in this chapter. It is worth repeating: "The failure to balance the tensions between strategy and operations is pervasive: Various studies done in the past 25 years indicate that 60% to 80% of companies fall short of the success predicted from their new strategies" (Kaplan and Norton, 2008: 64).

Step 2: Understand organization

This may appear to be an obvious step; however many organizations do not spend enough time being reflective as to the context in which they operate. There are two main reasons for this:

1. executives think they know enough about the organization and just want to start changing, often resulting in fighting symptoms rather than root causes;
2. executives don't want to know about the current situation, as this might be too confronting or embarrassing for them.

Truly understanding the organization's context is an essential part of any strategy.

If you wish to design and build a new house, you need to have a clear understanding upfront of the size, shape and type of the land upon which you need to build. You will need to take into consideration if it is a suburban or rural setting, the surrounding properties and houses, as well as the constraints of your financial situation. Once the house is built, the furniture for the various rooms will need to reflect the size and shape of the rooms and the style of house constructed; refer to Winchester House earlier in this chapter.

Organizations are no different except the organization is already a going concern and is evolving all the time. The strategy is the wish to change the organization in some way. For the strategy execution to be effective, from a process perspective, it will need to take into consideration:

• What type of organization is it: one that excels in operations; marketing (e.g., has a distinct product advantage); or excels in customer intimacy? Refer to Figure 13.19.

• How mature is the organization from a BPM or process perspective, as this is a key contributor in the performance of organizations?

• Has the BPM journey commenced or is this the initial stage? What have been the results and lessons learned from earlier BPM activities?

• What is driving the BPM and strategic changes?

• How ambitious is the strategy and program?

• What do you want the organization to look and function like after you have competed the journey?

These are fundamental questions that must be answered and understood for the BPM journey to deliver the strategy of the organization.

Each of these will now be considered.

Organization focus

Treacy and Wiersma (1997) suggest that a company must choose between three strategic options (refer to Figure 13.19):

• customer intimacy—the best total solution for the customer

• operational excellence—the lowest total costs

• product leadership—the best product.

Treacy and Wiersma (1997) suggest that it is impossible for an organization to be a leader in all three strategic options. Organizations must make a choice of one of these dimensions, otherwise they become "stuck in the middle" (Porter, 1980) and will eventually not survive.

Some of the characteristics of each strategic option are shown in Table 13.2.

While this is not an easy model for organizations to perfectly fit into, it does have significant implications for the way processes are oriented and designed. Different parts of an organization may choose, or have imposed upon them, a different strategic choice.

For example, think of a fully integrated energy business. The retail part of the business most probably will require a customer intimacy focus (selling and retaining customers); while the part of the business that operates the infrastructure (power stations, distribution networks, etc.) will or perhaps should have a product excellence perspective (after all, power outages can have a significant impact upon the business); and the shared services or transaction

Figure 13.19 What is the organization's core value proposition?

Source: Treacy and Wiersma (1997).

processing back-office of the business probably should have an operational excellence perspective.

From a process perspective understanding and linking to the strategic choice has a significant impact on individual business processes, the way they will be designed and the expected outcomes.

Reviewing and (re)designing processes will be suboptimal without this choice, because processes are all about making the right choices to achieve the desired results via the chosen strategy. Without the clear formulation of this strategy it becomes unclear how the processes should contribute to the organizational results, leading to inconsistent choices at lower management levels and, eventually, the inability of the executive management to steer the direction of the processes, organization and people.

Strategic choice should be analyzed from a business process perspective. It is important to obtain upfront consensus on the strategic choices, because only then can agreement be achieved on the processes to support the strategic choice.

The case study example in Figure 13.20 is of the claims department of a large insurance organization. It clearly shows that the various managers indicated have different views on the strategic choices within the organization both at an individual score level (right-hand side of the figure) and the average scores of the management team on each strategy aspect (left-hand side of the figure). The general manager (operational excellence), the call center manager (customer intimacy) and the marketing manager (product leadership) have very different ideas about the strategy. The implications of these varying views will be significant for the business processes. Once the visual results were presented, they realized why their previous improvement projects had failed.

Table 13.2 Strategic options characteristics

Operational Excellence	Customer Intimacy	Product Leadership
Best price	*Best friend*	*Best product (or service)*
• Reliability	• Empathy/contact	• Innovation
• Speed	• Experience	• Full product/service range
• Price	• Information	• Full service
• No errors	• Customization	• Leading role in market
• Value for money	• Fast response to changes	• Creative
	• Unique service	

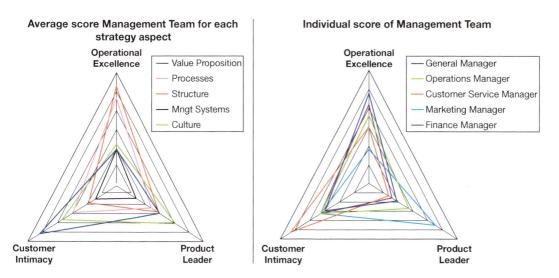

Figure 13.20 Case study of an organization's perception of core value proposition

BPM maturity

Understanding the BPM maturity of the organization will provide assistance to the organization in becoming more successful with BPM implementations. When the BPM maturity level is analyzed and understood it will provide the ability to create a future roadmap to increase the organization's business competency, capability, governance and level of sophistication of process performance management and measurement.

Chapters 29 and 30 provide a detailed discussion on a Business Process Management Maturity (BPMM) model.

This is because key stakeholder engagement will be more difficult if senior managers do not clearly understand and are active in the BPM program. Certainly starting from a lower level of maturity will result in BPM being more difficult to "sell" within the organization.

> ## BPM INSIGHT
>
> The critical aspect to clearly understand at this stage of the BPM journey is that if the organization attempts to implement a BPM program that is beyond its current level of BPM maturity, it is high risk and may move the organization backwards in its buy-in to BPM.

Increasing the BPM maturity in an organization requires a number of activities to be executed; Chapter 29 will outline these. Table 13.3 shows the suggested five levels of BPM maturity from Chapter 29 and then a metaphor for the progression in maturity level.

Progressing from one level of maturity to the next is not about continuing to execute the same activities better; it is about adding new activities on a continual basis to enable maturity progression.

BPM journey so far

Determining the BPM journey so far is not a complex aspect of the framework. It is simply about gathering together information about all of the existing process improvement activities throughout the organization. Once understood, these activities should be brought under the management and control of the one BPM team. This will enable a coordinated and focused approach to the management of business processes within the organization. Building upon the current projects and process improvement activities will be important, however, once focused and managed they will yield high returns to the business.

For this consolidation of activities to be successful some managers and process team members may need to give up their own expectations for the benefit of the overall potential organizational gains.

A critical analysis needs to be completed of the results and lessons learned from previous BPM activities. Only an honest review of previous activities will provide the right path to success: ignoring previous mistakes will most likely result in making the same mistake again.

Insanity is doing the same thing over and over again and expecting different results.

(Albert Einstein)

BPM drivers

In Chapter 4 we discussed the typical BPM drivers. During the Foundations phase it is critical to clearly understand what is driving the organization towards the implementation of a BPM-focused organization transformation program or large-scale program of BPM work.

If you start with the end in mind, you will have a better chance of delivering upon the desired end state. Many of the BPM drivers should already be well understood within the organization as a result of the strategy development process.

We will discuss how to further understand and articulate these drivers a little further on in this chapter when the Red Wine Test is described.

Table 13.3 BPM maturity metaphor

BPMM maturity stages	Characteristics	Metaphor (a large orchestra)
1 Initial state	No or very uncoordinated and unstructured attempts towards BPM. Organization working as individuals.	**Individual heroes**: world class musicians scattered all over the orchestra hall playing the same music. Musicians playing by themselves for themselves. Individually they sound fantastic, as they are world class musicians. Collectively it would sound uncoordinated and terrible.
2 Repeatable	Starting to build up BPM capability and increasing the number of people who look at the organization from a process perspective. Consistency in a team (organizational departments) environment.	**Individual teams**: group similar musicians into four different teams—strings, brass, woodwind, and percussion. It is the interrelationship between the four groups that matters. Music would improve but not be world class.
3 Defined	Experiencing increasing momentum in its quest to develop BPM capability and expand the number of people looking at the organization from a process perspective. Consistency within and across teams.	**Organizational teams**: musicians working more as teams across the orchestra; seeing, listening to and communicating with the conductor. The whole orchestra is now starting to work together and the music improves significantly.
4 Managed	Enjoying the benefits of having BPM entrenched in the strategic make-up of the organization. Capability of teams is measurable to a predictable performance level.	**Play as one**: up until this point the music is dull, robotic and needs to be more dynamic. It needs soul and to be played with feeling. This requires measurement, feedback and people helping each other. Fine tuning, finding the best players and practicing to make them even better will enable the orchestra to play as one.
5 Optimizing	Enjoying the benefits of having BPM entrenched as a core part of both strategic and operational management within the organization. Change will be predictable and determinable enabling the organization's capability to grow to world class standards. You won't see departments or silos or people working for their own gain. You will see transparency, visibility and a one delivery component which is a world class service to customers. Takes a complete end-to-end view on customers, suppliers, partners and employees.	**Being the best we can be**: this requires transparency and visibility of actions. It requires excitement and intensity in a relaxed environment. There is trust in your own ability and the ability of your fellow musicians.

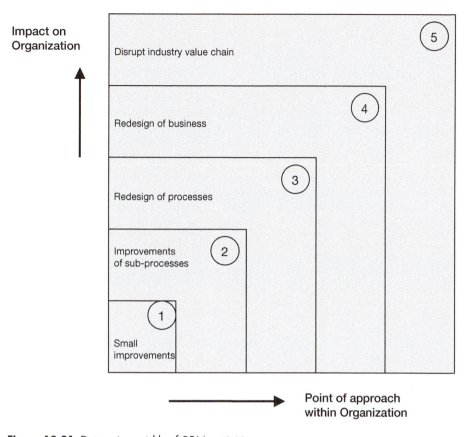

Impact on
Organization

Point of approach
within Organization

Figure 13.21 Determine width of BPM activities

BPM activity width

The "width" of the BPM activities again needs to be agreed and clearly understood. Figure 13.21 provides an indication of several possible approaches.

The organization needs to determine the purpose of the BPM activities. Does the business:

1. simply want incremental or small improvements in its business processes?
2. wish to look at the improvement of the sub-processes?
3. want to redesign an entire department by taking the existing processes and making them better (more efficient, effective, improved quality, reduced costs)?
4. want to take the opportunity of totally redesigning the entire business by the use of process innovation?
5. wish to disrupt the industry by fundamentally changing the industry value chain?

Only options 4 and 5 require this Foundations phase, as the others should go straight to the Launch pad phase.

Table 13.4 BPM width implications

BPM width	Delivers	Who cares?
BPM point solution (widths 1, 2 or 3)	Delivers departmental efficiencies	Management will get better performance out of their existing processes. However: *you can't save your way to market dominance.* E.g., perfecting your payroll processes will not lead to a pre-eminent position in the marketplace
Enterprise wide BPM (width 4)	Delivers organizational efficiencies across the cross-functional processes. Visibility, compliance and sustainability	This is your "dashboard" for continuous improvement and what is going on inside the organization
Value chain innovation (width 5)	Delivers industry disruption across the value chain and should structurally and fundamentally change the organization and the customer value proposition	Your "throttle"; setting the pace for competitive advantage innovation; and staving off competition

As the width increases, from 1 up to 5, the scope and complexity also increases. Table 13.4 shows some of the high level deliverables from each width and who cares about delivering a benefit to the business.

The impact upon the organization escalates with the "width" of the option selected.

BPM INSIGHT

Once the "width" of the BPM activities has been determined, the organization will need to look at (if this has not been done already) the driving forces behind the need for process innovation.

Is the width choice selected because the organization:

- *must* change—external or internal forces are demanding process change?
- *wants* to change—there is a realization that unless the processes change, the organization may not survive in its current form; or, there needs to be a substantial increase in the level of customer service; or, there needs to be a significant reduction in the cost model or increase in quality?
- *can* change—the maturity of the organization is such that managers now understand that it can change and, perhaps, for the first time, know how to achieve change successfully on a repeatable scale.

Forced to change by the market

A large organization was forced by the market to implement an Enterprise Resource Planning (ERP) system. The project director believed he was implementing an ERP application (a technology solution only with no process changes outside the technology),[4] while others on the project believed they were implementing organizational change. The project width figure was discussed in detail at the management workshop of senior executives. It was agreed that the organization wished to use the project to trigger business transformation to redesign the entire business (number 4 in Figure 13.21). It was however agreed that the "width" of the ERP implementation project was 3.5 in Figure 13.21. This shocked the project director and changed the project implementation approach.

Message: Without a common understanding and agreement of project width, the project may be trying to solve the wrong problem and there will be a mismatch of project expectations among the key stakeholders.

KEY POINT

While the discussions surrounding the BPM activity width can appear to be simplistic, the agreement and outcome can be far-reaching and may have a significant impact upon the approach and delivery to stakeholder expectations of BPM within the organization.

Red Wine Test

The BPM drivers, width and Red Wine Test outcomes have the potential to intertwine and overlap with each other. Certainly they need to be consistent across all three aspects. The Red Wine Test is about ensuring that there is agreement among the key stakeholders that the expectations of the BPM activities are consistent, agreed, understood and clearly documented.

The Red Wine Test is not about "envisioning" the future. This is a difficult activity for many people to achieve as it requires people to look into the future from now and describe what the future will be like after BPM.

The Red Wine Test is about mentally putting people into the future and explaining what it is like now (in the future).

KEY POINT

Clients have said that, when delivered well, the Red Wine Test can have a critical and far-reaching impact upon stakeholder expectation management and program alignment. It is a critical step in setting up the BPM activities for success.

From a BPM activity and business perspective, it is critical to understand what must be achieved for it to be successful. To apply the Red Wine Test ask this question:

It is a year after the completion of the BPM activities and you are sitting back at home in front of your fireplace in your favorite armchair on a freezing winter evening feeling warm and comfortable, having a glass of your favorite red wine, and reflecting upon the BPM activities. You decide that the BPM program was outstandingly successful in delivering for the business. What does the business look like now as a result of the BPM program?

The answers to this question will provide the success checklist and end state of what the business will be at the conclusion of the BPM activities. The Red Wine Test is conducted during an executive workshop with all key stakeholders being present. There are two steps:

Step 1: Answers to the above question are captured and displayed to attendees during the workshop. There should be no filtering of the answers and once captured the facilitator must review the answers with all attendees and ensure that *everyone* is in agreement with them. If not, the answers captured in step 1 must be changed until all are in agreement.

Step 2: for each answer (or line) it must be agreed who has the primary responsibility to deliver it—the BPM team or the business. This is recorded by placing a tick in the appropriate column. It is rare that an answer will be delivered by both.

Table 13.5 is an example from a real project where the BPM "width" was to "disrupt the industry value chain."

There are four critical outcomes from the Red Wine Test:

1. This may be the first time that executives have discussed the BPM activity deliverables/outcomes. The workshop facilitator must not complete this activity until *all* attendees agree with the list in front of them.

2. As mentioned above, for each answer either the columns headed BPM Team or Business must be "ticked." The tick indicates who will be primarily responsible for delivering the outcome—the BPM team or the business. This is a critical step because many business managers believe that the BPM team is responsible for delivering "everything" when they cannot. For example, the BPM team may not be able to deliver fast and accurate decision making as shown in the case study. This is the responsibility for the business to deliver. The BPM team may provide some of the "tools" to assist the business, but business managers are ultimately responsible for delivering the decision making within the organization. Sometimes both are responsible, although this should be the exception.

3. The items which have been "ticked" as a BPM team responsibility should be compared against the BPM activity scope—they need to align. If they do not align, then the BPM scope may be incorrect and needs to be either updated or the expectations should be reset!

Table 13.5 Case study example of Red Wine Test outcomes

	Step 1	*Step 2*	
		Delivered by	
	Business will have:	*BPM Team*	*Business*
1	Fast and accurate decision making		✓
2	Deep client insight		✓
3	Deep focus on cost	✓	
4	Not people dependent, but process dependent	✓	
5	Process focused not silo focused	✓	✓
6	Collaborative planning with our customers		✓
7	Just in time capacity	✓	
8	Efficient and effective business processes	✓	
9	Easy and fast access to accurate information	✓	
10	Agile and scalable business processes	✓	
11	Faster time to market		✓
12	Standardized worldwide business processes	✓	
13	Achieve our strategic objectives easier	✓	✓
14	Superior cross-functional teamwork and collaboration	✓	✓
15	Employee engagement		✓
16	Alignment with strategy	✓	✓
17	Beat our main competitor		✓
18	Retain and build our people		✓
19	Anticipate customer needs		✓

4. The business must appoint a business program manager who is accountable for the delivery of the items "ticked" as a business deliverable. The business program manager should develop a project plan for this to be achieved and ensure it is in alignment, where appropriate, with the BPM team plans. BPM programs are not solely delivered by project teams; business must be intimately involved and committed.

When organizations start to think about a program or project of any description, one of the first things they want to do is to write a statement of scope. The scope refers to what will be delivered by the program or project team to the business as a result of the successful completion of the program/project. While a scope statement is very important, it is also one of the most difficult things to get right. The business unit and program/project managers are trying to write a description of what will be delivered to the business in the future (sometimes up to 12, 18 or 24 months in the future). The reason for the difficulty is that organizations

Table 13.6 BPM activities and BPM approach

Type of BPM activity	Typical BPM initiator	Activity	Drivers/triggers
Bottom-up			
1 Simple low impact BPM project	• BPM passionate person	• Pilot project • Small to medium project	• Specific trigger
2 High impact BPM project	• BPM passionate person • Business manager	• Projects • Small programs	• Specific and/or general trigger(s)
Top-down			
3 Large-scale BPM program	• Senior executive • Divisional manager • CEO	• Medium to large projects/program	• Many triggers—maybe a cumulative effect • Divisional business drivers
4 Enterprise-wide business transformation program	• CEO • Board	• Organization transformation program	• Strategic business drivers, heavily linked to strategy

and businesses don't stand still, and the scope statement is looking into the future trying to predict business needs.

The reason the Red Wine Test is useful is not so much about the test or question itself, it is to do with a NLP (neuro-linguistic programming) technique of setting the scene by placing the stakeholders in the future and reflecting on the success of the program/project and determining what the business now looks like because of the success of the BPM activity. The Red Wine Test is *not* about mentally being in the present and endeavoring to envision the future state as this is very difficult for many people.

Step 3: Determine BPM approach

The approach adopted by an organization will have a critical impact upon the success of the BPM activity commenced.

In Chapter 3 (Table 3.1) the four types of BPM activities were discussed. Chapter 5 (Table 5.1) took each of these four BPM activities and linked them to the appropriate approach, or way to start. The table has been repeated here as a reminder (Table 13.6).

The likely BPM approach to be adopted will be linked to the BPM drivers and process maturity level. The more BPM mature the organization, the higher likelihood the approach adopted will be a top-down approach.

If the top-down approach is adopted, the Table 3.2 (BPM critical success factors) and Table 3.3 (Successful BPM organizations and who drove BPM) will be very important aspects to consider.

The top-down approach will require all aspects of the first step of the Foundations phase to be in alignment. For example:

- Strategic objectives will be linked to strategic themes
- There will be a clear understanding of the associated and impacted level 2 processes
- There will be an agreed set of programs
- There will be a clear understanding of the key executive responsibilities (who is delivering what and when)
- There will be a clear linkage to the target operating model components.

If the approach adopted is bottom-up, then as mentioned earlier, this Foundations phase will probably not be highly relevant.

Step 4: Agree Target Operating Model (TOM)

The Target Operating Model (TOM) represents a high level view of the future state of an organization's business-as-usual operating model. It represents the optimal method by which an organization's processes operate across the TOM components in order to align with and assist in the delivery of corporate strategy.

The TOM model depicted in Figure 13.22 comprises seven core components that must operate synchronously to enable BPM to be effective and successful within the organization. These components work together to enable a faster, more controlled and yet agile lower cost, higher service model for the business. The seven core components will be described in detail in Chapter 14 (Enablement phase) and include:

- the organization's strategy and linkage to the current BPM activities;
- process governance, with clearly defined roles and responsibilities;

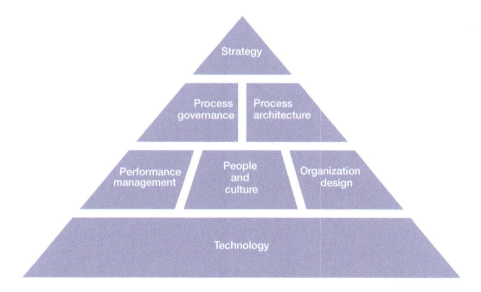

Figure 13.22 Components of a BPM target operating model

- process architecture, laying the foundations for creating an asset of your business processes;

- performance management framework;

- organization design supporting the strategy, process governance and performance management framework;

- people and cultural aspects supporting all components of the TOM;

- technology required to support all of the TOM components.

Table 13.7 shows each of the components and their corresponding sub-component that will be described in more detail in Chapter 14.

The critical requirement of this step in the Foundations phase is to gain complete agreement of the target operating model components and sub-components. If there is a desire to add or delete from the components specified in Figure 13.22 it must be justified and the impact clearly understood.

Once agreed, the TOM components and sub-components must be documented and made visible to the entire organization, especially all management and BPM team members. This documentation will assist in driving the alignment of the TOM components across the organization.

It is important to ensure that the TOM is not totally internally focused and takes into account the appropriate externals aspects and stakeholders, including customers, suppliers and business partners.

KEY POINT

A target operating model will provide stability to a BPM activity by agreeing a set of "rules" from which to launch programs and projects.

Chapter 14 will build upon the TOM components agreed during this step and further detail the sub-components and the guiding principles behind them.

Step 5: Communications

This is the only framework phase where communications is the last step in the phase. The reason for this is that once the Foundations and TOM have been created it will need to be clear, concise and widely communicated to the entire organization.

However, it is important to clearly communicate the purpose and approach during the first steps of this phase. The Communication step relates to communicating the findings and decisions of the earlier steps during this phase.

Communications could be achieved by:

- CEO announcements and presentations

- road shows and information sessions throughout the organization

- Web and IT access to the information

Table 13.7 TOM components

TOM component	Sub-component	Relevant 7FE Phase or Essential
Strategy	• Alignment with corporate strategy • Value drivers • Strategic themes and decisions • Regulatory constraints and requirements • Risk appetite statement	• Foundation
Process governance	• Establishment of process governance structure • Roles and responsibilities of process owners/stewards and executives • Process standards and controls • Controlled and informed decision making	• Enablement • Innovate • Sustainable performance
Process architecture	• Establish the standards for the process architecture • Documentation of the levels of business processes • Creation of the process asset • Maintenance of the process asset • Process guidelines and principles • Benefits management framework	• Enablement • Understand • Innovate • Realize value
Performance management	• Linking metrics with performance • Process performance measuring, monitoring and responses • Maintaining regular process performance reporting • Performance management guidelines • Benchmarking with other organizations	• People • Realize value • Sustainable performance
People and culture	• Building people process capability—skills and capabilities • Access to learning and development • Performance and service culture • People performance management framework • Code of behavior—acceptable and unacceptable behaviors	• People • People Change Management
Organization design	• Defined process-focused roles and responsibilities • Job families and descriptions • Organizational design alignment • Operational governance • Achieving organizational collaboration • Aligning processes with customers and stakeholders • Improving responsiveness to change	• People • People Change Management
Technology	• Enablement of process design, modeling and execution • Ability to build a process asset • Enablement of process control, governance, measurement and management • Online process and operational documentation and learning	• Develop phase • Enablement phase

- posters should be created expressing the purpose and approach of the BPM activity and placed in all parts of the business—lunch rooms, factories, coffee stops, foyers, and so on

- it should be continually referenced in correspondence and presentations.

FOUNDATIONS PHASE OUTPUTS

The Foundations phase outputs (Figure 13.23) will provide critical input into other phases of the framework. The Foundation phase provides the structure and components for the execution of the Enablement phase.

The input for the other phases will include:

- the TOM components agreed during the Foundations phase will be the cornerstone for its detailed development during the Enablement phase;

- when establishing the project or program scope and writing the initial business case during the Launch pad phase the BPM team and business must ensure that the project and programs are in alignment with, and adding value to, the organization strategy;

- all the phases of the framework will need to reference and clearly understand the outcomes of the Foundations phase to ensure each step in the project is adding value to the organization's objectives.

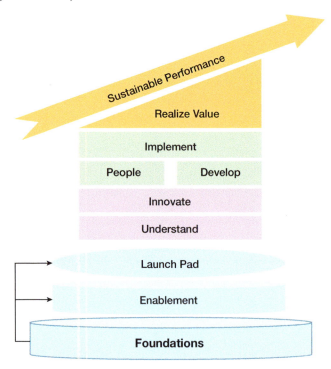

Figure 13.23 Foundation phase outputs to other phases

FOUNDATIONS PHASE RISKS

A few of the common risks involved in the Foundations phase are listed in Table 13.8.

Table 13.8 Foundations phase risks and mitigation strategies

	Risk	Mitigation strategy
1	Reinventing the organization's strategy	It is not the role of any BPM activity to create the organization's strategy. If during the Foundations phase there are significant findings that indicate that the strategy cannot be fully delivered, then that feedback should be made to the executive team.
2	No commitment from the senior executive team to the creation of the necessary BPM foundations	If this is the case you will need to revisit the organization's commitment to the BPM activity. Communicate with the major BPM sponsor to ensure the executives and organization are fully committed to BPM. It is better to postpone or scale back the scope of the BPM activity and be successful; rather than pursue it and fail or achieve suboptimal results.

SUMMARY

Without a robust and adequate set of foundations a house can be started but it just will not stand up or not allow for any additions to it. The BPM House is no different. If you are simply executing various individual BPM projects, then foundations are not nearly as essential as when you are executing a process-focused organizational business transformation via a BPM program of work. This chapter explored the creation and maintenance of the BPM Foundations which included:

- The mutual impact of strategy on BPM and BPM on strategy

- The importance of the execution of strategy was discussed

- Improving operational efficiency processes is important, but will not provide a sustainable competitive advantage; management effectiveness processes will

- The strategic choices associated with the Tracey and Wiersma (1997) model was discussed and the impact of this choice on BPM

- BPM maturity was shown to have an important impact on how BPM should be implemented in the organization; as was the determination and agreement of the BPM activities width

- Understanding the desired "end state" (what success looks like) was elicited by the Red Wine Test
- The TOM components were agreed by the senior executives and communicated to the organization.

SELF-TEST

1 Describe the strategy execution void and the relative importance of strategy versus execution.

2 Provide a brief explanation of why strategy should be involved with BPM activities.

3 Provide a brief explanation of why BPM should be involved in the creation of the strategy.

4 Describe the difference between "project execution" and "operational execution."

6 Describe the difference between "operational efficiency" and "management effectiveness" processes.

7 Provide six examples of management effectiveness processes.

8 How will the Tracey and Wiersma (1997) strategic choices selected by the organization influence process design and the impact on people, process and technology?

9 Will the BPM maturity of the organization impact the implementation of BPM and if so, why?

10 Is it necessary to understand the organization's business drivers for BPM and if so, why?

11 How will BPM activity width impact a BPM approach?

12 What are the benefits of conducting the Red Wine Test?

13 How will the selected BPM approach impact the likelihood of success?

14 The selection of the BPM target operating model components will impact how BPM is implemented within the organization. Why?

ASSIGNMENT

The new Chancellor, John Steward has outlined his strategy to regain the number one spot in the State within the next four years. The strategy includes the following aspects:

- Attract thought leaders as lecturers in key focus areas; increase the quantity and quality of publications; which should improve the profile of the university.
- Improve university collaboration with key organizations within the State, including joint research, guest lectures and internships.
- Expand the reach of the university, leveraging online channels, open a university in Asia and work more closely with renowned feeder high schools, including inter-state high schools.
- Improve the operational performance of the internal organization: obtain more results with less effort (and costs). This will include the purchase of a new single Finance and Student Administration solution.

John Steward has requested you, a respected independent external process consultant, to drive a process improvement program to improve operational performance and to implement the new solutions.

Prior to taking on this role, you have separate discussions with the key stakeholders and realize that the organization has a low level of process (BPM) maturity. You conduct a workshop where you perform the Red Wine Test. This highlights clearly that the key stakeholders have high ambitions and expect much from this program. You make clear that in order to be successful all key stakeholders need to be united and in agreement with the desired business outcomes; they need to demonstrate this by making time for the program; and all communications must show university staff and students that they are behind the program.

The first challenge you face with regard to this becomes evident when you start planning the workshop for the completion of the target operating model; many of the key stakeholder attendees are too busy to attend.

Outcome of the Red Wine Test:

- Kate Redmond (Board member)—wants to be part of the global top ten universities and become part of more corporate Boards of renowned organizations to promote the university even further
- John Steward (Chancellor)—wants the BPM initiative they are undertaking to be used in the MBA course as a textbook example of how to conduct a process improvement program
- Peter Ant (Operations Manager)—wants the university to be one of the top ten best places to work, thus overcoming the current low morale
- Kylie Sands (Vice Chancellor)—wants the university to maintain its identity and to increase the number of professors celebrating the completion of their 25, 30 and 40 years at the university
- Mark Spike (Head of Marketing)—wants the university to gain recognition for its successful recruitment drive and wants to increase student intake by 100 percent in three years
- Sue Splash (CFO)—wants to make the university the most profitable one in the country.

A high-level value chain is derived during the first workshop, as shown in Figure 13.24.

Figure 13.24 Assignment high level value chain

Assignment guiding questions

1 What key information did you require during this phase and what source did you use?
2 How did you resolve the challenge of ensuring all key stakeholders attended the workshop to determine the components of the target operating model?
3 How did you approach this project—using Table 5.1 and Figure 13.21?
4 What components did you decide to include in your target operating model and why?

Foundations phase checklist

This checklist provides a generic overview of possible inputs, deliverables and gates of this phase.

Possible inputs

See Table 13.9.

Deliverables

See Table 13.10.

Possible gates

- Stakeholder analysis
- Understanding magnitude of change
- Organization's capacity to change
- Organization's acceptance of change
- Availability of participants for workshops
- Inability to hold the executive workshops to gain clarity of the above expected phase outcomes.

Table 13.9 Foundations phase—possible inputs

✓	Source	Deliverable

	Other information	• Existing information on:
		  o mission
		  o vision
		  o values

		• Corporate brochures, websites, annual report and so on to determine the image of the organization
		• Induction program to provide input into the key values of the implementation strategy of the organization
		• Organization chart to assist in the identification of the main internal stakeholders
		• Product portfolio mix to determine the main products
		• List of key customer groups/types
		• Business model to determine main external partners

Table 13.10 Foundations phase—deliverables

✓	Deliverable	Used in phase
	Organization's core value proposition	• All phases
	BPM maturity of the organization	• All phases
	BPM drivers	• All phases
	BPM activity width	• All phases
	Red Wine Test outcomes	• All phases
	BPM approach	• All phases
	Components of the target operating model	• All phases

ENABLEMENT PHASE

OVERVIEW

The purpose of the Enablement phase is to build on the Foundations phase. It will develop the organizational guidelines and rules for the implementation of BPM activities throughout the organization. It is a prerequisite for any top-down BPM activity which will usually comprise either a large-scale BPM program(s) or an enterprise-wide business transformation program.

OVERALL LEARNING OUTCOME

By the end of this chapter you will be able to describe:

- Where the target operating model (TOM) fits with an organization's strategy
- Where the TOM fits with an enterprise architecture
- What the sub-components of the TOM are and how they are typically created
- Why it is useful and necessary to have process-view of the organization that complements the organization chart (the organizational functional view)
- The five levels of process structure
- The sub-components of process governance and why they are critical to BPM activity success
- What is process architecture and why process guidelines, a process asset, business rules library and benefits management framework add significant value to an organization

- Why all business processes should not necessarily be standardized
- Why measuring and performance management are critical to any successful organization
- Where people and culture fit into BPM activities
- How organization design is required to optimize process performance
- How technology can support BPM activities.

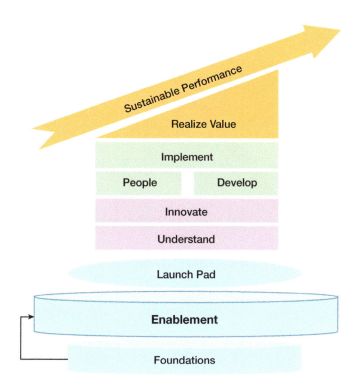

Figure 14.1 Enablement phase

WHY?

This chapter builds upon the BPM Foundations established and agreed in the last phase. BPM Enablement refers to the provision of the key architectures, detailed elements and guidelines that must be provided to support and enable business capabilities to enhance the successful delivery of all components of the BPM strategy.

It provides the link between the organization's strategy, the BPM Foundations supporting the strategy and the Launch pad phase where programs and projects are initiated.

This phase is a prerequisite for any top-down BPM program which usually comprises either large-scale BPM programs or an enterprise-wide business transformation program.

Enablement will provide the basis for a sustainable and agile BPM program, and one that will allow the organization to continuously meet the objectives of the organization in changing circumstances.

This phase would not normally be required for a bottom-up type of BPM activity which usually comprises simple low impact BPM projects or high impact BPM projects, however the deliverables of the Foundations phase can be used as a reference for these projects.

As discussed in Chapter 11, in order for a business strategy to be implemented the organization's management must establish a set of rules, guidelines or principles related to how the business will be conducted. The target operating model (TOM), described in the previous chapter on the BPM Foundations phase, will have determined the organization's view of the TOM components. Some call this Business Architecture and others Enterprise Architecture. Whatever it is called it must always remain holistic and pragmatic. Figure 14.2 shows the relationship of the various aspects.

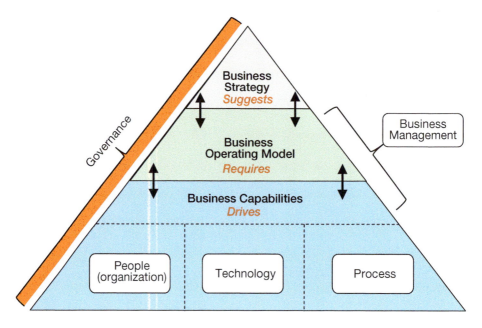

Figure 14.2 Organizational alignment

The execution of a TOM will *require* the creation, or further development, of specific Business Capabilities and it is these required capabilities that drive the creation of the components:

- people (organizational structure, culture and accountability);
- process (approach and architecture); and
- technology (IT strategy and capability) within the business.

It is the combination of the business operating model and the three components of business capability that is often referred to as business management.

It is governance that brings all aspects of Figure 14.2 together and provides the alignment between an organization's strategy and its ultimate execution.

Gartner have defined enterprise architecture as:

the process of translating business vision and strategy into effective enterprise change by creating, communicating and improving the key requirements, principles and models that describe the enterprise's future state and enable its evolution.[1]

Others have suggested:

An enterprise architecture (EA) is a conceptual blueprint that defines the structure and operation of an organization. The intent of enterprise architecture is to determine how an organization can most effectively achieve its current and future objectives.[2]

Even though it was stated in Chapter 13 it is important to restate it.

BPM INSIGHT

The establishment of basic Foundations and Enablement models and principles need not take months or cost a large amount of money if approached in a pragmatic way.

In fact, it is essential that establishing Foundations and Enablement components does not take too much time or cost too much money.

Once basic Foundations and Enablement components have been established and agreed, BPM activities should commence and start yielding value to the business. If the basic Foundations and Enablement have been established in an appropriate way, each subsequent BPM activity will add more value to them and they will grow and become more robust over time while delivering business value. It is this balance that is critical.

While there are basic concepts that work in most situations, they need to be tailored for each organization's business and process maturity, ensuring that they are fit-for-purpose.

Once the Foundations and Enablement principles have been established, and prior to the commencement of any BPM activities, the organization executive team needs to ensure that sufficient resources have been allocated to yield the desired outcomes. Resources include not only money, but people and particularly management focus and commitment.

RESULTS

At the completion of the Enablement phase, the TOM will have been agreed and documented. This will comprise:

- level 1 and level 2 process views;
- process governance structure—roles and responsibilities;
- process architecture, including:
  o process guidelines
  o process asset repository
  o business rules library
  o benefits management framework;
- methods by which people process capability will be built;
- organizational culture behavioral changes by the establishment of appropriate targets (KPIs) and linked rewards; and the code of behavior;
- a process-focused organizational design;
- the technology approach.

HOW?

The TOM components model, introduced in the last chapter and shown in Figure 14.3, shows there are four layers in the figure: strategy, process, people and technology.

The first layer is the strategy layer and shows that the organization's strategy is the driver for the business, and is at the top of the model as it is the driver of the three layers below.

The following three layers take each of the business capabilities components of process, people and technology, shown in Figure 14.2, and introduce their sub-components.

The second layer is process and is divided into the sub-components of process governance and process architecture.

The third layer is people and is divided into the sub-components of performance management, people and culture, and organization design.

The fourth component is the technology layer and, if introduced intelligently, it will provide a substantial and ideally optimizing enablement component for the business.

While each of the components, and their sub-components, will be individually discussed in detail shortly, it is important for the organization to reconcile the current state of the organization with the desired end state depicted in the TOM. This reconciliation will assist in creating the roadmap to the future.

How are the TOM sub-components created?

One or a series of senior executive workshops is the best way to achieve executive buy-in and commitment to the TOM sub-components and their subsequent guidelines. If the workshops

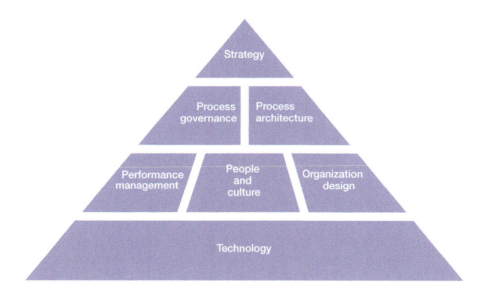

Figure 14.3 Components of a BPM target operating model

are well structured and prepared, they will not take a huge amount of time of the executive team. The case study in Chapter 13 is an illustration of this.

DETAILED STEPS

Figure 14.3 translates into the steps shown in Figure 14.4.

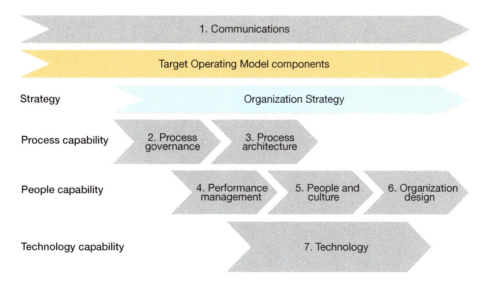

Figure 14.4 Enablement phase steps

Target Operating Model Components

Strategy

Strategy and its alignment with the BPM execution activities have been discussed in great detail in the last chapter. To briefly recap, strategy is very important and is the visionary state that the organization is endeavoring to move towards. Without a strategy the organization will not be moving forward and will ultimately wither and die. All BPM programs of work and projects must add value towards the achievement of the strategy.

Organizational alignment is an essential part of getting results within an organization, and there are many elements that need to be brought, or kept, in alignment.

Process capability

In the final paragraph of the Foreword to this book, written in 2006, Thomas H. Davenport states:

> **Process management doesn't replace everything else in organizations, and it's not a panacea. There have been other authors and publications that have strongly suggested that all an organization needs to do to be successful is process improvement. This book does not make that mistake; it simply argues that process management must become one of the abiding approaches to managing organizations. It must augment and align with strategy, human resource management, financial management, information management and the other traditional management disciplines. This and other perspectives within the book may appear to be only common sense. They are indeed sensible, but they are not sufficiently common.**

The reason for restating this now is that the following section may seem common sense. It may seem like an obvious thing to consider, but organizations generally do not.

Figure 14.5 shows a simple example of how a bank may be structured, which is similar to many other organizations.

Almost all organizations in the world are structured along the military "chain of command" approach which is called functional or geographical responsibilities and sometimes functional silos. This structure is depicted or represented as an organization chart (Figure 14.6).

Yet organizations do not work this way. Businesses operate via the execution of its end-to-end business processes as depicted in Figure 14.7.

These end-to-end business processes will have process goals (say to satisfy a customer's need). The critical aspect shown in Figure 14.7 is that often, perhaps mostly, business processes operate across the functional responsibilities or silos within an organization.

The question is, "who manages, controls and continuously improves these end-to-end processes on a day to day basis?" Do the individual function (or line) managers complete these tasks for their functional area within the process? If yes, then how do they know that the changes to improve a process in their functional area will not adversely impact efficient operations of the process in another part of the business?

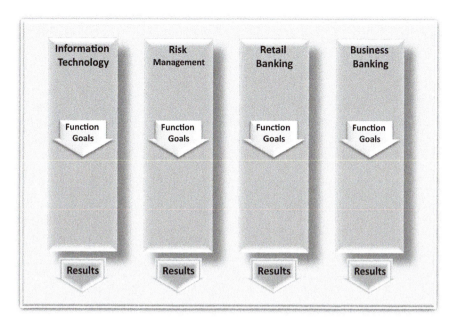

Figure 14.5 Functional organizational structure

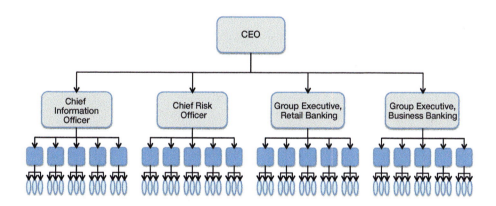

Figure 14.6 Functional organizational representation

While business managers and organizations understand that the horizontal nature of process flows is the way their business operates, there is rarely a diagrammatic representation of this within an organization. Perhaps there should be!

The organization process view represents the highest level view of the organization from a "process perspective." This is known as a level 0 or level 1 process view. The numbering depends upon the organization's preference. The process levels will be explained in detail a little later in this chapter.

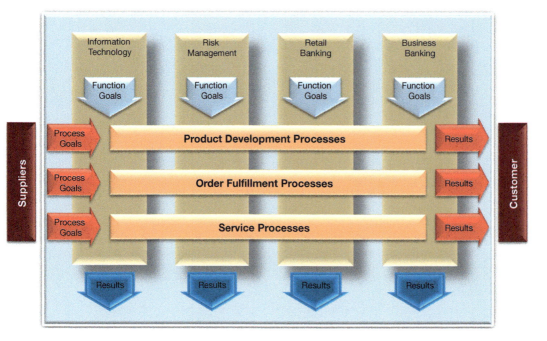

Figure 14.7 An end-to-end process perspective

BPM INSIGHT

The difference between a functional view and a process-focused view is critical. Often functional-based organizations have serious process problems due to the hand-offs (or lack thereof) between the various functional silos. This issue can become even more of a problem if projects are established with a scope that only takes into account a single functional silo.

Figures 14.8 and 14.9 show how two organizations have represented their organizations from a process perspective.

Figure 14.8 shows the 13 global processes within the Air Products and Chemical, Inc. organization. The organization preferred one word descriptions based on the Supply Chain Operations Reference (SCOR) model to illustrate its level 1 processes. The figure shows the seven customer-facing processes, which are the processes of the supply chain plus two additional processes. *Innovate* begins with new ideas and ends with a new marketplace offering. *Sell* starts with a sales opportunity, through proposal and contract and ends when a customer is on-stream. Once on-stream, the customer is served by the five supply chain processes.

As each of these 13 processes was too large to be managed globally by one person (designated a process executive in Figure 14.12), Air Products divided each process into three or four sub-processes which were managed by process stewards (owners).

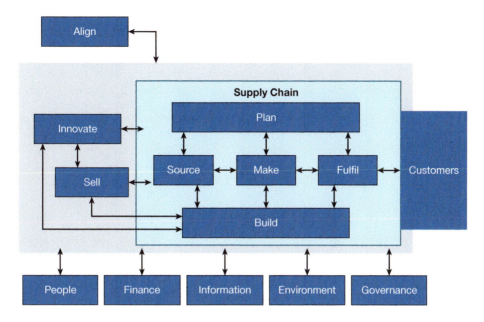

Figure 14.8 Process representation of Air Products

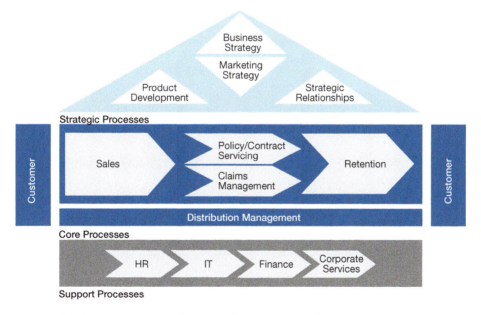

Figure 14.9 Process representation of an insurance organization

Figure 14.9 is an example of an insurance organization. The depiction or grouping of the processes is shown in three levels in this example:

1. *Strategic processes*—this level represents the strategic processes, which ensure that the underlying processes are meeting, and continue to meet, the specified organizational objectives.

2. *Core processes*—this level represents the core, or main, business activities of the organization.

3. *Support processes*—this level represents the non-core processes, which support the core processes of the organization.

The organization process view diagram has several uses:

- it should be used to describe the processes of the organization to all staff members and stakeholders;

- it should be placed in a prominent position throughout the organization and perhaps on the organization's intranet site (some organizations have used it as their intranet home page);

- it will assist in getting the senior executives and all management staff to understand the main activities and priorities for the organization, from a process perspective, and provides focus for BPM activities within the organization;

- providing the structure for all of the underlying processes to link back to these high level processes, thus ensuring that each process fits within the overall structure. This also assists in identifying process interfaces and linkages.

The benefits of an organizational process diagram are only achievable when the high level view has relevant underlying information and is adopted *and* used throughout the organization.

KEY POINT

The benefit of the development of an organization process view is that you not only have a high level model of the organization that can be used to link to the lower level processes, but it can also be used to engage with management in the modeling process.

The most visible difference between a process enterprise and a traditional organization is arguably the existence of process owners.[3] In a traditional organization, a geographical or functional manager oversees both the operations and the people performing them. In a process-oriented organization, it is the process owner who is responsible for the effectiveness and efficient execution of a process.

(Reijers and Peeters, 2010)

The high level process view (level 1 and 2 process representations) enables the organization's managers to define the critical process areas upon which they may wish to focus. It will also assist in ensuring that all key executives, stakeholders and participants in BPM activities have a common language and understanding.

As shown in the Chapter 13 case study, having a diagrammatic view of the level 1 (or level 0) processes within the organization enables a clear linkage between strategy and the strategy execution, via programs and projects.

Figure 14.10 shows the complete view of the process level structures which are typically numbered from level 1 to level 5 (which is used in this book). Others use numbering from 0 (zero) to 4. Figure 14.10 shows a brief description of each level and Table 14.1 provides a more detailed description and the context for later discussion.

BPM INSIGHT

One of the critical challenges an organization will face during the creation of the enterprise or organizational view (level 0/1) is ensuring it ONLY represents the "process" view. A common mistake is to take a functional view or a combination of process and functional views, which dilutes the focus on process and may distract from a more useful outcome.

For example, a bank may start to create a process view within the Retail division of the bank; and have another view for the Corporate division of the bank. This may not necessarily be incorrect, but always start with a "process" view, ignoring the functional way the organization is segregated or managed. Pursue this "process" view for as long as you can. If in the end the best organizational solution is a process view within a function (division), then maybe this is the best solution for your organization.

Each organization is different and good common sense must prevail as to the best solution. However, always start from the "pure" process view and see if this works for the organization.

Step 1: Communications

KEY POINT

A useful target operating model is one that is understood, transparent, supported and is actually used as a basis for BPM activities and decision making within the organization.

This will be facilitated by communicating the TOM and its benefits to all the people within the organization. It will also be of benefit to ensure that suppliers and perhaps key customers have an understanding of the TOM.

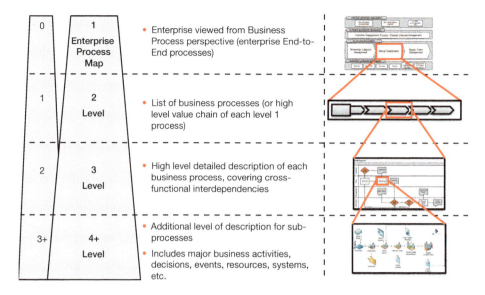

Figure 14.10 Process level structure

Table 14.1 Process level structure details

Levels		Level description
0	1	An enterprise or organizational view of the highest level end-to-end business processes in an organization. This typically consists of from 8 to 14 processes. Figures 14.8 and 14.9 are examples of this level.
1	2	This level often comprises two aspects: • a high level value chain of each of the processes depicted in the level 1 diagram. The high level value chain will typically comprise from 5 to 8 steps, although this could vary • a complete list of all the processes within an organization.
2	3	This level is the first "real" process model or map. It will comprise the high level detailed description of a process. Typically it should be able to fit onto an A4 sheet of paper (maybe an A3 at most). If aspects of the process need to be more detailed, this should be captured in the level 4 as sub-processes of level 3. Generally this will be the level that business managers will review or become involved with.
3	4	This level will generally comprise the sub-processes of the level 3 processes. It will usually contain business activities, decisions, events, roles, business rules and IT systems.
4	5	The last level is generally reserved for either procedures and/or requirements for the IT area. It will be too detailed for business managers to review and manage.

Ways of achieving this include the following:

- displaying posters of the TOM throughout the organization;
- communication sessions that are cascaded throughout the organization, and relevant business partners;
- ensuring that all relevant organization communications and activities use the TOM in their BPM activities and decision making.

Step 2: Process Governance

Governance could be defined as "the roles that individuals or committees undertake to manage accountability for decisions made (enabling success); manage business risk; and ensuring performance management expectations are achieved."

KEY POINT

Process Governance is arguably the most important dimension for the continued sustainability and long-term success in creating a process-focused high performance management organization.

Without a level of leadership commitment to the establishment of a governance structure based around business processes, it will be extremely difficult to achieve anything except isolated business process improvement projects and activities.

Figure 14.11 shows a simple and yet effective view of the desired governance within an organization, and is described from a process perspective.

KEY POINT

Governance is not just about the areas described in each of the oval shapes (organization, program/project, and business processes), it is also critical to ensure that the lines that join each of the areas are governed.

It is important to make a distinction between documented governance and embedded governance. Governance is only effective if it is being followed. Some organizations rely on the assurance that it is documented, regardless of whether or not employees are following the documentations.

The governance associated with the strategy and the organization's board is dealt with at a very high level, usually within board committees or subcommittees and is supported by the Strategy Office. Organizations are generally well managed in this area.

Program and project governance is usually managed by the Program Management Office (PMO) and, at a project level, by the various widely accepted project management methodologies, like PRINCE2™ and PMBOK™. Organizations vary widely in the acceptance and success of a PMO, however, the structures, roles and responsibilities for governance in this area are well documented and accepted.

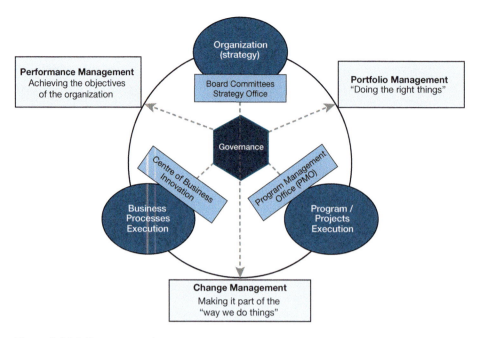

Figure 14.11 Strategic and execution governance

BPM INSIGHT

The best test of whether process governance is embedded or not is to see what behavior and actions are exhibited when things go wrong in a process. Ask:

- is the problem escalated to the process steward (owner)?
- is the process documentation used as a basis for understanding how and why the problem arose?
- is the root cause identified and addressed?
- have the relevant people been held accountable?
- is the process documentation updated and communicated, if necessary?
- is the process monitored to see if the problem arises again?

Processes are truly governed correctly if the answer to all these questions is "yes."

One of the critical outcomes of executing these two aspects of governance well will be the selection of the "right" projects to deliver the organization's strategy. Simply put, the organization will be "doing the right things." This is an extremely important management process, as described in the last chapter.

The "business processes" shape in Figure 14.11 describes the normal operations or business-as-usual part of the business; business processes play a critical part in the delivery of business outcomes. This is the area where most organizations do not manage well from a governance perspective.

If these two aspects (program/project and business processes) of governance are executed well, a critical outcome will be the handover/takeover of projects into the business operations, making it part of the "way we do things around here." The description "handover" and "takeover" are individually important aspects. The project must "hand over" the project in such a way that allows the new business benefits (processes) to be easily integrated into the business. The project must have someone to hand it over to. Equally, the business must be prepared to "take over" responsibility for the changes to business operations, see more in Chapter 20 on the Implement phase.

As we will discuss later in the Launch pad phase (Chapter 15) the business person who will take over responsibility for the project outcomes must be identified and engaged very early in the project to ensure this smooth transition. The people in the business who are responsible for the new processes, or changes to existing processes, being delivered by the project are often described as process owners, process champions or, preferably, process stewards (for reasons described later).

If business processes are governed effectively, and this will be described in more detail shortly, it will result in the achievement of the organization's objectives or strategy. Clearly, process governance is not the only component to the delivery of an organization's strategy. It is, however, potentially an extremely important component.

While this completes the description of the strategy and execution governance circle shown in Figure 14.11, it must be remembered that this is a continuous activity that must never end and, indeed, must continually mature in its execution.

The structure shown in Figure 14.12 provides the opportunity to both manage and increase the maturity of the process journey in an organization.

A description of the figure will be provided first and then some commentary of how this will, or ideally should, evolve within the organization.

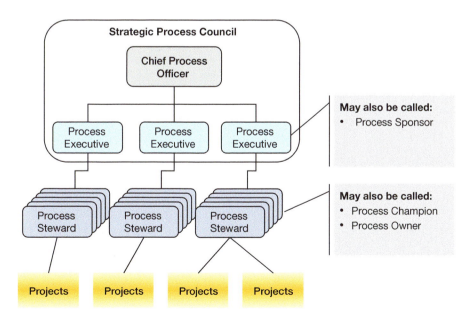

Figure 14.12 Sample organizational process governance structure

The Strategic Process Council is the primary governing body for an organization's business processes, both from an investment and management perspective. The Chief Process Officer (CPO) is the senior executive responsible for business processes across the organization. The CPO is responsible for the management of business processes through the Process Executive(s), who have Process Stewards (Owners) responsible for individual end-to-end processes.

It is the responsibility of Process Stewards to manage the performance of the process(es) they are responsible for and to continuously improve them. This continuous improvement could be via small incremental improvements, or for improvements or changes that require a larger effort, to spawn off business process improvement projects.[4]

The structure shown in Figure 14.12 could be described as an ideal state. However, there are a number of comments that should be made:

- The role of the Chief Process Officer (CPO) has been mentioned in literature many times over the years and yet in practice very few organizations have created this role. On one hand this could be considered to be a reflection on the lack of process maturity, and the understanding of the importance of business processes within organizations. On the other hand, perhaps it is a growing understanding that business processes are the responsibility of all executives within an organization. Either way, there have been very few CPOs appointed.

- Similar statements could be made about the Strategic Process Council; however, more organizations are taking process architecture and enterprise architecture seriously and have used these committees to start looking at this.

- The appointment of Process Stewards (Owners) is an essential role to ensuring BPM success. Research by Roel Peeters (Reijers and Peeters, 2010) showed that the appointment of a person in this role was a key factor in both the success of BPM within the organization and the increasing level of BPM maturity, and that "the fulfilment of the process owner role on the individual level can be very different from the organizational level. In other words, process owners do different things than what they are supposed to do. This insight follows most clearly from our case studies, where distinctive discrepancies were noted between the organizational and individual levels. It seems prudent that process ownership should be assigned to the best and most motivated people in an organization, as they may be expected to look for the maximal leverage they can get out this position."

For process governance to work effectively there will be a need to agree and document a list of process governance principles as part of the TOM. Examples could include:

- process governance will be matched to the organization's process maturity;
- process governance will align with and support the organizational design;
- there will be a consistent process governance structure;
- key stakeholders will have defined process governance responsibilities as part of their role;
- processes will comply with the rules covering internal controls and the segregation of duty.

The first bullet point above is critical. If the organization attempts to implement a process governance environment that is beyond the organization's process maturity, the likelihood is the attempts to implement BPM within the organization may not only be delayed, but could also have a negative impact upon its acceptance.

Process governance summary

While process governance, and indeed organizational governance, is about risk management and regulatory compliance, it is also about increasing an organization's efficiency, measurement, performance management, accountability for decisions made and the alignment between the major components (for example, business strategy, business processes and IT).

However, it is important to note that the establishment of an effective governance framework is not an end in itself, nor are there templates or out-of-the-box solutions that suit every organization. There simply is no "perfect" solution that suits every organization.

> ## BPM INSIGHT
>
> An effective governance framework is a multifaceted and complex implementation. It requires careful planning and matching to an organization's culture and process maturity and will require continual review, measurement and maintenance.

Unless the process governance has support from the executive leadership, management, appropriate staff and indeed, the organization as a whole, then it will be a significant challenge to make it work effectively.

In the remainder of this chapter, and throughout the book, when we refer to governance, we will be referring to process governance, unless otherwise specifically stated.

In summary, process governance provides a means for the alignment of business strategy and the high performance management of the organization via its business processes.

Step 3: Process Architecture

What is process architecture?

Listed below are the attributes that should be included in process architecture. These will include:

1. There must be a set of rules, principles, guidelines and models for the processes.

    Examples include:

    –   ownership of the processes (process governance)

    –   scope of the processes (end-to-end or not)

    –   how will processes be selected for improvement and the sequencing of the improvement activities?

- what structure will our process model levels take; how will they be populated; how much detail will they contain; how will they be maintained?

- will we use existing reference models, such as, SCOR, eTOM, any of the various APQC models?

While formulating principles it is important to specify the following elements as well:

- rationale: the description of the reason for the principle and this should link to the organization's objectives. It is often assumed that people will *"automatically"* understand the reasons that might lead to different interpretations and actions

- implications: description of what the future situation/way of working looks like. This is required to avoid any misunderstandings and make people realize how they need to behave and work in future

- impact: describes the change required to implement the principle successfully.

2. There must be a basis for design and for the execution of processes within the organization.

Refer to the Unification example provided at the end of this topic for examples of the basis for process design and execution.

3. Processes must be related to and support the organization strategy and objectives.

The organization must be able to provide a direct link between a process and how it supports or adds value to the organization's strategy in order for it to expend resources and money on improving it. Where there is not a direct link, and this will be the case for some business processes within the organization, then it could be argued that it may not be worthwhile spending any resources or effort in improving these processes.

4. Processes must be aligned with the business architecture, and information and technical architecture, which will equate to an organization-driven enterprise architecture or target operating model.

This will ensure that management understand the interrelatedness and dependencies between various business processes; and the impact of changing one process will have on another; or the changing of technology applications on processes. This relates to the processes not only within the organization but also to the processes of partners and customers. The impact on customer experience needs to be considered.

5. Processes must be easy to understand and applied by all relevant stakeholders.

Process models within the process asset must be able to be understood by all employees. They should provide clarity and understanding. While more complex technical process models may be necessary for the technology division of the organization, these should be stored separately for the technologists, and perhaps not be available for the normal business employees.

6. The process architecture must be dynamic, that is easily adaptable to the evolving changes in process, business and the organization.

A process architecture should be an evolving thing. While every effort is made at the start to "get it right," there is a balance between perfection, usefulness and the need to "start." Always ensure that feedback is provided to the business team who are responsible for the process architecture and that it evolves with the business and process maturity and BPM activities.

Process architecture has been referred to as the bridge between the business strategy and the IT strategy (refer to Figure 14.16).

KEY POINT

Business Architecture should provide guidance to executives and the business at the time of decision making. It should not document things after critical decisions have been made. Business Architecture should be Just in Time.

What are the components of process architecture?

A process architecture will provide a platform to enable:

- the execution of the organizational strategy
- delivery of BPM activities within the organization
- an ability to understand the impact of change.

The components typically include the development of:

- process guidelines
- a process asset
- a business rules library or repository
- a benefits management framework.

We will now describe each of these elements

Process guidelines

Process guidelines will often include standards, methods, rules and policies. They are the guidelines that must be formulated for the processes and comprise:

1. Ownership of the process
2. Scope of the processes—processes are end-to-end or are related to a function or organization entity
3. Process modeling conventions
4. Selection of a modeling method
5. Selection of a process asset tool
6. Method of governance of the processes.

BPM INSIGHT

Process guidelines are the translation of general business principles to the process domain. They provide concrete guidance for process innovation (redesign) and any subsequent IT development.

Creating the process guidelines must be a conscious and informed process.

Figure 14.13 shows the interaction between an organization's need for low and high business process integration and business process standardization. The categories are shown in Table 14.2. The information contained with Figure 14.13 is not duplicated in the table and the likely business outcomes are highlighted.

Figure 14.13 and Table 14.2 must be examined to determine the type of organization you are and the implications upon whether business processes should be standardized or not.

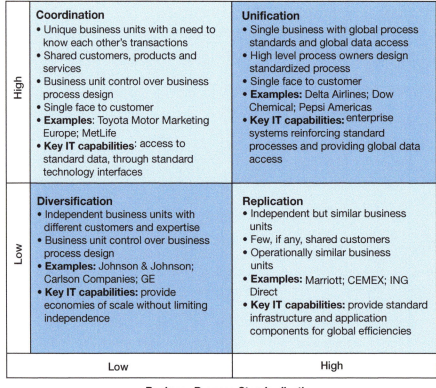

	Low	High
High	**Coordination** • Unique business units with a need to know each other's transactions • Shared customers, products and services • Business unit control over business process design • Single face to customer • **Examples**: Toyota Motor Marketing Europe; MetLife • **Key IT capabilities**: access to standard data, through standard technology interfaces	**Unification** • Single business with global process standards and global data access • High level process owners design standardized process • Single face to customer • **Examples:** Delta Airlines; Dow Chemical; Pepsi Americas • **Key IT capabilities:** enterprise systems reinforcing standard processes and providing global data access
Low	**Diversification** • Independent business units with different customers and expertise • Business unit control over business process design • **Examples:** Johnson & Johnson; Carlson Companies; GE • **Key IT capabilities:** provide economies of scale without limiting independence	**Replication** • Independent but similar business units • Few, if any, shared customers • Operationally similar business units • **Examples:** Marriott; CEMEX; ING Direct • **Key IT capabilities:** provide standard infrastructure and application components for global efficiencies

Business Process Integration (vertical axis label)

Business Process Standardization

Figure 14.13 Business capabilities delivered by processes

Source: Ross et al. (2006).

Table 14.2 Business integration and standardization categories

Category	Business Process Integration	Business Process Standard-ization	Impacts
Diversification	Low	Low	• Independent business units with different customers and expertise • Business unit control over business process design Business Outcome—there is no need for: • standardized or integrated business processes • IT systems (e.g., a data warehouse) to integrate organizational information • provides economies of scale without limiting independence Examples: GE and Johnson & Johnson
Coordination	High	Low	• Unique business units with a need to know each other's transactions • Shared customers, products & services • Business unit control over business process design • Single face to customer Business outcome—there is no need for: • standardized business processes Business outcome—there may be a need for: • an integrated IT system (e.g., a data warehouse) to consolidate and share information • an exception to the need for no standardized business processes may be a need for a single interface with the customer Example: Toyota and MetLife
Replication	Low	High	• Independent but similar business units • Few, if any, shared customers • Operationally similar business units Business outcome—there is no need for: • a common management information system (e.g., a data warehouse) Business outcome—there may be a need for: • standardized business processes Examples: ING Direct and Marriott
Unification	High	High	• Single business with global process standards and global data access • High level process owners design standardized process • Single face to customer Business outcome—there will be a need for: • standardized business processes • an integrated management information system Examples: Delta Airlines and Pepsi

BPM INSIGHT

Typically process analysts and many managers believe that all processes within an organization must be standardized. This may or may not be the case and will depend upon the organization.

CASE STUDY

A global organization with a low level of maturity wished to move from Diversification straight to fully fledged Unification. This would involve significant costs and be high risk, given their current low maturity level. They were advised to first identify and introduce some quick wins to gain momentum, then to commence streamlining and standardizing its processes. Subsequently, it could stop and assess whether business process Unification was viable.

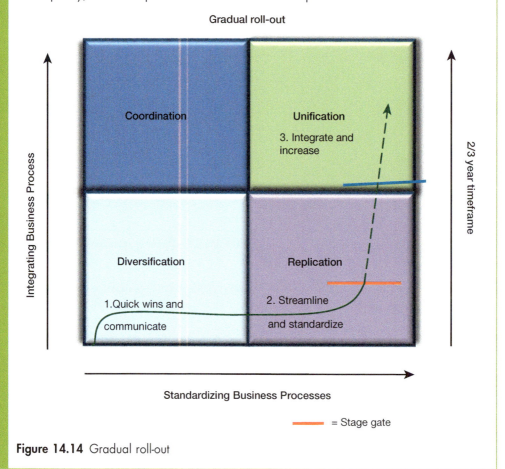

Figure 14.14 Gradual roll-out

Example

If there is a conscious and informed decision that the organization falls within the Unification category, then the type of process guidelines required for the TOM could include statements such as:

We will *always*:

- consider processes from an end-to-end perspective;
- have only *one* default process for each business function, exceptions require Board approval;
- have no customized processes for individual customers, if requested, we will evaluate them on an as-required basis and require Board approval
- be customer-focused;
- processes will be simplified; have minimal process handovers; and have clear and concise work boundaries;
- automate activities where possible, while ensuring business agility and flexibility;
- establish process performance management and measurement to support the business process and customer focus;
- have performance indicators or targets for each process; they should be available for everyone to see;
- have a process governance structure which will require a process steward (owner) for all key processes, The process steward will have a clearly defined and agreed role and responsibilities;
- have process models that are current and available on the intranet.

Process asset

What is a process asset?

An essential aspect of process architecture is the creation of an organization-wide, single strategic process asset.

A process asset is a central repository of all the information the business needs to capture and use regarding its business processes. Business processes are documented using process models which are a visual representation of the steps and activities in business processes as well as the high level links between processes.

CMMI–ACQ 1.2[5] states that:

> **organizational process assets enable consistent process performance across the organization and provide a basis for cumulative, long-term benefits to the organization.**

The organization's process asset library is a collection of items maintained by the organization for use by the organization's people and projects. This collection of items includes descriptions of processes and process elements, descriptions of lifecycle models, process tailoring guidelines, process-related documentation, and data. The organization's process asset library supports organizational learning and process improvement by allowing the sharing of best practices and lessons learned across the organization.

BPM INSIGHT

The process asset is a method by which an organization treats its business processes as a genuine strategic asset[6] within the organization.

The organization's set of standard processes also describes standard interactions with suppliers. Supplier interactions are characterized by the following typical items: deliverables expected from suppliers, acceptance criteria applicable to those deliverables, standards (for example, architecture and technology standards), and standard milestone and progress reviews.

A standard process is composed of other processes (i.e. sub-processes) or process elements. A *process element* is the fundamental (i.e. atomic) unit of process definition that describes activities and tasks to consistently perform work. The process architecture provides rules for connecting the process elements of a standard process.

The use of a technology tool is essential for the building of a useful strategic process asset which is used throughout the organization. This tool must include a central relational database where all processes are stored, may be re-used, shared and published. Refer to Chapter 27 Extra Reading section for a process modeling tool selection checklist.

What are the benefits of a process asset?

The creation of an organization-wide process asset will provide benefits to a business and the ability to:

- have a clear and concise repository of all the important business processes in the organization. This will include:
  o a list of processes
  o a definition of the purpose of each process
  o a brief overview of each process
  o graphical (process models/maps) of each process
  o have a graphical rendering of the process architectures of each process and process component, for example, each process event or function could have the associated: organizational role, business rules, IT application, data field identification, dependencies, interdependency, risk, compliance point, audit point (refer to Figure 14.17);
- re-use processes and sub-processes;

BPM INSIGHT

A process asset creates a consistent and maintainable strategic business asset that enables the re-use of business processes and facilitates a reduction of rework, increase in quality, consistency of process execution and an ability to manage your processes.

- identify the process steward (owner) and process executive;
- have performance metrics (cost, time, Key Performance Indicators (KPIs), service level agreements);
- publish details of processes to enable:
    o process creation and enhancement collaboration (even over time zones) with complete version control and roll-back to previous version capability
    o training
    o online help and guidance during process execution;
- transparency, consistency and efficiency with regard to risk, compliance and audit:
    o gain insight into ownership of risk
    o understand and identify all compliance and audit points and controls
    o easily analyze the impact of new laws and regulations on business processes and KPIs enabling the organization to comply quickly and with confidence
    o increase transparency with automated alerts of ineffective controls
    o report quickly on the organization's real-time compliance status
    o contain audit costs;
- adapt faster to new requirements by merging overlapping laws and regulations into a common set of business requirements, business processes, compliance requirements and reports;
- link to information systems documentation;
- demonstrate the customer experience.

Figure 14.15 shows a summary of these benefits and the purpose of the process asset. It indicates the necessity of starting with a solid BPM execution framework, of how to start structuring and populating the process asset and then a summary of the results or benefits.

When change occurs within the business and organization, Figure 14.16 indicates some of the questions that the process asset will assist in answering for the organization.

Where does the process asset fit into Enterprise Architecture?

Figure 14.17 shows that process architecture, and specifically the creation of a process asset, is the link, or bridge, between the business strategy and the IT architecture.

The process asset provides these links by having the various components of a process documented within the process models as shown in Figure 14.18. An example of some of these process components is given in Chapter 7 (Figure 7.2).

If the information shown within Figure 14.18 is collected for each appropriate event or activity it will create the necessary links between the business strategy and the IT architecture. For example each appropriate event or activity will show:

- the product or service involved in the event or activity
- the role within the organization structure executing the event or activity
- the application system that services this event or activity

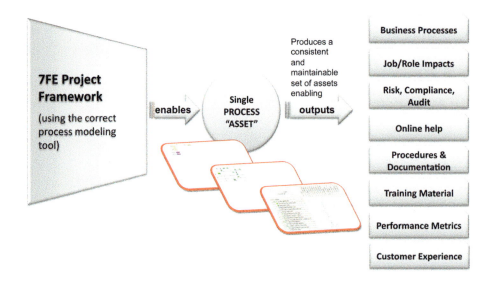

Figure 14.15 Process asset components

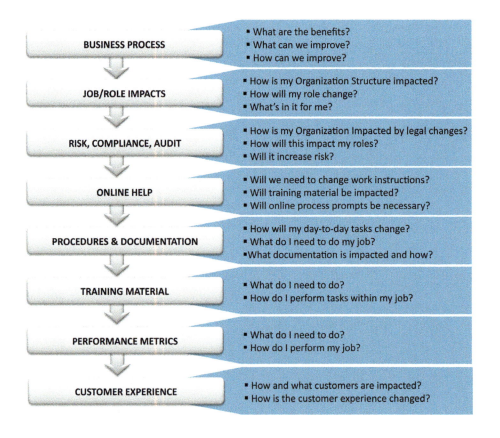

Figure 14.16 Process asset and change impact

- any data fields supporting it
- the associated business rules
- the risk and compliance points.

This information will not be necessary or appropriate for every single process event or activity.

As part of the Enablement phase the process modeling guidelines must be established to ensure that the information shown in Figure 14.18 is captured.

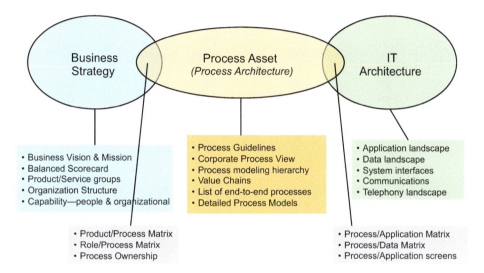

Figure 14.17 Process Architecture, link between business and IT

Figure 14.18 Process model information links

How do we start creating the process asset?

The following steps should be considered:

1. Create and agree the process guidelines.

2. Create and agree the process level structure that is appropriate for your organization, as shown in Figure 14.10.

3. Create and agree the structure that is appropriate for your implementation of a process asset. Many organizations spend far too much time and money laying these "foundations" rather than providing a broad outline of what is required and then refining it as the asset is built and populated.

4. Populate the process asset with the level 1 and ideally level 2 processes after they have been agreed. Level 2 processes can and will evolve as the BPM activities are executed. The Foundations phase in the previous chapter will assist with this step. There are also several process frameworks that are available. For example, SCOR for supply chain management; eTOM for the telecommunications industry; ITIL for Information Technology; APQC for general business requirements.[7] APQC also have process frameworks for specific industries.[8] Unless you have a specific business requirement because of your industry, consider using the APQC Process Framework as a starting point. It is available free and online.

5. The specific level 3 and 4 process models should be populated and evolved as the BPM activities are executed through projects.

How do we maintain the process asset?

The key to maintaining the relevance and integrity of the process asset is the process governance structure.

The various roles within the process governance structure must be charged with the task of maintaining the process asset. The responsibilities must include the maintenance of the process asset by ensuring the process models and documentation is managed and current, relevant, up-to-date, easy to use, in the central process asset repository, published, and meets all modeling, process architecture and compliance standards.

The best way to maintain the process asset is by ensuring that people are using it and that there is an easy way to flag any items that need to be changed. It is very challenging for a limited number of individuals to maintain the vast process asset.

The process asset will be leveraged during the Understand phase and updated during the Innovate, People and Develop phases.

Embedding process governance and architecture

A useful way to embed process governance and process architecture in the organization is the establishment of a business process governance and architecture committee, some organizations may call this a Strategic Process Council.

This committee should have the responsibility for maintaining an overview of the entire organization's processes and the process architecture. It should establish and maintain the link between the organization's strategic objectives and the process goals. It should also know the extent to which each process supports a defined strategic goal. When the strategic objectives of the organization change, this committee analyzes the impact of the change and then directs and changes the business processes to fulfill these new strategic objectives. If this impacts the process architecture, then the changes should be given as feedback for its ongoing maintenance and relevance. If the changes impact the process governance structure, then the required changes must be made. Remember, alignment of organization strategic objectives and the supporting processes doesn't just happen, it must be planned.

The business process governance and architecture committee is an ongoing committee, and is not formed just for a particular BPM activity.

Business rules

Business rules could be defined as "a statement that defines or constrains some aspect of a business. It is intended to assert business structure or to control or influence the behavior of the business."

Business rules are a component of, and support, business processes. In fact, they are so critically important in an organization and its business processes that it should be discussed in its own right.

Capturing, reviewing for applicability and periodically maintaining the business rules are essential. To achieve this it will be necessary to record the business rules within the process asset, as discussed in the previous section, and within its own repository (or database). It is important that the various technology systems are integrated so that all information is only entered once, avoiding outdated or incorrect rules.

Focusing on business rules in this way will provide the kind of agility that the organizations of today need. Business rules need to be:

- recorded and made transparent;
- reviewed to ensure that they are currently applicable for the organization. Business rules can sometimes be made "on the fly" and evolve over time, sometimes to the point where they are no longer visible within the organization and applicable. For example, in one investment bank the number of signatories to approve a payment had evolved over time to seven senior managers. No one knew this until the analysis was completed and made visible. This required fulltime staff to keep track of payment approvals;
- reviewed on a regular and formal basis (say every six to twelve months) to ensure their relevance.

Do not forget that business rules include the delegations associated with various activities. These must also be made visible and transparent by recording them in the business rules repository and reviewed at least once per annum to ensure they are still valid and appropriate.

Refer to Chapter 8 for more details.

Benefits management framework

A benefits management framework establishes a structure for the organization to approach, target, measure and realize project business benefits, and it should be incorporated into the process architecture.

These standards and templates should include, but not be limited to, the following:

- how the organization identifies benefits and links them to the organization strategy;
- how the organization defines and measures benefits;
- benefit roles, responsibilities and ownership;
- benefit planning procedures—milestone/benefits network matrices, delivery, assessment and review points, dependencies, risks, business impacts;
- the determination of what, when and by whom;
- guidelines on how to take advantage of opportunities for unplanned benefits;
- identification of any dis-benefits[9];
- identification of who is responsible for base lining and how, and who signs off on the baseline;
- a benefits realization register format—What is the benefit? How much it is worth? Who is accountable for the delivery or realization of the benefit(s)? When will it be delivered—timeframe? Where will it impact on the business?

BPM INSIGHT

The establishment of the benefits management framework will not only create the strategy and structure for managing business benefits realization, but also the organization's standards and templates and how benefits management will be communicated throughout the organization.

Regular benefit management meetings should be established to ensure there is a continual focus on the management and realization of the organizational benefits associated with the various business cases used to justify projects. These meetings will also assist in the creation and maintenance of a benefits-focused project culture. Decisions need to be made as to who should attend, how often the meetings will be held, and a standard agenda established, which should include:

- lessons learned
- benefits realized (Is it enough? Is there more?)
- benefits not realized—why? Adjust plans/mitigation and remediation strategies.

This framework will be used in Chapter 21, Realize value phase.

People capability

People capability comprises the three areas of performance management, people and culture, and organization design. Each of these three areas is heavily intertwined and is necessary to support the execution of high performance business processes.

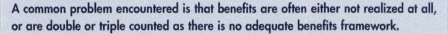

BPM INSIGHT

A common problem encountered is that benefits are often either not realized at all, or are double or triple counted as there is no adequate benefits framework.

An adequate Benefits Management framework ensures that benefits are related to the right BPM activity, even if multiple projects are undertaken.

Step 4: Performance Management

Unless you are treating these high performance differentiators as an asset and managing their performance, then they could become not a differentiator but a liability.

Performance management is about the establishment of a structure, goals and culture of accountability and responsibility for the management of an organization's strategic business processes in a sustainable way.

There is an acknowledged truism that few people would argue with:

if you are not *measuring* performance, you are simply not *managing* your business

and yet few organizations effectively and meaningfully measure the performance of business processes and their people, and even fewer organizations relate rewards clearly to the outcome of the performance of these business processes.

By effective and meaningful measurement, we are referring to the provision of information that will enable immediate decisions to be made on how to react to a given situation. What corrective action is required? How should we do it next time? Without effective and meaningful measurement it is impossible to manage your business operations, and it is difficult, if not impossible, to optimize the continuous improvement of your business processes.

The creation of a performance management environment is not a stand-alone activity as it is heavily intertwined with other aspects of the target operating model. For example:

- process governance—will establish some of the roles and responsibilities of how processes will be measured;
- people and culture—will create a culture in which the people in the organization understand and accept that measurement is part of the responsibility and accountability they have as employees;
- organization design—will support the performance management with the correct organization structures, or roles to optimize execution;
- technology—will support performance management with both proactive and predictive measurements.

KEY POINT

At a time when companies in many industries offer similar products and use comparable technology, high-performance business processes are among the last remaining points of differentiation.

(Davenport and Harris, 2007: 8)

It is the responsibility of management, during the Enablement phase, to establish the framework by which its business processes will be performance managed. There will be a need to agree the set of performance management guidelines. For example:

- performance management and metrics will manage, monitor and enable ongoing improvement of our key business processes;

- performance management will:
  - o report results against targets
  - o provide predictive performance analytics
  - o provide central reporting available to all appropriate employees via both soft and hard reporting; inquiries; and dashboards;

- performance measures will be specified, communicated and be the responsibility of a designated person(s) in the business. This designated person(s) will have been defined and agreed as part of the process governance activities;

- the performance measures will provide management with sufficient information to enable them to deal with uncertainty and changes in the business;

- business and people process performance measures (targets) will be established, agreed, documented, communicated and implemented;

- the organization will have a clear understanding of which of the organization's key business processes they wish to measure;

- there will be mechanisms in place to monitor the actual performance of the key business processes and employees, including managers, staff and teams, against the agreed targets;

- there will be recognition of good performance with matching and appropriate rewards.

Perhaps a performance management team will be established to proactively work with the business to provide the required performance management reporting.

It must be understood that the setting of targets or establishing a measurement environment alone will not ensure the organization establishes an effective performance management environment. The behavior of individuals and especially executives/managers within an organization is not only a reflection of the organization's culture, but will be significantly influenced (in fact, often driven) by the targets (KPIs) set by executive leadership. The expression, "you get what you set" is very true. Leadership needs to very carefully think through the consequences and expected behaviors that various KPIs will elicit.

Once agreed, performance targets must be fully supported by an appropriate rewards system. Behavioral shifts are less likely to occur unless there are clearly established links between targets and rewards. It is an interesting phenomenon that while executive leadership understands that targets (and especially financial rewards) drive executives and management behavior, and yet there appears to be reluctance within most organizations to change the targets and reward systems to support the required process-focused performance behavior.

This will be discussed further in the People phase.

Step 5: People and Culture

When striving towards a process-focused high performance organization the people within the organization are a critical component in the execution towards this objective. In fact, people are the focal point of a process-focused organization and any BPM program of work. This does not mean only having a high number of outstanding people or individual heroes. As the former basketball star Michael Jordan said: "talent wins games, but teamwork and intelligence wins championships."

Chapter 7 discussed the importance of not just assisting employees to develop their skills and capabilities, but to create the right working environment and the right attitude. Employees need to understand and believe that their employer (leadership team and managers) cares about them.

The Enablement phase is the opportunity to visit the "process" aspects of building people capability and ensure they are built into the target operating model. This will be discussed from two perspectives:

1. building people process capability by increasing skill, awareness and process (BPM) maturity.
2. organizational culture.

Building people process capability

Perhaps one of the first decisions for the organization as part of its BPM activities is to determine if a BPM Center of Excellence (or Center of Business Innovation) should be established and what form it should take.[10]

If the decision is made to establish the BPM Center of Excellence (BPM CoE) then, as part of the Enablement phase, there will be a need to have leadership commitment to:

- select a project implementation framework (for example, the 7FE Framework);
- train team members (and business people) in the selected framework and to have a process-focused understanding;
- provide coaching and mentoring services to both the BPM CoE team members and to the project and business people, as it is important that as many people as possible are process aware.

All these activities will be essential to building the internal capability of the BPM CoE team members and increasing the BPM maturity of the organization. It is critical to gain agreement and commitment from the leadership of the organization towards this goal and have the agreed aspects documented as part of the TOM.

People process capability is included in the People phase.

Organizational culture

The collective behavior of each person in an organization creates the organization's culture. It is shaped by the way they go about their daily activities, how they interact with each other and how they handle customer and colleague relationships.

If the senior executives and management, in particular, do not "live" the values the organization aspires to, then do not be surprised when the organization does not achieve the culture it aspires towards.

If culture is the collective behavior of each person in the organization, then how can an organization shape behavior?

KEY POINT

While culture will be caught from senior executives and managers,

> culture is built or destroyed each time people have a conversation, make a decision, choose a behavior and ignite ideas within others. At its very essence it is the way we treat each other when working with each other to achieve business outcomes.
>
> (Holloway, 2011: 13)

Chapter 25 will provide a suggested list of the various detailed aspects that lead to an outstanding culture and will build on Figure 14.19. This figure depicts behavior as the key component in culture. It suggests that behavior may be significantly influenced by:

- the targets and KPIs set for people (especially executives and managers) and the linked rewards for successfully achieving the targets;
- the creation of a code of behavior.

The starting point is always with the leadership team. To change the culture of an organization, the leadership team's behavior and culture *must* change first. As Stephen Covey said, "Motivation is a fire from within. If someone else tries to light that fire under you, chances are it will burn briefly."[11] If you try to change an organization's culture without starting with the leadership team then the fire will burn briefly with employees. All leaders can do is to *invite* employees to change the culture, because people love change, just so long as it is their own idea.

If a code of behavior is created and rewards are provided that are received only as a result of successful performance, then execution will improve. The code of behavior should create a culture of integrity and honesty, while rewards influence the culture to move toward the successful execution of objectives, targets and goals. It is suggested that as part of the creating of the target operating model, the organization ensure that a code of conduct is created.

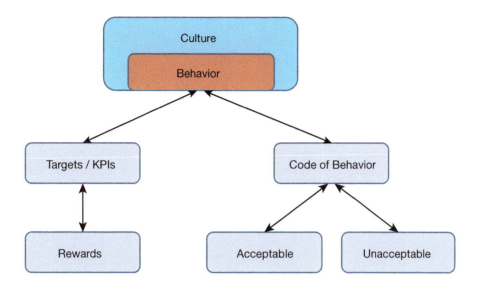

Figure 14.19 Changing behavior and culture

KEY POINT

Remember "culture is caught, not taught."

This will be further discussed in Chapter 25, People Change Management.

Step 6: Organization Design

Organization design could be defined as: a formal, guided process for integrating the people, information and technology of an organization. It is used to match the *form* of the organization as closely as possible to the purpose(s) the organization seeks to achieve. Through the design process, organizations act to improve the probability that the collective efforts of members will be successful.

Key aspects of organizational design include:

- organizational culture and maturity;
- people capability—building internal capability;
- complement and support the execution of the business processes;
- support business operational governance;
- support and enable performance management;
- ensure that organizational business and departmental collaboration is encouraged and maximized.

Many organizations and managers are quick to criticize and blame the people in the organization for any lack of performance. This is rarely the fault of the personnel on the "workshop floor" who execute the processes. An organization should approach an improvement program in the following sequence:

1. *Processes*—ensure the processes are efficient and effective and add value to the organization strategy.

2. *Structure*—ensure the organizational design (structure of roles and responsibilities) is appropriate, or as close to appropriate as you can, to support the new processes.

3. *People*—only after the processes and structure steps have been addressed, optimized and implemented can you evaluate the performance of the people.

In establishing the organization design sub-component of the target operating model there are a number of decisions to be made and guidelines established; for example, the organization design will:

- be process-led—takes into account the reality that the organization's end-to-end business processes are executed horizontally across the organization and may cut across several or many organization business units or departments. The organization structure will take this into account to allow the process to be optimized;

- be based on geographical and/or customer needs as appropriate;

- group similar processes to be managed under the one role. This will enable the organization to simplify the organization design by having fewer layers of management looking after similar activities;

- take into consideration the span of control. Note: for routine and transactional roles there can be a greater span of control;

- ensure that accountability is devolved to the lowest level possible;

- enable the performance management system (objectives, KPIs and rewards) to be optimized;

- ensure that the business operational governance is considered and accommodated in the design;

- ensure that organizational business and departmental collaboration is encouraged and maximized.

Step 7: Technology

The technology component of the target operating model does not require an explanation here. The organization will (or certainly should) already have an IT strategy, an IT plan and an IT architecture. The TOM, and especially the process asset, must link into these artifacts which contain the necessary guidelines regarding technology.

In Chapter 8 we described the technology components of a Business Process Management System (BPMS). If a BPMS has been implemented, or is being implemented, then it will need to comply with the IT architecture, or have the IT architecture enhanced to take it into consideration.

The selection of a BPMS toolset is *not* one of the first activities or steps in the implementation of BPM activities. Certainly a tool to assist in the creation of a process asset and business rules library can be useful. As a general statement 70 percent of the benefits to be made by optimizing business process performance will be achieved by process innovation/redesign and business rule improvement, before the engagement or support of technology. Obviously this will depend upon your strategy, business model and type of business/industry.

Technology will be discussed in the Develop phase.

ENABLEMENT PHASE OUTPUTS

The Enablement phase outputs (Figure 14.20) will provide critical input into other phases of the framework, including the following few examples:

- the TOM will provide the guidelines as to how the project should be scoped and established during the Launch pad phase;
- the TOM will also provide the guidelines for nearly all the phases in the framework;
- it will also provide feedback about the appropriateness of the Foundation phase components and the ability of the organization to deliver the strategy via its current business processes.

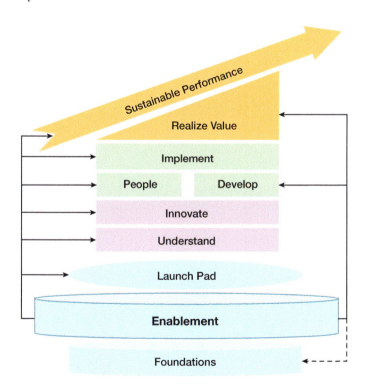

Figure 14.20 Enablement phase outputs to other phases

ENABLEMENT PHASE RISKS

A few of the common risks involved in the Enablement phase are listed in Table 14.3.

Table 14.3 Enablement phase risks and mitigation strategies

	Risk	Mitigation strategy
1	The is no, or insufficient, agreement of the TOM by the executive and management team	Consult with the CEO and/or BPM program sponsor to create a plan to overcome this risk. It is essential that this is resolved before proceeding with any major BPM activity.
2	The TOM has insufficient detail	Consult with the CEO and/or BPM program sponsor to create a plan to overcome this risk. It is essential that this is resolved before proceeding with any major BPM activity, unless the BPM team and sponsor are confident the missing details can be completed during the initial BPM activities.
3	The TOM takes too long to create and/or is in too much detail	This can delay the commencement of BPM activities and therefore has the potential of creating the impression within the business that BPM is delivering no value to the business. This is a risk that can frequently occur.
		Ensure that both the BPM sponsor and BPM manager takes control to ensure this does not occur.

SUMMARY

The Enablement phase has built on the outcomes of the Foundations phase. It has developed and agreed the organizational guidelines and rules for the implementation of BPM activities throughout the organization. Enablement is a prerequisite for any top-down BPM activity which will usually comprise either a large-scale BPM program(s) or an enterprise-wide business transformation program.

The TOM components and their sub-components have been defined.

The most critical aspect for the organization to understand is that the establishment of basic Foundations and Enablement models and principles need not take months or cost a large amount of money if approached in a pragmatic way.

SELF-TEST

1 The Enablement phase is only necessary in certain BPM circumstances. What are these circumstances and why is it necessary?

2 What is usually the best method to create the TOM components?

3 What are the five levels of a process structure? Provide a brief description of each level.

4. Describe the six aspects of strategy and execution governance.

5 Describe a sample organizational process governance structure.

6 What is process architecture and what are the typical aspects?

7 Why is process standardization not always the right choice?

8 What is a process asset and what are the benefits of having it?

9 Describe a benefits management framework and list five aspects.

10 What is the purpose and benefit of performance management guidelines?

11 How can people process capability be built and why is it important?

12 Why is matching the organizational design to business processes important?

13 How does technology contribute to BPM enablement?

ASSIGNMENT

Pete Ant (Operations Manager—comparable with a Chief Operation Officer) has been selected by John and you to be the main Business Lead for the BPM program. Pete has been complaining about the lack of performance, but never felt empowered to undertake a major initiative to correct this.

Pete and John run workshops to complete the details of the Target Operating Model, as well as the Benefit Framework.

Key aspects of the Target Operating Model are:

- **Process Framework**

  During the discussion it became evident that the following aspects need to be added/adjusted:

  o Marketing and Sales to ensure that a Marketing Strategy is formulated, including SMART objectives (Specific, Measurable, Achievable, Realistic and Timely) and that all Public Relations (PR) and Sales activities (including online) are contributing towards achieving these objectives

  o Student Management must look more broadly than just the administration, and review the entire student lifecycle o Partner Management—the executives realize that they need to work together with partners to more effectively achieve the objectives

o Alumni Management—work closely with the student alumni

o Strategy—needs to be recognized as a key process to establish the direction of the university and then track progress

o Corporate Support—run the university as a corporate entity.

- **Performance Management**
  The following principle will be used:

  Principle: All processes will have process owners assigned to them and they will be held accountable for the execution of the processes. The process owner's accountabilities and responsibilities will be considered during their performance review.
  Rationale: To achieve performance, people need to be held accountable.
  Implication: Process owners need to be considered during any change to the process or the underlying systems.
  Impact: this will be a major change in the organization and require excellent communication and explanation. Process owners will require training and coaching.

- **People Capability**
  The following principle will be used:

  Principle: All employees will be empowered to make more decisions and take ownership of their activities.
  Rationale: Employees must be actively engaged and committed to provide more value.
  Implication: Staff will be able to be able to make more decisions and become actively involved in relevant aspects of the business.
  Impact: Staff need to be trained and coached. Special attention must be given to middle management to enable them to support and facilitate staff members.

- **Organization Design**
  The following principles will be used:

  Principle: Common supporting processes will be centralized in a Shared Service department.
  Rationale: Provide more effective and efficient services by achieving economies of scale, overflow mechanisms and centers of expertise.
  Implication: Each faculty must now use the Shared Service business unit.
  Impact: Reorganization and reallocation of staff and the introduction of internal Service Level Agreements.

- **Target Operating Model**
  The executives have expressed a desire for the following outcomes:

  o Need for consistent student-related processes (including alumni) to achieve economies of scale and provide all students with a consistent and seamless service with streamlined processes. Minor variations will only be allowed for truly unique different circumstances (e.g., online or overseas). All variations will require the approval of the Chancellor.

ASSIGNMENT

o Have a single access portal of all partners as many have complained that they have had to provide similar data multiple times and that some data were outdated. Faculties will have the ability to define their own suitable process for tight collaboration with their partners. The executives encourage the faculties to share their best practices with each other and that they learn and adopt from each other.

o The Chancellor has assured the research staff that they would still have freedom to perform their research following their own processes. Some faculties have been very protective of their research data, while others are keen to share their data on a quid pro quo basis. The Chancellor has indicated that research stage gates may be included to assist in universal reporting.

ASSIGNMENT

Assignment guiding questions

1 How would you update the Value Chain and what is your rationale?
2 Please provide at least one more principle for each dimension of the Target Operating Model.
3 Please specify which part of Figure 14.13 and Table 14.2 should be chosen for:
   • Student administration processes
   • Partner processes
   • Research processes.

Please provide reasons.

Enablement phase checklist

This checklist provides a generic overview of possible inputs, deliverables and gates of this phase.

Possible inputs

See Table 14.4.

Deliverables

See Table 14.5.

Possible gates

• Stakeholder analysis
• Understanding magnitude of change
• Organization's capacity to change
• Organization's acceptance of change
• Availability of participants for workshops
• Inability to gain sufficient time and attention of the executive and senior management to gain clarity of the above expected phase outcomes.

Table 14.4 Enablement phase—possible inputs

✓	Source	Deliverable
	Foundations phase	• Organization's core value proposition
		• BPM maturity of the organization
		• BPM drivers
		• BPM activities width
		• Red Wine Test outcomes
		• BPM approach
		• Components of the target operating model

Table 14.5 Enablement phase—deliverables

✓	Deliverable	Used in phase
	Level 1 and level 2 process views	• All phases
	Process Governance structure—roles and responsibilities	• All phases
	Process architecture, including: • Process guidelines • Process asset repository • Business rules library • Benefits management framework	• All phases
	Methods by which people process capability will be built	• All phases
	Organizational culture behavior changes by the establishment of appropriate targets (KPIs) and linked rewards	• All phases
	Code of behavior	• All phases
	Technology approach	• All phases

CHAPTER 15

LAUNCH PAD PHASE

OVERVIEW

The Launch pad phase is the aspect of a BPM activity from which one or more BPM projects are launched. This chapter covers how to identify how to start the BPM activities; how to ensure you have identified and engaged with key stakeholders; how to ensure that all stakeholders and their expectations are matched and understood by all.

It is about ensuring that you have done all you can to establish the BPM activity for success, minimizing and managing business risk.

OVERALL LEARNING OUTCOME

By the end of this chapter you will be able to understand:

- The importance of the Launch pad phase and the main steps
- When to complete a high level process walkthrough
- The purpose of stakeholder identification and engagement
- Where and how to start the BPM activity (assuming a process-driven project)
- The drivers for your stakeholders and team members—the Red Wine Test
- Why early identification of the likely implementation approach is important
- Why the agreement of the process governance approach is important at this stage of the project

- The importance of an initial business case and its purpose throughout the project
- How to define and establish a typical BPM team
- How to develop the initial plan (schedule).

WHY?

It is often very difficult for organizations to determine where to start a BPM activity. The organization may know it has operational inefficiencies and issues within a particular business unit; however, how and where to start can be a very difficult decision. This can particularly be the case in a business transformation program of work.

The Launch pad phase (Figure 15.1) is the platform from which BPM activities are scoped, established and launched (see Figure 15.2).

In the case of a business- or process-issue led project, sufficient high level business and process analysis needs to be completed during this phase to enable the organization to determine a logical place to start, as well as determine the required effort to execute the BPM activity and the possible benefits. The analysis completed during the Foundations phase in

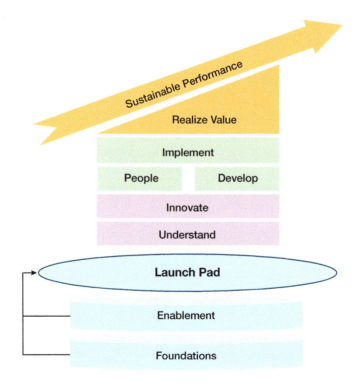

Figure 15.1 Launch pad phase

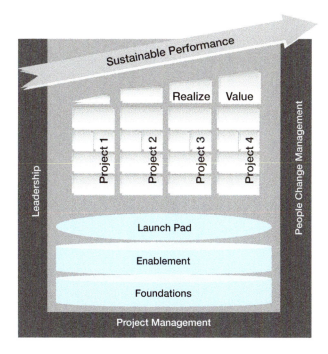

Figure 15.2 BPM Launch pad

the creation of a process asset will assist. In the case of the strategy led project, the starting point will predominantly be known (although it may require some refining).

This phase will not only provide a way of starting; it will also complete the steps necessary to establish the BPM activity for success. These steps include: BPM scope; project team selection and structure; stakeholder expectations, establishment and engagement; and the establishment of the initial process goals. Each subsequent project launched from this Launch pad will be able to benefit from synergies and lessons learned from previous BPM activities, rather than starting from scratch and/or reinventing the wheel every time. For an organization to progress, it is crucial that lessons learned are systematically and structurally embedded within the approach.

RESULTS

The results that should be expected from the Launch pad phase will include:

1. Identification of stakeholders involved or associated with the BPM activity.
2. Stakeholder engagement and commitment; and documented and agreed expectations.
3. Process selection matrix (if appropriate).
4. A list of identified high level business processes and initial metrics.
5. A list of agreed process goals.

6. Agreement of the process governance for the processes in the BPM activity.

7. Prioritized processes for the Understand phase.

8. An initial implementation approach.

9. Project management:

   - project charter document

   - project scope document

   - initial draft of the project plan/schedule (the Understand phase plan/schedule will be completed in detail)

   - determination and documentation of the initial communications strategy

   - initial risk analysis.

10. Development of the initial business case.

HOW?

To have a successful outcome from the Launch pad phase, there are several high level steps that must be followed (see Figure 15.3). How the BPM activity has been selected will assist in determining the approach to using the 7FE Framework and this will be discussed as each step is described.

All steps will still need to be covered; however, the BPM activity selection method will determine the depth of some of the steps. This will be mentioned as each step is described.

DETAILED STEPS

Step 1: Communications

Prior to the phase commencing, people within the organization should be informed of the BPM activity, its goals, its initial or likely scope, and indicative timeframes. Within some organizations, BPM activities still have a stigma attached to them from the business process reengineering (BPR) days—the view is that BPR equals downsizing, and people will be retrenched. This issue needs to be handled at the start with appropriate communication, informing personnel why BPM is different.

Communication must then continue throughout the phase, and the entire BPM activities, as the scope and plans/schedules are refined. This communication must include continual updates on:

- scope and desired outcome

- how the project will impact on employees

- how employees can expect management to conduct themselves

- how employees/people will be treated as a result of the change. How information will be shared with them, how often, and details of opportunities for people to participate (always be open and honest).

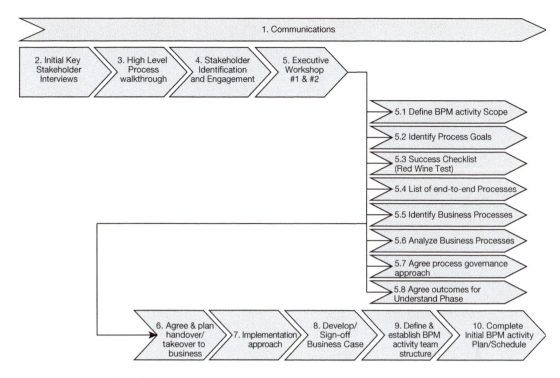

Figure 15.3 Launch pad phase steps

Always anticipate questions and objections and handle them in a proactive way. Perform analysis of the targeted stakeholder groups and tailor the communications to them, ensuring consistency.

Identify a person to be responsible for communications and people change management, and make that person accountable for this task. The individual should be engaged at this early stage of the project; a communications strategy and plan should be drafted and its execution commenced. (Refer to Chapter 24 for suggestions regarding the contents of the communications plan and how to address change management issues.)

Step 2: Initial key stakeholder interviews

After discussion with the project or business sponsor, a series of interviews with a small number of key internal business stakeholders should be conducted. The purpose of these interviews is to gain an overview of the current business and process environment, and to gather these stakeholders' views of the key areas of process and operational issues. This is not a long drawn-out process, but short and to the point. In the strategy led method, the interviews will also cover the communication of how this particular BPM activity will contribute towards the successful implementation of the organization strategy.

The outcome of the interviews will be:

- building rapport with the stakeholders (part of stakeholder management). This is a critical activity;
- obtaining a high level understanding of the issues from a stakeholder perspective;
- identification of quick wins, which the stakeholders are passionate about.

This step should not be confused with Step 4, where all BPM activity stakeholders are identified for input into the stakeholder management strategies as outlined in Chapter 23.

Step 3: High level process walkthrough

If the initial members of the BPM team are not familiar with the processes within the business unit, it can be extremely useful to spend a small amount of time speaking to the people who execute the processes in the physical area that the work is conducted, and following the processes within the business unit on an end-to-end basis. This provides an excellent overview of how the business is conducted, and provides an opportunity to identify process similarities and differences.

Similarly, a discussion with the IT department is useful to provide a high level overview of how the business applications and infrastructure (IT architecture) interact with and support the business processes. At this stage not a great deal is needed from IT as this step is about very high level business walkthroughs to gain an overview of the business area being reviewed.

The interviews typically will take 30–45 minutes each or half to a few days in total depending upon the scope of BPM activity. This review is not in great detail nor are you meant to comment or be critical of the current state. It is only to gather a high level overview of these processes within the business, as it now stands.

These walkthroughs must not replace the activities in the Understand phase, as these provide a more in-depth analysis and understanding.

Step 4: Stakeholder identification and engagement

This is a simple step to brainstorm who the key BPM activity stakeholders are from both an internal and external perspective. External, in this instance, could include stakeholders outside the business unit and still within the organization who will be impacted by the activity, as well as stakeholders external to the organization—such as customers, partners and suppliers. Do not forget to include "extended" stakeholders. By this we are referring to suppliers of suppliers, and further back in the supply chain. It can also apply to the customer of a customer, especially if the customer is a business or an intermediary.

Once this has been completed, the stakeholders who must contribute to the BPM activity are identified and must be kept informed. Important stakeholders (such as customers or suppliers) may need to be not only informed but also involved in and committed to the activity. Effort invested in redesigning, developing and implementing new process(es) would be wasted if customers or suppliers refuse to use them.

Stakeholder engagement is covered in detail in Chapter 23.

Premature implementation

The Managing Director insisted that the project was implemented on a certain date, even though the project manager, IT Director and Operational Director all insisted it was three months too early and implementation at this time would cause significant chaos within the operations area of the business.

The implementation proceeded as instructed by the Managing Director; it did cause operational chaos, and the project team subsequently discovered that the Managing Director "did" get his substantial bonus for implementing the project "on time"!

Message: Stakeholder analysis and gaining an understanding of stakeholder drivers is essential to a successful project outcome. Of course, it also shows that setting the wrong KPIs can lead to inappropriate behavior and ultimately inappropriate outcomes.

Step 5: Executive workshops

The agenda for these workshops typically comprises two three-hour sessions, and covers:

- definition and agreement of the BPM activity scope;
- identification of the initial process goals;
- agreement of the success checklist for the activity (you need to agree on what success looks like);
- stakeholder identification and categorization;
- creation of the initial list of end-to-end processes;
- identification of the individual business processes;
- an initial analysis of the processes, including high level metrics;
- agreement on the implementation plan and process governance for the processes in the activity;
- agreement of the outcomes for the Understand phase.

Each of these is examined in further detail below.

The business attendees of the management workshops usually comprise:

- the project sponsor
- senior managers within the business area/unit.

They will be decision makers and managers with a reasonably detailed understanding of the business area/unit.

CASE STUDY

Where to start?

A Managing Director gave directions to the Process Manager: "Go and find significant process improvements and identify where I can make large cost savings within the organization." The Process Manager was newly appointed to the task, and did not know where to start. He established several process project teams to process-model various parts of the business in their current state. There was no high level analysis completed to determine the likely areas of savings and focused activity, little or no executive support for the project(s), and no BPM coaching provided to the inexperienced Process Manager. The project largely failed to deliver to stakeholders' expectations, and was substantially dismantled a year later.

Message: Without an experienced person leading the project team and a structured approach, the team will find it difficult to know where to start in a disciplined way that will maximize potential effort.

Step 5.1: Define BPM activity scope

This is the normal scope referred to during the establishment of a project. As described previously, we do not propose to outline a project management methodology within this text. There is, however, one overriding question that needs to be answered: Do we feel confident that, with the initially planned scope, we can deliver the expected results for the stakeholders?

In many situations the business will already have determined the scope of the BPM activity—for example, in the strategy led method. At the very least, this "initial" scope should be revisited within the executive workshop and confirmed as still being appropriate to the business and other stakeholders. If the operational business wishes to change the scope of a strategy led method activity, it will be necessary to take this back to the project sponsor and executive leadership, as it may have an impact upon the organization strategy. It is important also to make it clear what is *not* included in the scope.

There are a number of considerations:

- If there are very clearly understood and defined business issues, the BPM activity scope may be clear and will not change as it progresses.

- The business may request the BPM/project team to solve a particular operational business process issue, but the "root cause" may be outside the requested scope. For example, the debt collections department of an energy company may be having issues

BPM INSIGHT

However, it is important to recognize that the scope of a BPM activity may be difficult to firmly bed down at this early stage. This will make it necessary to fine-tune the scope during the subsequent phases.

collecting debts within the agreed timeframes; however, the issue may not be with the collections department, it may be that the electricity meter billing process has significant errors. So if the BPM activity scope only covers the processes within the collection department, you will never solve the processing issues. The scope will need to be extended to include the end-to-end process and out into the billing process(es).

- In an organizational business transformation program of work, the high level business outcomes will, or should be, defined, but specific BPM activities and outcomes will need to be determined. In this situation, the scope may evolve during the execution of the Launch pad and Understand phases.

If this requires crossing departmental, business unit, stakeholder, or even organizational boundaries, then this should be done. The Understand workshops discussed in the next chapter must be conducted for the end-to-end process, and not be concerned about departmental, structural or organizational boundaries. For example, if a particular department is being examined (represented by the oval shape in Figure 15.4) and the process proceeds outside this department, it should be examined in the other "adjacent" departments—thus covering the "upstream" and "downstream" aspects of the process.

BPM INSIGHT

It is essential that the process(es) within the scope and being discussed during the management workshop are completed on a true end-to-end basis.

It is, however, necessary to have a common understanding of the "BPM activity width," which will have a significant impact on the scope.

BPM activity width

The management workshop must also determine or reaffirm the "width" of the BPM activity agreed in Chapter 13, the Foundations phase. As discussed in Chapter 13, Figure 15.5 provides an indication of several possible approaches.

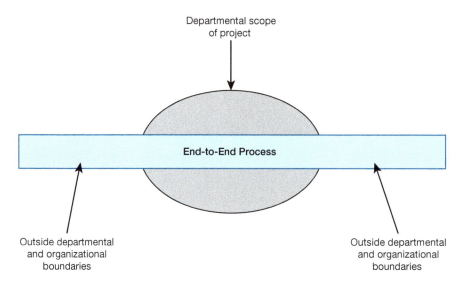

Figure 15.4 End-to-end process

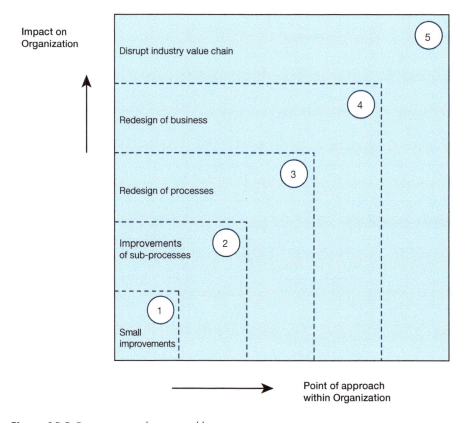

Figure 15.5 Determine redesign width

Agreement on this width is critical to determining what are the desired outcomes and approach during the Innovate phase of the project.

If you require more information on this aspect, refer to Chapter 13, step 2.

Step 5.2: Identify process goals

It is necessary to develop the process goals at this point so that the project can be planned appropriately. Unless you know the process goals and the BPM activity width, the organization does not have sufficient information to define and establish the BPM activity adequately. In a strategy led approach, it would be expected that the high level goals may already be known and dictated by executive management. In an operational initiative method, the goals will be determined during this workshop.

The process goals will need to be linked to the organization strategy and objectives (as identified in the Foundations phase). They must take into account:

- stakeholder needs
- benchmarking against competitors.

There are several inputs in the determination of the process goals, including:

- defining the measurement indicators used to evaluate the process performance today and planned to be used in the future;
- targeting the degree of performance improvement needed based on potential and risk;
- determining the level of improvement expected—targeting an 80 percent improvement is *totally* different to targeting a 10 percent improvement, and the approach will be substantially different. Perhaps the time taken for the process needs to be longer, in order to increase the quality? This needs to be very clearly documented, understood and agreed by all project stakeholders;
- identifying process performance measures starts with the expected performance measures of the stakeholders and then works backwards to derive the process performance measures;
- assessing the performance management and measures—for the individuals executing them (refer to Chapter 17 for more details);
- assessing for measures of: effectiveness, efficiency and adaptability;
- keeping the number of performance measures low—certainly no more than five;
- looking for an opportunity to establish "stretch goals."

Also, look at the change you would like to take place in the behavior of the employees involved in the process(es)—in managers, team leaders and staff.

All project goals should be made SMART (Specific, Measurable, Achievable, Realistic and Time-related).

Step 5.3: Success checklist (Red Wine Test)

This is an important step in the management of stakeholder expectations and validation of the required outcomes from this particular BPM activity.

From a BPM activity and business perspective, it is important to understand what must be achieved for it to be successful. While the high level success checklist, for a strategy led approach, will have been set by the executive, the details will be determined during this step. For an operational initiative method, all the success checklist criteria will be determined here. For details of how to conduct the Red Wine test, refer to Chapter 13, step 2.

BPM INSIGHT

Remember, now the Red Wine Test is being applied to a specific BPM project or group of projects, so the delivery and wording of the specific Red Wine Test question may require modifying.

CASE STUDY

The need to follow the framework steps

An executive workshop comprising the project steering committee members was conducted and the project scope (as agreed with the project sponsor) was presented. All steering committee members agreed with the scope. Later in the workshop, we asked the "red wine test" question to elicit the success checklist. During this it became obvious that the steering committee members did not agree with the project scope, as the success checklist described was inconsistent with the proposed scope.

Message: Without completing the success checklist (Red Wine Test) step, the project would have commenced with a scope that was inconsistent with the desired business outcomes, as expressed by the steering committee. If the project had been completed, it would not have satisfied all stakeholder needs and would have been a waste of time and money.

Step 5.4: List of end-to-end processes

The end-to-end process list provides an overview of the main processes of the organization and may already have been created during the Foundations phase. If it has already been created, then review it to confirm its relevance for this business unit. If it does not exist, then create one.

For an individual project, the completion of an end-to-end process list will provide assistance with the completion of the next step. An excellent way to obtain this information is via the executive workshop. A suggested agenda and approach is detailed in the Extra Reading section at the end of this chapter.

The Project Asset should be used to obtain this information as well as the business processes in step 5.5. Any modifications to the list of end-to-end processes and business processes need to be updated.

Step 5.5: Identify business processes

Prior to commencing a BPM activity, there is a need to identify all the relevant individual business processes within the business unit being examined.

> ## BPM INSIGHT
>
> **It is important to ensure that the processes identified as part of a BPM activity cover the end-to-end business processes.**

While there are many methods to achieve this, we have outlined only one here, the Process Selection Matrix, as it is one that is often used with great success.

The Process Selection Matrix (PSM) is a way of showing, usually on one page, all the business processes within a business unit. Figure 15.6 provides an example. Furthermore, the PSM is an ideal way of understanding and showing the level of process complexity, the number of processes, and the high level process metrics within the business.

The vertical axis (main processes) comes from the end-to-end processes developed as part of step 5.4. The horizontal axis (scenarios) represents the dimension that provides more detailed analysis of the processes listed on the vertical axis. This will vary from situation to situation: it might be represented by the products of the organization, payment methods, distribution methods, geographical locations, business units and so forth. The important consideration is to ensure that the cell at the intersection of the horizontal and vertical axes represents an individual business process.

If a process step is unique, the process object should be specified under that scenario (as in Process 1—Market A, Product 1 and Main Process A in Figure 15.6). If there is no process step under a scenario, then no process object should be specified (for example, Market A, Product 1 does not have a process associated with Main Process C). In the case where the process step is the same for several scenarios, the process object should spread across these scenarios (as in Process 5, where Market A, Product 1 and Product 2 share the same process related to Main Process B). This is normally the case when:

- the scenarios have no impact on the uniqueness of the process step;
- processes are carried out by the same business units/roles;
- processes are supported by the same IT applications.

Again, the best way to obtain this information is via a executive workshop with appropriate process managers and team leaders in attendance.

The PSM provides an excellent starting point for the project. It can and will be modified during the project, due to increased insight or changed circumstances.

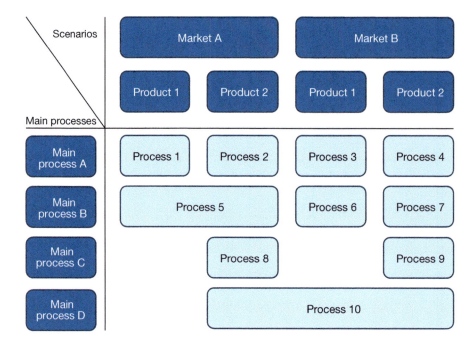

Figure 15.6 Process Selection Matrix

Step 5.6: Analyze business processes

The selection of which processes to include in the scope of a BPM activity sounds easy and yet it is critical and sometimes difficult to get correct the first time. Most organizations select processes intuitively, based on the problems a process appears to cause the organization or the guesstimated benefits to be derived from the redesign. While this is often a sensible starting point, adding some objective analysis around metrics to the selection process is important if for no other reason than validating the "gut feelings" of staff and management.

During the completion of the Process Selection Matrix, it is important to gather metrics of appropriate parts of the value chain and processes. Metrics useful for each process/market/product include:

- the number of people involved in executing a process;
- the number, value and profitability of transactions;
- the figures on quality (for example, customer satisfaction, errors, rework, complaints and so forth) which equates to process problem areas;
- the metrics on processing time, throughput time and waiting time, which can equate to process bottlenecks (sometimes compared to service level agreements—SLAs).

These will provide guidance for where to commence the more detailed analysis. For example, if Processes 3 and 5 in Figure 15.6 take 70 percent of the process resources, then any improvement in these processes can make a substantial difference to the costs of, and perhaps service provided by, the business unit. On the other hand, if Process 2 only occupies 4 percent of the resources, then process improvements here might not make a contribution to the cost within the business unit. The metrics collected should be recorded on the PSM, which becomes a powerful "picture" for management and the project.

If the project has been initiated as a strategy led approach, while all this information will be useful, the processes to be included in the BPM activity scope may already have been determined.

Figure 15.7 shows a real case study example of a completed PSM for an insurance organization in its "receipting" process area. You can see that there are a large number of processes and it is complex. This is particularly the case when you consider that there were only six main sub-processes (the vertical axis):

- receive payment
- reconcile payment to insurance policy
- receipt payment to insurance policy
- banking
- reconcile bank accounts
- collection control.

The horizontal axis in this case was relatively complex:

- the business unit (or distribution channel)
- payment cycle (annual or monthly insurance premiums payment method)
- geographical region (state or province)
- payment channel or method (cash; credit card; check; electronic funds transfer; direct debit).

In the current state the organization had over 54 individual processes when best practice would suggest six processes should be sufficient. This was even more interesting when there were only 122 employees in the business unit.

This lack of consistency of processes created plenty of potential for process standardization and, therefore, improvement.

This figure was shown to the chief financial officer (CFO) and it was all the "selling" that was necessary. It was obvious from the figure that there was plenty of opportunity for process improvement. He immediately commenced a BPM activity to rectify the situation.

The PSM is not the only method available to assist in the prioritization of process improvement opportunities. Quality of processing and rework are also key inputs.

Another matrix that will add an interesting dimension to the analysis of the business processes is the Keen Process Worth Matrix (Keen, 1997: 26), shown in Table 15.1.

This matrix provides a useful way of determining what business processes to invest in; however, it is not always an easy matrix to complete—processes can be difficult to categorize, and the categorization is often a qualitative decision. We have provided an example of a

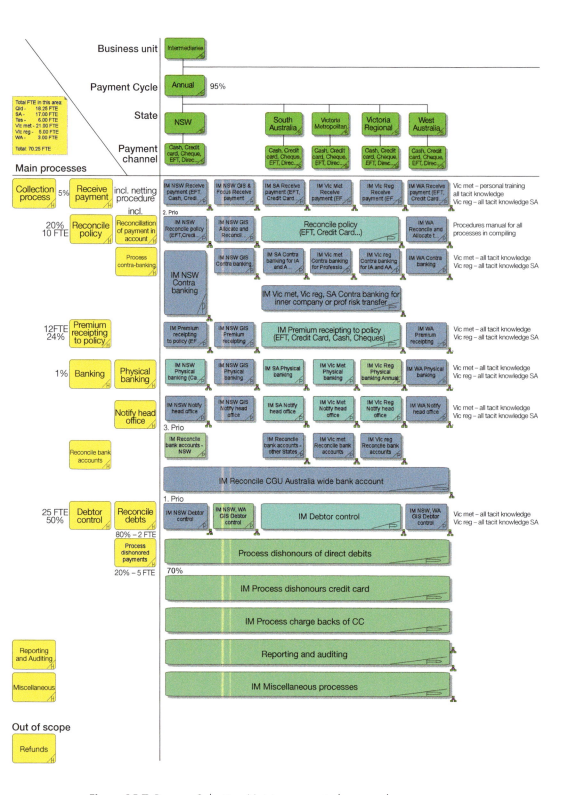

Figure 15.7 Process Selection Matrix—case study example

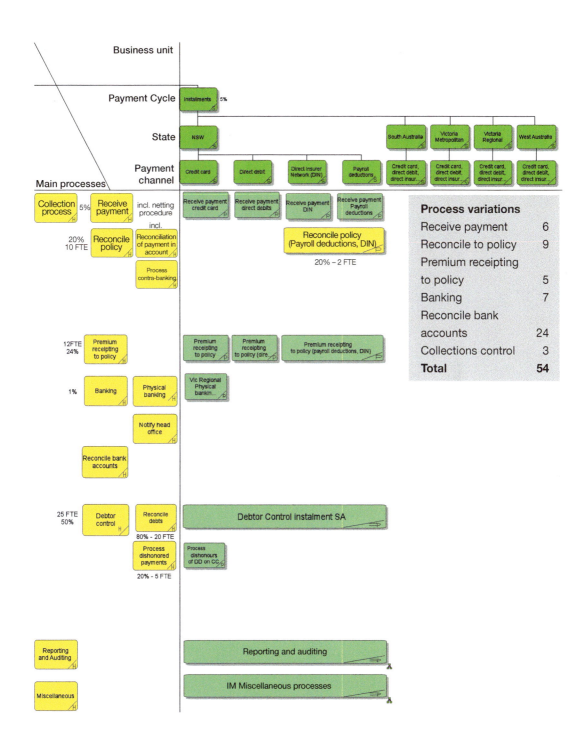

Figure 15.7 *continued*

completed matrix in Table 15.1 based upon the claims processes within an insurance organization. The definitions Keen uses are:

* *Asset*—"any process that returns more money to the firm than it costs is an asset" (Keen, 1997: 25). However, you must ensure that the determination of cost is correctly calculated—certainly do not use the traditional accounting definition.

* *Liability*—the opposite of an asset.

* *Identity*—defines the organization for itself, its customers and stakeholders. It differentiates the organization from its competitors. For example, McDonald's has a reputation based on fast, consistent service; similarly, Singapore Airlines' reputation is for friendly personalized service. These are the marketing perceptions that these processes *must* deliver. They are processes that define the organization's identity. These identity processes are a subset of the "core" processes referred to previously in Figure 14.9.

* *Priority*—these processes strongly support the effectiveness of the identity processes. Customers don't usually see them, but if they fail then the impact is immediate and visible to the stakeholders, especially customers. In the example of McDonald's above, these processes would include those that are part of the supply chain to deliver the raw materials for the products sold.

* *Background*—these processes support the daily activities of operations within the organization, and include those such as administration, HR and document management. Sometimes they are highly visible and therefore have the attention of management. It is a mistake to invest in these processes ahead of identity and priority processes. Most organizations target these processes for BPM projects, because they can be easy wins. This can be a mistake unless the economic cost/benefit stacks up, and even when it does there is usually greater value to the organization by first working on the asset processes.

* *Mandated*—these are processes imposed on the organization by external factors, such as legislation and compliance. The organization does not have any choice but to perform them. Usually these are liability processes, and rarely add direct value to the organization.

Other processes that can exist but don't appear in the matrix are "folklore" processes. Staff usually describe them as, "we have always done this." If you find any, challenge staff to assess their value and necessity, and then either add them to the list of processes or eliminate them.

While the initial Process Worth Matrix may be created during a BPM activity, it should not be a one-time exercise. A potentially useful time to revisit the matrix is at the end of the Understand phase.

The matrix should be added to the process asset repository and process architecture. It should be continually refined during the Understand phase, future BPM activities and business-as-usual activities. Processes may move from one category to another over time. This is usually caused by the business environment, management decisions, behavior of staff and the organization, and could also be caused by unintentional neglect of a process.

Having gathered the information in the PSM, the Process Worth Matrix, the associated metrics and the process goals, this is all brought together in order to eliminate, select and prioritize the order in which the processes will be addressed within the Understand phase.

Table 15.1 Process Worth Matrix

Salience*	Worth	
	Asset	*Liability*
Identity processes	• Claims notification • Claims approval	
Priority processes	• Claims assessment	
Background processes		• Claims payment • Customer change of address • Customer change of banking details
Mandated processes reporting		• GST/VAT/Sales tax

Note: * Salience is an intrinsic rule property that specifies a rule's priority relative to all other rules. In this example, it refers to the importance of one process over another, for example, an identity process will have more value or a higher priority to an organization than, say, a background process.

KEY POINT

When completing this analysis the organization must focus on the creation of value—creating benefits from the redesign of a process does not necessarily create value: "Benefit is a managerial concept; Value is an economic concept" (Keen, 1997: 75).

There are examples of organizations that gained substantial benefits from the redesign of their processes and yet their profit declined. Improvements in processes do not necessarily translate into business benefit. For example, a process may be redesigned to be more efficient, and yet it is of little benefit to the customer or adds no value/profit to the business.

CASE STUDY

Working on the right process?

A Process Worth Matrix for an organization early in the project showed that two business processes represented 52 percent of the people executing the process. One process (32 percent) was classified as a priority/asset process and the other (20 percent) as a priority/liability process. Of all the process people in the operational area of the business, 20 percent were involved in the execution of a process that had a negative impact on the value to the organization! Consideration was given, once further analysis had been completed, to outsource this process.

Message: The completion of the Process Worth Matrix is an extremely useful technique, as it helps management to understand and categorize the organization's processes and thus enable more informed decisions to be made.

BPM INSIGHT

The processes that should be selected for a BPM redesign activity are those that will add value to the organization.

Step 5.7: Agree process governance approach

The earlier the BPM project team agrees with the business who will be the "owner" of the business process in the business once it is implemented, the better. This business owner then needs to be intimately involved in the execution of the BPM activity. The management workshop provides a unique opportunity of addressing this issue.

While this activity is part of the business-as-usual process governance structure, it could be considered as part of the development and agreement of the business handover/takeover plan.

If it is a BPM program being implemented, then you should start the future process governance discussions in the executive workshop and perhaps agree the initial structure.

If it is an individual BPM project being implemented, then you should identify the person(s) who will be responsible for the process(es) after the project is handed over to the business. If the process owner/steward is not identified, agreed and engaged early, the project risk will increase. If the process owner/steward is only engaged during or after project implementation they may wish to change the process design or method of implementation which may require project rework.

BPM INSIGHT

The process governance structure (roles and responsibilities) must be discussed and agreed at the "right" time. If the organization is not ready for this (lacks process maturity) then it can significantly impact the success of BPM within the organization.

Step 5.8: Agree outcomes for Understand phase

Again, this is about stakeholder expectation management. It is much better to inform (and thus set expectations for) the appropriate stakeholders of the deliverables before the Understand phase commences, rather than complete the phase and not deliver to their expectations. If the project team does not set the expectations, the stakeholders will make up their own and the two rarely coincide.

The deliverables for the Understand phase will include:

1. A list of end-to-end process model(s).
2. A list of end-to-end sub-processes.

3. Models of the current processes to a level of detail sufficient to enable the Innovate phase to be completed.

4. Appropriate metrics, sufficient to establish a baseline for future process comparative measurements.

5. A list of major process issues, as determined by the business.

6. Identification of innovate priorities.

7. Identification of opportunities for quick wins.

8. Validation and handover of quick wins for implementation, if appropriate at this stage.

9. A report on the phase.

Step 6: Agree and plan the handover/takeover with the business

Before doing any further steps it is important to agree and plan the "handover" to the business. Equally as important is the business agreeing and establishing a "takeover" plan. The "handover" is from the BPM activity or project perspective and needs to be planned. The "takeover" plan is created by the business to ensure they are ready and willing to take over the BPM activities outcomes and deliverables, for example, new or changed processes.

Most projects fail the ultimate test: that the business is able and willing to take over the project as part of business-as-usual.

This step also serves as a good testing ground to see how the stakeholder management should be completed during this phase.

Stakeholder management is always a tough issue, but it is always better to receive feedback early in the project rather than later. This feedback will enable adjustments to be made to the approach.

When creating and agreeing a business handover/takeover plan the following issues need to be addressed:

- Project costs;
- Required support from subject matter experts during the project, the handover and the operational costs;
- Risks and issues;
- Ongoing costs and benefits;
- Timing of handover/takeover to the business;
- Implementation fall-back scenarios or contingency plans;
- Communication and implementation plan;
- Governance and escalation;
- Impact on customer experience.

The following situations are common:

- *Business does not see the handover/takeover as important nor something that needs to be addressed at this stage of the project.* Many business managers are still focused on the short term and want to address today's issues and worry about what are perceived as future issues, in the future. However, addressing the business handover/takeover plan is necessary at this stage. It would be easy for the BPM team to delay it to a later stage, but this will only aggravate the situation. Unless the business is fully involved and committed, and understands how it will be handling the project outcomes once the project is completed, then it is a reason to put the project on hold until this can be resolved.

- *Initial handover/takeover arrangements are modified without adequate change control.* If an initial handover and/or takeover plan has been completed and agreed, chances are that these arrangements will be changed in the future, either due to changes in the organization or due to changes in the BPM activity or the perception of the BPM activity (as the business gains a better understanding of the activity and its outcomes). Apply standard project management change control to any changes in the handover/takeover plans as this may impact the overall success of the BPM activity.

CASE STUDY

To celebrate the successful implementation of a BPM activity it was announced by the sponsor that the responsibility for benefit realization was to be one of the business managers. He was shocked and stated "if I had known this before, I would have been more realistic regarding the benefits and I would have worked harder to make the project more successful."

Message: Always appoint the business person responsible for the realization of the business benefits at the start of the project and ensure they are involved throughout the project.

Step 7: Develop implementation plan

The importance of implementation cannot be overemphasized. A common question is, "what benefit does the project get by spending more time and money on implementation?" The answer is simple, and sometimes the upfront proof is difficult to calculate. A good implementation will ensure that the proposed solution is optimal for the organization and that the organization uses this solution in the best manner and does so in the shortest possible time. If implementation is not completed smoothly, then one or more of the following situations may arise:

- the chosen solution is not optimal for the organization—this can be due to incorrect, incomplete or inconsistent gathering of the requirements; however, it is mostly caused by insufficient participation of the stakeholders and users of the process;

- the organization does not use the solution in the best manner because the users are not properly informed, trained and motivated;

- the solution cannot be implemented immediately because it needs some modifications, resulting in a longer timeframe for the realization of the benefits—which will not be as great as they should be.

A traditional implementation is characterized by little upfront effort and investment. By the time the solution is implemented, last minute changes have to be made resulting in significant, unforeseen, additional investment and lower sustainable results (see Figure 15.8).

If implementation preparation is started during the Launch pad phase of the BPM activities, it will initially result in a higher investment; however, once implemented, the solution will be off to a flying start, resulting in quicker and better sustainable results (see Figure 15.9).

> ## BPM INSIGHT
>
> If the two approaches are compared, it can clearly be seen that despite the early additional investment in implementation thinking, the benefits of this approach are substantially higher than the traditional approach (see Figure 15.10).

Forrester Research (2003) stated that: "How much you spend on IT doesn't matter, which technologies you buy does matter, how you implement matters the most." This comes from a recognition that more and more organizations are purchasing and implementing standard packages, which means that the competitive advantage does not come from the technology but from business processes. This advantage manifests itself in how the technology is configured and implemented within the organization; together with the process governance and management structures.

The Implement phase discusses the various options that should be considered during this step. The purpose of this step is to think through the implementation options and select one appropriate for the BPM activity, which will provide guidance for the other phases and steps in the framework as the activity progresses.

Step 8: Develop/sign-off business case

The standard organization business case template should be used. A sample BPM business case template is described in detail in the Extra Reading section at the end of this chapter.

The BPM team should *never* defend recommendations; only make them and explain the options in a neutral and objective manner.

Part of the business case development will include the identification of the business person(s) who will be responsible for the process(es) once the project has transitioned from a "BPM activity" to an "operational" situation. This is to ensure their engagement in the project and project decision-making activities so they have a level of ownership and responsibility for the project outcomes. Refer to step 5.7 earlier in this chapter for the

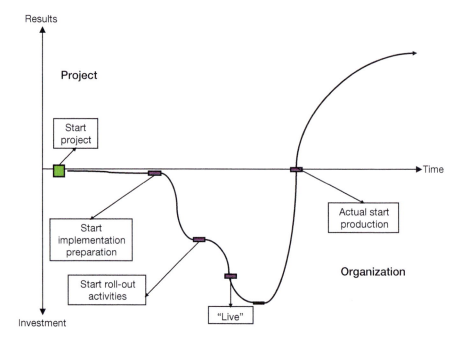

Figure 15.8 Traditional implementation

Source: Regatta® from Sogeti Nederland, reproduced with permission.

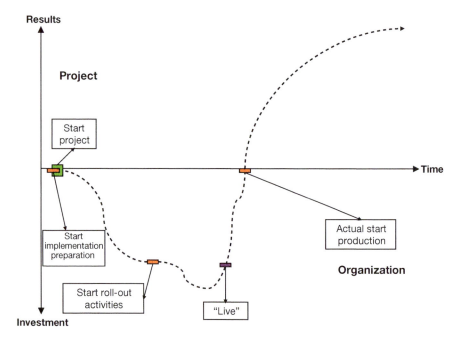

Figure 15.9 Involve implementation from the start of the project

Source: Regatta® from Sogeti Nederland, reproduced with permission.

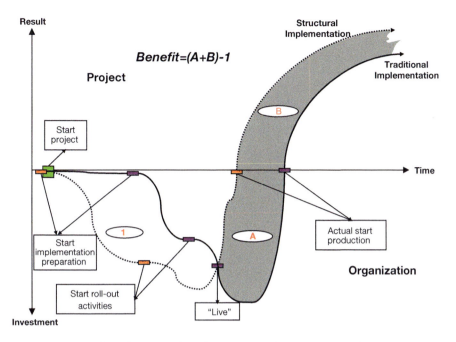

Figure 15.10 Benefits of Structural Implementation above Traditional Implementation

Source: Regatta® from Sogeti Nederland, reproduced with permission.

agreement of the process governance approach and step 6 for the handover/takeover plan creation and agreement.

Remember that this is only an initial business case, which may either justify the entire BPM activity or provide funding for further investigation to enable the development of a detailed business case for the full BPM activities. The business case will need to be updated or completed in the Innovate phase to justify the continuation of the BPM activity (refer to step 15: Identify benefits and update business case, in Chapter 16).

Step 9: Define and establish the BPM activity team structure

Having decided upon the sequence in which processes will be examined during the Understand phase, the initial BPM activity and business team will be in a position to create the BPM activity team structure and assemble the team. The structure of a BPM activity can be somewhat different to a "normal" IT or business project. The sample structure shown in Figure 15.11 assumes that an integrated document management system is being implemented simultaneously with the BPM implementation. Roles are discussed in more detail in the Extra Reading section at the end of this chapter.

This sample team structure is designed for a large-scale BPM implementation activity, and will need to be modified to suit the particular organizational and project requirements. Rarely does the team start off this size in the Launch pad phase. However, the future project team structure needs to be determined and planned. The number and make-up of the workstreams shown in Figure 15.11 will depend upon the BPM activity and the technology

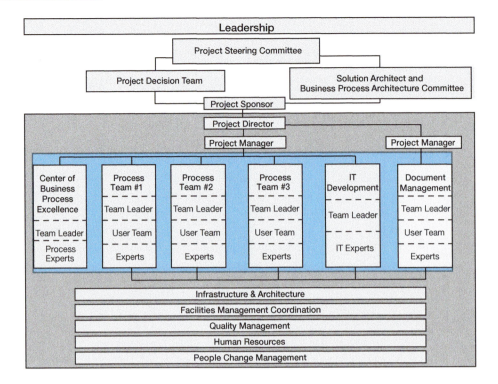

Figure 15.11 Sample BPM activity team structure for a large-scale BPM project

components involved. We have shown one workstream for a document management component; clearly, there could be others for process work management and business rules implementations. This is, however, a structure that has been particularly effective, so modifying it too much may lead to compromising the effectiveness of the BPM activity.

Project Steering Committee, project director and project manager

The roles and responsibilities of the Project Steering Committee, project director, project manager and team leaders are close to the normal functions these roles would have in any project. For a detailed list of their roles and responsibilities, refer to the Extra Reading section at the end of this chapter. The project manager's role is worth commenting on, as are a couple of the other roles.

It is highly recommend to have two key leadership positions within the team structure:

1. The business unit should have its own BPM activity (project) manager with overall responsibility for the entire program/project. This is, after all, a business activity, not an IT activity. This position is crucial to ensure that the *business* requirements are met and are of primary importance. IT, vendor and all other project components should report to this business BPM activity (project) manager. Ideally, this business manager will be an experienced project manager with BPM expertise. If the BPM activity (project) manager does not have BPM expertise (and this means having implemented several BPM activities), then a senior and experienced BPM consultant is required.

2. A senior and experienced BPM consultant is highly recommended, not only to coach the business manager, if BPM expertise is lacking, but also to assist with:

- objectively managing situations when process or project compromises need to be made during the course of the BPM activity as they inevitably will be. Such decisions can have very serious repercussions, and an expert BPM specialist can manage this risk to prevent the BPM activity turning into an expensive business process improvement activity that yields limited benefits;

- ensuring that the BPM activity remains focused and self-funding (unless compliance related), and continues to deliver real business value;

- identifying additional business opportunities that could be enabled through BPM;

- ensuring that the required people change management elements are correctly built into the BPM activity (project) plan/schedule and thereby managed as an essential part of the activity;

- adding value to the stakeholder management and providing the expertise necessary to ensure that stakeholders remain continually engaged and focused towards a successful BPM delivery.

While some of these may sound like the responsibilities of the project director or project manager, we have found that an independent consultant is often able to make judgment calls and express opinions that are politically difficult for an internal person to make. In this instance, the "independent" consultant could be a person within the organization and outside of the business units impacted.

Need for a business-based project manager with BPM experience

An organization insisted on appointing a project manager whose responsibility was to bridge the gap between the business and IT. However, the project manager reported to the IT department and had little knowledge of BPM implementation. When the project started to miss scheduled milestones, we were asked to provide a project health check. An outcome of this was coaching and mentoring for the project manager, and an external senior consulting manager participated on the Project Steering Committee to provide continual comment and advice to the committee and directly to the business project sponsor.

Had the organization spent more time in the first place carefully selecting an appropriate business project manager with BPM experience, the project delays and cost overrun could have been avoided.

Message: The selection of an experienced BPM business project manager is one of the most important decisions with regard to a BPM project. Spend the necessary time and money to ensure that the right person is appointed; it will pay for itself throughout the life of the project.

Project decision team

The project decision team should resolve as many questions as possible to avoid the necessity of referring them to the Project Steering Committee. It should comprise the user leaders of each of the user teams, and be chaired by the chief process officer or the designated process sponsor. The responsibilities for each of these roles are outlined in the Extra Reading section at the end of this chapter.

The project structure for smaller BPM projects may require some of the roles to be amalgamated; however, leadership is extremely important in any project and particularly important in a BPM project, so never compromise in this area of the project. We will cover leadership in more detail in Chapter 26.

The Steering Committee fulfills the normal role expected from this committee within a project. It usually comprises the project sponsor, project manager, business owner, CIO or senior IT person (where there is a large technology component in the BPM activity), and one or two people who represent the organizational aspects to ensure synergy can be gained across the organization.

Business Process Architecture Committee

This has been discussed in Chapter 14 on Enablement phase.

Process teams

The BPM activity team will be broken up into various teams (often referred to as workstreams). Whether the project has one or multiple workstreams will depend upon its size and complexity. In a large BPM activity involving technology, there would be an expectation that the teams would comprise a small team of process experts (probably from the Center of Business Process Excellence); an IT team handling interfacing and other development activities; and a team with document management expertise that will consult to all the team(s) and especially those completing the process analysis and innovation activities. Depending upon the size of the BPM activity, each team could comprise the following:

- team leader
- user leader
- user team representatives
- process experts.

Each of these roles is briefly described here, and the Extra Reading section at the end of this chapter describes them in more detail.

1. *Team leader.* This is the normal project team leader role. The leader will lead the team (workstream) and ensure that appropriate workshops are organized, the project plan is developed (in conjunction with the project manager), the timetable adhered to, budgets met, etc.

2. *User leader.* This individual is a business resource appointed by the business management, and has the authority to make (or obtain) decisions on behalf of the business.

3. *User team representatives.* These are the technical or subject matter experts from the business, and are selected by the user leader.

4. *Process experts.* This group will come from the organization's Center of Business Process Excellence, and will provide the expertise for:

   • process design and redesign

   • process design tool(s) used in the project

   • activity-based costing

   • process simulation

   • capacity planning

   • process interfacing.

If the organization does not have a Center of Business Process Excellence or internal expertise, then these resources may come from an external specialist BPM consultancy.

IT development team

This group predominantly comprises IT experts in systems interfacing. They will provide the expertise and work with each of the other teams to ensure that process interfaces to the various host systems are executed successfully.

Document management team

This group will comprise experts in document management, and business staff who understand how documents flow and are used with the processes in their area of business. This team will work with and provide expertise to all the other process teams in the project, to ensure that documents and images are successfully integrated with each process.

Step 10: Complete initial BPM activity plan/schedule

The initial BPM activity plan/schedule must cover the Understand phase in detail, with the Innovate phase steps included but with no timeframes against them at this stage.

Experience has shown that Understand phase workshops should comprise no more than three three-hour workshops per week, with the time in between scheduled to tidy up the models, review and analyze the findings within the business (including root-cause analysis) and gather and complete metrics analysis. This will be discussed in more detail in Chapter 16.

The number of processes modeled per workshop will depend upon their complexity and size.

Always remember to build contingency into your plan, and remember that the writing of the report at the end of this phase will always take longer than you think so allow an appropriate amount of time as this should not be rushed. In fact, always start populating the report as the project progresses to avoid the rush at the end. A sample report structure and project plan/schedule are provided in the Extra Reading section at the end of this chapter.

REALIZE VALUE

Potential benefits must be identified and planned as part of this phase. For details refer to step 2 of Chapter 21, where it is described in the context of realizing value within a project.

LAUNCH PAD PHASE OUTPUTS

The information being developed during the Launch pad phase will have inputs into the various phases shown in Figure 15.12.

The obvious input is into the Understand phase, where the BPM activity plan/schedule is further developed and refined, processes prioritized via the Process Selection Matrix, initial metrics and business case decided, and the project documentation established. Much of this information will also flow over into the Innovate phase, for example process goals.

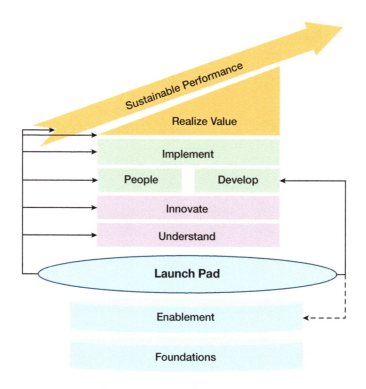

Figure 15.12 Launch pad phase outputs to other phases

LAUNCH PAD PHASE RISKS

This phase provides the platform from which BPM activities (projects/programs) are launched. Like any project, unless it is established correctly in the first place it will be difficult to get "back on track." There are several risks that must be considered, and mitigation strategies should be implemented to eliminate (or at least reduce) them. Some of these risks include those listed in Table 15.2.

Table 15.2 Launch pad phase risks and mitigation strategies

Risk		Mitigation strategy
1	BPM activity stakeholders are not all identified and/or engaged in the project	This is a critical function for the project manager and the project sponsor, and every attempt must be made to identify all the stakeholders and engage them. Stakeholders will be identified during the project, and Chapter 24 explains how to deal with this situation. Engagement is essential, and unless critical stakeholders are fully engaged, then the BPM activity risk is increased and consideration should be given to the continuation of the activity.
2	The BPM activity (project) manager is not experienced in BPM implementations and projects	There are three options available here: (1) replace the project manager with an experienced BPM person; (2) provide coaching and mentoring for the project manager from an experienced BPM project manager; and (3) continue with the inexperienced project manager, recognizing the significant increase in risk to the project.
3	The project scope is ill-defined and/or not clear and agreed	The project manager must clarify the scope with the project sponsor, and the project should not proceed until the scope is well defined, agreed and signed off.
4	The project is not sufficiently funded	Refer to the project sponsor for further funding. Consider stopping the project until adequate funding is available.
5	The business handover/takeover is not sufficiently planned, agreed and accepted	Ensure that basic arrangements are made in order to proceed. Consider stopping the project until you have complete business buy-in and support.

SUMMARY

The Launch pad phase is the aspect of a BPM activity from which one or more BPM projects is launched. The chapter discussed:

- how to identify a BPM opportunity and how to start the BPM activity
- how to ensure you have identified and engaged with key stakeholders
- how to ensure that all stakeholders and their expectations are matched and understood by all
- the completion of the executive workshop and the creation and agreement of: process goals; the likely process governance structure or approach; and the priorities for the Understand phase.

The phase is fundamentally about ensuring that you have done all you can to establish the BPM activity for success, minimizing and managing business risk.

SELF-TEST

1 What is the purpose of communicating at this stage of the BPM activity?

2 What is the purpose of the team completing the initial stakeholder interviews?

3 Is it important for the BPM team to have a high level understanding of the business processes in, or potentially in, scope?

4 Define an agenda for the executive workshop and the purpose and outcomes from each agenda item.

5 What are the potential benefits of the Process Selection Matrix and the Process Worth Matrix?

6 Do you need to develop a high level implementation plan at this stage, and if yes, why?

7 Create an example of a BPM activity (project) team structure, and briefly explain the various roles within the team.

You are running an executive workshop(s) to obtain the high level process view and identify key areas for improvement and areas impacted by the move to a single Student and Finance solution.

During the workshop the following aspects are discussed for the benefits:

- the number of students taking up study at BuProMan should increase as the university will provide an earlier response to student applications
- students are more positive about the university and write more positively in social media
- more tighter revenue collection processes and better reporting
- reduction in admin support by making fewer mistakes and simplifying the tasks
- increase in corporate sponsorship and reduced turnover of sponsors.

The executives hope that the employee satisfaction will increase and the employee churn will decrease.

Assignment guiding questions

1. Which seven people/roles would you invite for the Executive Workshop and why?
2. What are the six key outcomes you would like to achieve from this workshop?
3. How would you classify the processes from the value chain into the Process Worth Matrix (use Table 15.2) and why?
4. How would you quantify the benefits?
5. What high level metrics have you determined will be useful and why?

Launch pad phase checklist

This checklist provides a generic overview of possible inputs, deliverables and gates of this phase.

Possible inputs

See Table 15.3.

Deliverables

See Table 15.4.

Possible gates

- Stakeholder analysis
- Understanding magnitude of change
- Organization's capacity to change
- Organization's acceptance of change
- Availability of participants for workshops.

Table 15.3 Launch pad phase—possible inputs

✓	Source	Deliverable
	Foundations phase	• Organization's core value proposition • BPM maturity of the organization • BPM drivers • BPM activities width • Red Wine Test outcomes • BPM approach • Components of the target operating model
	Establishment phase	• An agreed target operating model • Level 1 and 2 process views • Process architecture, including: o Process guidelines o Process asset repository o Business rules repository o Benefits management framework • Methods by which the people process capability will be built • Organizational cultural behavior changes by the establishment of appropriate targets (KPIs) and linked rewards • Code of behavior • The process-focused organizational design • The technology approach to BPM
	Other inputs	• Business case template • High level metrics to assist in the determination of the main processes and bottlenecks • List of existing projects to determine synergy and overlaps

EXTRA READING

Project team structure and roles

The project team structure and roles are shown in Figure 15.11.

This section provides details of a "strawman" project team structure. This is usually modified to suit the particular organizational requirements. It is, however, a structure that has worked in an effective and workable manner, so modifying it too much may lead to compromising the effectiveness of the project. Obviously, the size of the BPM activity is important in considering the team structure.

BPM activity (program/project) sponsor

The BPM activity sponsor has the normal role of a sponsor in a business project. Often the sponsor is a leading business manager. The sponsor will be the BPM activity champion, and will be responsible and accountable for:

Table 15.4 Launch pad phase—deliverables

✓	Deliverable	Used in phase
	Identification of stakeholders involved and associated with the BPM activity	• All phases
	Stakeholder engagement involved and commitment; and documented and agreed expectations	• All phases
	Process selection matrix (if appropriate)	• Understand phase • Innovate phase • People phase
	A list of identified high level business processes and initial metrics	• Understand phase • Innovate phase • People phase
	A list of agreed process goals	• Understand phase • Innovate phase • People phase
	Agreement of the process governance for the processes in the BPM activity	• Innovate phase • People phase • Develop phase • Implement phase • Sustainable performance phase
	Prioritized processes for the Understand phase	• Understand phase
	An initial implementation approach	• Innovate phase • People phase • Develop phase • Implement phase
	Project management: • Project charter document • Project scope document • Initial draft of the project schedule (plan) • Determination and documentation of the initial communications strategy • Initial risk analysis	• All phases
	Development of the initial business case	• Understand phase • Innovate phase

- defining and approving the goals, objectives, constraints and success criteria of the BPM activity;
- signing off the scope;
- signing off the BPM activity definition document;
- signing off the BPM activity schedule/plan (GANTT chart);
- authorizing or obtaining authorization for resources and expenditure for the BPM activity;
- approving or rejecting any change requests that fall outside the previously agreed scope;
- approval of BPM activity budget;
- signing off that the BPM activity is complete, once the defined scope has been achieved and the benefits realized.

BPM activity (program/project) director

The BPM activity director is responsible for all activities associated with the project. The project manager(s) and/or process workstream leaders will report directly to the project director.

This role ensures that the implementation of the various project(s) is running smoothly and meeting stakeholders' expectations. The project director must also maintain the relationships with all stakeholders and ensure that the framework described herein is being applied appropriately for the particular organization. Other project-related responsibilities include:

- infrastructure and architecture;
- facilities management coordination;
- quality management and the satisfactory involvement of the employees;
- human resources;
- people change management and the satisfactory involvement of employees—this area in particular should not be underestimated, as it is possibly the largest component and one of the most important of any BPM activity;
- supporting project manager(s) and team members, especially in gaining action or agreement from other parts of the organization;
- ensuring that adequate resources and facilities, of all kinds, are available to the project team.

While it is the responsibility of the project manager(s) to ensure the day-to-day running and coordination of the above functions, the project director must take a "big picture" view of the strategic running and alignment of the project.

BPM activity (project) manager(s)

Project managers are responsible for the execution and coordination of the project, which includes:

- day-to-day management and execution of their part of the project;
- development of the policies and plans to ensure commonality of processes and systems wherever possible;
- ensuring that all people change management, human resources and training issues are addressed and implemented;
- management of all activities associated with the project to deliver the requirements of stakeholders in the planned timeframe, budget and quality;
- preparation and tracking of their part of the budget;
- gaining commitment from all stakeholders;
- coordinating and gaining agreement for project plans;
- establishing and using project control mechanisms to ensure agreed timescale and budgets are managed;
- reporting project progress to all stakeholders on the agreed timeframes;
- ongoing communication to the organization (business) and IT management;
- identifying and establishing communication links with related projects, and managing the risks that any interdependencies may pose;
- identifying, managing and elevating, if appropriate, potential or existing issues that may, if left unchecked, impact the project;
- monitoring the risks associated with the project and advising the project director and project sponsor.

Process teams

The process teams (often referred to as workstreams) will comprise various groups:

1. The team leader.
2. The user leader.
3. User team representatives.
4. Process experts.

Each of these roles will be briefly described here.

Team leader

This is the normal project team leader role. The team leader will lead his or her team (workstream) and ensure that appropriate workshops are organized, the project schedule/plan is developed (in conjunction with the project manager) and the timetable is adhered to, budgets are met, and so on. Furthermore, the role includes:

- managing assigned tasks by either completing them or delegating them to team members;
- undertaking periodic team reviews;
- completing periodic team status reports for inclusion in the overall project status reports;
- participating in periodic project review meetings;
- assisting in the resolution of project or business issues;
- ensuring that all issues are logged in the issues log and promptly dealt with and/or raised with the project manager and project team;
- managing development of the user acceptance testing (UAT) plan and test cases, and executing the testing successfully;
- obtaining sign-off for UAT within their area of responsibility;
- completing the implementation plan for their area of responsibility.

User leader

The user leader is a business resource who is appointed by the business management and has the authority to make decisions on behalf of the business. The role includes:

- selecting user team members (departmental and across departments);
- technical quality assurance and decisions on process design;
- regulation of any conflicts that may arise;
- representing the user team on the project decision team;
- participating in project meetings of all user leaders;
- working with other user leaders to ensure interfaces, hand-offs, etc. are correct and that there are no disconnects.

User team representatives

User team representatives are the technical or subject matter experts from the business, and are selected by the user leader. Their responsibilities include:

- participating in workshops and interviews;
- creating team-specific approaches to project activities;
- designing various Innovate phase approaches;
- ensuring that quality, compliance and technical assurance issues are addressed;
- seeking agreement with other teams on process interfaces and hand-offs, to ensure there are no disconnects;
- participating in user acceptance testing planning;
- participating in the writing of test plans and cases for user acceptance testing;

- participating in the execution of user acceptance testing;
- participating in implementation planning and execution.

Process experts

This group will come from the organization's Center of Business Process Excellence (CBPE), and will provide the expertise for:

- process design and redesign
- process design tool(s) used in the project
- activity-based costing
- process simulation
- process interfacing.

Sample report structure

This is a list of the possible topics that could be included in the report of the BPM activity. While the report will ultimately include the Launch pad, Understand and Innovate phases, it could (and probably should) be populated as each phase is conducted. Sections 2 and 3 should be completed at the conclusion of the Launch pad phase, section 4 at the conclusion of the Understand phase, and the remainder of the report at the conclusion of the Innovate phase. There is an overlap between the information in this report and the business case. The report is aimed at the management of the organization, and the business case can be used to populate several of the sections of the report. The business case is aimed at the project sponsor and steering committee as part of the project approval process. It is imperative that these two documents are consistent.

This report is often used at the end of the Innovate phase to justify the continuance of the project into the People, Develop and Implement phases.

Having stated all this, it is not essential that a report is completed. It will depend upon the needs of the BPM activity and the organization.

A sample report structure is as follows:

1. *Executive summary*
    1.1 Background
    1.2 Scope
    1.3 Approach
    1.4 Findings
    1.5 Recommendations
2. *Project*
    2.1 Background
    2.2 Scope
    2.3 Success checklist

Project plan schedule

The project plan schedule will provide an outline of a possible list of tasks and estimated length of time for completion for a smallish BPM activity.[1] The project manager will need to modify this to suit the particular BPM project.

Phase 1—Launch pad phase (~1 to 2 weeks)

Purpose

The Launch pad phase is the platform from which operational initiative approach BPM projects are selected, scoped, established and launched. While the strategy-driven approach projects will be initiated at the Foundations phase, the initial project effort will still need to be estimated. The purpose of this step is to gain an understanding of the effort involved in the completion of these activities.

Step and Duration

See Table 15.5.

Phase 2—Understand phase (4 to 8 weeks)

Purpose

The purpose of the Understand phase is for the project team members and the business to gain sufficient understanding of the current business processes to enable the Innovate phase to commence. The steps are outlined in Chapter 16.

This phase will lay the foundation for the Innovate phase. The current situation, with its requirements and restrictions, is assessed and analyzed. Quick wins may be identified and implemented.

Steps

The Understand phase will predominantly be conducted in a number of workshops. The duration and number of workshops depends on the scope of the project and the understanding gathered in the Launch pad phase.

A rough estimate suggests planning one week (comprising three half-day workshops) for four to six processes to be documented with metrics and timing. (See Table 15.6.)

Table 15.5 Steps

Step	Duration
Revalidate the scope	0.25 day
Understand workshops: • gather process flows • gather metrics (time, staff, volumes) • gather costs • document outcomes	A function of the number of processes
Complete metrics analysis	A function of the number of processes
Root-cause analysis	A function of the number of processes
People capability matrix	1 day
Identify knowledge and information needs	1 day
Identify priorities for Innovate phase	1 day
Identify quick wins (obvious ones, identified in the workshops): • discuss with business • select quick wins for implementation • prioritize	1 day
Options for implementation (not part of this project): • hand over to business to implement • spawn off separate project(s) (with separate team) • have a time-out for current project team to implement quick wins and then return to the current project	2 days
Complete report and present to management, including: • list of end-to-end process(es) • documentation of current processes with metrics • people capability matrix • knowledge and information needs • quick wins	4–6 days
Develop and deliver phase presentation for management	2 days
Project plan for the Innovate phase, including: • duration • cost • project team structure (any changes and estimation of all resources required)	2 days

Table 15.6 Step and duration

Step	Duration
Overview of the organization—usually delivered by a senior executive	0.5 day
Initial interviews with stakeholders	2 days
High level process walkthrough	2–3 days
Executive kick-off workshop(s): • identify process goals • define project scope • design success checklist • make list of end-to-end high level process model(s) • identify business processes • high level—analyze business processes • agree outcomes for understand phase	2 days (2 x 0.5 day workshops; plus 2 x 0.5 days for documentation)
Match processes to criteria and prioritize	1 day
Produce initial project plan (for Understand phase): • duration • cost	1 day
Define and establish project team structure—discuss with business and seek agreement of structure and team members. Document team member roles and responsibilities	3 days
Create Understand workshop presentation	0.5 days
Develop/sign off business case	Depends upon project, could be significant time
Complete report and present to management: • project scope • process goals • list of end-to-end process(es) • list of business processes • next steps	2–4 days

Phase 3—Innovate phase (6~10 weeks)

Purpose

The purpose of this phase is to make the process(es) within the scope of the BPM activity as efficient and effective as possible to meet stakeholders' current and/or future expectations. This phase also provides a unique opportunity to quantify further, in a more empirical manner, the benefits outlined in the business case.

The Innovate phase is to develop new solutions for the business. The effort and duration will very much depend on the scope and objectives—for example, whether system changes are in scope or not, the timeframe (short term, mid-term or long term), and whether revolutionary changes or incremental improvements are desired. (See Table 15.7.)

Table 15.7 Innovate phase steps and duration

Step	Duration
Executive kick-off workshop: • process goals • determine overall approach (automation, non-automation, etc.)	1 day
External stakeholder focus group	1 day
Initial Innovate workshop	1 day
Future process metrics projections	5–8 days
Simulation, assumes that: • metrics data gathering comes from both the metrics step and additional information gathering during this step • the process model has been created with simulation in mind	Depends upon the number of processes —as a guide allow 1–3 days per process
Update to people capability matrix for new skills required as a result of new processes	1 day
Capacity planning	5–10 days
Workshop proposed solutions	Depends upon the number of processes —refer to comments at the start of this phase
Demonstrate feasibility of proposed solutions: • with compliance • with audit	3 days
Process gap analysis	3–5 days
Identify and update business case	5–8 days
Complete report and presentation and present to management, could include: • list of the agreed process goals • documentation of redesigned processes • key findings and an analysis of the process touchpoints • agreed success checklist • business requirements specification, if appropriate • list of recommendations (including more quick wins) • a preliminary risk analysis • cost–benefit overview • suggested next steps • final list of recommendations	5–10 days
Obtain approval to go ahead	Depends upon the organization
Create business requirements document(s)	Depends upon the number of processes and the level of detail required

Table 15.7—*continued*

Step	Duration
Communications plan development	3 days
Communications implementation	Over life of project
Project management activities: • duration • cost • project team structure (all resources required)	Depends upon the scope and size of the project

Overall project management

Project management must be planned to ensure that there is enough time and enough resources in the budget. Activities include:

- risk management

- project change management

- communication plan

- project status (report for project sponsor)

- project team meetings.

The time needed for these activities depends on the size of the project and the project team.

It is also very important to include enough contingency in the project plan to be able to meet deadlines and budget.

CHAPTER 16

UNDERSTAND PHASE

OVERVIEW

The Understand phase is the first phase after the launch of a BPM activity and is required to obtain sufficient information and metrics to innovate the processes. This chapter covers the key steps to be completed to understand the current situation, the key challenges, methods and risks.

It is about ensuring that key metrics and root causes are identified so that a fundamental and significant change can be made.

OVERALL LEARNING OUTCOME

By the end of this chapter you will be able to understand the:

- Importance of the Understand phase and the main steps
- Need and method for communication
- Necessity of revalidating scope
- Importance and structure of Understand workshops
- Pros and cons of modeling the current process
- Essentiality of metrics and typical metrics required
- Need to perform root-cause analysis supported by metrics
- Necessity to identify impact on people
- Importance of identifying key information and documentation
- Importance of identifying and realizing quick wins at this early stage in the project/program
- Need for an Understand report and key elements to be included
- Outputs and risks for this phase.

WHY?

There are four clear and fundamental reasons why the Understand phase (as shown in Figure 16.1) is necessary:

1. For the BPM activity team members and the business to gain sufficient understanding of the current business processes to enable them to be redesigned during the Innovate phase.
2. The collection and baseline of appropriate metrics: for comparative purposes with the new processes to enable input into the business case; to clarify the 20 percent of functionality that delivers the 80 percent of business value; to gain further understanding, and assist in the establishment of the prioritization for innovation/redesign (Innovate phase).
3. Baseline the skills required to execute the current process(es), compare with the skills required for the future redesigned process(es) and enable training requirements.
4. To commence the people change management journey of unfreezing people and have them understand the need to change.

The project team must also understand what the business wishes to achieve from this phase. The process models created may be used for more than input into the Innovate phase, as the business may wish to use the models for documentation and training purposes while the innovation and implementation is taking place.

The Understand phase will also validate the current process reality within the organization and define improvement priorities within the project scope. It will assist in determining changes, if indeed changes to process(es) are necessary at all.

BPM INSIGHT

The crucial point here is that the BPM team and business are seeking to understand the current processes—not to document them in excruciating detail.

Once a process is clearly understood and documented, stop: this is enough detail. If it has been agreed with the business that the process models may be used for documentation and training purposes, then be sure also to agree the level of detail to be recorded within the process models.

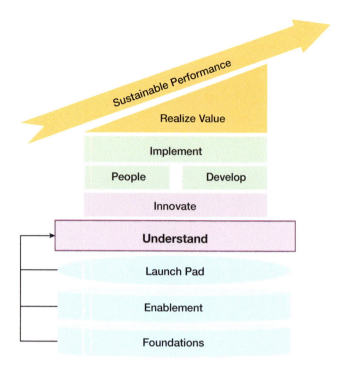

Figure 16.1 Understand phase

RESULTS

There will be a number of results and outputs that the business can expect from this phase, including:

1. Process models of the current processes.

2. Appropriate metrics sufficient to establish a baseline for future process improvement measurement, prioritization and selection in the Innovate phase.

3. Measurement and documentation of the current or actual performance levels.

4. Documentation of what works well (for taking into the Innovate phase) and what could work better (including root causes).

5. Identification of any "quick wins" that could be implemented within a four to eight week period.

6. A report on the phase.

HOW?

First, let's spend a few moments to overview the depth and approach for this phase. As stated previously, the Understand modeling should only be completed to the point where all participants (project team and business) have a common understanding of what is going on in the current business process(es) and there is enough information and metrics to commence the Innovate phase. There are several situations to keep in mind during this phase:

- "understand" what actually goes on, and ensure that what is documented reflects the actual "as is" situation and not an "as if" (or "should be") situation;
- ensure that the process(es) being understood (modeled) are completed on a true "end-to-end" basis (we will discuss this in more detail in step 3 of this phase);
- identify key pain points and their root causes. This will help with the engagement of staff as they feel that they are being listened to. It is important to include metrics as this ensures that facts determine what is important. Specifying the consequences of the pain points is useful as it will assist in building the business case;
- ensure that staff are comfortable within the workshops and do not feel as though they are being evaluated; unless staff are comfortable, participants may tell you what they think you want to hear, will not impart their knowledge, or may provide you with incorrect information;
- ensure that timeframes are set regarding the amount of time to be spent on understanding or modeling a particular process, and deliver to this timeframe—in other words, set some milestones and "time-box" activities. If you don't set milestones, you risk overruns of workshop time and the waste of valuable business subject matter expert time by going into too much detail. Workshops can be fun, and there is a risk of a workshop becoming an end in its own right, which is clearly not the purpose. Alternatively, participants can become bored and start to fail to show up for the workshops;
- use the Pareto principle (80/20 rule) to decide when you are reaching the point of diminishing returns. Always ask, "Do we have sufficient information now and can stop?"

CASE STUDY

Having the correct participants in workshops is crucial

We have been in workshops where the business experts came from different regions within the organization and actually "negotiated" the process in the workshop, in front of us, as we modeled it, until we realized what was happening. Participants then mutually acknowledged what was happening, and they were asked to explain the process one at a time.

Message: Always have people who know the detailed process in the workshop, and if they come from varying offices or regions where the process(es) could be different, request that the process be modeled for one area at a time until there is confidence that there is a common process(es).

A few of the reasons for and against process modeling in the Understand phase are listed here.

Reasons *for* process modeling in the Understand phase include:

1. To gain a common understanding of, and common language for, the problems.
2. To demonstrate the shortcomings of the current situation.
3. To support acceptance for the "unfreezing" for the BPM activities.
4. To allow evaluation of the completeness of the innovate process.
5. Models produced may be used as documentation of the process if there is little need to change the process(es).
6. People become used to process thinking and the process modeling.
7. To establish a baseline for the relationship of processes with the organization, IT and personnel.

Reasons *against* process modeling in the Understand phase include:

1. The current situation as modeled becomes obsolete as soon as the innovate processes are designed and implemented.
2. There is always the danger of having a "narrow focus" process design, thus putting constraints on the thinking for the innovate process. Perhaps a shortcoming of using Six Sigma.
3. It takes time, requires commitment of busy business resources and costs money; in most cases this will be a complicated procedure with a steep learning curve in the first instance.
4. There is a danger of doing too much and drowning in the details.
5. Momentum may be lost in the BPM activity.

In the past there have been numerous organizations that have spent a significant amount of time in mapping out all their processes in unnecessary detail, ignoring the reasons as outlined above as to the desired outcomes of this activity. However, in recent years an increasing number of organizations are limiting their Understand phase (current state) process modeling activities to purely understanding key processes only and the interfaces with other processes.

Key drivers for these trends are:

- Organizations are leveraging industry best practice models;
- Need to reduce the timelines of projects and the time to benefits;
- Better documentation of the current processes.

Indulska and colleagues (2009) conducted research of the current issues and future challenges for process modeling. The study made a distinction between practitioners, vendors and academics and highlights a clear distinction between the views of the three groups. The BPM Maturity model aspects described in Chapter 29 have been used in Tables 16.1 and 16.2.

In Tables 16.1 and 16.2 the practitioners score the BPM aspects of Governance, Strategic Alignment, People and Culture high for both current issues and future challenges. Information Technology and Method score higher with vendors and academics compared to practitioners. Interestingly, culture has been listed three times with practitioners as future challenges, while vendors and academics don't have any culture points in their top ten.

Table 16.1 Current issues of process modeling

Rank	Practitioners issue Mean rating (score) (BPMM aspect)	Vendors issue Mean rating (score) (BPMM aspect)	Academics issue Mean rating (score) (BPMM aspect)
1	Standardization —14.316 (Governance)	Model-driven process execution —12.222 (Information Technology)	Service orientation —8.440 (Information Technology)
2	Value of process modeling —12.105 (Strategic Alignment)	Value of process modeling —12.167 (Strategic Alignment)	Model-driven process execution —8.400 (Information Technology)
3	Buy-in —9.500 (Culture)	Business–IT divide —8.833 (Strategic Alignment)	Flexibility —7.480 (Method)
4	Expectation management —8.474 (Strategic Alignment)	Standardization —8.778 (Governance)	Compliance —6.880 (Governance)
5	Training —8.316 (People)	Process orientation —8.667 (Culture)	Methodology —5.960 (Method)
6	Governance —7.132 (Governance)	Modeling level of detail —8.222 (Method)	Modeling views —5.880 (Method)
7	Modeling level of detail —6.579 (Method)	Methodology —8.111 (Method)	Standardization —5.480 (Governance)
8	Model management —6.368 (Method)	Multi-perspective modeling —7.333 (Method)	Model management —5.040 (Method)
9	Adoption —6.263 (Culture)	Model management —5.778 (Method)	Ease of use —4.920 (People)
10	Model integration —5.632 (Information Technology)	Governance —5.444 (Governance)	View integration —4.640 (Method)

Source: Indulska et al. (2009).

Table 16.2 Future challenges of process modeling

Rank	Practitioners challenge Mean rating (score) (BPMM aspect)	Vendors challenge Mean rating (score) (BPMM aspect)	Academics challenge Mean rating (score) (BPMM aspect)
1	Value of process modeling —16.632 (Strategic Alignment)	Model-driven process execution —16.222 (Information Technology)	Model-driven process execution —10.960 (Information Technology)
2	Buy-in —12.342 (Culture)	Business–IT alignment —15.333 (Strategic Alignment)	Methodology —8.800 (Method)
3	Standardization —8.632 (Governance)	Value of process modeling —14.889 (Strategic Alignment)	Service orientation —8.560 (Information Technology)
4	Expectations management —7.842 (Strategic Alignment)	Ease of use —0.944 (People)	View integration —8.560 (Method)
5	Governance —7.079 (Governance)	Standardization —9.389 (Governance)	Value of process modeling —7.160 (Strategic Alignment)
6	Training —6.684 (People)	Collaborative modeling —9.000 (Method)	Standardization —7.000 (Governance)
7	Process architecture —6.316 (Strategic Alignment)	Training —6.944 (People)	Model management —6.960 (Method)
8	Model integration —6.289 (Information Technology)	Service orientation —6.556 (Information Technology)	Data-centric process modeling —6.560 (Method)
9	Adoption —6.132 (Culture)	Model management —5.833 (Method)	Compliance —6.160 (Governance)
10	Re-use —5.868 (Culture)	Ontology —4.889 (Method)	Tool support —6.080 (Information Technology)

Source: Indulska et al. (2009).

Considering the top three of practitioners (for both current issues and future challenges) in relation to the understand phase:

- *Standardization*: will assist in obtaining a consistent view of the organization and enable functional silos to be broken down;
- *Value of process modeling*: relates to the point made at the start of this chapter: process models need to be fit-for-purpose and provide tangible value to the organization, otherwise the business will not fund process modeling activities;

- *Buy-in*: process models only derive value from people committed to using them in their day-to-day work and providing feedback and suggestions for improvement.

DETAILED STEPS

The various steps to be completed within the Understand phase are shown in Figure 16.2.

Step 1: Communications

In this phase, the main communication activities relate to providing information to the stakeholders and people within the organization about the project, its objectives, and how and when people will be involved in the Understand phase. For example, it is during this phase that the project starts to have more visibility within the organization, because personnel are starting to be specifically engaged in BPM activity workshops and asked questions regarding their current process activities and associated metrics. This can raise concerns among some employees regarding their future role within the organization, and whether or not their employment will continue. If these concerns are not addressed early and satisfactorily, it will be difficult to obtain the support of the organization and its people.

The BPM team needs to create an atmosphere in which people feel at ease in providing the information necessary in the workshops. People should be comfortable in sharing their real issues and problems without fear of any blame.

By now communication should be an established part of the BPM activity. It is important to balance between consistency in the communication and ensuring that sufficiently new and up-to-date communication is prepared. Communication just for the sake of communication should be avoided.

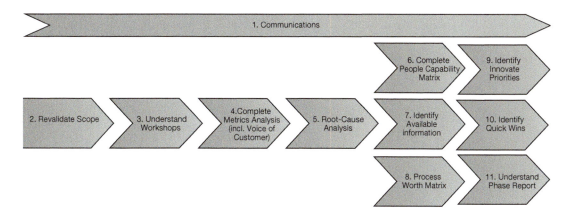

Figure 16.2 Understand phase steps

Step 2: Revalidate scope

It is essential to revalidate the scope of a BPM activity on a continual basis, and now is an ideal time—prior to the commencement of the Understand workshops. Key documents from the Launch pad phase (Chapter 15) can be leveraged, such as the Process Selection Matrix, the project scope document and Process Worth Matrix.

It may be useful to go into the various stakeholder organizations (suppliers, customers and distribution channels) and model their processes to understand how they fit in with yours, and how your processes can enhance their business processes. The benefits of revalidating scope include:

- helping the organization to gain a clearer understanding of the end-to-end process, thus allowing it to be more effective in the innovation of the process;

- providing the ability to suggest to the stakeholder(s) that their process(es) should be redesigned as well, and work with them to understand how this could be accomplished and fully integrated with your process(es);

- enabling the organization to minimize duplications and disconnects, and reduce and improve the hand-offs between your organizational processes and those of your stakeholders;

- if there has been a delay in commencing this phase from the Launch pad phase, then revalidate the scope to ensure it is still valid.

Step 3: Understand workshops

It is important that the project sponsor and business have a clear understanding of why this phase is necessary. It is unusual to encounter resistance to the Understand phase, however sometimes executives think that "it will only take a couple of hours to model all the processes!"

Should you encounter resistance and need to explain why the Understand phase is necessary, here are a few reasons:

1. To ensure a common understanding of the *facts* about the current process(es), not what management *thinks* happens.

2. To analyze whether improvement is possible, or even necessary. Some processes may need improvement (small changes); others may need to be redesigned using basically the same approach but just more efficiently; others may need innovation using a totally new approach (perhaps from different industries, or taking out steps in the value chain); and yet others will not warrant any change at all.

3. To assist with an understanding of the process interactions and impacts upon other processes within the organization—for example, from one department to another (hand-offs).

4. To understand and document the interfaces to existing legacy systems and applications, which will be essential for the Innovate phase—especially if process automation is involved.

5. Obtain key metrics that will assist in quantifying benefits and prioritizing activities.

Some of the drivers to complete process models, rather than take linear notes, could include: documentation, cost, simulation, improvement, compliance (for example, Sarbanes-Oxley, Basel II), software (selection, evaluation, configuration and development), assistance with the redesign of enterprise architecture, HR capacity planning, project management, knowledge management, document management and relationship management (Rosemann, 2005).

Prior to the commencement of the workshops it is important to have a clear understanding of why you are carrying out process modeling, to ensure that upon completion the models are relevant for the desired purpose. Don't strive for perfection; strive to have models that are sufficiently complete and relevant, and "fit for purpose." Always keep in mind Pareto's principle (the 80/20 rule), because "perfection is the enemy of good." Perfection at this stage can be an extremely expensive state to obtain, which can be an issue with the complete Six Sigma approach.

Questions that should be considered on a continual basis during workshops include:

1. Is the process fit for the purpose it is designed to serve?
2. Does the process satisfy the business requirements for which it is designed?
3. Is the process critical to the business outcomes or objectives?

When organizing the Understand process workshops, there are three steps necessary to ensure that they run smoothly:

1. Schedule the workshops early, and conveniently for the business participants (step 3.1).
2. Ensure that the participants' minds are "framed" appropriately before the workshop commences, to establish the correct expectations (step 3.2).
3. Conduct the workshops in a structured and controlled manner (step 3.3).

Step 3.1: Schedule workshops early and conveniently

The Understand workshops can be very time-consuming, and could require the subject matter experts (SMEs) to be away from the business for quite some time. This will interrupt the SMEs' ability to do their normal role, and take some of the best people out of the day-to-day activities of "running" the business.

It is always a challenge for the business to take some of their best resources "out" of the business for a significant amount of time to attend the workshops. Project team members need to be very sympathetic and sensitive to this, and to schedule workshops to best suit the business while still delivering the project to the business within the agreed timeframes. It is important to have the best people in the workshops, and not just people who are available, if the project and business are to obtain optimized results. This is why commitment from the business is important.

The workshop schedule should be agreed with the business executives and project sponsor as early as possible, with all necessary rooms and equipment scheduled. Workshop preparation is critical, and must include:

- scheduling them well ahead to ensure that SMEs are available;
- allowing some contingency in the number of workshops scheduled, as things will always take longer than expected;
- specifying the length of workshops (usually no longer than three hours).

BPM INSIGHT

The most capable people are quite heavily booked and managers are tempted to place the available, rather than the capable, people on projects as Subject Matter Experts. This seriously limits the potential to innovate, especially in transformation projects.

Step 3.2: "Framing" participants

It is necessary to set the expectations of the BPM activity sponsor and participants as early as possible, and certainly well before they walk into the first workshop. If *you* do not set the expectations for the participants, *they* will set their own—and their expectations may not be appropriate for the circumstances.

The format and purpose of the workshops should be discussed and agreed with the BPM activity sponsor and/or business owner, an agenda established, and a pre-workshop meeting held with all participants. The project sponsor should chair this meeting with the workshop facilitator.

The BPM activity sponsor should inform the participants of the importance of the activity, their role, and how important it is for them to attend. The workshop facilitator should outline the broad format of the workshops, the role of the participants, what is expected from them and the purpose of the workshops, from the BPM activity's perspective.

Step 3.3: Conduct the workshops—structured and controlled

Who should attend?

It is recommended that the following attend the workshops:

- the people who actually execute the processes—not the managers who *think* they know how the process works;
- team leaders, if they know the process(es) well.

It is always useful for the BPM activity sponsor to drop in on the workshops occasionally, so long as the sponsor takes a low profile and listens rather than participates. It is recommended that the BPM activity sponsor kicks off the first session to emphasize the importance of the activity and how it will contribute to the strategic objectives.

Workshop agenda

At the beginning of the first workshop, a presentation should be given to the participants informing them in more detail of the BPM activity and how the workshops will be conducted. The agenda, format and suggested presentation outline for the workshop is outlined in detail in the Extra Reading section at the end of this chapter; however, there are a few points to be made here:

1. There is no single correct way to complete process modeling; everyone will have a preferred method. You can use a process modeling toolset on a laptop, connected to a projector that can show the model on a screen or wall as it is being created. Using such a process modeling tool promotes discussion, by allowing participants to see and understand the process as it is created in front of them. It also allows participants to become familiar with the tool—in fact, it often gets to the point where the business subject matter experts want to "take over" the modeling tool. As soon as this happens, you know the business has started to "own" the process and you have significant buy-in, which is obviously an excellent outcome. We do not plan to cover modeling methods here, as there are many other books on this topic; we will only cover the steps in the Understand phase.

2. Always keep to the scheduled times and timeframe. Completing models for the current processes can be fun, and it is essential to keep to the BPM activity plan/schedule and ensure that the SME participants do not become bored.

3. Avoid "the power of one"—the dominance of a single person within the workshops. There are various techniques for handling this situation and it is largely a facilitation activity. For example, the facilitator could take the person aside during a break and request them to let others contribute as well. If this is not possible, or considered the best technique, the facilitator can let people talk in turns or point out the need for everyone to be provided with an opportunity of contributing during the workshop.

4. As mentioned earlier, the Understand modeling should only be completed to the point where you understand what is going on and you have enough information to commence the Innovate phase. What does this actually mean? How much detail should be modeled? This obviously will depend upon the particular organization and goals of the project. The simplest way is to always ask yourself, "Can we stop modeling now?" If the answer is yes, then *stop*.

Don't believe everything you hear. Challenge the information presented to get to the true situation if it does not make sense. People may be tempted to tell you what they think you want to hear, or management may tell you what they "think" happens. An extremely useful method of understanding the true situation is to take the process(es) modeled within the workshops and validate it in the workplace with "walkthroughs."

Furthermore, ask for facts when people make generic statements, for example, "our customers always complain about our services." Questions to ask are:

- How many complaints have you received?
- What do they complain about?
- What analysis has been performed?

End-to-end processes are critical

An insurance organization was reviewing the workloads and practices within the finance area. One of the staff commented that a particular process could be "so much better if only the underwriting area did their job correctly." It was found that in excess of 50 percent of the finance work effort in this process was attributable to "fixing up" the "errors" from the underwriting area. Underwriting simply had no idea of the impact it was having on finance. A joint workshop of both finance and underwriting was conducted to model the process (end-to-end), thus enabling the underwriting area to understand the critical nature of key process steps. Once corrected, this significantly diminished the work effort in the finance department.

In this instance, the "process" of conducting the workshop, to gain a common understanding and realization, was more important than the actual modeling. Modeling was simply a method of demonstrating the impacts of the way specific process steps were being completed.

Message: Always model a process on an end-to-end basis with all participants in the workshops at the same time. Sometimes the "journey" is more important than the documented outcomes (models).

It is useful to capture the ideas (opportunities) and issues raised during the Understand workshops and log them in an Issues and Opportunities register. This register should be maintained throughout the BPM activity, and a suggested layout of this register is shown in the Extra Reading section at the end of this chapter.

It is important to regularly communicate progress and findings from the workshop. Also, sometimes it is necessary to report attendance at the workshops to the Steering Committee if non-attendance is an issue.

Step 4: Complete metrics analysis, including Voice of Customer

Business process metrics are critical for the Understand phase. Metrics are defined as "a standard measure to assess your performance in a particular area" (Kureemun and Fantina, 2011: 124).

The purpose of gathering the business process metrics is two-fold:

1. to assist in the understanding of the process(es) and their impact upon the organization, and to provide prioritization for further investigation.

2. to provide a baseline for comparative purposes with the Innovate phase of the BPM activity. This can assist greatly in the completion of the business case and determination of expected productivity, cost and service level improvements.

People like to discuss exceptions or even exceptional exceptions, mostly to demonstrate either their insight or block attempts to change the process.

An Understand workshop participant was questioned when she raised an exception. She was asked how often this exception occurred. When the participant needed a long time to think, she was asked: "when is the last time this exception happened" and the response: *"I'm not sure, it was either last year or the year before."* It's quite obvious the value of having this clarified before a process is changed to accommodate the exception.

Message: Metrics are an objective basis to make informed decision and setting priorities.

Why complete a metrics analysis? Some of the reasons will include the need to:

- assist in the understanding of an organization's processes;
- produce an analytical view of the organization;
- reconcile the organization's process costs against departmental budgets to ensure that all major processes are either captured or intentionally excluded;
- aid the BPM activity team members in creating remedial, not just opportunist, solutions;
- aid in the prioritization of processes for further investigation during the Innovate phase;
- provide a baseline for comparative purposes with any future changes, allowing for the forecast of future potential benefits from any newly designed process environment, and to measure the impact of actual changes;
- input into the focus for the redesign effort, indicating areas that have the potential to provide the largest impacts;
- allow benchmarking of process data (task times, volumes and costs) between different organizations.

Prior to the commencement of the Understand workshops, a number of initial metrics will be gathered and analyzed. This task will include:

- gathering broad costing information—for example, budgets, organization charts and staff listings;
- reconciliation of the organization charts and HR staff listings;
- restructuring the budget if the budget is for a larger area of the organization than is being analyzed. In this case, the budget must be dissected and allocated to the specific area within the project scope. For example, staff costs could be determined by the number of staff in each department, while the other costs are more likely to be calculated by proportioning the non-productive personnel's staff costs across the productive resources costs.

During the workshops, as many relevant metrics as possible should be collected. At a minimum, the following must be included:

- transactional information—volumes, which role completes the tasks, and the process time;

- transactional data to reconcile against the resourcing levels within each process area for reasonability of processing times and volumes, and to identify any additional processes;

- direct labor cost per process, which is calculated based on task time, process transactions and labor recovery rates;

- IT costs and other overheads allocated to the process, based on daily task time.

A sample costing matrix is shown in Figure 16.3.

The department concerned only processes two types of transactions: receipting and policy updates. The number of transactions per day is shown in Figure 16.3, as is the estimated processing time (in minutes) per transaction (process). The hourly labor rate has been calculated, as has the non-labor hourly allocation. This allows the calculation of the average cost per transaction (process), and the annual cost per transaction (process) based on 250 working days per year.

Depending on the standard day used for calculation, different utilization levels will be acceptable in this reconciliation. For example, based upon a 7.5-hour day, a utilization level of between 80 percent and 85 percent could be considered reasonable. If an organization chose a 6.25 hour day, however, 100 percent utilization would be expected. *Note*: be careful with the percentages selected for use in the project, and ensure they are well socialized and agreed with the business.

An alternate way of examining process metrics is worth considering. This is especially useful where it is not possible to consider the cost of business processes on a departmental level. If individual staff members or staff within a department are involved in the processing of more than one process and it is difficult to allocate budgetary costing to the process, then an alternate method needs to be used. It is important that the method used is as simple as possible. Figure 16.4 shows such an analysis method.

This is an example of a large government health department which had approximately 35,000 nursing staff. Nurses were notified of their rosters (when they would be working) six weeks in advance. Recent experience revealed that the pattern of roster adjustment requests had changed from being received relatively evenly over the six-week period, to the majority being received in the last three days before they were scheduled to commence the shift. This created a spike in workload for the processing staff. Over a year, 9m roster adjustment forms were manually received by the central shared services processing area.

The purpose of the analysis was to gather the metrics (costs) associated with this manual processing state and assist in the business case to justify automation.

A range of central processing times were estimated, from 2 minutes per transaction up to 15 minutes per transaction. These estimates were then multiplied by the average annual salary of transaction processing staff, $60,000.

Analysis in the workplace indicated that 5 minutes per transaction appeared to be the likely average processing time. This equated to $25m per annum processing costs.

A	B	C	D	E	F	G	H	I	J	K	L
Process Name	Average Number of Transactions (per day)	Time per transaction (minutes)	Daily Time (minutes)	Labor Hourly Rate $	Labor Costs (Productive Labor) $	Non Labor Hourly Allocation (proportioned over processes by daily time) $	Non Labor Costs (proportioned over processes by daily time) $	Cost (per day) $	Average Cost per transaction $	Annual Cost (per annum) $	Annual Effort %
Receipting	3,000	10	30,000	$25.00	$12,500	$17.00	$8,500	$21,000	$7.00	$5,250,000	55%
Policy updates	3,500	7	24,500	$25.00	$10,208	$17.00	$6,942	$17,150	$4.90	$4,287,500	45%
			(B x C)		(D x E / 60)		(D x G / 60)	(F + H)	(I / B)	(I x 250)	(D / X)
Totals			54,500 (X)		$22,708		$15,442			$9,537,500	
Total time available (based on FTE times standard day)			20,000								
			(Y)								
Utilization %			272.5% (X / Y)								

Figure 16.3 Sample Simplified Costing Matrix

Health Department estimate — 9m Roster adjustment forms raised per annum

Estimated time to enter a Roster Adjustment (mins)	FTEs Required	Estimated Cost (per annum)
2	167	$10m
3	250	$15m
4	333	$20m
5	417	$25m
10	833	$50m
15	1250	$75m

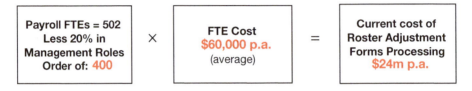

Figure 16.4 Alternate costing analysis

To validate this, the number of staff in the roster adjustment section was found to be 502. It was estimated that 20 percent were management and supervisory staff, which left 400 actual processing staff. This 400 was multiplied by the average cost of staff, $60,000, and this equated to $24m per annum.

It was believed that this comparison was adequate for the business case.

There are many ways to gather and analyze process metrics and it is suggested that metrics should be collected at all levels. Examples that may be useful include the following (although there is no expectation that all of these will be collected or used).

Process selection matrix level:

1. Sales and staffing levels at the business unit level.

2. Dissection of the organization (sales $ and volume) across the various segments of the business unit and/or project scope.

3. At a process and sub-process level, the percentage split of volumes.

4. The cost to the business of transacting this volume of business (for example, annual budgets).

Process level:

1. Determination of which part of the process(es) to measure.

2. Collection of estimated processing times per process or sub-process—if costs can be attributed to a given process, this is ideal; activity-based costing, if implemented within an organization, can supply a great deal of information.

3. Determination of process performance measures, for example, SLAs, KPIs, then sub-process KPIs, including lead times, processing time and errors/rework.

4. Details of how the accuracy of the process is currently measured—is there any error tracking?

5. Measurement of wherever bottlenecks occur.

Examples of the types of metrics that may be worth gathering include:

- number of transactions by payment method or region (monthly for last eight to twelve months, to indicate monthly trends or peak periods)
- process times for major process(es), particularly date-sensitive activities
- error numbers and types
- backlog reports, status and volumes (amount and numbers)—trends for last twelve months
- volumes and values of the various transaction types
- labor costs for key positions, including labor on-costs
- overtime/casual/contract hours worked—history for the last twelve months
- cost per hour, including labor on-costs for overtime
- complaints register—numbers and trends over the past twelve months, plus a sample analysis
- extent, percentage of transaction volume, time and labor impact of rework
- value of transactions "written off" monthly, for the last twelve months
- percentage of time spent on out-of-scope processes.

Management level:

1. Customer satisfaction surveys could provide interesting information.

2. For quality or effectiveness measures, use:
   - efficiency—how much resource is used doing what needs to be done?
   - adaptability—how easy is it for the organization to change?
   - common denominators, which are time, cost, customer satisfaction
   - customer retention rate, by division and/or distribution channel (monthly for the last twelve months, including monthly trends).

3. Productivity trend studies.

4. Headcount report by position, matched with the organization chart to discover any discrepancies.

5. Copy of management performance measurement reports for the last twelve months.

6. ISO and/or audit reports, both internal and external.

7. Current provision level for write-offs.

8. Staff turnover for the last twelve months.

9. Staff length of service.

BPM INSIGHT

Metrics are essential to ensure that decisions are made on the basis of tangible and relevant numbers or facts, rather than on the basis of the decibels produced by people in workshops.

How are these metrics gathered?

The metrics may be gathered:

- during workshops;
- by interviewing management and staff to validate the information gained during workshops;
- by various surveys and questionnaires;
- from management reports.

If it is difficult to collect process timings during the process modeling workshops, you could complete the process modeling and then hold another workshop or two to go through the models to collect the timing data; alternatively, other people within the organization may have the information. The data can then be extrapolated to ensure it makes sense.

For example, a spreadsheet created to multiply process times by the volume of transactions in order to calculate overall processing times, and extrapolated into the "expected" number of staff, can then be compared to the "actual" number of staff currently employed in the processes. If this is accurate to within 15—20 percent, it is close enough at this stage. When completing this exercise, make sure that all processes and activities are covered.

It is essential to understand the various executive, management and team leader performance measures to ensure that they are complementary to the process, and not working against it.

CASE STUDY

An Understand workshop requested the participating managers to rank their organization among the top 12 in their industry on basis of customer feedback. The general consensus from the workshop participants indicated that they were in about second or third place. They believed that with some minor adjustments they could reach first place, and had created a project with limited process change to achieve this. When they were informed that an independent customer survey ranked them 11 out of 12, they suddenly realized that they needed a completely different approach to even make it into the top three.

Message: Listening to the facts from customers is critical to understanding the facts and guiding BPM activities. This may create a burning platform required to initiate change.

Remember, the major purpose of collecting the metrics during the Understand phase is to enable the establishment of a baseline for comparative purposes with the Innovate phase, which informs the business case.

Many organizations forget to obtain information from a key source: the customer. Customers need to be listened to, and the organization must not assume that they know what customers want without validating it.

We define Voice of Customer as a process used to capture the stated and unstated requirements/feedback from the customer (internal or external) to provide the customers with the best in class service/product quality. This process is all about being proactive and constantly innovative to capture the changing requirements of the customers.[1]

It is important to realize the Voice of Customer requires obtaining both quantitative and qualitative data. The quantitative information can be used to evaluate and select various process improvement alternatives. The qualitative information will provide more insights in the rationale behind the data and will assist in eliminating misconceptions.

Figure 16.5 provides a sample Critical to Quality tree from a customer point of view. Critical to Quality is a useful way of ensuring that customers receive a fit-for-purpose service and the organization avoids under- or over-servicing customers. The Critical to Quality tree helps in obtaining tangible and measurable items. This is important as people will have different ideas around "value for money" and it is important that the customer's perception is understood in more granular detail.

It is important to ensure that the right approach is used when involving customers. Obtaining the Voice of Customer can be a good way to demonstrate the willingness to engage with and listen to the customer. This information can be obtained through surveys, interviews and focus groups. The BPM team needs to clearly establish the scope of the BPM activity with customers to ensure they have the correct expectations. After the initial interviews it is

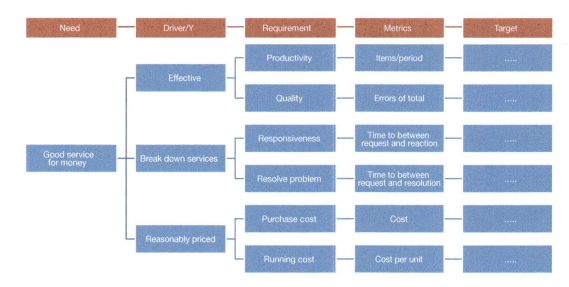

Figure 16.5 Critical to Quality tree

> ## BPM INSIGHT
>
> All business processes are geared towards providing value to customers. Hence, it is crucial to obtain insight about customers' expectations and perceptions rather than second guessing.

important to keep the customer informed about the progress. Customers that have initially participated will also be good pilot sites.

Step 5: Root-cause analysis

It is essential to determine the actual "root" cause of an issue or non-performing process. If you do not fully understand the root cause, you are not in a position to commence the Innovate phase of a process. You cannot be certain that once the redesign has been completed, the reason for the process non-performance has been addressed. It is like a medical doctor treating the symptom and not determining or understanding the actual cause of the disease. Process pain points may be obtained as part of the workshop activities.

What is the best way to perform root-cause analysis? This will vary from organization to organization. In some organizations the Understand workshops will flush out the root cause, while in other organizations the BPM team will need to go into the business and analyze the root cause themselves. The latter case will require observation, investigation, analysis, and speaking to the people who execute the processes on a day-to-day basis. Do not forget to talk to people outside the main processing team, because the root cause may be either upstream or downstream of the part of the process currently being analyzed. This is an example of why it is essential to examine processes on a true end-to-end basis, otherwise you cannot be certain that you have covered all aspects of the process. While it is essential to speak to management, it is unusual (depending upon the type of error) that they will know the root cause.

Suggested questions to keep in mind when conducting the root-cause analysis include:

- Where are the errors or rework coming from?
- Is this being caused by other process(es)?
- Is the information being received correctly?
- If not, what can be done to rectify the situation?
- Does the staff executing this process have the skills to complete it?
- Could the forms being used be better designed?
- Does the organization have sufficient capacity to complete this process to the desired standard?
- Are staff idle?
- Do the steps in the process add value to the stakeholder requirements and goals of the process?
- Are the steps in the process being completed in the appropriate sequence?

Ref#	Process	Failure Mode	Failure Effects	Sev	Occurrence	Occ	Current Detection	Det	Score	Action
1	Account Payable	Lack of controls on invoice reference	Invoices get paid double	2	2% of all invoices	1	Manual check only	8	16	Keep track of invoices already paid
2	Account Payable	Lack of segregation of duty	Possible fraud	8	less than 1%	1	Dependent on individuals	9	72	Implement segregation of duty
3	Accounts Receivables	Lack of control on outstanding payments	Late payments by debtors	3	30% of invoices are paid late	3	Manual check only	6	54	Keep track of outstanding payments

Figure 16.6 Sample Failure Mode Effect Analysis (FMEA)

It may be useful to use metrics during the root-cause analysis to ensure that the key issues are being addressed. One method of achieving this is by the use of the Failure Mode Effect Analysis (FMEA), see Figure 16.6. This method includes:

- Process reference

- Failure mode—what can go wrong?

- Root cause—why does it go wrong?

- Failure effect—impact of error

- Metrics for severity, frequency and detectability resulting in total score (product of the three metrics)

- Action to address issue

- If required the residual risk can be captured.

The score in the FMEA can be used for a process heat map, as all failures relate to a process (step).

BPM INSIGHT

The FMEA method will ensure that the key root causes are identified, prioritized and used to effect in the BPM activity.

Step 6: Complete People Capability Matrix

The People Capability Matrix will provide useful information about both the current and the future environment. It is, however, the future that is the most important. If the future is substantially different from the current situation, as it often is during large transformation programs, then it may not be appropriate to complete the matrix for the current environment other than for understanding the gap between the skills now in the organization and how they will need to change in the future. In some cases, analysis of the current skills can provide useful information about the root causes of particular process aberrations.

This gap analysis is important, and needs to be well documented and understood at a high level at this stage. It is during the Innovate and People phases that this will be analyzed

Knowledge capabilities/ skills required Key processes	Ability to sell to customers	Communication skills	Data entry skills	Dealing with difficult customers
Notification	Recommended (2)	Recommended (2)	Desired (3)	Mandatory (1)
Assessment	Mandatory (1)	Mandatory (1)	Desired (3)	Mandatory (1)
Approval	Desired (3)	Recommended (2)	Desired (3)	Mandatory (1)
Payment	Recommended (2)	Recommended (2)	Desired (3)	Recommended (2)
Finalization	Recommended (2)	Desired (3)	Mandatory (1)	Mandatory (1)

Figure 16.7 People Capability Matrix

in far more detail and linked to individual roles, specific action plans and potential changes to the organization structure.

Figure 16.7 provides an example of how this matrix could be completed. The horizontal axis represents the core skills or competencies required by each of the processes to complete the tasks or activities. The vertical axis represents the end-to-end process model, group of processes or individual processes. These core competencies are then rated on the simple basis of 1, 2 or 3, where 1 is a mandatory core competency, 2 is a recommended skill set and 3 is desirable but not essential.

Remember to:

• look at the current capability versus the future needs;

• do it from a "big picture" level, not at a person level, at this phase of the project;

• review role description areas at a high level;

• review people core competency enhancement requirements.

Step 7: Identify available information

The purpose of this step is to gain an understanding, within the BPM activity scope, of the currently available information within the organization. This step should only be completed if it will be of use within the BPM activity. The best way to identify the available process information or knowledge is via a workshop and/or discussions with people within the business, HR and training departments.

Within the Understand workshops, a matrix can be developed in a similar format to the Process Selection Matrix. An example is shown in Figure 16.8.

The key processes for which you wish to complete this matrix are displayed on the vertical axis—in this case, an end-to-end claims process comprising notification, assessment, approval, payment and finalization. The types of knowledge that the business deem to be available or desirable within the organization are shown on the horizontal axis.

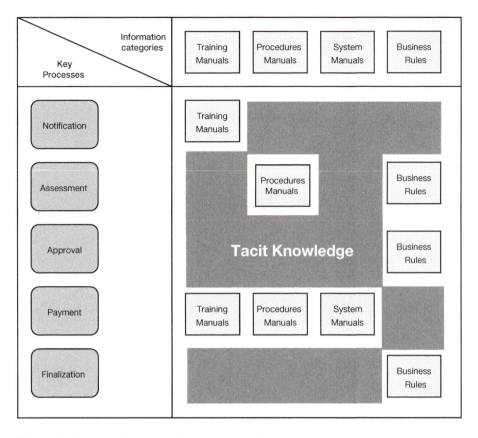

Figure 16.8 Knowledge and information needs map

Knowledge is usually categorized into two classifications:

1. Tacit human, education, experience (basically, in people's "heads" and not documented within the organization).

2. Explicit documented knowledge within the organization. Documentation can include the knowledge built into automated solutions, such as workflow or application systems.

The matrix can then be completed in a similar manner to that shown in Figure 16.8. The grey areas in this figure are all tacit knowledge areas.

It is particularly useful to clearly identify the knowledge available for the "identity" and "priority" processes of the organization; that is, the most valuable processes. Refer to step 8 Process Worth Matrix.

It is equally important to be clear about what type of documentation is needed for the satisfactory delivery of products and services to stakeholders (internal and external). Clearly, the more process knowledge is explicit (documented or systematized) the better it is for the organization and the less likely it is that knowledge will "walk" if staff leave the organization.

As part of this step it is important to obtain insight into the key IT applications that are used in the processes in scope of the BPM activity. Documentation that could be useful includes:

- IT Strategy and plan
- IT Architecture
- Application landscape
- Data landscape and Master Data Management
- Communication and Telephony landscape
- System interface.

This information should be available from the Enablement phase, see Chapter 14.

Step 8: Process Worth Matrix

The Process Worth Matrix was discussed in step 5.6 of the Launch pad phase. This analysis method could now be revisited if it is considered useful. The reason for revisiting it is to overlay the process metrics determined during this Understand phase over the matrix.

For example, one organizational department had 20 different business processes within it. The Understand phase determined that six processes cost 65 percent of the departmental budget. That was considered useful information for the business; however, the Process Worth Matrix revealed that four of these six processes were "liability" processes.

This raises the potential to consider outsourcing these liability processes if a business case can be made.

Step 9: Identify Innovate priorities

Identification of Innovate priorities should be an outcome of the Understand modeling, metrics gathering and root-cause analysis steps. During these steps, it should become obvious which areas of the business, and which process(es), provide an opportunity for improvement and quick wins.

The prioritization should be based upon the analysis completed during the workshops, the metrics, stakeholders' views, and the choices made for each process. These could include:

1. leaving the process(es) as it is—it is good enough.
2. improving—which means the process(es) needs "tweaking" or small changes only.
3. amalgamating with other process(es).
4. redesigning—starting with a blank sheet of paper.
5. total innovation—thinking outside the "box" and making radical changes.
6. outsourcing—the contracting out of a business process, which an organization may have previously performed internally or has a new need for, to an independent organization from which the process is purchased back as a service.

7. in-sourcing—is the opposite of outsourcing and relates to the cessation of outsourcing by an organization and the commencement of performing the activity internally.

8. eliminating the process.

In identifying redesign and quick win opportunities, it is essential to ensure that they are consistent with and contribute towards the process goals, organizational strategic objectives and stakeholders' expectations established during the Process architecture phase. Spend some time linking or mapping them back to these goals, objectives and expectations.

It may be necessary to complete a business case (including a cost–benefit and/or economic value analysis) within some organizations before the management grants approval to continue the project. This may be achieved by updating the business case developed earlier.

A useful way to visualize the priorities for the Innovate phase is to produce a "heat map" using the FMEA scores overlaid on the Process Selection Matrix identifying the key areas for improvement. Refer to Figure 16.9.

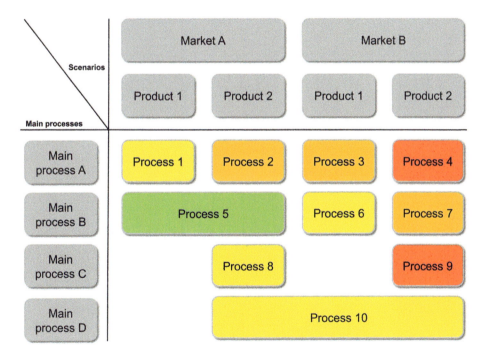

Figure 16.9 Process Selection Matrix heat map using FMEA scores

Step 10: Identify quick wins

As mentioned previously, most organizations insist that process improvement projects are self-funding—so it is essential to find quick wins to implement. It is also highly recommended that some of the suggested quick wins come from the front-line personnel who execute the processes, even if the benefits are not great, because it shows you are listening to them. Ensure that the front-line personnel are given credit in a public way for the ideas and success of these quick win implementations. This contributes towards the change management process essential to any BPM project.

The activities to be performed at this phase of the project are as follows:

- to revisit these quick wins via workshops with the business, to validate them in more detail and to prioritize them for implementation;
- to validate the feasibility of implementation; ensuring that the quick wins are cost-effective (that is, the cost of development and implementation does not outweigh the benefits to be gained), and that they will be useful and efficient solutions for the business;
- once this has been validated, to document the proposed solution(s) for approval by stakeholders (internal and external);
- after approval is obtained, to finalize and execute a more detailed development and implementation plan.

Consideration should be given to forming a sub-project team to implement these quick wins. This has the advantage of not distracting the core project team from the Innovate phase.

If the quick wins are given to a separate team or the business to implement, the main project team should *not* completely outsource this implementation, nor abdicate responsibility and take no further part in the implementation. The main project team *must* still take ultimate responsibility for the implementation, because if there are any issues regarding not realizing the projected benefits outlined in the business case or quick win documentation, the main team will be deemed responsible—even if this was caused by poor implementation. The main team should set the project scope, assist in the development of the project plans/schedules, quality assure the project continually throughout its life, and ensure that the designated benefits are realized.

Step 11: Understand phase report

At the completion of this phase, the project team should deliver a report to the business and project sponsor documenting the phase outcomes and findings. This report should contain at least the following information:

1. The purpose of the Understand phase.
2. The process issues found during the workshops and analysis within the business.
3. A list of stakeholders and their relevance to the project.
4. Findings:
    - current process(es)
    - metrics
    - identified quick wins.
5. A suggested Innovate phase prioritization.
6. Appendix should include list of workshop participants and documents used.

REALIZE VALUE

Baseline and comparative measurements must be established as part of this phase. For details, refer to step 3 of Chapter 21, where it is described in the context of realizing value within a project.

UNDERSTAND PHASE OUTPUTS

The Understand phase will provide valuable input into other phases of the framework (see Figure 16.10), including the following few examples:

- knowledge may be gained that will be useful to the process architecture in modifying or enhancing the standards or guidelines for the organization;

- certainly there will be input into the Innovate phase—baseline metrics, innovate priorities and so forth;

- there will be outcomes that will assist in the potential development of new roles in the People phase, or indications of what may be required in the development of solutions and how a solution may be rolled out across the organization, for example, the People Capability Matrix.

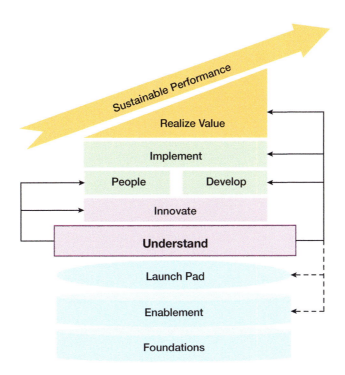

Figure 16.10 Understand phase outputs to other phases

UNDERSTAND PHASE RISKS

During the execution of the Understand phase there are a number of high level risks that must be considered. Table 16.3 is not meant to be a complete list; just the beginning of a list of risks that the project team members can use to start their own project risk analysis:

Table 16.3 Understand phase risks and mitigation strategies

Risk		Mitigation strategy
1	Processes are not reviewed on a genuine end-to-end basis	This risks compromising the common level of understanding of a process(es) and the ability to ensure all aspects of a process are covered during the Innovate phase. Ensure that the project scope is for an end-to-end situation, and if in doubt go back to the project sponsor for clarification and amendment.
2	The workshops overrun time	Plan the workshops carefully before you commence and keep to the plan. The plan does not need to work perfectly to the minute; however, the overall plan must be achieved. The plan must be constantly reviewed throughout the phase. Keep focused on the purpose and avoid the "power of one."
3	The workshop modeling is in too much detail	The purpose of the Understand phase must always be kept in mind, and modeling must only be in sufficient detail to enable a common understanding and to enable the Innovate phase to commence. Remember to always ask the question, "Can we stop modeling now?" This applies to each process and the entire Understand phase.
4	Workshop participants do not understand the actual workings of the current processes	Go back to the business and if necessary to the project sponsor for discussions. This should be addressed before the workshops commence, to minimize the chance of it occurring. Change workshop participants if necessary.
5	The metrics analysis is completed in too much detail	Again, the purpose of analyzing the process metrics is to provide prioritization for the Innovate phase and a baseline for comparison with the outcomes of the Innovate phase. The project manager (or a delegated person) needs to monitor this and ensure that the metrics analysis does not analyze in too much detail.
6	No metrics gathered	This is a critical aspect of the Understand phase to enable the establishment of a baseline for future comparative purposes. If there is push-back on the completion of metrics, gain the support of the project sponsor.
7	Insufficient participation of business SMEs	Explain importance of Understand phase activities. Start rolling out quick wins.

SUMMARY

This chapter highlighted the key steps of the Understand phase. It highlighted the following:

- The importance of the Understand phase to revalidate scope and keep the stakeholders informed and engaged.

- The need to get insight in current processes and pain points through analysis and workshops.

- Obtaining the Voice of Customer is a good way to get relevant metrics that the process improvement can be evaluated and prioritized against.

- The necessity to perform root-cause analysis and obtain metrics to ensure well-informed decision making and to prioritize.

- Get key information regarding the people and their capabilities, so that at a later stage the change impact can be measured.

- It is strongly recommended to achieve some quick wins at this early stage in the project/program to gain momentum.

SELF-TEST

1 What are the pros and cons of modeling the current process?

2 What are typical agenda items in an Understand workshop?

3 Prepare a Critical to Quality tree for a service.

4 What are the deliverables of the Understand phase?

5 What are key risks of the Understand phase?

You elect to conduct several Understand phase workshops to process model (map) the current processes; gather high level metrics; and complete the People Capability Matrix.

You have also elected to conduct a Voice of Customer exercise from a student point of view. You may wish to complete Figure 16.11 for the on-boarding of new students.

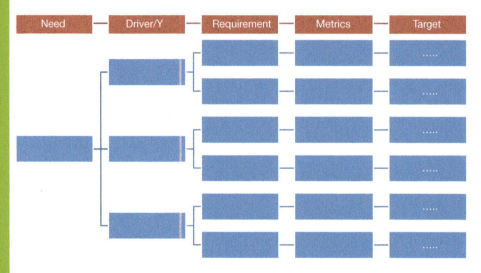

Figure 16.11 Voice of Customer for on-boarding of new students process(es)

During a workshop the process consultant requested the participants to specify their key problems and the root causes of the student on-boarding process which is considered to be lengthy with many errors and delays.

Ref#	Process	Failure Mode	Failure Effects
1	On-boarding of students	....	.....
2	On-boarding of students	....	.....

Figure 16.12 Voice of Customer for on-boarding of new students process issues

ASSIGNMENT

Assignment guiding questions
1. Which processes did you complete process models for?
2. What high level metrics did you collect and what did you learn from this?
3. For which processes did you complete the People Capability Matrix and what did you learn from this?
5. What quick wins can you identify based on your analysis so far?

Understand phase checklist

This checklist provides a generic overview of possible inputs, deliverables and gates of this phase.

Possible inputs

See Table 16.4.

Deliverables

See Table 16.5.

Possible gates

- Unable to obtain satisfactory baseline metrics
- Subject matter experts unavailable.

EXTRA READING

Overview of Process Models

The Understand phase chapter has provided an overview of the key process models, including the Process Selection Matrix, and the various levels. In this section we will provide an additional model, as the usefulness of each model is determined by its purpose and audience.

Five-column (SIPOC) process model (levels 3 and/or 4)

The five-column process model provides an overview of the source, input, action, output and destination for each activity. It can be specified as a flow chart or as text, see Table 16.6.

Table 16.4 Understand phase—possible inputs

✓	Source	Deliverable
	Foundations phase	• Organization's core value proposition • BPM maturity of the organization • BPM drivers • BPM activities width • Red Wine Test outcomes • BPM approach • Components of the target operating model
	Establishment phase	• An agreed target operating model • Level 1 and 2 process views • Process architecture, including: o Process guidelines o Process asset repository o Business rules repository o Benefits management framework • Methods by which the people process capability will be built • Organizational cultural behavior changes by the establishment of appropriate targets (KPIs) and linked rewards • Code of behavior • The process-focused organizational design • The technology approach to BPM
	Launch pad phase	• Stakeholders defined in, involved in or associated with the BPM • Stakeholder engagement, commitment, and documented and agreed expectations • Process Selection Matrix and initial metrics • A list of identified high level business processes and initial metrics • A list of agreed process goals • Agreement of the process governance for the processes in the BPM activity • Prioritized processes for the Understand phase • An initial implementation approach • Project management: o Project charter documents o Project scope (initial) document o Initial draft of the project schedule (plan) o Determination and documentation on the initial communications strategy o Initial risk analysis • Potential project benefits and realization plan • Initial business case

Table 16.5 Understand phase—deliverables

✓	Deliverable	Used in phase
	Revalidated scope	• Innovate phase
	Process models of current processes	• Innovate phase • People phase • Develop phase
	Metrics baseline (including voice of customer)	• Innovate phase
	Prioritized quick wins	• Innovate phase
	People capability matrix	• Innovate phase • People phase
	Knowledge and information needs	• Innovate phase • People phase • Develop phase • Implement phase
	List of priorities for Innovate phase	• Innovate phase
	Project plan (in detail) for Innovate phase	• Innovate phase
	Baseline and comparative measurement (from Realize value phase)	• Realize value phase
	Report to management	• Innovate phase
	Presentation to management	• Innovate phase
	Initial communications plan	• Innovate phase • Implement phase

Table 16.6 Sample SIPOC diagram

Source	Input	Action	Output	Destination
Customer Billing system	Complaint that invoice is not correct	Validate the invoice (customer service representative)	Invoice is not correct: request to correct invoice	Customer service manager
			Invoice is correct: explain invoice to customer	Customer
Customer service representative	Request to correct invoice	Correct invoice (customer service manager)	Corrected invoice	Customer billing system

The columns are defined as follows:

1. **Source:** the origin of the input for the action.

2. **Input:** the necessary resource (document or information) for the action.

3. **P**rocess: the activities and choices (it should also be specified who is executing this action).

4. **O**utput: the result (document or information) of the action.

5. **C**lient: the destination of the output generated by the action; this could be an archive or a subsequent action.

The main benefit of the five-column process model is that it is the best text-based way of describing processes in the case where there is no process modeling and management tool available.

Some people use a three-column structure (input, activity and output) or a four-column structure (activity, person, document and system), but these models do not provide a clear view on how the various actions are related to each other—which is one of the most important issues when preparing models.

Understand Workshop—Initial Workshop Presentation

One of the first steps in the Understand phase workshop is to provide a frame for the various workshops that will be conducted. This framing is usually managed by a presentation to the business and certain members of the project team. The following provides a sample of the possible contents of such a presentation.

1. Agenda
   a) Introduction:
      i. How the Understand workshops will run (including rules and guidelines)
      ii. Roles and responsibilities of participants
      iii. Scope of the project and this phase
      iv What is Business Process Management? (Not all participants will understand it, so a brief explanation or presentation will assist)
   b) Agreed list of end-to-end processes
   c) Organization Process Selection Matrix.

2. Workshop participants' expectations (the facilitator needs to understand whether the participants' expectations are different from those planned, and, if so, to reset the expectations).

3. Project scope—reaffirm the scope and ensure that all participants understand it.

4. BPM Activity objectives—ensure that all participants understand the objectives of the BPM activity.

5. Understand phase outcomes—ensure that all participants understand what is expected at the end of the workshops.

6. Perhaps show a few slides on the modeling tool that will be used, describing how models will be created and the types of models that will be used (it is not necessary to provide a demonstration of the tool in detail, as the workshops will commence using it in practice).

7. Individual workshop agenda—each workshop should have an agreed agenda or format, and we suggest the following:

   a) Recap and review of the previously completed workshop sessions

      i.   Discuss and review work completed after workshop end by the BPM activity

      ii   Follow-up action items from previous workshop

   b) Complete session modeling and discussion of processes

   c) Business subject matter experts to present a summary of the sessions

   d) Actions to complete outside the workshop, before the next workshop

   e) Agree agenda and business processes to be modeled and discussed at the next workshop.

Modeling guidelines

Guidelines to be considered when modeling processes are as follows.

- *Purpose and audience of the model*: before modeling, it is important to specify the purpose and audience for that process model. Process models are often used by more people and for more purposes than initially envisaged.

- *Approval and governance*: prior to modeling, it is important to specify who will approve and maintain the process models. Do not have people at the end of the project say: "If I had known that I would be the person formally approving these process models, I would have been more intensively involved."

- *The BIG picture*: the first step in process modeling is to specify how the process fits into the overall processes of the organization, and then to drill down to the more detailed processes; this provides the participants with the required BIG picture.

- *Process model steps*: it is crucial that a clear set of steps for this is outlined specifying how the process model is to be developed, reviewed, approved and maintained, and what the roles and responsibilities of the various people will be.

- *Standards and reference models*: ascertain the standards and reference models that are applicable.

The following modeling principles are listed (Davis, 2001):

- *Principle of correctness.* A model must have the correct semantics and syntax. The method must be complete and consistent, and the model must comply with the method. Only then can the model be validated against the real world, using the modeling tools, and shared with other modelers and business users. Stick to the modeling method (well, mostly).

- *Principle of relevance.* Items should only be modeled if they are relevant to the model's purpose. Modeling in too much detail wastes time and money, and confuses people. In general, if your model is larger than two A4 pages, you are modeling at too detailed a level. Don't model the universe.

- *Principle of cost versus benefit.* The amount of effort to gather the data and produce the model must balance with the expected benefit. In general, 80 percent of the benefit comes from 20 percent of the effort. Getting the last 20 percent will cost you another 80 percent in effort. Know when you've done enough.

- *Principle of clarity.* The model should be understandable and usable. Business process models are complex, so break the models down into understandable chunks that fit into an overall structure. Keep it simple—clever models often confuse.

- *Principle of comparability.* A modeling tool can be very powerful. It can be used in lots of different ways to achieve the same end. The real benefit comes from communication and sharing. To do this, you must take a common approach to modeling within the modeling tool. Define standards and stick to them.

- *Principle of systematic structure.* Models produced in different views should be capable of integration. Again, stick to the method, stick to the common naming conventions, and produce and re-use libraries of common objects. Don't reinvent the wheel, re-use whenever you can.

Issues and Opportunities register

An extremely important part of the Understand phase is the capture of ideas, opportunities and issues, and registering them in the Issues and Opportunities register. This register should be maintained throughout the Understand phase (and other phases), and contain the following information:

- Issue number
- Process name
- Description of the issue
- Consequence (is it broad or narrow?)
- Priority
- Does it affect the strategy, business, organization, architecture (including compliance) or IT?
- What is the solution?
- Is it a short- or long-term issue?
- Responsibility (whose?)
- Likely benefits:
  - o   description
  - o   amount ($)
  - o   how derived?
  - o   constraints
  - o   assumptions
  - o   qualitative/quantitative impact
- Associated costs?

CHAPTER 17

INNOVATE PHASE

OVERVIEW

The Innovate phase is the critical group of steps where the final solution is designed. It is often the most challenging phase as it requires people to think creatively and break existing barriers. However it is also the most exciting phase because of the opportunity to be creative and innovative. The magnitude of change in this phase will be driven by the type of BPM activity being undertaken.

OVERALL LEARNING OUTCOME

By the end of this chapter you will be able to understand the:

- Importance of the Innovate phase and the main steps
- Need and approach for communication
- Criticality of involvement and commitment from executive management
- Necessity to obtain input from internal and external stakeholders (including customers and suppliers)
- Preparation and outline of the innovate sessions/workshops and the various techniques that can be used
- Involvement in innovate workshops of the type of people who will assist in the People change management effort
- Approach to validation and simulation of the newly designed processes
- Need to obtain formal approval and commitment to the new process designs.

WHY?

The purpose of the Innovate phase (Figure 17.1) is to make the process(es) within the scope of the BPM activity as efficient and effective as possible, to meet stakeholders' current and future expectations. This phase also provides a unique opportunity to quantify, in a more rigorous manner, the benefits outlined in the original business case.

Setting the directions and goals for the Innovate phase is a critical step, and one that needs to be addressed early in the phase. The Innovate phase is like starting a new game—unless you know the rules of the game before you start, it is difficult to play and win. Setting the rules is therefore one of the initial critical steps in the phase.

Innovation is all about being inspired to think and act differently.

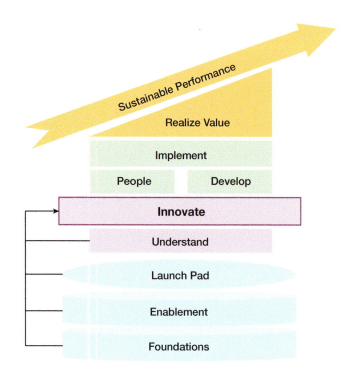

Figure 17.1 Innovate phase

RESULTS

The various documents that may be created as a result of this phase could include:

1. Redesigned process models and supporting documentation.
2. High level business requirements of the new process options.
3. Simulation models and activity-based costing details.
4. Capacity planning information.

5. Confirmation that the new process option alternatives will meet stakeholder expectations.

6. Confirmation that the new process options are consistent with the organization strategy and will achieve the designated process goals.

7. A process gap analysis report.

8. A BPM activity plan or schedule in detail for the People and Develop phases.

9. Detailed cost–benefit analysis may be produced and be input into the business case.

10. An updated business case with more detailed and quantifiable benefits and costs, and assessment of impact on the organization; these should reflect the tangible and intangible benefits.

11. A detailed report outlining the steps taken, alternatives and options considered, analysis, findings and recommendations.

12. A presentation to senior management supporting the business case and direction recommended.

13. An initial communications plan for informing all stakeholders for the next phases.

KEY MISUNDERSTANDINGS ABOUT INNOVATION

True innovation requires an organization to be brave. It is useful to gain some knowledge of the common misunderstandings surrounding innovation before the "how" to achieve innovation is explored.

Innovation is done through continuous improvement

"Why are we doing this Innovate phase, and to what degree of innovation?" is a fundamental question that must be answered before you commence. According to Paul O'Neill, Chairman of Alcoa 1991, in a worldwide letter to Alcoa staff in November 1991:

> **Continuous improvement is exactly the right idea if you are the world leader in everything you do. It is a terrible idea if you are lagging the world leadership benchmark. It is probably a disastrous idea if you are far behind the world standard—in which case you may need rapid quantum-leap improvement.**

Innovation is about doing things completely differently

When innovation is taking place it is important for the organization to be able to continue to operate profitably. An example of innovation was the British Comet, the first production commercial jetliner. It was a true innovation but suffered severely from a flawed window design that provided unnecessarily large windows, which were not an essential component of the airliner's innovation. The organization's competitive advantage was effectively eliminated after several crashes caused by the faulty window design.

Another example of the innovation was Henry Ford, who allegedly stated: "If I'd asked people what they wanted, they would have asked for a faster horse." The motor vehicle he produced was an example of true transformational thinking. At the same time, to reduce production time and costs, he limited choice by stating "a customer can have a car painted any color he wants so long as it is black."

Only a specialist can do innovation!

Process innovation can be achieved by anyone with an open mind. The most effective process innovations are often reapplying ideas and concepts from other areas and industries.

> **Discovery consists of looking at the same thing as everyone else and thinking something different.**
>
> **(Albert von Szent-Gyorgyi)**

> **Creativity consists largely of rearranging what we know in order to find out what we do not know. Hence, to think creatively, we must be able to look afresh at what we normally take for granted.**
>
> **(George Kneller)**

Innovation is automation

Should the BPM activity consider automation as part of this phase? There is a great comment attributable to Bill Gates, CEO of Microsoft, in relation to automation:

> **The first rule of any technology is that automation applied to an efficient operation will magnify the efficiency.**

> **The second is that automation applied to an inefficient operation will magnify the inefficiency.**

CASE STUDY

Figure 17.2 shows the current process on the left slide and the redesigned process on the right. The only metric the BPM project team was allowed to collect was the number of times an employee handled an activity in the process (a "touchpoint"). The current process was costing the organization many millions of dollars per annum to execute.

The redesign on the right side was the result of a two-hour workshop. The first time the process was redesigned the number of "touchpoints" was reduced to five. The facilitator then stated that participants would have a brief coffee break (to create a mental break from the new redesigned process) and after the break the participants would make the process even better. The second redesign brought the number of "touchpoints" to three. The Chief Financial Officer stated that this improvement would "save the organization $6–7m per annum."

Message: Innovation is more than just making minor improvements to the current process it requires fundamentally rethinking the way the processes get executed. During workshops it is important to challenge the participants and provide them with the opportunity of demonstrating their creativity and genius, and look at the results in Figure 17.2.

Getting the processes "right" before automation should definitely be a goal and this was discussed in Chapter 6.

Innovation requires a fundamentally different way of thinking, not just tweaking the existing way. Figure 17.2 gives an example of significant innovative thinking.

HOW?

The best way to develop the new process options and alternatives is through the use of workshops. These workshops are different in structure and approach to the Understand workshops, and it is essential that this is understood upfront and planned for appropriately. The workshops need to ensure that the processes being redesigned are completed on a true end-to-end basis. If this means crossing departmental or business unit boundaries, or even organization boundaries, then this should be done.

In the case of a process led transformation, large BPM program or project the Innovate workshops should not be concerned about the current organization structure; if it needs changing, then recommend this. In the case of a small BPM initiative it will be more difficult to change the current organization structure and recommend changes. Organizational structure change should be addressed separately and later in the BPM activity, during the People phase; however, there are key analyses required here to support and provide input into the People phase. This will be discussed in more detail in step 2, Executive kick-off workshop.

It is crucial to realize that true innovation requires different thinking:

We can't solve problems by using the same kind of thinking we used when we created them.

(Albert Einstein)

Every act of creation is first of all an act of destruction.

(Picasso)

KEY POINT

Innovation is not about having a workshop with lots of people or to have a competition (with a great prize for the winner) asking people for their ideas. Innovation typically goes through the following phases:

* get people in the right frame of mind (steps 1 to 5)
* implement the creativity or innovative activities, engaging with employees to tap into their genius (steps 6 and 7)
* select and fine-tune (steps 8 to 12)
* prepare the potential solutions and determine a course of action (steps 13 to 17)
* execute (subsequent phases).

Current process

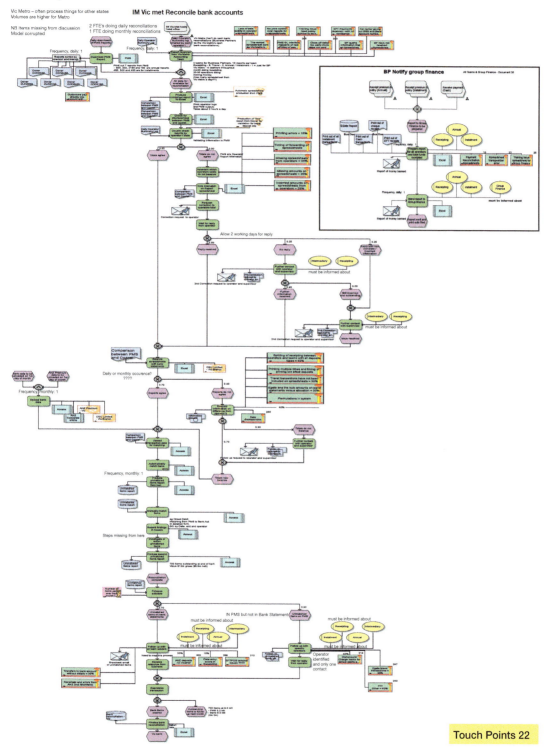

Figure 17.2 An example of innovation

Redesign Opportunity

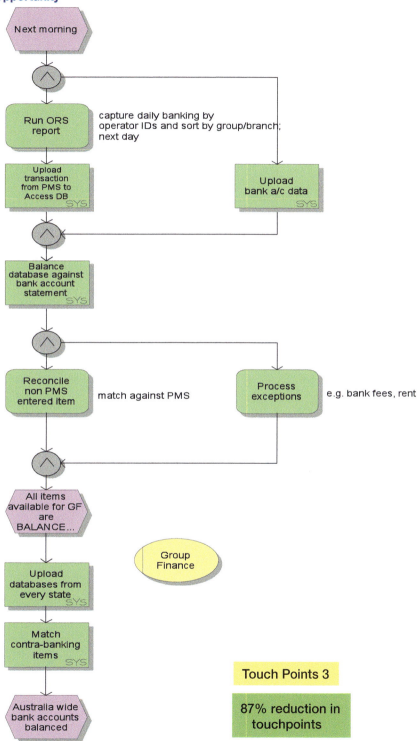

Figure 17.2 *continued*

One of the key challenges with regard to providing process innovation to an organization is the mismatch between conventional organization structure (vertical or pyramid basis) and the way "work" (transactions) are received and processed within an organization. Figure 17.3 shows the conventional organization structure.

The vertical lines represent the division of the organization into departments, with process workers providing hand-offs to each other across the various departments. Work is processed horizontally, as in Figure 17.4, passing through various departments within the end-to-end process model of the organization. It is the hand-offs between departments that often provide the greatest opportunities for improvements in processes.

The goals or objectives (key result areas and key performance indicators) of the various organizational departments, and the transaction passing through them, may be at odds with the efficient and effective processing of the transaction. This mismatch is one of the key challenges for the business and the BPM activity team to overcome.

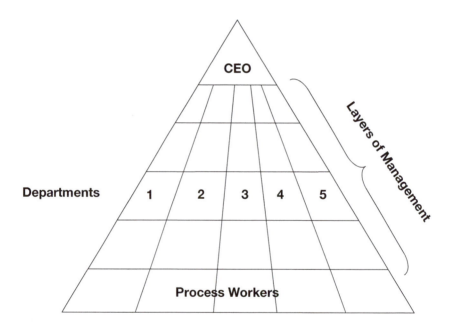

Figure 17.3 Conventional organization structure

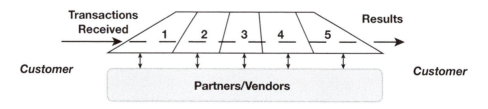

Figure 17.4 Transaction processing

Prior to commencing workshops and the innovation of process(es), there are two critical questions that must be asked:

1. How much innovation is required?
2. How do we know what we have designed and propose to implement is what our customers/suppliers/partners need to achieve a high level of satisfaction and effective service?

We have already discussed the first question in Chapters 12 and 13, and Figure 13.21 described the width of the BPM activities and Figure 12.3 highlighted the importance of matching ambition and mandate.

The second question must be answered or the BPM activity may not be successful—even if it reduces costs or increases quality levels.

CASE STUDY

Examples of traditional and end-to-end process management can be found in the automotive industry process of bringing a new automobile into existence, and how the manufacturing process is conducted.

Traditionally, a simplistic view is that the design department will create the concept design of the new automobile. They then request the engineering department to create a detailed design, and obtain the engine and other appropriate parts. Procurement is then involved in sourcing the parts, and finally the factory manufactures it.

The Japanese (and a few other automobile manufacturers) have adopted a horizontal approach to this process. They have placed one person in charge of the entire process, from the creation to the building of the new automobile. This person has responsibility for the design, engineering, sourcing of parts, manufacturing and so forth, and is truly responsible for the end-to-end process of the new automobile. This individual must work through the "matrix" reporting structure, while having the responsibility and power to "make things happen."

Message: Process management is far more effective when understood and managed from an end-to-end perspective. Process interfaces and hand-offs are typical areas with significant process improvement opportunities.

Figure 17.5 shows how customers' levels of service and satisfaction can be measured. It is important to understand that "service" and "satisfaction" are different. A customer can receive a high level of service and still be dissatisfied.

Organizations continually speak of the "wow" factor, and how they need to "exceed customers' expectations" and "delight" them. This "wow" factor can come in the form of product features, or an unexpected pleasant surprise in the way customers have been serviced. "Wow" factors can be extremely effective and build customer loyalty, provided customers are not irritated or annoyed overall. Samples of customer irritations include: incorrect customer data, overcharging and not leveraging customer information. Customer irritation can have far more impact upon how a customer thinks of the organization than any "wow" factor.

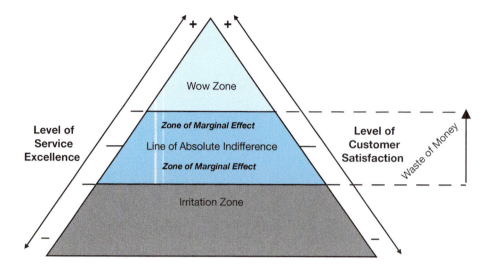

Figure 17.5 Customer levels of service and satisfaction

There is also the area between the irritation zone and the "wow" zone that should not be addressed by any BPM activity or business case, if the goals of innovation are increased customer service and customer satisfaction. Spending funds on this area will provide no benefit to the customer and must be avoided.

It is interesting that the time spent by organizations on the "wow" and irritation zones is disproportional to the benefits to be gained from them, as depicted in Figure 17.6.

The inverse triangle in Figure 17.6 depicts the amount of effort organizations traditionally spend upon these aspects of service. Organizations often spend a great deal of time trying to differentiate themselves from competitors by developing "wow" factors in their products and services. Conversely, less time is spent upon eliminating the "irritation" factors of customers. This is the exact opposite of what should be happening.

It's the process that matters

One of the authors purchased a laptop computer from a well-known, very large computer manufacturer. The plastic carry bag fell apart for the second time, and when the manufacturer was contacted again, it believed it exceeded expectations by providing a new leather carry case at no cost as a "sign of good faith." However, in order to hear about the new leather case he had to wait 30 minutes on the telephone, being transferred multiple times, and was then told that a "manager" would call back in the next week or so and this "irritated" the author to a far greater extent than he'd been "wowed" by having his expectations exceeded in getting a leather case for nothing.

Message: The organization must understand the difference between excellent service and customer satisfaction. The "wow" factor can be easily wiped out by poor service. It is important that the typical "hygiene" factors are taken care of before any "wow" factors become effective.

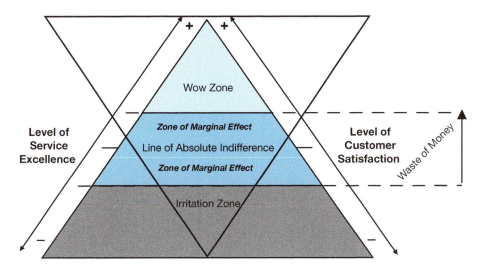

Figure 17.6 Organization effort

If organizations spent more time eliminating the irritation factors, they would find that customers would have higher levels of service and satisfaction. In general, most of the irritation factors are caused by processes that do not function properly.

When looking at the factors that are critical to a BPM initiative's success, research must be conducted into understanding the above to assist in the appropriateness and direction of the BPM activity; and to know that if certain process changes are implemented then customers will have increased satisfaction levels, thus contributing towards customer retention.

Participants could be inspired about the benefits that technology can provide, see Chapter 7 for more details.

Before we move on to the steps associated with the Innovate phase, there are several essential elements that must always be addressed in the innovate workshops. The BPM activity must ensure that:

- all disconnects in the organizational functional structure are identified (the organizational relationship map and the list of end-to-end process model(s) assist in this process);
- the new process alternatives are reasonable, practical and simple;
- stakeholder expectations are understood and met;
- all opportunities for automation are identified;
- all interdependencies with other processes or sub-processes are considered and addressed.

DETAILED STEPS

To have a successful outcome for the Innovate phase there is a number of high level steps that should be followed (see Figure 17.7).

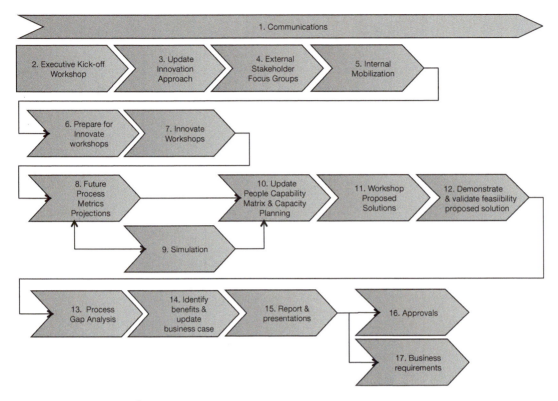

Figure 17.7 Innovate phase steps

Step 1: Communications

It is important to keep the relevant stakeholders informed about the scope of the Innovate phase, the options being considered, and their status. This is the phase where ideas may be gathered from a wide group of people. However, it is important to ensure that the ideas fall within the scope of the BPM activity.

The communications must ensure that stakeholder input is not lost in the detail, and that stakeholders are always kept informed as to the status of their input. If their suggestions cannot be accommodated, it is important to inform them of the reasons why. This will also assist in them gaining greater understanding of the objectives of, and choices made by, the business on behalf of the BPM activity. The development of the initial communications plan will assist with this.

Step 2: Executive kick-off workshop

It is necessary to start this phase with a workshop involving the BPM activity sponsor and other senior business leaders, to determine and understand the process goals associated with the BPM activity, and the area of the business being redesigned. The information gathered as part of the Launch pad phase will provide some baseline information for this workshop. Thought should be given to conducting this workshop towards the end of the Understand phase, to ensure that there is no delay in the commencement of the Innovate phase.

There is usually one "key" person in this workshop who is the primary stakeholder within the BPM activity. It is this person who should be primarily involved in the decision making within the Innovate executive workshop.

Timeframes

It is during this workshop that the critical questions relating to the Innovate options are asked and answered—questions regarding the timeframes and the options to be considered. The timeframes from the Launch pad phase need confirmation.

These options are some of the rules of the Innovate phase "game," and the rules by which we will "play." It is important to have one or two open-minded individuals who have detailed knowledge of the current processes and who participated in the Understand phase process modeling workshops.

Process goals

While "workshopping" the Innovate options, be clear about the establishment of the goals. It is interesting that if the sole focus of the options and phase is cost reduction, then quality often suffers. This is especially so if the reduced cost focus is supported by performance measures that reward cost-reduction behavior. The resulting behavior can result in quality issues as employees, team leaders and management focus on driving transactions through the process as fast as possible in order to reduce costs. This is a short-sighted approach, because a drive for "speed" will result in decreased quality and increasing rework, and thus

---

CASE STUDY

Drive for reduced processing costs

A financial services organization was not meeting its processing service level agreements (SLAs) by a long way (achieving less than 50 percent of what they should be), so staff and management were motivated to increase throughput with incentives. To address quality they introduced 100 percent checking, thinking that this would solve any quality issues.

The results were further reduced SLAs and a decrease in quality. An analysis of quality issues revealed the conflict between the need for speed, and checking. The processing staff's aim was to process the transaction as quickly as possible, because if there were any errors they would be picked up by the checker. The checkers' view was that the original processor would have processed the transaction correctly, so it would only need a quick check.

These were not complex transactions, and errors should not have resulted from processing. In addition, the supporting workflow system did not have sufficient business rules and built-in knowledge, which only added to the quality issue.

Checking was costing the organization 24 percent of the overall processing costs, and yielding little benefit. There was a general lack of ownership and accountability across the processing staff and team leaders.

Message: By changing the culture to one of ownership and accountability, supported by feedback loops and appropriate performance measurement and rewards, great gains were made on quality, and reduced costs, at the same time—thus embedding quality in the process.

increased costs. It is important that during this phase personnel are thinking "outside the box." This will provide an opportunity for the processes to be better, faster and cheaper by accepting different ways of working. However, the executive management team should list its requirements and the order of priority.

On the other hand, if the focus is on quality, then reduced cost is a likely result as it will reduce errors and rework. It is expected that the Launch pad phase already has clear objectives included. The process goals need to be related to these objectives.

Questions that must be answered in order to determine the process goals include the following.

Strategic

1. Is this an evolutionary or revolutionary (substantial innovation) BPM activity? Do you want to make incremental change, or radical change involving technology, or no technology? The answer to these questions will substantially change the approach to, and expected outcomes from, the Innovate phase.

2. How does the BPM activity fit into the organization strategy?

3. How does the BPM activity support the plans for the next year or two?

Planning

1. What is the business rationale for this BPM activity?

2. Why are you doing this BPM activity (determine the ranking for these options)?

   - to resolve bottlenecks—both current and future?
   - to provide an ability to implement new products and services?
   - to improve customer service?
   - to cut operating costs?
   - to decrease customer irritation?
   - to improve quality?
   - for compliance purposes?

3. What are the specific goals and process performance measures associated with this phase of the BPM activity? The customer should be used as the focus for the development of these goals. Compare what the customer and organization think, because they can be at odds, so research is critical.

4. Do we have the necessary resources to undertake this BPM activity?

5. What do you want to happen as a result of this BPM activity?

6. Will it add to the capacity of the organization?

7. What are the "no-go" conditions?

Constraints

1. What timeframes should you be working to—3, 6, 12 or 24 months?

2. What are the barriers and constraints to be built into the Innovate phase (for example, are changes allowed to IT systems)?

3. Are there change management or people constraints?

Success

Some of the following will already have been addressed in the Launch pad phase, if this is the case then update the information with the new knowledge gained during the Understand phase.

1. How will the organization know when it has achieved milestones or completion of the BPM activity?
2. What will this involve the organization doing?
3. What do different stakeholders (internal and external) expect from the BPM activity?
4. How will the organization know when it has been successful? Success criteria should be built in, understood and documented upfront.

How to inspire the organization

As mentioned before, innovation requires people to think differently. However, most of us are quite set in our way of working. Ideally the executive workshop will be able to outline the burning business platform that will get people outside their comfort zone and thinking differently.

The two case studies (on the facing page) provide examples of the process goals established as a result of executive kick-off workshops. You will note the differences, which are largely attributable to each organization's BPM maturity (more on BPM maturity can be found in Chapters 29 and 30).

Automation

When reviewing the possible future options available to the organization and the BPM initiative, BPM automation, and especially workflow, is often raised as a possible, or desirable, option.

CASE STUDY

Government department

This organization was on the lowest level of BPM maturity and unable to envision where it should be in two years' time. A six-month horizon was all that could be agreed on and implemented at any one time. It also had no track record in the successful delivery of projects, and therefore lacked confidence in the organization's ability to succeed.

The organization was assisted in moving towards the point of agreeing that workflow and imaging, in a very limited capacity, would be the six-month horizon. This would provide the foundations from which further improvement projects could be made once the organization was comfortable with the workflow and imaging implementation and could focus on the next "vision."

Message: The options selected must match the organization's BPM maturity and ability to implement.

Financial services organization with a higher level of BPM maturity

A financial services organization had already installed a workflow system that was used in a very rudimentary manner. During the executive kick-off workshop, the managers understood clearly what a "full" BPM implementation would entail and how they would benefit from it. They therefore set three scenarios that would potentially assist in building a business case and taking them on the journey to a "full" BPM implementation:

1. Six months of quick wins with minimal system changes.
2. Eighteen months with full BPM and image processing.
3. Eighteen months with enhancements to the existing workflow system, no full BPM and no image processing.

The establishment of these three scenarios worked extremely well and, together with significant work on the metrics side, provided excellent information to populate the business case.

Message: As the maturity of the organization increases, the options available, and their sophistication, will increase.

While workflow can be a significant benefit in the right circumstances, it is not necessarily the most important aspect for improved process performance. The single most important aspect is to focus on people—creating the right culture, motivation, responsibility, ownership, accountability, performance measures, feedback and rewards.

Much BPM hype can lead us to think that BPM software solutions can provide the most important benefits. While they can provide an appropriate and beneficial enabler, it is the culture and people aspects that can be significant constraints if not handled correctly, or significant enablers if handled well.

Even though automation can be extremely useful in making processes more effective, the people aspects of a BPM initiative should not be ignored.

Key system or application questions to be answered are:

• Re-use, buy, make, outsource or put in the Cloud?
• Make business processes fit system; or make the system fit the business processes?

Success checklist

It is essential that the process success evaluation criteria are agreed before the Innovate phase process workshops commence, and that the workshops build on the agreed and defined stakeholder expectations. When conducting the workshops, always ensure that the proposed new process is consistently related back to these stakeholder outcomes, the success checklist, the key performance indicators and the performance measures.

Government department and staff constraint

The organization embarked upon the implementation of a workflow and image processing system. The system was completed, worked well in the testing environment and was implemented. The staff hated it and refused to use it, and the implementation failed.

There was no effort to involve the staff throughout the project. There was nothing wrong with the software; it was just that the change management issues were not addressed. The staff had never been measured or held accountable before, and they saw the implementation as a threat and refused to use it. The system was abandoned.

Message: If you do not handle the people issues (change management), then the risk of failure will be very high. Hence, it is important that during the innovation phase all aspects are holistically considered.

Executive workshop preparation

The preparation for this workshop should include the distribution to participants of the following information. This information should have already been developed.

- the organization process view;
- the organizational relationship map;
- the end-to-end process model for the business area being examined within the BPM activity;
- the Process Selection Matrix for the business area being examined within the BPM activity;
- a list of all the issues and opportunities developed during the Understand phase;
- a list of all the processes, by name and function;
- appropriate metrics that are relevant to the discussion.

Other useful information to have available includes the business plans and budgets for the current and coming year, and a list of the organization's BPM activity portfolio (to review overlapping and related BPM initiatives).

Outcomes

As a minimum, the outcomes from this executive workshop must provide a clear way forward (set of rules) for the Innovate phase. This will include:

1. An understanding of how and where the BPM activity and new process(es) link with the organizational strategy; refer to Chapter 13 Foundations, step 2, Red Wine Test.
2. A documented understanding of the proposed or desired goals for the new process(es) and the associated process performance measurements.
3. An agreed list of constraints to be placed upon the innovate process.

4. Agreed timeframes for the innovate options.

5. An agreed "width" for the BPM initiative; refer to Chapter 13 Foundations, step 2 BPM activity width.

6. Approach to automation.

7. Agreed approach to engagement and communication.

Unless at least these aspects are clear the BPM activity outcomes and success are at risk. You will have started playing the "game" when you don't know, or fully understand, the rules (i.e., whether you are scoring points or are heading in the right direction). These rules are provided by the executives during the executive kick-off workshop.

The workshop should provide the required results and should typically not take more than half a day to a full one day to conduct. The exception will be for a (global) transformation program where many of the above questions will be time-consuming because of the complexity, interdependencies and sheer magnitude.

The facilitator in this workshop is crucial, as he/she needs to drive the right outcome and needs to push the participants, if required, to make clear and unambiguous decisions.

KEY POINT

The involvement and commitment of executive management is essential in this phase, first to ensure that a clear vision to inspire people to innovate the process adequately is provided; and second, to provide clear guidance with regard to the magnitude of change required.

Step 3: Update innovation approach

This step requires a quick review of the current BPM activity plan (or schedule) to ensure that, as a result of step 2, you have the correct people in the Innovate workshops. The different types of people that should be involved in the various Innovate workshops are covered in a later step. The executive workshop ideally should have created an understanding of why process innovation is necessary in the organization.

As a result of the executive workshop, it is necessary to ensure that all the BPM activity requirements, as outlined in the BPM activity plan, are consistent with the organization strategy and process goals. Refer to the Extra Reading section at the end of this chapter for a sample plan. The agreed timeframes and approach (options) to the Innovate phase may also have an impact upon the BPM activity plan. The plan also needs to be reviewed and updated as a result of the number of new process scenarios proposed—for example, there may have been a decision to develop new process options for several of the following: 3-month horizon; 12-month horizon; 24-month horizon; automated and non-automated.

Step 4: External stakeholder focus groups

External stakeholders are defined as being "external" to the business unit/area being reviewed within the BPM activity. They may include stakeholders within the organization but external to the business unit/area, and stakeholders external to the organization, such as vendors, partners and customers.

Prior to conducting the initial innovate workshops, it is often useful to gather appropriate external stakeholders together into a focus group(s) to inform them of the proposed plans and their expected involvement in the process. They should then be asked to input their thoughts regarding the current process(es) (shortcomings and issues) and how they would like to conduct business with the organization. This will provide valuable input into the process redesign activities.

At this early stage, all discussions should be kept at a high level with the detail to come later after the detailed Innovate workshops. The external stakeholders should again be involved at a later stage. The purpose, at this moment, is to gain direction from them and to make them feel involved. It is part of stakeholder management (refer to Chapter 24).

These stakeholder focus groups should also provide input into the earlier discussions regarding customer service excellence and satisfaction.

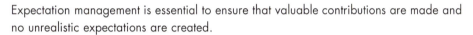

KEY POINT

To make innovation fit-for-purpose it is crucial to invite to the focus groups the ultimate beneficiaries of these improvements, for example customers or suppliers.

Expectation management is essential to ensure that valuable contributions are made and no unrealistic expectations are created.

Step 5: Internal mobilization

It is important to gather any innovative ideas internally as well. Quality of ideas will be more critical than quantity, so at this stage it is important to clearly articulate the type of ideas the BPM activity is looking for.

Suggestions on how to gain involvement could include:

* run a competition for new and innovative ideas;
* identify ideas from previous BPM activities or competitions;
* workshop participants could share workshop outcomes (ideas) with their colleagues and to further stimulate new ideas;
* surveys about current challenges, root causes and possible solutions.

Step 6: Prepare for Innovate workshops

The Innovate workshops are critical as they lay the foundations for the new way of working in the organization. So workshop preparation is critical and everything should be done to make sure that the workshops are successful. Simply bringing lots of people together in a room does not necessarily ensure success.

The timeframes associated with each redesign scenario in the Innovate workshop should have been clearly agreed during the executive workshop.

Where timeframes of 6 and/or 12 months have been chosen, the participants in the workshops should be people from the business with the detailed knowledge of the process(es). Longer-term timeframes of say, 18 to 24 months, should include more senior managers/executives who are able to make decisions relating to more strategic issues, such as changes in the way business is conducted, changes in application systems, whether various methods of payment should be dropped from the payment options, and whether new methods of payment should be introduced, and similarly for the various distribution channels within the organization.

Innovate workshops are often significantly different from Understand workshops, as the discussion moves from recording what currently happens (Understand) to being creative and innovative (Innovate). This means that the workshop participants will generally comprise managers and decision makers.

For specific details on how to run the Innovate workshops, refer to the Extra Reading section at the end of this chapter.

The following preparation must be undertaken prior to the workshops:

- brief participants well ahead of time about the workshop, their contribution and any necessary preparation;
- provide relevant material to them, including:
    o relevant BPM activity documentation, for example scope and process goals
    o key documents from the Understand phase, for example high level process models and root-cause analysis;
    o relevant background information.

Initial workshop

The initial workshop is unique as it introduces the entire Innovate phase and a typical agenda could comprise:

- an introduction from the executive sponsor:
    o thanking participants for the involvement with encouragement about how they are assisting to create the future
    o outlining the goals and vision, as well as constraints, as agreed during the executive workshop;
- the key facilitators may then introduce the BPM activity team, their roles and then explain the role of and expectations from, participants.

This information may be presented as part of the initial workshop or, if there are many participants in various workshops, then it may be more effective to have an Innovate phase kick-off session for this purpose.

> ## BPM INSIGHT
>
> Care must be taken in selecting the right participants for the Innovate workshop. Be careful not to just send the people that are available, rather than the people who are most capable. This is tempting for the business because it is the latter that are considered too valuable to take out of the day-to-day running of the business. The final results always reflect any poor decision making surrounding workshop participants.
>
> Key characteristics of participants should include:
>
> * change champions who are willing and able to drive change
> * people who can think creatively
> * people with an understanding of the end-to-end process
> * people with process and customer thinking capacity.

Step 7: Innovate workshops

This is where the BPM Innovate activity changes from analysis (as undertaken in the Understand phase) to creativity (synthesis of new ideas, and being innovative). However, be careful: the approach you undertake in the Innovate phase will very much depend upon the outcomes you wish to achieve. When looking at improving a process, the workshop participants will need to ensure that they do not limit themselves by only looking at fixing the current process problems, unless that is clearly the desired goal. Looking at the current process issues will potentially limit thinking and the possibilities of process innovation and/or redesign.

The setting of the Innovate options or scenarios in the executive workshop will set the scene for breaking away from this constraint and towards process innovation. Innovate options should not be based upon the Understand phase situation or individual processes.

This step has been divided into two sections on how to conduct the workshops from an:

* administrative perspective;
* creativity perspective.

Step 7.1: Workshop administration

Generally process redesign goes through a small number of steps on its way to being redesigned and agreed and signed-off by business management. The most effective route is a three-stage phase:

1. *Initial redesign workshop*—this is where the process redesign activities commence. At the completion of the workshop and subsequent documentation tasks, described below, it is expected to have the new process at about 70 percent completion.

2. *Confirmation workshop*—the purpose of this workshop is to review the redesigned process from the initial workshops and build in:

    • any suggestions as a result of the review and reflection from the initial workshop and distributed documentation;

    • new ideas and corrections from stakeholders who may not have attended the initial workshop.

    By the end of this workshop and subsequent documentation tasks, described below, it is expected to have the new process at about 95 percent plus completion.

3. *Finalization workshop* (step 11, Workshop proposed solutions)—this is where the "final" process is presented to a wider audience of stakeholders for their agreement and sign-off. This workshop may have many processes presented at once. It is always an excellent idea to have the workshop participants (business) create several "real" examples of how the process will work in practice in the business to make the presentation concrete for attendees. Business staff should present these examples rather than BPM activity team members.

The workshop agenda will depend upon the outcomes required during the Innovate phase activities and the specific goals and objectives for each individual process, however, a typical agenda could include:

1. A review of the purpose, goals and desired outcomes for the specific process.

2. Perhaps a discussion of the shortcoming of the current process, although, if the process is to be totally redesigned, then this may or may not be appropriate.

3. Start with the "process triggers" (what various activities initiate this process) and then redesign the process, using a process modeling tool projected onto a screen in front of the participants.[1]

4. How many times should the process be redesigned? This will depend upon the scenarios agreed during the executive workshop. If it has been agreed that there will be:

    • *Scenario 1*: 12-month timeframe; a small amount of technology; no or little organizational redesign

    • *Scenarios 2*: 18-month timeframe; full business process management system (or application); organizational redesign is an option, together with a change in culture then the process should be redesigned at least twice, once for each scenario. The next question is do you start with scenario 1 or 2? Always start with the process that provides the most opportunity for change and innovation; in this instance it is scenario 2. This scenario allows the opportunity for the most creativity. Once scenario 2 has been redesigned, then take a "copy" of the process model created and ask how this must be changed in order to accommodate scenario 1.

If you start the redesign process with scenario 1, there is the potential of limiting participants' creativity by becoming "stuck" in the smaller scenario constraints and mindset.

Never be afraid of redesigning a process multiple times as it invariably becomes better with each redesign effort.

5. Provide participants with an opportunity of presenting the process back to the group. This will provide an opportunity of thinking through the process once more.

After the workshops

Once a workshop has been completed there are a number of tasks that the BPM activity team needs to complete:

- compare any notes taken in the workshop with the process model created to ensure there are no gaps or omissions;

- ensure that the process model is enhanced and improved from a presentation and documentation perspective. It is not the role of the BPM activity team to improve the process, at this stage;

- further investigate the technical feasibility of the various alternatives;

- reapply the design and evaluation criteria in more detail to ensure consistency;

- send the process models and supporting documentation to workshop participants to comment. Placing the new processes on common building walls, perhaps near the coffee area, and inviting employees to write on them may provide excellent ideas and ensure employees feel included in the process;

- receive the comments back from participants; build them into the process models and documentation in preparation for the Confirmation workshop or Finalization workshop (step 11, Workshop proposed solutions).

As mentioned above, part of the after workshop activities is to create additional documentation to support and enhance the process models. Suggested content of this documentation could include:

1. for each process:
   - process name
   - date
   - version number
   - process purpose
   - assumptions and dependencies.

2. details of process:
   - triggers/process reference number—the process model must have each event or activity uniquely numbered to allow identification and reference to this documentation;
   - activity/event/sub-process name—should be the same name as in the process model, for reference purposes;
   - description—a more detailed description of the activity/event/sub-process;
   - business rules—record or create the business rules. This is useful for transferring to the business rules repository (refer to the Enablement phase);

- business requirements—describe what the business requires and/or the business outcomes from this activity/event/sub-process;

- area—the section or department of the business;

- system(s)—what technology application systems support this activity/event/sub-process;

- notes—anything else that may be useful to record;

- decisions—what decisions are required; approved; rejected. This may be, or support, any decision logs maintained by the BPM activity team;

- responsibility/date—who is responsible for making a required decision; who made or rejected a requested decision and what date.

If this documentation is recorded in a product such as Microsoft Excel, then additional columns may be added by the technical member of the BPM activity team to document any technical build requirements and specifications.

Step 7.2: Workshop creativity

If you want to improve or redesign your process(es), then synthesizing new creative ideas is important. If the proposed outcome is to implement process innovation, the creativity process should not be limited to internal ideas but should also include external ideas from different industries and perhaps some radical thoughts with regard to the future process structure. Innovation will involve significant questioning of the current paradigm, and thinking outside the tradition for your industry.

Certainly there will be the need to use the knowledge gained from the previous Understand phase, and to rethink the current approach to the process. The obvious question to ask is, "Is there a better way of approaching/doing this process?" A strengths and weaknesses analysis of the current process may be useful. This could, at the very least, provide a starting point for discussion.

So what techniques can you employ? Workshops and discussion with the business is definitely the best approach. Employing creativity and innovation techniques by experienced BPM facilitators can be very productive. The use of external facilitators with considerable BPM experience provides the best outcomes in the Innovate phase. (The reason for "external" facilitators is so that there is no "baggage" brought to the sessions by people who work in the area being examined. "External" can mean the organization's internal facilitators who are experienced in BPM and facilitation but do not work within the business area undergoing process innovation, or facilitators external to the organization. Facilitators who are external to the organization can bring experience from other industry sectors.)

There is a wide variety of innovation activities. The value of an experienced BPM facilitator is that the most valuable results are obtained by executing the right activity in the right way. Table 17.1 provides an overview of some of the potential innovation activities.

During the workshops, concentrate first on getting a quantity of ideas. Don't filter these ideas too much at this stage; this will come later. Initially:

- include divergence of ideas—that is, try to get as many ideas (including radical ones) as possible;

- cover right-brain or creative ideas—employ lateral thinking ability;

- ensure there is no judgment—it is essential that neither the facilitator nor the workshop participants pass judgment on any idea put forward at this stage; there must be an openness to all ideas put forward;

- look for opportunities—especially outside the norm (traditional thinking);

- look from the other side—view the organization from the perspective of customers, suppliers, partners or competitors.

Table 17.1 Innovation activities

Type of activity	Definition	Rationale
Brainstorm	People provide ideas based on a specific statement.	– This is an excellent technique to gather a number of free flowing ideas – Especially appropriate in case a significant change is required – This activity requires a good facilitator to get the right outcome and keep participants focused and involved
Role play	Look from a different perspective.	– How would you look at this problem if you were a customer or a vendor? – Especially appropriate if participants have an inside-out view rather than an outside-in and customer centric view. – This activity requires meaningful role-play to achieve the intended benefit
Magic wand	What would you do if you had a "magic wand"?	– This assists people in identifying and eliminating obstacles. – Especially appropriate if participants seem to feel constraint in developing new solutions – This activity requires a good facilitator to ensure that people know how to use this exercise correctly
End state	Ask people to describe their ultimate outcome. "Start with the end in mind."	– This helps people focus on their ultimate outcome and then work back to see how this can be achieved – Especially appropriate if participants require a tangible outcome and are well informed about the possible solutions – This activity requires the participants to be innovative enough and not just address today's problems and tomorrows wishes
Demonstration	Get various vendors to present various technology options.	– This assists with "opening" people's minds to possibilities and becoming inspired about new functionality that is available from the various vendors – Especially appropriate if participants are struggling to visualize the new solution – This requires good support to obtain the right business requirements and involvement of the vendors

It is important to realize that there are different techniques to get people to think creatively. Different people will relate to some techniques more than others, so it is advisable to use multiple techniques in workshops. Table 17.2 provides an overview of the various techniques.

Other useful ideas for innovation include:

- empower employees to make more decisions themselves and combine logical tasks together, which reduces the waiting time;
- build quality control into the process rather than having it as a separate activity at the end of the process;
- technology enables information to be available from multiple places, so people can be involved in the process without the requirement to have a physical document present;
- telecommunication can be more integrated with IT—for example field-staff having access to up-to-date information and making bookings from the client site;
- RFID (Radio Frequency Identification) makes it possible to track more economically—for example tracking the progress of an express parcel;
- leverage social networking;
- do not create complex processes to handle the exceptions; only look at the mainstream and deal with exceptions separately—for example a mortgage company was able to reduce the processing time for 95 percent of their mortgages from three weeks to three minutes by separating the odd 5 percent that require substantial additional checking;
- availability of real-time information—for example pricing of airline tickets is now on the basis of real-time availability of information;
- integrate processes with suppliers, partners and clients;
- reorganize your processes so that they are much more geared to dealing with customizations—for example Dell has its whole process geared towards customization;
- use agent technology to trigger events on the basis of predefined situations—for example clients specifying the maximum amount they want to purchase for an airline ticket.

Remember to brainstorm and get lots of ideas first. At a later stage it will be possible to converge to suitable solutions.

A proven workshop technique to achieve this is to ask people what their key stakeholders (for example customers, partners and management) expect from the improved process and

BPM INSIGHT

Innovate workshops are also a key step in the People change management activities. It is important to inspire people to think and act differently: to think from an end-to-end customer perspective rather than from an isolated team perspective.

Table 17.2 Innovation techniques

Type	Definition	Example
Transposition	Moving established ideas or solutions to a new domain	Leverage similar functionality as check-in service by airlines
Combination	Create something new by combining existing ideas	Cirque de Soleil combined the idea of circus, performance and dining as a unique, high value entertainment
Abstraction	Look at a broader pattern	Give clients more say in their choices, rather than just their self-service
Discovery	Find new things	The initial idea of using the Internet for customer self-service
Transmogrification	Changing the rules of the game	The iTunes business model changes the rules in music game
Distillation	Simplifications to the bare essentials	Reduce all unnecessary steps in the process
Specialization	Leverage key strengths of the organization	Organization that is good in processing for example Accounts Payable, can provide this service to other companies (in-sourcing)
Opposition	Opposing an existing paradigm or competitor	It is rumored that Steve Jobs launched the touch-based iPhone/iPad because he heard his competitors talk about keyboard-based applications
Provocation	Create problems, then offer the solution	If a client-related activity takes at the moment 5 days, ask why this cannot be completed instantly. This highlights the key bottlenecks for which a solution needs to be found. Another way of using this is by asking how they will manage the process if volume increases by 10 or 100 fold
Tantalization	Suggest that a solution exists, often without proof	Challenge people to think differently by stating "wouldn't it be nice if we could do . . . "
Constraint	Limiting resources to promote efficiency	Constraint can be used in two ways: • how to make the end-to-end process more efficient by optimizing the effort of the most constraint resources (see Goldratt's Theory of Constraints) • ask people how they will do their work if their time is constrained. They will be forced to describe their key tasks and leave out any non-value added tasks*
Audacity	Embrace the impossible. Aim for an ideal goal without the slightest hindrance of reason or feasibility. Envision how the problem would be solved with magic	The statement of Virgin Galactic that they wanted to go into space travel and invited designers to show how to do it

Source: http://arcball.com/2010/05/forms-of-innovation/ (accessed 28 August 2012).
Note: * Goldratt (1999).

create a big poster with this information. There is only one catch: they are not allowed to use any words. This will force the participants to think deeper and be more creative. Once completed, the other participants have to guess what the symbols and drawings mean. This allows for some good discussion.

This is a great exercise to break the ice in workshops, provide some fun and establish an excellent basis for the remainder of the sessions. If during the workshops people tend to defend their current way of working, you can go back to the posters and ask if that will satisfy the requirements of the stakeholders.

Another dimension that may be reviewed, and is often discussed by organizations, is "best practice." This can be an excellent starting point for a BPM activity if an industry best practice can be found. Some commonly available best practices are:

- eTOM model (in the telecommunications industry)—see www.tmforum.org
- ITIL (for information technology)—see www.itsmf.org.au
- SCOR (for supply chain management)—see www.supply-chain.org
- APQC covering various industries.—see www.apqc.org

However, be careful, because there will be a need to look at the appropriate "best practice" in its entirety—not just the "raw" process model or flow. What surrounds a process model can be as important as (or more important than) the actual processes themselves. Surrounding factors include: culture, performance management and measures, people motivation, people empowerment, business rules, organization policies and so forth. It is therefore important to customize these reference models and best practice models to the individual objectives and context of the organization. If this approach is considered important, it should have been reviewed in the Enablement phase as part of a possible process architecture.

It is extremely difficult and high risk for a BPM activity team to simply take what is considered to be best practice and expect this to translate into success for the particular organization.

Once this initial step has been completed, start to bring the ideas together into groups and begin to apply the evaluation criteria developed and agreed earlier. This is where the left-brain logical thinking starts to be applied. As ideas and options are narrowed down, start to gain general acceptance of ideas and options. Start also to look at the feasibility of the

KEY POINT

The Innovate workshops are the key phase in the project to design the new way of working. Hence it is crucial that the following factors are taken into account:

- executive involvement and commitment
- the right people in the room for the workshops and executive meetings
- the right facilitator
- the right approach and attitude.

options—at least at a high level. Detailed feasibility will come in the following steps. One of the key questions to ask is, "How will these ideas meet stakeholder expectations/needs?" This is because you must always ensure that the options take into account the ideas and thoughts from the external stakeholder focus group discussions. They also need to satisfy the process goals established during the executive workshop.

As the Innovate process workshop is conducted, it can be useful to maintain an "issues and opportunities" register to record items that must be dealt with, and opportunities to follow up. This register can be populated from the workshop scribe's notes.

The number of iterations or options developed for each process will depend upon the timeframes, constraints and width agreed in the executive workshop. The Extra Reading section at the end of this chapter contains information about the organization of the workshop.

Potential results

What results can you expect from these innovate workshops? Obviously, this will depend upon the organization; however, some examples are provided by way of case studies.

Once a new process option has been completed (or nearly completed), it is useful to conduct a "what if?" walkthrough with the business, or even build a prototype if a technology solution is required.

Step 8: Future process metrics projections

Having completed the Innovate workshops and modeled the new processes, it is time to ensure that there is an understanding of the potential operational costs for these new processes and then include them in the business case. This is also the time to determine whether there are additional benefits and opportunities for the business.

This metrics analysis is not just about the business case cost–benefit analysis, or the calculation of the cost of implementing the new processes. This is also about projecting the potential ongoing operational costs for the business.

CASE STUDY

Toyota

Toyota is acknowledged as one of, if not the most efficient, automobile manufacturers in the world. Many other automobile manufacturers have toured Toyota manufacturing plants, witnessed the "process flows" and tried to emulate them. So why does Toyota continue to be the best?

It is not just about copying the "process flow." Toyota has a complex number of aspects to its production techniques. The company has goals for its customers, employees and itself, which are supported by detailed strategies and continuous improvement programs. This is a way of life for Toyota and its employees, not just a one-time project.

Unless other manufacturers can emulate the "entire" system and culture, they will not be able to "copy" Toyota's best practice.

Message: World's best practice is a complex thing, and not easily duplicated.

Human touchpoints significantly reduced

This organization wanted two scenarios for the Innovate workshops: first, a non-automated and 6-month horizon; and second, an automated and 12-month horizon. The end-to-end high level process model was redesigned to move from a reactive to a proactive basis. The number of processes redesigned was 13, and they were consolidated into 7 processes during the workshops. In this particular example, the improvements were measured by the reduction in human touchpoints associated with the processes (see table below).

Number of original touchpoints, and reductions achieved

Process	Original	Non-automated	Automated
1	53	23 (57%)	9 (83%)
2	15	15 (0%)	1 (93%)
3	46	46 (0%)	5 (89%)
4	47	18 (62%)	17 (64%)
5	4	4 (0%)	1 (75%)
6	14	10 (29%)	1 (93%)

The reason for using human touchpoints was that the timeframe allowed for the workshops did not provide sufficient time for metrics analysis—which is not an ideal situation. However, the potential reduction in human involvement in the process was impressive.

While "touchpoint" measurement need not translate into time and cost savings for the organization, it does show a significant reduction in the handling by the people in the organization. Since the people involved in the process were professional, high salaried people, the costs and customer service did improve dramatically.

Message: Analysis without supporting detailed metrics is very difficult to justify in a business case. An analysis of process "touchpoints," while indicative, is not enough to justify funding. Always insist on having enough time for detailed metrics analysis.

One way of approaching this costing is to allocate one or more workshops to the discussion of the expected new process timing for each individual process. This will involve reviewing the current process and timing from the Understand phase and, if appropriate, comparing it to the new process to assist in the determination of expected process timings.

If the current process and timings are not applicable, estimates will need to be made of the expected process execution times. Simulation may sometimes be of assistance with this determination (refer to step 9). The use of minutes as the common denominator for process metrics measurement will focus attention on the primary objective and allow conversion into any other measure that is useful (hours, work days, number of FTE (number of employees required to execute the process)).

The next step is to extrapolate the expected future transaction volumes. If the option being considered is 18 months in the future, then the business will need to estimate any increase or decrease in transaction volumes, by process.

> ## BPM INSIGHT
>
> It is crucial to have a reliable model that incorporates the volumes, efficiency and key assumptions. Often the models used for this purpose contain data and calculation errors that can significantly impact the outcomes. It is strongly recommended to:
>
> - have clear visibility on the formulas and assumptions
> - obtain sign-off on each individual assumption, volume and productivity measure (and hold people accountable for this)
> - review the various scenarios being considered.

The expected process timings can then be multiplied by the future transaction volumes to derive the future total processing minutes. This will be achieved by completing the spreadsheet shown in Figure 16.3 (Simplified Costing Matrix).

The next step is a review of the departmental budget. The forecast budget is amended to allow costs to be calculated for the various Innovate scenarios selected:

1. Based upon the new resource utilization, the number of FTEs is forecast and a new staff cost calculated (total of salaries for the new number of FTEs). "Other staff costs" are calculated on a FTE proportional basis.

2. "Other budget" costs are discussed with the business to identify which ones are impacted by a change in FTE count. These costs are proportioned based on the new FTE count. Remaining costs are adjusted according to the business input.

3. The current and the projected IT costs are assessed. An automated BPM solution could increase the IT costs; however, a more streamlined automated BPM solution may reduce IT costs. This occurs when inefficient and high maintenance systems can be replaced by better, more cost-effective solutions.

The level of process modeling and the recalculation of transaction volumes and times available will determine the accuracy of the cost allocations.

This will result in a new forecast budget which should be used in the future process costing metrics analysis.

Step 9: Simulation

Simulation is one method of determining the feasibility and efficiency of the proposed redesigned process options. Simulation can also be used to test the logic and consistency of processes before their implementation. What if our demand doubles or quadruples? What if we increase the number of people in one area of the process? Various scenarios should be run to test the metrics and assumptions.

Simulation requires a significant amount of effort and should not be underestimated or undertaken lightly. There will be a need to gather the necessary metrics and assumptions to run the simulations.

Financial services organization

The business drivers for process innovation were:

- an inability to meet service levels
- issues with quality
- an inability to provide "tiered" levels of service.

After completing the Understand and Innovate phases of the 7FE Framework and detailed metrics analysis, the organization understood that a phased implementation of the new processes, which included image processing, would yield a reduction in their annual operational budget of 40 percent and an FTE reduction of 45 percent.

Message: Without the detailed metrics analysis, it would have been difficult to quantify the overall potential for budget reduction and provide sufficient business case detailed analysis (on the benefits side of the equation) to justify the way forward.

Once completed, the simulated "runs" should be evaluated and, ultimately, activity-based costing and capacity planning estimates completed, if necessary. This will assist in the determination of performance management and measurement for the process options.

Options should be narrowed down to the most feasible at this stage, and it is these options that should be "workshopped" with the various stakeholders in the next step. Simulation allows, even requires, that many assumptions be made (for example, frequency and distribution of demand, effective work rates, number of errors and so on). It is crucial that these assumptions are documented and provided to the stakeholders, including the context in which they were determined.

The suggested solutions, together with supporting evidence, should be documented, and process models completed for distribution prior to the next workshops. A detailed example of how simulation can fit into the Innovate phase is provided in Chapter 28, Citibank case study.

KEY POINT

Simulation can be very useful. However, it is solely dependent on reliable data and assumptions. Furthermore, it is important that upfront a clear assessment is made of the usefulness of simulation, because sometimes organizations become lost in an analysis frenzy and lose sight of the original objectives.

Step 10: Update People Capability Matrix and capacity planning

Step 6 in the Understand phase discussed the need to create a People Capability Matrix. The matrix (Figure 16.7) needs to be reviewed, or created, for the future new process(es). This information will then be used in the People phase, to be compared with the matrix of the current people capabilities developed in the Understand phase. A gap analysis will also be completed and linked to individuals, with specific action plans (training or up-skilling), and potential changes to the organization structure.

Capacity planning can be useful from two different perspectives. First, it is about planning to ensure that the right number of appropriately skilled people is available at the right time to meet customer and organization needs. Second, it will provide input into the establishment of the performance management and measurement goals to be established in the People phase for individuals, teams and management.

Rather than delve into this here, refer to the case study of Citibank in Chapter 28, which shows how capacity planning links with simulation, activity-based costing and work-routing.

Step 11: Workshop proposed solutions

The BPM activity team should have narrowed down the process options to a smaller number by this step, and the purpose of the next set of workshops is to gather all the stakeholders together to determine whether the proposed options meet all the stakeholder needs. This step was also discussed as part of step 7.1 and referred to as the "finalization" workshop.

The stakeholders should include:

- business
- external stakeholders (customers, distribution channels, vendors, suppliers, perhaps investors)
- compliance staff
- information technology
- operational risk
- internal audit
- (perhaps) external audit, depending upon the processes.

This is where the documented process options are presented, together with the outcomes of the various simulation runs, the activity-based costing and other supporting evidence.

All these stakeholders should probably not be involved in the one workshop, due to the potential competing requirements.

There is always a debate as to whether a process should be designed around the audit, compliance and risk requirements or not. We suggest that you should consider redesigning the process to be as efficient and effective as possible, to meet the business and primary stakeholder needs, and then consider the audit, compliance and operational risk requirements in a second pass. Audit, compliance and operational risk should not be driving the redesign, but also must not be ignored: the organization simply has to meet these requirements. Another approach is to outline the basic rules from an audit, compliance and operational risk perspective, and endeavor to include these in the process as it is designed.

We strongly recommended that the business and critical external stakeholders participate in the workshops to ensure that the redesigned processes meet their needs and are not fundamentally changed by other, competing requirements. Only once this has taken place should compliance, operational risk, and internal and external auditors be included.

However, sometimes compliance or operational risk is the initial driving force behind business process initiatives. This has certainly been the case in several banks, where it has been compliance and operational risk that has provided the initial funding because of external requirements (such as Sarbanes–Oxley). Once these requirements have been addressed, the business can then take an interest and expand the original BPM activities to take a BPM improvement direction.

The outcomes of these workshops are the agreement and sign-off of the new process options to take forward to the feasibility step.

Step 12: Demonstrate and validate feasibility of proposed solutions

If not already completed, further analysis may be necessary to ensure that the redesigned options are operationally viable (or feasible):

- Will the new process be able to be supported from an IT perspective?
- Will the business be able to function efficiently and effectively as a result of the new process?

If the new process is to be automated, it is often an excellent idea to build a demonstration or prototype of the proposed process. Vendors often refer to this as a "proof of concept." If the process is to be manual, then walkthroughs within the business should be conducted. When conducting these automated demonstrations or walkthroughs, ask the "testers" to come up with exceptions. Role-playing will assist here. Remember always to go back and evaluate the new options against the process goals agreed in the executive kick-off workshop.

It may be necessary, as a result of this step, to go back to the Innovate workshop step if you find that some aspects of the process are not feasible or cannot be implemented.

Step 13: Process gap analysis

In certain circumstances it is useful to develop a gap analysis between the Understand and new Innovate processes. Waiting until the new process option has been selected during steps 11 or 12 will save the development of several versions of this document. A heat map with the level of change can provide a useful visual representation of the magnitude of change.

The purpose of completing this step is to provide a comparison between the new and the old processes for the business, IT department and developers of the training material. This analysis also provides an indication of the magnitude of change for the People Change component. The process gap analysis should cover the following topics for each process:

- a brief overview of the current process
- a brief overview of the new redesigned process
- key changes between the two processes
- process issues
- relevant metrics

- business and process impact comments
- new (business) opportunities
- required changes (for example, IT changes).

The process gap analysis could also comment on training, occupational health and safety and organizational structural issues, and will assist in the change management aspects of the BPM activity. An example of a process gap analysis is included in the Extra Reading section at the end of this chapter.

Step 14: Identify benefits and update business case

The initial business case written during the Launch pad phase will have identified some of the estimated benefits. During the Innovate phase of the BPM activity, after the redesign options have been finalized, there will be more detailed information available to enable the re-forecasting of the benefits in a more defined manner.

The business case should be able to be far more definitive at this stage because of the work completed during the simulation, activity-based costing and metrics steps: the benefits (for example, improved processes) and the costs (for example, implementation costs) are much clearer. (Sometimes, however, it is difficult to obtain the costs at this stage of the BPM activity. Once the new process options have been determined and the BPM activity progresses to the Develop phase, the development and implementation costs can be determined more accurately.) The organization may understandably require a signed-off business case before any development is commenced.

These new costs and metrics will be able to be compared against the metrics gathered during the Understand phase. A comparison between the two (baseline Understand and Innovate) will provide quantifiable benefits for the redesigned processes. This will provide more robust evidence to support the business case. (Refer to Figure 21.5 for an example.)

Furthermore, the business case should aim for a smooth implementation and transition from BPM activity to business-as-usual operations. As much as possible, it should also include the known information regarding the proposed new operational organization design, and the impact upon the people.

Step 15: Report and presentations

This is where the reports and/or presentations are developed to:

- inform the business of the activities, findings and decisions from the Innovate phase;
- support the business case.

The report should be presented and delivered to senior management for approval. Approval is important, and every effort should be put into the development of the report and/or presentations. This presentation should have been planned and scheduled during the initial communications step, and be directed at the senior management or executives. The report should also include the key discrepancies from earlier assumptions and findings.

The purpose of the report is to provide the BPM activity status, outcomes and recommendations from the Innovate phase. This is the BPM activity team's and sponsor's opportunity to "sell" the recommendations to the executive for funding (if not already approved).

Step 16: Approvals

This is the step where the organization approves the recommended options. Each organization will have its own process to follow for the approval of a business case, and this should have been clarified and taken into account during the Launch pad phase of the BPM activity.

KEY POINT

Approvals are not just about the BPM activity asking for funding for the next phase, it is also where the BPM activity requests reconfirmation of the involvement and commitment of the executive team.

Step 17: Business requirements

This step may not be necessary as it may have already been completed as part of the Innovate workshops, as described in step 7.1.

If not already completed, then writing the business requirements is simply the further development of the documentation supporting the process models. This is to be provided to the Develop phase. It may be necessary to provide this to a separate implementation team and/or IT development team if systems development or changes are required.

Each organization will have its preferred method and required documentation, so we do not propose to define it here, although a useful example was provided in step 7.1. Suffice to say, the documentation should be written from a business and process perspective.

In the Citibank case study in Chapter 28 we have provided a detailed case study of how one organization went about substantially changing the way it conducted its business by changing business processes and reducing its operating costs significantly, using the activities outlined in this chapter.

KEY POINT

It is important that business requirements are created as part of the process redesign activities and not independently gathered. Business requirements are not "just listing the needs of the users," they need to be elicited. A useful technique is to always answer or structure business requirements using these statements:

- As a <role>,
- I want <requirement>
- In order to <benefit>.

If you cannot identify the benefits, then perhaps it is not required.

The success of the Innovate phase will be judged not on the standard of the process models (do they follow the organization's agreed process architecture and model conventions?) nor on the efficiency or effectiveness of the process models "on paper," but on how well they can be translated into implemented processes, functioning business processes. Creating new process models can be great fun, but until they translate into implemented, efficient, effective and appropriate processes, adding value to the organization strategy, objectives and all stakeholders, they are just "interesting" models.

REALIZE VALUE

The benefits mix must be refined and optimized as part of this phase. For details, refer to step 4 of Chapter 21, where it is described in the context of realizing value within a BPM initiative.

INNOVATE PHASE OUTPUTS

The Innovate phase will provide valuable input into other phases of the framework (see Figure 17.8). A few examples are listed here:

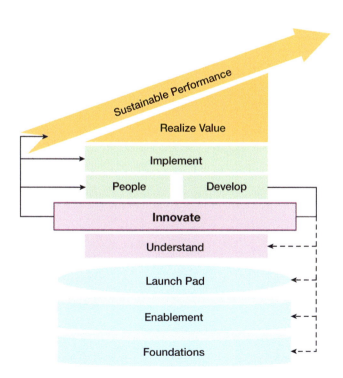

Figure 17.8 Innovate phase outputs to other phases

- knowledge may be gained that will be useful to the process architecture in modifying or enhancing the standards or guidelines for the organization;

- opportunities may arise that provide feedback into modifying the organization strategy (or Foundations and Enablement phases)—for example, in-sourcing for processes where the organization is operationally excellent;

- further knowledge of how to structure roles will unfold in the People phase;

- innovation is the primary input into the People and Develop phases, and will provide more ideas on how the proposed changes may be implemented.

Table 17.3 Innovate phase risks and mitigation strategies

Risk	Mitigation strategy
Unsure where to start	Follow the 7FE Framework
The organization is too ambitious and tries too hard (that is, tries to make too many changes at once)	Step 2 (Executive kick-off workshop) needs to provide practical BPM process goals and scenarios. Experienced external facilitators can often ensure the scope is practical without fear of internal conflict.
Too many innovate options are selected—for example, 3, 6, 12 and 24 month options for both automated and non-automated	Step 2 (Executive kick-off workshop) needs to provide practical BPM process goals. Experienced external facilitators can often ensure the scope is practical without fear of internal conflict.
The organization does not have a vision for the Innovate phase and is unable to establish process goals	The Enablement phase provides direction for this phase; however it is step 2 (Executive kick-off workshop) that provides the detail. Again, an experienced facilitator can assist in overcoming this risk.
The scope for the Innovate phase is too small	The scope is initially defined in Launch pad phase and is refined for the Innovate phase during step 2 (Executive kick-off workshop). The scope needs to provide a level of business benefits to make it worthwhile completing the BPM activity.
Stakeholders' expectations and needs are not considered	Step 2 (Executive kick-off workshop) and step 4 (External stakeholders) are important in establishing stakeholder expectations and needs, while steps 11 (Workshop proposed solutions) and 12 (Demonstrate and validate feasibility of proposed solutions) need to revisit these expectations.
BPM tool (or its vendor) is heading the Innovate phase, leading to the business not being optimally supported	The business must lead the process innovation activities and may be inspired by the opportunities that the BPM tool may provide.

INNOVATE PHASE RISKS

This phase provides an opportunity for innovation to occur; however, there are several risks that must be considered and mitigation strategies implemented to eliminate, or at least reduce, them. These risks include those listed in Table 17.3.

SUMMARY

In this chapter you have learned the:

- Importance of the Innovate phase and the main steps.
- Need and approach for communication.
- Criticality of involvement and commitment from executive management.
- Necessity to obtain input from internal and external stakeholders (including customers).
- Preparation and outline of the Innovate workshops and the various techniques that may be used.
- Involvement in Innovate workshops will assist in the People change management effort.
- Approach to validation and simulation of the newly designed processes.
- Need to obtain formal approval and communication regarding the decisions.

SELF-TEST

1 What is unique about the Innovate phase?
2 What should executive management agree prior to the Innovate workshops?
3 What type of involvement is required from internal and external stakeholders?
4 How can Innovate workshops be structured?
5 What validation needs to be completed prior to approval?

You have been asked to perform some Innovate workshops.

It is important to leverage the information you obtained in the previous phases.

Assignment guiding questions

- Who would you invite to the Innovate workshops and why?
- What workshop techniques have you chosen to use (see Tables 17.1 and 17.2) and why?
- What improvement, leveraging existing IT applications and functionality, would you recommend?

Innovate phase checklist

This checklist provides a generic overview of possible inputs, deliverables and gates of this phase.

Possible inputs

See Table 17.4.

Deliverables

See Table 17.5.

Possible gates

- Stakeholder analysis
- Understanding magnitude of change
- Organization's capacity to change
- Organization acceptance of BPM
- Technical review
- Compliance issues
- Risk management issues
- Expectations not achieved.

EXTRA READING

Innovate executive kick-off workshop

Objectives

1. To provide an update on the project status.
2. To provide a context for the Innovate phase of the project:
    - ensuring that the outcomes are consistent with the strategic objectives of the organization
    - providing written guides for the process goals for the various processes
    - providing guidelines for constraints, issues and timeframes.

Outcomes

We will have an agreed written list of:

- process goals;
- guidelines for the Innovate phase, in terms of the constraints from the business, business issues and desired timeframes to implement the redesigned processes.

Format

See Table 17.6.

Steps of an Innovate workshop

This section provides a suggested structure and organization for the Innovate phase workshops.

Structure of Innovate workshop

Workshop organization will vary depending upon many factors—the size of the organization, the number of workshops and workshop participants, and the complexity of the processes being reviewed, to name but a few of the variables. The best configuration of roles, assuming a reasonably large organization and complex processes, is as follows:

- "Facilitator"—this is the person who controls the workshop, ensuring that the direction and guidelines are strictly adhered to and that the timeframe and outcomes are kept in mind at all times.
- "Process modeler"—this assumes that the process modeling will be conducted online, using a process modeling and management tool during the workshop and projected onto a screen for all participants to view. We have found this to be the best approach as it allows the participants to become intimately involved. The process modeler not only "creates" the models for all to see during the workshop, but also participates in the workshop discussion.

Table 17.4 Innovate phase—possible inputs

✓	Phase	Deliverable
	Foundations phase	• Organization's core value proposition • BPM maturity of the organization • BPM drivers • BPM activities width • Red Wine Test outcomes • BPM approach • Components of the target operating model

	Establishment phase	An agreed target operating model Level 1 and 2 process views
		• Process architecture, including:
		  o Process guidelines
		  o Process asset repository
		  o Business rules repository
		  o Benefits management framework
		• Methods by which the people process capability will be built
		• Organizational cultural behavior changes by the establishment of appropriate targets (KPIs) and linked rewards
		• Code of behavior
		• The process-focused organizational design
		• The technology approach to BPM

	Launch pad phase	• Stakeholders defined in, involved in or associated with the BPM
		• Stakeholder engagement, commitment, and documented and agreed expectations
		• Process selection matrix and initial metrics
		• A list of identified high level business processes and initial metrics
		• A list of agreed process goals
		• Agreement of the process governance for the processes in the BPM activity
		• Prioritized processes for the Understand phase
		• An initial implementation approach
		• Project management:
		  o Project charter documents
		  o Project scope (initial) document
		  o Initial draft of the project schedule (plan)
		  o Determination and documentation on the initial communications strategy
		  o Initial risk analysis
		• Potential project benefits and realization plan
		• Initial business case

✓	From Understand phase	• Revalidated scope • Process models of current processes • Metrics baseline (including Voice of Customer) • Prioritized quick wins • People Capability Matrix • Knowledge and information needs • List of priorities for Innovate phase • Project plan (in detail) for Innovate phase • Report to management • Presentation to management • Initial communications plan
	Other input	• List of relevant projects to determine synergy and overlap

- "Scribe"—this person takes notes of the discussion; collects metrics, issues, opportunities, thoughts and ideas; and notes any "parked" ideas for future consideration. Individual team members (especially from the business) should be tasked, after a workshop has been completed, to investigate ideas back in the business and present back to the workshop—for example an improvement opportunity may require further investigation to ensure that there are no impacts on other business areas, IT systems, suppliers or customers. The scribe needs to keep track of these tasks, as well as taking detailed notes from the workshop. Our experience is that the scribe provides added value; however, the necessity for the role will depend upon the size and complexity of the workshop.

Table 17.5 Innovate phase—deliverables

✓	Deliverable	Used in phase
	List of agreed process goals	• Develop phase • People phase • Implement phase
	New process models and documentation	• Develop phase • People phase • Implement phase • Sustainable performance phase
	Simulation models	• Develop phase
	Activity-based costing information	• Realize value phase
	Capacity planning information	• People phase • Implement phase
	Stakeholder engagement, commitment, and documented and agreed expectations	• People phase
	Process gap analysis	• Develop phase • People phase • Implement phase
	Updated Process Selection Matrix	• Launch pad phase
	Metrics for the various innovate scenarios	• Develop phase
	Benefits side of a cost–benefit analysis for the business case	• Used in Innovation phase
	Project plan (in detail) for People and Develop phases	• Develop phase • People phase
	Updated communications plan	• People phase
	People Capability Matrix for new processes	• People phase • Implement phase
	Initial business requirements	• Develop phase
	Refined and optimized benefits mix (from Realize value phase)	• Develop phase • People phase • Implement phase • Realize value phase
	Communication of the results	• Used in Innovation phase

The behavior of the facilitator and other project team members should reflect the difference between the Understand and Innovate phase workshops. An experienced BPM workshop facilitator will understand these differences and be aware of the following:

- Business participants may feel threatened by suggested changes to the processes and their possible future roles; the facilitator and group need to be sensitive to this.

- Whether an issue or suggestion fits within the timeframe is being considered.

- The facilitator (and the non-business participants) must remain neutral for as long as possible during the discussions. Business participants must be given the opportunity of making the processes better. This also ensures that the business owns, and is committed to, "its" ideas for process improvement.

Table 17.6 Format of workshop

Item	Topic	Who
1	Project status report • project plan—to date and future • findings to date	
2	Project scope review	
3	Business process innovation versus design	
4	Guidelines for the Innovate phase ("rules of the game"): • Opportunities • Constraints: o people o applications o cultural • Issues • Timeframes (3, 6, 12 or 24 months?)	
5	Establish future process goals—where do you want to take the business from a process perspective?	
6	How do the goals for the redesigned processes relate to organization strategic objectives?	
7	Review Process Worth Matrix	
8	Success checklist agreed at the initial executive workshop; ensure items are still consistent with the decisions of this workshop	
9	Project deliverables for this Innovate phase	
10	Other business	

- The facilitator must create an environment where there can be lots of questions asked—this is achieved by the facilitator asking lots of questions, and keeping criticism and negative comments to a minimum and under control.

- There must be lots of "why?" questions asked.

- There must be no significant disagreement from non-business/project team members within the workshop.

- There may be a high level of passionate disagreement between the business participants as to how a process should be modified or totally changed. While this is good because it promotes better outcomes, it does need to be sensitively handled by the facilitator.

- The facilitator must work on the creative members of the group and perhaps guide them to make suggestions first, ensuring that all workshop participants contribute and have an opportunity to have their say.

- Very detailed information should be avoided. For example, if there is a need for a new business "form," then agree on this, but do not go into the detail of "form" design.

- Always ensure that all business participants are recognized and praised for their contributions.

- At the conclusion, it must be business that owns the new process options, not the project team members or facilitators.

- It is important that the participants get challenged to ensure that they provide truly innovative ideas and make significant improvements.

- Finally, the improvements must also be considered from a client perspective.

Short-term horizon

Below is a sample workshop agenda for 3- and 12-month timeframe scenarios.

Introduction

Request a senior executive to open the session and describe the following:

- the objectives to be achieved

- the goals and vision for the workshop(s)—these will have been agreed in the executive workshop

- the constraints to be taken into consideration during the workshops—for example the timeframes are 3 and 12 months; are changes to IT applications, to distribution channels or to product configurations allowed?

Sequence

1. Review the list of end-to-end processes developed for the area under consideration during the Understand workshops. If necessary, this should then be redesigned.

2. Present the top two items selected during the strengths and weaknesses (strengths represents opportunities) discussion in the Understand phase workshops. Ensure that these are placed in a prominent position (such as on a whiteboard or wall), are referred to on a regular basis and are taken into account during the Innovate phase discussions.

3. Review the process goals and organization objectives to ensure that the new processes take account of them.

4. There are then two ways to commence the Innovate process discussion:
   - discuss the shortcomings of the current process and improve it
   - completely redesign the process.

5. Commence the creative Innovate work. If it is warranted, during the modeling of the Innovate process ensure that model components are color coded, highlight the differences from the old process (if appropriate) and represent the timeframes involved in the introduction of the suggested improvements. Differing timeframes may also be shown by separate process models.

6. Capture ideas and tasks that need to be checked regarding feasibility.

   Team members should then be tasked with the responsibility of going back into the business and validating the feasibility of the suggestions. They should then return to the group and present their findings.

7. At various stages during the workshops, it is essential that a business participant "presents" the suggestions back to the group and invites managers to ensure or consolidate the business ownership of the new processes. The facilitator should ensure that the business participants are credited with the ideas.

8. Several new process scenarios should be developed; do not stop at one and think you have done a good job. The first one or two redesigned processes only start the creative flow, and it is the later innovative processes that are the most creative and efficient.

After workshop activities

- Immediately after the workshop, the Innovate workshop project team must complete a review of the model(s) against the notes taken by the scribe to ensure that the notes and the model(s) record all aspects discussed and are consistent;
- Expand details to shortlist alternatives;
- Further investigate the technical feasibility of the alternatives;
- Reapply the evaluation criteria in more detail to ensure consistency;
- Select no more than three options for management consideration;
- Build a plan (next steps).

Long-term horizon

The details and agenda for this workshop are mainly the same as those for the short-term horizon, with the following exceptions:

1. Rather than starting with the process created during the Understand workshops and slightly or significantly modifying it, you start with a "clean sheet of paper."

2. Clearly, there is an opportunity "totally" to rethink how the business is to operate. Radical ideas and process innovation should be considered. A useful approach is to brainstorm "outside the box" ideas:

- the facilitator should ask the participants for radical ideas and there should be no criticism or comment from the group at this stage; ideas should be written on Post-it notes and placed on a whiteboard;
- the next step is to have participants place the ideas into groups;
- discussion should then take place to eliminate the ideas that are outside the criteria set by the executive workshop for this Innovate phase;
- ideas can then be debated on their merit.

3. These ideas and suggestions can be used in the design of the new process.

Workshop preparation

It is essential that the team members involved in conducting the Innovate workshops prepare in advance. Preparation should include the following:

- reviewing the Understand models being addressed during the workshop to ensure a common understanding;
- if necessary, confirming aspects of the Understand process in the initial workshop;
- thinking through possible innovation process solutions so that the workshop may be "directed," if appropriate, by the facilitator.

Workshop execution

How to start the workshops? Clearly, the obvious way to commence an Innovate workshop would be to ask the business participants to think of a new, more efficient process that will meet the timeframe and other constraints agreed at the start. Sometimes this approach meets with blank faces and no response.

Other methods to enable this process to commence in a more structured and clear manner could include the following:

1. *Control points.* If the process to be modeled is a financial or control process, then you could brainstorm the various control points that are required within the process. For example, in a receipting and bank reconciliation process, the control points might be the following:
   - ensure all data have been entered by operators into the application system;
   - a single person collects audit trails of the information entered into the application system;
   - balance these audit trails to the application system;
   - combine all these audit trails into one report;
   - balance audit trails to bank statements to ensure physical banking has been completed and ensure that the bank statements are correct;
   - review bank statements for items that have been deposited directly into the bank and must be entered into the application system;

- send reports (audit trails or consolidated reports) to the finance department for completion of the bank reconciliation;
- ensure all reports reach the finance department.

Once these control points have been agreed, the development of the process can be relatively quick and easy because you have agreed the essential steps that must be met by the process.

2. *Critical activities.* For a non-financial process, a list of critical activities could be brainstormed and written on a whiteboard or Post-it notes. Again, the process could be relatively quickly and easily developed. Always question the critical activities to ensure they are really necessary. Process innovation may allow the circumvention of some of the current critical activities.

3. *Business participants' resistance and push-back.* If you are experiencing this within the session—for example the business participants believe their Understand (current) process is "perfect" and cannot be improved, or do not wish it to be improved—then do not start by trying to redesign the current process. Ask for suggestions for improvement activity by activity in the current process, and brainstorm the issues and areas that could be improved. The new process could then be developed from these brainstormed suggestions and shown to the business participants.

Questions for an Innovate workshop

This section contains the most important questions to be considered before redesigning a process. It is best if these questions are discussed at the start of the workshop.

This document is based on the belief that a business process and the related process models are not goals in themselves, but a means to achieving a business objective within a given context. Therefore, before commencing the Innovate workshop process and indulging in process modeling, it is important to have the correct focus and context on which the modeling should be based. Furthermore, these considerations should be discussed and made explicit.

It is important to understand that everyone has implicit assumptions about the possibilities and limitations of process innovation. The potential for the Innovate workshops will be hampered by these implicit assumptions unless they are addressed, shared, understood and agreed upon. The questionnaire below only relates to process-oriented redesign, and not to system- or organizational-oriented redesign.

How to use this document

Prior to the commencement of the Innovate phase, the questions listed in the table below should be discussed. It is crucial that the scope of the Innovate phase is specified before conducting the workshop. Then the modeling can start.

Questionnaire

SCOPING

1. What is the scope and extent of the process(es) to be redesigned?
2. What is out of scope?

BUSINESS

2. To which overall business objective do these processes contribute? (WHAT?)
3. Which strategy should be used as a basis for the processes? (HOW?)
   - Customer intimacy
   - Product leadership
   - Operational excellence.
4. What are the main driver(s) of process change? (WHY change?)

CUSTOMERS AND PARTNERS

5. What do the clients currently want?
6. What are the aspects that our partners can and want to provide?
7. What are additional services and products that we can provide?

PROCESS

8. What is good in the current process(es)?
9. What are the bottlenecks/issues to be overcome in the current process(es)?
10. Which best practices can be included? This can be done on the basis of reference models, ideal models, industry practices and benchmarking.
11. What are the most significant improvements that can be made to the process(es)?
12. What are the performance indicators/SLAs (quality and quantity)?
13. What are other relevant metrics associated with the process(es)—including relevant decompositions?
14. How are the process(es) monitored and by whom, and which variables can be used to adjust the process(es)?
15. What rules and regulations must this process comply with (internal and external)?
16. What significant interfaces does this process have with other process(es)?

ORGANIZATION

17. What organizational units are involved, and what criteria do they impose on the process?
18. What positions and people are involved in the process, and do we need to take this into consideration in the innovate workshops?

INFORMATION SYSTEMS

19. What information systems are involved, and what restrictions and opportunities does this provide?

DOCUMENTS

20. What outputs and/or documents must be generated, and must they comply with any particular requirements (e.g., legal)?

Sample process gap analysis

The process gap analysis documents the differences between the Understand phase findings and the Innovate phase, and should contain the following information:

1. An overall analysis of the impact of the changes in processes on the organization;
2. Implementation options and comments;
3. Per individual process:;
   - a brief description of the Understand process
   - a brief description of the selected new Innovate process
   - a summary of the key changes between the two
   - any process issues
   - the impact of appropriate metrics
   - general impact discussion and comments;
4. An identified general impact assessment;
5. Identified project timelines;
6. Identified training impacts and requirements;
7. Identified change management issues;
8. Identified organization structure impact and requirements;
9. Process and implementation.

Quick wins—Kaizen

This book has described the key activities that need to be performed from small BPM projects to large-scale transformations. However, some process challenges are relatively small and do not need to follow all the steps and phases of the 7FE Framework.

Below is an example of a quick win approach that can improve relatively small process challenges within a week, provided that there are no IT changes required. This quick win approach leverages the key steps and tools from the 7FE Framework. It works as a "pressure cooker" whereby key people will be put together and inspired to produce appropriate solutions within a short time-boxed period.

This approach is based on Kaizen, which has the following principles:

- Open-minded
- Positive attitude
- Keep asking questions (five whys)
- Everyone's contribution is valued
- Everyone is equal
- Take action
- Full support by management and strong commitment from the business.

Table 17.7 Sample schedule for realizing quick wins

When	What	Input	How	Who	Deliverable	Phase
Monday morning	Select & define BPM activity	Opportunities register	Meeting with Project sponsor	Process lead Project sponsor	STAGE GATE Signed Project Charter	Launch pad
Monday afternoon	Review high level process	Process models	Understand workshop	Process lead Project sponsor Key SMEs & managers	SIPOC view of process List of pain points and opportunities	Understand
Tuesday morning	Analyze key metrics	Key metrics & reports Issue logs Customer complaints Audit reports	Analysis Observations	Process lead Key SMEs	Draft Root-Cause analysis Draft FMEA Draft Pareto	Understand
Tuesday afternoon	Validate key metrics	Input from customers and SMEs	Interview key SMEs Interview customer(s)	Process lead Customer Selected managers	STAGE GATE Final Root-Cause analysis Final FMEA Final Pareto	Understand
Wednesday morning	Brainstorm solutions	Root-cause analysis FMEA Pareto	Innovate workshop	Process lead Project sponsor Key SMEs & managers	List of potential ideas Updated opportunities register	Innovate
Wednesday afternoon	Prepare solution	List of potential ideas	Work on process models and solution	Process lead Key SME	Draft solution Draft updated process models	Innovate
Thursday morning	Present solution and discuss implications	Draft solution Draft updated process models	Implementation workshop	Process lead Project sponsor	Updated solution Updated process models Implementation considerations	Innovate People
Thursday afternoon	Finalize solution	Updated solution Updated process models Implementation consideration Process metrics	Complete the documentation and obtain sign-off Produce draft benefits	Process lead Project sponsor	STAGE GATE Final solution Updated process models Agreed benefits Sign-off by project sponsor	Innovate People

Table 17.7 Sample schedule for realizing quick wins—*continued*

When	What	Input	How	Who	Deliverable	Phase
Friday morning	Communicate solution	Corporate communication template and strategy Final solution Updated process models Agreed benefits	Produce communication for relevant stakeholders, including: • Management • Employees • Partners/customers • Projects	Process lead Project sponsor	Relevant communication	Implement
Friday afternoon	Prepare implementation	Relevant communication Updated process models Final solution	Liaise with key stakeholders for implementation	Process lead Project sponsor	STAGE GATE Ready for roll-out	Implement
To be determined	Implement	Final solution Communication	Monitor correct implementation	Process lead	Updates to solution and process models Updates to benefits	Implement
Weekly/monthly after implementation	Monitor benefit realization	Agreed benefits Actual benefits	Assess discrepancies and take appropriate action	Process lead Project sponsor	Benefit tracking	Realize Benefit
1 month after implementation	Close activity	Benefit tracking Final solution	Close activity	Process lead Project sponsor Selected SMEs & managers	Lessons learned Updates to approach (if required)	Sustainable Performance

CHAPTER 18

PEOPLE PHASE

OVERVIEW

The People phase deals with the people and organization design aspects of the Target Operating Model (TOM). These are crucial to ensure that the new processes are understood and executed correctly. This chapter will cover role descriptions and role responsibilities; people capabilities; and organization structure. The supporting policies and performance measures will also be determined.

This phase is about ensuring that people are better placed, supported and motivated to be more productive and to increase the employee engagement and satisfaction.

OVERALL LEARNING OUTCOME

By the end of this chapter you will be able to understand the:

- Importance of the People phase and the main steps
- Need and method for communication
- Necessity of designing the people strategy
- Importance and approach of activity definitions and roles design
- Need and method for people core capabilities gap analysis
- Need to redesign organizational structure, including the reporting structures
- Necessity to identify fit-for-purpose performance management and measurement
- Importance of the correct corporate culture and critical success factor to achieve this
- Need to start developing training and updating human resources policies
- Outputs and risks for this phase.

WHY?

The People phase (Figure 18.1) is a crucial phase in any BPM process implementation, and unless it is handled thoroughly and to a high standard, the rest of the project will be put at risk. It is important to understand clearly that this is different from the Implement phase, which focuses on the roll-out of the solution. The People phase will determine the people aspects of the TOM while the People Change Management essential will focus on making the transition to the TOM, including the cultural aspects. The People phase will usually be conducted in parallel as the Develop phase of the project. The Develop phase creates the automated (or otherwise) solution, and People phase creates the roles and people measurement solutions.

The purpose of this phase is to ensure that the activities of the individuals who will be executing the new processes are in alignment with the agreed organization and process goals established in earlier phases of the project.

KEY POINT

At the end of the day, it is people that will make processes function effectively and efficiently, no matter how much processes are automated. If you do not get the people "on board" with the project and new processes, then they will find a way to ensure that the processes either do not work, or do not work efficiently.

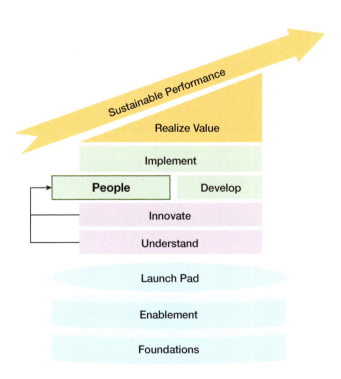

Figure 18.1 People phase

Note: While this statement is true, it has to be balanced with commercial reality, and we will cover this later in step 4 of this chapter.

This phase is where business staff and management have their job goals defined and job descriptions redesigned or created. The manner in which their performance will be measured and managed will also be changed or developed to match these process goals and organization structure. It provides the opportunity for the organization to make the roles more interesting and to increase the employability of the people. This relates not only to internal employability (ensuring that the people are capable of performing multiple roles, which means that they can continue with the organization in a variety of roles) but also external employability (boosting the confidence of staff as well as helping in the transition where retrenchment or outsourcing occurs).

BPM INSIGHT

The success of the assembly line in the beginning of the industrial revolution was by separating the workers on the assembly line and the engineering that constructed the assembly line. Robert Taylor with his Scientific Management optimized these operations.

Today there is a critical need to exchange information and ideas and every worker can contribute to the success of the organization, provided that they are motivated to do so and provided with the opportunity.

The results of this phase must work: failure is not an option. The phase is not a mechanical set of steps that the project just has to work through; it is where the project team needs to spend as much time as is necessary to ensure the results are successful.

RESULTS

How will you know that this phase has been effective? By the way people react to the change, changed roles, new processes and new role performance management and measurement targets. There are a number of practical steps and documents to produce during this phase, but at the end of the day it is the people who will show, by their behavior, whether or not this phase has been successful.

Some of the activities and reports that will be produced during this phase include:

1. The dissection and amalgamation of the new processes and their component tasks into activities.

2. Redesigned role descriptions and goals that have been discussed and agreed with the people who will be executing them.

3. Performance management and measures for appropriate roles, which have also been discussed and agreed with the people who will be executing them.

4. A plan and set of tasks to enable the organization to "transform" from where it currently is to where it needs to be. This will include a thorough understanding of the existing and future core competencies and capabilities of the people, at a role level. This will be overlaid on the process gap analysis produced earlier to enable the appropriate training plan to be developed for individuals and teams of people.

5. A new process-based organization structure for the business area involved in the project.

6. Updated policies, including HR policies.

7. Steps towards a new organization culture.

HOW?

Many organizations and managers are quick to criticize and blame the people for the lack of performance in an organization. In our experience, this is rarely the fault of the personnel on the "workshop floor" who execute the processes. An organization should approach an improvement program in the following sequence:

1. *Processes*—get the processes efficient and effective and adding value to the organization strategy.

2. *Structure*—get the roles and structure right, or as close to right as you can, to support the new processes.

3. *People*—only after the processes and structure steps have been addressed and implemented can you evaluate their performance.

> **if you put a good performance against a bad system, the system will win almost every time.**
>
> **(Keen, 1997: 65)**

In most organizations the people executing the business processes are good people, doing the best they can with the systems and processes with which they have been provided by management. In many cases, these people do exceptional jobs, putting in long and dedicated hours to service customers. It is management's responsibility to provide these people with the environment and "tools" (processes, culture, infrastructure, systems and support) to complete their job in an effective and efficient manner.

At the BPM activity level, in order to meet the agreed process goals, the organization will need to design roles to support the processes and sub-processes and ensure that the work environment is structured to enable people to maximize their contribution. Even if the organization has their structure optimized, people are the ones who execute the processes and make things happen. Without them, you have nothing.

The areas that must be covered during the People phase of the BPM activity are: a decision on how to execute this phase; the establishment of activities, roles or jobs and performance measurements for the people who are executing the process(es); ensure that the interface between the process(es) is managed to ensure there are no "gaps" and ensure that the right supporting culture is in place. This assumes that you have provided an appropriate level of resources and that they have been allocated appropriately to enable the people to be effective and efficient.

Before the People phase steps are described it is important to recognize the enormous shifts that have taken place in the workplace. These shifts need to be considered during the execution of the People phase steps. The workplace shifts include:

- the need and demand by employees for flexible working hours, including early or late start times, part-time work, and working from home;
- the increasing number of contractors and temporary employees performing roles and the growing outsourcing of business activities;
- increasing globalization of the workforce driven by migration, global expansion and outsourcing;
- the wide variation of worker expectations and ambitions which are influenced by a variety of reasons;
- the expanding use of mobile technology and social media is blurring the boundaries between work and leisure time.

Without taking these aspects into account it is impossible to arrive to a fit-for-purpose people solution.

KEY POINT

In a world where employees and organizations have a wide and, potentially, varying set of expectations, demands and needs, the challenge is for management to ensure that all aspects are addressed in the set of organizational policies and strategies.

DETAILED STEPS

The steps associated with the People phase of the project are shown in Figure 18.2.

Step 1: Communications

This phase revolves around the people in the organization and to achieve the best outcomes they should be involved and informed throughout the process. Expect to be asked:

- What is proposed?
- How will it be completed?
- How will it affect me?
- What input will I have into the outcomes?
- What if I do not like the outcomes?

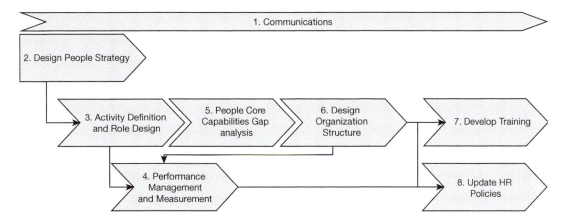

Figure 18.2 People phase steps

These are just some of the questions that will need to be answered. The BPM activity team will need to ensure that it has a proactive approach to communicating with the business and the affected people.

It is important to ensure that the right channels are used as sensitive items are covered during this phase of the project. Furthermore, it is also the time that the executives, BPM activity sponsors and project managers are required to be accessible to answer questions from those concerned. Social media, the intranet and face-to-face information sessions may be used quite effectively, in addition to the traditional communication methods.

KEY POINT

Most people derive consciously or unconsciously great value out of their job; it provides them income for their family, money for their interests, social status, friends and sense of belonging and even power. Making any change to their job or the risk of losing it, will be quite unsettling for many people. It is crucial that this is considered in all communications and BPM activities.

Step 2: Design people strategy

While the project team must take accountability for the delivery of this step, the Human Resources department of the organization should be significantly involved in the strategizing and planning of how the People phase of the project will be approached (the people strategy). The level of involvement of the HR department is dependent on the scenario selected: in case of an enterprise-wide transformation program the HR department will be more heavily involved due to the significant and structural changes compared to an isolated BPM project.

Key elements of a people strategy could include:

- relevant corporate values
- guidelines that supports an organization structure (for example team size, hierarchy levels)

- guidelines supporting and directing the creating of job structures and descriptions
- leadership and management development
- reward and recognition
- learning and development
- performance management
- staff engagement
- recruitment and retrenchment policies.

The agreed people strategy must be tailored to the BPM activity being undertaken, then documented and signed off by the appropriate stakeholders. These stakeholders may include: management and leadership, unions, the people themselves, and perhaps even customers and suppliers. It is counterproductive to reorganize in a way that will not be supported by unions, customers or suppliers.

If a change in organizational culture is required to support the BPM activity, then the impact on the BPM team will depend on the type of BPM activity and the BPM approach adopted. The strength of this relationship (BPM activity and the BPM approach) will determine the effort required on the cultural activity. Table 18.1 indicates the magnitude of the cultural activity.

Table 18.1 Relationship between the extent of cultural activity and the various BPM approaches

BPM activity initiation approach	Type of BPM activity		
	Large-scale program or enterprise-wide transformation	BPM program or portfolio of projects	Isolated BPM projects
Strategy led	Critical	Critical	Significant
Business Issue led	Critical	Significant	Moderate
Process led	Critical	Significant	Moderate

Step 3: Activity definition and role design

An activity may be an entire process or parts (tasks) of a process. Either way, an activity must contribute, or add value, to the process goals established and documented earlier in the BPM activity. An activity (collection of tasks) must be clearly defined and communicated to the people who will be executing the tasks, to ensure that they understand what is expected of them, how well (performance measurement) they are expected to perform the tasks, and with what aim they are expected to do this (performance measurement is covered in step 4).

The process models created during the Innovate phase will indicate the tasks associated with each process, so reviewing these models is an essential step in creating the definition of the activities. This step is about collecting process tasks into appropriate activities, as shown in Figure 18.3.

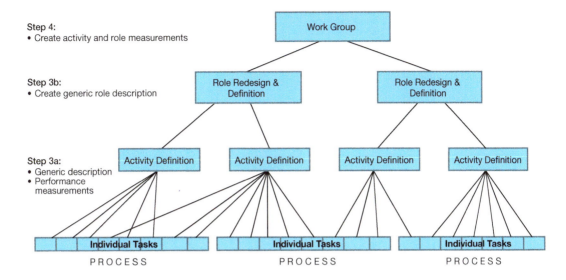

Step 4:
• Create activity and role measurements

Step 3b:
• Create generic role description

Step 3a:
• Generic description
• Performance measurements

Figure 18.3 Activity, job and structure creation

Once you are satisfied that the task groupings into activities are correct, then you can start to group the activities into generic "roles." They have been called roles, rather than jobs, because they are of a generic nature at this point, and the word "job" seems to imply a specific role for an individual.

At this step of the People phase, a role is defined at a higher level than the individual person or job description; it is a generic role, such as receipting clerk or claims assessor. (*Note*: It is recognized that a particular person's "job" may comprise several roles, depending upon the size of the organization or department; however, in the example provided we have assumed that this is not the case.)

This may be an iterative process of grouping the various activities into roles, discussing them with management and the people who will be involved in their execution, and then regrouping them, until you and all the stakeholders are satisfied with the outcome of the new role definitions.

Once this has been achieved, you are in the position to write the new role description. Most large organizations have their own templates for a role description, and we will not provide examples here. We will, however, mention a couple of specific process-related considerations.

It is worth taking a few moments to show some of the key components that must be addressed during the creation of activities and roles. The well-known RACI (or RASCI or RASIC) model is a useful method of helping to identify activities, roles and responsibilities during the People phase of a project.[1] This model may assist in describing clearly what should be done by whom to make a new process able to be executed by the people.

RACI/RASCI is an abbreviation for:

- **R** = Responsibility—the person who owns the problem or activity.
- **A** = to whom "R" is Accountable—who must sign off (Approve) the work before it is effective.
- **(S** = Supportive—can provide resources or other information in a supporting role in the completion of the process or activity).
- **C** = to be Consulted—has information and/or capability that is necessary to complete the process or activity.
- **I** = to be Informed—must be notified of the results of the process or activity, but need not be consulted during execution.

Some people have added "G" (Governance) to highlight the person who has to ensure that the RA(S)CI elements are being applied and enforced.

These key components (as abbreviations) can be shown in a chart for a particular generic role. Table 18.2 is an example of how five roles interact with the generic role.

Table 18.2 Sample RASCI model

	Business unit manager	Manager	Business unit head	Team leader	Compliance advisor
Activity 1	R		A		
Activity 2	A	R		S	C
Activity 3	RA		I		I
Activity 4	RA				C
Activity 5	A	R		S	

The sequence in completing this table is:

1. Identify all the activities as defined in step 3 (activity definition) of the People phase, and list them on the vertical axis.

2. Identify all the likely future roles, list them on the horizontal axis and complete the cells in the table with an R, A, S, C, I for each activity.

3. Resolve gaps and overlaps. The situation could occur where there are no "Rs," multiple "Rs" or no "As" for an activity. As a general rule, every activity should have only one "R" and at least one "A." These need resolution or completion before the role is finalized.

In reviewing the generic roles of people, the organization has a unique opportunity for management not only to empower staff and make people's jobs more interesting, but also to reward them in more interesting ways (other than financial) and provide promotional opportunities. The more this can be taken into account, the easier it will be for this to be "sold" to people and therefore implemented.

Most role descriptions must include authority levels, policies and procedures, allocation of responsibilities, delegations and environmental considerations. However, a process-related role description must also include performance measures for each part of the end-to-end process or sub-process, which brings us to step 4.

Step 4: Performance management and measurement

There is a frequently stated comment in process work—"you get what you measure" or put another way, "you get what you set." Without measurement you are not managing, whereas if you measure at least the critical parts of the process, and use that information in an intelligent way, then the results will be significantly enhanced.

Performance management covers both the performance of the individual process(es) and the performance of the people. This chapter covers the people aspects only. Process performance will be addressed in the Sustainable performance phase chapter (22).

Louis Gerstner (2002) said that "since people don't do what you expect but what you inspect . . . you need to create a way to measure results."

BPM INSIGHT

When establishing performance measures it is critical to focus on the desired outcomes because the key performance indicators (KPIs) can, and most often will, change behavior.

In a call center, management decided that creating customer intimacy was an important outcome they wished to achieve and rewarded consultants for the duration of their phone calls. Subsequently, call center staff did everything they could to extend telephone calls, even when it was clear that the customer was not interested in buying anything and was becoming annoyed with the call. Setting the wrong KPIs can actually be counterproductive.

Before you commence the people performance management and measurement step there needs to be a clear understanding of the capacity of the business unit or organization. Is the business unit over- or understaffed, or are the staff numbers at the correct level? The reason for completing the capacity planning models, in this context, is to ensure that the performance targets established by management are realistic and do not exceed the capacity of the available staffing levels to deliver. Capacity planning should have been completed during the Innovate phase, and the outcomes should be referenced. The use of process simulation may be helpful to validate that capacity is sufficient.

The creation of a performance management system and performance measures throughout the organization is a critical step. If not implemented correctly, BPM will not be as successful as it could be. The general BPM literature states that it is critical that the performance measures for all people (leadership, senior executives, managers and process execution people) be linked to the organization strategy, targets and process goals. If these links are not tight, then performance and outcomes will become fragmented. In practice, it is only about the first three levels of management that should or are able to have their KPIs directly linked to organizational strategy (balanced score card). Cascading the complete balanced score card (BSC) all the way down the organization does not work. The lower levels of the organization staff need selected aspects of the balanced score card that are simple goals, such as the number of widgets produced per day. Obviously, these can be created in such a way that they add to the organization strategy and objectives. The introduction of Strategy Maps may assist in ensuring that the elements of the balanced score card are aligned to achieve the overall objectives.

KEY POINT

As stated earlier, establishing the wrong KPIs has a high probability of creating undesirable behavior. To overcome this, some organizations are establishing group or team-based KPIs rather than individual-based KPIs. This can influence behavior to become more collaborative.

Figure 18.4 shows that performance measurement is not something that can wait until this People phase before it commences; it must be started at the very beginning of a project and considered at every phase, as follows:

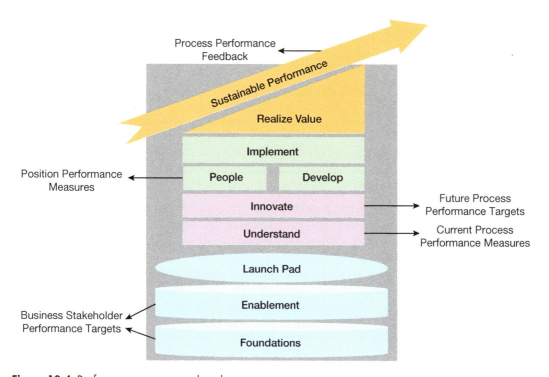

Figure 18.4 Performance measures by phase

- *Foundations and Enablement phases*—obtain a clear understanding of the required outcomes and objectives of the stakeholders. These must be met by the ongoing performance of the people and process(es), which contribute towards these outcomes and objectives.

KEY POINT

If the organization's strategy is linked to individuals' or group/team performance measures, performance bonuses and ability to be promoted, a powerful synergistic relationship is created.

A balanced score card approach may assist in achieving this.

- *Understand phase*—obtain a clear understanding of the current performance measures and how successful they are, and any lessons to be learned from their implementation.

- *Innovate phase*—capacity planning is completed and will contribute towards establishing and validating the future performance targets or goals; targets will be established as part of the process goal-setting.

- *People phase*—all the information collected will be brought together to link to the performance targets established for individual people, teams and management.

- *Sustainable performance phase*—the performance management system will become part of "what we do around here." It will become sustainable by continual feedback and improvement.

If performance management and measurement is new to an organization, start with a few measures only, and keep them simple. If necessary, the number and complexity of management reports and measures can grow with time and experience. Obviously, these measures must not be in conflict with the goals of other processes and departmental measures. In practice, this is a critical and difficult implementation issue.

Once the new roles and their related activities are understood by the employees, the organization is in a position to set the performance measures. These usually take the form of key result areas (KRAs) and key performance indicators (KPIs) (Kaplan and Norton, 1996).

Measuring role performance is of limited and dubious value unless the organization ensures that people understand why the measures have been established and are important to the organization.

When establishing role description performance measures, you must ensure that they satisfy, and add value to, the goals of the end-to-end process and organization strategy. This will included the needs of the various process stakeholders.

There are many organizations where the employees do not clearly understand their roles, what is expected of them and how they are being measured. *If you do not understand the rules of the game, how can you be expected to play well, let alone win?!* This seems such a basic and fundamental step, and yet organizations continually fail to complete this well. This can often be a large part of the process problems.

KEY POINT

It is management's role to create an environment where people can perform effectively. For this to occur, people must have a clear understanding and agreement as to their role and how their performance in that role will be measured. They need to have a written and well-communicated role description, clarity of the performance levels expected from them, and a feedback mechanism. It is management's role to provide these.

Furthermore, it is also management's role to listen to the people who are executing the processes. The people are the experts and knowledge holders who will provide excellent suggestions for process improvement. Management should provide the spark of inspiration for ideas outside the detailed level that the people work in. Management must constantly review processes themselves and establish mechanisms (internal and external) for this to take place. This will be covered in more detail within the Sustainable performance phase.

It is worthwhile at this point to stop and place all of this in perspective. While consultation with and inclusion of the people executing the processes is essential if the desire is to create a "process factory," the organization is not a democracy. It is management role to make decisions about "how things need to get done around here," and people (employees) are the ones who execute them. It is appropriate for management to say "no" to the people who execute the processes—just make sure they are informed why the answer is "no," which will provide more insight on what the organization requires. Once management decisions have been made, people are not in a position to wake up one morning and decide that today they are going to execute the process in a different way. This would ultimately lead to process and operational chaos at worst, or ineffective and inefficient processes at best.

After all these needs have been established, it is imperative that management uses the performance management and measurement information in the correct way. It should never be used as punishment. It should always be used as a means of coaching and enhancing performance, and improving the decision-making ability, of management and the people.

In fact, ideally managers should not be the ones to provide the performance measurement reporting to the people; it should come directly, or be available, to the people themselves. People must be able to measure their own performance. This will enable them to be able to remedy any situation, in a proactive way, before it becomes a management or business issue.

People should never be surprised with any performance measurement information coming from management. This performance measurement information should be readily available to all people within the business unit or process team. A little competition, by making the team goals and all individual team members' performance visible, is an important management technique.

The very last question that management should ask is: "Are the individual people up to the tasks allocated to them?" Management should not "jump to conclusions" about the capability of staff until all the prior points have been addressed.

CASE STUDY 1: PERFORMANCE MANAGEMENT

The following is an example of how the performance management might work within an organization. This example is based upon an actual implementation within a financial services organization.

An organization completed a review of its processes, the competency requirements of the people required to execute them and capacity planning of the business unit. It was decided to create new roles (not more people) to provide more focus on the desired performance outcomes. Two new roles were created: a relationship specialist and a specialist administration role. Previously, a single role had covered both these two roles of relationship and administration activities.

Process activities were examined and new job descriptions created to reflect the processes to be completed and the desired outcomes. The new suggested performance targets were to continue to be based on a balanced score card approach that the organization already employed. The targets at the lower levels would add towards the achievement of targets at the next higher level, and cumulatively upwards (for example administration staff targets would add to team leader's targets; team leader's targets to manager's targets; and so forth). Figure 18.5 shows an example of this approach.

The capacity planning assisted management and staff to understand that the targets set for the various roles were realistic and achievable and that the business unit was not over-

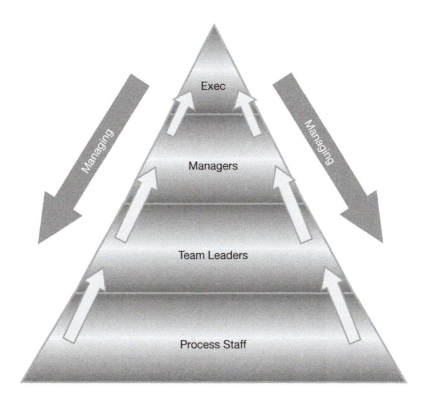

Figure 18.5 Pyramid of performance targets

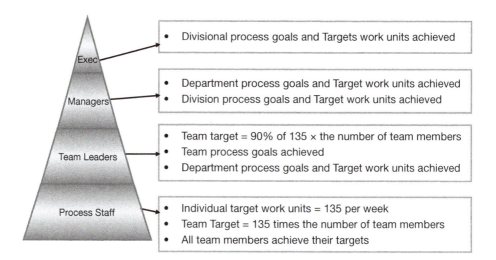

Figure 18.6 Sample throughput and service targets

or understaffed. The performance targets were to reflect throughput and quality, and each of these is discussed separately here.

A suggested structure and approach for the administration role and the associated performance targets is shown in Figure 18.6. This was reviewed to ensure that it was in alignment with the organization strategy and objectives, and departmental objectives and goals. Targets for the administration role included both individual and team targets. The individual targets, for example, would be the number of work units processed within a defined time period. A unit of work (or work unit) was set at 15 minutes. The reason for using "work units" instead of a "number of transactions" completed per time period was that it provided a means of overcoming the difference in processing times between various transaction types— for example some transactions required 15 minutes to process, while others took several hours.

The "work unit" approach required that each transaction type be examined to determine the number of work units of effort to process it. Much of this information was available from the project work completed during the Understand and Innovate phases. For example process A was 1.25 work units and transaction type B was 2.5 work units. All processes were rounded to the nearest 0.25. Using a standard effective day of 6.25 hours, this equated to 25 work units per day per person. (Staff worked an 8:30 a.m. to 5:00 p.m. day, which is 8.5 hours; allowing 1 hour for lunch and 15 minutes for morning and afternoon breaks, and an allowance for bathroom breaks and other activities, the organization settled on a 6.25-hour effective day.)

At a detailed level, in the case study organization, the administration role and team were given the targets as shown in Table 18.3.

Targets for team leaders included:

- the same team targets as the administration role, to encourage the management of the team in a way that benefits everybody (the organization, management, team leaders and team members);

Table 18.3 Sample performance targets

Objective	Measure	Target	Comment
Productivity	Individual Performance	135 units per week	This was 25 per day (6.25 hours divided by 15 minutes) or 125 per week; the additional 10 were established as a stretch target. When the individual was involved in team meetings, training courses and so forth, this time was recorded and counted towards the number of work units.
Productivity	Team Performance	1,350 units per week (for 10 team members)	This was the individual target of 135 multiplied by the number of team members. The team targetencouraged staff to help other members of their team who may have been struggling because of inexperience or being flooded with work.
Quality	Individual Quality	1 error per 100	Individuals were initially allowed a small allowance for processing errors per week (this progressed to zero tolerance for errors with experience).
Quality	Team Quality	0 error per 100	The team as a whole was allowed zero "external" errors. In other words, team members had to check each other's work to ensure that "zero" errors reached customers or other stakeholders.

- meeting the process goal timeframes in 90 percent of cases, which ensured that team leaders would manage their teams proactively to ensure that the workload was spread evenly to avoid backlogs;
- a target to meet the process goals of the overall department, which encouraged cooperation between team leaders in the same department.

This accumulation and building of targets proceeded up the hierarchy to each level of management.

To raise the level of quality within the team staff were required to always route errors back to the staff member who caused them in the first place. This ensured feedback to the team member on his or her performance. No additional work units were to be credited for the rework.

In the case study organization, team members recorded their performance on a daily basis, and had access to other team members' performance reports and the team performance report on a continual basis.

The team leader and team members also had access to a report that provided information on the number of transactions in the pipeline and any backlog. This was needed to ensure that the process goals were met. The data needed to measure the above throughput targets were included in the report shown in Figure 18.7.

These data were available for any given time period, by person, team, department and division.

A review of the performance of a department within an organization found that invoicing was late and often incorrect. The Billing and Statement team were blamed for this poor performance. The provision of additional staff was considered as the team could not cope with the enormous workload. A root-cause analysis revealed that a new manager in the Order Entry team had relaxed the quality criteria for his team and was just focused on clearing the order backlog, as this was related to his bonus. It took the Billing and Statement team considerable time to correct even the smallest mistake of the Order Entry team. From the moment the principle that whoever makes the mistake has to correct it was introduced, the quality of order entry improved significantly and the invoices could be sent out again on time with rarely an error.

Key message: Always determine and address the true root cause first and ensure the person or team who created the error fixes it.

Transaction type	Brought Forward	New Transactions	Completed Transactions		Carried Forward (days left in SLA)				
			within SLA	OOS	OOS	1	3	5	10

Figure 18.7 Process performance report

For each transaction type the information included:

1. The number of transactions brought forward from the last period.

2. The number of transactions received during the period (new transactions).

3. The number of transactions completed during the period that:

    a. met the respective SLAs (service level agreement) (process goals)

    b. were Out of Standard (OOS).

4. The number of transactions carried forward into the next period, including the number of days left in the SLA (process goals) or whether it was already out of standard.

Note: It should always be remembered that performance targets only provide benefit if they are recorded, if feedback is provided to all performers, and if the outcome is measured and rewarded.

KEY POINT

Providing transparency and even some level of competition can truly improve the drive and performance of teams. Some organizations publish the performance of teams in frequently accessed places, such as canteens or the intranet. Other organizations publish their safety records (e.g., last accident requiring work to stop) for the public to see.

Step 5: People core capabilities gap analysis

This step analyses the gap in the skills required to execute the current processes (from the Understand phase) and those required in the new redesigned processes (from the Innovate phase), to determine the necessary action. Refer to figure 18.8. The Human Resource department must be intimately involved in this step, as it should in this entire phase.

Figure 18.8 represents an example of this gap analysis (between the current state matrix created in the Understand phase and the redesigned processes created in the Innovate phase).

The gap will indicate the necessary course of action. For example train people in new skills; provide on-the-job coaching for existing people; replace people with more, less or different skills. Do not underestimate how long it may take to change attitudes and behaviors. Considerable effort, time and resource should be devoted to this activity.

Key processes \ Knowledge capabilities/ skills required	Ability to sell to customers	Communication skills	Data Entry skills	Dealing with difficult customers
Notification	Recommended (2)	Recommended (2)	Desired (3)	Mandatory (1)
Assessment	Mandatory (1)	Mandatory (1)	Desired (3)	Mandatory (1)
Approval	Recommended (2)	Recommended (2)	Desired (3)	Mandatory (1)
Payment	Recommended (2)	Recommended (2)	Desired (3)	Recommended (2)
Finalization	Recommended (2)	Desired (3)	Mandatory (1)	Mandatory (1)

Significant under qualified
Under qualified
Qualified
Over qualified

Figure 18.8 People Capability Matrix with Gaps

BPM INSIGHT

Automating a process as part of an improvement initiative has often more far-reaching people consequences than normally considered, as automation will require less data entry but typically more data analysis skills. These latter skills are not necessarily available or can be taught to data-entry staff.

Step 6: Design organization structure

This step looks at the impact of the role and process changes on the existing organization structure. If the current organization structure does not support or optimize the changes brought about by the BPM activity, then the organization structure will need to be changed or redesigned and the first activity is to understand the impact and place it in perspective. Organization structures are usually created in one of several ways, and these can be linked back to the selected BPM activity. The three possible scenarios for the implementation of BPM were described as:

- Large-scale BPM activities, such as a large program or enterprise-wide transformation
- BPM program or portfolio of projects
- isolated or small-scale BPM projects.

Only the first and second scenarios are likely to have any immediate impact on the organization's structure; the last one is more likely to impact the wider structure of the organization over time or perhaps will have an impact upon an individual section or department in the business. Figure 18.9 shows how an organization's structure can be created.

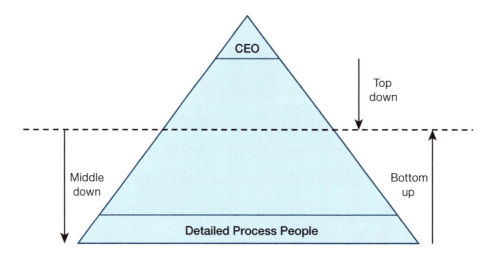

Figure 18.9 Organization structure creation

Figure 18.9 shows that the organization's structure is usually created in two sections. The CEO determines the upper echelons of the organization—his or her direct reports and the areas of responsibility. These areas of responsibility might be broken down by product, customers, distribution channels and so forth. This component of the structure is about service and reporting lines, and may or may not relate to the organization's processes. It is referred to as being "top down."

The lower half of the organization may be created either from the "bottom up" (based upon a process-focus approach) or "middle down" (based upon the CEO and their direct reports deciding the structure, usually on a functional basis). The middle-down method is the usual way an organization's structure is created, whereas a process-focused organization will favor the bottom-up approach. In the bottom-up approach, it is important to start with a decomposition of the processes into activities (as described in step 3 onwards). Then there is a need to distinguish between the "core" processes of the organization and the "supporting" and "strategic" or "management" processes, with the roles and structure reflecting this split.

KEY POINT

Changing the structure of the organization, including changing the reporting lines, often causes or results in much anxiety in the organization. Typically, people will become distracted from their job and start engaging in discussions and rumors. It is critical that communication and the flow of information is controlled and executed swiftly.

Do not be careless with confidential information. Do not leave new organization charts lying around; erase whiteboards after you have finished; and be careful what you say in public places (for example coffee shops).

Functionally based organizational structures create a tension between various organizational departments or business units, because processes are end-to-end and cross-departmental boundaries. To assist in overcoming this tension many organizations today are creating matrix-based organization structures, where functional managers are responsible for the traditional areas of sales, manufacturing, marketing, etc., and process owners are responsible for the value chain or high level end-to-end processes. Where this is the case, there needs to be a facilitated communications process that allows conflicts to be resolved.

Process owners usually have a hierarchy that allocates responsibility from the high level processes and value chains, down to the sub-processes. The role of a chief process officer is to coordinate all the process owners. Where matrix organizational structures have been created, it is essential that the reward and compensation systems are linked to the structure.

In all cases, the organization's structure is about ensuring that:

*   the proposed new structure is designed to support the organization strategy and process goals;
*   process gaps between departments are minimized—they will never be eliminated, but there is a great deal that can be achieved in minimizing them. In a true end-to-end process redesign and process-focused organization structure, these process gaps should be non-existent—or very close to it.

The way to achieve this is to approach organization structure creation as a process. Complete a high level model and then progressively model the restructured organizational design in more detail. Complete a new organizational relationship model to ensure that the process gaps are minimized as much as possible.

The organizational chart should:

*   minimize departmental interfaces;
*   maximize process effectiveness and efficiency;
*   minimize the layers of management;
*   most importantly, maximize clarity.

Table 18.4 Span of Control (team size) distribution chart

Team size (incl. vacancies)	1	2	3	4	5	6	7	8	9	10	11	12	13	14	15	16	17	18	19	20
As Is (frequency)	39	42	41	34	28	21	12	17	11	9	1	4	0	1	0	1	0	0	1	0
To Be (frequency)	12	15	18	21	20	23	20	18	15	12	6	2	2	2	1	2	1	0	0	0

Another important organization challenge is the direct reporting lines, especially in the case of an enterprise-wide transformation program. Many organizations have, over time, created a complex structure with a high number of small teams. This can result in the need for a relatively high amount of time spent on coordination activities. The People phase is an opportunity to formulate and execute new guidelines relating to the span of control, reporting lines and hierarchies.

It is recommended to populate a Span of Control distribution chart. This tallies the occurrence (or frequency) for each size of team, both for the Understand phase (As Is) and the Innovate (To Be) situation. For example the sample in Table 18.4 reflects an organization that has currently (As Is) 39 teams with a size of 1 and 42 teams of 2, etc.

Figure 18.10 shows the information gain in the Understand phase (As Is) (data from Table 18.4) as the red lines. A similar table to 18.4 should be produced during the Innovate phase (To Be) and a hypothetical example is shown in Figure 18.10 as the green lines. The purpose of the graph in Figure 18.10 is to demonstrate that there has been an improvement of 25 percent fewer team leader positions, with the same number of total staff.

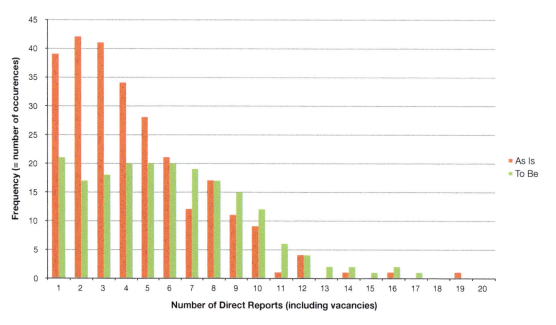

Figure 18.10 Sample Span of Control distribution chart

BPM INSIGHT

Team structure and sizes are important for the optimization of business process execution. Many errors can be traced back to hand-offs and mis-communications between teams; so having a process-focused structure is important.

Remember that structure follows strategy and process redesign.

Organizational structure can, however, be significant in the optimization of the working of an organization. If it is incorrectly designed it can cause process and management disconnects (from a process perspective). It is more important to get things right at the "bottom" of the organization structure, because this is where organizations "get the work done."

As part of the process of determining the ideal organizational structure, the new redesigned process environment must be considered, including how it is to be measured and managed. In fact, the way the processes are to be measured may well provide the answer as to how the organization should be structured. In an operations area, the management exists to "manage" the processes and people, requiring the ability to measure both process and people performance.

Process-focused structured organizations are more difficult to manage because the degree of management skill required is higher. Management need to pay substantial attention to performance measurement, motivation, rewards and culture.

There is no one right solution for an organization's structure; it will depend upon the requirements and circumstances of each organization. However,

there is clearly a wrong solution. The wrong solution places all the power and control with departmental managers and creates incentives for managers based on departmental goals. This almost always results in sub-optimization of overall process improvement and corporate performance.

(Harmon, 2005b)

Organizations have to be adaptable and flexible in order to survive in the long term. This is especially true when change is unpredictable and happening faster and faster. An organization's structure should therefore be fluid and capable of changing in an agile way, continually adapting to the business environment and organization demands.

KEY POINT

Cultural misalignment is one of the key causes when employees are disengaged with their work and employer, especially in the case of contracting or outsourcing arrangements. It is important that the hygiene and motivator factors as outlined in Chapter 7 are identified and adequately addressed.

Step 7: Develop training

During the Understand phase, the organization will have started to identify the information and knowledge needs and to build a capability matrix, which is then extended and completed in the core capability gap analysis step in this phase. This, together with the People Capability Gap Matrix, should be used to develop the training strategy and plan.

It is best to ensure that, as soon as possible, the training department is engaged in the development, and fully informed, of the new activity definitions and role description changes that are taking place. Training and HR need to liaise on a continual basis and should assist in this process.

The activity here is to plan and write the training requirements from a process perspective. The process requirements documentation written during the Develop phase will provide input into this step.

To complete the development of the training, the organization will also need to complete:

* a training needs analysis;
* a training media analysis (how will training be documented and delivered?);
* training material development;
* population of just-in-time training delivery vehicles—it is no use training people well ahead of time and then having them forget the lessons learned.

The development of a process gap analysis between the current processes, modeled during the Understand phase, and the new processes, developed and modeled during the Innovate phase, is extremely useful in developing the training requirements.

Activities to consider during the development of the training include the following:

1. How is the training to be delivered:
   * by professional trainers?
   * by trained "super" users from within the business (this has benefits because of their specialist knowledge of the business and processes, and will allow the internal trainers to go on to be "coaches" during the Implement phase)?
   * via a pilot(s) training session(s), using this as an opportunity to gain feedback and provide "train the trainer" skills?
   * include the "gaps" discovered during the people core capability matrix gap analysis?
   * via computer?

2. Who should be involved in developing the training:
   * project team?
   * HR and training departments?
   * process staff representatives (those who execute the processes)?
   * management?
   * suppliers/vendors?

> ## BPM INSIGHT
>
> It is important to consider all relevant stakeholders for the training. For example an organization in the finance industry was struggling to achieve the desired outcomes with its transformation program because it failed to train the suppliers in the new accounts payable process; especially in the online registration of invoices.

3. What format should be used:

    • classroom?

    • train-the-trainer?

    • online computer-based self-study?

    • on-the-job training?

    • paper-based self-study?

Ensure that the initial training sessions and material include feedback forms that can be used to improve the training as it is rolled out across the organization. Training staff and coaches should also provide feedback.

It should be remembered that training should be accessible for any new personnel as well as refresh courses for existing staff. Incorporating the training as part of online help may assist in meeting this need.

KEY POINT

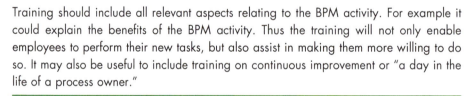

Training should include all relevant aspects relating to the BPM activity. For example it could explain the benefits of the BPM activity. Thus the training will not only enable employees to perform their new tasks, but also assist in making them more willing to do so. It may also be useful to include training on continuous improvement or "a day in the life of a process owner."

Step 8: Update HR policies

Once all the above details have been finalized, the various policy and procedural manuals, job families/groups (roles), remuneration structures and other HR documentation must be updated or written. When considering how to approach the development of these policies, consider the use of a process modeling tool to attach the new policies and procedures documentation at the appropriate points in the processes. This documentation could then be made available over the organization's intranet. Other documentation that may require updating might include remuneration incentive schemes; these must be tied directly to performance measurement and customer satisfaction.

KEY POINT

It is important that policies are completed correctly, especially the monetary related aspects, such as incentive schemes or employee terms and conditions (in case of a merger or acquisition), and sufficient effort is given to address any misconceptions. It is critical to success that staff are not disgruntled or believe they have been disenfranchised by the new HR policies.

REALIZE VALUE

Benefits must be defined in detail in order to gain agreement as part of this phase. For details refer to step 5 of Chapter 21, where it is described in the context of realizing value within a project.

PEOPLE PHASE OUTPUTS

The People phase will provide valuable input into other phases of the framework (refer to Figure 18.11), including the following few examples:

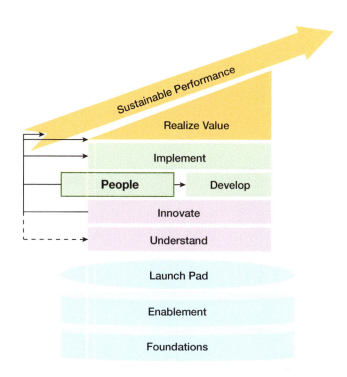

Figure 18.11 People phase outputs to other phases

- working through the performance measurement could indicate that changes are required in the new processes, which will provide feedback, and possible rework, in the Innovate phase;

- how the roles, performance management systems and training are designed will have an impact upon how they are to be implemented; they could also impact how the benefits are to be realized;

- the way the performance management systems have been established will impact their sustainability.

PEOPLE PHASE RISKS

In this phase there are several risks that must be considered and mitigation strategies implemented to eliminate (or at least reduce) them. These risks include those listed in Table 18.5.

SUMMARY

This chapter highlighted the key steps of the People phase. It highlighted the following:

- The importance of the People phase to develop the people and organization aspects of the Target Operating Model.

- The need and method for communication as this phase deals with people's career and job satisfaction.

- The necessity of designing people strategy and determining the guidelines for the organization structure and culture.

- The approach towards defining activities and designing roles.

- Updating the people core capabilities gap analysis.

- The need to (re)design organizational structure, including the reporting structures.

- The approach to develop fit-for-purpose performance management and measurement.

- The considerations for training and updating HR policies.

- The outputs and risks for this phase.

Table 18.5 People phase risks and mitigation strategies

Risk	Mitigation strategy
1. Communications to people within the organization are not adequate	Communication is the responsibility of the project manager, who should seek the assistance of HR and communications specialists within the organization and the business. Employees and stakeholders should be fully informed at all times.
2. Judging the performance of people within the organization before the process and structural issues have been addressed	Define the processes, new roles, understand and update the People Capability Matrix, provide appropriate and targeted training and create performance measures and implement them, before the people are evaluated regarding their performance.
3. Capacity planning is not complete	Schedule this into the project plan and convince stakeholders and management of its importance.
4. Staff performance targets are unrealistic, as the business unit is understaffed	Capacity planning will provide this information.
5. People not being consulted or engaged in the performance measurement establishment	Change management is a critical aspect to any project. Unless people are part of the journey, they may refuse to accept the changes and use them.
6. HR is not being engaged early enough or at all	If HR is not involved, the impact, rework and delay could be considerable. HR's involvement must be a task in the project plan at a very early stage. Allocate the responsibility for this, and the project manager is to ensure the task is achieved. Provide as much notice as possible to HR of their required time involvement.
7. Communication regarding restructuring is "leaked" prior to official release	Make sure to have controlled communication and ensure that all people involved understand their role and responsibilities.

SELF-TEST

1 Which aspects of the Target Operating Model are covered in this stage and why are they important?

2 What are the elements of the people strategy?

3 What steps are taken to derive the organization structure?

4 Which considerations should be taken into account for training?

ASSIGNMENT

During the Launch pad and Understand phases it became evident that major changes will occur for the staff. For example there will be less focus on data entry and more on providing student service.

Assignment guiding questions

1. Determine the relationship between the extent of cultural activity and the chosen BPM approach and describe its impact.
2. Describe the key roles for a student on-boarding officer and their required skills.
3. What type of training would you recommend and why?

People phase checklist

This checklist provides a generic overview of possible inputs, deliverables and gates of this phase.

Possible inputs

See Table 18.6.

Deliverables

See Table 18.7.

Possible gates

- HR policy inflexibility
- Employee council or trade union inflexibility
- Stakeholder analysis
- Understanding magnitude of change
- Organization's capacity to change
- Organization's acceptance of BPM.

Table 18.6 People phase—possible inputs

✓	Source	Deliverable
	Foundation phase	• Organization's core value proposition • BPM maturity of the organization • BPM drivers • BPM activities width • Red Wine Test outcomes • BPM approach • Components of the target operating model
	Enablement phase	• An agreed target operating model • Level 1 and 2 process views • Process architecture, including: o Process guidelines o Process asset repository o Business rules repository o Benefits management framework • Methods by which the people process capability will be built • Organizational cultural behavior changes by the establishment of appropriate targets (KPIs) and linked rewards • Code of behavior • The process-focused organizational design • The technology approach to BPM
	Launch pad phase	• Stakeholders defined in, involved in or associated with the BPM • Stakeholder engagement, commitment, and documented and agreed expectations • Process selection matrix and initial metrics • A list of identified high level business processes and initial metrics • A list of agreed process goals • Agreement of the process governance for the processes in the BPM activity • Prioritized processes for the Understand phase • An initial implementation approach: o Project management o Project charter documents o Project scope (initial) document o Initial draft of the project schedule (plan) o Determination and documentation on the initial communications strategy o Initial risk analysis • Potential project benefits and realization plan • Initial business case
	Understand phase	• Process models of current processes • People Capability Matrix • Knowledge and information needs

continued . . .

Table 18.6 People phase—possible inputs—*continued*

✓	Source	Deliverable
	From Innovate phase	• A list of agreed process goals • New process models and documentation • Capacity planning information • Stakeholder engagement, commitment, and documented and agreed expectations • Process gap analysis • Project plan (in detail) for Develop phase • Updated communications plan • People Capability Matrix for new processes • Refined and optimized benefits mix
	From Develop phase	• High level overview of the solution • Detailed business requirements
	Other input	• HR policies and guidelines • Existing job descriptions and roles

Table 18.7 People phase—deliverables

✓	Deliverable	Used in phase
	People strategy documentation	• Implement phase • Sustainable performance phase
	New roles descriptions	• Implement phase • Sustainable performance phase
	Role measurement (goals) creation	• Develop phase • Implement phase • Sustainable performance phase
	Performance measures	• Develop phase • Implement phase • Sustainable performance phase
	People core capabilities gap analysis	• Implement phase • Sustainable performance phase
	Redesigned organization structure	• Implement phase • Sustainable performance phase
	Updated HR policies	• Implement phase • Sustainable performance phase
	Training documentation	• Develop phase • Implement phase • Sustainable performance phase
	Defined benefits details (from Realize value phase)	• Implement phase • Sustainable performance phase
	Communication of the results	• Used in People phase

CHAPTER 19

DEVELOP PHASE

OVERVIEW

During the Develop phase the automation components of the solution are developed. This chapter explains the key questions that need to be asked when developing the solution: it covers the age-old question of whether to re-use, make or buy as well as the more recent question of choosing waterfall versus agile. Finally it also addresses aspects of testing.

OVERALL LEARNING OUTCOME

By the end of this chapter you will be able to understand the:

- Importance of the Develop phase and the related steps
- Key decisions to be made regarding automation
- Need for updated functional and technical specification
- Various options available, such as re-use, buy, build, outsource or Business Process as a Service (BPaaS)
- Key decisions that need to be made regarding approach: waterfall versus agile and business (process) requirements versus system driven
- Software development approach
- Need for hardware deployment
- Need for the various testing.

WHY?

It has previously been stressed that a BPM project need not involve a technology solution in order to be successful, and in fact in Chapter 6 it was argued that it is important to improve business processes before automating them. Chapter 7 introduced the various technology components of a BPMS. The Develop phase (Figure 19.1) includes the steps necessary to take the newly redesigned or improved processes from the Innovate phase to the Implement phase. The standard development steps will not be described in detail, as most of these steps will be generally standard to an IT department and the BPM activity team. This chapter will concentrate on describing the development of an automated BPM solution (that will have been selected in the previous phases) and the specific topics around an automated BPM solution versus a "standard" automated solution.

This is the phase where the preparations must be completed and the solution prepared. It is then followed by the Implement phase. It is important to understand that "develop" in this context should be completed in parallel with the People phase in which the people component is elaborated.

Care should be taken when developing a new system; it should provide sufficient flexibility to meet business changes in the near future and over its lifetime, and to cater for the frequent changes of the business processes. Furthermore, it is important to understand that during the time it takes to develop the BPM system during this phase, the business processes can also change. The systems development methodology used must be able to

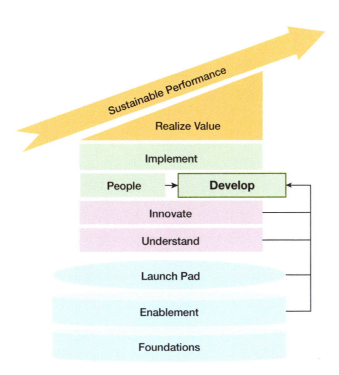

Figure 19.1 Develop phase

CASE STUDY

An audit was conducted of a troubled enterprise resource planning (ERP) implementation. The business ran at an acceptable 95 percent plus on time delivery and after introducing the ERP system it dropped to as low as around 30 percent. The volume of calls was so large that the entire call center called in sick for three days. It became obvious that the implementation was flawed. The business had taken a global functional view, where all the BPM activity streams were working in silos leveraging the technical perspective, while no one looked at the end-to-end customer view, and many orders were being lost in the interfaces between the functional silos.

Message: It is crucial to always look at the end-to-end process view, even when you are automating the processes and using standard ERP packages.

The devil is in the detail

A telecommunications organization had an ambitious marketing department that introduced a new bonus incentive, but forgot to inform the systems department. As a result, the manager of the systems department had to read an advertisement in a newspaper to become aware that his department was required to enhance systems to be able to deliver the promises of the advertisement. In an emergency meeting, it was decided that the required changes would be made within 24 hours. The marketing department stated: "We don't care what it costs, just make the change to enable us to provide the features that we have promised in our advertisement." A programmer made the changes to the system overnight, and everything seemed to work nicely. However, because of choices made to provide this quick fix, more than half of all the future marketing activities could not be supported by the system—a clear case of organizational suboptimization.

Message: Reflect on system changes and their impact before making them, and ensure that all stakeholders are involved.

accommodate this situation. Unless this is the case, the delivered system may become a legacy system upon implementation, and will seriously hamper the agility of the organization and its business processes.

KEY POINT

The key limitations in most systems are not due to technology constraints, but due to incorrect design decisions that do not leverage the technology used.

The concept behind a BPM automation solution is that with BPM technology it is now possible for the business rules and process components of an application to be extracted into their own "layers." Smith and Fingar (2002) believe that a BPM system comprises three broad areas, as shown in Figure 19.2:

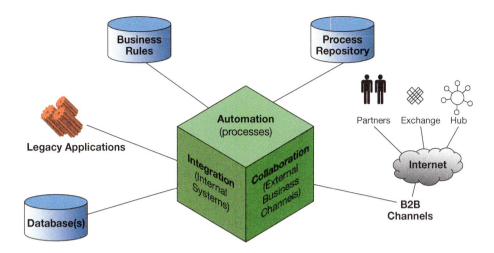

Figure 19.2 Business Process Management System

1. Integration of internal systems (EAI component).

2. Automation of what they refer to as processes (business rules and process repositories—a process asset).

3. Collaboration with external entities—customers, business partners, distribution channels, hubs and business exchanges of information.

While the individual technology components have been around for some time, it is the integration of these various components, together with the growing process-focused thinking, that have made the difference.

If we could look into the future, it is arguable that the legacy application systems that have served large organizations so well, and yet provided significant constraints on them, will have the potential of "only" being:

- large data storage and management repositories;

- large batch processing modules, for the batch jobs that large organizations require (for example renewals processing within an insurance organization);

- large batch or volume reporting and printing drivers (for example, again, printing renewals for insurance organizations, if they are not already outsourced, or large volumes of reports).

Recent changes in technology mean that it is easier to develop and implement an automated BPM solution than in the past (assuming that it is approached correctly). Furthermore, current technology allows the business to become more directly involved with the development and management of these systems. In other words, the business can drive the automation of a BPM system.

Business Process as a Service (BPaaS) combines Business Process Outsourcing (BPO) and Software as a Service (SaaS). They provide an alternate model where existing offerings can be leveraged and various payment types can be offered, including pay as you go. This provides not just another option to an organization regarding their automation, it fundamentally changes the way requirements are gathered.

RESULTS

The deliverables for this phase are:

1. a high-level overview of the solution
2. detailed business requirements, unless already completed earlier
3. finalized software selection documentation
4. software specification/design
5. software development/configuration
6. software test scripts and results
7. hardware specification
8. hardware availability
9. hardware test scripts and results
10. integration test scripts and results.

HOW?

There are basically two ways to develop an automated BPM solution: the traditional waterfall approach of Software Development Life Cycle (SDLC) or the iterative and agile approach of Rapid Application Development (RAD). This chapter will be approached differently from the other phases, as we will provide a few high level steps (Figure 19.3) that should be considered when implementing an automated BPM solution. Detailed steps for SDLC and RAD are well covered in other publications, and are outside the scope of this book.

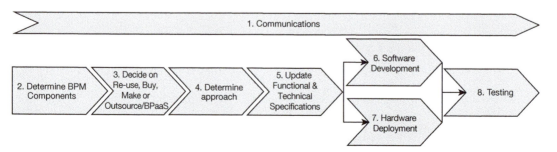

Figure 19.3 Develop phase steps

DETAILED STEPS

Step 1: Communications

During the Develop phase it is important to communicate the scope and proposed extent of the automation to all stakeholders. It is also important to address the main questions that arise in the case of automation:

- Will I keep my job?
- What new skills will I need?
- How will my job change?

Automation might also influence the interaction with suppliers, partners and customers. With web services and service-oriented architecture, it becomes much easier to integrate processes across the borders of the organization. If this is the case, the communication should also extend to the related parties, ensuring that not only the benefits and impact of automation are specified, but also the progress, issues and potential delays.

Step 2: Determine BPM components

One of the first decisions in the Develop phase is which automated BPM components are required—this is about making a decision regarding the "tools" that will be required (see Figure 19.4). This may well be a point where it is not so much about making the decision as finalizing it. Several of the tools may already have been purchased for earlier phases of the project (such as process modeling and design components, for the process asset repository), and others may have been addressed during the Innovate phase (such as use of business rules engine and/or a work management module).

An automated solution may consist of the components shown and discussed in detail in Chapter 7.

KEY POINT

It is important to realize that benefits for a BPM activity can be multiplied if multiple modules are used.

Work management effectiveness can be increased if a business rules engine is used, integrated with a document management system that includes the automated handling of documents. While at the same time business analytics could be used to handle exceptions.

When automating parts of a process, the major challenge that a BPM activity will face is obtaining the data that the process requires. These data may be scattered over multiple legacy systems. Based on the ease of gathering the data, the BPM activity needs to determine which automated BPM components it intends to use during the development of the solution.

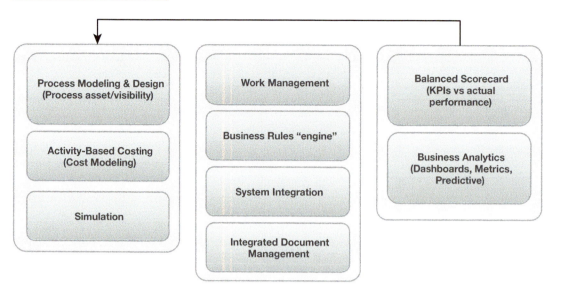

Figure 19.4 BPM components of an automated solution

Number of systems

An automated solution will more than likely involve more than one component—for example a work management system, an automated business rules engine and an integrated document management system. In a situation with multiple automated components, consideration should be given how best to integrate the various components.

> ## BPM INSIGHT
>
> Some organizations wish to have the "best of breed" for all the applications in the business to achieve the required functionality perfectly without realizing that this requires a very high capability for integration within the organization's IT department.
>
> Organizations that do not have a high integration capability will be much better served settling for a limited number of different applications to reduce the dependency on integration, even if this means settling for an 80–90 percent match to the required functionality.

Step 3: Decide on re-use, buy, make, outsource or BPaaS

The next decision for the project is what approach it wishes to adopt with regard to make or buy for the various software components. The following options are available.

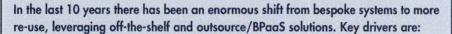

BPM INSIGHT

In the last 10 years there has been an enormous shift from bespoke systems to more re-use, leveraging off-the-shelf and outsource/BPaaS solutions. Key drivers are:

- high cost of developing your own systems
- high risks of developing your own systems
- limited flexibility of bespoke systems (including challenges in upgrading solution).

Re-use of an existing system

Many organizations have a wide variety of systems in their IT landscape. Hence, before considering any other options, it is worthwhile to assess whether any of the existing systems can be re-used. This includes solutions in other regions, business units and merged and acquired organizations.

Main advantages:

- synergy and economies of scale;
- the system is known and has proved itself.

Main disadvantage or issue:

- the system may not meet all the current requirements or doesn't provide sufficient flexibility for likely new requirements.

Buy an off-the-shelf product that can be configured

Many BPM vendors are now offering "skeletons" of applications that are designed to be significant starting points for an organization. Some have even developed full "vanilla" service offerings for specific industries and domains.

They are not expected to provide a total solution, but can supply a simple framework that the organization can enhance (configure) to meet its specific requirements. This can be a significant advantage to an organization (and BPM activity) if one is available for the desired application and that predominantly meets the requirements of the business. Examples of these "skeleton" solutions include: insurance claims processing, various telecommunications applications and loan processing.

Main advantages:

- the chance to obtain a suitable product or starting point at lower cost and development risk;
- a solution that meets a specific situation of the organization and marketplace;
- product support is available.

Main disadvantages or issues:

- additional upfront costs for modification, although it could end up saving costs;
- it is essential that the initial skeleton configuration predominantly meets the requirements of the organization, otherwise it will become an instant legacy system (configuration of a new package is like pouring concrete—when applying it is very flexible, but afterwards it sets rock solid);
- development of a system against immature requirements, which may limit future flexibility.

Develop a new system

This is the development of a bespoke system, and as a general rule should be avoided if at all possible.

Main advantage:

- the system can be fully customized and configured for the organization.

Main disadvantages or issues:

- considerable development cost and time and ongoing operating costs;
- project risks include late delivery, low quality and higher costs.

Outsource the application

This is increasingly an option for an organization, and should be seriously considered, especially with the possibility that Cloud computing provides.

Main advantages:

- makes use of the existing knowledge and processes of the in-sourcer;
- use of economies of scale and synergy.

Main disadvantages or issues:

- cost involved in the handover to the outsourcer;
- lack of flexibility.

Business Process as a Service (BPaaS)

This is a recent phenomenon which combines Business Process Outsourcing and Software as a Service. With BPaaS an agreed service is provided by either the internal IT department or by an outsourcer, the underlying process is like a black box and the relevant business rules are agreed. For example with a credit check the company can choose to leverage BPaaS where it provides real-time electronic credit card details in an agreed format and will get instant feedback regarding the credit worthiness of the concerned individual or company. This uses agreed business rules.

Some people see service as fundamentally different from process, see Figure 19.5. Others believe that service is the end-result of the process, seen in Figure 19.6.

Figure 19.5
Process and Service seem different

Figure 19.6
Service is the result of the Process

Main advantages:

- makes use of existing systems, knowledge and process of the in-sourcer;
- flexible pricing and options of "pay as you go";
- use of economies of scale and synergy.

Main disadvantage or issue:

- ensure right credentials of parties concerned.

Step 4: Determine approach

The two key approaches that need to be decided upon are:

1. waterfall versus agile;
2. requirements (process) led or system led.

Waterfall

Waterfall is the traditional way of development. The scope is specified upfront and the development time and budget are subsequently specified. Typically, there is one main release, but there could be several.

Typical advantages:

- upfront clarity around what will be delivered;
- people are familiar with this approach;
- seemingly easy to manage.

Typical disadvantages or pitfalls:

- big scope of work to concentrate on throughout the project
- cost and time overruns are difficult to compensate as the BPM activity needs to be completed to deliver release
- delays typically hold up the complete release
- budget and window of opportunity could be completed prior to delivery of the deliverables, increasing likelihood of terminating the project without any tangible outcome
- difficult to make any changes to the scope due to changes in internal and external focus.

Agile or Rapid Application Development (RAD)

Agile is an iterative way of development. The budget and times are specified upfront and the required functionality is delivered in multiple releases (delivered through sprints), where the high value release is developed first. The productivity is measured and managed throughout the BPM activity.

Typical advantages:

- the first release is comparatively quick and there is an ability to correct things during subsequent releases (sprints);
- ability to re-prioritize during the BPM activity;
- each release (sprint) has limited (or small) scope, enabling people to concentrate;
- if the BPM activity is terminated earlier (e.g., budget cuts) the highest value releases have already been delivered.

Typical disadvantages or pitfalls:

- many people don't understand agile as they think it is more like development on the fly and has less documentation (which is not true as agile requires significant discipline);
- upfront there is no confirmation that can be provided of the complete scope of all sprints.

Agile method is often mistakenly seen as a method that does not require good documentation or stringent software development discipline. It is the opposite: agile provides flexibility in the outcome provided that the documentation and development method is strictly adhered to.

KEY POINT

Agile provides a lot of benefits. However, it is critically important that the agile methodology is followed correctly. BPM activities can fail with agile because of the incorrect execution of the agile methodology.

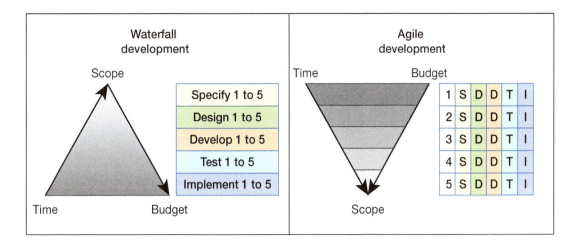

Figure 19.7 Visualization of Waterfall and Agile development

Requirements (process) led approach

The business determines the requirements based on the strategic objectives and optimized processes.

The next step is to determine the most suitable solution, including the selection of the solution.

Main advantages:

- complete freedom to determine the most suitable business requirements;
- most suitable solution is selected.

Main disadvantages:

- can lead to increased costs as much needs to be developed;
- can take longer time to complete.

Most suited for:

- development of own solution;
- buy off-shelf product/outsource/BPaaS (after product selection).

System led approach

The organization has already selected the system to be used, for example re-use of existing system, or global system. Especially as many systems have no out-of-the box solutions and industry and domain reference models.

The next step is to determine fit-gap analysis where the offered functionality is validated against the desired business requirements.

Main advantages:

* can be faster;
* leverage existing system functionality resulting in lower costs.

Main disadvantages:

* may result in not selecting the most suitable solution;
* system can become more dominant than the business process requirements.

Most suited for:

* Re-use of existing system;
* Outsource/BPaaS to pre-selected vendor.

CASE STUDY

Wrong project approach

An audit was completed on a project where the costs had blown-out by over 50 percent resulting in a $20-million cost overrun. It became quite evident that the project had started from a requirements led approach where they were planning to build their own system. During the course of the project they decided to buy a best of breed billing solution which had many processes readily available. However, the project did not change their approach as they spent a great deal of money and time customizing the solution with little or no benefit and they ended up with a system that was not fit for their purpose. In hindsight, they would have been much better off using the standard functionality and just changed the business rules.

Message: Choosing the development method is critical and needs to be followed throughout all steps of the Develop phase. Any change to the development method needs to be realistically assessed, agreed, communicated and adhered to.

Step 5: Update functional and technical specifications

There must be a structured approach to the specifications (functional, technical and system or design) development and testing of the BPM solution, and this is shown in Figure 19.8. The V-diagram provides the "missing links" between the specifications themselves and the specifications and testing. The missing links shown in this figure are often the root cause of why many development projects have failed in the past.

The left-hand side of the figure shows the business requirements and related design documents, and the right-hand side shows the testing to verify that what is produced by the

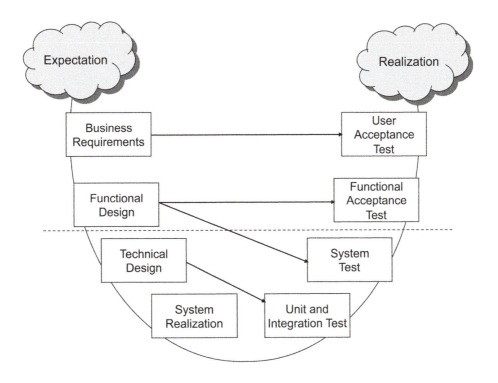

Figure 19.8 V-diagram: linking specification, development and testing of software

development team conforms to these requirements and designs. The challenge is to ensure that the expectations are fulfilled from a business perspective, and it is the business that decides whether this has been achieved. The boxes above the dotted line relate to the functionality, while the boxes below the dotted line refer to the technical aspects.

A common problem during the Develop phase is conflict between what the business wants and how the developers interpret the requirements. This is often a function of how these two stakeholders work together and understand the implications of this working relationship.

How many times have we all heard of situations where the business writes a specification of its requirements, technical staff then rewrite this into a technically based functional specification, predominantly in terms that the business finds difficult to understand, and in order to meet the delivery timeframe gives the business three days to sign it off? The business not only has difficulty in understanding the technical language used, but at the same time has a business to run—and so the three-day timeframe is extremely difficult to meet. To avoid delays, the business signs off on the functional specification without fully understanding the consequences. The development team now designs the new BPM system and delivers it to the business. During the testing phase the stakeholders complain that the system does not meet their expectations, saying, "this is not what we wanted!" The development team's response is, "yes it is, refer to page 179 of the signed-off technical design specification." The business then replies, "well, it is not what we meant!" The project is then in rework mode, resulting in longer times, greater costs and potential business opportunity losses.

This is the traditional SDLC approach, and it generates a higher risk situation in a BPM activity than is desirable.

These risks can be minimized in several ways, including the following:

1. Perform "what if?" analysis.
2. Perform simulations.
3. Specify what is out of scope.
4. The business requirements should be developed as part of the Innovate phase and the functional design written during the Develop step. However, it is extremely important to have the business working closely with technical development staff and to write the functional design document jointly. The business needs to be able to sign off on the document, clearly understanding the consequences and ensuring that the requirements are consistent with and add value to the business strategy and objectives. A good way to ensure that the business understands the business requirements is to write them from a process perspective.
5. Separate the functional design and the technical design.
6. Specify and seek agreement on the consequences of the development.
7. As described in Chapter 14, it is important to use the architecture in a flexible way—for example what do you do if there is an urgent business requirement and the solution does not fit in the architecture? One of the options that could be considered is to allow the requirement to be developed and to make clear rules on how to deal with this exception—such as the solution should be phased out after a small number of months, or the solution should comply with the architecture within a defined number of months. This "pressure cooker" mechanism is very important, as the ultimate test of an architecture is how it deals with exceptions. Ignoring or rejecting all exceptions may appear to win but will eventually lose the war as people ignore the architecture on an increasing basis.
8. It is crucial to include both the software and hardware requirements, as in most cases there is a dependency between the two.

An important issue when dealing with software is the use of relevant standards. With the growing technical possibilities, such as XML, web services and service-oriented architecture (SOA), it is becoming increasingly possible to extend process automation possibilities well beyond the boundaries of the organization and to suppliers, customers and partners. This will provide more efficiency and speed.

For a brief discussion on standards refer to Chapter 7.

Traceability

While updating the requirements it is crucial that traceability of the business requirements to the strategic objectives, pain points, process and solution is maintained. This applies to both a waterfall and agile approach, although some agile projects seem to neglect thorough documentation.

Stringent application of traceability ensures that integrity is maintained. Without traceability it becomes difficult to:

- track initial strategic and pain-point analysis to business requirements;
- link business requirements to process aspects;
- link requirements to benefits;
- provide audit trails;
- streamline sign-off of requirements.

BPM INSIGHT

BPM activities with good traceability have typically less issues with conflicting requirements and software because there is an increased understanding of the business requirements. Traceability is only achieved if it is adhered to throughout all the steps of the BPM activity.

Business Process Architecture Committee

During this phase of the BPM activity many decisions and interpretations have to be made. These decisions need to be considered not just from the BPM activity point of view, but also from an organization point of view, as the BPM activity needs to fit in with the overall systems landscape.

The Business Process Architecture Committee has been explained in Chapters 14 and 15.

During the Develop Phase the committee is responsible for the completion of the target operating model and execution of the TOM during the course of the BPM activity. They will make more detailed content decisions than the Steering Committee.

BPM INSIGHT

Some BPM activities use the Steering Committee for all decision making, including detailed design issues. Most Steering Committee members don't have the required insight, knowledge or time to make the right decisions. It is better to have a separate Business Process Architecture Committee looking at this on behalf of the Steering Committee.

Step 6: Software development

Basically, any automated BPM solution will have three layers to consider:

1. Presentation layer of the solution to the user.

2. Processing layer containing the automated tasks.

3. Integration layer to other systems and databases containing the data.

It is crucial to understand that each of these three layers needs a different approach to both development and testing, as it involves different groups of people.

1. The *presentation layer* is focused on the end-users and represents their view to the system. Issues to consider are:

   • is it a view that end-users are familiar with and revolves around does the solution have a logical look and feel (that is, is it similar to existing/other systems or does it have a logical flow of the screens)?

   • different types of users will have different needs and ways of interacting with the systems (for example employees, controllers, managers, etc.).

2. The *processing layer* deals with the activities that the system needs to perform. This should be completed with people who have a good understanding of the business as well as the objectives of the BPM activity. An important issue to consider is the documentation; with the growing popularity of pilots, RAD and BPM tools development, there is a growing tendency not to document at all, or not in as much detail as is required. The developers' argument is that the documentation is implicit in the configuration of the system and can be reviewed there. Looking at the system will provide an overview of *what* has been configured, but will not provide the information on *why* this configuration has been chosen. Without the insight into the decisions behind the configuration, it becomes difficult to make changes in the future with any degree of certainty that they will be consistent with the original choices.

> ## BPM INSIGHT
>
> Many people struggle to visualize the new solution and find it hard to talk in more abstract and conceptual terms. It is strongly recommend using pilots or prototypes as a way to communicate new concepts with the key stakeholders. This is especially applicable in case of large and fundamental change.

3. The *integration/data layer* is more technical, as it deals with the interfaces with other systems. A deep technical knowledge is required, as well as a clear understanding of the systems to which the automated BPM solutions link.

One of the most challenging aspects of the software development phase of a BPM activity is not just related to the actual development, but also with the migration to the new system. The road to failure is scattered with projects that have underestimated the issues involved with migration and interfaces. It looks so easy, but is deceptively complicated.

Migration from a lay perspective can look easy, as the business models, processes and data have to be transferred from one system to another and it seems that matching the various fields to each system is all that is required. However, it is critical to ensure that the business models, processes and data in the existing system are correct. Experienced practitioners know that users will have been using the system in different ways, and this will mean that the system (and data) contains far more (systematic) errors than thought at first glance.

Should the organization first migrate the current system to the new system and then make the changes, or should it make the changes first in the current system and then migrate to the new system? Often the latter is the preferred solution, as many projects and organizations find themselves unable to make changes in the new system once it is populated.

While doing this targeted analysis, it is important to differentiate between the importance that stakeholders place on their various requirements. The MoSCoW approach (Dynamic Systems Development Method[1]) is a useful approach. This approach breaks down the priority of the requirements into the following categories:

- **M**ust have
- **S**hould have if at all possible
- **C**ould have this if it does not affect anything else
- **W**on't have (in this release), but would like to have it later.

As mentioned before there are two main development approaches: Traditional (SDLC) Waterfall and Agile/RAD approach, described earlier in step 4. Here we will briefly explain the key steps in the actual software development

Option 1: Traditional SDLC approach to development

Figure 19.9 shows the likely steps involved in following a traditional Software Development Life Cycle (SDLC) approach to the development of a BPM activity.

While this approach is a tried, tested and proven way of developing solutions, it is not necessarily the best or most appropriate approach. The most appropriate approach will depend upon the scenario, organization and scale of BPM activity.

The traditional SDLC approach to technology projects requires the project manager to monitor the project at regular intervals to ensure that it is still on track to meet the specified requirements and that the business still supports the original specifications. Too often, the project delivers a software solution after a long period of development and testing, only to find that the business requirements have changed.

Perhaps a more successful approach is the Agile or Rapid Application Development approach.

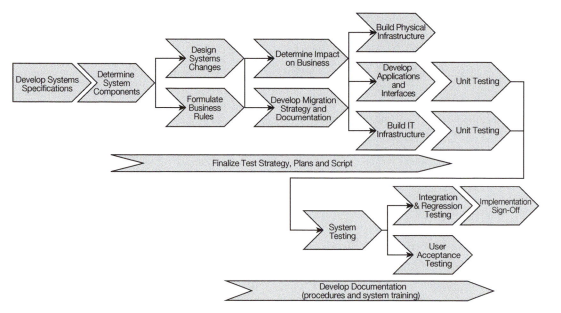

Figure 19.9 Traditional SDLC approach to development of a BPM solution

Option 2: Agile or Rapid Application Development (RAD)

As mentioned previously Agile or RAD approach is based on close interaction between the business and the developers. It is based on an iterative approach where deliverables are produced typically within a one to two week cycle (sprint). This is especially useful in a pilot situation to explore the opportunities that a new BPM solution offers. It will also provide the business with a quick look and feel of how the solution will look and operate. However, when modeling the entire solution it is crucial that the previous 7FE Framework phases are followed, proper specifications are still completed to enable testing and documentation is created for future reference.

Business should be actively involved from the beginning. Waiting passively to just check the end product will not provide the right result, as the agile approach requires active participation.

It is essential that the business provides the information on the processes. Whoever is responsible for the processes needs to be fully aware of the configuration, its place within the larger context of the system, and the consequences of the choices they make. If this is unclear to them, it will inevitably lead to an IT-dominated development and solution. This will result in the business having insufficient knowledge or influence regarding its development and outcomes.

Everyone needs to have an open mind and continue to look for further improvements. Prioritization will ensure that the highest priority activities will be taken up.

Agile's close management helps identify and address issues quickly. They could include:

- daily stand-up ("scrum") to ensure that everyone knows what they are doing, what others are doing and what key impediments need to be addressed;

Figure 19.10 Sample Burn Chart

- daily update of the Burn Chart (actual outstanding work mapped versus ideal outstanding work) provides a good visual regarding progress and improves productivity and team work (see Figure 19.10);
- focus on the velocity of the team (this is an indication of the productivity);
- clear roles around the scrum master, BPM team and business process owner (makes the decision on behalf of the project sponsor).

Many people have a misconception that agile development requires less discipline or less documentation. However, this is not true. Traceability and testing demand appropriate documentation. Furthermore, most failures with agile can be traced back to a lack of either understanding and/or adherence to the method.

As BPM technology improves further, this approach will gain significant momentum and business benefits.

Step 7: Hardware deployment

Hardware can include the following aspects: computers for users, servers, networks, cloud offerings, and related appliances such as laptops, smartphones, printers, scanners and storage media. Preparing for Service Activation needs to be considered in this step as well.

The issues that should be considered include:

- compatibility—are all the systems able to communicate with each other, particularly the interfaces and platforms?
- increases in transaction volumes

- maintenance and support—are all the hardware components assigned to skilled people who can maintain the particular component (including back-up and restore facilities) and provide or arrange for support for users?

Finally, always ensure that the hardware test environment is *exactly* the same as the future production environment. Many systems have tested perfectly in the "laboratory," only to fail in a production environment because the two were not exactly the same.

It is important to note that hardware deployment in the case of Outsourcing or BPaaS is mainly outsourced.

An increasing number of organizations are deploying a Bring Your Own Device (BYOD) policy. This is an option when considering any hardware and software deployment. BYOD has become popular due to an increase of short-term contractors and the fact that many employees have personally more advanced devices than in their office.

BYOD typically brings challenges to organizations to support a multitude of devices and operating systems as well as security issues. The first challenge is typically encountered by supporting a number of devices but not all devices. The second challenge requires strict policy and procedures and could result in insisting on additional software to improve security.

Step 8: Testing

Testing is a crucial step in the Develop phase and has been discussed previously. Testing is the activity when the developed application systems are compared with the original business requirements, assuming the test plans and scripts have been developed appropriately. The International Standards Organization (ISO) describes testing as a:

> **Technical operation that consists of the determination of one or more characteristics of a given product, process or services according to a specified procedure.**[2]

A simpler and arguably more appropriate definition for testing of a software application is:

> **A process of planning, preparing, executing and analyzing, aimed at establishing the characteristics of an information system, and demonstrating the difference between the actual status and the required status.**
>
> **(Pol et al., 2002)**

Testing becomes more critical in circumstances of fundamental business, or large-scale, changes than in shorter or smaller development times. Testing is a crucial activity that must be planned appropriately and in detail, and must not be left too late in the project. Writing test plans and scripts is an activity that should be completed, in detail, at the time of writing the business and functional specifications. If test scenarios and test scripts are completed at this time, it will provide the business and developers with a clearer understanding of the business requirement. The developers will understand the basis upon which their new system will be evaluated, which should further diminish the risks associated with a misunderstanding between the business requirements and the developers' outcomes.

Important issues to consider include the following:

- it is important to remember that more than half the time involved in the testing activities is required to be spent on the preparation and planning, and the remainder on the actual execution of the testing;

- it is nearly impossible and highly undesirable to complete a full 100 percent test, as the costs and timeframes involved will be prohibitive. It is better to complete a structured approach to testing, maximizing the effectiveness and minimizing the effort. The person in charge of testing should always specify the extent of testing, the number of errors and the "test coverage."

It is important to distinguish between the following types of testing (Pol et al., 2002):

- A *unit test* is a test executed by the developers in a laboratory environment that should demonstrate that a particular activity or step of the automated BPM solution meets the requirements established in the design specifications.

- An *integration test* is a test executed by the developer in a laboratory environment that should demonstrate that a function or an aspect of the automated BPM solution meets the requirements established in the design specifications.

- A *system test* is a test executed by the developer in a (properly controlled) laboratory environment that should demonstrate that the automated BPM solution or its components meets the requirements established in the functional and quality specifications.

- A *functional acceptance test* is a test executed by the system manager(s) and test team in an environment simulating the operational environment to the greatest possible extent, which should demonstrate that the automated BPM solution meets the functional and quality requirements as specified in the functional requirements.

- A *user acceptance test* (UAT) is a test executed by the users of the system where, in a shadow operational environment, the automated BPM solution will be tested to demonstrate that it meets the business requirements. This is included in the Implement phase.

- A *regression test* aims to check that all parts of the system still function correctly after the implementation or modification of an automated BPM solution. Regression is a phenomenon to ensure that the quality of the system as a whole has not declined due to individual modifications.

Obviously, the normal testing process should be followed. The usual sequence is as follows:

1. *Determine a test objective*. Testing always involves a balance between the benefits of testing and its associated costs: 100 percent testing is nearly impossible and extremely expensive.

KEY POINT

Regression testing aims to check that all parts of the system still function after any changes. Given the fact that existing systems can be complex and new BPM activities may deal with significant change, regression testing is crucial.

It is strongly recommended to use automated testing for regression testing, as it allows the execution of similar test scripts over and over again in a relatively short time span.

2. *Determine and write a test strategy.* This is a strategy describing how the organization wishes to approach testing. It should include unit testing, user acceptance testing (UAT), integration testing, regression testing and so forth. Consideration should be given to the infrastructure to be employed. *Note*: always try to ensure that an exact copy of the live infrastructure environment is used during the testing stage. Also, remember that not all testing relates to application systems. In a process environment, much of the testing will revolve around "walking" the process through the business and determining that it is fit for purpose.

3. *Write a test plan.* This is where the organization decides on the number and type of test cases to be applied. Remember to ensure that all appropriate stakeholders and other project teams are involved.

4. *Write the various test cases.* The volume of test cases will depend upon the size and complexity of the project. The most important aspect is to cover all of the likely scenarios.

5. *Execute the testing.* The test cases and test scripts are completed.

6. *Review the results and decide on how to proceed.* The options are to go ahead with the implementation; to stop the implementation until the errors are solved; to go ahead with implementation and ensure that changes can be incorporated along the way; or a combination of these three.

Not all these tests are actually performed in this phase, but they will have to be considered here. The user acceptance testing, for example, is prepared and performed as part of steps 3 and 5 in the Implement phase.

REALIZE VALUE

Benefits must be defined in detail in order to gain agreement as part of this phase. For details refer to step 5 of Chapter 21, where it is described in the context of realizing value within a project.

DEVELOP PHASE OUTPUTS

The Develop phase will provide valuable input into other phases of the framework (see Figure 19.11), and a few examples are mentioned here:

- the proposed solution could impose requirements on the people who have to work with the system;

- the Develop phase will provide input for the training during the Implementation phase;

- the proposed system might provide functionality that gives the business additional opportunities; alternatively, the development might not be able to provide all the requested functionality as specified in the Innovate phase, in which case the same people who prepared the specification after the Innovate phase must be involved;

- the Develop phase should ensure that sustainable performance is created;

- the development of software could impact changes in the process architecture (especially the relevant information and technology).

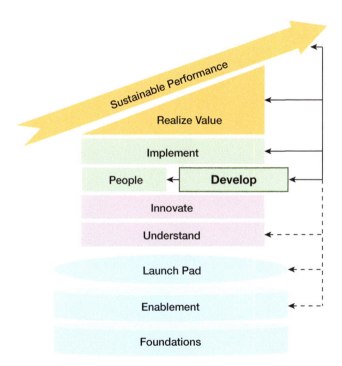

Figure 19.11 Develop phase outputs to other phases

DEVELOP PHASE RISKS

In this phase there are several risks that must be considered and mitigation strategies implemented to eliminate (or at least reduce) them. These risks include those listed in Table 19.1.

Table 19.1 Develop phase risks and mitigation strategies

Risk	Mitigation strategy
1. Developed solution does not meet the business requirements	Ensure that the stakeholders are involved throughout the BPM activity and that they fully understand all the decisions made and the resulting consequences. Work on the basis of the agreed process architecture and business case (deviations from both should be agreed with all those concerned).
2. Some applications work, however, the overall solution does not work	For example a cause could be that one or more of the interfaces do not work correctly. Ensure that the initial design takes all interfaces and interoperability into account.
3. Testing finds too many errors	Ensure that the requirements (functional and technical design) are explicit and clear enough to be used as a basis for the systems development, as well as preparing the test scripts.
4. Cost of the solution becomes too high	Manage deviations and customization in a thorough and transparent manner.

SUMMARY

In this chapter you have learned:

- The importance of the Develop phase and the related steps.
- Key decisions to be made regarding automation.
- The need for updated functional and technical specification.
- The various options available, such as re-use, buy, build, outsource or BPaaS.
- Key decisions that need to be made regarding approach: waterfall versus agile; and requirements led versus system driven.
- Software development approach.
- The need for hardware deployment.
- The need for the various testing approaches.

SELF-TEST

1 What are the various solution options regarding system development?

2 What are the main differences between agile and waterfall?

3 What are the main differences between requirements led and system led development?

4 Why is traceability of requirement important?

5 What are the various test scenarios that need to be performed?

ASSIGNMENT

Only answer these questions if you are completing the Option 3 approach to the assignment.

Assignment guiding questions

1. What would be the three IT components that you recommend for the student administration system and why?
2. Would you re-use, buy, make, outsource or BPaaS the student administration and why?
3. Would you use an agile or waterfall approach for the development?

Develop phase checklist

This checklist provides a generic overview of possible inputs, deliverables and gates of this phase.

Possible inputs

See Table 19.2.

Deliverables

See Table 19.3.

Possible gates

- Development and testing hardware and software configuration not the same as it will be in the live environment
- Stakeholder analysis
- Understanding magnitude of change
- Organization's capacity to change
- Organization's acceptance of BPM
- Technical difficulties
- Testing difficulties.

Table 19.2 Develop phase—possible inputs

✓	Source	Deliverable
	Foundation phase	• Organization's core value proposition • BPM maturity of the organization • BPM drivers • BPM activities width • Red Wine Test outcomes • BPM approach • Components of the target operating model
	Enablement phase	• An agreed target operating model • Level 1 and 2 process views • Process architecture, including: o Process guidelines o Process asset repository o Business rules repository o Benefits management framework • Methods by which the people process capability will be built • Organizational cultural behavior changes by the establishment of appropriate targets (KPIs) and linked rewards • Code of behavior • The process-focused organizational design • The technology approach to BPM
	Launch pad phase	• Stakeholders defined in, involved in or associated with the BPM • Stakeholder engagement, commitment, and documented and agreed expectations • Process selection matrix and initial metrics • A list of identified high level business processes and initial metrics • A list of agreed process goals • Agreement of the process governance for the processes in the BPM activity • Prioritized processes for the Understand phase • An initial implementation approach • Project management: o Project charter documents o Project scope (initial) document o Initial draft of the project schedule (plan) o Determination and documentation on the initial communications strategy o Initial risk analysis • Potential project benefits and realization plan • Initial business case
	Understand phase	• Process models of current processes • Knowledge and information needs
	Innovate phase	• List of agreed process goals • New process models and documentation

Table 19.2 Develop phase—possible inputs—*continued*

✓	Source	Deliverable
		• Simulation models • Process gap analysis • Updated process selection matrix • Metrics for the various Innovate scenarios • Project plan (in detail) for People and Develop phases • Initial business requirements • Refined and optimized benefits mix (from Realize value phase)
	From People phase	• Role measurement (goals) creation • Training documentation • Performance measures
	Other input	• List of relevant projects to determine synergy and overlap • Enterprise or IT Architecture

Table 19.3 Develop phase—deliverables

✓	Deliverable	Used in phase
	High level overview of the solution	• People phase • Implement phase • Sustainable performance phase
	Detailed business requirements	• People phase • Implement phase
	Software selection documentation	• For Develop phase only
	Software specification and design	• For Develop phase only
	Software development and configuration	• For Develop phase only
	Software test scripts and results	• Implement phase
	Hardware specifications and availability	• For Develop phase only
	Hardware test scripts and results	• For Develop phase only
	Integration test scripts and results	• Implement phase
	Defined benefits details (from Realize value phase)	• Realize value phase • Sustainable performance phase
	Communication of the results.	• For Develop phase only

CHAPTER 20

IMPLEMENT PHASE

OVERVIEW

The Implement phase deals with the actual roll-out of the new processes, the updated people design and, if appropriate, any developed IT solutions. This is the phase where a start is made of realizing the benefits outlined in the business case.

OVERALL LEARNING OUTCOME

By the end of this chapter you will be able to understand the:

- Importance of the Implement phase and the main steps
- Importance and approach for communication
- Necessity to market the project internally and its benefits to clients and vendors
- Approach to user acceptance testing and training
- Need to update deliverables and complete planning
- Importance of monitoring, adjusting and providing feedback
- Risks involved in the implementation and the possible mitigation strategies.

WHY?

The Implement phase (Figure 20.1) is the phase where all the designed process improvements, people and organizational design, and developed system solutions will actually be "brought to life." It is also the phase where many of the people change management activities come together. Although this is one of the last parts of the framework and project cycle, it needs

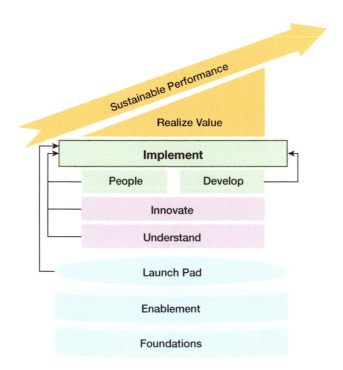

Figure 20.1 Implement phase

to be considered at the very start of each project and as early as the Launch pad phase, for it is at the start of the BPM activity that the decision should be made regarding how the implementation will take place within the business (see Chapter 15 for details). The implementation decision will impact upon many facets of the BPM activity—areas such as how processes are designed or redesigned, how development and testing may be conducted and so forth. The decision will be continually reviewed during the life of the BPM activity, recognizing that the method of implementation may change.

KEY POINT

BPM activities are challenging, especially transformation programs, as the organization still needs to function effectively during the execution of the BPM activity.

The Implement phase is crucial as it is not just a test of whether the designed people, process and technology solution delivered by the BPM activity is fit for purpose, allowing business-as-usual to be conducted. But also if the benefits designated in the business case can be realized.

It is like a supply ship that aims to meet a cruiser somewhere on the ocean. The timing and the determination of the target state (where they will cross paths) need to align to make sure that both arrive at the same place at the same time.

CASE STUDY

Implementation too little too late

A review of a failed BPM project was conducted. The project sponsor was surprised that his project had failed; all metrics were established at the start, the technology worked, the main stakeholders received weekly briefings, and the users were informed through a massive poster campaign, email bombardment and extensive training.

Users were interviewed and it was found that they were not consulted about the proposed changes, which were built on incorrect assumptions and would not work in practice. When we asked the BPM activity sponsor at what stage of the project the users were consulted and informed about the changes, we found that the project only did this after the redesigned processes had been created, with the assistance of an external consultant.

Message: Business users must be included very early in a BPM activity, as indeed must all stakeholders, and then continually throughout.

RESULTS

When the Implement phase is completed well, the organization can expect to have:

- trained and motivated staff;
- improved or new processes that work satisfactorily, according to the identified stakeholders' requirements and needs, and as outlined in the business case;
- the specified benefits in the business case realized.

HOW?

BPM activities often fail because implementation is merely restricted to being one of the closing steps, and mainly being centered on one-way communication to inform the staff and other stakeholders of the benefits of the new solution for the organization. Moreover, most activities are focused on ensuring that users of the processes can use the new solution (for example, training), and not on whether users want to use the new processes (that is motivation of staff).

The best way to ensure a smooth implementation is to start considering implementation issues at the initiation of the BPM activity. Only then will the Implement phase be focused on updating the information and performing the tasks, rather than thinking of last-minute ways to appease the users.

The coffee machine test

Involvement of users and stakeholders is frequently spoken about but is not often achieved. There is a test to assess, in a simple and non-scientific way, the involvement of users.

Just go and ask people at the coffee machine about the proposed process improvements. If you receive answers like:

- "I have no idea what they are doing"
- "they gave a pep talk, but I have not heard any more details"
- "they never inform us anyway"

you know you have clear signs of non-involvement of users and insufficient or ineffective communication.

Occasionally BPM activities occur where the people involved in the BPM activity do not defend it when their colleagues speak negatively about it. This is often a clear indication of lack of confidence and pride in the BPM activity. This can stem from the lack of people change management activities and resulting commitment of these people.

Message: It doesn't matter how large the benefits are that you expect to gain from the BPM activity; if you don't communicate these benefits to stakeholders and users, you will find it difficult or impossible to realize these benefits.

DETAILED STEPS

Figure 20.2 illustrates the steps that are applicable in the Implement phase, and these are discussed below.

Step 1: Update implementation strategy and plan

At the beginning of the project the implementation strategy should have been determined. When the Implement phase is reached, it is crucial to complete a review of the original implementation strategy because:

- the project team and the organization will have a much better understanding of the proposed changes;
- the implementation strategy has to take the current situation into account, and this may (and probably will) have changed since the initial determination of the implementation strategy.

Table 20.1 gives examples of the types of strategies that should be considered.

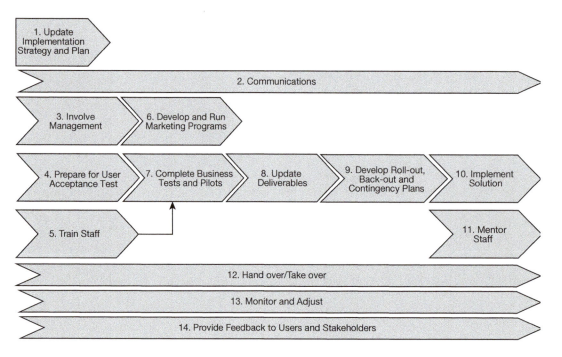

Figure 20.2 Implement phase steps

Step 2: Communications

Successful implementations require good communication, and this involves true two-way communication. Inviting active participation of users in a project will lead to excellent suggestions, and it may also lead to some "interesting" (critical) comments and unsuitable suggestions. However, when users are informed why their comments or suggestions are not contributing to the overall project objective, this leads to more insight on what the project could achieve. It is better to deal with this feedback rather than ignoring it and thus causing lack of interest or apathy. It is also interesting and important to understand that some communication actually increases, rather than decreases, the resistance to change—so always monitor your communication methods and activities.

BPM INSIGHT

After many months of preparing for an implementation, it could be thought that it is the final hurdle and that once implemented, people can go back to just doing their work. However, it is important to clearly communicate that the implementation is only the beginning of a new way of working and that people need to be continually alert for further improvements.

Table 20.1 Implementation scenarios

Implementation scenario	Advantages	Disadvantages	Typical use
Big Bang The proposed change is introduced in one major overhaul  Big Bang	• Fast to implement • Minimal overhead	• Risk of disruption to the business is high • Any errors may not be picked up and could have a high impact on the business	• Isolated BPM projects (pilot project and small to medium projects), typically with limited number of business units, regions or people involved
Parallel The proposed change is introduced step-by-step (e.g., by location or business unit), with the next roll-out starting before the previous one is finished  Parallel	• A relatively faster implementation • Ability to make use of lessons learned from preceding implementations	• Additional resources will be required to assist with overlapping implementations • Coordination of simultaneous roll-outs will be high and potentially complex	• Large-scale projects where there is a great level of similarities across the various regions and business units • Portfolio of projects, where projects will run in parallel
Relay The proposed change is introduced step-by-step with each roll-out only starting once the previous one has been completed  Relay	• Opportunity for a higher quality implementation as the lessons learned from the preceding roll-out(s) can be fully taken into account and the same implementation team can be used	• Lack of speed, as the implementation could, depending on the circumstances, take some time to complete • High costs related to the duration of the project	• Large-scale projects where specialist skills are in high demand, leveraging the same implementation team over and over again • Portfolio of projects where there is a strong interdependency of the projects
Combination A combination of the above mentioned implementation approaches—perhaps a small pilot and then building up to larger implementation  Combination	• Provides the organization with the benefits of tailoring the roll-out to the specific situation • Flexible yet manageable	• Pitfall could be lack of communicating the rationale of this approach, as it might seem chaotic to some	• Can be used in any project type • Typically used in case of a transformation project, where a small project is used as a testing ground and then expanded to large and more critical parts of the organization

Step 3: Involve management

Management must be kept up to date with developments (good and bad) at all times. Honest communication is the only type of communication that is acceptable. Make sure there is plenty of it.

It is management's responsibility to continually inform staff and external stakeholders of the latest developments on the BPM activity. Management can be involved via:

- People change management practices (refer to Chapter 25)

- Professional training development (refer to People phase in Chapter 18)

- Off-site workshop retreats (it is best to conduct workshops off-site to minimize distractions for managers); it is often best to have external facilitators to conduct these workshops.

If necessary, include a public relations firm or in-house facilities to assist in this process. Effective promotion and communication is too important to try to learn on the job.

When dealing with management, remember that it is crucial to ensure that they go through their own personal change first, especially if the proposed changes have a major impact upon them. Only then can the managers help others.

BPM INSIGHT

Management has a critical role in the smooth implementation of the solution. In a BPM activity an executive manager kept moving the goalposts, just to demonstrate the power he had. This became detrimental for the staff and the outcome of the project. After escalation to the Steering Committee the executive manager was corrected and the project implementation could continue smoothly.

Step 4: Prepare for user acceptance testing

During this step, if applicable, the test cases for business testing are prepared. The actual business users are required to test the solution in step 7 (complete business tests and pilots). They will be able to test the completed solution from a "normal practice" perspective. To this stage in the project the solution will have only been tested against the written specifications of the business requirements, while now the solution must also be tested for integration with the daily routine of the business users, as well as the implicit assumptions and expectations.

Ideally, the preparation for business testing should have started during the design of the new process(es). This could have occurred during either the Innovate or the Develop phase of the project, depending upon the particular circumstances. If the test cases are developed at this early stage, the organization has the ability to compare the test case expected outcomes with the business and technical specifications and design, to ensure there are no gaps in the requirements. This is an excellent "checking" activity to avoid costly mistakes being made. Refer to Figure 19.8.

Step 5: Train staff

In the Innovate phase, the new processes will have been designed. The organization will have developed them, and will have defined any changes to the organization's structure, job roles and job descriptions during the Develop and People phases. It is now time to train the people who will be executing these processes.

Just as the test scenarios can be developed based on the redesigned processes, the training materials can be created from the process documentation of the redesigned processes.

Training can take the form of formal courses or on-the-job training (in situ) (see Table 20.2). Mentoring and coaching should continue during the business testing, pilot steps and initial implementation.

Obviously, the training materials used should be consistent and the training should not be conducted too far in advance. In fact it is best to train just before the skills are needed, to avoid loss of knowledge (if people learn new skills too early and then do not use them, they will forget the new skills). Suggestions regarding training are:

- small doses of just-in-time training;
- provide individual training schedules, ensuring that people know when their session is scheduled (this builds confidence and inclusion);
- test competencies after training;
- monitor job performance after an appropriate period of time.

One of the outcomes of the people training step can be the development and training of "super users" in the new processes. These will be the "front-line" people who will be available during the implementation steps. It is important that these "super users" are not just focused on the mechanical aspects but are also key proponents of the intended change (see Kotter, 2012).

Training should be focused on more than just the key activities or any automated solution; it should also cover aspects such as:

- impacts of the proposed solution;
- which existing bottlenecks will be tackled;
- any new bottlenecks the participants expect to arise during the implementation period;
- the benefits and possibilities of the proposed solution.

KEY POINT

Training is often the first time people become involved, in a detailed way, with the new way of working, so attention should not just be given to "how" to do things, but also "why." It is recommended to have key stakeholders and BPM activity sponsors involved in the initial training kick-off sessions to reiterate the importance and benefits of the BPM activity.

Table 20.2 Types of training

Type of training	Advantage	Disadvantage	Application
On-the-job coaching	• Full support • Ability to personalize the training • Ability to include change management activities	• Expensive	• For key people that face fundamental changes
Classroom training	• Large number of people in one session • Ability to have team assignments • Ability to include change management activities	• Relatively expensive	• For a larger group that requires team activities and/or change management activities
eTraining (can be based on Internet or CD training)	• Ability to be anywhere or anytime training • Can be re-used for new employees	• More challenging to include change management activities	• For a larger group that focuses especially on "mechanical" or compliance changes

Step 6: Develop and run marketing programs

Think about the applicability of running formal marketing campaigns in the marketplace, specifically targeting external stakeholders. The organization may even wish to publish the innovation program, with the new strengths and competitive advantages that it will bring to the general marketplace. If this latter course of action is chosen, whatever implementation date is announced to the market must be realistic and achieved or the organization risks losing credibility with its stakeholders.

Often individual or small group meetings with key stakeholders can make them feel special, and can result in significant benefits. Plans can be shared, under non-disclosure agreements, with important customers and suppliers as early as possible.

Certainly, whatever method the organization selects, use multiple approaches to marketing and have your top customers informed by senior executives as much as possible.

KEY POINT

The BPM activity should take a broader view that is not limited to the boundaries of the business unit or organization. If relevant, market it to a wider audience, including addressing the age-old question "What's In It For Me?" For example a process was redesigned to introduce electronic logging of sub-contractor claims. Initially the sub-contractors viewed this as a burden until they understood that it would lead to their invoices being paid on time, provided the contractors had followed the right process. The change was welcomed and embraced.

Step 7: Complete business tests and pilots

This is where the user acceptance testing test cases are executed by the business. It could range from executing data or transactions through an automated BPM solution to manually simulating the "process" transactions through the business. The staff will need to have been trained in the system and or processes prior to commencing the test cases.

BPM INSIGHT

Most BPM activities are focused on streamlining the end-to-end process, including the interfaces with vendors and customers. It is crucial that key customers and vendors have been involved sufficiently in the proposed solution and that during the implementation they have been given an opportunity to test the new solution. This will apply to the interfaces with their organization, but also any modifications they had to make internally to their systems.

It is essential that the organization:

- involves customers and suppliers, where appropriate;
- has strong project management of the testing steps;
- has a feedback mechanism that is easy to use;
- listens and communicates honestly—feedback and listening to the feedback is absolutely essential; there can be a great deal to learn from this step;
- has a mechanism to measure and share the results of the tests;
- is always prepared to accommodate changes, provided that they follow the right triage and prioritization processes;
- communicates results of pilots and testing—shows success to stakeholders, especially any wins; however, always be honest about any challenges associated with the testing;
- obtain testimonials from staff, customers and suppliers;
- celebrates success and rewards team members (project team and business).

KEY POINT

User acceptance testing should be completed against the business requirements as agreed in the earlier phase of the project. Any testing incidents identified need to be linked to these business requirements. If the incident was not included in the original business requirements it should be raised as a change request. This approach should ensure that users are not changing the system on the fly.

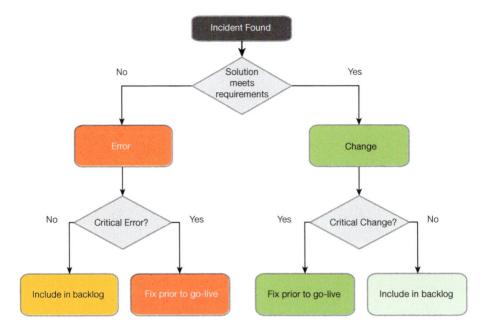

Figure 20.3 Classification of incidents during user acceptance testing

User acceptance testing usually involves a broader group of users who typically don't have a testing background. So it is important that clear guidelines are provided on how to categorize issues arising from this testing. Furthermore, the project needs to have a triage process for these issues, and an established escalation path. Figure 20.3 provides a sample of incident classification.

Step 8: Update deliverables

This covers the feedback from the training and testing steps. It is important to continually update the expected deliverables and ensure that they have stakeholder acceptance and buy-in. The organization must constantly double-check that all stakeholders, management and BPM activity team members still have a consistent set of expectations. Also make sure, again, that the roll-out scope is understood and agreed.

KEY POINT

All project deliverables, such as training material, communication collateral, manuals, etc., need to be reflective of any modifications made during the Implement phase. This is especially applicable in the case of changes made during testing and as a result of a phased implementation approach. Ensuring that deliverables are up to date also ensures that the material will be used throughout the use of the new solution, for example if new people join the organization.

Step 9: Develop roll-out, back-out and contingency plans

Normal project management skills are required, and we will not explore the requirements further here other than to say that we suggest the following points are taken into consideration:

- complete individual plans for each business unit involved in the roll-out;
- develop plans collaboratively with management and staff;
- plan for multiple planning sessions, ensuring that the BPM activity accommodates mistakes and continually learns and adjusts the plans accordingly;
- ensure that individual expectations of people are crystal clear, so there is no room for any misunderstanding;
- have a "dry" run (practice) of the back-out or roll-back and contingency plans, make sure that they work and continue these "dry" runs until any doubt is removed.

A *back-out plan* is required in case the implementation needs to be reversed. Typically this could happen where the validation testing indicates that the solution has critical problem areas.

A *contingency plan* is required to deal with unforeseen circumstances, such as a flow-on impact from another system(s), especially in the case of a replacement of legacy system(s).

These plans need to be developed in great detail, especially in the case of a large project and/or transformation. It is recommended that a play-book is developed with the timings to the relevant level of detail.

BPM INSIGHT

Rolling back an implementation is not just a tick box activity. There are many examples of horror stories of how an organization's systems became negatively impacted as a roll-back did not perform successfully. If rolling back the solution is required it is important to realize that rolling back nearly takes as much effort as implementing the new solution, and includes, but is not limited to:

- activities that need to be performed to restore the original situation
- time and effort that is required (this should not be underestimated)
- validating that the original position is correct and working
- sign-off of the roll-back to the original state
- communications about the roll-back.

Step 10: Implement solution

Once the roll-out of the new processes has been implemented effectively, you must ensure that the "old" processes and supporting systems are no longer available to staff. It is also essential that a continuous improvement mechanism is put in place. This is discussed in more detail in Chapter 22.

Reporting relationships and organizational structure changes will also require implementation, as will the initiation of any new roles and incentive schemes based on performance results. Do not underestimate the complexity of this, or the time it will take.

KEY POINT

In the past many organizations ran parallel or shadow production instances, where the data entry would be completed twice, once in each system (the old and the new). This was implemented because the business did not completely trust the new systems and the testing. With improved testing and system functionality the need to run actual parallel or shadow production systems is significantly reduced. Much of the validation and comparison between the old and new can be done in the back-office. It is more important to monitor the data entry, the outcomes and validate against expectations.

Step 11: Mentor staff

As mentioned previously in the training step, if selected people are trained as "super users" first, they may then be used to train the remaining people and provide mentoring during the early period after going "live."

It is important that the "super users"/mentors are available full-time during the initial implementation phase, and do not resume their business-as-usual roles until the implementation has settled down to everyone's satisfaction. It is important to provide these people with incentives to break from their daily work and invest time and energy in the BPM activity. These incentives should not necessarily be monetary, but could include a new challenging role for these people and a way of proving their ability to handle projects that may lead to a promotion or recognition within the organization

BPM INSIGHT

Sometimes the difference between success and failure is a handful of dedicated people who work hard to make it work. These people go beyond what is expected from them. It is important to recognize and reward these people.

Step 12: Handover and takeover

Once the solution is operational and the initial issues are resolved the team needs to hand over the BPM activity to the business, which must be prepared to take it over.

There is a distinct difference between the two activities of "handover" and "takeover"; this needs to be acknowledged and addressed by the BPM team and the business.

The BPM team must prepare all documentation, training and impart knowledge to ensure the business will be able to understand and support the new processes—this is the "handover."

"Takeover" refers to the business preparing for the handover. The business will need to allocate roles and responsibilities, and allocate sufficient time for the business staff to learn about the new processes or systems.

Both of these activities should have been planned during the Launch pad phase.

The formal handover/takeover means that from that moment onwards the final responsibility and accountability lies firmly within the business, which will need to address any further or new issues with the new processes. This is an important step and it is recommended to have clear criteria that must be met before the processes are officially handed over.

Examples of criteria:

- no outstanding level 1 issues;
- have completed a month end process, if appropriate;
- all project tasks and documentation have been completed.

It is important that the handover/takeover is not executed too soon. It is crucial that the new solution is stable prior to handover/takeover and the BPM team has built adequate capability to deal with the migration. The BPM team needs to ensure that sufficient time is spent in handing over to the business and the business spends adequate time taking over from the BPM team. This will assist the business in becoming comfortable in their new responsibilities.

KEY POINT

Creating a formal step to hand over and especially take over ensures that there is a clear moment in time in which the responsibility and accountability shifts back to the business. The timing of the handover/takeover is important (when it will take place), as well as having a clear set of criteria as to when it is ready to take over/hand over.

Step 13: Monitor and adjust

During the roll-out of the changes, ample effort should be devoted to monitoring the progress of the roll-out and the progress towards achieving the business results.

BPM INSIGHT

Social media are a good barometer to assess how people feel about the change. Care should be given that criticism is not overruled but that people can freely provide their opinion. It needs to be monitored to address any factual inaccuracies.

The BPM activity sponsor could have a blog to invite people to ask questions and provide feedback.

It is important to have established performance indicators to monitor progress. Examples of this include the:

- number of questions in the first week(s);
- number of errors in the first week(s);
- percentage of staff working with new processes;
- level of overtime required to get the work done.

Step 14: Provide feedback to users and stakeholders

During the entire project, and especially in the Implement phase, a great deal is required from the business, business users and stakeholders—their commitment, involvement and participation. Sufficient care should be taken to thank the business, business users and stakeholders for this, and to ensure that they are continually kept informed about the progress of the project and the various lessons learned.

REALIZE VALUE

Just as in the Develop and People phases, the benefits must be defined in detail in order to gain agreement as part of this phase. For details refer to step 5 of Chapter 21, where it is described in the context of realizing value within a project.

IMPLEMENT PHASE OUTPUTS

The Implement phase will provide valuable input into other phases of the framework (see Figure 20.4), and a few examples are mentioned here:

- how the project is implemented will have an impact upon how the realization of the BPM activity value (benefits) will take place;
- implementation will also provide input into the Sustainable performance phase;
- the review and finalization of the implementation approach may necessitate changes to the People and Develop phases—for example it may not be possible to change immediately to the newly created roles; there may be a need to stage such implementation.

IMPLEMENT PHASE RISKS

There are several risks that must be considered in this phase, and mitigation strategies implemented to eliminate (or at least reduce) them. These are listed in Table 20.3.

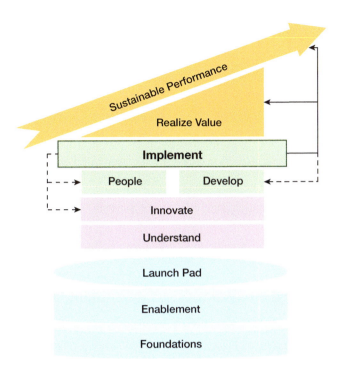

Figure 20.4 Implement phase outputs to other phases

Table 20.3 Implement phase risks and mitigation strategies

	Risk	Mitigation strategy
1.	Business testing and/or training becomes a show-stopper	Ensure that the requirements are discussed and agreed with the business, key users and stakeholders as early as possible and the related expectations and implications of these requirements. Stop unnecessary change requests.
2.	The core BPM activity team is unable to deal with all the problems and inquiries at the start of the implementation	Involve "super users" and ensure that they are capable (via training), available (full-time on the project) and willing (through motivation and involvement). In addition, a "flying squad" could be helpful, especially for more detailed and technical assistance.
3.	Stakeholders are not kept informed about the BPM activity	Communicate, communicate and communicate. There can never be too much of it (as long as it is right). Ensure that these tasks are allocated to a specific person or team to coordinate, and that they have sufficient time to complete the tasks.
4.	The business does not have sufficient expertise or	The business many need some coaching in how to complete a test plan or write test scripts, and on the

Table 20.3 Implement phase risks and mitigation strategies—*continued*

	Risk	Mitigation strategy
	resources to complete user acceptance testing	execution of these. The BPM activity team must take care not to "take over" these tasks and only provide coaching and guidance. The level of resources required must be discussed and agreed early in the BPM activity with the business to ensure they allocate sufficient people.
		The BPM activity needs to get the right resources for the testing. The business can look at back filling their day-job.
5.	If time is tight on a project, testing is always one of the first things to be cut or minimized	Testing is one of the most crucial aspects of a BPM activity, and should never be compromised. If necessary, extend the implementation date or go to a phased implementation, but never cut back on testing, the BPM activity and business will pay for it later if it is cut.
6.	Business is not ready to take over project	Ensuring the planning for the transfer from the BPM team to the business is commenced in the Launch pad phase will assist in mitigating this risk. The business team needs to be continually engaged throughout the BPM activity.

SUMMARY

In this chapter you have learned the:

- Importance of the Implement phase and the main steps.
- Importance and approach for communication.
- Necessity to market the BPM activity and its benefits to clients and vendors.
- Approach to testing and training.
- Need to update deliverables and complete planning.
- Importance of monitoring and adjusting and providing feedback.
- Risks involved in the implementation and the possible mitigation.

SELF-TEST

1 What are the four implementation scenarios and when would you use them?

2 How would you use social media during the Implement phase?

3 How will you involve clients and vendors in marketing and testing?

4 What is the necessity of a roll-back plan?

5 Why and how will you monitor and adjust the implementation?

ASSIGNMENT

You are about to implement the improvements highlighted in the previous phases.

Assignment guiding questions

1. What approach do you recommend to implement the proposed improvements?
2. What communication have you already used to inform the stakeholders about the implementation?
3. What communication will you now use to inform the stakeholders about the implementation?
4. What are the key risks for implementing the proposed changes and how will you mitigate against them?

CHAPTER 21

REALIZE VALUE PHASE

OVERVIEW

The purpose of the Realize value phase is to ensure that the benefit outcomes outlined in the project business case are realized. This phase comprises the delivery of the benefits realization management process and benefits realization reporting. Although this is described as the ninth phase of the framework, it is in fact not a discrete phase in its own right because many of the steps are executed in previous phases. The steps have been grouped together in this chapter to provide an end-to-end insight into the role of realizing value in a BPM activity and to ensure that the BPM project team takes time after the Implement phase to realize the benefits specified in the business case.

OVERALL LEARNING OUTCOME

By the end of this chapter you will be able to:

* Understand the importance of an end-to-end approach to benefit realization
* Realize the importance of assigning benefit owners to specific benefits
* Relate how the benefit steps of the previous phases intertwine with the end-to-end benefit approach
* Understand the need for a benefits management framework
* Identify potential benefits
* Establish baseline and comparative measurement
* Refine and optimize benefits mix
* Define benefit details
* Perform benefits delivery and tracking
* Monitor and maximize value
* Communicate benefit approach and results.

WHY?

Many project managers and organizations believe that a project is finished after it has successfully gone live and the users are happy. Nothing could be further from the truth. A project is only complete once the reason for its existence has been achieved and it has been handed over to the business in such a way that the business can now sustain the project outcomes.

Why is a project brought into existence in the first place? The business case should tell you. It should contain the business value or benefits that are expected to be achieved at the completion of the project.

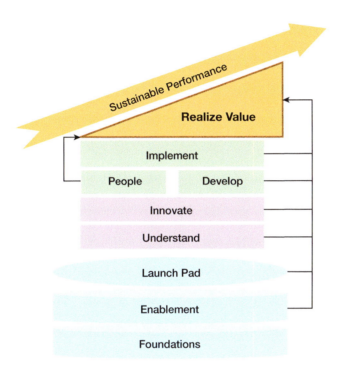

Figure 21.1 Realize value phase

Business value doesn't just "drop out" of projects with no effort. Benefits need to be planned, owned, tracked, worked for and monitored in order for them to emerge. The realization of this business value (Figure 21.1) rarely happens immediately after the project implementation; sometimes there can be a delay from three to six months, as shown in Figure 21.2.

There is often a transition period where operational costs actually increase for a short period of time after implementation, and then the benefits start to be realized and the operational costs decrease.

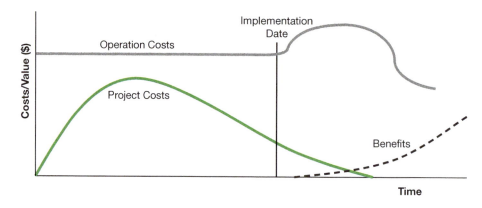

Figure 21.2 Project cost/benefits payback period

There is also an overlap in the project costs and the start of the business value realization, because some part of the project must continue until the benefits begin to be realized and it is handed over to the business as an ongoing activity.

While we have provided steps in each of the other phases that will contribute towards the realization of business value, the purpose of this chapter is to bring all the value realization steps and management framework together to ensure that it is thoroughly understood and the project value is ultimately realized.

If it is discovered during a project that the expected business value cannot be realized, or has gone away, the project should be stopped. If the business case is maintained and updated throughout the project (at each phase), this will become apparent.

The ability of projects to maximize benefits realization will be increased on a BPM project if the framework steps are followed.

The generally accepted term for the control, management and realization of business value is benefits management. Benefits management translates business objectives into benefits that can be measured, tracked and realized.

If an organization chooses not to execute benefits management diligently, the risk of projects not meeting stakeholder expectations is increased. A sample of these risks is shown at the end of this chapter.

KEY POINT

To realize benefits it is crucial that benefits are considered throughout all phases in the BPM activity.

It is impossible to realize benefits for a BPM activity just by stating them in the business case without any further tracking or consideration.

Benefits management can also act as a catalyst for further change if the project is not realizing the expected benefits. This can force the project and organization to complete a review that can lead to changes in the approach to the project, and thus to subsequent realization of the expected value.

RESULTS

There will be a number of results and outputs that the business can expect from the steps described in this phase, including:

- a benefits register (from the Enablement phase)
- a benefits summary plan (from Launch pad phase)
- a benefits milestone network matrix (from Innovate phase)
- a benefits delivery matrix (from Develop, People and Implement phases).

HOW?

If business value is to be realized, there must be a structured process throughout the BPM activity and entire organization. This is the benefits side of the cost–benefit analysis. Figure 21.3 shows the context for benefits management.

The business will have various drivers that are directed by the organization strategy and objectives together with customer needs and the types of benefits that are available to the organization. Another significant influencer is the type of process change project(s) being undertaken within the organization. Are these organizational changes driven by the culture of the organization, people skill levels, or changing from a functional to a process-based structure? These are the critical people change management issues associated with the project.

When executed well, the benefits will be more easily obtained from a BPM activity and feed back into the initial business drivers and organization strategies.

It is essential for the BPM activity sponsor and project manager to understand that benefits management is not outside the BPM activity. It is their responsibility to plan,

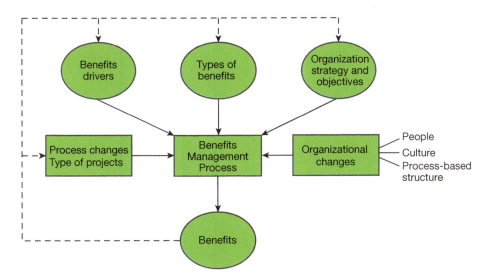

Figure 21.3 Benefits management context

manage and ensure accountability within the BPM activity team, and ultimately to deliver on the business value outlined in the business case.

KEY POINT

Traceability of benefits throughout the BPM activity and related to process is crucial to be successful in realizing the stated benefits.

Some organizations will use the benefits outlined in the business case only to obtain the funding for a BPM activity. Ignoring the realization of the benefits is very much a short-term viewpoint and poor management.

The Realize value steps ensure that throughout the project the benefits are considered, managed, refined and monitored.

DETAILED STEPS

Realizing business value is a progressive process throughout the project, and the framework shows you how to achieve this by completing the steps outlined in Figure 21.4.

While each of these steps will be described in this chapter, they must be executed in the appropriate nominated phase.

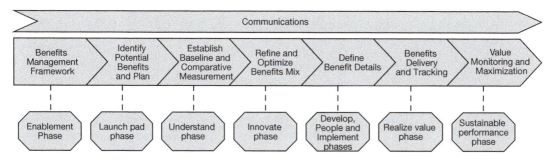

Figure 21.4 Realize value phase steps

Step 1: Communications

Communicating the benefits is crucial throughout all phases of the BPM initiative and hence all steps of benefits realization as business benefits are the reason why initiatives are started in the first place.

As mentioned before benefits are a key benchmark throughout the initiative to determine which ideas, requirements or aspects should be in-scope and which should be ruled out-of-scope.

Communication ensures that participants in the workshops and other activities feel that they know where the project is heading and are involved and being listened to.

It is important that benefits communication considers all key aspects of the communication activities, especially if people are impacted, by, for example, reduction in

> ## BPM INSIGHT
>
> Communication is critical during the specification and realization of the benefits. First, a better communicated benefit provides better transparency and better ability for an organization to track and realize the benefits. Second, better communicated benefits will get more buy-in from the employees and a better understanding regarding how to realize the benefits.

employee numbers; changes to KPIs and bonuses of employees; and impacts on profitability levels.

It is important to communicate quick wins as soon as possible as this provides belief and generates momentum. Don't wait until the project is completed to communicate positive outcomes and benefits.

Step 2: Benefits management framework (Enablement phase)

As indicated earlier, this step (step 3: Process Architecture of the Enablement phase in Chapter 14) is about establishing a benefits management structure for the organization to approach, target, measure and realize project business benefits, and it should be incorporated into the process architecture.

This step is where not only the benefits management structure is created, but also the organization's standards and templates are established and communicated throughout the organization as part of the Target Operating Model and the Process Architecture.

These standards and templates should include, but not be limited to, the following:

- how the organization identifies benefits and links them to the organization strategy;
- how the organization defines and measures benefits;
- benefit roles, responsibilities and ownership;
- benefit planning procedures—milestone/benefits network matrices, delivery, assessment and review points, dependencies, risks, business impacts;
- the determination of what, when and by whom;
- guidelines on how to take advantage of opportunities for unplanned benefits;
- identification of any dis-benefits;
- identification of who is responsible for baselining and how, and who signs off on the baseline;
- a benefits register format—What is the benefit? How much it is worth? Who is accountable for the delivery or realization of the benefit(s)? When will it be delivered—timeframe? Where will it impact on the business?

Regular benefit management meetings should be established to ensure there is a continual focus on the management and realization of the organizational benefits associated with the various business cases used to justify BPM activities. These meetings will also assist in the creation and maintenance of a benefits-focused project culture. Decisions need to be made as to who should attend, how often the meetings will be held, and a standard agenda established, which should include:

- lessons learned
- benefits realized (Is it enough? Is there more?)
- benefits not realized—why? Adjust plans/mitigation and remediation strategies.

Step 3: Identify potential benefits and enter in benefits register (Launch pad phase)

The initial business case will have been delivered as part of the Launch pad phase (step 5.6: Analyze business processes. and step 6: Agree and plan the handover/takeover with the business, in Chapter 15), and will have identified the likely initial benefits associated with the project. The benefits will be further identified and confirmed as the BPM activity progresses through subsequent phases of the 7FE Framework. The benefits register must be used to record, for each identified and defined benefit, the following information:

- a description of the benefit to be achieved;
- the person responsible for realizing the benefit (benefit owner);
- a description of the current situation or performance of the business process;
- the current cost or performance measure of the business process;
- the target cost or performance measure of the business process after the planned change;
- the target date for the benefit to be realized;
- the trigger or event that will cause the benefit to be realized;
- the type of contribution to the business;
- process impacted;
- the assessed value of the benefit or saving;
- dependencies and assumptions;
- potential risks and barriers;
- comments about the assessed value of the benefit or saving;
- the organization strategy and objectives supported by the benefit;
- how this benefit will contribute to the achievement of the strategic objective (for example, effectiveness in the billing process will reduce revenue leakage and increase earnings before income tax (EBIT)).

Benefit owners are crucial in ensuring that benefits are realized, as the accountability rests with them. Benefits owners are:

- responsible for the realization of the specified benefit;
- responsible to manage and deliver the benefits, changes and measures;

- kept informed about any changes to the BPM activity or business settings that will impact the benefit realization, including changes affecting the assumption, dependencies, potential risks and barriers;
- able to influence the outcomes given their position;
- typically a (senior) manager in the area affected by the BPM activity with authority, credibility and influence with the employees and stakeholders and who understands process;
- accountable to the project sponsor and steering committee for achieving the benefits.

The BPM activity sponsor is:

- responsible for the achievement of the overall benefits;
- responsible for managing the BPM activity and benefits in such a way that the benefits are maximized and support the business in the best possible way;
- consulted and/or requested to make decisions that impact the BPM activity and benefits;
- able to influence the organization, BPM activity and benefits given their position;
- typically an executive with a passion for process;
- accountable to the steering committee.

BPM INSIGHT

Passion for process is critical for the BPM activity sponsor. He/she needs to convince and lead by example the benefit owners and the BPM activity team to realization of the business benefits.

The benefits may also be summarized in the benefit summary plan (see Table 21.1) for executive presentation. This plan records the benefit, who is responsible for the delivery (realization) of the benefits, the expected value, when the benefit will start to accrue and end (if appropriate, as some benefits continue into the future), and any dependencies and risks associated with the benefit.

This step involves identifying, documenting and planning for the management of the benefits that are expected to be delivered by the BPM activity. These are the benefits that will be monitored and updated (if and when required) throughout the life of the BPM activity, and achievement of these benefits will be measured and reported upon at the end. They must also be compared to the business case.

KEY POINT

The benefits register needs to be kept up to date during the course of the BPM activity as new information and insights become available.

Table 21.1 Benefit summary plan

Benefit description	Benefit owner (who)	Benefit amount ($)	Expected benefit Realization date		Dependencies	Risks
			Start	End		

As processes may go across functional areas, this may make the measurement of the BPM benefits more difficult to measure. This, however, does not excuse the organization or BPM activity from making the measurement. Remember, it is better to have rough estimates than having no data at all.

The BPM activity team must take into account that a single BPM activity may have both quantifiable and non-quantifiable benefits associated with its implementation.

BPM INSIGHT

It is important to try to quantify the benefits as much as possible. For example reduction of risk can be quantified as the reduction of unnecessary costs or revenue leakage; or an improvement in employee satisfaction will reduce employee churn and the associated costs of finding and training new staff.

It should be noted that a productivity improvement by itself does not deliver a tangible cost reduction unless it can be translated into actual savings of staff numbers, avoidance of extra costs, reduced resource requirements or additional revenue. Savings of small time increments that cannot be aggregated across many staff to provide realizable savings should not be treated as tangible benefits.

In consultation with the affected business units, benefit targets should be identified as relevant to the project. The targets should also set a timeframe for achievement, and an outline of the action necessary to reach the targets set. The BPM activity sponsor is responsible for the realization of these benefit targets, and for adherence to the timeframes and actions.

Often people are concerned about providing high benefits estimates as they feel they will be locked in to achieve the projected amount. In this situation, it is recommended to deploy one or more of the following approaches:

- Specify the key benefits drivers, without stating an immediate amount figure. For example reducing revenue leakage can be broken down as follows:

o   how many items are produced and charged

o   how much revenue leakage takes place per item (percentage of total revenue)

o   how much can this revenue leakage be reduced (percentage of leakage).

- Allow the initial estimate to have a wide range of margin (e.g., +50 percent at the initial business case) and later refine it (e.g., +10 percent at the time of the final business case sign-off).
- Specify the assumptions, dependencies and risks that are at the base of these benefits, as it is often difficult to state a figure without many assumptions and dependencies.

A comprehensive plan of action, and register of benefits to be achieved, should now have been prepared and accepted by the responsible business managers (benefit owners) and approved by the BPM activity sponsor.

Step 4: Establish baseline and comparative measurement (Understand phase)

As discussed in the Understand phase (see step 4: Complete metrics analysis, including Voice of Customer, and step 11: Understand phase report, in Chapter 16), the completion of metrics is an essential step at the time of modeling the current processes, and it is this baseline from which improvements are measured. Therefore, in establishing the baseline, ensure that it is solid and will stand up to scrutiny by others, and that it is aligned with the business case. Ideally, all baseline measurement techniques should be consistent at an agreed institutionalized organization level. This should have formed part of the Benefits Management Framework that will have been agreed in the process architecture.

BPM INSIGHT

It is important that the underlying drivers of the baseline metrics are captured, as the circumstances might have changed during the course of the BPM activity, for example change in volumes; a merger or acquisition; or a more competitive environment. This could be achieved by the monthly costs being broken down by item and volume, so that a change in volume still allows a comparative assessment of the change in the cost price.

Step 5: Refine and optimize benefits mix (Innovate phase)

During the Innovate phase (step 8: Future process metrics projections, and step 14: Identify benefits and update business case, in Chapter 17), the processes will be redesigned based upon criteria determined during the Innovate executive workshop. These newly redesigned processes should have process metrics calculated for them, to estimate their impact on increased processing efficiency.

Confirmation of the benefits should include reviewing the original baseline measures for accuracy and validity, and updating them using the latest rates for business expenses

BPM INSIGHT

As part of the validation, it is important that the impact of any change in scope on the benefits is determined. Hence, traceability of benefits to processes is important as process should be one of the scope dimensions.

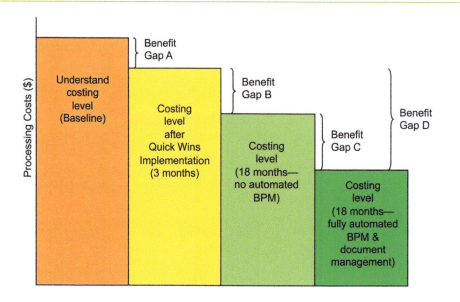

Figure 21.5 Scenario comparisons to baseline costing

In the example shown in Figure 21.5, the BPM activity requested, during the Innovate executive workshop, to complete three redesign scenarios:

1. Three months (what can be implemented without any IT system changes—these were called Quick Wins)
2. Eighteen months (with no BPM automation; existing application changes were allowed)
3. Eighteen months (with full BPM automation and document management implementation, and changes to existing applications).

The BPM activity sponsor has stated that she does not know whether a fully automated BPM and document management system implementation can be cost justified, so she has requested that the BPM activity redesign processes be based upon the two 18-month options (one automated and the other not automated) in order to determine the additional benefits.

Benefit gap A will show the cost reduction to be gained as a result of implementing the quick wins, and this will assist in their justification. Benefit gap B shows the additional measurable benefits to be gained from the 18-month non-automated solution. Benefit gap D shows the measurable cost reduction of the fully automated solution.

It is benefit gap C that the project sponsor is interested in—the additional benefits to be gained from the fully automated solution. It is this gap that needs to be included within the business case to justify the potential additional costs associated with the BPM and a document management solution.

(A note of caution: a fully automated BPM solution should not only use the measurable benefits as justification; there are many non-financial benefits to implementing this type of solution, such as business agility, increased staff satisfaction and an ability to interface with suppliers and customers.)

This comparison will prompt the following question for the BPM activity steering committee: Do the calculated benefits meet the expectations outlined in the business plan? If the answer is no, then the BPM activity should either be terminated or go back to the Launch pad phase, where a different set of processes will be selected for the project.

(e.g., salaries)—especially if there has been some delay or time period between phases, or the scope has changed.

A comparison should then be made between these new Innovate phase metrics and the updated baseline metrics from the Understand phase. In reviewing the various redesign process options, consideration should be given to the "mix" of options and their impact upon the benefits. Effort should be made to maximize the benefits by selecting the appropriate process options. As a result of this, process options and the updated business case can be finalized.

Once all of the above analysis has been completed, the benefit milestone matrix (Figure 21.6) can be finalized.

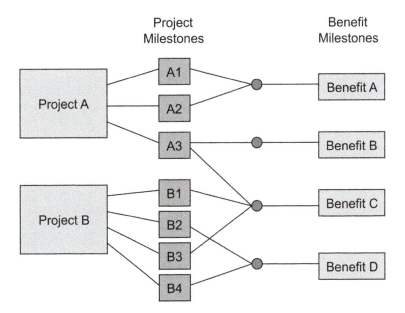

Figure 21.6 Benefit Milestone Matrix

This network matrix shows the relationship between various projects, project milestones and specific benefits. Unless you can show this relationship continuously throughout the project, linking milestones directly to benefits, then the benefit may have gone away and the project, or part of the project, should be stopped. All project team members and business people must understand this relationship—especially the project sponsor, project manager and business owner.

It is necessary to ensure that business change issues are identified so that their progress can be monitored in terms of benefits realization. Some of these will have been identified in the benefits realization plan, whilst others will emerge as more detailed people change management plans are developed. Equally, hidden benefits identified during implementation should also be incorporated into the benefit realization plan. It will be necessary to develop milestones and targets for benefits realization associated with the people change management activities so that it will be possible to monitor the progress of benefits realization amongst these change activities.

Step 6: Define benefit details (Develop, People and Implement phases)

At the commencement of the Develop phase, after updating the project plan, the benefits delivery matrix (Figure 21.7) must be completed. This matrix shows the relationships of the project milestones and benefits as outlined in the benefits milestone matrix. The difference here is that the milestones and benefits are time-lined and then adjusted on a continual basis for changes in the delivery dates for the project milestone tasks. Note that there can be a delay between a milestone being completed and the realization of a benefit such as benefit D in Figure 21.7.

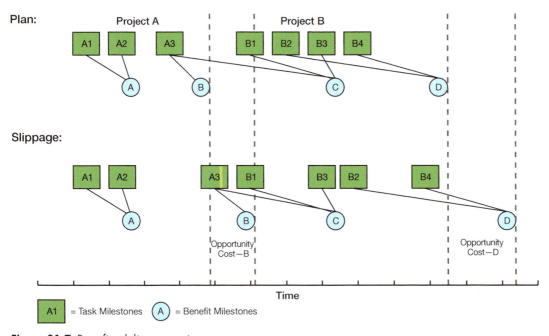

Figure 21.7 Benefits delivery matrix

In this example:

- milestones A1 and A2 have been delivered according to schedule, resulting in benefit A being realized on the planned date;
- milestone A3 has slipped while B1 and B3 are on schedule, which has resulted in benefit B being delivered late and benefit C being on time; the slippage of benefit B will have a cost associated with the delay;
- both milestone B2 and B4 are late and have caused the slippage of benefit D, which also has a cost associated with the delay.

It is important to track slippages, as the impacts on the organization can be several-fold. A few of the impacts are as follows:

- the smallest cost is the cost of funds associated with not releasing the cash benefit earlier, such as interest and cash flow impact;
- missed business opportunities (unable to capitalize on a business opportunity because of the non-delivery of a project or project milestones on time); some business opportunities have a limited window of opportunity;
- additional cost of the project, including the cost of resources for a longer period of time;
- missed profit targets for the organization (may slip from one financial year or quarter to another);
- lack of capacity for a new contract.

Understanding the relationship of milestones and benefits, when a slippage is looming, will direct the business and project team as to where to place resources to yield the maximum benefits for the organization. Perhaps resources should be taken away from other tasks or projects (whose benefits are of less value) and placed on tasks with high benefit value.

Monitoring of progress against benefits realization milestones should be an integral part of project reporting, and incorporated as a segment in the regular reports to the BPM activity sponsor and steering committee.

The benefit milestone matrix and benefit delivery matrix must continue to be updated during the development phase, and taken into account during the completion of the People phase.

BPM INSIGHT

When specifying benefits, it is important to look beyond the typical employee reduction savings. Three options could be presented:

- **Pure employee reduction savings**
- **No employee reduction savings but an uplift in revenue and reduction in costs**
- **Combination of employee reduction savings, uplift in revenue and reduction in costs.**

Step 7: Benefits delivery and tracking (Realize value phase)

It is the responsibility of the benefits owner to ensure that:

- all activities identified in the benefits summary plan are realized
- the appropriate control structures necessary for benefits realization are in place.

People change management planning is regarded as a crucial element in project success; it should be undertaken in parallel with BPM activity implementation planning and, in fact, the entire project. The BPM activity sponsor and benefits owner should ensure that any dependencies between the implementation, the people change management and the benefits realization activities are in the plans.

Once benefits are realized, obtain a formal sign-off, put them in the register and "tell people" (celebrate).

Step 8: Value monitoring and maximization (Sustainable performance phase)

As the achievement of some benefit targets will rely on activities occurring after project completion, it will be necessary to ensure that post-implementation reviews check that the benefit targets are being realized and continue to be realized. Checks should include:

- an internal audit of compliance against benefit targets in the benefit realization register;
- a review of project plans and registers to ensure all the benefits realization-related activities were successfully completed;
- a review of benefits realization related to major people change management activities.

This does not mean that the BPM activity should wait until completion to commence monitoring the realization of the value expected from it. Monitoring, via the various matrices outlined previously, together with compliance or project office audits, should take place during the project lifecycle. Monitoring should also include the realization of the dependencies and assumptions.

At the completion of the BPM activity, a full report on the achievement of benefits should be provided to the BPM activity sponsor and business project owner. Where benefits were fully achieved, or targets exceeded, it will only be necessary to record that occurrence.

Where benefits failed to reach targets by a margin of greater than 10 percent, the report should analyze the circumstances that caused the shortfall and recommend whether remedial action is appropriate. A full analysis will facilitate more accurate future benefit estimates and will provide input to the Launch pad phase for future BPM activities.

As part of the handover to the business, these areas should be followed up with the responsible business managers to validate the findings and identify areas where remedial action may be appropriate. Where the business managers identify that benefits may still be achieved, new targets should be established in consultation with them.

For each of the benefit areas where new targets have been agreed, an action plan should be developed in conjunction with the responsible business manager. Responsibility for the implementation of this action plan should be assigned to the business manager in charge of the area in which the benefits will be realized. The benefits realization register should be updated, subject to approval by the project sponsor, to reflect the newly agreed benefits targets.

The organization should be confident that it has achieved the maximum possible benefit from the investment it has made. If this benefit has fallen short of the original expectation, there should at least be an understanding of the causes and possibly a plan for future remedies.

BPM INSIGHT

The level of detail and rigor that is applied in the identification, specification, delivery and monitoring of the benefits will depend on the maturity of the organization in this area. Typically this benefit maturity is roughly related to the process management maturity. Understanding this will avoid frustration by the BPM team and their stakeholders when unrealistic expectations are set. It is recommended that over time (and over multiple projects) the maturity in benefits is increased by increasing detail and rigor leading to better tracking and management of benefit realization.

CRITICAL SUCCESS FACTORS

How does an organization ensure that it maximizes the benefits from its BPM activities? We have outlined an approach within this chapter, and list some of the more important critical success factors below:

- need for communication as outlined by Kotter (1995);
- an understanding that the realization of value needs to be intricately intertwined with, and a critical part of, the project and organization culture;
- it is necessary to plan benefit delivery—timeframes and costs;
- there must be agreement of the roles, responsibilities and accountabilities associated with the realization of value;
- there must be complete identification of the risks associated with the non-delivery of the value, and appropriate remediation strategies;
- the staff involved in the realization of the value must be trained in benefits identification, analysis and review;
- relevant measures and management must be in place to track and act on the results;
- unexpected benefits must be recognized and recorded;
- if it is possible to benchmark against other organizations within your industry, or appropriate other industries, then do so;

- never underestimate the importance of the people change management aspect of the project on realizing value; if you do not have the support of the people, it will be extremely challenging to meet the project benefit expectations;
- make value realization part of a broader organization governance structure, e.g., ask the external auditor to assess the planned outcomes and monitor the actual realization.

CASE STUDY

A CFO wanted to replace a legacy Finance System and initiated a Finance Transformation program to obtain the funding. However, once the money was approved, the focus was only on the system and not on achieving the business benefits. To counter this, the project requested the Risk Board committee to engage the external auditor to monitor the specification and realization of the benefits. The CFO was highly critical of the report and requested fundamental watering down of the findings and recommendations. However, the external auditors refused as they were only responsible to the Risk Board committee and they could make the necessary changes in the project so that the business benefits could be realized.

Message: It was evident that without the appointment of the external auditors through the Risk Board committee the project would have never achieved any of the business benefits.

REALIZE VALUE PHASE OUTPUTS

The Realize value phase will provide valuable input into other phases of the framework (see Figure 21.8), and we provide a few examples here:

- feedback may be provided to suggest changes in the way implementation is completed to maximize the future benefits; this could assist where a staged roll-out is being completed, to ensure that subsequent roll-outs are changed to maximize the benefits;
- changes to the people change management could also be suggested;
- it may be realized that changes are needed in the way the new processes have been designed and developed to again maximize benefits;
- knowledge will also be gained that will contribute towards ensuring the sustainability of the BPM activity outcomes.

REALIZE VALUE PHASE RISKS

An overview of the high level risks that must be considered during the Realize value phase is given in Table 21.2.

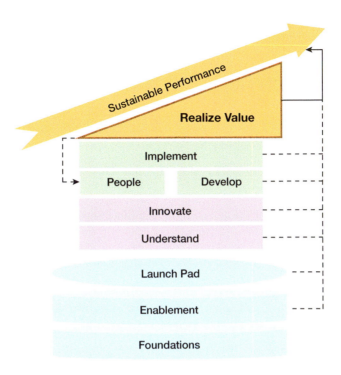

Figure 21.8 Realize value phase outputs to other phases

Table 21.2 Realize value phase risks and mitigation strategies

	Risk	Mitigation strategy
1.	Business may not commit to the realization of the benefits	Project manager, process architecture team and BPM activity sponsor are responsible for the benefit management system
2.	Lack of focus on realizing the business value as outlined in the business case	Project manager, process architecture team and BPM activity sponsor are responsible for the focus
3.	Unrealistic benefit expectations, making it difficult to realize with any level of certainty	Only record realistic benefits in the business case and reporting matrices
4.	Lack of a structured approach to the realization of the business value (benefits)	Establish a benefits management system as part of the process architecture of the organization

SUMMARY

The Realize value phase is the benefits thread that runs throughout all aspects of the BPM activity and 7FE Framework that ensures focus, traceability and ultimately realization of the stated benefits. The chapter discussed:

- The importance of an end-to-end approach to benefit realization.
- The importance of assigning benefit owners to specific benefits.
- How the benefit steps of the previous phases intertwine with the end-to-end benefit approach.
- Need for a benefits management framework.
- Identification of potential benefits.
- Establishment of a baseline and comparative measurement.
- Refinement and optimization of the benefits mix.
- Definition of benefit details.
- Benefits delivery and tracking.
- Monitoring and maximizing value.
- Communication of benefit approach and results.

SELF-TEST

1 Why is benefit realization essential for any BPM activity?

2 Why has each BPM activity phase a benefit step included?

3 Why does the benefit management framework relate to the process architecture?

4 What are the key elements in a benefits register?

5 What are the roles and responsibilities of the benefit owner and BPM activity sponsor?

6 Why would you use multiple scenarios while refining and optimizing the benefit mix?

7 What is a benefit delivery matrix and how does it assist in the benefit realization?

8 What are the key steps in relation to benefits while handing the project over to the business?

ASSIGNMENT

You are completing the Realize value phase steps during each of the phases of the assignment.

Assignment guiding questions

1. Ensure that you complete for each phase the related Realize value step. How did you achieve this?
2. Complete the benefit summary plan as much as possible.

CHAPTER 22

SUSTAINABLE PERFORMANCE PHASE

OVERVIEW

This chapter describes how a BPM activity moves from a BPM activity (project or program) basis to a business environment. That is, how the BPM activity links in with the Operate, Manage, Sustain aspect of the BPM House. This will then further link to the Organization Sustainability and Performance Management "roof" of the BPM House.

This chapter should be read in conjunction with Chapter 29 (BPM maturity) and Chapter 27 (Embedding BPM within the organization). The reason is that the activities conducted within this chapter must match the current level of BPM or process maturity within the organization and contribute towards a growing maturity level.

OVERALL LEARNING OUTCOME

By the end of this chapter you will be able to:

- Understand why sustainability is critical to an organization's ability to create and deliver value
- List the steps involved in moving from the Sustainable performance phase to ensure organizational sustainability
- Institutionalize process governance
- Review the transfer to sustainability and fine-tune the organizational sustainability and performance management aspects, if required.

This chapter describes the Sustainable performance phase (Figure 22.1), the last phase of the 7FE Framework, which relates to the need to move from the BPM activity to a business environment. While this is the last phase of the 7FE Framework, it is the first phase of BPM as a business-as-usual activity.

KEY POINT

As Stephen Schwartz of IBM is purported to have said,

> **We had improvement programs, but the real difference came when we decided it was no longer a program, it was a business strategy.**

WHY?

Without sustainability, the expectations that have been built with the stakeholders will not be met over the long term, which in turn will make it more difficult to obtain their commitment and trust for future BPM activities.

The purpose of this phase is to ensure the ongoing sustainability of the process improvements that have been completed as part of a specific BPM activity and make them part of business-as-usual. The considerable investment made in the specific BPM activity must be maintained and enhanced over time—certainly not diminished or depreciated. The organization must understand that processes have a limited life and can continue to be improved after the BPM activity targeted improvements have been realized.

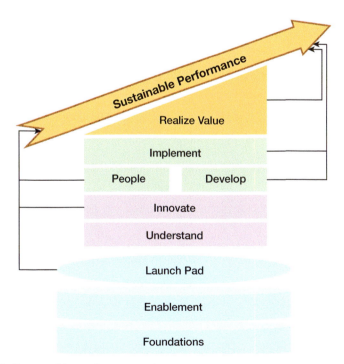

Figure 22.1 Sustainable performance phase

BPM INSIGHT

Process improvements without sustainability are arguably not worth the effort as the improved practices quickly fade away as the business grows and changes.

If this doesn't happen, the organization will simply be running its processes in a suboptimal fashion.

In other words, sustainable performance is about the continual management of processes aimed at achieving the specified organizational objectives. This chapter will outline the steps involved in moving the process(es) involved in the BPM activity from a project-based set of tasks into the Operate, Manage, Sustain aspect of the BPM House, always ensuring they link in, and are consistent, with the Organization Sustainability and Performance Management "roof" of the BPM House shown in Figure 22.2).

Figure 22.2 shows how this phase and phase 9 (Realize value) are referenced back to the BPM House described in Chapter 1; this is shown by the area surrounded by the red box in Figure 22.2.

The red box area of Operate Manage Sustain covers the realization of the benefits accruing as a result of the BPM activity; and the establishment or linking into the process governance and performance management aspects that specifically relate to the process(es) involved in the current BPM activity. Process governance and performance management will

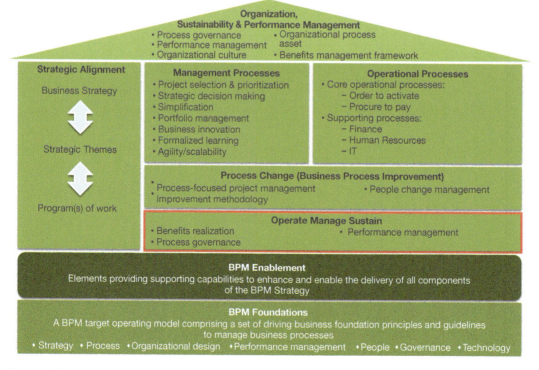

Figure 22.2 BPM House and the Sustainable performance phase

> ## BPM INSIGHT
>
> Sustainability is determined by an organization's ability to create and deliver value for all stakeholders on a continuing basis. It is about understanding what customers value, now and in the future, which will influence organizational strategy, design and call to action. Processes must continually be improved and redesigned to reflect this call to action.

then link in with the "roof" of the BPM House—Organization Sustainability and Performance Management.

RESULTS

The results that will be delivered during this phase specifically relate to the business processes involved in the BPM activity undertaken and will include the following:

1. Mechanisms (a set of practical steps) to manage these specific business processes, and identify and realize opportunities for process improvements.
2. Managed and continuously improved processes.
3. Specific links into the BPM House roof aspects to support BPM-focused sustainability within the organization.

HOW?

Before the steps involved in this phase are described, there are a number of activities that must have been completed before this phase of the 7FE Framework can be commenced. These completed activities include the:

- handover/takeover must have been adequately completed at this stage (part of Implement phase);
- business process steward(s)/owner(s) identified early in the BPM activity (Launch pad phase) will have taken over responsibility for the process(es);
- performance metrics for the "people" involved in the execution of the process(es) will have been agreed (part of the People phase);
- business benefits described in the business case must have either been completely realized (although this is unlikely at this stage of the BPM activity) or at least planned and being executed (Realize value phase).

DETAILED STEPS

With the above assumptions in mind, this phase will involve the steps shown in Figure 22.3. These steps will ensure that the process(es) are fully handed over to the business and have

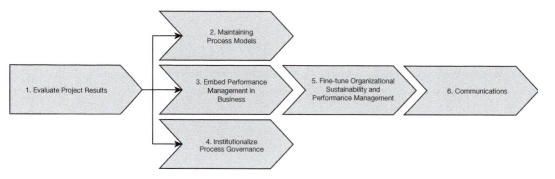

Figure 22.3 Sustainable performance phase steps

all the necessary tasks completed to enable them to be part of the organization-wide sustainability and performance management activities (the "roof" of the BPM House).

Note: This will only apply to processes that are important enough to the organization to require them to be part of the organization-wide sustainability and performance management activities.

Step 1: Evaluate project results

During this step, the initial business case (along with any modifications) should be compared to the actual outcomes of the project (which will include the value that has been, and is currently being, realized). The original baseline and benefit realization matrix are reviewed to determine the following:

- how much faster the processes are executed
- by how much errors, rework and backlogs have been reduced
- how efficient are the processes being performed
- how much customer satisfaction has improved
- how much employee satisfaction has improved
- the overall cost–benefit analysis for this project
- whether benefits have started to flow as expected.

The results of this evaluation have two purposes, to:

1. make the necessary changes to the current environment to correct any shortcomings; and
2. include lessons learned in the relevant aspects of the BPM Foundations, Enablement and the Launch pad phases for later BPM activities—in other words, to see process improvement as a process to improve the execution of BPM activities.

Refer to Chapter 24 (Project management—section on Continuous Active Project Review) for additional ways of continually reviewing project performance.

Steps 2, 3 and 4 may be completed simultaneously.

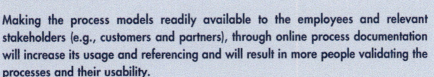

BPM INSIGHT

Making the process models readily available to the employees and relevant stakeholders (e.g., customers and partners), through online process documentation will increase its usage and referencing and will result in more people validating the processes and their usability.

Step 2: Maintaining process models

Processes are not static but dynamic and they will most likely have changed as a result of the BPM activity just completed. This step will ensure that the processes will already have been updated into the process repository to maintain the process asset as discussed in Chapter 14, the Enablement phase. Process documentation, including the business rules repository, will also require modification to reflect changes.

Step 3: Embed performance management in business

To achieve sustainable performance it is crucial that processes are managed, and managing processes requires continuous measurement of their performance.

This step covers ensuring that all the process-related performance management activities have been completed previously within the 7FE Framework phases, and that business employees and management understand them and the related management reporting available to them. The business (employees and management) must be in a position to "performance manage" the process(es) at the completion of this step.

KEY POINT

Measuring should ideally be linked to a higher level organization objective to ensure that the processes are geared towards and evaluated by their contribution to this objective.

Furthermore, measuring processes should also relate to evaluating the performance of the people involved. In other words, good process performance should be rewarded.

If business processes are important enough to manage, then they will require a set of performance targets (KPIs). It is usual to have both a dollar (cost) and timeframe performance set of measures; however, every process is unique and the measures need to meet the particular requirements of the process. This was discussed in Chapter 17, the Innovate phase.

The employees who execute the process(es) should also have appropriate performance targets, and these were discussed in Chapter 18, People phase.

In this step, review the process and employees targets again to ensure they are still appropriate for the circumstances and adjust if necessary.

The frequency of reporting against the measures (KPIs) will depend upon the particular process and its importance to the organization. Reporting could be via printed reports, reports viewed on a computer, laptop, tablet or smartphone, exception reporting, dashboards and so forth.

Reporting on operational processes (for example bank deposits, insurance claim processing, loan applications and welfare payments) could need to be provided to a process steward (owner) many times a day. Indeed, it could be a real-time alert. Other processes may only require daily, weekly or monthly reporting.

Monitoring frequency needs to strike a reasonable compromise or balance between being too expensive because of too much monitoring and too little. It needs to be comprehensive and cost-effective. The litmus test is that information is only useful if action can be taken as a result of receiving the information. If it is just interesting to know, it is probably a waste of time receiving it.

From an organizational perspective, the Balanced Scorecard is an excellent way to measure the processes, as it not only deals with the short-term financial aspects but also covers the customer perspective and the internal view. In fact, it is important that all stakeholder needs and expectations are covered in any scorecard that is established. Another benefit of the Balanced Scorecard approach is that it explicitly links the performance of the processes to the objectives of the organization, as well as linking initiatives to the specified objectives. This highlights the importance of carefully selecting the scorecard indices.

The Balanced Scorecard approach does not necessarily need to be cascaded all the way down the organization. It is an extremely useful mechanism for the first three or so layers within an organization, but beyond these levels, the performance measures need to be simple (and able to be clearly understood by employees) and not necessarily directly linked to higher level objectives.

Remember that when process performance measures are determined there are several components to be taken into account. These include effectiveness (including quality), efficiency (including cost and time), adaptability, risk, customer satisfaction and many more. There will be different drivers in different parts of the organization.

Continual measurement must be a key component in the establishment of process measures and performance targets. The targeted measurements must be capable of being compared to the actual outcomes of the process. There are, however, several ways or levels of measurement, including the measurement of:

- stakeholder visions and expectations;

- management expectations (although "management" is obviously a stakeholder, it is a "special" stakeholder and its needs must be met). Management expectations, however, must be articulated in quantitative terms, and the usual way of expressing this is via KPIs. Qualitative measures can also be measured through KPIs;

- customer experience throughout the process.

The measures, once established, should allow the organizations' supervisors, team leaders and area managers to act in a proactive way, changing staffing levels, redirecting staff and resources to immediately eliminate bottlenecks, and providing input into process changes that are necessary.

Other measures that can be made are the following:

- comparative measurements within the organization's industry, against competitors, and outside the industry, where this can be sensibly achieved and meaningful measures obtained;

- ensuring that the process stewards (owners) understand their role in detail and have accepted it (remember, not every process needs to have a steward (owner); some are too small and others are simply not important enough to warrant a steward);

- providing the process stewards with written job descriptions and KPIs;

- ensuring that the people change management process has empowered the people for change;

- centrally monitoring, in detail, that this continuous improvement strategy is working;

- adjusting the approach from the lessons learned;

- continually re-evaluating the applicability of the performance measures established, as the business changes and moves on, which will lead to a change in the way of measuring.

Benchmarking

When organizations start measuring the performance of their processes, they often wonder how they compare across business units within their organization or with competitors. Benchmarking processes allows this comparison to take place. Before comparing figures with other organizations, it is crucial to understand all the considerations and definitions used in the comparison to ensure that the figures are comparable. Organizations often compare figures without understanding the difference in scope, complexity or culture. This will make the benchmarking a waste of time and money.

Benchmarking can be related to throughput times, processing times, costs, quality, customer satisfaction, and profitability. Benchmarking can also be completed at different levels, such as product level, process level, business unit level and organization level.

Step 4: Institutionalize process governance

Process governance has been discussed in Chapter 14 (Enablement phase) and this step is about ensuring that at the completion of this BPM activity, the process(es) have process steward(s) appointed, and all other governance principles have been adhered to.

Governance is a major requirement in most organizations and business communities. The governance of processes is defined as "managing, controlling and reporting of processes within an organization." Governance forces organizations to consider all the relevant stakeholders, such as employees, financiers, shareholders, government, customers, suppliers and the community at large.

Governance is not a new phenomenon; it has been around for many years within organizations. However, it has shifted radically from being voluntary (as in a voluntary code of conduct between organizations or an industry) to becoming more rigid and far-reaching based on legislation (such as the Sarbanes–Oxley Act of 2002). This has been accelerated by the recent collapse of large billion-dollar organizations, which has shown that self-regulation is difficult for organizations. Furthermore, an increasing number of organizations are adopting good governance practices, even though they are not legally required to do so, or voluntary regulations such as EFQM and ISO.

What is the impact of governance on BPM? There are two levels of impact: impact on the:

- processes;
- management of the business processes.

Impact on the processes refers to the increasing number of rules and regulations applying to processes. The best way to address this is to ensure that governance is included within the process architecture as discussed in Chapter 14, Enablement phase. The process architecture must ensure that the processes are:

- transparent;
- accountable for all individual process steps and for the entire end-to-end process;
- able to produce the required reporting.

Impact on the management of the business processes refers to the fact that governance forces organizations to take all the necessary measures to ensure that the processes are managed and under control, and that they are properly administered. This could include the following:

- ensuring that the processes are properly followed;
- ensuring that exceptions and undesirable outcomes are identified and dealt with by the business;
- ensuring that the reporting and audit trail of the actions taken are properly recorded;
- identifying the non-compliancy, risk and weak points in the process and taking appropriate measures.

When completing a BPM activity, the project manager must ensure that governance is taken into account at each of the framework phases—thus further embedding governance as part of the organization's process management approach.

From a governance perspective, the following points should be considered (Bloem and van Doorn, 2004):

1. *Keep measuring.* This involves the cycle of ensuring that the expected outcomes are specified at the start of the project, measuring the progress in achieving the expected outcomes, and evaluating the extent to which the outcomes have been achieved. Lessons learned should also be evaluated and applied to future projects. Remember, measuring only makes sense when management applies what is learned from the measures and ensures that the roles and tasks are properly allocated to apply these lessons.

2. *Divide the leadership.* Many managers strive to have all aspects of a process fully under their control; however, many of these managers fall into the same trap—the more they want to control, the more time it takes and the less effective they are, so they become more and more their own major bottleneck. Managers should move to a form of distributed leadership (delegated responsibility), ensuring that all aspects of a process are taken care of, rather than having to understand every detailed aspect. Thus, only when everyone understands what is expected of them in a process and what they are accountable for can the managers really manage a process.

3. *Almost any governance structure is good.* The most important thing is that a governance structure is selected and used. It is not important to select the most complete or up-to-date model; what is crucial is that it fits with the organization's needs, meets the organization's objectives and is consistently applied. In fact, a suitable solution can evolve over time as a result of the increasing process maturity of those involved.

4. *Encourage the desired behavior.* Ensure that the people are supported and encouraged to do the right things correctly. Management has a large range of measures that can be used to achieve this, from incentives to sanctions. Senior management has the important role of setting the right example. Furthermore, the right behavior should be included in performance reviews.

5. *People are allergic to excessive control.* Excessive control does not improve the performance of people. Appropriate control measures should become an integral part of everyone's working environment, and should also be delegated just like leadership.

6. *Keep it simple.* Management often falls into the trap of preparing models that are too complex, which inevitably leads to complications. If a control model is too difficult to understand, it becomes less effective.

Step 5: Fine-tune organizational sustainability and performance management

There is a need when transitioning the completed BPM activity from a project status to business-as-usual, to review the principles and mechanisms established as part of the Foundations and Enablement phases and the organizational sustainability and performance management aspect of the BPM House. Lessons will have been learned during the execution of the BPM activity and transition that may require enhancements to be made.

KEY POINT

Lessons are not learned until changed action and behavior occurs.

This step is about updating the principles and mechanisms in the organizational sustainability and performance management aspect of the BPM House.

The organization's, customers', suppliers'—in fact, all stakeholders'—expectations and needs change over time. The organization's sustainability strategy will have established several formal mechanisms to ensure that it will not only maintain the investment made in these processes, but also continually review the applicability of the processes to the current, and expected future, operating environment.

The organization must continue to reassess the relationship between the business and process stakeholders, and the organization's evolving strategies and plans, and understand the gaps as they emerge. A mechanism must then be available to fill these gaps, adjust processes, handle the change management issues arising out of these gaps and update the organization's sustainability strategy.

The sustainable performance strategy should answer questions such as:

- What are the objectives of sustainable performance?
- What is in the scope of sustainable performance and what is out of scope?
- What are the roles and responsibilities regarding sustainable performance?
- How are people rewarded for their contribution towards a sustainable environment?

Step 6: Communications

When the BPM activity moves from the project phase to business-as-usual, it must focus its communication on the actual benefits that have been realized and motivate employees to identify other areas to explore, as well as ensuring that people work according to the new process(es). It is important to emphasize that each completed BPM activity should bring the organization one step closer to a more process-focused way of thinking and working.

REALIZE VALUE

The business value expected to be gained as part of the BPM activity must be monitored and maximized as part of this phase. For details refer to step 7 of Chapter 21, where it is described in the context of realizing value within a BPM activity.

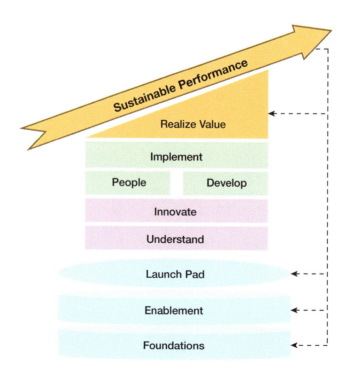

Figure 22.4 Sustainable performance phase outputs to other phases

SUSTAINABLE PERFORMANCE PHASE OUTPUTS

The Sustainable performance phase will provide valuable input into other phases of the 7FE Framework (Figure 22.4). The main outputs will be to the Foundations and Enablement phases, with lessons learned being taken into future Launch pad phases. The knowledge gained from the ongoing business activities will provide information that could change both these phases for subsequent projects and the further business-as-usual activities.

SUSTAINABLE PERFORMANCE PHASE RISKS

Table 22.1 highlights the most common risks involved in ensuring sustainable performance.

Table 22.1 Sustainable performance risks and mitigation strategies

	Risk	Mitigation strategy
1.	No one takes ownership of the processes and the management of the processes	Discuss with senior management, as ownership has already been specified at the Launch pad phase—this is one of the most critical success factors in BPM.
2.	People are not following the new way of working	Find out why people are not working in the new way and address the issue. If people are not motivated, "sell" the benefits to them. If people have forgotten how to use the new way, provide additional training and guidance.
3.	Processes are not updated into the process asset repository	Ensure that people are using the process models and can detect any issues that are outdated, and ensure that processes are reviewed on a regular basis.
4.	No further process improvements are identified or initiated from employees and line management	Encourage employees and line management to provide suggestions. Explain what happens to their suggestions, explain why certain suggestions are not viable, and communicate successes initiated by employees.
5.	Difficulty in keeping up with the pace at which governance requirements are formulated	Approach governance holistically, rather than piece by piece.

SUMMARY

This chapter described how a BPM activity moves from a project or program basis to a business environment. That is how the BPM activity links in with the Operate, Manage, Sustain aspect of the BPM House, and then subsequently on to the Organization Sustainability and Performance Management "roof" of the BPM House. However, there are a number of activities that must be completed before this phase can be commenced.

SELF-TEST

1 Describe in one brief paragraph the purpose of this phase of the 7FE Framework.

2 Why is sustainability important?

3 List the four activities that must be completed before this phase is commenced.

4 Briefly list and describe the six steps in this phase.

5 Briefly describe how this phase links with the Foundations and Enablement phases, and with the BPM House.

ASSIGNMENT

You now wish to inform the executives how you will embed the benefits of this BPM activity into the organization.

Assignment guiding questions

1. How have you evaluated the project results (New Student Enrolment)?
2. How have you embedded process governance for the student on-boarding process?

Sustainable performance phase checklist

This checklist provides a generic overview of possible inputs, deliverables and gates of this phase.

Possible inputs

See Table 22.2.

Deliverables

See Table 22.3.

Possible gates

- Development strategy does not deliver benefits
- Implementation strategy does not deliver benefits
- Stakeholder analysis
- Understanding magnitude of change
- Organization's capacity to change
- Organization's acceptance of BPM
- Technical review.

Table 22.2 Sustainable performance phase—possible inputs

✓	Phase	Deliverable
	Foundations phase	• Organization's core value proposition • BPM maturity of the organization • BPM drivers • BPM activities width • Red Wine Test outcomes • BPM approach • Components of the target operating model
	Establishment phase	• An agreed target operating model • Level 1 and 2 process views • Process architecture, including: o Process guidelines o Process asset repository o Business rules repository o Benefits management framework • Methods by which the people process capability will be built • Organizational cultural behavior changes by the establishment of appropriate targets (KPIs) and linked rewards • Code of behavior • The process-focused organizational design • The technology approach to BPM
	Launch pad phase	• Stakeholders defined in, involved in or associated with the BPM • Stakeholder engagement, commitment, and documented and agreed expectations • Process selection matrix and initial metrics • A list of identified high level business processes and initial metrics • A list of agreed process goals

Table 22.2 Sustainable performance phase—possible inputs—*continued*

✓	Phase	Deliverable

		• Agreement of the process governance for the processes in the BPM activity
		• Prioritized processes for the Understand phase
		• An initial implementation approach
		• Project management:
		  o Project charter documents
		  o Project scope (initial) document
		  o Initial draft of the project schedule (plan)
		  o Determination and documentation on the initial communications strategy
		  o Initial risk analysis
		• Potential project benefits and realization plan
		• Initial business case

	From Understand phase	• Revalidated scope • Process models of current processes • Metrics baseline (including Voice of Customer) • Prioritized quick wins • People capability matrix • Knowledge and information needs • List of priorities for Innovate phase • Project plan (in detail) for Innovate phase • Report to management • Presentation to management • Initial communications plan
	From Innovate phase	• New process models and documentation
	From People phase	• People strategy documentation • New roles descriptions • Role measurement (goals) creation • Performance measures • People core capabilities gap analysis • Redesigned organization structure • Updated HR policies • Training documentation • Defined benefits details (from Realize value phase)
	Develop phase	• High level overview of the solution • Defined benefits details (from Realize value phase)
	Implement phase	• Trained and motivated staff • Implemented solution • Final defined benefits details (from Realize value phase)
	Realize value phase	• Benefits delivery and tracking

Table 22.3 Sustainable performance phase—deliverables

✓	Deliverable	Used in phase
	Mechanism to manage business process, and identify and realize opportunities for process improvement	• Used in Sustain performance phase
	Managed and improved processes	• Used in Sustain performance phase
	Value monitoring and maximization	• Used in Sustain performance phase
	Updates of process models to the process asset repository	• Enablement
	Updates to the business rules repository	• Enablement
	Refine the organizational approach to: • Benefits management framework • Process governance structures and roles and responsibilities • Performance management approach • Organizational structure	• Enablement
	Refine and provide feedback to: • Organization strategy • Organization core value proposition • Suggestions on how BPM maturity is being, or may be, increased • Effectiveness of the current BPM approach • Refinements to the target operating model	• Foundations

CHAPTER 23

ESSENTIALS INTRODUCTION

OVERVIEW

The three essentials—Leadership, BPM Project Management and People Change Management—are critical for each BPM activity and should be considered during each of the phases. They are referred to as "essentials" because that is what they are–essential. BPM cannot be delivered without these aspects permeating every phase and activity of the 7FE Framework and hence a BPM activity.

OVERALL LEARNING OUTCOME

By the end of this chapter you will be able to:
- Understand the importance of the essentials
- Name the three essentials.

WHY?

The ten specified phases are not sufficient to ensure the success of a BPM project, as a BPM project requires many aspects and facets to be covered. Without the three essentials of project management, people change management and leadership being an integral part of a BPM activity the likelihood of success is significantly diminished and certainly risk is much higher.

The Cambridge Dictionary defines the word essential as: "necessary; needed; a basic thing that you cannot live without." A BPM activity cannot "live" without these three essentials.

The essentials required for any BPM activity are:

- *Project management:* aimed at ensuring that the resources, budget, timelines, stake-holders and output are managed.

- *Leadership:* aimed at ensuring that the leaders of the organization provide the necessary support and guidance to ensure that the BPM activity and organization are aligned and deliver the right business outcomes.

- *People change management:* aimed at ensuring that all concerned stakeholders are able (for example, through training) and willing (through change management) to embrace and contribute to the future solution.

HOW?

An essential is an aspect of a BPM activity that is considered extremely important, in fact crucial, to ensuring the success of the project, but it does not occur as a sequential activity or at a certain time within a BPM activity. An essential occurs on a continual basis throughout the entire BPM activity, and this is why essentials have been represented differently to the other phases in Figure 23.1.

- While the ten phases of the framework are not rigid sequential activities either, as they overlap and intertwine, they predominantly occur in the sequence shown. The method of approach and scenarios described throughout Part II provide examples of how the framework could be used and sequenced.

- An essential is considered to be fundamental to the success of the entire project, and an aspect that permeates and occurs throughout every phase. Essentials are the foundations

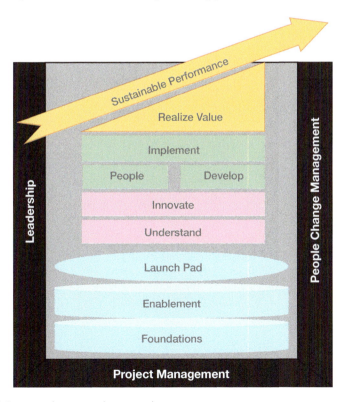

Figure 23.1 Project phases and essentials

> ## BPM INSIGHT
>
> Too often BPM programs and large projects have been broken down into multiple streams: e.g., change management, project management, process, and technology streams. Each stream has its own methodology and approach, resulting in silos that do not provide a holistic solution, resulting in increasing frustrations, diminishing benefits and increasing risk of failure.
>
> To maximize the likelihood of success, and therefore decrease risk, every BPM activity needs a holistic and consistent approach.

upon which any successful BPM activity rests. When executed well, these foundations will be rock solid; when executed poorly, they will act like quicksand and the BPM project "stool" (see Chapter 11) will tilt, sink or collapse.

WHAT ARE THE THREE ESSENTIALS?

The three *essential* components upon which any successful BPM activity rests are:

1. *Project management.* The question is often asked, "Can a normal application or business project manager implement a BPM project?" The answer is a qualified "Yes, but nowhere nearly as well as an experienced BPM project manager." The risks will be significantly higher, and the organization risks missing out on many of the potential benefits that can be achieved from BPM. Can a person without significant project management experience implement a BPM project? This answer is easy—"No." Project management is a fundamental skill or requirement for any project and a BPM activity is no different. In fact, the requirement is even higher because of the increased complexity of BPM activities. The reason for these answers is that BPM adds significant complexity to programs and projects and increased skill levels are required. We will discuss these additional skills in Chapter 24.

2. *People change management.* The importance of the change management process as it specifically relates to the implementation of the employee aspects of a BPM activity are discussed in Chapter 25. There have been many articles written on why process improvement and BPM activity failures occur, and we do not propose to mention all the reasons. However, there is a growing belief that the employee aspects of an improvement project have not always been addressed in sufficient detail. As Michael Hammer stated in 1993, "coming up with the ideas is the easy part, but getting things done is the tough part. The place where these reforms die is . . . down in the trenches"— and who "owns" the trenches? The people in the organization. We would suggest that people change management aspects of any BPM activity is in excess of 60 percent of the effort. Unless this is addressed extremely well throughout every BPM activity (phase and steps) the initiative will suffer.

3. *Leadership*. A point acknowledged by all business process change experts is that any change program must have the support of senior leadership/management to be successful. According to Keen (1997: 119), "These people's commitment to change matters more than the details of the plan for change." The extent to which executive leaders "delegate" responsibility is crucial to the effectiveness of the outcomes of BPM activities. There have been extremely successful BPM implementations and some poor ones, and the common thread in both types has always been the commitment, attention and process maturity of the executive leaders. The successful BPM activities had excellent executive commitment, attention and understanding, while the poor ones did not (more details are given in Chapter 26).

Project management, people change management and leadership are topics that have been written about in significant detail in countless articles and books. We will not describe all the aspects of a successful project management methodology, or the framework of how to complete an organization-wide people change program, or what makes a great leader. We will, however, describe the aspects of each that are considered essential to a BPM activity—the aspects that, if missing or executed poorly, will have a significant impact on the success of BPM projects. We will cover the parts of each of these that the business and BPM activity team must address during a project/program to ensure success.

KEY POINT

The following three chapters describing the essentials will focus on the specific BPM aspects rather than provide all aspects for these essentials.

SUMMARY

- This chapter outlined the importance of essentials and the need to consider them for each BPM activity and throughout each phase and step.
- A brief overview has been provided about the three essentials: project management, people change management and leadership.

SELF-TEST

- What are the three essentials?
- Why are the three essentials crucial for each BPM activity?

CHAPTER 24

PROJECT MANAGEMENT

OVERVIEW

This chapter provides an overview of the key aspects of one of the essentials: project management.

It focuses on the key Project Management aspects that are unique for BPM activities and looks at the role and profile of the Project Manager.

It describes key gates that the BPM activity needs to pass through to be successful; as well as covering key stakeholder management methods.

OVERALL LEARNING OUTCOME

By the end of this chapter you will be able to:

- Understand the difference between traditional project management and BPM project management
- Recognize the importance of project stages
- Know the various project stages and their criteria
- Understand the importance of stakeholder management
- Be able to apply the stakeholder management framework
- Be aware of the project management risks.

WHY?

This chapter is not intended as a guide to project management. It is assumed that project management discipline is already understood. The intention is to focus on the aspects of project management that require particular attention in a BPM activity in order to increase the chances of delivering success.

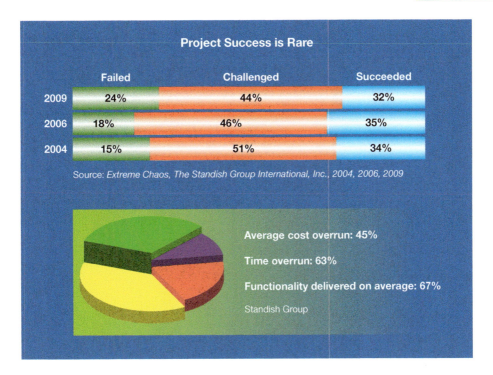

Figure 24.1 The myth of project management methodology success

Source: Statistics from The Standish Group, 2004, 2006 and 2009 (www.standishgroup.com).

Notes: Failed: a project that is cancelled at some point during the development cycle. Challenged: projects that are completed and operational but over-budget, over time estimate and offer fewer features and functions than originally specified. Succeeded: projects that are completed on-time and on-budget, with all features and functions as initially specified.

Before BPM project management is discussed, there is a need to look at standard project management methodologies, examples are PRINCE2® and PMBOK® (Project Management Body of Knowledge).[1] Conventional thinking is that if an organization employs one of these project management methodologies (or a similarly recognized methodology), then its projects will more likely be successful. Figure 24.1 shows research conducted by The Standish Group that clearly shows this is not always the case.

Standish's research shows that in 2004, 15 percent of all projects failed outright and progressively this figure became worse until in 2009 the figure was 24 percent.

If failed and challenged projects are combined, then a whopping 68 percent (2009) of projects are not successful. Further analysis[2] shows that:

- The average cost overrun was 178 percent for large companies ($500m plus revenue);
- One-third of projects experienced time overruns of 200 to 300 percent;
- Time overruns for large companies was 222 percent.

Standish surveyed IT executive managers to endeavor to elicit why projects succeed or fail. The top three project success factors were:

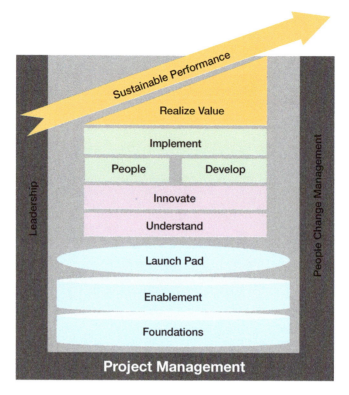

Figure 24.2 Project management essential

- User involvement—15.9 percent
- Executive management support—13.9 percent
- Clear statement of requirements—13.0 percent.

The purpose of highlighting these statistics is not to critique current project management methodologies, but to highlight that by themselves they are simply not enough. While the use of a project management methodology in any BPM activity is essential, it is not enough and will not guarantee success. The 7FE Framework plus the additional aspects considered in this chapter will assist projects in becoming more successful (from a BPM perspective).

These statistics emphasize that merely completing activities according to a methodology is never sufficient to be successful. Each project and initiative is unique and requires a person who truly understands the business objectives and how to address the challenges, supported by the methodology. The project manager/director is a critical role in achieving the business objectives and therefore success.

Project management is considered to be one of the three essentials in the BPM project framework (Figure 24.2). Without excellent project management, an organization and project team cannot deliver a successful project. Is being a good project manager enough? We would say no. Being a good project manager is no longer about having the skills and knowledge inherent in using traditional project management methodologies. BPM project managers must include in their repertoire significant additional or deeper skills with regard to:

- people change management;
- stakeholder management;
- in a BPM project, in-depth knowledge and experience in the implementation of BPM activities/projects.

It could be argued that good project management has always required the first two of these skills; it is just that BPM projects require this knowledge to be deeper and better executed than in the past. Traditionally, projects delivered under project management methodologies have targeted the technology-based or low-resistance business changes. This enables a certainty of delivery that project sponsors like to have. BPM changes are different in one very important aspect: they almost always require a large element of people and/or cultural change, especially in case of large transformation programs.

Why is this? Consider any manager in a large organization who is in control of inefficient processes. Nine times out of ten the manager is well aware of the inefficient operation—as indeed are his or her superior managers and most of the employees (process workers). Once a BPM practitioner is brought in to improve the situation and recognizes that stakeholders understand that the processes are inefficient, the obvious assumption to make is that the implementation job will be easy. This, of course, is not the case. The difference with BPM activities is the people and cultural impact of process changes. The underlying causes, interests and agendas that require the operation to change are often not recognized, understood or addressed. We are now deep in territory where a traditional project manager does not want to be—this world is uncertain, high risk and not easily controlled, especially as an increasing number of BPM activities involve customers, partners and suppliers. A BPM project manager needs to be skilled enough to succeed in this type of environment. Program managers that have in the past delivered successful transformations will be well placed to manage and direct large-scale BPM programs. Table 24.1 provides some guidelines for this.

The question is, can a normal application or business project manager implement a BPM project and be successful? The answer is a qualified yes (probably), but nowhere nearly as well as an experienced BPM project manager. With an inexperienced BPM project manager, or a project manager with limited BPM experience, the project risks will simply be significantly higher and the organization risks forgoing potential benefits that can be achieved via BPM. As stated before, successful transformation program managers will be well placed to be successful with a large-scale BPM activity.

It is important for the organization to appoint its own project manager with overall responsibility for the entire project, even if the project manager is inexperienced in BPM implementation. If this is the case, it is crucial that the project manager is a business person and not an IT appointee; IT, vendor and all other project components must report to this business BPM project manager. To support an inexperienced BPM project manager, a senior and experienced BPM consultant (internal or external) will be required to coach the project manager throughout the project. In addition, the consultant can add value to the project by:

Table 24.1 Traditional versus BPM project management

Traditional project management	BPM project management
Ensure scope provides certainty for delivery	Ensure scope delivers the business objective required by improved processes; understand that scope will evolve over the life of the BPM activity (project)
Stakeholder management to deliver implementation only	Stakeholder management to deliver implementation and long-term behavioral change and sustainability for the business
Contingency planning is only for recognized and easily defined risks	Cultural change hurdles (require sometimes up to 60 percent of total effort) and contingency for unrecognized and difficult to define risks must be built into the plans
Works with sponsor/steering committee/ project board to deliver defined outcomes	Works with the sponsor, steering committee, project board, business, users and partners to manage uncertainty and deliver uncertain outcomes while delivering to meet the organization's strategy and objectives
Project success criteria are driven by quantifiable goals only	Project success criteria are driven equally by quantifiable and qualitative goals
Focus on the outcome and let content be managed by experts	Outcomes are integrated in all aspects of project management. Process selection and prioritization are important elements of BPM project management

- objectively managing situations when process compromises need to be made during the course of the project (as they inevitably will be); such decisions can have very serious repercussions, and a BPM specialist should be able to manage these risks appropriately to prevent the BPM activity turning into an expensive, small incremental improvement activity;

- ensuring that the BPM activity remains focused and as self-funding as possible, and continues to deliver real business value;

- ensuring that the required people change management and cultural elements are correctly built into the project plan/schedule and managed as an essential part of the project;

- adding value to stakeholder management and providing the expertise necessary to ensure that stakeholders remain continually engaged, have their needs met and are focused towards a successful BPM delivery.

Can a person without significant project management experience implement a BPM project? The answer to this question is easy—no. Project management is a fundamental skill or requirement for any project, and a BPM activity is no different—in fact, the requirement is even greater because of the increased complexity.

Table 24.2 Type of project and type of project manager

Type of project	Type of project manager
Pilot BPM project	Traditional project manager with eagerness to understand process, supported by an experienced process consultant
Large BPM program	A project manager who has been involved in various BPM projects
	A traditional project manager is highly unlikely to be successful
Transformation program	A program director with substantial BPM experience in large-scale process changes

During this chapter, there is an assumption that BPM project management covers all the different types of BPM activities, from the program management activities for the large transformation program to the small-scale process improvements.

RESULTS

When project management is executed well, the risks of the project are significantly diminished and the likelihood of achieving the organization's initiative objectives and realization of the benefits is enhanced.

All projects must be subject to the normal organizational project governance requirements throughout their life, and these will be covered in the project methodology used by the project manager.

HOW?

There are many project management methodologies, and there have been many books written on the subject, so we do not propose to outline a new methodology here. We will, however, examine two key aspects of project management from a BPM perspective. These two key aspects are:

- that there are several key "gates" that must be passed satisfactorily if your BPM project is to be a success or indeed continue;
- stakeholder management.

PROJECT "GATES"

A project "gate" represents a critical checkpoint, milestone or risk in the journey of the project. When this milestone is reached, the gate is always assumed to be closed until the project manager and project sponsor are satisfied that there is sufficient information available to

BPM INSIGHT

Not handling these project gates in a disciplined manner is an error that many inexperienced BPM practitioners make. They assume that "having a good discussion" is a substitute for the formal sign-off of relevant project gates, for example scope. The reason is often the desire to continue as soon as possible, as they do not wish to hold up the process by these formalities, only to find out later that there is less agreement on scope than they thought.

It is essential, in fact critical, to adhere to the relevant project gates.

"open" the gate and continue the project. If the gate is to remain closed, because the available information is not satisfactory, then the project should be stopped until information is available to allow the gate to be opened. A partially closed gate means that the information is incomplete and the project should be paused or slowed down until more information is gained in order to open or close the gate fully.

A few of the potential gates that the project may encounter along the way have been identified and will be discussed. All the possible gates that a project may encounter will not be identified and discussed as each project is unique and will encounter its own unique set of gates.

These gates need to be incorporated in the project life cycle. Critical gates should be identified as early as possible in the project planning, and should be:

- at points where the business can exit or pause the project, if necessary, with reduced risk and costs to the organization; exit strategies should be planned and agreed when gates are identified;

- placed strategically to ensure that value has been created for the organization up to this time, regardless of the exit point.

We have numbered the gates here so that we can refer to them. The reader should not interpret the numbers as an order of occurrence within a project.

KEY POINT

It is important to validate that the conditions that opened a gate are still in place. Changes in personnel, circumstances or market environment need to be assessed and it needs to be determined if any of the project stages need to be revisited.

Gate 1: Stakeholder analysis[3]

One of the first steps in a project should be the identification and subsequent analysis of the project stakeholders. The analysis should include:

- leadership styles of the stakeholders (refer to Chapter 26 for a more detailed examination and categorization of leadership styles);
- an understanding of where the internal stakeholders are placed within the organization and the organization hierarchy;
- an understanding of the internal stakeholder's business (organization) and personal drivers—the business drivers are usually reflected in the individual key result areas and key performance indicators; however, the personal drivers (ambition) of the internal stakeholders can be an extremely important motivator for an individual.

This gate is often closed until the stakeholder environment has been assessed and is deemed to be in alignment with the project goals. Are the stakeholders generally aligned to the proposed changes (project)? Is there misalignment? Are most of the stakeholders aligned, but not the major decision makers or influencers? This is also related to the BPM maturity of the individual(s) and to organization BPM maturity. If the change is large and the stakeholder environment is not fully aligned to support the change, the project is unlikely to succeed.

This gate is often opened by:

- confirmation that the stakeholder environment, BPM maturity and BPM activity objectives are consistent (aligned) with achieving a successful outcome;
- planning the steps necessary to achieve stakeholder alignment so that they are adequately completed and under control. This may mean additional time, cost, multiple project checkpoints and the creation of additional gates.

This will be covered in more detail in the next section of this chapter (Stakeholder management).

BPM INSIGHT

Many organizations start a finance transformation in isolation from the business, as they see that it is mainly focused on the finance function. However, the finance function is often closely intertwined with the business. If this is not fully understood or not adequately addressed the project gate should remain closed.

Transformation programs that proceed anyway have a higher failure rate or will increase project cost considerably.

Gate 2: Understand magnitude of change[4]

The level of change and alignment of the stakeholders will, to some extent, be linked to the type of BPM activity.

In the early planning stages of the project, during the Launch pad phase, the project team will need to determine and document the magnitude of change and stakeholder alignment required during the project—as it is known at that stage. The magnitude of change will be further refined during the Innovate phase, once there is additional knowledge of how processes are to change, and once the people capability matrices have been completed.

There needs to be a very clear understanding of the magnitude of change required by the organization. It is strongly recommended to use the models outlined in Figure 12.3 (Scenarios for process improvement) and Figure 13.21 (Determine width of BPM activities). Until this is understood and agreed the project should not proceed, because an understanding of this leads directly into the next project gate—the capacity of the organization to change.

This gate is often closed because:

* the scope of the change is not understood and/or agreed by the business and/or project team, due to unclear baseline processes, lack of information regarding organizational operations, differing stakeholder needs, etc.;
* the total impact to the organization is unknown: that is, the size of the immediate change is understood, but the impact to related processes and to the organization is not.

This gate is often opened by:

* scoping agreement
* impact assessment.

CASE STUDY

Business problem definition

An organization was planning a multimillion-dollar project to implement a Customer Relationship Management system (to address Call Center issues), a data warehouse, data mining, a major data cleansing operation for data integrity reasons, and a document management system.

A stakeholder workshop was held for the primary purpose of defining the business problem the project was expected to resolve. After three hours, the problem could not be defined by the stakeholders. The stakeholders (management) simply "wanted" the new system, and external consultants had recommended it. It was a technical solution looking for a business problem.

It was recommended that the project be broken down into smaller components and a business case be built for each component.

This advice was ignored, and the project manager spent the next year canvassing the stakeholders and trying to build a business case. The project did not proceed.

Message: Workshop, with all relevant stakeholders, the reason for the project and the business problem that it will solve prior to building, or at least finalizing, the business case.

The difficulties with scope can often be because the business problem that the organization is trying to resolve has not yet been adequately defined and agreed upon by the business and stakeholders. This is a critical step, and one that must be addressed and agreed upon before the business case can be finalized.

Gate 3: The organization's capacity to change[5]

The nature of a BPM activity is such that it will no doubt cause change within the organization. The level of change can range from small to significant; however, in most BPM activities the level of change will be from the middle to the high end of the change scale.

An organization's ability to (and capacity for) change will be put to the test in a BPM activity. This ability and capacity for change within an organization needs to be determined very early on in the project, because if the project requires significant change and the organization maturity is unable to cope with the level of change required, the project is doomed to failure from the outset. In this instance, the project manager should go back to the project sponsor to discuss and decide upon a course of action. This could mean walking away from, or stopping, the project. It is far better to establish this at an early start in a project than to spend time and money, only to discover later that the organization is incapable of changing to the extent necessary.

Chapter 29 will assist the project sponsor and project manager to gauge the organization's maturity to cope with change.

This gate is often closed because of:

- overconfidence—organizations tend to have an insatiable appetite to "want the universe," and yet they are only capable of changing their world at a limited rate. BPM project managers need to identify the gap between an organization's desire for change, and reality;

- lack of confidence—an organization may not clearly understand its capability to change and tend to underestimate its capacity to absorb change.

This gate is often opened by:

- assessing and understanding organizational BPM maturity;

- assessing capacity for change (reviewing similar past projects may assist in this regard);

- planning for the rate of change. Ambitious objectives can often be broken down into smaller stages—that is instead of one large step change, you may plan for a smaller step

> ## BPM INSIGHT
>
> It is important to consider all impacted people when assessing the readiness for change. Larger BPM projects and transformation programs are often head-office centric and forget to consider the pressures and changes that are impacting the various operational divisions and geographical regions.

change with specific milestones, followed by further incremental improvements, followed by another smaller step change, followed by further incremental improvements, and so on.

Gate 4: Organization's acceptance of BPM[6]

Organization BPM maturity also relates to the organization's understanding of the importance of business processes and how process improvement can make a substantial difference in meeting the organization's strategy and objectives.

It is a combination of organizational BPM maturity and executive understanding of BPM, and the executive's attention to process, that will determine an organization's process-focused view.

This gate is often closed because:

- executives are too busy "fighting fires";
- executives do not understand the importance of business processes to their organizational effectiveness.

This gate is often opened by:

- market pressures forcing organizations to look at cost reductions, and thus focus upon business processes;
- growing maturity and successful case studies of BPM implementations within other organizations;
- just one executive within the organization implementing one or a small number of pilot BPM activities that is successful. This is sometimes enough to demonstrate the benefits of BPM to the organization.

Gate 5: Technical review[7]

Where a BPM project is to involve automation and interfacing to existing infrastructure (hardware, networks, legacy application systems), there needs to be a technical review conducted early in the project to ensure that the selected BPM solution can indeed interface with the required infrastructure and systems. This can be a "show-stopper" if it either is not technically possible or will involve significant expenditure to achieve.

This may seem obvious; however, it is disappointing how often a review of this nature does not occur early in a project.

This gate is often closed because:

- the existing technical infrastructure is unknown, poorly documented, the interfaces are not understood, technologies are incompatible, etc.

This gate is often opened by:

- technical analysis at an early stage;
- consideration in the selection of the BPM automation toolset (and a vendor "proof of concept" demonstration during the selection process).

STAKEHOLDER MANAGEMENT

The first consideration is to understand who is a stakeholder. A stakeholder is an individual, or group of individuals, who have (or believe they have) a "stake" (positive or negative) in the project. They can be as diverse as: individual managers, employees, vendors, other internal business units, suppliers, customers, distribution channels, the community, the environment and the marketplace.

Stakeholder management is important—in fact crucial—in a BPM initiative for a number of reasons:

- Without key internal stakeholders, the project will not have funding;
- In the Understand and Innovate phases, it has been suggested that processes need to be examined on an end-to-end basis—which means that in all likelihood they will cross

CASE STUDY

Infrastructure "show-stopper"

The systems and infrastructure of an organization had grown piecemeal over time as the organization grew. It was now attempting to implement an automated BPM solution. This left some interesting challenges with regard to the existing infrastructure.

The organization was informed that the project should temporarily pause to review and pilot how the selected BPM solution was going to interface with the existing infrastructure, as there were concerns that the legacy applications may require substantial changes to accommodate the BPM solution. The CEO ignored this advice and insisted on proceeding because of business imperatives to implement.

A couple of months later the project was *forced* to halt because the infrastructure could not be interfaced without significant rewriting of some legacy applications. Had the project paused when originally suggested, the rework could have taken place in parallel with other aspects of the BPM project—thus avoiding the delay and costs.

Message: If there are potential major issues with infrastructure, address them early in the project to ensure that the impact is known and understood, to save time and money.

External stakeholder involvement

The majority of the organization's business was distributed via intermediaries. The organization wished to redesign its processes that were executed and generated by these intermediaries.

It was suggested that a small number of stakeholder focus groups should be established to inform the intermediaries of what the organization wished to achieve. This would allow the organization to listen to their concerns and ensure that the intermediaries would ultimately use the new processes. This was met with resistance by the sales team and a belief that this was simply not necessary.

Once the organization understood the opportunity and need for the meeting, it proceeded to engage the intermediaries and the outcomes were excellent.

Message: If external stakeholders of processes are not involved in their creation, how can you expect them to use the processes once introduced?

departmental and perhaps organizational boundaries. Without key stakeholder support, both internal and external, this end-to-end perspective cannot be achieved in any meaningful way;

- Without stakeholder support it will be extremely difficult to realize the business benefits set out in the business case;

- There are many parties to a BPM activity—the business, project team members, vendors, suppliers, customers and so forth—and without their support and enthusiasm; the project simply becomes more difficult. Many of these parties may not have direct contact with the project, but rely on what others are saying about the BPM activity;

- Certain external stakeholders, e.g., key customers, regulators, key partners, etc., can be crucial to the success of a BPM activity, and these must be identified.

Communications must be targeted specifically to the various groups.

Stakeholder management is all about relationship management. It is a structured process approach for handling the necessary relationships involved in the project. Owing to the complexity of BPM activities, this stakeholder management needs to be a more formal process than in traditional projects.

How do you create this more formal stakeholder management structured process? There are two types of stakeholder management usually required for successful BPM activities. The first is called "managing stakeholders for successful delivery." This is a more formal method of ensuring that stakeholders do the tasks asked of them to ensure delivery of the project. This is based on more traditional project management delivery-focused techniques. It is adversarial based, and recognizes that most organizations are still an adversarial environment. It is a "get things done" environment. This approach will assist with delivery; however, it is unlikely to affect any long-term behavioral change, which can influence the people change management aspects of a project.

> ## BPM INSIGHT
>
> The larger the BPM activity is, the more people who are impacted, and the more crucial stakeholder management will be. However, it is important to realize that in a large BPM activity the project team may not directly communicate with a large percentage of those people who are impacted. It is crucial that these stakeholders receive a consistent message throughout the project.
>
> Message: Project management also has to ensure that all relevant feedback is captured and acted upon.

The second is "interest-based" stakeholder management, and this is based on cooperative problem-solving techniques. This is where relationships are made and maintained that progress towards permanent change in individual and group behavior and is more conducive to cultural change.

Both techniques will need to be used for the significant organizational change that is necessary for BPM initiatives. For small changes or large projects with minimal cultural change impact, the key technique to use is "managing stakeholders for successful delivery."

The topic of managing stakeholders and the detail of the theories and these techniques is too vast a topic to discuss in this book. We will provide a summarized practical stakeholder management framework of how to utilize these techniques within a BPM activity.

MANAGING STAKEHOLDERS FOR SUCCESSFUL DELIVERY

The steps are:

1. Establish the internal project or business team to build the stakeholder management structure, plan, engagement and execution.
2. Identify all stakeholders and their relationship to the BPM activity.
3. Profile the role key stakeholders will play in the BPM activity.
4. Map stakeholders to determine the individual stakeholder requirements or the outcomes that they need from the BPM activity.
5. Determine the best strategies to engage and manage each stakeholder, to satisfy their needs and ensure a safe delivery of the BPM activity.

Each of these steps is discussed below in more detail.

Step 1: Establish the internal stakeholder team

In this step, it is essential that the project manager involves the business owners to ensure that they are fully engaged in the building of the stakeholder management structure (the how are we going to do this step), and the detailed planning, engagement and execution.

Who from the business needs to be involved? Usually this includes the project business owner, the project sponsor and all other business stakeholders who have to advise or propose a final solution.

The project manager and business stakeholder leader will have overall responsibility for stakeholder management, and need to be persons who:

- are well respected by the executives across the organization
- have credibility throughout the organization
- are comfortable in speaking their mind, even if it goes against the current organization's culture
- are able to deliver both good and bad news in a sensitive and yet honest manner
- are considered to be agents for change within the organization
- are able to get things done.

It is the responsibility of the project manager to "move" stakeholders to where they need to be in supporting the BPM activity, and to control and manage the stakeholder relations. The project manager will need to have confidence that he or she has the support and assistance of the project sponsor, and that the two of them can have confidential conversations about stakeholder management issues.

The project manager will need to provide project team members with the messages to deliver to specific stakeholders to assist in gaining individual stakeholders' support. The message needs to be delivered consistently by all project team members.

Activities need to be allocated by the project manager to other key project and business team members. These activities will be developed during the next steps.

Step 2: Identify all the stakeholders and their relationship to the project

A detailed list of stakeholders needs must be compiled. The starting point for this list will be the list of stakeholders compiled during the Launch pad phase, step 4: Stakeholder identification (Chapter 15). A sample list of stakeholders identified during this step of a BPM activity includes:

Internal:	*External:*
Staff	Intermediaries
Management	Clients
Executive management	Clients of clients
Board	Press
Finance	Funds managers
Facilities management	External audit
Compliance	Vendors
Risk management	Legislative bodies
Information technology	Partners
Human resources	
Internal audit	
Business development	

As can be seen from this list of possible stakeholder groups, there may be many stakeholders to manage—probably more than you have time for, or it is appropriate to manage, within the BPM activity. The above are stakeholder groups and it will be necessary to identify individuals within these groups who are important stakeholders. It is essential for the project team to understand that the organization's staff are one of the key stakeholders, and without their support and enthusiasm the project will either not be a success or be severely challenged. Refer to Chapter 25 for a more detailed discussion on this aspect.

In order to determine which stakeholders to manage, the project manager and business stakeholder leader should complete one or both of the matrices in step 3. Both these will assist in the identification of which stakeholders it is appropriate to manage. It should be updated, as required, after each stakeholder meeting.

Step 3: Profile the role key stakeholders will play in the project

Once stakeholders have been identified, the project manager needs to profile them. A form such as that shown in Table 24.3 can be used effectively for each key stakeholder. The individual stakeholder analysis should be reviewed by the project manager and/or business stakeholder leader prior to meeting with a stakeholder, to provide a reminder of the issues regarding the stakeholder and what the BPM activity wants to achieve with that particular stakeholder's assistance.

In order to identify key stakeholders and to facilitate the stakeholder mapping step, it is often useful to document further stakeholder information in a matrix as in Table 24.3. Do not interpret from the perceived sequence that one of these tables should be completed before the other; often both will happen concurrently and are constantly maintained throughout the BPM activity.

Table 24.3 shows similar summarized information for all identified stakeholders.

The first step in the completion of a stakeholder analysis matrix is to categorize the stakeholders by type or group and individual name. The next step is to distinguish between the power the stakeholder has now, in relation to the BPM activity, and the power the stakeholder will have after the completion of the BPM activity implementation. It is essential to distinguish those stakeholders that are critical to the progress of the project from those that simply have an interest in the project. Use Table 24.3 to assist in understanding the categorization.

A brief explanation of the columns of Table 24.4 follows (except where the columns are self-explanatory).

- *Power today*, and *Power after implementation* of BPM activity: *Source* refers to position, personality (aggressive, charismatic), knowledge or expertise (maturity) regarding BPM, resource control (ability to grant or withhold resources to the BPM activity), and whether the stakeholder has the power of veto over the BPM activity. *Relative strength* should simply be ranked as high, medium or low.

- *Ability to influence project and other stakeholders*: there is a need to understand how great the influence or power is that the stakeholder can exert over the BPM activity and other stakeholder(s). Who is able to influence whom, and how is this achieved? As the BPM

KEY POINT

Stakeholder management needs to focus on the key individuals. However, with larger BPM activities it is important to continue focusing on the key individuals, and to also start grouping the various underlying stakeholders to keep it manageable. The individual analysis should have at most about 30 to 50 names for large BPM initiatives.

Table 24.3 Individual stakeholder analysis

Name:	Position:
Ability to impact BPM activity:	View of BPM activity (commitment level):
High —|—|—|—|—|— Low (circle position on the line)	Positive —|—|—|—|—|— Negative (circle position on the line)
Risks:	(What risks does this stakeholder bring to the BPM activity? What risks are associated with the stakeholder?)
Strengths:	(What strengths does this stakeholder bring to the BPM activity?)
Weaknesses:	(What weaknesses are associated with this stakeholder being involved with the BPM activity?)
WIIFM	(What's in it for stakeholder?)
What turns him/her off?	(What does the stakeholder like/dislike about the BPM activity, their role, organization, personal interests, and so forth?)
What actions do I need to take?	
Action:	Timeframe:

activity is executed, will the reaction of stakeholders change—and how? In Chapter 25, we mention the "gatekeepers" of change. These are the people who potentially "filter" information before it is passed on to other stakeholders or stakeholder groups. It is necessary to understand whether a stakeholder is a "gatekeeper" or not and, if so, how the stakeholder will behave and possibly filter information onwards. The impact this could (or will) have on the BPM activity must also be understood.

- *View of project (interest level)*: not all stakeholders have a view on or interest in the outcomes of the BPM activity; some are only interested in what happens during the execution of the BPM activity. However, it is important always to be vigilant and on the lookout for new stakeholders; some may only start to pay attention to the BPM activity once it starts to have an impact upon them. These stakeholders need to be identified and managed as early as possible.

- *WIIFM. "What's In It For Me"* is a critical area to understand. If you do not understand what is in it for a particular stakeholder, how can you direct communication and outcomes? WIIFM is not only about the impact of the immediate outcomes of the BPM activity, but also about the impact of the BPM activity on the future of the stakeholder and what they get out of it at a personal and a professional level.

Table 24.4 Stakeholder analysis matrix

Type	Name	Power Today		Power after implementation		Ability to influence project and other stake-holders	View of project (interest level)	WIIFM
		Source	Relative Strength	Source	Relative Strength			

Stakeholder no longer has a role as a result of the BPM activity

A BPM activity was commenced with the usual Launch pad phase. By the time the Innovate report was completed, a significant recommendation was the reorganization of the department's structure. The recommendations were that the department staff numbers decrease by half, and that there be a reduction from one departmental manager with four sub-managers to one manager for the entire department. The project sponsor was the departmental manager so the implementation of the BPM activity could result in the sponsor not having a role within the organization. Without careful and sensitive stakeholder management, this could have resulted in a difficult situation.

Message: Always complete stakeholder analysis and understand the possible future impacts for key stakeholders, and handle this with care and sensitivity.

Predicting outcomes is part of stakeholder analysis and management. The likely impacts must be maintained on a continual basis throughout the BPM activity.

Some of this information will be difficult to obtain, will be subjective, and could be extremely confidential and sensitive. The culture and maturity of the organization and individual stakeholders will determine how open the project manager can be with this information. There is an emerging trend in some countries to be far more open about stakeholder management and individual stakeholder positions on projects. It is based upon an understanding that stakeholder management is not "manipulation," but openly influencing them with an integrity that endeavors to understand the stakeholders' underlying interests and address these interests. This approach will build trust.

However, openness is not always possible in all organizations due to the level of organizational maturity and the maturity of individual stakeholders. Where this is the case, the project manager must respect this information and keep it absolutely confidential.

Great care must be taken regarding where this information is stored in project documentation and to whom access is given.

KEY POINT

The information gathered during the stakeholder analysis is extremely sensitive and it is crucial that this information is shared with only a limited number of people and stored securely. If this sensitive information was to become public it may result in an adverse impact on the project and its team members.

Step 4: Map stakeholders

Taking the information gathered so far, the next step is to map the stakeholders onto two separate matrices that bring out subtle differences which will enable decisions to be made as to how to engage with the stakeholders. The purpose of this mapping is to determine where the stakeholders are now, and then to understand where they need to be, from a project perspective.

The first matrix (stakeholder project impact and view analysis—Figure 24.3) will show the project manager a stakeholder's ability to impact the BPM activity (project), and view of the BPM activity (project).

The "ability to impact project" axis refers to the power a stakeholder may have over the BPM activity. The stakeholder may have the power of veto or approval. Stakeholders can also overtly or subtly have significant power and impact over a project, at the BPM activity commencement, during the activity and at the implementation stage.

Coupled with this impact is the "view of project" axis. Stakeholders may be vitally interested in the BPM activity, as it will have a positive or negative impact upon their ability to meet their business and personal objectives, or they may have no view or interest at all. It is important for the project manager to recognize that individual stakeholders may also develop a "view" during the BPM activity as they come to realize the impact of the project upon themselves. This new view may be as a result of the project manager's stakeholder management, or stakeholders may have more information and come to the conclusion themselves; either way, the project manager must recognize this, re-map it and manage it.

The circles in Figures 24.3 and 24.4 represent the current position of an individual stakeholder, and the arrow indicates the position to which the stakeholder needs to be moved. The circles without arrows mean that the stakeholder is in a position that the project manager thinks is correct and therefore does not need to be moved. As can be seen in Figure 24.3, one

BPM INSIGHT

The "relative strength" and "ability to influence project" refers to not only the formal authority of a person, but also the informal authority: the ability to influence. Hence, it is not sufficient to cover only the key boxes in the organization chart. It is important to find out who the key drivers are behind the scene, exploring the informal and social networks to influence key decisions.

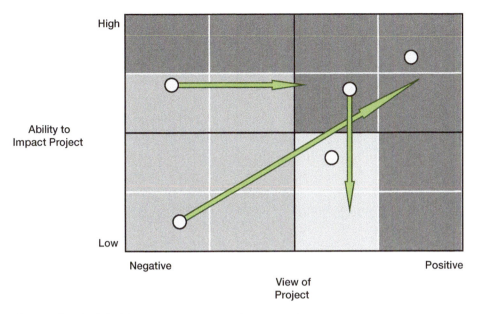

Figure 24.3 Stakeholder project impact and view analysis

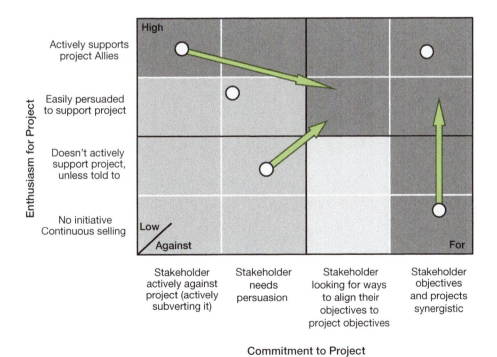

Figure 24.4 Stakeholder enthusiasm and interest analysis

of the stakeholders currently has a low ability to impact the project and a negative view of the BPM activity. The project manager has determined that this is an important stakeholder who needs to be moved from the current position to one of having a positive view of, and high influence over, the BPM activity. There will need to be a number of tasks established to make this occur.

While Figure 24.4 is very similar to Figure 24.3, there are subtle differences that can be elicited and explored.

A stakeholder can have low commitment to the project and yet a high level of enthusiasm. Equally, a stakeholder may have a high level of enthusiasm for the project and yet it could be at odds with their business or personal objectives, and therefore their commitment level is "against" it (the organizational silo effect).

If movement of a stakeholder is to take place, the project manager will need to develop a strategy for each arrow in these two figures. The strategy will be a set of tasks that will, once executed, move the stakeholder to the desired position on the matrices. This brings us to the last step to be completed in gathering stakeholder information before planning the stakeholder strategy and engagement. This is the need to document the outcomes or objectives that each stakeholder will want from the BPM activity, and map these to the actual project outcomes and objectives. This will provide obvious evidence of where the objectives are synergistic or otherwise.

Step 5: Determine the best strategy to engage and manage the stakeholder

This last step in stakeholder management is about creating a strategic plan (or pathway) towards successful stakeholder engagement.

The strategic plan must be completed at BPM activity and individual stakeholder levels, and must provide a pathway from the individual stakeholder's objectives and outcomes to the BPM activity objectives and outcomes. It must show how the project manager will manage those stakeholders for and against the BPM activity, and how the project manager plans to encourage low-enthusiasm stakeholders to be highly enthusiastic (or at least neutral) towards the BPM activity.

The plan should show:

- where the stakeholder is in his or her thinking with regard to project delivery effectiveness;
- where the stakeholder needs to be in order to contribute to successful delivery of the BPM activity;
- using identified stakeholder drivers, how the project manager will move stakeholder interests to support project delivery appropriately;
- continuous review periods—this should be every time a project manager meets a stakeholder, whether it is in a formal meeting or for an informal chat in a hallway.

This stage should link with the communications plan developed as part of the BPM activity. It should also link with the aspects discussed in Chapter 26.

"Interest-based" stakeholder management

Managing stakeholders to deliver projects can create adversarial conflict, which can not only damage relationships but also ensure only short-term behavioral change. Here, once the project is closed, behavior reverts back to previous patterns and potential benefits to the organization can be lost. If this is the case, it is very important to use other techniques that ensure the maintenance of relationships throughout the ups and downs of project delivery pressure and also to ensure that behavior change is an ongoing and permanent outcome of the BPM activity. The best way to achieve this is to utilize interest-based stakeholder management, which involves cooperative problem-solving techniques. The process of interest-based stakeholder management is detailed in Figure 24.5.

Interest-based stakeholder management is about:

- assessing the problems, defining the issues and setting the stage for win–win solutions—these are necessary steps prior to identifying individual underlying interests;
- the underlying interests that need to be identified, which are those that cause individuals to take positions relating to the problem;
- analyzing any areas of disagreement, using techniques such as brainstorming to develop win–win solutions. BATNA is one such negotiation technique, where you determine your Best Alternative To a Negotiated Agreement. This allows you to understand your negotiating boundaries and reduces the chances of holding an entrenched position to the detriment of all concerned.

The skills required for cooperative problem-solving, as described by Wertheim et al. (1998), are the ability to:

- identify underlying interests in relation to needs, wants, concerns and fears; this is done by understanding why you are taking a certain position in the conflict;
- examine all interests, including the use of empathy;
- listen actively, using skills such as reflection, communicating by taking turns, utilizing attentive body language and not behaving defensively;
- separate the people from the problem;
- brainstorm;
- find creative new alternatives;
- assess whether the solution satisfies the resolution of all the underlying issues.

Multi-party interest-based stakeholder management

The same principles used in cooperative problem-solving between two parties can also be used for organizational multi-party problem solving. The resolution process must take into account the organizational structure, and be aware of dealing with coalitions, factions and alliances of stakeholders in addition to individuals. The principle is still the same, whereby win–win solutions are sought to resolve underlying issues.

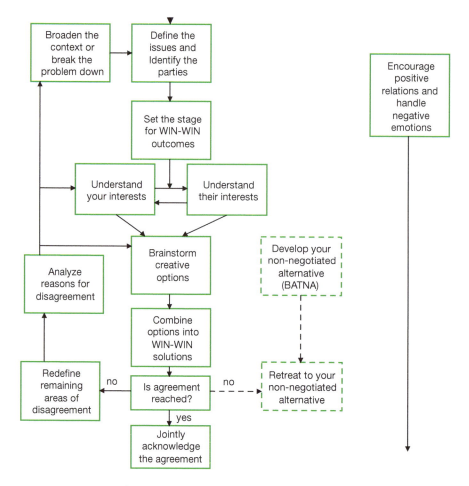

Figure 24.5 Basic conflict resolution model
Source: Wertheim et al. (1998).

An example of this is described by Gray (1989), who explains a collaborative approach to multi-party conflict resolution. This approach seeks to explore the differences between stakeholders over an issue in order to create new solutions to solve the problem. The skills required to apply this collaborative approach to conflict resolution include the ability to:

- define the problem
- commit to solve the problem
- identify all stakeholders impacted by the problem
- assess stakeholder interests
- identify available resources to solve the problem
- establish ground rules
- set agendas

- organize sub-groups working on the problem resolution
- share information
- explore multiple options
- reach agreements with other stakeholders
- implement the agreement.

Third-party intervention

Third-party intervention takes into account mediation, conciliation, arbitration and adjudication. These approaches are a mixture of adversarial and cooperative approaches to managing stakeholders, and involve the introduction of a third party with a specific role in order to guide parties in conflict towards some sort of agreement or settlement. The skills required when using these methods are the ability to:

- know when to introduce a third party into a conflict resolution process
- define clearly the role of the third party
- agree the process for resolution under these approaches
- agree to the final outcome of the process.

Putting it into practice

Stakeholder management during a BPM activity is often handled on an intuitive (rather than formal) basis. While project managers often speak of the need for stakeholder management and spend a great deal of time on this aspect of project management, it is rarely systematically analyzed, planned and executed and yet relationships are the basis for everything we do.

The critical aspects of stakeholder management are to:

- understand who the stakeholders are
- understand their relationships to the BPM activity and each other
- determine what role they are playing, or will play, in the BPM activity
- determine their requirements from the BPM activity
- determine how best to engage with them to satisfy their needs.

It is best if the business owners (project sponsor and business owner) are engaged in and actively support the stakeholder planning, engagement and execution processes.

It is important for the project manager and sponsor to recognize that stakeholder management is about dealing with people, and because of this there are no guarantees of the outcomes. The project manager can complete the stakeholder management to a very high standard and still not achieve the desired outcomes, because a stakeholder has either provided the wrong signals (on purpose or unintentionally) or simply changed his or her mind.

CONTINUOUS ACTIVE PROJECT REVIEW

As part of the project management activities, or during the Sustainable performance phase, a Post Implementation Review (PIR) may be performed if the organization, project team or business requires it. However, completing a PIR at this stage of a project is too late! It is a little like completing a PIR for a medical surgical operation after the patient has died or is very ill. It is too late to change anything.

The reason most organizations complete PIRs is to learn what worked well and what could have worked better, so that new projects will have a higher level of success. Yet, most organizations complete the PIR, document it and then file it away. Little sharing takes place.

Perhaps a better approach is to learn as the project is executed and behavior changed as you go. Such an approach is the "Continuous Active Project Review" (CAPR) approach. The military refer to this as an After Action Review. Figure 24.6 depicts the process.

The purpose of the CAPR is to learn and adjust as the project is executed.

The process starts before the project is commenced, and continues throughout the project, to prepare, execute well and review the actions taken and results obtained. This enables the explicit linking of lessons learned to future actions,

The process is as follows:

1. The project/program director meets with the project managers and team leaders to explain what needs to be achieved as a result of the next milestone.

2. The project manager(s) and team leaders go and plan:

    a. all the activities necessary to achieve the project milestone

    b. identify the challenges (risks) that are likely to occur

    c. build ways of mitigating these challenges to minimize the impact or the likelihood of them occurring.

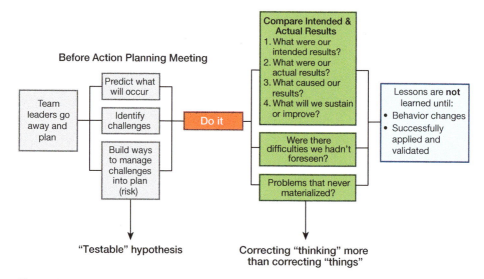

Figure 24.6 Continuous active project review

3. The project team then meet again with the project/program director to:

    a. inform the project director of the objectives to achieve at the milestone (this ensures there has been no mis-communication between the key project members)

    b. present and agree the actions.

4. Once this has occurred and all are in agreement, the project has a "testable hypothesis"—something that the results can be compared to.

5. The project team then execute all activities to achieve the milestone.

6. After the milestone has been reached and all results are complete, the project team meet again to compare the intended results with the actual results. During this meeting it is critical that "all" people in the meeting are treated equally. That is, there are **no** bosses. The most junior person in the meeting is allowed to tell the most senior person that they have made a mistake or not done their job properly, and there must be no recriminations. Remember, the purpose is for all to learn. The questions to review in the meeting include:

    • What were our intended results?

    • What were our actual results?

    • What caused our results?

    • What will we sustain or improve?

    Further questions are:

    • Were there difficulties we had not foreseen?

    • Did we identify challenges/risks that never materialized?

7. The outcomes from this meeting are about correcting "thinking" more than correcting "things."

8. The final outcome of this CAPR is about learning as the project is executed, however, it is critical to understand that a lesson is not learned until behavior is changed and it has been successfully applied and validated. This should be known by the end of the next CAPR.

These activities occur before *and* after each significant phase/milestone in the project.

The benefits of completing a CAPR activity include:

• The improved care and precision that goes into before-action planning

• Higher quality outcomes

• Reduced risk

• Clarity of:

    o Business intent

    o Desired result

    o What is required

• Clear accountability/responsibilities for actions.

PROJECT MANAGEMENT RISKS

In this essential part of the BPM activity, there are several risks that must be considered and mitigation strategies implemented to eliminate or at least reduce them. Table 24.5 shows some of these.

Table 24.5 Project management risks and mitigation strategies

	Risk	Mitigation strategy
1.	All "gates" are not identified and managed	During the Launch pad phase, and continually throughout the other phases of the project, potential gates must be identified and managed as early as possible in the project. Stop or pause the project if a gate has not been satisfactorily addressed.
2.	Stakeholder analysis and management are not addressed thoroughly	Ensure that the stakeholder management steps are included in the project plan and continually addressed proactively throughout the project.
3.	There is no appointed business project manager	BPM is a critical activity for the business and one that has the potential for substantial benefits and some risk. The business project manager is not the business expert, but needs to have both substantial project management and BPM experience.
4.	Insufficient BPM expertise is available to the project team	Ensure that the project has both specialist BPM project management and process analyst skills available.
5.	The governance, as outlined in the Launch pad phase, is not working	Escalate to the relevant people when the governance structure doesn't address key issues, e.g., project stages, gates or conflicts. If this doesn't work the BPM activity should be put on hold.

SUMMARY

This chapter highlighted the project management aspects that are unique or specifically relevant to BPM activities:

- It highlighted the difference between traditional project management and BPM project management.
- It described the importance of project gates and provided several examples of project gates, including their criteria.
- Stakeholder management was explained as well as several techniques that may be used to manage stakeholders.
- The key project management risks were provided, including mitigations that can be undertaken.

SELF-TEST

1 Why are project gates important?

2 Can you name five project gates?

3. Why is stakeholder management important?

4 What are the key steps in stakeholder management?

5 What models can be used to map current and desired states for stakeholders?

6 What are the key project management risks?

ASSIGNMENT

Project management is being performed throughout the project.

Assignment guiding questions

1 How have you incorporated BPM project management into the project?

2 What are the differences with 'normal' project management?

CHAPTER 25

PEOPLE CHANGE MANAGEMENT

OVERVIEW

When first written, this chapter was simply called "Change management," and we found that many reviewers thought it was about change management as is referred to in a project management methodology, that is, How do you change the scope of a project to include additional deliverables for the project? So the title was changed by adding in the word "people" to make it more specific.

This chapter is about what is often referred to as "organization change management" which is arguably the most important aspect of any BPM activity. Where BPM is a large program or organizational transition activity then it will play a crucial role. If it's a smaller BPM activity, then people change management may only play a small role. The importance of an organization's culture and trust levels is discussed, together with providing two potential approaches to change management.

OVERALL LEARNING OUTCOME

By the end of this chapter you will be able to:

- Understand the importance of people change management in any type of BPM activity
- Appreciate the importance that an organization's culture plays in its success
- Understand cultural influencers and the typical aspects of an outstanding organizational culture
- Outline two approaches to people change management: a traditional approach, with its challenges; and the more recent Appreciative Inquiry approach
- Provide an overview of the criticality that trust plays in the success or an organization.

Good companies react quickly to change;
Great companies create change.
Move before the wave; change before you have to.

(Hriegel and Brandt, 1996)

If there was ever an event that validates this quote it was the global financial crisis and years that followed it. Change is not something that is desirable; it is a necessity for survival.

Opinions on the importance of people change management vary enormously. Various writers and leaders have stated differing views, such as:

transforming the corporation is not just a dream but an urgent necessity.

(Keen, 1997: 15)

There is no such thing as luck in business. If you are in the business of continuous change you must have a process, applied in a very disciplined way, that tells you where you are heading. You need to understand what you are trying to achieve and make sure that when you do it, you do it right.

**(Don Argus, Former CEO, National
Australia Bank, in Cavanagh, 1999)**

Jim Collins's (2001) research led him to state that:

The good-to-great companies paid scant attention to managing change, motivating people, or creating alignment. Under the right conditions, the problems of commitment, alignment, motivation, and change largely melt away.

The interesting phrase in this last quotation is *under the right conditions*. It is the responsibility of the leadership of the organization to "create" the right conditions, and these do not happen by accident. As Don Argus said, "you must have a process, applied in a very disciplined way."

As stated earlier, people change management is arguably the most critical aspect of BPM, at least 60 percent of BPM activity effort should be spent on people change management and communications.

KEY POINT

Without people in an organization, you have nothing. Without the people in the organization having the right attitude, motivation, work ethic, focus and customer care, the challenges may be insurmountable, or at the very least it is not a very nice place to work.

Yet, many BPM activities, and other projects for that matter, pay little or no attention to it.

This is why people change management is one of the three essentials of a BPM project (Figure 25.1). It is the process of applying the changes planned for in the BPM activities being undertaken. It is about moving towards a high performing organization.

During a BPM activity, unless it is an extremely small and isolated activity, organizational culture will need to be dealt with, especially as part of the People phase. However, be careful not to listen to the people within the organization who use culture as an excuse and tell

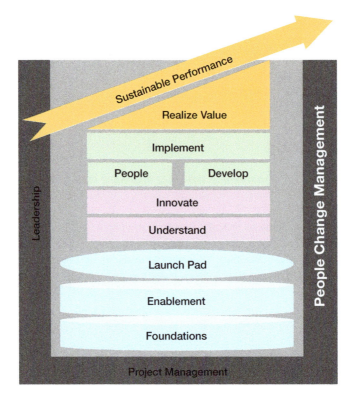

Figure 25.1 People change management essential

you that this is "just the way we do things around here," or this is "just the way things are." If culture needs improving, then it will always be as a result of some part of the organization's processes, structure or people management systems (including leadership) not functioning as they should. It could be incorrect role descriptions or performance measurement targets; lack of appropriate management reporting or structure; lack of skills or capacity; inappropriate leadership style; lack of transparency; or external forces imposing change on the organization and the organization's processes, structure or people management systems not responding or changing as required.

The case for people change management is highlighted in Figure 25.2 which provides evidence that projects with effective change management have:

- nearly a six times higher rate of success—16 percent versus 95 percent
- a four times higher Return on Investment (ROI)—35 percent (expected) versus 143 percent (actual).

Within a BPM activity, always remember that the BPM activity outcome is the goal, and any cultural change that may be necessary is a result of the BPM activity goals. In a large BPM program or transformation cultural change is essential for success; however, cultural change is not an end in itself. It will however significantly influence the desired business goals.

Before we proceed to discuss people change management in detail, organizational culture will be explored in a little more detail.

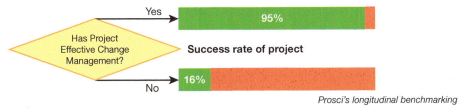

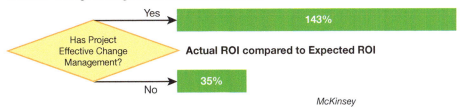

Figure 25.2 Benefits from change management

Source: Prosci (2011); McKinsey (2002).

> ## BPM INSIGHT
>
> Change management is often the most difficult challenge in a BPM activity. Sometimes BPM and business team members wonder "What is required to make people change?" Sometimes team members try to find a burning issue and sell the change on the assumption that if people's careers were dependent on change they would change. However, a recent study (Kegan and Leahy, 2009) showed that people don't change, even if their life depends on it!
>
> The results of the study demonstrate that even when doctors tell heart patients they will die if they don't change their habits, *only one in seven will be able to follow through successfully*. Desire and motivation aren't enough: even when it's literally a matter of life or death, the ability to change remains frustratingly elusive. Given that the status quo is so ingrained in our psyches, how can we change ourselves and our organizations?

ORGANIZATIONAL CULTURE

Marvin Weisbord (1992: 8–9) stated that "to implement effectively we need a shared picture of the 'whole system'—future vision, values, policies and procedures in a *global* context." This requires an organization to have a vision, values, mission statements shared and understood by all. To take these and "implement" them requires common sense.

KEY POINT

Weisbord suggests that the common-sense equation goes something like this:

THE RIGHT TASK + THE RIGHT PEOPLE + THE RIGHT SETTING
= UNPRECEDENTED ACTIONS

The right task—relates to linking strategy to the actions within the organization. This has been discussed in Chapters 13 (Foundations phase) and 14 (Enablement phase).

The right people—relates not only to an organization's employment policies, but also to ongoing training, skills development and capability enhancement, among other things. It includes key partners and vendors as well.

The right setting—relates to the organizational environment, which will be significantly influenced and shaped by an organization's culture. It is about engendering the right "attitude" and creating the right environment for employees to work in. Employees need to understand and appreciate that their employer and managers care about them. Managers need to empower staff and be servant leaders by supporting, facilitating and coaching. Managers need to be proactive and anticipate potential issues and roadblocks. They should let employees attempt to solve issues themselves and only step in to support and assist when necessary.[1] Remember FAIL stands for First Attempt In Learning and failing at the second attempt stands for Forgot to Apply Its Learning.

To understand the importance that *the right setting* or organizational culture plays in the effectiveness of an organization, 100 companies were studied over an eight-year period.[2] This research showed that an organizational strategy accounted for 2 percent of performance variability while organizational culture accounted for 17 percent of performance variability.

With culture accounting for a 17 percent influence on performance variation, the effectiveness of an organization's strategy mix becomes very vulnerable in an unaligned culture. For example, if an organization values profit, productivity and quality it will prefer to operate in a way that prioritizes action and behavior that reflects those values. Another organization that values innovation, research and learning will prefer to operate in a way that prioritizes action and behavior that reflects those values. For either organization, if the values that are influencing daily behavior and actions are not aligned with the strategies then their performance and results will suffer (Henderson and Thompson, 2004).

So where does culture come from and what is it? Culture is the collective behavior of all employees and significant stakeholders. It is shaped by the way they go about their daily activities, how they interact with each other and how they handle customer relationships.

Culture is built or destroyed each time people have a conversation, make a decision, choose a behavior and ignite ideas within others. At its very essence it is the way we treat each other when working with each other to achieve business outcomes.

(Holloway, 2011: 13)

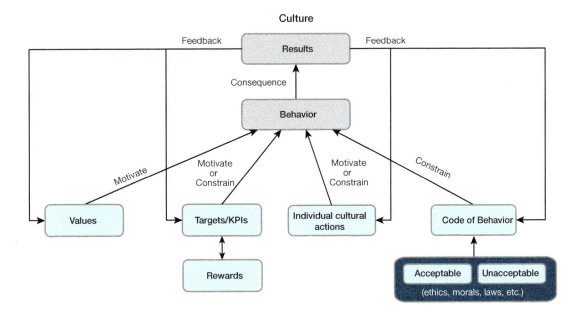

Figure 25.3 Organizational culture

If we take Figure 14.19 from the chapter on Enablement and further develop it, it will look like Figure 25.3.

While this is a simple view of the influences on an organization's culture, it does provide four of the major influencers.

How employees, from the most senior executive to the most junior employee, behave will deliver the result of the organization. The four major influencers on employee behavior are depicted as: values, targets or KPIs, individual cultural actions and code of behavior.

KEY POINT

Values are the things that are most important to a person in a given context. Values lie behind all the choices we make. Here it is both an individual person's values and the collective values of the organization that are being referred to. If an organization predominantly employs people with similar values to the organizational collective values, then there will be "value alignment" and a person will be motivated to contribute towards the desired organization strategic outcomes being targeted.

Targets/KPIs—can be both a motivator or, if implemented poorly, a constraint. If both the target/KPI and the reward are linked and tailored to the individual or group of individuals in an appropriate way, then they can be a significant motivator. *Remember*: You get what you set; so be very careful in the setting of targets and KPIs.

Individual cultural actions—the list of individual actions or activities that senior management may choose to implement as part of setting the culture within the organization. These individual actions can be both a motivator or, if implemented poorly or not at all, a constraint.

Code of behavior—the constraints that ethics, morals, laws, etc. provide to us all. Because we live in a society, we cannot live our values in any way we want. The impact of how we live our values on other people and the environment must be considered. Organizations will also often develop a specific code of behavior of how all employees are expected to behave—what is acceptable and what is not acceptable. While these codes are predominantly constraints on behavior, they could also provide a motivator if they, for example, include expectations of innovation and an acceptance of failure.

Once behavior is established and actioned it will deliver a result for the individual and the organization and provide feedback. In the case of targets/KPIs, individual cultural actions and code of behavior, the feedback will provide information for management to change the various components if necessary.

However, in the case of values, management needs to understand that when people engage in a behavior that has been motivated by their values, they don't see the actual consequences of their actions (results). Rather, the results of their actions are filtered through their values—they see what matches their values, and don't see what does not match. The factors that shape, and result in, our values include: the media; emotion; family; age and education; gender; peers; skills and abilities; nature; created nature (for example technology and science); the cultural environment in which we were raised; and brain preferences. It is suggested that "what you are, is what you were, when you were ten years of age."

This means that, as a generalization, our values are locked in by the time we are 10; and only a significant event (emotion) can change them.

This is why it is so important for an organization to understand the values that work for it, and employ people with similar values.

When leaders are capable of ensuring that strategy (the organization's plans for moving forward in a chosen direction) and the culture (the organization's values, beliefs and behaviors) are in alignment with one another then they can make a positive impact on moving the organization towards its vision.

Management can significantly assist in the creation of the organization's culture by implementing the *individual cultural actions* referred to previously; or the variations of the suggested individual actions that are applicable to your organization.

Rosabeth Moss Kanter[3] provides an insight into why an organization's culture is important (Kanter, 2009). She explains that while capitalism has worked well in the past it has now hit the wall: "In its place must arise a new model of the company, one that serves society as well as rewarding shareholders and employees." It must codify a "set of values and principles as a strategic guidance system." Organizations "gain advantages from actions they take based on the societal responsibility these statements imply both in terms of external constituencies in their extended family of partners and stakeholders and with regard to their employees."

Organizations who ground their "strategy in a sense of wider societal purpose provide many significant advantages and only a few potential disadvantages. Values and principles of this sort not only speak to high standards of conduct but also stretch the enterprise beyond its own formal boundaries to include the extended family of customers, suppliers, distributors, business partners, financial stakeholders, and the rest of society." These "companies gain both a moral compass and an entire guidance system."

The advantages for these "companies through their strategic use of values and principles include":

- Competitive differentiation;
- Public accountability via end-to-end responsibility;
- Rationale for thinking long term—as IBM CEO Sam Palmisano said "management is temporary; returns are cyclical." Longer term thinking and the values based approach will avoid "short-termism";
- Common vocabulary and guidance for consistent decisions—"clear articulation of values and principles helps employees choose among alternatives in a consistent manner";
- Talent magnets and motivation machines—"businesses are a network of people working toward the same end. And everyone has to be proud of what they're doing";
- Human control systems—peer review and self-control system—these organizations' "belief in the purpose and embracing the values generate self-guidance, self-policing, and peer responsibility for keeping one another aligned with the core set of principles. This kind of human control system does not work perfectly by itself, but it certainly reduces the need for rules and thus helps people feel autonomous."

KEY POINT

Remember, when looking at an organization's culture that:

Culture is caught, not taught.

If the senior executives and management do not "live" the culture they wish to have, do not be surprised when you do not get the culture you want.

Culture will be caught from these senior executives and managers, so behavior and attitude matter, and matter a lot.

PROCESS OF PEOPLE CHANGE MANAGEMENT

The importance of the change process as it specifically relates to the implementation of a BPM activity will now be discussed. BPM activities are about changing the processes and the way business is conducted within an organization and, if you think about it, cultural change is

BPM INSIGHT

People change management is a core essential of successful BPM, and an area that must be focused upon throughout the entire BPM activity.

"just" another process itself. We will discuss this "process," how it can be implemented and, most importantly, how it can be sustained over time.

In this chapter we will outline two approaches towards achieving the change desired within an organization. The first approach is the more traditional method and is shown in Figure 25.4. The second approach is commonly known as the Appreciative Inquiry method.

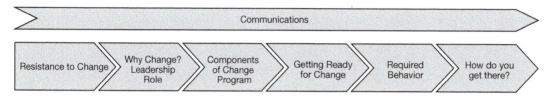

Figure 25.4 People change management steps

Whichever approach is adopted, it must be linked with the ten phases of the 7FE Framework and executed throughout the BPM activity.

The traditional approach is about providing a "process" of how to assist these "ordinary managers and workers" to become prepared for, and accept, change.

The communications step has not been described separately but is discussed throughout the various steps, especially Step 3.

Step 1: Resistance to change

Mark Twain is purported to have said that "the only person who likes change is a baby with a wet diaper," and you know, he is probably right.

If Mark Twain is correct, why do people dislike change so much? Some of the reasons include the following:

1. *Fear.* This is the most common cause of resistance, and one of the most powerful. This is often because change is uncertain, uncomfortable, unpredictable and unsafe. Communication and honesty are powerful ways of overcoming this fear factor.

2. *Feeling powerless.* This is often because the BPM activity team and business management have not involved the people enough. Provide people with the opportunity to participate and feel they have power to influence the change process.

3. *Too much effort and pain is involved.* It takes a great deal of effort and often pain to achieve change, and then to become comfortable with it. Most people will avoid pain and move towards pleasure, and in this instance pleasure equals the status quo.

4. *Absence of self-interest.* People need to understand what is in it for them, or that they will not be any worse off. If it is the latter, then they will ask, "Why change?" and this needs to be clearly articulated. In step 2, we will discuss why people should understand the need for change.

Resistance must be anticipated as much as possible, and research, via surveys and questionnaires, should be conducted. An understanding of the type and level of change should be determined for the project. The project sponsor and project team should be aware that resistance often increases towards the end of the project as more information becomes available. Plans should be developed to contend with this increase.

Step 2: Why change? and leadership role

In traditional BPR projects, "the focus of change is on work processes, new technology . . . and decentralized service rather than on the people who must implement change" (Goldsmith, 1995). As Michael Hammer stated in 1993,

coming up with the ideas is the easy part, but getting things done is the tough part. The place where these reforms die is . . . down in the trenches—and who "owns" the trenches? People.

It is the "people" who are the gatekeepers of change, and again Michael Hammer (1995) expressed it well when he said that people are "the most perplexing, annoying, distressing, and confusing part" of BPR. Whether or not people are annoying and distressing does not matter; the fact is, they are a critical part of the success of any BPM project, and if you do not get this part of the project right, the project will either fail or have only limited success. The BPM team can create the best processes and BPM systems, but if people refuse to use them, or use them poorly, then the project will not be successful.

CASE STUDY

Workflow and image implementation

An organization was extremely conservative. The organization built a business case for the implementation of a workflow and imaging system; it was stated that it would not work!

Why? Investigation revealed that the organization had tried it five years previously and it was a failure, and management was nervous about trying again. Further investigation revealed that no people change management had been included in the project.

The organization's people were extremely fearful and uninformed of the new system, and when it was implemented they simply refused to use it. Management had to un-install the system and go back to the old, costly, manual processes.

Message: If you expect a change in people's behavior, then they must be listened to and included within the planning for the change process.

While the role of leadership is covered further in Chapter 26, it is important to briefly state here the function that leadership must play in the people change management events.

KEY POINT

People do not like change and will not implement or participate in a change program, unless they believe it is necessary.

Simplistically, there are two methods of convincing people to change. The method selected will depend upon the organization, the particular situation and the leadership style of the leader.

The first ("burning platform") method suggests that:

there must be a crisis, and it is the job of the CEO to define and communicate that crisis, its magnitude, its severity, and its impact. Just as important, the CEO must also be able to communicate how to end the crisis—the new strategy, the new company model, the new culture.

(Gerstner, 2002)

In communicating the crisis, or the reasons why change is necessary, it is imperative that the CEO or change leader formally informs the people that *no change is not an option*, so that they are fully aware that the change program *is* going to take place and it is their role to decide how and when to come on the journey. If a crisis exists, then openness, honesty and the maintenance of integrity is essential in communicating the crisis and way forward. If a crisis is "manufactured" to instigate change, then this has the potential to conflict with the required honesty and integrity required of leadership.

The second method is more subtle, and requires leadership to have people understand that there is a "problem" and inform them of the magnitude of the problem and why it is essential to change. People will need to understand the impact upon the organization and themselves if the problem is not addressed.

The people within the organization do not need "rah-rah" speeches; they need leadership—direction, consistency, momentum and persistence. They want leaders who will focus on solutions and actions. If there are hard decisions to make, as there often are in any change program, make them as early as possible in the program, and make sure everyone (management, employees and stakeholders) knows about it and why it was necessary; then implement it.

As one unknown person purportedly stated, "Reengineering is like starting a fire on your head and putting it out with a hammer"—that is, it's painful and boring.

While the CEO does not, and should not, need to be the leader of all people change management programs, especially in the case of a small BPM activity, the program does need to have a primary leader or sponsor who will guide the change process. This person's role will include providing the answers to the following questions, always remembering to keep this within the bounds of your BPM activity (Scheer et al., 2003: 26):

- What is the change intended to achieve?
- Why the changes are necessary?
- What will be the consequences of these changes to both the organization and the individuals?

The latter point must cover not only outcomes of the change process, but also what will happen if we do not change.

Change takes a great deal of time and considerable commitment by leadership at all levels within the organization and project team. It cannot only be led by the CEO—we will cover the three suggested levels of "leadership" in Chapter 26.

When leadership commences the communication process of motivating people for the change, leaders must show them the way forward—the "reality" of the situation. Truth, however, is critical in showing and telling people the facts.

If the leadership and management of the organization say they do not have time for this, they need to understand that this *is their job!* It is they who must change first and then be the role models for the rest of the organization. In other words, *walk the talk* for everyone to see. Trust will be discussed later in this chapter.

While it is not the leadership's role to provide a detailed project plan of the people change management steps, the leadership must ensure that the project/program manager has taken responsibility for this. The project/program manager needs to work with the project/program sponsor, organization leadership and the human resources department to ensure that all the steps are addressed and the project/program plan is completed and implemented.

Leaders, and in this context we are referring to anyone providing a role model for others, need to understand that people are different and take different amounts of time and effort to change. Some will change fast and get on board, others will be slower, and still others will never change and will need to be accommodated in an appropriate way, as mapped in the adoption curve, see Figure 25.5. It is the leader's role to understand this and to provide people with the necessary time and support.

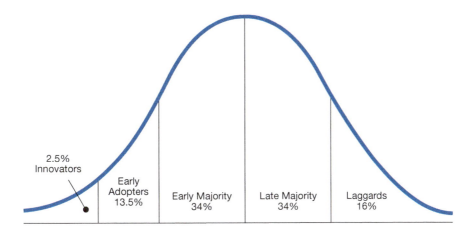

Figure 25.5 Adoption curve

Source: Rogers (1962).

Successful change programs have three important qualities: passion, enthusiasm and intense excitement. It is the leader's responsibility to ignite each of these and find others to keep the "fire burning."

Step 3: Components of the change program

Before we launch into the components of a people change management program, it is important to make it clear that it is the responsibility of the BPM Activity Steering Committee, together with the project manager and business sponsor, to deliver the results of this program. The change program cannot be outsourced, or totally (or significantly) delegated to any of the following:

1. *Another area*. Sometimes there can be a temptation to "hand it over" to the human resources department. While there is no question that HR should be intimately involved in the program, the coordination of activities is such that the project manager needs to involve all aspects of the BPM activity—for example the People phase will have a significant impact upon and input to the people change management program.

2. *Consultants*. Change is an "inside job" that cannot be given to an outside group to complete. Certainly, consultants can contribute ideas, structure and learning from their other engagements, but the responsibility must lie with the project manager and business to plan, execute and deliver.

The essential components of this approach to people change management include the following:

1. Planning a detailed project plan.
2. Selection of key personnel to be involved in the program.
3. A clear understanding of the program's links to: strategy, culture, structure, new people roles, new processes and the overall BPM activity.
4. A detailed communications plan, outlining the way information will be delivered to all stakeholders. This must link in with the BPM activities communications plan.

We will take each of these and briefly describe its role in the change program, and the important issues to consider.

Planning

The people change management program can be a significant program of effort in its own right, and will have many activities and tasks that must be integrated with and form part of the overall BPM project plan. The plan should obviously contain all the steps involved in the change program, responsibilities, and deliver dates. It must include steps specifically designed to show how the organization or business unit proposes to unfreeze, move and refreeze the organization.

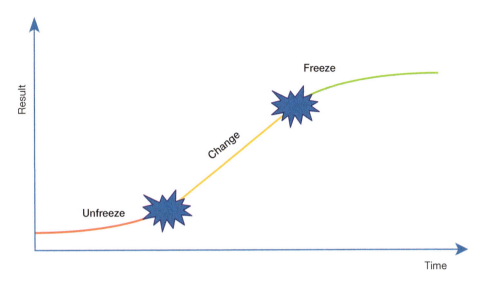

Figure 25.6 Unfreeze–change–freeze method
Source: Lewin (1930s).

Unfreezing is about creating the awareness and need for change, and creating a climate that is receptive for change. *Change* the organization focuses on the changing forces and changing behavior from the old to the new. *Refreezing* is the reinforcement process that occurs, leading to the institutionalization of the change making it sustainable and part of "business as usual" (Lewin, undated).

The basic questions of who, what, which and how need to be answered. Examples of these questions are as follows:

1. Who will be involved in the change program—customers, suppliers, investors, management, people within the organization (organization-wide or localized to one or more departments)? Obviously, this will depend upon the BPM activity selected.

2. What is going to change and what new information will be needed or produced?

3. Which new deliverables or outcomes can be expected?

4. How do the changes fit together and influence the new expected state for the organization?

These questions need to be answered before the planning process can be completed.

Selection of key personnel

This refers to the selection of the change champions—those members of the organization who will be the leaders of the change program. These people will come from all levels within the organization and project team. Chapter 26 will outline three levels of "leadership," and the change champions should be carefully selected from all of these levels.

Understanding of links

The change program will impact, and be impacted by, all phases and aspects of the BPM activity. We have discussed many of these links throughout the book, but they include links to:

- organization strategy
- culture of the organization
- any proposed new organization structure, people roles and processes.

As described in the introduction to the essential aspects, these links are why people change management is shown as an essential in the framework and not as a phase.

Communications plan

The completion of a communications strategy and plan is an essential aspect of any BPM activity and change program. It needs to be thought through in a thorough way, and continually adjusted throughout its life as feedback is received and an understanding of what has worked well and what could have worked better is obtained.

Here follows an outline summary of general guidelines regarding how to go about the construction of a communications plan, and what should it address (Scheer et al., 2003: 7–8).

Actions for communication plan

1. Segment the audience or different groups who will be receiving the messages.
2. Plan to use multiple channels for the delivery of the messages, ensuring that all personal communication modalities of people are addressed—visual, auditory and kinesthetic.[4]
3. Use multiple people to deliver messages—different people will have different styles; however, you must ensure that the message is consistent and never contradictory.
4. Be clear and communicate simple messages, always ensuring that the change program is setting the expectations and never leaving expectations to be set by the recipients.
5. There should be a small number of key, simple messages for the entire program. People will not remember, nor want to hear, a large number of complex reasons or messages. The more senior the manager, the more simple and consistent the message needs to be.
6. Honesty is the *only* policy—sooner or later people will find out the truth anyway, and the program and deliverer will then lose all credibility if an honest approach has not been adopted.
7. Play to people's emotions; logic alone will not be accepted, nor will it work.
8. Empathize and acknowledge that change is difficult, for the problem is not so much the new state of where you expect people to end up, but the pain of the transition to get there.
9. Make the message tangible and simple—tell people how and what will change specifically for them and their work area (team). Change must address the specifics of how it will affect individuals.
10. Match key project plan milestones to communication events.
11. The most crucial aspect is *Listen, Listen, Listen*—and learn from and react to what you hear.

Step 4: Getting ready for change

Simplistically, getting ready for change falls into two categories:

1. Create an environment that will allow and encourage people to change.
2. Ensure that there is feedback regarding performance and the change program.

Create an environment

There are essentially three broad components involved in creating the environment that allows people to change: trust, caring and ownership.

KEY POINT

Trust is critical. People must feel they can trust their leaders and the environment within which they function, at all levels within the organization. They must believe that leaders are honest with them, have high levels of integrity and are reliable and open. People must believe that they can ask any question and get an honest answer.

Table 25.1 shows a number of actions that do and do not fulfill these criteria. The criticality of trust will be further discussed at the end of this step.

Caring is about respect and empathy for others. It is about acknowledging and thanking people for their contribution and effort. Respect includes many of the trust builders mentioned in Table 25.1. People will feel they have respect from leaders when the leaders always tell the truth, keep their word and respect each other.

Ownership is about providing people with as much control over their own destiny as is possible. It is about empowering people with information that will allow them to be responsible for their own decisions and actions, and to be held accountable for them. Clarify expectations (what the organization expects from its people) and responsibility (how the organization expects its people to be responsible in their actions and behavior)—don't delegate, elevate. Provide a sense of ownership by providing people with access to feedback (performance reporting) before the boss gets it, thus allowing people to make corrections themselves before the boss provides the feedback. This leads us to the next point.

Provide performance feedback

Leadership cannot expect behavior change until people have been provided with an appropriate environment for work (systems and processes, as well as the human environment), and until they are provided with feedback on their performance via appropriate performance measurement systems linked to rewards. This was covered in detail in Chapter 18.

Table 25.1 Trust builders and busters

Trust builder	Trust buster
"Walk the talk"—that is attitudes and actions are consistent with the words spoken or written	Talking, but not "walking the talk"
Openness and honesty—there is no substitute for communication, communication, communication, as long as it is "open and honest" communication. Always ensure you address the "grapevine talk"	Not telling the truth (if communication is poor, then the organization "grapevine" will create rumors and meaning that may have absolutely no resemblance to the truth). How important is telling the truth? In the 1980s, AT&T confided to Wall Street analysts that there would be retrenchments. Obviously word leaked out, and some employees even read about it in the newspapers. Work almost came to a standstill while employees worried about their future. At least two employees killed themselves (*Fortune*, 18 October 1993: 67). Change and the truth is a serious thing. It may hurt, but people deserve and have the right to the truth
Use the word "we" and not "me"—create a team environment	A more senior person who takes the credit stealing an idea from an employee and taking credit for it or, conversely, blames another for his or her mistakes
	Nothing will demotivate people and break down trust and teamwork faster than these activities
Over-communication goes a long way towards eliminating gossip	"Loose lips sink ships"
	"What people don't know, they make up"

Source: Hriegel and Brandt (1996: 161–169).

CASE STUDY

How useful is employee training?

An organization stated: "We trained the staff six months ago in customer care and telephone skills to increase service levels and we have not changed much at all."

They were asked, "What measures do you have in place to provide feedback to staff and management on the level of customer service and telephone calls informing customers of the status of their processing?" The reply was, "We monitor it by the customer complaints register."

As stated earlier in this book, "since people don't do what you expect but what you inspect . . . you need to create a way to measure results" (Gerstner, 2002). The organization changed and established a set of simple people performance measures to provide immediate feedback to people and change their behavior.

Message: You cannot expect people to change unless you provide them with performance feedback measures and link the achievement of these measures to rewards.

Criticality of trust

In a very real sense, the level of trust is a thermometer of individual and group (organization) health. With trust, we all function naturally and directly.

The research and findings of neuroeconomists (Zak, 2008) are causing other economists to rethink theories that have been based on the assumptions that people act in pure self-interest. Zak discovered that our brains are wired to guide us towards both socially and individually beneficial behavior and that this motivation to cooperate happens on an unconscious level.[5]

KEY POINT

Trust is among the strongest known predictors of a country's wealth; nations with low levels tend to be poor. Our model showed that societies with low levels are poor because the inhabitants undertake too few of the long-term investments that create jobs and raise incomes. Such investments depend on mutual trust that both parties will fulfill their contractual obligations.

(Zak, 2008: 88)

Figure 25.7 shows the results, by country, of the answer to a simple question: "Do you think most people can be trusted?"

Why should we be concerned about trust at a cultural level? It turns out that the standard of living in a country is directly related to the degree to which people in the country trust each other. That is, wealth is correlated to the trust levels. Why? Because when trust levels are high, financial transactions costs are low and efficient—there is no need for elaborate contracts to protect the parties involved. Whereas, in low trust environments, elaborate, inefficient means are necessary to protect the parties, making transaction costs high.

Personal income will rise 1 percent for every 15 percent increase in the proportion of people in the country who think others are trustworthy; the reverse is also true. Trust begets trust; fear escalates fear.

The national or country relationship with trust translates to individuals and organizations.

Step 5: Required behavior

Having discussed why we must change, why people are resistant to change, leadership's role in the change process, the various components of the change process and how we should get ready for it, what exactly is it?

What behavioral changes does the organization expect and demand from its people?

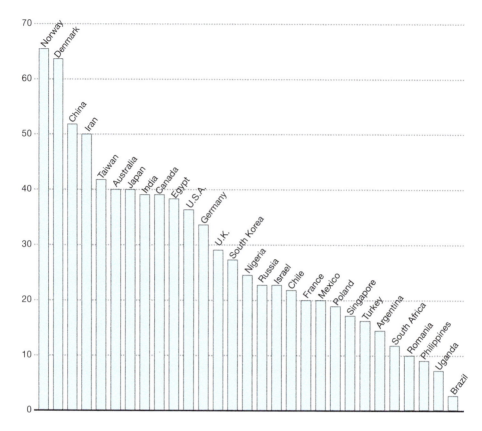

Figure 25.7 National trust: trust level by country

Source: Zak (2008: 95).

CASE STUDY

Increasing a division's ranking in an organization employee survey

The division was not performing well in the annual corporate employee cultural survey and the head of the division requested an investigation into why and then engaged a consultant to ensure that the ranking increased at the next survey.

One-on-one interviews were conducted with direct reports and focus groups for 25 percent of the divisional staff. Confidentiality was insisted upon by the consultant and promised to the staff.

The first step was to establish a baseline understanding of where the division was currently (the survey did not provide this in enough detail), what the employees saw as the issues, and where the employees and management wanted to be in two years' time.

A pathway was devised with in excess of 30 recommendations regarding actions required in order to achieve the desired outcome.

Message: Unless people are listened to and included in the process of creating their own pathway to a changed environment, you cannot expect them to participate passionately.

The impact of a small BPM activity on the organization-wide culture

Many years ago a banking system was implemented into a multi-branch building society. The organization, now privatized, was still emerging from its government bureaucratic heritage.

The organization's employees on the project had relatively low productivity and motivation compared to similar organizations in the private sector. The project team instituted a "fun" and "empowering" environment within the team. Not only did the project employees' productivity increase to 200–300 percent above the norm within the organization; the culture also started to permeate the rest of the organization in a positive way.

While this BPM project team involved a comparatively small number of people, it influenced the entire organization.

Message: You cannot not influence other people with whom you come into contact.

There is much talk in management literature of corporate culture and the role it plays in an organization. What type of culture is best, what type does your organization want or already have, and do you wish to change it?

Louis Gerstner (2002) made a very profound and practical statement with regard to culture when he said: "I came to see, in my time at IBM, that culture isn't just one aspect of the game—it is the game. In the end, an organization is nothing more than the collective capacity of its people to create value."

What he is really saying is that we all must make the culture we want in the organization into part of the organization's DNA.

How much influence will the BPM activity have over the organization's culture? Obviously, this will depend upon the type of BPM activity selected. However, never underestimate the impact a reasonably small-sized BPM activity can have on the culture of an organization.

There are three simple steps that, if published widely, can assist the people change management process:

1. A short, clear uncomplicated message needs to be developed. "Win, execute, and team" (Gerstner, 2002) provides an example of how short, clear and powerful this message can be.

2. A behavioral charter needs to be developed showing the behavioral change required for change from the current to the new behavior.

3. A set of *principles* that we will all live by within the organization must be developed.

It is essential that these are documented and widely communicated to all the people within the organization.

Step 6: How do you get there?

Many of the "how to's" have been explained in earlier steps in this chapter, and they will not be repeated here.

It is important to understand that you should never underestimate the time and effort involved in a change program. It will take a minimum of three years for a smaller organization and five years plus for a multinational-sized organization to "move" culture, and there are no guarantees. The leader plays a pivotal role, imparting the consistent message to all senior management, team leaders and people within the organization. The role or impact the current BPM activity will have on the people change management requirements of the organization will depend upon the length of the BPM activity (project). If the BPM activity is a shorter time period than the three to five years mentioned above, then it will need to link into the larger people change management activities/program of the organization.

Some of the challenges with this traditional approach include:

- It primarily relies on a few people trying to convince many people of the need for change.
- Often the employees are less informed and ultimately this leads to a less effective change effort.
- Employees do not believe they are responsible for the necessary change—it is someone else's (leadership's) job or issue.
- Change often occurs sequentially.
- Change is perceived as a disruption of the "real work" that needs to be done.
- The pace of change is often too slow.
- It can lead to a substantial change in part of the organization and modest change in the entire organization.
- It is the execution that is critical and the traditional approach can break down at the time of implementation.

While there are many excellent aspects to this style of approach, it is predominantly based upon a *deficiency* model, which if stated simply is:

- Identify the problem(s)
- Conduct root-cause analysis
- Brainstorm solutions and analyze
- Develop action plans/interventions.

KEY POINT

The traditional approach is based upon the unwritten rule:

Let's fix what's wrong and let the strengths take care of themselves.

Whereas the second approach, the Appreciative Inquiry (AI) model, is based upon the assumptions that the questions we ask will tend to focus our attention in a particular direction. It is the questions we ask that are critical. Organizations move in the direction of what they study; and what they study is based upon the question(s) being asked.

KEY POINT

Human systems tend to move in the direction of what they most frequently and persistently ask questions about.

What you study—grows.

If an organization completes a survey of the moments of highest engagement and enthusiasm of the employees and the organization, they have an opportunity of taking these moments, magnifying them and learning.

APPRECIATIVE INQUIRY APPROACH

Appreciative Inquiry (AI) is an "asset-based approach" that starts with the belief that every organization, and every person in the organization, has positive aspects that can be built upon.

If you analyze the two words, the definitions in the *Oxford English Dictionary* are:

Ap-pre'ci-ate: verb, 1. Valuing; the act of recognizing the best in people or the world around us; affirming past and present strengths, successes, and potentials; to perceive those things that give life (health, vitality, excellence) to living systems. 2. To increase in value, e.g. the economy has appreciated in value. Synonyms: valuing, prizing, esteeming, and honoring.

In-quire' (kwir), verb, 1. The act of exploring and discovery. 2. To ask questions; to be open to seeing new possibilities. Synonyms: discovery, search, and systematic exploration, study.

In an interview, Peter Drucker stated that "the task of leadership is to create an alignment of strengths, making our weaknesses irrelevant." AI is an approach or model that is based around an organization's strengths.

"Some researchers believe that excessive focus on dysfunctions (problems in an organization) can actually cause them to become worse or fail to become better" (*Time Magazine*, 2005). By contrast, from an AI approach, when all members of an organization are motivated to understand and value the most favorable features of its culture, it can make rapid improvements.[6,7]

It is about promoting change by amplifying the best of 'what is' rather than attempting to fix 'what isn't' working.

Table 25.2 Distinguishing AI from traditional problem solving

Traditional problem solving (deficit-based change)	Appreciative Inquiry (strength-based innovation)	Basic assumptions
Identify the problem(s)	Identify current successes and strengths. Value (appreciate) the Best of What Is	What we focus on becomes our reality
Analyze the causes of the problems	Identify the factors that enable our success and envision our desired future. Envisioning what might be	In every ongoing team/group/organization some things work
Treat the problem. Analyze possible solutions	Innovate to build more support for those factors that enable success	People have more confidence and comfort to journey to the future (the unknown) when they carry forward parts of the past (the known)
We get better by solving our problems. Develop the action plan	We get better by enabling our best work	The mode and language of inquiry affects the organization being observed

AI often relies on interviews to qualitatively understand the organization's potential strengths by looking at an organization's experience and its potential; with the objective of eliciting the assets and personal motivations that are its strengths.

Table 25.2 provides a contrast between the traditional problem-solving approach and the AI approach, together with some basic assumptions applying to AI.

In summary, the traditional approach:

- Only involves a top few experts to provide the answers;

- Focuses on what is wrong;

- Searches for the root causes of these failures—if you look for problems, you will find (and create) more problems;

- Endeavors to "fix" the past;

- Obstacles are treated as barriers.

These all combine into a very negatively based point of view and perhaps this highlights why it is so difficult to motivate employees to "take the change journey."

By contrast, a summary of the AI approach:

- All (or all levels in the organization) are involved;

- The solutions come from within; not from experts, who are often outside the organization;

- The focus is on what works;

- Searching for the root cause of success—if you look for successes, you will find (and create) more successes, leading to an amplification of further successes;

- Endeavors to create the future;

- Obstacles are treated as ramps to new territory and opportunities.

KEY POINT

These aspects combine into a positive-based approach that generates significant energy and enthusiasm within the organization. Organizations work best when they are vibrant, alive and fun. Employees will sense that the spirit in the organization is vital and healthy and people take pride in their work. The organization is a place where everyone builds on each other's successes. Where people have a positive can-do attitude that is infectious. A place where the glow of success is shared, embraced and celebrated.

Applied research has demonstrated that the AI method can enhance an organization's internal capacity for collaboration and change (Whitney and Trosten-Bloom, 2003). It is powered by the type and quality of the questions asked. It has been suggested by many that we live in a world that is created by the quality of the questions we ask. Once again a comparison is provided between the two approaches (Table 25.3).

The AI step approach is based upon the 4-D Cycle model shown in Figure 25.8 and a brief explanation of the four steps follows.

Step 1: Discovery

Begins with a grounded observation of the best of what is inside the organization. It looks for examples of excellence and "peak" experiences. The types of questions that may be asked are:

- What is happening now?

- What impact is it having?

- Who else is involved?

- How much? How many?

- What has happened up to now?

- When have you felt energized? Why?

- When has your team really excelled? What factors enabled this to occur?

- Think of a time when you were part of a revolutionary partnership, a time in your life— at work, or in your personal or community life, when you not only met the other person(s) half way, but met and exceeded needs on both sides. Describe the situation in detail:

  o What made it feel radically different?

  o Who was involved?

Table 25.3 The art of the question in leadership and change

Traditional problem solving (deficit-based change)	Appreciative inquiry (strength-based innovation)
• What is the biggest problem here?	• What possibilities exist that we have not yet considered?
• Why did I have to be in this problem organization or department?	• What's the smallest change that could make the biggest impact?
• Why do you make so many mistakes?	• What solutions would have us both win?
• What do we need to do to fix this?	
• Why do we still have those problems?	

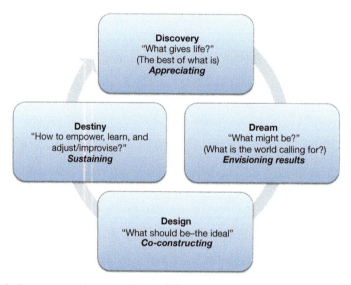

Figure 25.8 Appreciative Inquiry 4-D model

   o   How did you interact differently?

   o   What were the outcomes and benefits you experienced?

Step 2: Dream

This step provides a vision of the future by envisioning the perfect state. Through this vision and logic it will enable employees to collaboratively state what might be. The types of questions that could be asked are:

- What is the world calling for you/your team/your department/organization to become?
- What would success look like?
- What will be different?
- What is the best that could happen?

Step 3: Design

This determines how to achieve the vision and encourages employees to think "outside the box." It starts to elicit what should be. The types of questions that could be asked are:

- What could you/your team/your department/organization do?
- What are your options?
- Who could assist you?
- What may support the vision?
- What processes, structures and relationships do you need to create or change to make the vision a reality?

Step 4: Destiny

This aligns the way forward to enable employees to collaboratively commit to what can be. It is more inspirational than a detailed action plan. It creates a sense of being engaged by a compelling vision. The types of questions that could be asked are:

- What will you do to contribute towards this?
- What will you do first?
- How will you do this?
- When will you start?

It is the promotion of employee and management successes and not employee and management failures that can motivate. It is building upon these successes that makes employees proud and develop the desire to do even better.

Whichever approach is adopted as part of the people change management strategy there are two things that must be kept in mind:

1. The first step is to analyze the needs of the BPM activity, because deciding what and how to change is critical:
   - Does the BPM activity require the entire organization to change, or only parts of it?
   - Once this is agreed, determine the depth and breadth of the change program;
   - Always have "depth" rather than a "shallow" change effort; understanding this will take longer and require more effort, but will yield significantly better sustainable results;
   - Always match the change program to the various aspects of the People phase of the framework.
2. Consistency, persistency and communication are the bywords of an organization culturally and the change management program.

As Albert Einstein said: "There are only two ways to live your life. One is as though nothing is a miracle. The other is as though everything is a miracle."

We all spend a great deal of our waking time at work. So make our environment (physical, emotional), our business processes, our colleagues, our stakeholders, our customers, our business partners, our society, a better place and a fun and rewarding place to be. The change starts with you.

SUMMARY

During this chapter it was suggested that people change management is arguably the most important aspect of any BPM activity. Where BPM is a large program or organizational transition activity then it will play a large and crucial role. If it is a smaller BPM activity, then people change management may only play a small role. The importance of an organization's culture and trust levels was discussed; together with providing two potential approaches to change management. The chapter also provided an:

- Appreciation of the importance that an organization's culture plays in its success.

- Understanding of the cultural influencers and the typical aspects of an outstanding organizational culture.

- Outlined the two approaches to people change management: the more traditional approach, with its challenges; and the more recent Appreciative Inquiry approach with its emphasis on strength-based innovation.

SELF-TEST

1 Briefly describe the importance of people change management in BPM activities.

2 Briefly describe why an organization's culture will significantly influence its performance.

3 List the four main influencers of behavior noting if they are a motivator or constraint and why.

4 List the eight major groupings of culture actions, and provide some examples for each group (refer to the Extra reading section and Kotter's change model in Table 25.4).

5 List out the steps in the traditional approach to change management with a brief description of each step.

6 Name some of the challenges with this traditional approach.

7 Briefly describe why organizational trust is critical.

8 List four trust builders and four trust busters.

9 Briefly describe the Appreciative Inquiry (AI) approach.

10 List and describe the four steps in the AI approach, listing some of the questions that may be asked in each step.

11 Provide a brief comparison between these two approaches.

ASSIGNMENT

During the BPM activity you have to look after People Change Management.

Assignment guiding questions

1. What type of communications did you undertake for each of the various stakeholders?
2. What action did you take to mobilize the forces of cultural change?

EXTRA READING

Drivers for cultural change

The forces of cultural change provide a useful framework to specify the roles of leadership, employees and management in the cultural change program and to assign specific project initiatives. It is only meant to be a simple document with bullet points under each "project initiative." It is a means of focusing stakeholders and gaining a simple level of consensus.

Figure 25.9, in conjunction with this chapter, shows the areas that will need to be addressed.

Need leads to movement—it increases the willingness to change. The ability to make the promise of a successful future tangible and realistic and stimulates the need to take action. It should not create fear (as fear paralyzes people), but it should create a sense of urgency.

Vision gives direction—it provides a goal and objective for the change. The leadership believes in this vision and "walks the talk" on the basis of the proposed new culture.

Forces of Cultural Change			Project initiatives
Purpose (Leadership)	Need	Makes people move	• •
	Vision	Gives direction	• •
	Success	Makes believe	• •
	Spirit	Gives strength	• •
Action (Management)	Structures	Challenges	• •
	Capacities	Makes it achievable	• •
	Systems	Enforces changes	• •

Figure 25.9 Forces for cultural change

Source: Published with permission of Berenschot.

Success creates belief—it will increase the confidence that the new culture is able to be achieved. Success must be propagated quickly and broadly. Success increases the motivation to participate.

Spirit gives power—it is the source of energy for change. It is about the dynamics of the change process itself. It is about providing people with the additional strength to break the existing barriers, to think outside the box and to make things happen.

Structure invites change—people's behavior will be influenced by changes in various aspects of the organization. Physical changes in the work environment could also trigger changes. It is important to mobilize all the available and potential willingness, within both the organization and the people, for change.

Capacities guarantee the change—providing the capacity for change will increase the confidence of employees. The required capacities will be achieved through training, education, information and promotional campaigns, and personal successes of employees in the change project.

Systems reinforce changes—feedback on results will provide further willingness to change. Performance review systems, remuneration systems and information systems play an important role. They must ensure that the new culture is reinforced.

Kotter's change model

John Kotter is regarded by many as the leading expert of organizational change. He has written many books and papers on the subject based upon his research and thinking.

We have compared the Kotter's (2012) change model to the 7FE Framework in Table 25.4. Kotter's model is specifically related to achieving organizational change. The 7FE Framework relates to project management and specifically relating to process change and process management, and therefore we do not cover every aspect of Kotter's model. However, many, perhaps most, of Kotter's steps and activities are covered either entirely or partially within the 7FE Framework. This highlights the need to ensure that the project team for your BPM activity must have a mix of the right resources and skills; this must include organizational change expertise.

Table 25.4 Kotter's change model and 7FE Framework

John Kotter's Leading Change (2012)	7FE Framework
Step 1: Create Urgency	Part of Launch pad phase and Leadership
For change to occur, it helps if the whole organization really wants it. There is a need to develop a sense of urgency around the need for change. This may help people spark the initial motivation to get things moving.	Covered in Leadership and Launch pad phases.
This isn't simply a matter of showing people poor sales statistics or talking about increased competition. Open an honest and convincing dialogue about what's happening in the marketplace and with your competition. If many people start talking about the change you propose, the urgency can build and feed on itself.	
What you can do:	
• Identify potential threats and develop scenarios showing what could happen in the future	Covered in Leadership and Launch pad phases.
• Examine opportunities that should be, or could be, exploited	Covered in Leadership and Launch pad phases.
• Start honest discussions, and give dynamic and convincing reasons to get people talking and thinking	Covered in Leadership and Launch pad phases.
• Request support from customers, outside stakeholders and industry people to strengthen your argument	Covered, including customers and partners
Note: Kotter suggests that for change to be successful, 75 percent of an organization's management needs to "buy into" the change. In other words, you have to work really hard on Step 1 and spend significant time and energy building urgency, before moving onto the next steps. Don't panic and jump in too fast because you don't want to risk further short-term losses— if you act without proper preparation, you could be in for a very bumpy ride.	

Table 25.4 Kotter's change model and 7FE Framework—*continued*

John Kotter's Leading Change (2012)	7FE Framework
Step 2: Form a Powerful Coalition	Launch pad phase Leadership and People change management
Convince people that change is necessary. This often takes strong leadership and visible support from key people within your organization. Managing change isn't enough—you have to lead it.	Covered in Communications steps, Leadership and People Change Management
You can find effective change leaders throughout your organization—they don't necessarily follow the traditional organization hierarchy. To lead change, you need to bring together a coalition, or team, of influential people whose power comes from a variety of sources, including job title, status, expertise, and political importance.	Covered in Leadership
Once formed, your "change coalition" needs to work as a team, continuing to build urgency and momentum around the need for change.	Covered in Stakeholder Management, Project Management Leadership
What you can do:	
• Identify the true leaders in your organization	Covered in Leadership
• Ask for an emotional commitment from these key people	Covered in People Change Management and Leadership
• Work on team building within your change coalition	Not explicitly covered, however, team building is a critical normal part of establishing any project team. Ensure the project manager/ organization change project team members address this
• Check your team for weak areas, and ensure that you have a good mix of people from different departments and different levels within your company	Not explicitly covered, however, should be a normal part of establishing any project team.
Step 3: Create a Vision for Change	Launch pad phase Innovate phase Leadership
When you first start thinking about change, there will probably be many great ideas and solutions floating around. Link these concepts to an overall vision that people can grasp easily and remember.	Covered in Innovate and the Red Wine Test
A clear vision can assist everyone understand why you're asking them to do something. When people see for themselves what you're trying to achieve, then the directives they're given tend to make more sense.	Communications is a critical step in each phase
What you can do:	
• Determine the values that are central to the change	Covered in Foundations and Innovate

Table 25.4 Kotter's change model and 7FE Framework—*continued*

John Kotter's Leading Change (2012)	7FE Framework
• Develop a short summary (one or two sentences) that captures what you "see" as the future of your organization	Similar to Red Wine Test
• Create a strategy to execute that vision	Covered in Innovate and from a Transformation perspective in Foundations and Enablement
• Ensure that your change coalition can describe the vision in five minutes or less	Organization change experts must ensure this is addressed as part of the Communications steps
• Practice your "vision speech" often	Organization change experts must ensure this is addressed as part of the Communications steps
Step 4: Communicate the Vision	Communicate step in all phases
What you do with your vision after you create it will determine your success. Your message will probably have strong competition from other day-to-day communications within the company, so you need to communicate it frequently and powerfully, and embed it within everything that you do.	Organization change experts must ensure this is addressed as part of the Communications steps
Don't just call special meetings to communicate your vision. Instead, talk about it every chance you get. Use the vision daily to make decisions and solve problems. When you keep it fresh on everyone's minds, they'll remember it and respond to it.	Covered in Communications as well as Leadership and People Change Management
It's also important to "walk the talk." What you do is far more important—and believable—than what you say. Demonstrate the kind of behavior that you want from others.	Covered in Communications as well as Leadership and People Change Management
What you can do:	
• Talk often about your change vision	Covered in Communicate steps
• Openly and honestly address peoples' concerns and anxieties	Covered in need for honest communication
• Apply your vision to all aspects of operations—from training to performance reviews. Tie everything back to the vision	Covered in several places within Framework
• Lead by example	Covered in Leadership
Step 5: Remove Obstacles	Launch pad Project management People change management
If you follow these steps and reach this point in the change process, you've been talking about your vision and building buy-in from all levels of the organization. Hopefully, your staff wants to get busy and achieve the benefits that you've been promoting.	Stakeholder management within Launch pad, Project management, People change management phases must address these issues
But is anyone resisting the change? And are there processes or structures that are getting in its way?	Covered in People Change Management and Project Management

Table 25.4 Kotter's change model and 7FE Framework—*continued*

John Kotter's *Leading Change* (2012)	7FE Framework
Put in place the structure for change, and continually check for barriers to it. Removing obstacles can empower the people you need to execute your vision, and it can help the change move forward.	Covered in People Change Management and Project Management
What you can do:	
• Identify, or hire, change leaders whose main roles are to deliver the change	Ensure the organization change team members address this
• Look at your organizational structure, job descriptions, and performance and compensation systems to ensure they're in line with your vision	Covered in People phase
• Recognize and reward people for making change happen	Covered in People phase
• Identify people who are resisting the change, and help them see what's needed	Covered in People phase and People change management
• Take action to quickly remove barriers (human or otherwise)	Covered in People phase, Project management, Leadership and People change management
Step 6: Create Short-term Wins	Innovate and Implement phases
Nothing motivates more than success. Give the organization a taste of victory early in the change process. Within a short timeframe (this could be a month or a year, depending on the type of change), you'll want to have results that your staff can see. Without this, critics and negative thinkers might hurt your progress.	Part of each Communications step
Create short-term targets, not just one long-term goal. Each smaller target must be achievable and achieved, with little room for failure. The organization change team may have to work very hard to come up with these targets, but each "win" that you produce can further motivate the entire staff.	Part of each Communications step
What you can do:	
• Look for projects that you can implement without help from any strong critics of the change	Project selection is a critical part of the Launch pad phase Leverage initial findings in Understand phase to drive quick wins
• Don't choose early targets that are expensive. You want to be able to justify the investment in each project	Covered in Understand and Innovate
• Thoroughly analyze the potential pros and cons of your targets. If you don't succeed with an early goal, it can hurt your entire change initiative	Covered in People Change Management and Leadership
• Reward the people who help you meet the targets	Covered in People Change Management and Leadership

Table 25.4 Kotter's change model and 7FE Framework—*continued*

John Kotter's Leading Change (2012)	7FE Framework
Step 7: Build on the Change	Realize value and Sustainable performance phases
Kotter argues that many change projects fail because victory is declared too early. Real change runs deep. Quick wins are only the beginning of what needs to be done to achieve long-term change.	Realize value phase will assist in demonstrating success Sustainable performance phase will provide longevity
Launching one new product using a new system is great. But if you can launch ten products, that means the new system is working. To reach that tenth success, you need to keep looking for improvements.	Sustainable performance phase reviews lessons learned and provides feedback into the Foundations, Enablement and Launch pad phases
Each success provides an opportunity to build on what went right and identify what you can improve.	
What you can do:	
• After every win, analyze what went right and what needs improving	Covered in Sustainable performance phase
• Set goals to continue building on the momentum you've achieved	Covered in Sustainable performance phase and each Communications step
• Learn about Kaizen, the idea of continuous improvement	Covered in Sustainable performance phase
• Keep ideas fresh by bringing in new change agents and leaders for your change coalition	Ensure the organization change team members address this
Step 8: Anchor the Changes in Corporate Culture	Realize value and Sustainable performance phases
Finally, to make any change stick (is permanent), it should become part of the core of the organization. Corporate culture often determines what gets done, so the values behind the vision must show in day-to-day work.	Covered in Sustainable performance and Foundations phases
Make continuous efforts to ensure that the change is seen in every aspect of your organization. This will help give change a solid place in the organization's culture.	Covered in People change management
It's also important that your organization's leaders continue to support the change. This includes existing staff and new leaders who are brought in. If you lose the support of these people, you might end up back where you started.	Covered in People change management and Leadership
What you can do:	
• Talk about progress every chance you get. Tell success stories about the change process, and repeat other stories that you hear	Covered in Leadership
• Include the change ideals and values when hiring and training new staff	Covered to some extent in People phase

Table 25.4 Kotter's change model and 7FE Framework—*continued*

John Kotter's Leading Change (2012)	7FE Framework
• Publicly recognize key members of your original change coalition, and make sure the rest of the staff—new and old—remembers their contributions	Ensure the organization change team members address this
• Create plans to replace key leaders of change as they move on. This will help ensure that their legacy is not lost or forgotten	Ensure the organization change team members address this

CHAPTER 26

LEADERSHIP

OVERVIEW

This chapter describes the last of the three essentials: Leadership.

Leadership is critical for the successful completion of any project, and this especially applies to BPM activities, as they often require significant change, both structurally and in a sustainable way, in the organization.

This chapter describes the different leadership levels that can be found in an organization, and the various leadership styles and their influence on BPM activities.

OVERALL LEARNING OUTCOME

By the end of this chapter you will be able to:

* Understand the difference between management and leadership
* Distinguish the different leadership styles
* Comprehend the different spheres of influence
* Understand the six leadership styles.

WHY?

Why is leadership (Figure 26.1) one of the essentials to a successful BPM project? This is an important question. In Chapter 3, four different types of BPM activities were outlined and Table 3.1 outlines these and the typical leader (sponsor and manager) who would drive the activity and an indication of the role they may fulfill. For convenience the table has been repeated here (Table 26.1).

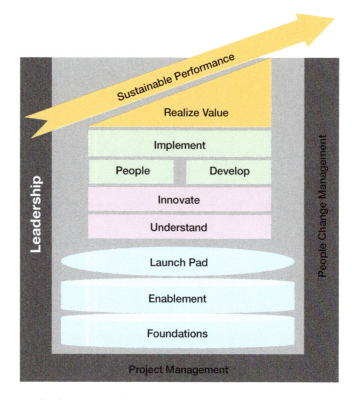

Figure 26.1 Leadership essential

Communications, "walking the talk" in the organization and the people change (organizational) management aspects are critical in all types of activities.

The first two types of BPM activities shown in Table 26.1 are often initiated or driven from the bottom-up as they are typically projects. Even if a BPM activity has a large impact upon a business unit it is often initiated by a knowledgeable and passionate process-focused manager or executive. It most probably will not have significant attention from the Chief Executive Officer (CEO).

However, the last two, program and transformation, activities shown in Table 26.1 will typically be top-down driven as they cannot be initiated or successful without the drive and detailed support of the CEO. Even if driven or sponsored by another senior executive, the success will depend upon the continued support of the CEO. (Refer to Chapter 5 for more detail on bottom-up and top-down approaches and why one approach will never (or rarely) work for an enterprise-wide BPM implementation.)

Table 26.1 BPM activities and the type of involvement

Type of BPM activity	Typical leaders	Role
Simple low impact BPM project	Sponsor: business unit leader Manager: Project Manager	• Deliver to the business case • Manage the project effectively
High impact BPM program	Sponsor: Divisional Leader; Senior Executive Manager: Project Director	• Deliver to the business case • Manage the project effectively • Ensure that the organizational change aspects of the project are effectively managed
Large-scale BPM program	Sponsor: CEO or another very senior executive Manager: Program Director	• Personal involvement (not just turning up to steering committee meetings once a month) • Publicly aligning program and individual projects with the organization strategy • Communications—formal and informal to all stakeholders • "Walk the talk"
Enterprise-wide business transformation program	Sponsor: CEO Manager: Transformation Program Director (usually a senior executive)	• Personal involvement (not just turning up to steering committee meetings once a month) • Publicly aligning program and individual projects with the organization strategy, especially to external stakeholders • Communications—formal and informal to all stakeholders • "Walk the talk"

HOW?

We will not be completing a series of steps for this BPM project essential, as it is not appropriate. Instead, we will discuss the following topics:

- what leadership means in the context of a BPM activity;
- leadership's sphere of influence;
- how organizational strategy and leadership are related;
- six leadership styles and how they will influence BPM activities;
- the importance of communications and the role leadership plays
- relationships—leadership at all levels within the organization is all about relationships.

We will then bring this all together into a leadership levels and components table.

> **Leaders should lead as far as they can and then vanish. Their ashes should not choke the fire they have lit.**
>
> (H. G. Wells)

WHAT IS LEADERSHIP IN THE CONTEXT OF A BPM ACTIVITY?

The essence of leadership is captured in this simple statement:

> **The yardstick to measure good leadership is the culture of enduring excellence which a leader leaves behind after he is gone from the scene.**
>
> **(Chibber, undated)**

An initial reading of this quotation leads you to think of the leader as the CEO; however, when you read it again, it can apply to any level of leadership within an organization. For the purpose of discussing leadership in the context of a BPM activity, we have devised three levels of leadership:

1   Chief executive officer (CEO), senior executive or business unit manager

2   Program/project sponsor, program director and project manager

3   People (project team members and business staff).

It is important to understand that each of these groups of people provides leadership to each other and to other stakeholders. They are role models and leaders of change within smaller parts of the organization, but they are leaders just the same.[1] The role each leader plays will depend, as stated previously, upon the type of BPM activity selected.

Table 26.2 shows some of the key differences between a leader and a manager. It is important to realize that in the twenty-first century the emergence of the "knowledge worker" has resulted in the blurring of the lines between a pure leader and a pure manager—it has become a merger of both. However, when we talk about leadership in the BPM context, we mean the person is much more a leader rather than just a manager.

A person is a true leader if they can get things done, without using positional authority and sanctions.

> **There is NO one right way to manage people. One does not "manage" people. The task is to lead people. And the goal is to make productive the specific strengths and knowledge of each individual.**
>
> **(Drucker, 1999: 21–22)**

Drucker also stated that: "Most of what we call management consists of making it difficult for people to get their work done."

Sphere of influence

The leadership levels can have varying degrees of influence over a BPM project, the organization, people and their environment. Figure 26.2 shows the sphere of influence of leadership in general terms.

Table 26.2 Differences between leaders and managers

Leader	Manager
Innovates	Administers
Develops	Maintains
Focuses on people	Focuses on systems and structure
Inspires trust	Relies on control
Has a long-range perspective	Has a short-range view
Asks what and why	Asks how and when
Eyes the horizon	Eyes the bottom line
Originates	Imitates
Challenges status quo	Accepts status quo
Is his or her own person	Typically is a classic good soldier
Does the right things	Does things right

Source: Murray (2010).

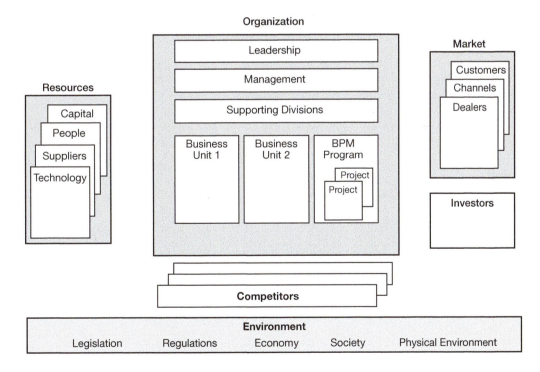

Figure 26.2 Leadership's sphere of influence

Source: Adapted from Rummler (2004), © International Society for Performance Improvement; reproduced with permission.

The three levels of leadership described earlier will have varying degrees of influence over the components of Figure 26.2:

- *Level 1 leaders* (CEO, senior executive or business unit manager) will have a sphere of influence over all or most of the various components of Figure 26.2.

- *Level 2 leaders* (program/project sponsor, program director and project manager) will have a sphere of influence that will vary depending upon the size and scenario of the BPM activity being undertaken by the organization. This influence will range from within the business unit only, to across most of the organization and perhaps several of the external stakeholders within the market and resources groupings. It is unlikely they will have much influence over the environment and investors or competitors, although a large BPM program could impact upon the value of the organization and have an impact upon investors and competitors. Some level 2 leaders can have an extensive network within and outside the organization due to their personal networks and/or length of service with the organization.

- *Level 3 leaders* (people—project team members and business staff) will invariably have a sphere of influence either within their business unit or confined to the organization.

No matter what your level of leadership, it could be argued simplistically that the most important quality of a leader is to have passion, closely followed by honesty and integrity, and the ability to genuinely listen. This is true of all levels of leadership, but obviously magnifies with seniority within the organization.

According to Hawley (1993):

> **One of the hardest things I have come to realize as a general manager is that my state of mind is really my primary tool ... My everyday life is spent dispensing energy, and keeping a mental focus is a full-time effort.**

KEY POINT

Providing inspiring leadership is a challenge. Much energy and focus needs to go into inspiring people to feel empowered and achieve.

Passion is about "the emotions as distinguished from reason; intense; driving, or overmastering feeling of conviction." Synonyms include: enthusiasm and zest ("energetic and

BPM INSIGHT

Some BPM initiatives need a Servant Leadership approach as it aims to build people and institutional capability to ensure that the changes are structural, significant and sustainable.

CASE STUDY

BPM, another project

A senior executive was being sold on the benefits of BPM when he stated that he had just been on a two-day planning session with his people and they had listed 67 projects for the next year. He was so impressed with the potential benefits of BPM for his organization that he was seriously considering making BPM the 68th project.

The suggestion was that he didn't, because it would not have his "attention."

Message: Ensure that the BPM activity (particularly if a large program) is one of the top priorities of the key person. If a CEO cannot provide sufficient attention for this, then perhaps a pilot or two should be considered.

unflagging pursuit of an aim or devotion to a cause"—*Merriam–Webster online dictionary*). Leadership, in this context, also includes "attention" to the various tasks at hand. If a significant BPM program or project does not have the attention and the passion of the leadership of the organization, then do not do it—it will be a battle all the way to completion, which will place the project at significant risk.

It is critical to understand and address the sphere of influence of level 1 and level 2 leaders. An example is the statement by Stephen Covey, that "the key to the ninety-nine is the one . . . how you treat the one reveals how you regard the ninety-nine because everyone is ultimately one" (Hawley, 1993). This comment refers to the need for leaders and all levels to "walk the talk"—people pick up in an instant on a mismatch between what has been said by someone and his or her behavior. This lack of congruency is a mismatch of integrity and honesty. Whenever leaders at all levels complain of the lack of commitment of people within the organization, it is usually a result of the commitment the leaders have to their people. The need for leaders at all levels to "walk the talk" is essential.

The success of a BPM activity is often determined by the right level of involvement of the right level of leadership, as outlined Table 26.3 (derived from Table 12.1).

Table 26.3 Relationship between leadership level, BPM activity and involvement

Type of BPM activity	Leadership		
	Level 1—CEO, senior executive, business unit manager	Level 2—program/ project sponsor, program director and project manager and management	Level 3—people (project team members and business staff)
Large-scale BPM program or enterprise-wide transformation	Key driver	Committed	Committed
BPM program or portfolio of projects	Committed	Key driver	Committed
Isolated BPM projects	Informed	Key driver	Committed

Organization strategy

This is about level 1 leaders developing a strategy for the organization. As stated in the Foundation and Enablement phases, we will not provide mechanisms or techniques for strategy creation; we do, however, think it is worth taking a few moments to understand what constitutes a strategy, and what use it is to an organization and, therefore, a BPM activity.

A strategy is not a plan, "it is a purposeful process of engaging people inside and outside the organization in scoping out new paths ahead" (Stace and Dunphy, 1996). There needs to be a link between the strategy and how it is to be implemented and "sold" to the people in the organization.

According to Blount (1999):

Leadership is about "bringing everyone along" in a balanced way, not just in their minds so they understand it, but emotionally as well, in their hearts, so they are really energized and identifying with it, and they themselves take part in the leadership.

A compelling strategy or vision rarely motivates people. People move away from pain and towards pleasure. Confronting reality can provide the pain to move. A leader must create a climate where "the truth is heard and the brutal facts confronted" (Collins, 2001).

As discussed in Chapter 25, looking at it simplistically there are two methods regarding how people can be convinced to change. The method selected will depend upon the organization, the particular situation and the leadership style of the leader.

The first method was used in turning around IBM in the 1990s, where Louis Gerstner (2002) stated that:

If employees do not believe a crisis exists, they will not make the sacrifices that are necessary to change. Nobody likes change. So there must be a crisis, and it is the job of the CEO to define and communicate that crisis, its magnitude, its severity, and its impact. Just as important, the CEO must be able to communicate how to end the crisis—the new strategy, the new company model, the new culture. All this takes enormous commitment from the CEO to communicate, communicate, and communicate some more. No institutional transformation takes place, without a multi-year commitment by the CEO to put himself or herself constantly in front of employees and speak plain, simple, compelling language that drives conviction and action throughout the organization.

BPM INSIGHT

Some CEOs take the ultimate step to convince their organization, customers, partners and other stakeholders about their intent to make fundamental changes: they announce large transformation programs, including their financial and other targets, to the market and show that they can be held accountable for achieving those targets.

The second method is more subtle, and requires leadership to enable people to understand that there is a "problem," and to inform them of the magnitude of the problem and why it is essential to change. People will need to understand what the impact will be upon the organization and themselves if the problem is not addressed.

Communication is not just with the people within the organization; the strategy must be "sold" to all stakeholders continually until it becomes inculcated in the culture of the organization. People need to take it up with a level of urgency and passion.

Having set the organization strategy and vision, and continuing to communicate it until it is inculcated within the culture, it is critical to review it continually along the journey. Rarely will a CEO "dream up" a strategy that is perfect, or indeed dream up the strategy on his or her own. Strategies usually provide a vision or broad way forward, with the detail being determined and implemented further down the organization's hierarchy. According to Stace and Dunphy (1996):

> **Strategy is the search for directions which energize the life of an organization; structures provide the social organization needed to facilitate the strategy ... Strategy and structure need to be constantly re-examined and realigned to be effective.**

However, having said how important strategy is, it must be seen in context—for it is important to understand that as a leader "your state of mind is more important than your well-knit strategies and perfectly laid plans" (Hawley, 1993). It is better to have a leader who exhibits great passion, honesty, integrity and an ability to listen, with no strategy, than the opposite of this.

Leadership style

Which type of BPM activity should be selected by the organization or business unit will be influenced by the leadership style of the organization. Leadership style "is not a strategy but an approach to strategy: it is defined by the role of a firm's leaders" (Keen, 1997).

Keen[2] has identified six leadership styles (he calls them "strategic styles") that we have found to be consistent with the leadership styles in the organizations we have engaged with:

1. Transformational leadership
2. Delegated mandate
3. Reactive urgency
4. Individual initiative
5. Sustained improvement
6. Opportunism.

We will briefly describe each of these, relating them to the likely BPM implementation scenarios.

Transformational leadership

This type of leadership style requires a unique leader who will be either a hero or a villain at the conclusion of the transformation. The leader (level 1 or 2) will personally lead the change program, selling it to all stakeholders, internal and external, and it is a high risk activity. Don't underestimate the time for transformational change; it can take from five to ten years. The level 2 project sponsor or project manager could provide this leadership style to the BPM activity, as long as this person has a strong enough personality to be able to "sell" the program to the rest of the organization.

For example, an Australian bank undertook such a program. The CEO initiated a $1.5-billion spend over three years to transform the operational processes of the bank to make it more customer-focused and efficient. He personally sold the program to the management, employees and investment community. In the initial phases the CEO received a great deal of criticism from the financial press and employees. The program is complete and the outcomes are perceived by the investment community and financial press as being a success.

Delegated mandate

Keen says that this leadership style is seen in about one-third of organizations. This style is where the leader (CEO) provides a clear mandate for the need for change but the strategy is only communicated in generalist terms—for example "we need to be more customer focused," "we need to be more competitive and therefore, need to cut our costs by $xx million."

The details of the execution are left up to the lower management levels. This can result in unclear messages, confusion and doubt regarding how to execute the strategy. For level 2 leaders, this could equate to the project sponsor or project manager telling the project team, in broad terms, what the desired outcome of the project is expected to be, and leaving it up to the project team leaders and members to deliver. The difficulty with this situation is matching the activities to the desired project goals, and the coordination between the various project team leaders—especially as the project manager has to ensure that the project's goals are met.

This style usually results in incremental programs and projects, such as BPR.

Reactive urgency

This is crisis management, and the most common leadership style. It is usually initiated as a reaction to competitor or market conditions. Reengineering, cost-cutting and downsizing are the typical approaches, and these are typically led by a tough senior executive with a reputation for "getting things done."

While a crisis can focus an organization and get results, it is far better to be proactive or predictive than reactive.

Project management (level 2) and project team members and business staff (level 3) acting in crisis mode can be counterproductive and compromise project outcomes, or at least add significant risk to projects, as too much pressure or urgency can lead to errors and omissions.

What do we do?

A CEO initiated a multiple-year program with the outcome to be a reduction in the cost level of the organization of $25m per annum. He launched this to the organization and told his direct reports to "go and make it happen."

The response, away from the CEO, was one of disbelief and confusion. They were confused as to the expectations—did the CEO want just cost reduction, which could have happened simply by retrenching staff; and cutting other costs? This obviously would have impacted growth, service levels and future business opportunities.

The program limped along for 18 months before, through trial and error, the direct reports gained an understanding of the CEO's expectations.

Message: A more transformational leadership style would have provided a common vision which would have allowed the organization to gain momentum much faster, with resulting benefits to the organization.

Individual initiative

This leadership style relies on a well-meaning leader who is in a position to make a change. It is usually started by the leader finding a "solution" that he or she thinks will be extremely useful to the organization, and then going looking for a problem.

When successful, the leader will be seen as having great initiative and the solution will start to spread throughout the organization. Never underestimate the impact that this style can have on an organization.

Level 2 and level 3 leaders can also initiate activities that lead to benefits (and risks) for the organization; the extent will simply be smaller the lower the level of leader.

Sometimes, when the time is right, the slightest variation can have explosive results within an organization. Part of a leader's role is to create an environment where this can take place—where an individual can take initiative, be empowered and be allowed to fail without recrimination.

Sustained improvement

This type of improvement program can only be tolerated if the organization is already best in class (the world leader). Paul O'Neill (1991), Chairman of Alcoa, made a great statement, which we quoted in Chapter 17; it is worth repeating here:

> **Continuous improvement is exactly the right idea if you are the world leader in everything you do. It is a terrible idea if you are lagging the world leadership benchmark. It is probably a disastrous idea if you are far behind the world standard—in which case you may need rapid quantum-leap improvement.**

Toyota is another great example of the sustained improvement program proponents. These organizations never rest on their laurels; they continually work hard at getting better and better.

Unless you are a world leader, then this is not the strategy style that should be adopted. In this case, it is not good enough to be better than you were last year, or even better than your competitors; there needs to be a significant leap forward in your productivity.

This leadership style should be adopted by all leadership levels within the organization. All people must contribute, on a continuous basis, towards sustained improvement of the organization.

Opportunism

This can be an extremely successful strategy for some organizations. It is not crisis management, like the "reactive urgency" style; however, it is also not predictive, and nor is it a sustained improvement strategy. Leaders who adopt this style tend to be proactive in the prevention of crises, but do not lead the industry or get too far ahead of their competitors. They can be a bit trendy, in the sense of trying the latest management fad.

Again, it is the responsibility of all levels to be continually on the lookout for opportunities for the organization. Level 1 and level 2 leaders must ensure that the culture of the organization promotes and encourages ideas from all people.

It is fair to say that leaders should adopt different strategy styles at different times within the organization. Sometimes a BPM activity needs to be incremental, and at other times it should be radical. Both can be appropriate at the same time within different business units. Organizational transformation is difficult and complex, and there is no single right way of doing it.

Communications

Even if a leader sets and communicates an excellent strategy, unless the leader can get the majority to follow, it is useless. People are therefore a critical component. As Jim Collins (2001) said, "the old adage 'people are your most important asset' turns out to be wrong. People are *not* your most important asset. The *right* people are." Get the "right" people on board and get the "wrong" people off, and then the "right" people can help build the strategy. There is nothing like involvement to get buy-in, ownership and commitment.

Thus, execute the *who* first (get the right people), and they will figure out the *how* and *what*.

Leadership is about "infecting" people with an exciting way forward, and a desire for results and a pride in attaining these results. It is about treating people with respect.

Great leaders understand the difference between providing people with an opportunity to be heard and providing them with an opportunity to have their say. Hierarchical organizations have difficulty in allowing people to have an opportunity to be heard. The "I am the boss" syndrome gets in the way. These days, you would expect this to be less of a problem—or is it? Unfortunately it is still alive and well within many organizations!

> **If organizations are machines, control makes sense. If organizations are process structures, then seeking to impose control through permanent structure is suicide. If we believe that acting responsibly means exerting control by having our hands in everything, then we cannot hope for anything except what we already have—a treadmill of effort and life-destroying stress.**
>
> **(Wheatley, 1994)**

Hierarchical management style

An organization had an extremely egalitarian culture and management style. The CEO regarded himself as simply having a different role to the other employees, and the culture allowed all personnel to be heard and respected. The organization grew rapidly, and consistently achieved a compounding 35 percent growth rate per annum.

With a change in leader came a change in the leadership style, so that it became more hierarchical and command-and-control. When decisions were made that the majority of the people disagreed with, and spoke out against, they were told just to worry about doing their job and to leave the running of the organization to those responsible for running it.

Growth suffered for many years, and in fact the organization shrank in size and underwent retrenchments. It took several years for the leadership to change and the organization to begin to recover both its culture and growth.

Message: It takes a long time and dedication, with a persistent and consistent approach, to implement the "correct" culture for an organization, and it is very easy to lose the "correct" culture rapidly with a change in leadership (at all levels within the organization).

We should be looking for *order* rather than *control*. However, we must understand that "*disorder* can be a source of *order*, and that growth is found in disequilibrium, not in balance" (Wheatley, 1994). Disequilibrium is extremely uncomfortable for people in general—even for some leaders. The normal reaction is to do whatever is necessary to quell the disturbance.

Some leaders create an overload and confusion on purpose (taking people outside their comfort zones), because they realize that from confusion emerges order and new and interesting ideas and possibilities that would rarely come from any other activity.

The important constant in this is for the leader (CEO) to have established a compelling vision or strategy that other internal organizational leaders can use as a reference point to maintain the focus.

From this *disorder* or *chaos* will come surprises. "Surprise *is* the only route to discovery" (Wheatley, 1994), and in order to discover, leaders need to create an environment where

BPM INSIGHT

The preference of *order* over *control* is crucial for organizations that move from a successful small BPM activity to a larger BPM activity, as some leaders managed their initial success with control rather than order. These leaders will typically struggle if the scope, size and magnitude of the BPM activity stretch beyond their control or ability and capacity to handle it.

mistakes are tolerated. Human beings learn by their mistakes, and unless we are allowed to try and fail we will simply stop trying. This applies to all three levels of leadership, from the CEO to team leaders within the business.

Relationships

Wheatley (1994) would argue that *relationships* are the basis for everything we do:

With relationships, we give up predictability for potentials ... None of us exists independent of our relationships with others. Different settings and people evoke some qualities from us and leave others dormant.

According to Chibber (undated), "Twelve percent of 'effective management' (which is the management terminology for leadership) is knowledge and eighty-eight percent is dealing appropriately with people."

So what has the more important influence on behavior—the system or the individual? Keen (1997:65) says "Put a good performer in a bad system, and the systems will win every time." The converse is also true—poor performers will still perform badly with a good system (although hopefully less so). Wheatley (1994) would argue that "It depends ... There is no need to decide between the two. What is critical is the *relationship* created between the person and the setting" (or system).

Obviously, if the reward and performance systems are aligned with the strategy, the synchronicity adds significant impetus to the execution and drive. However, while rewards are important, they will not achieve the results. Once you have the right people, they will infect the rest of the "right" people (a chain/change reaction) and pride in achieving will be a motivator; if the culture of the organization supports these "right" people. It is nice to receive rewards and recognition, and these will help in the sustainability over the longer term.

If you need rewards and compensation to get the "right" people, then you have the "wrong" people. The right people will not settle for second best; irrespective of the reward system, they will have a need to build something great.

So what should leaders do in relation to the implementation of BPM into their organization? First, leaders such as the project sponsor should facilitate relationships between the project manager, stakeholders (internal and external) and him or herself.

Second, how should they start? We like the saying, "eat the elephant one bite at a time."

Do not underestimate the impact of creating an incremental change environment within the organization. Many extremely successful large programs start small and progress to change an entire organization.

KEY POINT

Organizations with a relatively low process maturity or little success with large-scale BPM programs should start with an incremental BPM activity. This will provide the leadership with the ability to make the right modification before the initiative gets bigger and more spread throughout the organization.

OVERVIEW

In Table 26.4 we have brought the three leadership levels and the six components together to show the impact each level of leadership will (or can) have within a BPM project.

Table 26.4 Leadership levels and components table

Leadership component	Level 1—CEO, senior executive, business unit manager	Level 2—program/project sponsor, program director and project manager and management	Level 3—people (project team members and business staff)
Sphere of influence	• The entire organization and all its people and management • All components of the leadership sphere of influence (Figure 26.2) • The strategy can and will impact resources, markets, competitors and the environment	• People within the area of the project—this covers the end-to-end process(es), so it could and probably will cross business unit boundaries • Level 1 and 3 leadership levels—leadership • Stakeholders involved in and near the project • Supporting divisions within the organization • Market—customers, channels and dealers • Resources—people, suppliers and technology • Perhaps competitors	• Fellow employees • Level 2 leadership • Customers, suppliers and other
Organization strategy	• Responsible for strategic direction • What is strategy? Consistent direction, provides focus • Why it is important? • How does it contribute to a BPM program/project? • Strategic alignment—keep communicating the message of how the project is aligned with the organization strategy—how it fits with and contributes towards the strategy • Allocation of process owners • Allocation of funds to the project(s) • Creates project(s) for strategy execution • Responsible for selling strategy message throughout the organization and to all stakeholders	• Need to understand how the strategy was created and why • Provide feedback on the strategy • Provide detailed implementation plans for strategy execution • Responsible for delivering projects • Need to help "sell" the strategy to people (project, business and stakeholders)	• Need to understand the strategy and why it is important to the organization • Need to be passionate about implementing the strategy via project(s) and other means

Table 26.4 Leadership levels and components table—*continued*

Leadership component	Level 1—CEO, senior executive, business unit manager	Level 2—program/project sponsor, program director and project manager and management	Level 3—people (project team members and business staff)
Leadership style	• This is a personal thing. The CEO's style will probably come from the options provided in the Leadership style section of this chapter • Aware leaders adopt the leadership style for the particular occasion and change their style as the organization changes	• Work with the leadership style of the CEO and other senior level 1 leaders—understand it and accommodate it • Work with the leadership styles of colleagues • Be passionate about the delivery of the project(s) • Deliver project(s) on time and budget • Ensure value is realized from the project(s) • Be accessible to project team members and business staff	• There will be an individual style for each person
Communication	• Can never do too much of it • "Walk the talk" • Continually promote the strategy • Use formal and informal methods • Seek and be receptive to feedback • This is covered in detail in Chapter 25	• Can never do too much of it. • "Walk the talk" • Continually promote the project strategy and outcomes • Use formal and informal methods • Seek and be receptive to feedback • This is covered in detail in Chapter 25	• Ask questions • Provide feedback
Relationships	This will vary depending upon the role CEO: • Direct reports, management and rapport and trust from all people within the organization • Market, resources and competitors as defined in Figure 26.2 • Politicians, regulators, legislators, media and appropriate members of society Senior executives and business unit managers: • Direct reports, management and rapport and trust from all people within the organization • Market, resources and competitors as defined in Figure 26.2	• Level 1 leaders • Project sponsor, project director and project manager need to have a solid, trustworthy and honest relationship • Project team members • Business units members related to, and involved with, the project • Suppliers and vendors • Project stakeholders (customers, suppliers and business stakeholders)	• Level 2 leaders • Fellow employees and workers of the organization • Customers, suppliers and business stakeholders within their sphere of influence

SUMMARY

This chapter described the difference between management and leadership and the importance of leadership in BPM activities.

It described the six leadership styles and their impact on BPM activities and outlined the sphere of influence for the various leadership levels.

SELF-TEST

1 What are the key differences between leaders and managers?
2 Why is leadership important in a BPM activity?
3 What are the three levels of leadership?
4 Draw the sphere of influence.
5 What are the six leadership styles?

ASSIGNMENT

Assignment guiding questions

1. When you speak with the Board members, what are the key questions you will ask them and what would you request from them during the project?
2. If you want to initiate a business transformation program for the entire organization, who is the key sponsor you wish to have the support of?
3. What role does the program sponsor need to play?

CHAPTER 27

EMBEDDING BPM IN THE ORGANIZATION

OVERVIEW

This chapter will focus on how and where BPM should be embedded within the organization. Previous chapters have predominantly focused on the processes from a BPM activity (project or program) perspective. Here, the emphasis shifts to one of ongoing management and sustainability of processes from an organizational perspective.

This chapter takes the elements of the Foundations and Enablement phases, the BPM maturity of the organization and applies them to various organizational BPM structures. The chapter will deal with the "roof" of the BPM House—Organization Sustainability and Performance Management.

OVERALL LEARNING OUTCOME

By the end of this chapter you will be able to:

- Understand the importance of embedding BPM in the organization
- Distinguish between the activities and scope of BPM activities and those of embedding BPM in the organization
- Name the key components of embedding BPM in the organization
- Understand the three broad stages that organizations can be in
- Understand key steps that can be taken to improve BPM embedding within the organization.

Embedding BPM in an organization is a large and complex set of tasks. It is far too large and complex for just one chapter of a book. While this chapter will provide an overview of the topic, it cannot hope to cover all areas. If you wish to explore this topic in more detail, then please refer to: *Management by Process—A Roadmap to Sustainable Business Process Management* (Jeston and Nelis, 2008) which contains chapters covering:

- overview of the Management by Process framework
- process leadership
- process governance
- process performance
- strategic alignment
- people capability
- project execution

and six additional case studies.

As every organization is different in terms of its business and process maturity; its capabilities; and successful implementation of business capabilities; it is only possible to provide an overview of the "ideal" state for each of the six aspects of the Management by Process framework and then the individual components that should be present. It is up to the organization to determine how to implement and intertwine these components based upon its individual situation.

WHY?

The aim is to develop a business operational state that will continuously observe, manage and improve business processes; to create a culture and foundation that has process improvement at the forefront of business and people initiatives; to provide organization agility, continuous improvement and business opportunities that may not otherwise be available.

Improving processes and obtaining results is not the end but just the beginning of managing business processes. Previous chapters have outlined how to ensure that a culture is in place to continuously improve and monitor processes, but this is not sufficient; the organization should also have an appropriate structure to ensure that the benefits of BPM become clear to the organization and that these benefits are continuous. Process-focused organizations understand they need an appropriate BPM structure. Experience has shown that although an organization's BPM unit can start from a project, it requires a lasting and structural solution to provide continuous improvement.

As Miers (2005) says:

> **From an organizational structure perspective, most firms that have embraced process management have adopted a hybrid-style approach. It's not that the functional silos of the past are going to disappear overnight. Line of business managers will still run their operations, but for important processes, especially those that cross organizational boundaries, a "Process Owner" is usually appointed who is responsible for the way in which the process operates in each different business unit.**

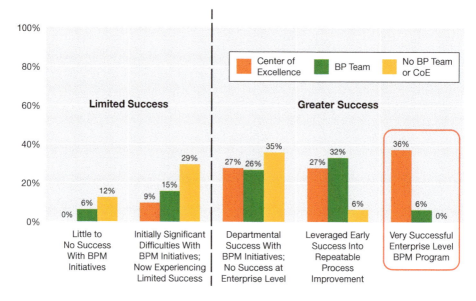

Figure 27.1 Organizational embedding of BPM influences success rate

Source: BP Trends research (www.bptrends.com).

KEY POINT

Embedding BPM in the organization is not focused on just providing a fancy title to staff or to convey the BPM vision and methodology, it is all about being in a position where process improvement and process execution (business-as-usual) provide the most value to the organization.

In Figure 27.1 BP Trends research shows the relation between the organizational position of BPM and the likelihood of success of BPM activities.

Figure 27.1 shows that organization's that have a BPM Center of Excellence (CoE) are much more likely to have greater success (91 percent) with BPM versus organizations that have only a Business Process Team (79 percent) or no BPM Center of Excellence or BPM Team (59 percent). Furthermore, six out of seven organizations that have very successful enterprise level BPM programs have a Center of Excellence (36 percent) and one out of seven organizations has a Business Process Team (6 percent).

WHAT ARE THE ELEMENTS OF EMBEDDING BPM IN THE ORGANIZATION?

Embedding BPM in an organization relates to the "roof" (Organization Sustainability and Performance Management) of the BPM House that was introduced in Chapter 1 (see Figure 27.2). The BPM House clearly distinguishes the activities for embedding BPM in the

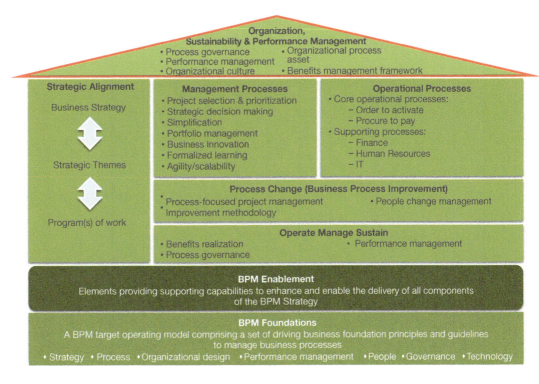

Figure 27.2 BPM House and embedding BPM within the organization

organization with those activities that relate to perform business process improvement as outlined in Part II of this book.

Embedding BPM within an organization requires an organizational structure that supports:

- organizational process assets and methods—relates to Methods and IT in the BPM Maturity model discussed in Chapter 29;

- organizational process governance—relates to Governance in the BPM Maturity model;

- organizational culture—relates to People and Culture in the BPM Maturity model;

- performance management—relates to parts of the Governance in the BPM Maturity model;

- benefits management framework—relates to parts of the Governance aspect in the BPM Maturity model.

The organizational structure aspects mentioned above relate predominantly to process stewardship (ownership). This will be discussed now before organizational embedding is discussed any further.

OWNERSHIP OF PROCESSES

One of the most challenging parts of business process management is to ensure that the accountability and responsibilities of the processes are clearly and appropriately assigned.

An organization has a number of choices with regard to process ownership. It could:

- make the functional managers responsible for their own part of the process only (part of an end-to-end process, that is a sub-process);

- appoint a functional manager (from one business unit) to be responsible for the entire end-to-end process;

- appoint a manager who has no functional responsibilities to be responsible for the entire end-to-end process.

Whichever choice is made, there are associated challenges and risks.

- *Functional sub-process owner.* The risk associated with this approach is that sub-process owners will only see their own part of the process (a silo perspective) and changes to this sub-process may negatively impact other parts of the end-to-end process which could in turn lead to a suboptimized end-to-end process.

- *Functional end-to-end process owner.* The difficulty with this approach is that there is a conflict of interest for the end-to-end process owner. Being responsible for both the end-to-end process and their particular functional silo (a sub-process), process owners may have to make changes that impact their own functional silo profitability and operational efficiency in order to benefit the end-to-end process. Management of processes in this manner has the potential to lead either to the end-to-end situation not being sufficiently considered, or to the functional managers using their responsibility for the end-to-end process to pursue their own functional objectives.

- *Process owner with no functional responsibilities.* While this approach does not suffer from the above issues, it can be extremely challenging to manage because of the need to gain consensus across functional managers. For this to work effectively, the person appointed must be a senior executive or manager with a high level of respect within the organization. This person must be able to provide the additional persuasion that functional managers sometimes need to look at an end-to-end process perspective. This person can also be called a process "steward," as he or she does not have the "normal" operational responsibilities but provides "stewardship" for the end-to-end process. The challenge is for the end-to-end process owner to be able to counter the suboptimization efforts of the functional managers and pursue the end-to-end process objectives. In this situation, it is often recommended to have the end-to-end process owner report to the COO (Chief Operations Officer) or a CPO (Chief Process Officer).

If an organization is extremely BPM mature (some would call it a process-focused organization), then the process responsibility can be arranged along end-to-end process lines. In other words, the organizational structure is totally along end-to-end processes lines, and the organization functional silo structure has been eliminated (or at least minimized). In this case, it is crucial that the various functional employees are still able to share their process expertise and experience.

The main activities for a process owner relate to:

- *Process documentation.* The process documentation of the relevant processes must be correct, up to date and easy to use. Furthermore, the process owner must ensure that the documentation meets all the relevant standards and requirements (e.g., compliance).

- *Process improvement.* The process owner is the focal point for proposals for process improvement, and will be responsible for the decisions, change management and implementation of these improvements. This includes liaison with relevant stakeholders.

- *Interface and boundary management.* The process owner has to ensure smooth transition between and across processes, as in many cases the end-to-end process problems arise at the interfaces of the individual processes. The process owner must ensure that the boundaries between various processes are well understood and documented.

- *Process automation.* The process owner has to be involved in all the relevant automation in relation to the process. It is important to remember that many IT applications span across various processes.

- *Process performance management.* The process owner must ensure that the performance of the processes and their contribution to the objectives and strategies of the organization are measured, and that the relevant people act on this information. In other words, the process owner must ensure that the processes are managed to ensure that they meet their objectives.

- *Process promotion.* The process owner must promote the proper use of the process itself, as well as the generic promotion of process thinking.

ORGANIZATIONAL STRUCTURE OF EMBEDDING BPM

As outlined in Figure 27.1 the organizational structure has a significant impact on how well BPM is embedded in an organization and eventually on the value that an organization will derive from BPM. The next section outlines three ways BPM may be positioned in an organization and these positions are linked to the level of BPM maturity in the organization (refer to Chapter 29). Each of the three types of BPM embedment will be described: Ad-hoc BPM; building BPM; and BPM enabled. Each of these is described below.

- *Ad-hoc BPM:* this is where there is no formal BPM group or program of work, other than individual BPM initiatives, ranging from small project to large programs. The most important characteristic is that BPM activities are typically only temporarily performed during the course of BPM initiative.

- *Building BPM:* there is a formal BPM Group or BPM Center of Excellence that reports to either the Business (Divisional or Departmental level), IT or other (Quality, Finance, HR or other). The two key characteristics are: a permanent BPM group, but no executive sponsorship yet.

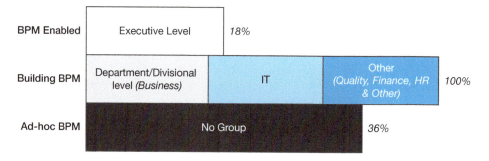

Figure 27.3 Positioning of formal BPM group

Source: Based on BP Trends, 2012 (www.bptrends.com).

- *BPM Enabled*: Process focus and enablement is placed at the Executive level, with the BPM Group or Center of Excellence reporting at this Executive level.

These three groups are visualized in Figure 27.3.

Interestingly enough, these percentages have hardly changed over the last six years that this research has been conducted; an indication that working on embedding BPM is a slow and difficult process.

The positioning of a formal BPM group in an organization is a clear indication of the maturity in the organization, as outlined in Table 27.1.

Each of these embedding choices will be discussed in detail.

Table 27.1 Relation between level of BPM embedded and BPM maturity

Level of BPM embedment	Initial state	Repeatable	Defined	Managed	Optimized	Position of BPM Group/Center of Excellence
Ad-hoc BPM	Likely	Less Likely				No formal BPM Group
Building BPM	Less Likely	Likely		Less Likely		Business, IT or other (e.g., HR, Quality, Finance)
BPM Enabled			Less Likely	Likely		Executive Level

AD-HOC BPM

Where is BPM placed?

There is no formal and permanent BPM group or official BPM manager in the organization. Typically, an organization will have:

- a number of BPM enthusiasts, some might even have a managerial role;
- some project and programs that have a strong process component which might not have been recognized as such by those involved;
- one or more BPM initiatives, with a more formal recognition of the role of process;
- some remains of a previous attempt to have a BPM Center of Excellence that was aborted.

How is it structured?

An organization that performs one or more BPM initiatives would typically have some of the following roles present in the organization:

- *BPM project manager*, who is the person responsible for achieving the specified project objectives by using BPM.
- *Process architect* (could be on a part-time basis), whose main responsibilities are to ensure that the project and process architecture align with the overall enterprise architecture, and that relevant people within the organization are informed and involved in the execution of the process architecture.
- *Process engineer*, who could be involved where an automated solution is to be used. Where the organization is implementing its first few BPM activities, the process engineer will ensure that the technical solution fits within the infrastructure of the organization.
- *BPM consultant*, who assists the business in identifying and realizing benefits that can be achieved through BPM, including new opportunities by changing processes and in coaching the relevant people in achieving them.
- *Process modeler*, whose main responsibilities include the process modeling during the Understand and Innovate phases.

In summary, BPM might be in multiple places within the organization, but there is no central coordination.

How does it work?

- *Organizational process assets and method:* Because of the fragmented nature of BPM across the organization there are piecemeal and ad-hoc approaches to improving and managing business processes: most of the methodologies, techniques and templates are provided by individuals and might range from the 7FE Framework, BPR, BPI, Lean and Six Sigma and vary by BPM initiative.

- Typically, various process modeling tools are used, with predominantly Visio and PowerPoint. This results in a range of inconsistent process assets that provide little or no ability to achieve cross-collaboration within the organization.

- *Process governance:* There may be embryonic or initial steps at process governance; unsophisticated attempts and steps to process management, where a different range of approaches are used. There may be some leverage from more generic governance framework. It is unlikely that there will be any process ownership.

- *Organizational process culture:* Is limited and fragmented, there may be some elements of process culture embedded in the generic culture, for example customer-focused work culture. There may be some process elements in training but nothing covering a holistic process view.

- *Performance management:* Is limited and not linked to processes.

- *Benefit management framework:* Is limited or non-existent, typically projects will not quantify any benefits nor have objectives specified.

How to drive value?

- Be successful in your job: either executing process, managing process or delivering the BPM activity.

- Leveraging successful process improvements, best practices and lessons learned will help to drive value as well as achieving economies of scale and synergies.

BPM INSIGHT

The challenge with BPM is that most organizations have heard and tried the promise of process improvement and continuous improvement before. The best way to convince them is not by presenting PowerPoint slides or making similar promises, but by actually demonstrating that process improvement and continuous improvement can provide significant and sustainable benefits, provided it is done correctly.

Key challenges?

- Obtain buy-in for business process improvement and management, recognizing that everyone is busy with their daily tasks. Hence, it is important to demonstrate how process improvement will reduce the workload.

- Many people will be keen to stay with their preferred BPI methodology; there is a need to agree at least some type of commonality and consistency.

- The BPM activity must generate awareness of BPM in the organization to ensure that there is sufficient support and commitment for it. It is important to balance the message between the general benefits of BPM and the specific results for the particular BPM activity itself.

- The BPM activity should not spend too much time on generating BPM awareness, as all project members should remember that their efforts will be predominantly judged by the realization of the project objectives, and not by well-intended awareness of BPM which is outside the scope of the BPM activity. The BPM activity should provide an excellent showcase of the business benefits of BPM. The best way to sell BPM is *not* through theories or textbook case studies, but through achieving results within the organization itself.

- As there is no overarching BPM group at this level of embedding, everything must be done through convincing people, rather than telling them what to do. Without a clear benefit management framework it will be difficult to state the success of BPM activities.

BPM INSIGHT

The business case for maintaining and building BPM expertise and experience in the form of a permanent BPM Group should be very strong.

Most of the effort of establishing such a group should have already taken place during the course of the initial BPM activities (assuming it has been a large BPM or transformation program).

The benefits are mainly driven by the ability to improve processes further as a result of the insights gained during these activities. In any medium to large organization, the BPM group should be able to generate annual benefits at least double the costs of the people within that group.

A key benefit of starting a BPM Group from a BPM activity is that everyone understands the need to realize benefits and value and should not get distracted by too many conceptual activities.

How to reach next phase?

- Leverage success achieved in processes and BPM initiatives.

- Include the establishment of a BPM Center of Excellence in any future target state. The key task could be the further improvement and fine-tuning of the organizational BPM activities and later grow to a broader scope outside the initial BPM activity.

- Demonstrate the value of consistent process, methods and tools.

- Explain to management how much more success can be achieved by creating a formal BPM Group or Center of Excellence.

- Build an internal BPM network or Community of Practice.

- Increase awareness by selling BPM as a way to be successful rather than BPM as a methodology.

- Training and coaching will be the most common form of external support, especially where this is the initial framework-driven BPM activity within the organization. It is important to ensure that BPM training is fit-for-purpose for the organization.

- Unless an organization is mature in BPM, external support will be crucial at this stage to ensure that the right approach is adopted. In the next phase BPM will be in the take-off phase and a false start at this stage will be extremely energy, time and money consuming. External experts can provide their knowledge and experience.

BUILDING BPM

Where is BPM placed?

The BPM Group or Center of Excellence can be placed in a variety of places:

- Departmental or Divisional level (business)
- IT
- Finance
- HR
- Quality
- Strategy.

This is the phase where there may be multiple formal BPM Groups or Centers of Excellence.

It is preferable to have a single Center of Business Process Excellence (CBPE) at the corporate level, as the CBPE exists to facilitate and support the activities of the various BPM activities (projects and programs). It is definitely best to have the group within the business.

How is it structured?

By now the organization has probably executed several large-scale BPM activities (project/programs) successfully, which means that BPM has gained momentum and the organization now wants to institutionalize their BPM expertise and experience by establishing a Center of Business Process Excellence (CBPE). A CBPE brings together people with different skills and experiences to solve complex business problems. It takes the traditional concept of project management far beyond its primary concern of the technical implementation of a project. Indeed, a CBPE demands a range of competencies to move BPM activities through several lifecycle phases of conception, development, implementation and review.

The CBPE aims to facilitate cooperation between the business and IT, giving business greater responsibility for the delivery of automated and non-automated BPM solutions. It will, in effect, pool resources in order to assist a wide range of business units to develop, implement and/or manage self-improvement BPM projects. A CBPE is a group of people who are the organization's experts in BPM. They are not the people who execute all the work associated with a project, as this will not lead to lasting and sustainable results. Rather, the CBPE is a centralized group whose members should provide expertise to facilitate the relevant organizational units to be successful in their BPM efforts. This will enable the organization to have the skills and knowledge to successfully repeat BPM activities.

Typically a BPM Group or Center of Business Process Excellence contains the following roles, in addition to the one mentioned above:

- A *CBPE manager*, whose main responsibility is to ensure that the CBPE is capable of assisting the business units of the organization in achieving success. It is crucial that the manager is capable of motivating and guiding staff rather than being the person with the most expertise. It is more important that the manager is capable of communicating and working with the other business managers and executive management.

- *Process quality assurers/senior process modelers*, who are required to ensure that the various BPM activities are meeting the desired (minimum) standards and are not "reinventing the wheel" every time. These people should guide the process modelers in the BPM activities and provide coaching in situ. They could also assist with some of the modeling—especially establishing the initial process framework.

- A *BPM consultant/account manager*, who works with the business to identify the opportunities for process improvement and process management within the organization and coordinate how the CBPE can be of assistance. The BPM consultant should be the first person to discuss the BPM opportunities with the business, and the role the CBPE will play. For organizations where the CBPE charges its customers, the BPM consultant is also the account manager for the services of the Center.

- A *process modeling and management tool administrator*—with a CBPE it is required that there is a process modeling and management tool (process asset repository). The administrator ensures that a minimum set of standards are being maintained.

- A *BPM trainer*, who is responsible for preparing and providing BPM training. With the number of people to be trained increasing, the trainer will also be responsible for customizing the training to the particular requirements of the organization, rather than just providing a standard course.

How does it work?

The BPM Group has typically a limited area of authority covering:

- *Organizational process assets and method:* There is more coordination and consistency, even though there may still be competing process tools. The CBPE will model processes, typically as part of a project and hence will cover the most important processes in the organization over time. Meeting global standards and requirements such as Sarbanes–Oxley might require the organization to model key processes.

- *Process governance:* If process ownership is present, it will likely be sub-functional process owners. Some might have already experimented with a more end-to-end approach to process ownership.

- *Organizational process culture:* People will start understanding the importance of process and will increasingly start to take a process-focused approach to solving problems.

- *Performance management and benefit management framework:* This is emerging. Typically, a framework is in place to measure the benefits of BPM activities and work is underway to achieve overall performance management.

How to drive value?

- Focus on achieving benefits for the business, by ensuring benefit traceability throughout the lifetime of a BPM activity.

- Highlight shortcomings in the management of processes and identify opportunities for improvement.

- Ensure that BPM activities are focusing on the right problems (through root-cause analysis) and that solving these problems will significantly contribute to the achievement of the overall organizational or departmental objectives.

KEY POINT

Having a BPM Group/Center of Excellence should not be taken for granted. It should be considered a program/cost center or profit center that has to meet expected financial and non-financial targets every period and apply the same rigor in achieving these benefits as is being imposed on the BPM activities that they are supporting.

Key challenges?

- Making sure that the BPM Group/CBPE achieves its expected targets and generates at least double the benefits that its costs.

- The CBPE has to maintain the balance between ensuring that the individual BPM activities are successful and the desire to have them comply with the emerging organizational standards and methods. These standards are crucial to the organization as more and more BPM activities are initiated and people become involved: if standards cannot be enforced during the program, they will certainly not be enforceable throughout the organization.

BPM INSIGHT

Do not allow the BPM Group/Center of Excellence to fall into the trap of feeling invincible. They typically become involved in too many activities that do not directly contribute to their targets and hence get distracted. This can often happen in relatively immature organizations where the BPM Group/ CBPE want to "make the organization run before it can walk" in the BPM space.

- The process owners might struggle with the limited scope of their ownership and the temptation is to ask for more advanced ownership, but it is strongly recommended first to obtain tangible benefits from the limited role responsibilities. Going too far too fast seldom provides the desired results.

How to reach next phase?

- Work closely with the other disciplines, such as Strategy, Project Management Office, Finance, IT and Audit;
- Highlight the benefits of having a Chief Process Officer;
- Continuously show that process is part of the solution rather than part of the problem.

BPM ENABLED

Where is BPM placed?

There is an Enterprise Center of Excellence reporting directly to the Executive, typically the Chief Process Officer (CPO), as process management is recognized for its strategic performance.

How is it structured?

The CPO will have the Center of Business Process Excellence reporting to him/her as well as the group of process owners. Refer to the previous sections for details on these two groups.

How does it work?

The CPO is responsible for ensuring that the processes are geared towards contributing efficiently and effectively to the objectives of the organization. This can be achieved by ensuring that the organization's process architecture is well embedded within the overall enterprise architecture, the processes are considered with any major change or initiative within the company, and the CBPE is accepted and well respected for its contribution to the business.

The CPO will be responsible for coordinating the various organizational strategies and aligning them with the specific process strategies to ensure that they support organizational goals. This involves the following aspects:

- Customer service
- New product development
- Procurement strategy
- Fulfillment strategy
- Human resource and training strategy
- Accounting and finance strategy
- Technology strategy.

The CPO will be responsible for all end-to-end processes within the organization, which may extend to the processes the organization has with its customers, suppliers and partners. This also involves the IT-related processes. As mentioned previously, IT is aimed at supporting the business processes; a separation between the two domains will lead to suboptimization.

The CPO will be responsible for:

- End-to-end processes within the organization.

- Achieving the process goals across the organization, and assuring the smooth flow of data, documents and information between sub-processes.

- Maintaining a customer focus, constantly working to assure that processes, as a whole, function to satisfy the customer.

- Ensuring that problems, disconnects or gaps that arise when processes cross departmental lines are resolved to the satisfaction of all stakeholders.

- Planning, managing and organizing processes as a whole.

- Ensuring that appropriate process measures are established, monitored and maintained.

- Establishing and maintaining the BPM project framework or methodology across the organization.

- Nurturing ongoing and continuous improvement programs for business processes.

- Smooth running of the Center of Business Process Excellence team.

- Establishing and maintaining the relationships with the BPM vendors.

- Ongoing knowledge management for BPM within the organization.

- Overall quality management.

At a more detailed level, a CPO has the following characteristics.

- *Organizational process assets and method:* CPO typically coordinates with Strategy Office and PMO to come up with an overall corporate method. The process assets, method and IT are aligned with the Strategy, IT and BPM activities.

- *Process governance:* Is typically from an end-to-end perspective by either functional managers or by process owners that do not have a functional responsibility.

- *Organizational process culture:* Process improvement and management are well embedded within the organization and it is included in all aspects of the organization, including in training, promotion criteria and the way they work together with clients and partners.

- *Performance management and benefit management framework:* Should be well embedded within the organizational way of working. Typically, the process performance management and benefit management framework are closely aligned with the other disciplines within the organization. Any planned BPM activity benefits will be reflected in the relevant budgets and financials plans.

How to drive value?

- Take a proactive approach by identifying strategic issues and themes and drive them from a process perspective.

- The efforts of the CPO should provide demonstrable value at the overall performance of the organization.

- Everyday focus on increasing value from process execution and process management, including the dealing with clients and partners by driving value chain improvements.

Key challenges?

- In order to obtain the buy-in from all process owners and senior management the CPO should clearly demonstrate his or her added value, as many process owners might consider the CPO to be an extra organization layer.

- The CPO must maintain a strategic orientation and not become too involved in the day-to-day running of the Center of Business Process Excellence, as this is a completely different role that should have a dedicated person with the right capabilities for that job.

- The CPO must be able to provide added value at the Executive Board level, as all other CxOs will have larger departments, more people and higher budgets. Thus the CPO must have the vision and capabilities to deliver this vision in tangible results, which should ensure that the other CxOs provide the necessary funding, resources and people to make use of BPM initiatives. It will be a challenge in itself to find a person like this, as the person must have a strategic view and also be able to have a detailed understanding of the operational processes, without becoming too involved in the detail.

- It is important to include a few words of warning. A CPO is especially helpful in a process-focused organization that is mature in its process dealings. If an organization is still evolving to this level of maturity, then the best alternative is to have a BPM program with buy-in from the CEO and senior executives to improve the processes, and then at a later stage appoint a CPO.

- Appointing a CPO or establishing a CBPE in an organization that is not mature enough to understand or sustain it will seriously impact the added value they can bring to the organization, and could lead to difficulty in achieving the high expectations of these roles.

- Keep it real and tangible, especially as a process methodology and governance at an enterprise level in a large organization becomes quite abstract and conceptual.

- Making it all come together not just from the different elements (e.g., method, people, benefits, IT, process) but also ensure that it is done at all the relevant levels (e.g., executive, operations, etc.).

How to maintain?

- Maintain the rage: continue looking for opportunities to improve and widen the message for BPM.

- Work closely with client and partners to continuously improve interactions, this is the best way to be competitive and leave a legacy.

SUMMARY

This chapter highlighted:

- The importance of embedding BPM in the organization.
- The difference between the activities and scope of BPM versus those of embedding BPM in the organization.
- The key components of embedding BPM in the organization, which includes the aspects of the "roof" of the BPM House.
- The role of process owners.
- The three broad stages that an organization can be in, relating to the levels of BPM maturity.
- The key challenges and the steps that can be taken to improve the BPM embedding process.

SELF-TEST

1 Why should organizations strive to embed BPM?

2 What are the key elements of embedding?

3 What are the three stages organizations can be in and progress through?

4 What are the key steps an organization needs to take to further embed BPM in the organization?

5 What is the role of process owners?

6 What are the activities of a Center of Business Process Excellence (CBPE)?

7 What is the role of a CPO?

EXTRA READING

How to position BPM in large organizations?

This is always considered by many to be a difficult question. To some extent it is, as it very much depends upon the organization's culture, process maturity, the strength of various positions (CEO, COO, head of HR, CIO, business heads), operating model (centralized or federated, or somewhere in between).

Earlier in this chapter we provided an overview of the structuring and positioning of BPM in the organization based on the process maturity of the organization and key stakeholders. Larger organizations with multiple business units/divisions and high process maturity need to consider whether they are using a federated or central operating model.

- *Federated Model*: Each business unit has a BPM Group that has ownership of BPM activities within their business unit and is supported by a central entity that drives synergies across the organizations.
- *Central Model*: The organization has a centralized BPM Group that drives the BPM methodology and instructs the BPM teams in the various business units.

Comparison of Federated versus Central Model

Tables 27.2 and 27.3 provide more details on these two models. It is important to state that the contents of Table 27.3 could easily change depending upon the organization. It is however based upon the authors' consulting experience and observations of organizations around the world that are attempting to implement BPM or already have.

Observations

1. There is not a huge difference between the two models (centralized and federated). If the CEO and Board wish to implement process management across the entire organization it will need the focus and commitment of all senior leaders.

2. Depending upon the size of the organization and its divisions, a leader or leaders within one or a small number of divisions may choose to implement process management without the entire organization commitment.

3. The authors have never seen the IT department drive BPM throughout an organization enterprise-wide in a sustainable way. It always requires CEO drive and commitment.

4. Similarly for HR. HR could, with the support of the CEO, establish KPIs for each level of management and employee in the organization to achieve process-related targets. However, it is then up to the CEO and divisional business leaders to drive it throughout the organization and make it sustainable.

Table 27.2 Difference between Federated and Central Model

	Federated Model	*Central Model*
Main advantages	• Provides flexibility for business units	• Consistency across business units
Main disadvantages	• Some duplication and variance across business units	• Lack of variance across the organization
Typical use	• In organizations with a wide variance in process maturity and need • Organizations with a holding company structure	• Integrated organization

Table 27.3 Where should BPM reside?

	Centralized				Federated			
	CEO	Business head	Human Resources	IT	CEO	Business head	Human Resources	IT
Focus	• Driver	• Main	• Support • Main (only with direct support of CEO)	• Support	• Driver	• Driver	• Support • Main (only with direct support of CEO)	• Support
Link to strategy	• Driver	• Main	• Support • Main (only with direct support of CEO)	• Cannot long term	• Driver	• Main	• Support • Main (only with direct support of CEO)	• Cannot long term
Funding support	• Driver	• Main	• Not HR's role	• Not IT's role	• Driver	• Main	• Not HR's role	• Not IT's role
Execution	• Driver • Support	• Driver	• Support	• Support	• Driver • Support	• Driver	• Support	• Support
Ongoing process management	• Driver • Support	• Driver	• Support	• Support	• Driver • Support	• Driver	• Support	• Support
Process governance	• Driver • Support	• Driver	• Support	• Support	• Driver • Support	• Driver	• Support	• Support

Notes:

Driver—primary driver or advocate. For example if the CEO, it needs to be across the organization; if a business divisional head, it needs to be within their sphere of management control and influence.

Main—primary person who is responsible to "make it happen."

Support—provides support to the Main person.

BPM interest group/community of practice

This chapter described the positioning of BPM within the organization structure. Many organizations have several people interested in, or even passionate about, BPM; however, they can often find it difficult to convince management to take any structural steps to embed BPM.

One way to ensure that the interest of BPM is captured and can expand within the organization is to establish a BPM interest group. This group can bring people from all over the organization (or even from partners and customers) together to discuss how BPM could provide opportunities for the organization.

The interest group should generate awareness within the organization regarding what BPM is (and what it is not), what the benefits will be for the organization and how each employee could contribute. The group should have clear, specific objectives and targets. The group could present examples on how the organization might benefit from BPM, and have people from various parts of the organization share experiences and ideas. It is recommended that the group distinguishes various focus points, as BPM is so broad and varied—for example the technical, regulatory and business aspects.

A BPM interest group is a great way to generate initial interest. Some organizations need some initial interest and results prior to taking the first steps to embed BPM within the organization.

If this group is initiated from a BPM project, it is crucial that the emphasis of the project remains on the achievement of the project objectives. It is recommended that the BPM interest group be coordinated by an enthusiastic sponsor from the business, to ensure that the project staff remains focused on the project and to obtain sufficient buy-in from the business.

The best way to balance multiple initiatives and at the same time have an overview of all these initiatives is to ensure that all initiatives are coordinated by a member of the BPM Center of Excellence.

It is strongly recommended to involve customers and partners in this group to look from an end-to-end view.

Leveraging intranet and social media is a good way to remain in touch and ask for specific assistance, especially in large organizations that are geographically spread.

Process modeling conventions

This section provides an outline of suggested process modeling conventions. The purpose of modeling conventions is that is aims to get consistency of process across projects, business units and make it independent of the modeler.

Modeling conventions should aim to address:

- *Uniformity.* Only a uniform presentation of information in the tool creates a communication basis for employees in different business units and departments. This communication basis is important if employees are to inform each other about the interfaces of various work areas, as part of process orientation, or if employees from different departments are to work together on projects. Uniformity in this sense applies to designing graphics, naming conventions and the envisaged degree of detail.

- *Reduce complexity and increase readability of process models.* Definition and documentation conventions will ensure that all employees involved in process modeling, as modelers or readers, will only be confronted with the information of importance for them and the organization. This is particularly important with the selection of models, objects, symbols and attributes, how the process structure will link, and formal settings of the master database. The benefits of reduced complexity and increased readability are especially noticeable during the familiarization of new employees and when carrying out new projects with the process modeling and management tool.

- *Integrity and re-usability.* Integrity and re-usability of information in the process management and modeling tool are prerequisites for a consistent overview of an organization and its structure and processes. This overview in turn is a prerequisite for being able to interpret the information already stored.

- *Consistency and analyzability.* The objective must be to enable the unambiguous, complete and accurate analysis of process database information across departments and project teams.

To achieve this, the modeling conventions should be

- *Practical*—the modeling conventions document itself must be useful for the modelers, while they model processes, and must provide practical information (not theoretical) on modeling with the selected tools and methods within the organization.

- *Accessible*—the reader should be able to access the required information easily and intuitively; the best way to achieve this is to have a clear and logical table of contents and use a list of diagrams, a glossary and an index.

- *"Fit for use"* for the modelers, and should not duplicate the training manuals or user guides; rather they should provide practical tips and guidelines for modeling with the selected process modeling and management tool within the organization.

Selecting a process modeling tool

An appropriate tool for an organization should not be determined solely by its functionality or price, but by the suitability of the tool for the purpose for which the organization chooses to use it. There are two commonly made mistakes in selecting a process modeling and management tool (Figure 27.4):

1. *Waste* (overpriced): The organization's requirements for a tool are quite basic and a state-of-the-art, high functionality tool is purchased. This results in higher than necessary costs (purchase and maintenance) and dissatisfied users (as the tool requires substantial training), and only limited use is made of the wide variety of functionality that the tool offers.

2. *Legacy* (underperform): The organization wants to start with a basic set of requirements and purchases a basic tool. The requirements evolve over time and the organization finds that the incumbent tool is unable to keep up with the new functionality required. This results in increased effort in process modeling, frustrated staff, and additional costs and rework when eventually migrating to another tool.

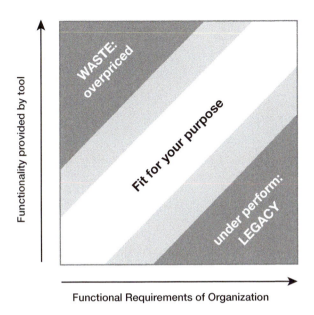

Figure 27.4 Mapping of functional requirements required and provided

If the organization's initial requirements are basic and it wishes to start with a simple tool, there are basically two strategies that could be employed:

a)   The *modular approach*: Select a tool that can either be extended at a later stage with additional modules or be initially configured in a limited manner and easily reconfigured later for wider use. These additional modules could either be part of the same suite or be modules from other vendors. Care should be taken that the tool is also scalable and usable with an increased number of users.

b)   The *tactical approach*: Select a tool that serves the initial purpose and make a conscious decision to replace the tool if and when your requirements increase. It is important to realize that the more effort put into the models in the tool, the harder and more expensive it becomes to migrate the tool to a new one—for example all process models will need to be recreated.

Issues to consider

*   Remember that most tools are used for longer and for more purposes than initially thought. Converting all the developed process models to another tool is a large task, which can involve significant effort and resources. Thus, it is important to specify whether the organization requires a short-term easy design tool or a more robust, architecturally based modeling and management tool.

*   Some vendors will promote features that will not be relevant to the organization; therefore it is important to ask vendors to showcase how they will meet your requirements and how will the tool work for you.

- Involve sufficiently the key stakeholders such as IT, BPM Center of Excellence, management, finance, HR, etc.

- Ensure that you do a proper reference check, where you look at all key aspects and roles that are impacted by the tool.

The key components that should be covered in a selection are:

- Functionality (each functionality module has its own set of questions)
- Integration with other BPM modules
- Technical aspects
- Usability
- Price
- Vendor fits organization need for support and guidance.

Part 3

CASE STUDIES AND BPM MATURITY

This part comprises three case studies from the USA, Asia and Europe and an explanation of the organizational aspects of BPM maturity.

There are many lessons to learn from observing an organization implement BPM and the three case studies provide some of these lessons.

A desire to obtain a certain BPM maturity level of itself should never be an objective. BPM maturity is a contributor to the achievement of the business objectives of an organization. However it is important to highlight the benefits of BPM maturity.

When considering BPM maturity consideration should be given to the benefits as well as the cost of achieving the desired maturity level. The costs of maintaining the desired maturity level must also be taken into account.

Many organizations only focus on project management maturity. As a consequence, change management, process management and performance management are largely ignored.

Many organizations perform a self-analysis on their maturity performance and typically make the following mistakes:

- the assessment is competed by people who are actually running the BPM Center of Excellence who may have a biased view compared to other people in the organization, or external advisors
- interpret the question in the most favorable way
- look at the way things are documented within the organization rather than how BPM is actually embedded and executed.

Chapter 28 provides a detailed discussion of the three case studies written by Andrew Spanyi, Jerry Dimos and John Jeston.

Chapter 29 is written by Michael Rosemann, Tonia de Bruin and Brad Power and describes in detail a BPM maturity model that has been developed for the evaluation and advancement of BPM effectiveness across organizations.

Chapter 30 is written by Dr Amy Van Looy who discusses her research into the selection of the appropriate BPM maturity assessment tool to enable the required outcomes for the organization. She also provides access to an online selection tool.

CHAPTER 28

CASE STUDIES FROM THE USA, ASIA AND EUROPE

OVERVIEW

In this chapter three case studies will be described from around the world. They will cover both successful and not so successful BPM implementations at an enterprise level within three very different organizations. Sometimes the lessons learned from failures or unsuccessful implementations are more valuable than from the successful implementations. Both will be covered.

Thanks should go to Andrew Spanyi for writing the USA-based case study and to Jerry Dimos for the Unilever case study. The case studies are from three continents:

USA—a global automotive components organization that used a process-focused approach to implementing an ERP and the challenges they faced.

Asia—Unilever, the global organization that had its origins in the 1890s with the advent of Sunlight soap. This is the story of how Unilever transformed itself into a more agile organization by establishing a common way of selling, making and delivering its goods globally.

Europe—Citibank Germany, had 300 retail branches and has been sold to another bank as a result of the rationalization of Citibank that was necessary as part of the global financial crisis. Yet it is a wonderful example of how a process-focused approach more than halved the bank's operating expenses within 3.5 years, while significantly increasing customer service and employee engagement. This case study is a detailed analysis of how Citibank went about achieving this wonderful result.

CASE STUDY 1: USA—WHEN BPM IS LOST IN TRANSFORMATION

A robust program of BPM combined with a global ERP implementation can be a powerful coalition. However, finding the right balance between an enduring focus on the improvement and management of an organization's value creating business processes and implementing the ERP system on time and on budget can be challenging as this case study illustrates.

Background

A global automotive components company (GACC), serving both original equipment manufacturers (OEM) and retail customers for aftermarket products, recognized the need to replace outdated legacy systems with a global single instance of an integrated Enterprise Resource Planning (ERP) system. At the outset, the plan appeared to be sound. The organization made a commitment to use a process-centric approach and implement a process enabling IT system to drive its business process management efforts.

There appeared to be a clear recognition of the complexity involved. The current business operating model was characterized by:

- Different business process operating models
- Multiple major system backbones with separate code bases
- Significant internal and external interfaces
- Fragmented processes
- Limited visibility
- Suboptimal performance.

The overarching objective was to implement a world-class enterprise system and business processes that would transform GACC's ability to grow global market share, ensure quality and cost leadership.

GACC had developed a successful program of continuous improvement (CI), focusing on projects of small scope, largely at the plant level, within the operations group.

Approach

The ERP program was launched with significant fanfare. An all-day meeting was held with the top three levels of management. The CEO and several senior vice presidents presented their views as to why this transformational effort was essential to GACC's future. The overall program was planned on a three-year timeframe, structured in phases, with a roll-out by geographic region, and details were outlined and reviewed.

In order to assure the tight integration between the new IT systems and a process focus, the former VP of the BPM Center of Excellence for US Operations was named to a new global staff position as the global VP of BPM. He was tasked to focus on the integration of process management principles and process-enabling IT systems and to emphasize:

- Process governance and process ownership
- Process metrics
- Process models.

The focus on governance, metrics and process models was planned to occur concurrently with the implementation of the ERP system roll-out to deeply embed a process orientation into the organization.

There was a clear intent to move towards process management. The VP BPM defined BPM as "the ongoing management and optimization of GACC's end-to-end business processes." He had a plan to build a small team of BPM experts, comprised of staff positions aligned with the ERP scope and focused on the end-to-end processes such as order to cash (OTC), procure to pay (PTP) and record to report (RTR).

Both global and regional process owners were to be appointed, again aligned with the ERP roll-out, for the key processes such as OTC, PTP and RTR. The importance of alignment with the group responsible for continuous improvement was recognized, as was the need to develop process models and metrics.

While the plan was sound on the surface, significant challenges occurred in execution.

Challenges

The principal challenges were organizational and cultural.

The VP BPM reported to the global VP Operations, and the VP IT who was accountable for the ERP implementation reported directly to the CEO at GACC. While the CEO was a vocal advocate of BPM, the VP IT had the advantage in terms of visibility and clout at the senior leadership team (SLT) level.

GACC's culture was dominated by a traditional focus on producing high quality products at the lowest possible cost. Regional VPs had significant clout, as did the Operations group. While lip service was paid to the importance of managing the firm's end-to-end processes, when push came to shove, regional and profit and loss (P&L) issues took priority.

The risk areas shown in Table 28.1 were recognized by both the VP IT and VP BPM.

The impact of these challenges and risk areas became clear as the program rolled out.

The first six months

The VP BPM had a clear idea of what he wanted to accomplish and took two concurrent actions to launch the program. He tasked human resources with recruiting a small group of business process specialists to support key areas such as OTC, PTP and RTR and he engaged a small consulting company (SCC) to develop a roadmap for BPM at GACC and provide leadership education on BPM to GACC's senior leadership team.

The SCC outlined the key elements of a roadmap to take GACC from managing individual processes to organization-wide process management. However, the VP BPM challenged some of the key concepts. For example he believed that many of the foundational elements such as creating an advocacy group, focusing on the right processes and establishing the right governance structure were already in place. Future events would reveal that the VP

Table 28.1 Executive risks and project risks

Executive risk	Project risk
Key executives must support the overall program	Project must be properly planned, scope managed and decisions made
Resource risk	*Functional risk*
Proper definition of resources needed for optimum performance	User requirements must remain closely aligned with project goals

BPM overestimated the extent to which these foundational elements were in place. Nevertheless, the SCC was directed to focus more on developing swim lane version maps of selected key processes such as OTC, PTP and RTR and deliver the planned educational session on BPM to the SLT.

The SCC recognized that the existing process maps were linear and had a significant IT bias and so they proceeded to develop swim lane version maps of selected key processes such as OTC, PTP and RTR. These swim lane maps showed the key activities, the departments involved, key performance measures and high level issues in each core process, thereby enabling the organization to ask and answer questions such as:

- What immediate opportunities might exist to capture "quick wins"?
- What performance measures will the ERP system provide and what metrics may need to be captured via other means?
- Which key activities require cross-departmental collaboration?

Concurrently with the development of these process maps in swim lane format, the SCC conducted interviews with members of the SLT to assist in preparing the educational sessions on BPM at the enterprise level.

The key messages delivered in the hour and a half session to three groups of executives stressed that GACC needs to emphasize:

- The development and use of simple, visually compelling models for key processes such as OTC, PTP and RTR. SLT members need to become comfortable with using these models to shift management mindset and link major performance issues to the need for cross-departmental collaboration.
- The monitoring of critical to customer metrics in terms of quality and time and make these part of the SLT scorecard.
- Aligning the BPM program with strategy.
- The increasing use of process-based governance for key decisions.
- The alignment of recognition and reward systems to visibly distinguish the people and teams who succeed in improving process performance.

These sessions were generally well received by the members of the SLT and the VP BPM was trained on delivering additional sessions to the management teams in the GACC regions. However, the global VP Operations was conspicuous by his absence and other cracks in the overall BPM program were beginning to appear. The recruitment of process specialists to support key areas such as OTC, PTP and RTR was well behind schedule, with only one of four positions filled in six months. Also, there were early signs of delays and budget overruns for the ERP system implementation, and changes to RICEFs (Reports, Interfaces, Conversions, Enhancements and Forms) began to take out the many meaningful customer-facing metrics.

SCC submitted its final report to the VP BPM and recommended that he:

- Develop the messaging and communication needed to differentiate BPM from the ERP roll-out.
- Champion the continued development and use of end-to-end swim lane process view.
- Provide near-term measurable value, 30–35 percent of BPM's efforts should focus on end-to-end process improvement.
- Place a greater emphasis on collaborating with the continuous improvement group.
- Continue to work with process owners to define the critical three or four metrics for each end-to-end process.

The VP BPM thanked SCC for their work, but it was clear that he was more concerned with taking immediate action on delays and budget concerns than the longer term, high level recommendations.

One year into the program

The ERP roll-out was by now known to be six months behind schedule and more than 30 percent over budget. While the recruitment of process specialists to support key areas such as OTC, PTP and RTR had been completed and the communication plan to differentiate BPM from the ERP system had been delivered, the overall BPM program was struggling.

Process owners were in place, but in name only, and these executives continued to focus predominantly on their functional responsibilities.

The anticipated collaboration between the BPM group and the CI group had not taken place as the CI group took pride in its success on projects of small scope, within functional boundaries, and its track record in producing measurable results and it was reluctant to address projects of much larger scope with the attendant challenges that cross-departmental issues held. Also, there were political issues that could not easily be overcome as the CI group did not report to the VP BPM and instead reported to the VP Operations in each region.

The program to develop the use of critical to customer metrics in terms of quality and time and make these part of the SLT scorecard stalled and it was not even possible to get agreement on a common definition of what "perfect order delivery" meant, with some regions defining this as "on-time and complete," while others defined it simply as "on-time" (e.g., when promised).

What could have been and might have been simply wasn't happening—or at least, not quickly enough. BPM risked getting lost in the ERP lead transformational effort.

Author's comments

Success with BPM at the enterprise level relies on a clear and compelling case for change, cross-departmental collaboration, attention to pacing, and an enduring focus on value creation. The VP BPM in this case seriously underestimated the impact of GACC's traditional culture and his reporting line was such that he did not have the needed clout to drive change.

Further, he made a number of classical errors in the three key areas of getting ready, taking action and sustaining gains as outlined in Table 28.2.

GACC never truly understood that BPM is a management discipline focused on using process-based thinking to improve and manage its end-to-end business processes, and the BPM program was lost in the ERP led transformational effort.

Table 28.2 Key pitfalls

Getting ready	Taking action	Sustaining gains
Fragile case for change. Failure to capture the heads and hearts of people who do the work.	Pacing is too slow. Bogged down in measurement, modeling and/or analysis.	The new, recommended performance measures are not incorporated into the senior leadership team's scorecard.
Failing to align BPM with strategy.	HR involvement is late or inconsistent, and the recommended training is low on the HR project priority list.	The recommended alignment of recognition and rewards is delayed or ignored.
Placing methods or tools before results. Too much fervor and zeal around the method or "system" (e.g., ERP).		Insufficient effort invested in establishing the infrastructure and governance for continuous improvement.

CASE STUDY 2: ASIA—THE UNILEVER TRANSFORMATION

Background

Unilever traces its origins back to the 1890s with the advent of Sunlight soap. By the 1980s it had evolved into a complex organization with various operating models across each country, as was typical of conglomerates at that time. In the 1990s, the firm moved to more closely align its operating models, exploit its natural synergies and sharpen its focus on fewer product categories, leading to the focusing of its portfolio and reduction in brand number by two-thirds. The firm also rationalized its many layers of management, streamlined reporting and adopted common operating standards globally. The shift from a largely decentralized organization to a more centrally managed one was a huge undertaking, especially whilst trying to maintain its entrepreneurial spirit and autonomy required at the country level.

The need for change

Unilever realized that the silo'ed, country-focused operations of the past 100 years did not allow the organization to capitalize on its scale nor support efficient growth. A project was conceived and established, amongst other things, to help develop a single supply chain across the European businesses. The project would take over four years and considerable manpower with commensurate investments in technology. SAP was used to drive standardization across the firm in pursuit of its promise to integrate the fragmented business across the organization. Major strategic decisions were made that led to:

- a series of disposals and acquisitions;
- a standard operating model; and
- a new organizational structure with a single CEO.

This was a major milestone and message to the market that Unilever was on track to becoming a more agile, globally integrated business.

Unilever's ambition was to establish a common way for how it would make, sell and deliver its goods globally; moving away from the departmental silos of the past to a globally process-focused organization.

To achieve a reasonable level of business agility, Unilever needed to be able to respond to changing conditions quickly and effectively. The ability to change quickly was distilled to three things:

- understanding the impact of the change on people, process and the technology;
- implementing the appropriate change effectively; and
- obtaining adequate information, monitoring and embedding the new processes.

All three required well-documented business processes and an understanding of how the underlying system applications and supporting technology work. Only with all this information can the Unilever team quickly assess, implement and communicate the changes effectively.

With these objectives in mind, in 2006, a second, similar project was launched across Asia, Africa, the Middle East and Turkey. It was considered to be a hugely ambitious undertaking to integrate Unilever's largely autonomous businesses across a geo-politically and socio-economically diverse region, spanning three-quarters of the globe. Reapplying the lessons learned from the European experience, the new project was based on three principles of:

- functional centralization;

- common processes and standards (commonality);

- operational efficacy—reducing costs and increasing quality simultaneously.

SAP was again chosen as the technology platform; however, it was set up as a separate instance to Europe.

Change is harder than it seems

Multinational multi-product organizations have inherently high levels of complexity and inertia to change. Unilever was no different. Two years into this five-year project, the team was experiencing this inertia and recognized the need to adopt a new approach to help manage the complexity and overcome the inertia. Simply implementing SAP does not solve the business issues.

A new approach was adopted that prioritized the business process design—this process-driven approach would enable the project team to:

- visualize their entire operating model and end-to-end processes;

- accelerate the remaining country deployments (they were 50 percent complete);

- retro-fit earlier deployments to the new process model gold standard;

- converge pre-existing SAP instances;

- reduce design risks and cost;

- deal with the ongoing business priorities such as business acquisitions and disposals;

- more easily manage process performance and governance.

The common prerequisite across all Unilever's project "business benefits" was the need for standard processes, which over time can be cost-effectively managed and optimized. For example the business benefits that arise from an agile supply chain—every FMCG (fast-moving consumer goods) firm's goal—that enables less inventory and waste, yet higher customer case fill on-time in-full (CCFOTIF), requires a standard and effectively managed Sales and Operations Planning (S&OP) process that integrates Demand Planning (Customer) with Supply Planning (Manufacturing), connected by Logistics, Warehousing and Distribution.

To achieve standard business processes across the organization entailed:

- common process standards and definitions;

- a single database containing all process designs;

- processes linked to the specific IT applications (i.e., SAP);

- connect all learning systems and materials to each process;

- tools that enable sustainable process performance monitoring, governance and change management workflow;

- an expressed goal to converge all processes towards one common design.

How adopting a holistic approach to BPM helped

The BPM approach adopted addressed the three levels of Enterprise Design that helped Unilever's leadership team achieve their objectives. The three levels are:

- *Operating Model design*—strategy layer that defined the business model and optimal legal entity structure (in the 7FE Framework this equates to the Foundations, Enablement and Launch pad phases).

- *Process Model design*—operations layer that sets out the one best way of executing end-to-end process such as Order to Cash, Procure to Pay, Hire to Retire, etc. (who does what, when and how—in 7FE Framework this is the Understand, Innovate and People phases).

- *Technology Model design*—automation layer (in 7FE Framework this is the Develop and Implement phases).

Unilever knew that the greatest value for them would come from the Operating Model design. At this level decisions were made about the organization's structure, the location and purpose of every legal entity, their level of risk taking. For example: should the factories be owned, if yes, should these factories be managed in country or regionally, and then what legal and process relationship do they have to each other? Answering these design questions makes a very material impact on processes, roles, governance, risk, service levels and of course the firm's bottom line.

Applied correctly, BPM goes beyond process design to address design decisions across the entire Enterprise Design stack. Starting at the top with the Operating Model layer and the firm's high level value drivers, the design cascades down to the process model design that addresses workflow, process and controls, end-user reports, forms and other requirements. It then continues down the lowest level of detail, which is the Technology Model design, addressing applications, test scripts, access controls, input/output data, and infrastructure. All these variables needed to be designed in an integrated manner across the entire Enterprise Model.

However, Unilever came to realize that, like most organizations, they had fallen into the trap of spending the majority of their time on process model design and spending most of the project budget on technology. In the absence of an integrated approach the project was challenged by the sheer design complexity. Past projects have experienced similar issues with the blame for delays and unmet goals unduly piled onto the project manager, the vendor and/or the technology platform in question.

Unilever recognized these potential pitfalls early and therefore the fundamental need to integrate all three design layers successfully if they were to have any chance of achieving their ambitious business change agenda.

They understood that business units/departments are useful constructs for organizing people with common skills and outputs, but inevitably this creates silos, interface and handover issues. End-to-end business processes were used to show how work steps connect to each other to add value and produce outcomes, across departments. Unilever's "regional process template" was created to set the (gold) "standard" for end-to-end processes. A common process baseline that follows an agreed "standard" was considered a prerequisite to achieving commonality across the business and therefore in delivering on the benefits of a major business transformation program. Reflecting back to the earlier integrated S&OP process example, it became obvious how important it is to have process standards in place. In one database, Unilever had defined its entire business Enterprise Model; the operating model; the process models, with respective performance measures and standards for commonality. The risk, governance and controls frameworks were embedded in this database, as well as the change management procedures. All of it interconnected so that any design change, at any level, on any element, could be quickly assessed for its cost, resource and business impact. This was considered an essential to enable the whole enterprise model to stay current and useful after the system go-live. This was also essential to enabling a behemoth like Unilever to perform like an agile organization.

This enterprise model is the single source of truth regarding Unilever's operations. Used effectively, this "process" becomes a strategic asset to the firm, and will in the future reduce Unilever's operations, training, compliance and technology costs. This is something that very few organizations achieve.

The BPM solution in summary

The following outlines some of the critical steps in the program:

- design the operating model to drive key business goals such as an agile supply chain; integrated sales and operations planning; improved customer satisfaction; and reduce structural costs;

- develop a high level process decomposition framework and modeling standards;

- using a centrally managed BPM platform (in Unilever's case it was ARIS[1]), create a central process repository that can be accessed by all parties based on their roles and user rights;

- establish process standards and structure for all workstreams with strong governance;

- set up an integrated change management process with role-based flexibility implementing the BPM platform workflow engine;

- review the design, training and organizational change management process to bring forward integration testing and training (e.g., using ARIS and HP Quality Center or similar);

- establish an approach that can manage all process information, not just those in SAP. Typically about 50 percent of an end-to-end process is SAP-based, the balance is other applications or manual/non-system steps;

- use the SAP Solution Manager features to support and expedite design, implementation and support/maintenance requirements;

- start early to help the management team implement the business transformation agenda (working with people to change their work habits and methods).

This process led approach to business transformation has since been adopted by Unilever globally. They have established a BPM Center of Excellence in London to drive the ongoing transition to globally managed business processes. At the time of writing, Unilever was rolling out the third regional project across the Americas.

BPM business benefits

Unilever spent less than 1 percent of the total project budget adopting a BPM approach and yet it has paid significant dividends. Explicitly, the business case showed an internal rate of return (IRR) of 150 percent. The intangible benefits are considered to be worth much more than that and include:

- a single process design with limited localizations that simplifies system maintenance, training and operations;

- zero corrective work in documentation after each country go-live;

- a standard regional risk controls framework. Over 1,000 risks and controls were reduced to just 120 standard risks across the business;

- re-use of the project documentation for other stakeholders such as internal and external audit and outsourced service providers. "One source of truth" for all processes, but with many uses for all parties;

- cost-effective way of sustaining the optimal Enterprise Design. Otherwise, after spending hundreds of millions of dollars on technology, what stops the people from regressing to their old work habits?

- a single process platform enables continuous improvement and the pursuit of commonality globally. Common process designs are cheaper to operate, maintain and control.

In closing, firm-wide standardization and control of process documentation will enable sustainable business improvement and realization of the project's business benefits for years after the SAP implementation. Many firms invest in technology to achieve a business improvement goal but in reality are not making the necessary business changes to take full advantage of the technology features. Unilever was the exception in that the process design and related business changes came first, with appropriate enabling technology designs being the secondary consideration.

Author's comments

Potential pitfalls of large transformation programs include spending too much time on the detailed process modeling and too much budget on technology. Furthermore, each roll-out in a global program needs to be assessed and monitored for key differences in the various regions. A global "one size fits all" approach rarely works. The case study shows that a pragmatic approach using a clearly defined target operating model provides the necessary guidance for process, technology and organization structure.

CASE STUDY 3: EUROPE—CITIBANK GERMANY: THE "INDUSTRIALIZATION" OF THE CONSUMER DIVISION

Most readers would be familiar with the developments in the manufacturing sector over the last 30 or more years. Manufacturing has spent considerable time and effort in the improvement of their production line processes to make them continually more efficient and effective. They have consolidated many manufacturing plants into one or a few, and implemented continuous process improvement programs, often to the level where it has become a significant part of the culture of the organization. Toyota is the classic case study of the quest for continuous improvement—they call it *Kaizan*.

The non-manufacturing sector, financial services (banks and insurance organizations), service utilities, government departments and instrumentalities have been much slower to adopt the approach and culture of the manufacturing sector and hence have not achieved the process improvement gains that the manufacturing sector has made.

In 2002 the consumer division of Citibank Germany embarked upon the "industrialization" of their organization. They adopted the term "industrialization" to align it with the thinking of the manufacturing sector. This is the story of the gains they have achieved in this part of their organization and it makes for a compelling business outcome.

Background

As many readers will know, Germany is a heavily unionized country, with the unions being extremely powerful and having a Workers' Council that works alongside the organization's Board of Directors. All decisions impacting workers need to be approved by the Workers' Council before they can be implemented.

The Bank was divided into two operating divisions: Consumer and Non-Consumer (investment and corporate). In the consumer division they had 300 branches spread throughout Germany that behaved much the same as most branches throughout the world's banks: they interacted with customers face to face, received transactions via the counter and mail. These transactions were largely administered within the branch or sent to one of the four processing centers throughout Germany for execution.

Each year the Bank's Consumer division received 11 million documents, made 160 million payments, 35 million home banking transactions and received 14 million telephone inquiries.

Business challenges

The Bank faced a number of organizational challenges which included:

- the need to significantly decrease their expense ratio (expense to revenue) as the initial levels were above the industry average and, in order to effectively compete, this needed to reduce to below the industry average to gain a competitive edge;

- the need to increase the time spent by branch staff with customers rather than on administrative activities (providing the opportunity of increasing customer services, satisfaction and revenue);

- the desire to build long and deep relationships with customers;

- better use of staff while increasing employee satisfaction and providing customers with stable service, even in peak periods;

- a need to compete in the marketplace and enter new markets.

Like the rest of the German banking community at the time, they were also facing a number of significant market and economic based challenges and these included:

- the demographics of the country, like most Western economies, was substantially changing to a significantly older population;

- this aging population meant a significant shift to a welfare society and the resulting alteration of banking habits;

- the impact of the country's labor laws (unions) was placing restrictions on the business that were proving difficult;

- banking products were becoming a commodity; and

- the ethnic population was also changing the way banking was being conducted.

Opportunities

The issue was not only to overcome these challenges, but also to turn them into business opportunities. For example:

- the aging population provided an opportunity for pension products;

- the labor laws provided an opportunity to create a relationship with the unions and make them partners in the business;

- the commoditization of products could create an opportunity of *truly* creating commodity products, for example the time to arrange personal loans from application to approval was reduced from two days to 20 minutes; and

- the ethnic population created an opportunity to enable this part of the society to *send money "home" quickly and easily.*

Results

In the first 3.5 years of the Bank's *industrialization* program the results have been nothing short of spectacular. The Consumer division of the Bank:

- reduced their expenses ratio by 50 basis points (bps); while

- increasing the customer facing time within the 300 branches to more than 70 percent. *Note*: a reputable consultancy completed an industry (German banks) review that determined that branch staff spent 17 percent of their time with customers. With the removal of the majority of the back-office processing, the Citibank's branch staff are now spending more than 70 percent of their time with customers;

- errors reduced significantly, from 25–30 percent to 3–5 percent, which is considered an acceptable level; and

- staff and customer satisfaction has increased significantly, as measured by surveys.

No matter how you wish to measure its achievement, the Bank has shown the way forward to other banks and industries and created what Michael Porter referred to as a *competitive advantage*.

Approach

It was with this background and attitude that the Chief Operating Officer (COO), and member of the Board, commenced the industrialization of their business. The COO always worked with the tenet, "perfection is the enemy of good." In other words, you do not need to obtain perfection in order to be successful. In fact, often a 20 percent effort will yield 80 percent of the benefit.

The Bank's industrialization process was seen, and understood, to be a *journey* that would take several years to achieve and would need to be addressed on a number of simultaneous fronts. These "fronts" were considered to be both *internal* and *external*. The *internal* front needed to address internal productivity. In order to create significant productivity gains, both the capacity of the organization and the skill base of the staff needed to be addressed. On the *external* front, the organization needed to address product features, channel features and behaviors.

In this case study we will only be observing the *internal* productivity approach and achievements.

The first step was to address the multiple back-office processing centers and over the period from 2002 to 2003 the Bank consolidated the existing three processing centers into the one service center. If you are wondering, there are sophisticated business continuity and disaster recovery plans in place within the group.

It should be noted that the Central Service Center (central processing back-office) is a separate legal entity, and the Bank has outsourced its back-office processing to this separate organization.

The Central Service Center comprised 2,000 staff members, approximately 900 of whom are on the telephones (inward and outward bound call centers; collections; and tele-marketing).

There was a large component of part-time staff and a goal to significantly increase the current number to allow greater flexibility in workforce planning. Germany has maternity and paternity laws that allow for the mother or father to have three years off work after having a child. The Bank has found that many of the mothers wish to return to the workforce much earlier than the three years, but are understandably restricted because of the child. So the Bank provided the facility for staff to work during hours that suit the organization, the mother and the child.

One of the key goals was to relieve the branch staff from having to complete administrative activities. A few examples of these activities are:

- if a person attends a branch to inform them of a customer's death, they are given a special business card and requested to get in touch with the Central Service Center and the matter is handled in a caring and sensitive manner by appropriately skilled staff;
- credit card limit adjustments;
- all contracts are scanned and centrally stored in an optical format.

The Bank has also negotiated with the Workers' Council and included them in the "industrialization" process to provide competitive salaries and working conditions. The Workers' Council agreed that the organization could monitor and measure the performance of individuals and provide individual incentives to staff. By mid-2006 this was at 75 percent roll-out and continuing and completed within one year.

This was considered a significant breakthrough with the Workers' Council and the Bank being the only organization that they know of within Germany that has achieved this. More details of this measurement and rewards will be described later in this case study.

The Central Service Center is also seen as the "center for innovation" for the business. It is where they develop and test new products, services and management paradigms.

They have created a department known as the *Engineering and Capacity Management* (ECM) group. The COO's first appointment to this department was a manager who proceeded to implement the "industrialization" process.

One of the first things the ECM manager and his team created was a *closed-loop industrialization model*. This comprised three components:

- Process and Organizational Development
- Resource Planning and Performance
- Command Center.

The department's organization structure and responsibilities are shown in Figure 28.1.

Figure 28.1 shows that the Process and Organizational Development division was responsible for the creation and maintenance of the Bank's business process models, the business process simulation function, the implementation of workflow and the continual optimization and improvement of the business processes. Most organizations think that once they have achieved this they have "done a great job" and only need to create or provide a continuous business process improvement program or culture.

The Bank realized that this is only the first step and that these activities need to be operationalized within the business if the full realization of operational cost savings is to be achieved, together with an increase in staff and customer satisfaction. This is where the other two divisions come into play.

The Planning division takes the information collected from the workflow system and marries it with the considerable knowledge that they have of their processes (cycle times, transaction volumes and so forth) and then projects staff utilization into the future. In fact this division forecasts business operational staff, which then is provided to operational management to action.

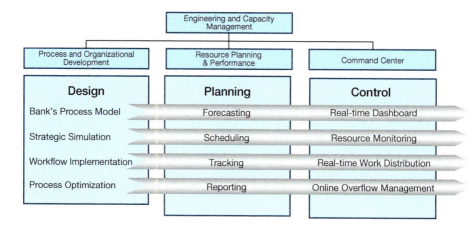

Figure 28.1 Engineering and capacity management structure

The Command Center division then provides the real-time feedback and support to operational management and staff. It monitors the inbound and outbound call centers by exception; the workflow system allocates work based upon transaction volumes (real and predicted), staff skill and performance levels and cross-skill factors. This will be discussed in more detail a little later.

Prior to starting their process journey, the Engineering and Capacity Management department created a vision for how this would be implemented. This resulted in the adoption of the *Industrialization Toolset* shown in Figure 28.2.

We will use this model as a means of tracking the evolution of the various phases in the Bank's journey towards the delivery of the desired increase in internal productivity. We will not describe this figure in any detail here as it will be described during the explanation of each phase.

Phase 1: Starting out

How did the consumer division of the Bank start this significant productivity improvement program of work?

Figure 28.3 shows that the first activities to be started included the commencement of the documentation of the current business processes which could then be used for process optimization improvements and simulated to determine both the accuracy of the documented processes and the validation of suggested process improvements prior to their implementation.

Figure 28.4 shows the timelines for these two activities.

Process management training

The first activities started in Q2 (May) 2003 was the creation of process awareness which commenced the process of "enabling our people."

Establishing true end-to-end
process transparency

Using integrated cost systems to
drive profitability

Enabling our people!

Analyzing, designing, and
operating complex process
environments

Eliminating paper-based
transactions

Achieving accurate and cost-effective
staffing for optimal performance

Figure 28.2 Industrialization toolset

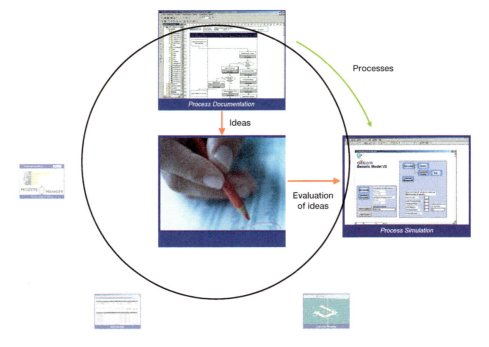

Processes

Ideas

Evaluation
of ideas

Figure 28.3 Process management training and simulation

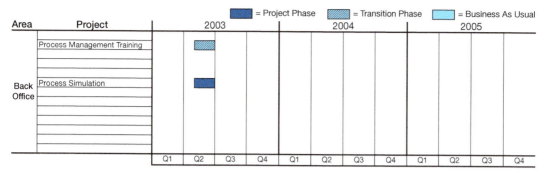

Figure 28.4 Phase 1: Evolution and status of industrialization in Central Service Center

The Bank would be the first to say that they did not get it perfect first time, but they were smart enough to learn and change the approach as required. In the first instance they provided training to show staff that they were part of a business process, but the day-to-day pressure of business-as-usual activities meant nothing changed nor happened.

So they changed tack and started to deliver half-day *process awareness* training across the organization. This provided staff with an understanding of the power that the improvement of their business processes would bring to the organization and decreased any fear factors that may have been present. They also used specific Bank examples of process improvement throughout the training. But management understood that this alone would not create the changes within the organization that they required. So they created the opportunity, within the half-day process awareness training, for staff to attend a five-day advanced training course. They were only looking for passionate (enthusiastic and ambitious) people to attend the advanced training, so they created specific targeted incentives.

First, staff can only be promoted within the Bank if they have completed the advanced training course.

Second, a staff member could only "apply" to attend the course and then needed to be accepted. The requirement for acceptance was that the applicant was required to think up a "breakthrough" project and write a short (one- or two-page) business case and have the process owner and the manager of the Process and Organization Development division sign it off. To achieve sign-off the business case needed to meet certain criteria which included:

- the project must be capable of being delivered in less than 100 working days;
- there must be more than 0.5 FTE savings and this must be sustainable.

The goal of this approach was to create urgency within the business, and obviously to achieve quick wins. It also provided funding, via the savings, for future business process improvement activities.

Once accepted, there were no more than eight or nine attendees on a course, with two trainers. During the course, the attendees further developed their project plan and became the project manager for their "breakthrough" project which commenced after the completion of the course. These projects were continuously tracked and the project managers were coached and supported to success during the 100 days of the project. After the successful completion of the course and the project, the success was celebrated and a presentation provided by a Board member.

This approach resulted in more than 85 certified process experts within the organization and in excess of 100 "breakthrough" projects initiated. These process experts were kept in the business after the completion of the projects to "spread the word." If necessary, they could be seconded to other projects in the future.

There were two other significant actions from a project and operational perspective once a project was completed:

- the savings signed-off in the project business case were withdrawn from future operational budgets; and
- the delivery of the savings (benefits realization) was very well controlled and monitored.

While these "breakthrough" projects started small, they yielded benefits (mainly in terms of free capacity through process enhancement and consequent workload reduction and cost avoidance) in excess of €5m over four years and provided the "cash cow" for the continued justification of business process improvement within the business. In fact, this led to an increase in the budget for the Engineering and Capacity Management department to grow and continue their work.

Process documentation

The modeling of the current business processes was seen as an investment in the future. They elected to document 100 percent of all the current business processes and sub-processes, in a common format in a central repository, across the business. They had 150 people across the business involved for 14 months in this exercise. It is important to also understand that they were not involved full-time on this documentation process. This activity was viewed as a pure investment for the future. It could, however, be justified by the quick wins provided by the "breakthrough" projects, many of which were identified during the course of process documentation.

What business benefits did the Bank gain from documenting their current business processes? They would say that it provided them with:

- a transparency and an end-to-end view of the business processes;
- the ability to provide training, reference material and improved staff induction because of the agreed common format (part of the process architecture and process asset);
- more clarity around IT development activities, especially for the implementation of the workrouting system, which came later;
- ability to identify and implement the concept of business process ownership (governance);
- a clear understanding of business process responsibilities;
- an ability to identify process optimization opportunities.

During the process documentation or modeling activities, they linked process steps to corporate policies. This provided the business with a clear understanding of the impact of policy changes and an ability to react quickly.

As part of identifying process optimization opportunities, "breakthrough projects" were initiated that resulted in quick wins, thereby justifying the investment.

Process simulation

The Bank wished not only to model the current processes, but also to validate the documented outcomes via running process simulations—"does it (the process) make sense?" This provided "evidence" that what had been documented was accurate and provided a level of analysis in a complex business process environment.

Process simulation was used as a strategic planning tool to capture the processing activities of a department, using key parameters such as average handling time, volumes, employee skills and availability. With the help of simulation, a department head was able to evaluate the different options (without needing to implement them individually) to arrive at the optimal solution for a given situation.

In short, process simulation provided a means to quantify the impact of the proposed redesign changes prior to their implementation within the business.

Process simulation was also used at a tactical level by running simulation periodically, using forecasted volumes and average handling times and thereby looking for early warnings, such as backlogs, periods of underutilization, etc.

Phase 2: Capacity planning

Phase 2 continued with phase 1 activities and commenced the development and understanding of capacity planning—Figure 28.5.

The timeframe for phase 2 is shown in Figure 28.6.

It is important to understand what is meant by "capacity planning" in this context. The Bank refers to capacity planning as projecting the future operational business capacity to meet service levels based upon expected future transaction volumes and mix.

This phase was where the Resource Planning and Performance division of the Engineering and Capacity Management department project future staff requirements. This was compared to planned staffing levels and provided to line managers, with commentary and recommendations, to "manage" their part of the business. The inputs into this capacity planning predictions included:

- the expected number of transactions by type
- the number of employees available
- service level targets data, that is desired handling time
- service level weakness points
- backlogs (in terms of both the number of FTEs and days effort)
- average handling time, by department or team
- staff experience, quality of their work, performance levels and cross-skilling factors.

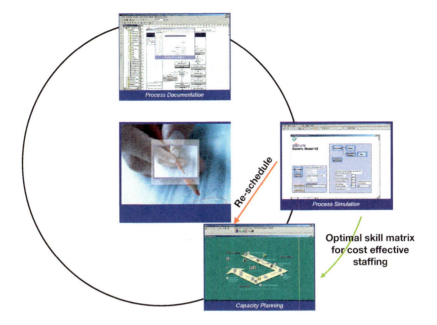

Figure 28.5 Capacity planning

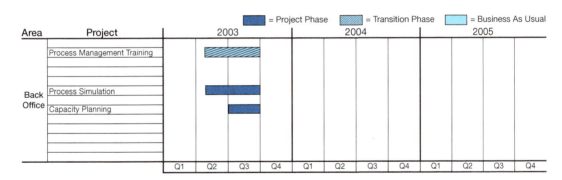

Figure 28.6 Phase 2: Evolution and status of industrialization in Central Service Center

As a result of this capacity planning activity, the staffing level of the capacity planning section has decreased from 30 staff members to 4 staff as at January 2005.

Capacity planning was so highly regarded by the Bank that the ECM manager stated that "process management is nothing without capacity management."

Phase 3: Workrouting (workflow)

This phase is where the Bank commenced the development and implementation of a workrouting (workflow) solution.

Data that provided input into this environment included the information gathered for both the capacity planning and process simulation activities. This information included:

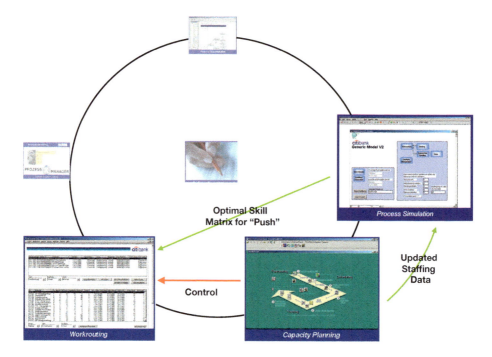

Figure 28.7 Workrouting

- a skill matrix that defined the optimal routing of work packets to employees;
- the availability of the employees—in terms of a Control.

Figure 28.8 shows the timeline for this phase.

When implementing workflow, simplistically, there are two traditional methods for allocating work to staff—the "pull" method or the "push" method. The "pull" method allows staff to "pull" down the number and type of work items that they choose to execute; whereas, the "push" method "pushes" individual work items automatically to staff based upon an established set of criteria. In the Bank's experience, the "push" method has yielded a considerably higher productivity gain compared to the "pull" method.

The set of criteria established by the Bank for the allocation of work items to staff included:

- processing priority of the transaction type;
- staff skill and experience level, which had an impact on, and was an indicator of, the average handling time;
- staff performance level, that is the quality of their work;
- cross-skilling factors.

Measures were developed and placed in a matrix for staff groups and transaction types. Based on discussions with the team leaders and department heads, transaction types were mapped to staff groups, incorporating a "priority factor" (priority with which the group of staff would work on that transaction type).

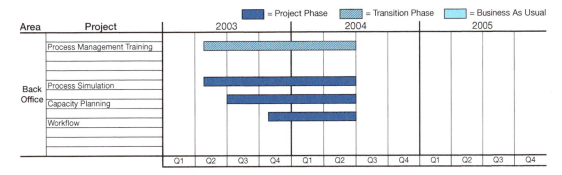

Figure 28.8 Phase 3: Evolution and status of industrialization in Central Service Center

This matrix, together with the current and expected transaction volumes and backlogs determine the allocation of work items to staff members.

The 11 million documents that the Bank received every year was also imaged, optically stored and attached to work items as they "move" around the organization.

Phase 4: The Bank's process model

Phase 4 developed the ability for gathering all the data from the previous activities collected into a data warehouse for use and feedback into the rest of the "toolset." Accurate processing data (times, backlogs, delays, staff performance levels and so forth) allow for more accurate and improved processes, together with an ability to continually improve business processes (refer to Figure 28.9).

The period from mid-2004 to the end of Q1 2005 saw the completion of the end-to-end process modeling across the organization (refer to Figure 28.10).

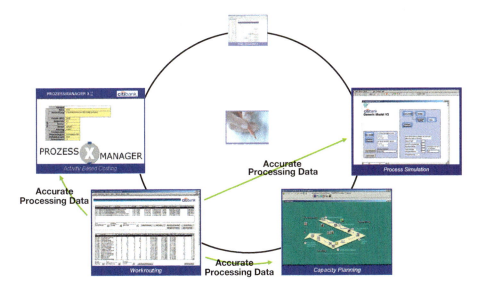

Figure 28.9 Accurate processing data

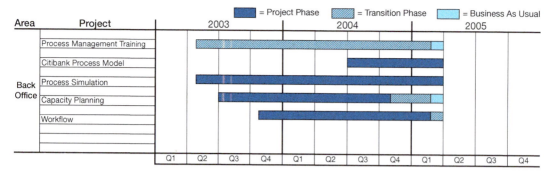

Figure 28.10 Phase 4: Evolution and status of industrialization in Central Service Center

This phase delivered:

- a transparency of the current end-to-end processes;
- a structured, consistent and complete process landscape;
- process documentation for the back-office was completed on an activity level.

As this information further evolved, the plan was to make it available in an integrated central web-based process portal (database) with version control and audit trails, along the lines shown in Figure 28.11.

Note: CPM in Figure 28.11 refers to the Bank's Process Management Asset Repository. As can be seen in Figure 28.11 the intranet portal included:

- the organization chart;
- all documented business processes. These will be split by operational, control and business processes;
- products and services offered by the business;
- policies;
- procedures;
- guidelines.

Phase 5: Activity-based costing

The remainder of 2005 (Q2 to Q4) (Figure 28.12) comprised the completion of activity-based costing on the business processes to:

- determine the true end-to-end process, product and channel costs;
- build the basis for future financial benchmarking with the intention to extend the Activity-Based Management for profitability analysis.

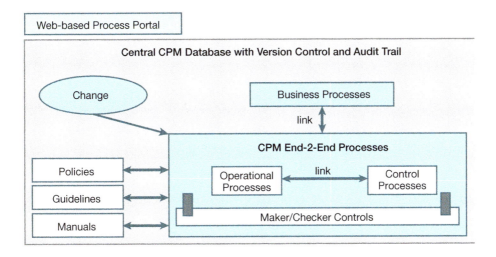

Figure 28.11 Future web-based process portal

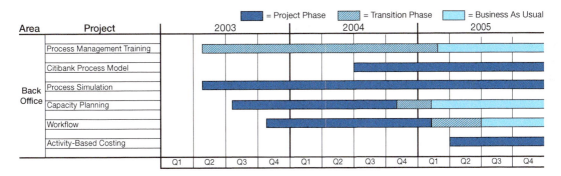

Figure 28.12 Phase 5: Evolution and status of industrialization in Central Service Center

Process activities were grouped, or boxed, into those activities that were to be measured. The Bank had been measuring many of the activities for some years and was able to match appropriate process models to the existing historical measures.

The costs of non-process activities (meetings, etc.) were distributed across all processes to provide a "true" cost. These non-process activity costs were regarded as costs over which they had no control. If a process was optimized and the cost changed, then the non-process costs were redistributed.

Note: The activity-based costs were calculated from the "bottom up" and, once accumulated, were checked (validated) back to the actual costs of a department. The Bank believed that the individual costing provided a reflection of the "true" cost of a process.

Ongoing monitoring

The ongoing monitoring of the business processes are handled, in the first instance, by the Command Center staff which was staffed from 8 a.m. to 9 p.m.

Two staff at a time sat at a desk surrounded by several computer screens. One staff member handled the inbound call center and the other the outbound call center. Only exceptions were displayed on the screens, where an exception is defined as an event outside the established goals or targets. Examples of these targets include the monitoring of:

- when a staff member logs on at the call center. This is compared to their official work start time. There is an allowance of eight minutes' grace and if they are not logged on by this time, the Command Center calls the case to the attention of the SPOC (single point of contact) within the respective department/area;

- length of call time. Again, if the call length was outside the normal call duration, a team leader was called to go and provide assistance to the staff member;

- call wrap-up time. This was handled in a similar manner to the above call length situation.

While this appears to be a little like "big brother," the aim was to assist staff and managers in the execution of their tasks and the management of their business and it was conducted and received in a positive manner.

Individual staff achievements of targets were reflected in the bonuses they received. These results were published only to the individual, his/her team leader and department head. With the performance-based bonus system, it could so happen that some staff received close to nothing whereas the high achievers almost doubled their salaries.

The targets include: quality, achieving service levels, selling products, selling appointments to a branch, did the customer actually attend at the branch, what did they buy, and so forth. Staff *and branches* are also provided with a disincentive in case of bad appointment quality or high cancellation rates. The reporting on these targets is fully automated.

Authors' comments

One of the authors spent some time with the "Industrialization" team in Germany and they were an impressive and intelligent team. The reason for the visit was to learn from their success and compare the organization's approach to the 7FE Framework outlined in this book.

The authors would like to reflect on the organization's obvious success and highlight a number of activities and approaches that we believe ensured the successful outcomes.

1. The initial process improvement team was small and built on their success.

2. The business process improvement program had the full support of the senior executive of the organization.

3. Process awareness workshops were held across the organization to "spread the word" of the benefits of managing by processes. When the initial training model was not as successful as expected, the team quickly adapted and created the short half-day session.

4. Providing an opportunity beyond these short sessions to a longer training course allowed ambitious and enthusiastic staff to contribute. Making applicants for these longer training courses apply (via a business case) by identifying a "real" business process improvement opportunity within the business meant that only committed staff applied.

5. Furthermore, coupling the process management training to the career path provided the right impetus among the staff of the organization.

6. The type of projects (100 days, no IT changes) meant that quick wins were implemented, thus justifying continued process improvement activities.

7. We like the fact that the applicant's managers signed off on the business case. This meant that only genuine business cases were approved and that the manager actually had to realize the business benefits identified in the business case.

These activities meant that the business process improvement program was commenced with a high probability of success and with significant commitment and support from the organization's managers and staff.

The project team, staff and entire organization should be very proud of themselves and their achievements.

SUMMARY

Three case studies from three different continents have been described. Each of the case studies included lessons learned on how to increase the likelihood and magnitude of the success of a BPM activity.

The critical elements across all three case studies were:

- Always obtain genuine commitment from senior executives and stakeholders; continually selling the benefits and validate BPM activity progress against the business objectives.

- Have a clear vision of the target state (via the target operating model described in Chapters 13 and 14).

- Need to understand the true BPM maturity of the organization and build further on it.

Demonstrating value by achieving early benefits is crucial, especially in long multi-year programs.

SELF-TEST

1 Describe the key challenges in each of the three case studies.

2 Describe the steps/phases in each of the three case studies.

3 Describe the key lessons learned in each of the three case studies.

CHAPTER 29

BPM MATURITY MODEL

Michael Rosemann, Tonia de Bruin and Brad Power

OVERVIEW

The chapter provides a brief and selective overview of the structure and components included in a holistic and contemporary model that facilitates the assessment of BPM maturity.

OVERALL LEARNING OUTCOME

By the end of this chapter you will be able to understand:

- the five levels of BPM maturity and the typical characteristics
- the six factors of BPM maturity
- the dimensions of the BPM maturity model
- how the BPM maturity model may be applied.

INTRODUCTION

As this entire book outlines, BPM is a holistic organizational management practice that requires top management understanding and involvement, clearly defined roles and decision processes as part of BPM governance, appropriate BPM methodologies, process-aware information systems, educated and well-trained people, and a culture receptive to business processes. BPM has its roots in a number of approaches, including BPR, quality management (e.g., TQM, Six Sigma), operations management (e.g., MRP II, CIM, Kanban), business process modeling and process-aware information systems (e.g., workflow management systems, service-oriented architectures). It is widely recognized as a foundation for contemporary management approaches as the analysis of business processes drives understanding to the roots of an organization. The popularity and significance of BPM leads to the question of how advanced different organizations are in their BPM development. The notion of "maturity" has been proposed for a number of management approaches as a way to evaluate "the state of being complete, perfect, or ready" or the "fullness or perfection of growth or development" (Oxford English Dictionary, 2004). This chapter describes a new business process management maturity (BPMM) model that has been developed for the evaluation and advancement of BPM effectiveness across organizations.

The structure of this chapter is as follows. The second section looks at the value proposition of a BPMM model and how different maturity stages can be represented within such a model. The third section presents a new maturity model developed specifically for BPM, and details the objectives and core framework of this model. A focus of this section is on the major characteristics of the model as represented by six critical success factors and their underlying capability areas. The fourth section discusses how this BPMM model can be applied within an organization to drive improved operational performance, whilst the fifth section provides the justification and support for the model development. The final section concludes with a brief summary.

BUSINESS PROCESS MANAGEMENT MATURITY

Business process management is a complex management practice that many organizations find difficult to implement and progress to higher stages of maturity. This is supported by research indicating that 97 percent of European organizations surveyed considered BPM to be important to the organization and only 3 percent had not commenced BPM practices. Despite this importance, 73 percent were considered to be only at the early stages of adoption (Pritchard and Armistead, 1999: 13). A review of CIOs by Gartner (2005) confirmed the importance of BPM, with the top issue identified for 2005 being BPM. For BPM practitioners, therefore, one concern is that the complexity of BPM may result in organizations being unable to achieve desired benefits of BPM.

Maturity models are used as an evaluative and comparative basis for improvement (Fisher, 2004; Harmon, 2004; Spanyi, 2004), and in order to derive an informed approach for increasing the capability of a specific area within an organization (Ahern et al., 2004; Hakes, 1996; Paulk et al., 1993). They have been designed to assess the maturity (i.e., competency, capability, level of sophistication) of a selected domain, based on a more or less comprehensive set of criteria. Therefore, a BPMM model is a tool that can assist organizations in becoming more successful with BPM, resulting in the achievement of greater operational and business performance benefits. In addition, the increased success of BPM adoptions will contribute to positioning BPM as an enduring management practice. In particular, maturity models can be used for three purposes:

1. As *a descriptive* tool enabling an "as-is" assessment of strengths and weaknesses.

2. As a *prescriptive* tool enabling the development of a roadmap for improvement.

3. As a *comparative* tool enabling benchmarking to assess against industry standards and other organizations.

Unlike other existing models, the BPMM model discussed in the following sections has been developed to enable each of these three purposes.

A typology of BPMM stages

Paulk et al. (1993: 5) stress that improved maturity results "in an increase in the process capability of the organization." Consequently, it is not a surprise that a number of models to measure the maturity of different facets of BPM have been proposed (Davenport, 2005). The common base for the majority of these models has been the Capability Maturity Model (CMM), where the most popular way of evaluating maturity is a five-point Likert scale with "5" representing the highest level of maturity. Among others, Harmon (2004) developed a BPMM model based on the CMM (see also Harmon, 2003). In a similar way, Fisher (2004) combined five "levers of change" with five states of maturity. Smith and Fingar (2004) argue that a CMM-based maturity model that postulates well-organized and repeatable processes cannot capture the need for business process innovation. Further BPM maturity models are offered by TeraQuest/Borland Software (Curtis et al., 2004) and the Business Process Management Group (BPMG). In addition to dedicated BPMM models, a number of models have been proposed that study single facets of a BPM maturity model. Examples are Luftman's (2003) maturity model for strategic alignment and McCormack's (1999) maturity model for process orientation which focuses on process performance.

An attempt to divide organizations into groups depending on their grade and progression of BPM implementation was made by Pritchard and Armistead (1999). Whilst trying to define maturity of BPR programs, Maull et al. (2003) encountered problems when attempting to use objective measures. They tried to define maturity using two dimensions: an objective measure (time, team size, etc.) and a "weighting for readiness to change" (Maull et al., 2003). However, this approach turned out to be too complex to measure. Therefore, they chose a phenomenological approach assessing the organization's perception of its maturity, using objective measures as a guideline. Another example of how to define maturity (or, in their case, "process condition") is provided by DeToro and McCabe (1997), who used two dimensions (effectiveness and efficiency) to rate a process's condition.

The comparison of low and high maturity in Figure 29.1 helps to clarify the comprehensiveness and range of BPMM. The idea of comparing low and high maturity derives from Paulk et al. (1993), who presented such a comparison to facilitate the understanding of the concept of process maturity.

The proposed BPMM model adopts the five maturity stages of CMM in an attempt to differentiate various levels of sophistication of a BPM initiative.

Stage 1: Initial state

An organization with a BPMM at Stage 1 will have made either no or very uncoordinated and unstructured attempts towards BPM. Typically, such an organization may display some combination of the following characteristics:

- ad hoc approaches
- individual efforts (IT or business)

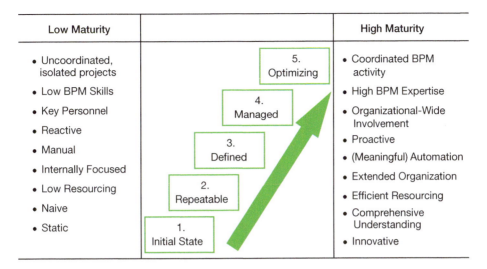

Figure 29.1 Comparison of low and high maturity and the five maturity stages

- various and non-consolidated approaches to methodology, tools and techniques
- limited scope of BPM initiatives
- minimal employee involvement
- low reliance on external BPM expertise
- high levels of manual interventions and workarounds.

Stage 2: Repeatable

An organization with a BPM maturity at Stage 2 will have progressed past making first BPM experiences and will be starting to build up BPM capability and increasing the number of people who look at the organization from a process perspective. Typically, such an organization may display some combination of the following characteristics:

- first documented processes
- recognition of the importance of BPM
- increased involvement of executives and top management
- one main purpose for exploring BPM
- extensive use of simple process modeling with simple repositories
- first attempts with a structured methodology and common standards
- increased reliance on external BPM expertise.

Stage 3: Defined

An organization with a BPM maturity at Stage 3 will experience increased momentum in its quest to develop BPM capability and expand the number of people looking at the organization from a process perspective. Typically, such an organization may display some combination of the following characteristics:

- focus on the management of the early phases of the process lifestyle
- use of elaborate tools (e.g., dynamic modeling, server-based applications, multiple and distributed users)
- a combination of different process management methods and tools (e.g., process redesign, workflow management and process-based risk management)
- more extensive use of technology for delivery and communication of BPM (e.g., process designs available to users via an intranet site)
- comprehensive and formal BPM training sessions
- less reliance on external expertise.

Stage 4: Managed

An organization with a BPM maturity at Stage 4 will enjoy the benefits of having BPM firmly entrenched in the strategic make-up of the organization. Typically, such an organization may display some combination of the following characteristics:

- an established Process Management Center of Excellence that maintains standards
- exploration of business process controlling methods and technologies
- merging of IT and business perspectives on process management (e.g., workflow management and activity-based costing)
- formal, designated process management positions
- widely accepted methods and technologies
- integrated process management purposes
- process orientation as a mandatory project component
- continuous extension and consolidation of process management initiatives
- minimal reliance on external expertise.

Stage 5: Optimized

An organization with a BPM maturity at Stage 5 will enjoy the benefits of having BPM firmly entrenched as a core part of both strategic and operational management within the organization. Typically, such an organization may display some combination of the following characteristics:

- process management is a part of managers' activities, accountabilities and performance measurements
- wide acceptance and use of standard methods and technologies
- one organization-wide approach to BPM that incorporates customers, suppliers, distributors and other stakeholders

- established business process lifecycle management

- Business Process Management Center of Excellence reduces in size as process management becomes simply the way business is done.

THE BPM MATURITY MODEL

Our BPM maturity model extends and updates earlier maturity models by addressing the requirements and complexities identified within BPM in a more holistic and contemporary way.

Objectives and framework

The development of our model was driven by the following requirements:

1. We wanted to develop a model with a *solid theoretical foundation*.

2. Consequently, we carefully studied previous research on BPM and the development of maturity models across a range of domains. Our proposed model has been heavily influenced by the consolidation of these previous research outcomes.

3. We wanted to design a *widely accepted global standard* rather than providing yet another competitive maturity model. As such, we approached authors and developers of previous BPM maturity models for collaboration. Over a period of six months, we conducted a series of Delphi studies designed to incorporate input of recognized thought leaders in the BPM domain. Each Delphi study related to a single factor of the model and used a moderated survey method, utilizing three or four rounds per factor to derive consensus on a number of issues (Rosemann and de Bruin, 2005). The proposed model is now not only a result of merging three reasonably advanced models, but also includes the contributions of more than 20 BPM thought leaders.

4. We were interested in developing a *holistic model* that captured the entire scope of BPM. The extensive literature review that provided us with a solid theoretical foundation also provided insights into the success factors of BPM including perceived barriers to BPM success and details of various implementation approaches for BPM initiatives. Thus our model incorporates factors covering such diverse areas as strategic alignment, information technology and culture.

5. The need to balance the theoretical development of the model with *high applicability* in practice. As a consequence, over the last two years our model was applied, at different stages of its development lifecycle, to a number of organizations in a range of industries. The continuous industry feedback has been used to ensure an industry-oriented structure and terminology throughout the entire model.

6. A main design paradigm was that the model should *support the individual information needs of different stakeholder groups*. As a consequence, the model has three levels: Level 1—the six success factors; Level 2—capability areas within each of these factors; and Level 3—detailed questions to measure each capability area. Essentially these levels

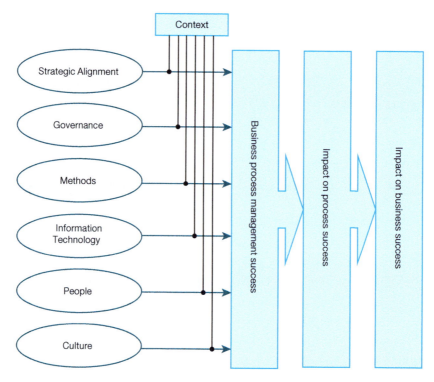

Figure 29.2 The underlying model

form a tree structure that can be expanded based on the reporting and analysis requirements of the individual stakeholder.

The resultant model is multidimensional, including a number of distinct components: factors, stages and scope (organizational entity and time). The underlying assumption of the theoretical model is that the factors (based on identified BPM critical success factors, barriers to BPM success, and implementation approaches for BPM initiatives) represent independent variables, and the dependent variable is BPM success. A further assumption is that higher maturity in each of these factors will be reflected in higher levels of success in the BPM initiative. Finally, the notion of "process success" has to be translated into relevant, BPM-independent success measures for the entire organization—that is actual business success (Figure 29.2).

The focus of our model is on the independent factors for two reasons. First, they provide insights into how process performance can actually be improved rather than measured. Second, a number of models and solutions are already available for the measurement of process performance (e.g., IDS Business Process Performance Measurement). A brief overview of the dimensions of our model, including definition, origin and purpose, is included in Table 29.1.

Factors are considered to be the primary dimension, as they represent the elements within organizations critical to the success of BPM. (Further insights into the detailed elements of the model can be found in Rosemann and de Bruin, 2004.)

Table 29.1 Dimensions of the BPM maturity model

Dimension	Definition	Origin	Purpose
Factor	A specific, measurable and independent element that reflects a fundamental and distinct characteristic of BPM. Each factor is further broken down in a 1-m hierarchy	Current factors have been derived from an extensive literature review of BPM critical success factors and barriers to successful BPM implementations	• To cluster important components of BPM and allow a separate evaluation of these factors, that is to enable identification of strengths and weaknesses within the organization that are most likely to impact on BPM success • To enable organizations to tailor specific BPM strategies with a view to improving BPM success • To enable future research into relationships and correlation between factors to improve understanding of BPM issues
Maturity stage	A predefined maturity stage ranging from 1 (low) to 5 (high)	Levels and names are based on those used in CMM	• To quantify and summarize evaluations in a consistent and comparable manner
Scope: organizational entity	The organizational entity which defines the unit of analysis and to which the model is being applied, for example a division, a business unit, a subsidiary	The organizational entity is defined on a case-by-case basis by the participating organization	• Acknowledgement that in reality BPM does not conform to any one implementation and adoption route • To enable internal comparison and assessment between entities • To enable specific strategies to be implemented • To identify and maximize leverage of internal knowledge sources and sharing
Scope: time	The point in time at which the model is applied	Variable aspect of the model that is selected by the organization applying the model	• To enable understanding of current position and the formation of an internal baseline • To enable the model to be reapplied over time to assess progress in a longitudinal study
Coverage	The extent to which BPM practices extend through the organizational entity being assessed	Based on existing practice where organizations can (and do) adopt different approaches to BPM implementation	• To recognize the fact that the standardized and consistent distribution of BPM capabilities deserves recognition
Proficiency	The perceived goodness of BPM practices in the organizational entity being assessed	Concept based on the notions of efficiency and effectiveness in similar models (DeToro and McCabe, 1997)	To recognize the fact that the quality of BPM capabilities deserves recognition

It will be important in our future research to identify relevant contextual factors—for example process-oriented incentive schema might be an indication for a mature organization, but such schema cannot be applied to public organizations. This leads to the important aspect that there is (most likely) not a common set of BPM best practices that are equally valid for all organizations. Consequently, we define the highest level of maturity (level 5) as the most sophisticated level of conducting BPM, which is *not* necessarily identical with the best way for all organizations. It is a case-by-case challenge to identify the most appropriate BPM maturity level for an organization, based on context, underlying objectives, related constraints, possible business cases and so on.

The six factors of BPM maturity

The consolidation of related literature, the merger of three existing BPM maturity models and the subsequent Delphi process led to the development of our maturity model, which contains at its core six factors. Each factor represents a critical success factor for BPM—that is this element has to go right in order for the organization to be successful with BPM. Each of these six factors has been expanded to a further level of detail, derived from the Delphi study. Our aim with using the Delphi technique was to access views on contemporary global BPM issues not easily identifiable through a review of existing literature. We call the resultant sub-elements of the factors *capability areas*. Table 29.2 shows the demographics of thought leaders that contributed to the Delphi studies.

Whilst the following sections provide further insights into each of the factors, Figure 29.3 provides an overview of the model incorporating the capability areas that were derived through the Delphi studies.

Strategic alignment

Strategic alignment as part of our BPM maturity model is defined as the tight linkage of organizational priorities and enterprise processes enabling continual and effective action to improve business performance. Through our Delphi study, we identified five principal

Table 29.2 Delphi study participants (I, industry; A, academia)

	Strategic alignment		Governance		Method		Information technology		People		Culture	
Category	I	A	I	A	I	A	I	A	I	A	I	A
Region:												
USA	8	6	10	6	10	5	9	4	9	5	8	5
Australia	2	1	2	1	2	1	2	1	2	1	2	1
Europe	1	–	1	–	1	1	1	1	1	–	1	–
Asia	–	–	–	1	–	1	–	–	–	–	–	–
Category total	11	7	13	8	13	8	12	6	12	6	11	6

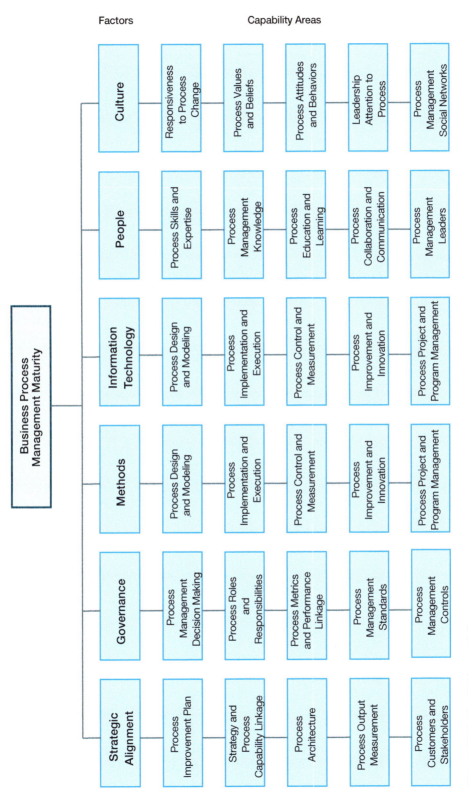

Figure 29.3 The BPM capability area

capability areas to be measured as part of an assessment of strategic alignment capabilities, as they relate to BPM. The sequence in which we present these capability areas reflects the average *perceived importance* weighting assigned by the experts participating in the Delphi study.

1. A strategy-driven *process improvement plan* captures the organization's overall approach towards the BPM initiative. The process improvement plan is derived directly from the organization's strategy, and outlines how process improvement initiatives are going to meet strategically prioritized goals. The process improvement plan provides information related to the targets for the process improvement project, together with planned review and monitoring processes.

2. A core element of strategic alignment, in the context of BPM, is the entire bi-directional *linkage between strategy and business processes*. Do the business processes directly contribute to the strategy, and do organizational strategies explicitly incorporate process capabilities? By way of example, do we know which processes are impacted by a change of the strategy and which processes could become a bottleneck in the execution of the strategy, is the strategy designed and continually reviewed in light of process capabilities, how are scarce resources to be allocated to perhaps competing processes, and which processes are we better off outsourcing or offshoring?

3. *An enterprise process architecture* is the name given to the highest level abstraction of the actual hierarchy of value-driving and enabling business processes. A well-defined enterprise process architecture clearly depicts which major business processes exist, how the industry-/company-specific value chain looks, and what major enabling processes support this value chain—for example finance, HR, IT. A well-designed process architecture derives from a sound understanding of organizational structures from a process viewpoint. In addition, it serves as the main process landscape and provides the starting point for more detailed process analysis.

4. In order to be able to evaluate actual process performance, it is important to have a well-defined understanding of *process outputs* and related KPIs. A hierarchy of cascading, process-oriented and cost-effectively measured KPIs provides a valuable source for translation of strategic objectives to process-specific goals, and facilitates effective process control. Relevant KPIs can be of differing nature, including financial, quantitative, qualitative or time-based, and may be dependent upon the strategic drivers for the specific enterprise process. Often equally important, but more difficult to measure, are KPIs related to characteristics of an entire process, such as flexibility or reliability.

5. Finally, we recognize that strategies are typically closely linked to individuals and influential stakeholder groups. Thus, how well BPM is aligned to the actual priorities of *key customers and other stakeholders such as senior management, shareholders, government bodies and so on* should be evaluated. For example, in practice it can be observed that a change of a CEO will have significant impact on the popularity (or not) of BPM even if the official strategy remains the same. Among others, this also includes investigation of how well processes with touchpoints to external parties are managed, how well external viewpoints have been considered in the process design, and what influence external stakeholders have on the process design.

Governance

Governance in the context of BPM establishes relevant and transparent accountability, decision-making and reward processes to guide actions. In the tradition of corporate or IT governance, a focus is on the decision-making processes of BPM and related roles and responsibilities:

- The clear definition and consistent execution of related BPM *decision-making processes* that guide actions in both anticipated and unanticipated circumstances is seen to be critical. In addition to *who* can make *what* decision, the speed of decision making and the ability to influence resource allocation and organizational reaction to process change is also important.

- Another core element is the definition of *process roles and responsibilities*. This covers the entire range of BPM-related roles, from business process analysts to business process owners up to chief process officers, and encompasses all related committees and involved decision boards, such as Process Councils and Process Steering Committees. The duties and responsibilities of each role need to be clearly specified, and precise reporting structures must be defined.

- Processes must exist to ensure the direct linkage of process performance with strategic goals. While the actual process output is measured and evaluated as part of the factor strategic alignment, the process for *collecting the required metrics* and linking them to performance criteria is regarded as being a part of BPM governance.

- *Process management standards* must be well defined and documented. This includes the coordination of process management initiatives across the organization, and guidelines for the establishment and management of process management components such as process measures, issue resolution, reward and remuneration structures and so on.

- *Process management controls* as part of BPM governance cover regular review cycles to maintain the quality and currency of process management principles, and compliance management related to process management standards. Such controls will include the degree to which BPM governance standards are complied with in order to encourage desired behaviors.

Methods

Methods, in the context of BPM, have been defined as the approaches and techniques that support and enable consistent process actions. Distinct methods can be applied to major, discrete stages of the process lifecycle. This characteristic, which is unique to the "methods" and "information technology" factors, has resulted in capability areas that reflect the process lifecycle stages rather than specific capabilities of potential process methods or information technology. Whilst, arguably, defining capability areas in this way is different from the way adopted for other factors, it is important to note that the capability areas have been derived using the same Delphi process. An advantage of associating the method capability with a specific process lifecycle stage is the resultant ability to assess methods that serve a particular purpose, rather than purely all methods relating to BPM. For example it is possible to assess the specific methods used for designing processes as distinct from those used for improving processes. This form of analysis is considered to be particularly beneficial, given the common practice of methods (and information technology) being developed, marketed and implemented to meet the needs of a specific process lifecycle stage. The methods maturity assessment therefore focuses on the specific needs of each process lifecycle, and considers elements such as the integration of process lifecycle methods with each other and also with other management methods, the support for methods provided by information technology, and the sophistication, suitability, accessibility and actual usage of methods within each stage.

- *Process design and modeling* is related to the methods used to identify and conceptualize current (as-is) business processes and future (to-be) processes. The core of such methods is process modeling techniques.

- *Process implementation and execution* covers the next stage in the lifecycle. Related methods help to transform process models into executable business process specifications. Methods related to the communication of these models and escalation methods facilitate the process execution.

- The *process control and measurement* stage of the process lifecycle is related to methods that provide guidance for the collection of process-related data. These data can be related to process control (e.g., risks or errors), or could be process performance measures.

- The *process improvement and innovation* stage includes all methods that facilitate the development of improved and more innovative business processes. This includes approaches such as process innovation, Six Sigma and so on.

- The assessment component *process project management and program management* evaluates the approaches that are used for the overall management of the BPM program or projects, including the management of process change.

Information technology

Information technology (IT) refers to the software, hardware and information management systems that enable and support process activities. As indicated, the assessment of IT capability areas is structured in a similar way to that of methods, and refers first to process lifecycle stages. Similarly to the methods maturity assessment, the IT components focus on the specific needs of each process lifecycle stage and are evaluated from viewpoints such as customizability, appropriateness of automation and integration with related IT solutions (e.g., data warehousing, enterprise systems, reporting), in addition to the more generic considerations such as the sophistication, suitability, accessibility and usage of such IT within each stage.

- *IT solutions for process design and modeling* covers IT that enables derivation of process models automatically from log files, and overall tool-support for business process modeling and analysis (e.g., process animation, process simulation).

- *IT-enabled process implementation and execution* focuses on the automated transformation of process models into executable specifications and the subsequent workflow-based process execution. This also includes related solutions such as document management systems or service-oriented architectures. This entire category of software is often labeled "process-aware information systems."

- *Process control and measurement* solutions facilitate (semi-)automated process escalation management, exception handling, workflow mining, performance visualization (e.g., dashboards), and controlling based on process log files.

- Tools for *process improvement and innovation* provide automated support for the generation of improved business processes. These could be solutions that provide agile (i.e., self-learning) tools that continuously adjust business processes based on contextual changes.

- *Process project management and program management* tools facilitate the overall program and project management. They are essential, but typically less BPM-specific.

People

While the information technology factor covered IT-related BPM resources, the factor "people" comprises the human resources. This factor is defined as the individuals and groups who continually enhance and apply their process skills and knowledge to improve business performance. The focus on skills and knowledge of people involved in a BPM initiative could be seen as the "hard facts" of people. The next capability area ("culture") covers the "soft side," including behaviors and attitudes leading to the overall appreciation of BPM within the organization.

- *Process skills and expertise* is concentrated on the comprehensiveness and depth of the capabilities of the involved stakeholders in light of the requirements as formulated by the allocated role or position (e.g., business process analyst, process owner).

- *Process management knowledge* consolidates the depths of knowledge about BPM principles and practices. It evaluates the level of understanding of BPM, including the knowledge of process management methods and information technology, and the impact these have on enterprise process outcomes.

- *Process education and learning* measures the commitment of the organization to the ongoing development and maintenance of the relevant process skills and knowledge. The assessment covers the existence, extent, appropriateness and actual success (as measured by the level of learning) of education programs. Further items are devoted to the qualification of the BPM educators and BPM certification programs.

- *Process collaboration and communication* considers the way in which individuals and groups work together in order to achieve desired process outcomes. This includes the related evaluation analysis of the communication patterns between process stakeholders, and the manner in which related process knowledge is discovered, explored and disseminated.

- The final "people" capability area is dedicated to *process management leaders*. The maturity assessment evaluates people's willingness to lead, take responsibility and be accountable for business processes. Among others, it also captures the degree to which desired process leadership skills and management styles are practiced.

Culture

Culture, the sixth and final factor, is the collective values and beliefs that shape process-related attitudes and behaviors to improve business performance. During the Delphi process, it was surprising to observe that consensus and mutual understanding of capability areas was reached within this factor with a greater degree of ease and considerably less discussion than had occurred in the earlier studies. Arguably, this phenomenon could be the result of "culture" being one of the last Delphi studies in the series; however, the study for "people" was run concurrently and similar findings were not present within this study.

- *Responsiveness to process change* is about the overall receptiveness of the organization to process change, the propensity of the organization to accept process change and adaptation, and the ability for process change to cross functional boundaries seamlessly and for people to act in the best interest of the process.

- *Process values and beliefs* investigates the broad process thinking within the organization—that is, do members of the organization see processes as the way things get done? Furthermore, this capability area concentrates on the commonly held beliefs and values on the roles and benefits of BPM. Among them is the longevity of BPM, expressed by the depth and breadth of ongoing commitment.

- The *process attitudes and behaviors* of those who are involved in and those who are affected by BPM are another assessment item in the "culture" factor. This includes, among others, the willingness to question existing practices in light of potential process improvements and actual process-related behavior.

- *Leadership attention to process management* covers the level of commitment and attention to processes and process management shown by senior executives, the degree of attention paid to process on all levels, and the quality of process leadership.

- Finally, *process management social networks* comprise the existence and influence of BPM communities of practice, the usage of social network techniques, and the recognition and use of informal BPM networks.

APPLICATION OF THE BPM MATURITY MODEL

The BPMM model can be applied within an organization in a number of ways, dependent upon the desired *breadth* and *depth* of application.

Breadth refers to the unit of analysis defined for assessment. A unit of analysis can be (in the extreme case) the entire organization, or specific lines of business within the organization. The model can be applied separately to multiple units of analysis, leading to valuable internal benchmarking data.

For each unit of analysis, the model can be applied in two ways: factor level, and capability level. This represents the *depth* of the model application.

A *factor-level* application provides a high-level analysis with results collated on the basis of the six factors contained within the model—that is strategic alignment, governance, methods, information technology, people and culture. Typically, this level of analysis is achieved by BPMM experts undertaking extensive one-on-one interviews with key executives providing complementary views on an organization's BPM initiatives. The BPM maturity experts then analyze the findings from these interviews, provide a detailed presentation and report back to the organization. This level of analysis is useful for providing a rough understanding of the "as-is" BPM position from an executive perspective, and provides a good first starting point for organizations in understanding the sophistication of their BPM activities.

A *capability-level* application provides a richer understanding of the "as-is" BPM position by conducting additional analysis into the five capability areas identified for each of the six factors. In addition to the factor interviews with key executives, this level of analysis involves in-depth workshops with relevant employees with specialist knowledge of BPM activities within each of the capability areas. In addition to a more thorough understanding of the "as-is" BPM position, this level of analysis enables future BPM strategies to be formulated and targeted to particular aspects of BPM. A further benefit of this level of analysis is that a comparison between BPM perceptions of executives and employees is possible. Moreover, a BPM maturity assessment on the capability level is complemented by an analysis of BPM-related documents (e.g., process models, job descriptions, definitions of process KPIs).

It is intended that future versions of the model will incorporate a self-assessment component that will enable an organization to achieve a limited maturity assessment without the need to seek external BPM maturity expertise in addition to being able to have a comprehensive assessment conducted by certified assessors.

RELATED WORK

More than 150 maturity models have been developed to measure, among others, the maturity of IT service capability, strategic alignment, innovation management, program management, enterprise architecture and knowledge management. Many of these models have been designed to assess the maturity (i.e., competency, capability, level of sophistication) of a selected domain based on a more or less comprehensive set of criteria. Unlike CMM, which has reached the level of a compliance standard for software development (Mutafelija and Stromberg, 2003), most of these models simply provide a means for positioning the selected unit of analysis on a predefined scale. Shortcomings of current BPM maturity models have been the simplifying focus on only one dimension for measuring BPMM and the lack of actual application of these models. Moreover, many existing BPM models do not always clearly differentiate between the evaluation of the maturity of a business process (as measured by its performance) and the maturity of the *management* of business processes. Further shortcomings of many available BPMM models are the missing rigor in the model development process, the limited scope and depth of single facets of BPM, their idiosyncratic nature due to a lack of foundation in related work, the missing consideration of relevant stakeholders, the lack of empirical tests for these models and, especially, the lack of sufficient depth in the assessment levels.

The proposed BPM maturity model addresses these shortcomings by combining a rigorous theoretical framework with multiple practical applications during the development process to ensure that the resultant model incorporates specific BPM requirements in a practical and useful manner.

SUMMARY

This chapter has provided a brief and selective overview of the structure and components included in a holistic and contemporary model that facilitates the assessment of BPM maturity. The actual BPM maturity assessment derived by applying this model can occur on various levels. In its most detailed and recommended form, such assessment takes place one level below the capability areas. The entire assessment kit is based on a maturity assessment questionnaire, semi-structured interviews with key BPM stakeholders, and the evaluation of related documents (e.g., process-related job descriptions, process incentive schema, process models). The triangulation of these three sources of evidence leads to the final assessment score. In analogy to the original CMM, separate evaluations (ranging from one to five) are calculated for each of the six factors. This provides the organization with an overview of its BPM initiatives, and helps to localize the immediate action points necessary for an increased BPM maturity. A corresponding tool semi-automates the data collection, analysis and presentation activities.

SELF-TEST

1 List the five levels of BPM maturity and each level's typical characteristics.

2 List the six factors of BPM maturity.

3 List the dimensions of the BPM maturity model and provide a brief description.

CHAPTER 30

BUSINESS PROCESS MATURITY MODELS

What's in a name?

Amy Van Looy

OVERVIEW

There are many maturity models around these days that claim to assess and improve business processes. However, there are also substantial differences between them. This chapter helps you see the wood for the trees, and gives you tips and tricks to identify a business process maturity model (BPMM) that best fits your needs.

OVERALL LEARNING OUTCOME

By the end of this chapter you will be able to:

- Have a working definition for a business process maturity model (BPMM)

- Appreciate that business process maturity affects process characteristics, but also organizational characteristics, and business (process) performance

- Understand the different types of business process maturity

- Understand the considerations that must be made when choosing a BPMM that best fits your organization

- Identify the benefits associated with BPMM.

Globalization, higher competitiveness, more demanding customers, growing IT possibilities, etc.; all these challenges put pressure on organizations to perform better, and thus to obtain mature (or excellent) business processes. Consequently, business process maturity models (BPMMs) have been designed to help organizations gradually assess and improve their business processes. Some well-known examples are CMMI (SEI, 2009) or OMG-BPMM (OMG, 2008), but many others exist. For instance, the previous chapter elaborated on the maturity model of de Bruin and Rosemann (2007).

In fact, there are so many BPMMs around these days that organizations cannot see the wood for the trees. Organizations risk selecting a BPMM that does not fit their needs, or a BPMM that might be of lower quality. Moreover, academics have frequently criticized maturity models for being consultancy speak as those models typically simplify the complex reality. Nevertheless, the essential process improvements are not easy to realize and organizations may need some practical guidance on their journey towards excellence. BPMMs remain important tools to help organizations, but they must be thoroughly examined to allow a critical view on the many BPMMs and to theoretically underpin them. For this purpose, this chapter gives you some tips and tricks to identify a BPMM that best fits your needs.

This chapter is based on the dissertation of Amy Van Looy, in which she gives a comprehensive overview of 69 existing BPMMs (also referred to as: N = 69). By including non-academic BPMMs, her sample is more comprehensive than other BPMM overviews. Further on, different process types are included, namely generic business processes, but also supply chains and collaboration processes to reflect end-to-end value chains. Hence, the sample suggests versatility which should facilitate transferability of the findings to other process types. A detailed overview of the 69 collected BPMMs is available in Van Looy et al. (2012) or at: http://www.amyvanlooy.eu/bpmm-sample-n-69.

First of all, the exact naming of BPMMs can vary. For instance, Harrington (2006) refers to a "process maturity grid," whereas de Bruin and Rosemann (2007) refer to a "business process management (BPM) maturity model" and McCormack and Johnson (2001) refer to a "business process orientation (BPO) maturity model." To better understand these different BPMM names, let's look at clear and accepted definitions for the three umbrella terms to which the models refer (Van Looy et al., 2012):

- a business process (BP)
- business process management (BPM)
- business process orientation (BPO).

First, definitions for a business process (BP) generally refer to a transformation of inputs to outputs. For instance, "a process is a series of interconnected activities that takes input, adds value to it, and produces output. It's how organizations work their day-to-day routines. Your organization's processes define how it operates" (Harrington, 2006: xxii). This transformational view originates from manufacturing and is less clear in service delivery. Hence, other definitions exist which emphasize more a coordination of activities (Gillot, 2008). Despite these different emphases (transformation or coordination), BP definitions implicitly focus on business process *modeling* and *deployment,* which are the first phases of a typical business process lifecycle. Deployment means running processes in real-life and is particularly underlined in Harrington's (2006) definition by the verbs "work" and "operate." Deployment is also central to the simple BP definition of this book: "it is the way things get done around here." However, deployment implicitly requires modeling or predefining business processes in textual or graphical descriptions to determine what the inputs, activities and outputs can be at run-time (Weske, 2010). These implicit assumptions of BP definitions are made explicit by BPM definitions.

As explained earlier in this book, *BPM* involves continuously managing and improving business processes, guided by process owners. Depending on their background, authors underline more the IT benefits or the management aspects. Gillot (2008) and Gulledge Jr. and Sommer (2002) summarize four general components in BPM definitions: (1) *modeling*, (2) *deployment*, (3) *optimization*, or improving business processes based on real metrics and (4) the *management* of business processes, each with a process owner and a cross-functional team. For instance, Weske (2010: 5) defines BPM as "concepts, methods, and techniques to support the [1] design, [4] administration, [2] configuration, enactment, and [3] analysis of business processes." BPM thus differs from BP by optimizing and managing one, more or all business processes. In other words, BPM includes BP, but BP does not necessarily include BPM. A business process can run without optimization or management efforts, albeit not in its most excellent way, but it always needs some (in)formal modeling. When translating these distinct components of BP definitions and BPM definitions to maturity, it seems appropriate to refer to *"BP maturity"* when process modeling and deployment are addressed by maturity models, and to *"BPM maturity"* when all four components are addressed, and this for one, more or all processes.

These BPM-specific components are also present in the BPM definition described in Chapter 1: "A management discipline focused on using business processes as a significant contributor to achieving an organization's objectives through the [3] improvement, ongoing performance management and [4] governance of essential business processes." However, when looking at the BPM House in Chapter 1, performance management and governance also seem to include some aspects that relate to the organization's culture and structure, instead of being limited to characteristics of business processes. The BPM House thus refers to an organization-wide realization of BPM. Indeed, some authors go beyond these four BPM components by explicitly referring to organization management. Particularly, by adopting two additional foci: (5) a process-oriented *culture*, e.g., with rewards linked to the performance of business processes instead of departments and (6) a process-oriented *structure*, e.g., with a horizontal or matrix chart instead of vertical departments. More specifically, McCormack and Johnson (2001: 185) define business process orientation (BPO) as an organization that "emphasizes process, a process oriented way of thinking, customers, and outcomes as opposed to hierarchies." Although the distinction between BPM and BPO is not always explicitly made (e.g., in de Bruin and Rosemann (2007) or in the previous chapters of this book), it allows separately examining the different nuances. Consequently, *"BPO maturity"* differentiates from "BPM maturity" by also covering a process-oriented culture and structure, besides the BPM-specific components.

BPM INSIGHT

The highest maturity levels and capability levels are not required for all organizations and all processes. Instead, an organization must strive towards optimal levels, by taking into account its organizational context.

Managers should decide for themselves which processes are important enough to invest up to the highest maturity levels (i.e., those that are critical to customers). Other processes may, for instance, end up with levels 2 or 3 as optimal level, and need not necessarily be improved towards level 5. That would be a needless over-investment of time, money, resources, etc.

A BPMM should not be blindly followed or misused. Its goal is not to get to level 5, but to help organizations obtain higher business (process) performance!

With the presented division in mind, we now define a BPMM as follows.

KEY POINT

A definition for a business process maturity model (BPMM) is given in Van Looy et al. (2011: 1132–1133):

A model to assess and/or to guide best practice improvements in organizational maturity and process capability, expressed in lifecycle levels, by taking into account an evolutionary roadmap regarding

1. process modeling,
2. process deployment,
3. process optimization,
4. process management,
5. the organizational culture and/or
6. the organizational structure.

It is important to have a common understanding of what we mean by each of the significant words in our BPMM definition. Therefore, each of them is discussed in Table 30.1.

In theory, all six theoretical capability areas must be assessed and improved to fully reach business process maturity. However, in practice, existing BPMMs do not necessarily address all of them. That's why the definition summed them up by using "and/or."

Of course, these findings are not only derived from the BP, BPM, and BPO definitions. These six main business process capability areas (necessary to reach excellence) can be broken down into 17 sub-areas, as illustrated in Figure 30.2. In Van Looy et al. (2012), it was shown that the first three main capability areas are primarily addressed by the traditional business process lifecycle theory (Weske, 2010), whereas the other three are supported by organization management theories regarding organizational change management (Waterman et al., 1980; Burke and Litwin, 1992), strategic management (Kaplan and Norton, 2000) and

Table 30.1a Definitions of terms used in BPMM definition

Assess	A BPMM should explain how to assess (i.e., evaluate or measure) the current degree of maturity (the As-Is lifecycle levels).
Guide	A BPMM should suggest possible improvement activities (as best practices) to improve from the current degree of maturity (the As-Is lifecycle levels) towards the desired degree of maturity (the To-Be lifecycle levels).
Organizational maturity	Business process maturity indicates the extent to which an organization has explicitly and consistently deployed its business processes, by taking into account the six BPMM components, as listed in the definition. It expresses the expected business process performance based on the actual capabilities, in order to predict the actual performance of business processes.
	Maturity is, however, a broader concept than capability. The former focuses on the whole assessment unit and the organizational strategy by taking into account all six components listed in the BPMM definition, whereas the latter relates to the associated parts and their specific purposes by improving an individual component. Consequently, the terms "organizational maturity" and "process capability" can be used to properly stress this difference in scope. Regarding "organizational maturity," an alternative and more specific naming is that of BP, BPM or BPO maturity, as discussed above.
Process capability	This refers to the skills and competences needed to achieve the targeted process results.
	The six components, listed in the BPMM definition, are areas of related skills and competences that are needed for a business process to perform excellently. As such, they are called "business process capability areas," and will be gradually assessed and improved when using a BPMM.
Lifecycle levels	A BPMM can define maturity levels, capability levels, or both.
	Maturity levels indicate an overall growth throughout all capability areas of a BPMM, whereas capability levels indicate a growth in an individual capability area. This illustrates why it is more accurate to refer to "organizational maturity" with regard to BP, BPM or BPO, and to "process capability" (or "process capability area").
	Lifecycle levels constitute a scale (mostly a 5-point scale), with the highest level representing excellence. In other words: the higher the levels, the better business processes can perform.

human resources management (Boswell et al., 2006). On the other hand, the first four main areas represent the characteristics of a specific business process, whereas the final two main areas represent the characteristics of organizations (with characteristics that impact their whole portfolio of business processes).

Figure 30.2 shows that the 17 sub-areas are mostly comparable with those covered by the BPMM of de Bruin and Rosemann (2007), as presented in the previous chapter. The capability areas of de Bruin and Rosemann (2007) rely on studies on critical success factors for BPM and empirical research (Delphi studies and case studies) in order to build a maturity model. On the other hand, the framework of Figure 30.1 is structured by the underlying theories, and validated by a large amount of maturity models (N = 69), instead of a single BPMM.

Table 30.1b Definitions of terms used in BPMM definition—continued

| Evolutionary roadmap | A step-by-step plan, which explains how to reach each consecutive lifecycle level. As such, you can compare a BPMM with a global navigation system or GPS, which explains where you are and which possibilities exist to gradually evolve to a desired level.

More specifically, the roadmap defines the criteria (i.e., goals and best practices) that must be satisfied before reaching each particular level and proposes possible improvement activities to go from the current level to the next, desired level. |
|---|---|
| Process modeling | A business process capability area, comprising methods and IT for the design and analysis of business processes. |
| Process deployment | A business process capability area, comprising methods and IT for the implementation and enactment of business processes, as well as their measurement and control during enactment. |
| Process optimization | A business process capability area, comprising methods and IT for the evaluation and improvement of business processes after enactment. Improvements vary from incremental (e.g., total quality management) to radical (e.g., reengineering, or referred to as innovation in earlier chapters). |
| Process management | A business process capability area, comprising the daily management of business processes, including the required roles and responsibilities with corresponding skills and training. It also involves linking process goals to the organizational strategy and the relationships with customers, suppliers and other stakeholders. |
| Organizational culture | A business process capability area, comprising values that favor business processes (e.g., empowerment, collaboration, or a customer focus), and their translation in attitudes and behaviors. It requires appraisals and rewards that consider process results and top management commitment. |
| Organizational structure | A business process capability area, comprising a shift in the organization chart to visualize horizontal business processes and specific governance bodies (e.g., a program office, assisted by a Center of Excellence) to coordinate the management of all business processes within an organization. |

Table 30.2 illustrates how the framework of Figure 30.1 is structured according to the underlying theories. For instance, the aspects regarding the organizational performance and management theories of Waterman et al. (1980) and Burke and Litwin (1992) affect the theoretical capability areas of Figure 30.1.

After mapping the capability areas of Figure 30.1 to the BPMM sample (N = 69), cluster analysis and discriminant analysis statistically revealed three maturity types:

- BPM maturity, primarily focusing on business process modeling (1), deployment (2), optimization (3) and management (4);

- BPO maturity, combining BPM maturity with a process-oriented culture (5) and structure (6);

- intermediate BPO maturity, limiting BPO maturity to some process-oriented aspects, usually cultural (5).

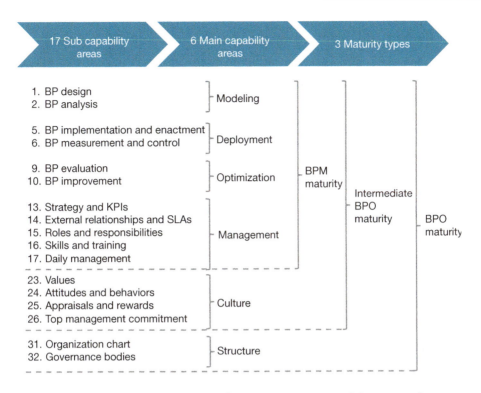

Figure 30.1 The conceptual framework of business process capability areas of Van Looy et al. (2012), based on definitions and theories

Source: Van Looy et al. (2012); © Amy Van Looy.

BP maturity was not present in the sample, given the importance of optimization and management to reach process excellence. Next, the number of business processes to which BPMMs literally refer can be added. This comes down to nine different maturity types being measured by the BPMM sample (N = 69).

KEY POINT

A BPMM can assess and improve no less than nine different maturity types (Van Looy et al., 2012):

- BPM maturity for one, more or all business processes
- Intermediate BPO maturity for one, more or all business processes
- BPO maturity for one, more or all business processes in the organization.

This key point refines the two maturity types of de Bruin and Rosemann (2007), which were limited to the maturity of managing specific processes versus the maturity of managing all processes in the organization.

Table 30.2 An illustrative mapping to organization management theories

Capability areas for organizational performance and change:		Capability areas for business process maturity (i.e., expected performance):	
7-S model (Waterman et al., 1980)	Burke–Litwin model (Burke and Litwin, 1992)	Main areas	Sub-areas
Systems	Systems (policies and procedures) (1)	Modeling	• Business process design • Business process analysis
		Deployment	• Business process implementation, enactment, measurement and control
		Optimization	• Business process evaluation • Business process improvement
Strategy	Mission and strategy	Management	• Strategy and Key Performance Indicators (KPIs)
	External environment		• External relationships and Service Level Agreements (SLAs)
Skills	Task and individual skills		• Roles and responsibilities • Skills, expertise, training
	Management practices		• Daily management
Super-ordinate goals	Organizational culture	Culture	• Values
Staff (soft aspects)	Motivation Work unit climate Individual needs and values		• Attitudes and behaviors
Staff (hard aspects)	Systems (2)		• Appraisals and rewards
Style	Leadership		• Top management commitment
Structure	Structure	Structure	• Organization chart • Bodies

Source: Van Looy et al. (2012); © Amy Van Looy.

What do these maturity types exactly mean for the BPMM names mentioned at the start of this chapter? Well, first, they allow a critical view on the many BPMMs. For instance, the model of McCormack and Johnson (2001) is called a "BPO maturity model," but our study has ranked it as measuring BPM maturity, albeit for all processes. The model of de Bruin and Rosemann (2007) is called "BPM maturity," whereas we have ranked it as BPO maturity for all processes (which is better than the name suggests). On the other hand, Harrington's "process maturity grid" (1991) is also classified as BPO maturity, but further analysis shows that it addresses a single business process, instead of all business processes.

This key point and BPM insight imply that the model of de Bruin and Rosemann (2007) is inherently more complete regarding its capability coverage and/or the number of business

	Capability areas in the BPMM of de Bruin and Rosemann	Capability areas in the conceptual framework of Van Looy *et al.*
Strategic alignment	Process improvement plan Strategy & process capability linkage Process architecture Process output measurement Process customers & stakeholders	1.1 Business process design 2.2 Business process measurement & contr 3.1 Business process evaluation 4.1 Strategy & KPIs 4.2 External relationships & SLAs
Governance	Process management decision making Process roles & responsibilities Process metrics & performance linkage Process management standards Process management controls	2.2 Business process measurement & contr 3.1 Business process evaluation 4.3 Roles & responsibilities 4.5 Daily management 5.3 Appraisals & rewards 6.2 Process-oriented management/governa
Methods Information technology	Process design & modeling Process implementation & execution Process control & measurement Process improvement & innovation Process project & program management Process design & modeling Process implementation & execution Process control & measurement Process improvement & innovation Process project & program management	1.1 Business process design 1.2 Business process analysis 2.1 Business process implementation & ena 2.2 Business process measurement & contr 3.1 Business process evaluation 3.2 Business process improvement 4.5 Daily management 6.2 Process-oriented management/governa
People	Process skills & expertise Process management knowledge Process education & learning Process collaboration & communication Process management leaders	4.4 Skills & training 4.5 Daily management 5.2 Attitudes & behaviors
Culture	Responsiveness to process change Process values & beliefs Process attitudes & behaviors Leadership attention to process Process management social networks	5.1 Values 5.2 Attitudes & behaviors 5.4 Top management commitment 6.1 Process-oriented organization chart

Figure 30.2 Mapping the capability areas of de Bruin and Rosemann (2007) to the capability areas of Van Looy et al. (2012)

Source: de Bruin and Rosemann (2007); Van Looy et al. (2012); © Amy Van Looy.

> ## BPM INSIGHT
>
> **One word of caution: don't be misled by the names given to BPMMs, because they often do not properly reflect their actual coverage of capability areas and the number of business processes addressed. Hence, take a few moments to look carefully at what is really being measured, because that will be the direction given by the model.**

processes addressed than, let's say, the models of McCormack and Johnson (2001) and Harrington's (1991). But, and here comes an important but, we do not assert that this model is necessarily better or worse than the other two models, because that depends on the direction a specific organization wants to take. For instance, it might depend on the degree of top management support, your IT background, prior BPM experience, organization size, degree of market competitiveness, etc.

Let me explain that with some examples. Organizations with local, bottom-up initiatives or with limited BPM experience might wish to start with BPM maturity, limited to the four areas of the traditional business process lifecycle. Additionally, the culture capability area requires a minimum level of management support to promote business processes and granting (financial) rewards to process performance. Finally, structural configurations inherently require top management support. The latter is particularly recommended if you already have some BPM experience or if your ambition is to standardize processes across large departments or divisions.

Moreover, many other BPMMs exist than that of de Bruin and Rosemann (2007). Therefore, the author currently works on a theoretical model for business process maturity. It would be nice if the authors of different BPMMs could collaborate in order to build that theory. Such a maturity theory must be independent of a particular BPMM, and can draw general conclusions regarding the performance outcomes of using BPMMs, as proposed in Figure 30.3.

The proposed maturity theory of Figure 30.3 could, for instance, demonstrate which combinations of capability areas (i.e., maturity types) contribute more to performance than others. Do the additional efforts of BPO maturity significantly increase business (process) performance, compared to the basic efforts of BPM maturity? Or does it depend on other context factors, such as the organization size?

Today, the proposed maturity theory is still in an immature state and we may come back to it in the next edition of this book. But what this book can already offer is more advice on good BPMM selection, that is when you want to start with a BPMM or when you just want to verify if the BPMM that you already use is indeed the right one for your organizational needs. Here are some 14 questions that are worth considering and strategically thinking through to find a BPMM that fits your needs. They were derived by an international Delphi study with 11 BPM academics and 11 BPM practitioners, each from five continents (Van Looy, 2013). The sequence of the questions reflects the average perceived importance, as weighted by the experts participating in the Delphi study.

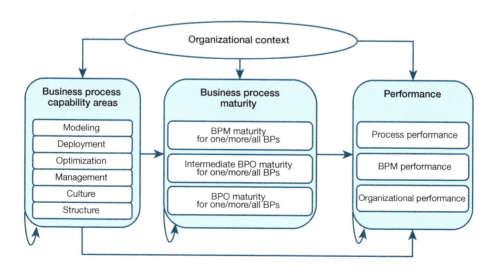

Figure 30.3 A theoretical model for business process maturity

Source: Van Looy et al. (2012); © Amy Van Looy.

1. Which capability areas must be assessed and improved according to your needs?

2. Must the BPMM define capability levels, maturity levels, or both?

3. How much guidance must the BPMM give on your journey towards higher maturity?

4. Must the BPMM be generic (i.e., for business processes in general) or domain-specific (e.g., for business processes in supply chains or collaboration situations)?

5. Which type of data must be collected during an assessment (qualitative or quantitative)?

6. How must information be collected during an assessment (objectively or subjectively)?

7. For which purpose must the BPMM be used (raising awareness, benchmarking or certification)?

8. Must evidence be explicitly given that the BPMM is able to assess maturity and helps to enhance the efficiency and effectiveness of business processes?

9. How many business processes must be assessed and improved?

10. How long must a particular assessment maximally take?

11. Must the assessment questions and corresponding level calculation be publicly available (instead of only known to the assessors)?

12. Must the BPMM explicitly recognize to include people from outside the assessed organization as respondents in the assessment?

13. How many questions must be maximally answered during an assessment?

14. Must the BPMM be free to access and use?

More information regarding these considerations and their trade-offs for BPMM selection can be found in the BPMM Smart-Selector. It concerns an online decision tool, which is freely available at: http://smart-selector.amyvanlooy.eu/. By answering the online questionnaire with these 14 questions, the BPMM Smart-Selector will propose a BPMM out of a large sample (N = 69) that best fits your organizational needs.

KEY POINT

If you want to start with a BPMM or verify whether the BPMM that you already use is right for your organization, then go to the BPMM Smart-Selector and fill out the questionnaire yourself.

Check it out at: http://smart-selector.amyvanlooy.eu/

Finally, the BPMM Smart-Selector offers a feedback form that you can fill out to share your experience of using the tool with the author (for further research).

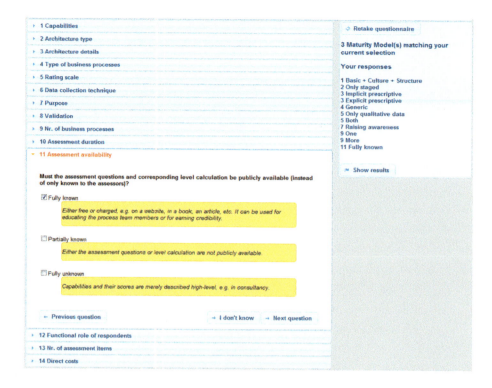

Figure 30.4 The BPMM Smart-Selector

Source: http://smart-selector.amyvanlooy.eu/ (© Amy Van Looy).

SUMMARY

A business process maturity model (BPMM) is:

- A guide for organizations wishing to improve their processes in a structured way.

- An assessment method and an improvement method.

- Possibly more than just process characteristics.

- Possibly more than a single process.

- An umbrella term for different maturity types, based on the capability areas and number of business processes addressed.

- The BPMM Smart-Selector provides an online questionnaire with 14 considerations and trade-offs to be made when selecting a BPMM that best fits your organizational needs.

SELF-TEST

1 How would you define a business process maturity model (BPMM) and explain each of the key words in your definition?

2 Can you describe what makes a maturity model a business process maturity model (BPMM)?

3 Name the different business process maturity types. Which one(s) would you choose for your organization?

4 Explain the different criteria and their trade-offs to be considered when choosing a BPMM that best fits your organizational needs. Which of them are most important to you? Are there any other criteria or trade-offs that apply to your organization, but that are not listed here?

NOTES

CHAPTER 3

1 For a detailed explanation of the role of process owners/stewards and process executives, together with their responsibilities, refer to Chapter 5 and appendix B Process Governance (online), in *Management by Process: A roadmap to sustainable Business Process Management*, by Jeston and Nelis, 2008.

CHAPTER 7

1 A "value network" is defined as "the links between an organization and its strategic and non-strategic partners that form its external value chain" (Chaffey and Smith, 2008: 499).

2 http://www.businessrulesgroup.org/defnbrg.shtml

3 https://www.oasis-open.org/committees/tc_home.php?wg_abbrev=wsbpel

CHAPTER 9

1 In an organization's target operating model there are aspects or components other than those that directly impact business processes and these have not been addressed here and will be mentioned in Chapters 13 and 14. These could include: products and services; market and/or customer segments; distribution channels; geographical operating areas; financial management; resource management; innovation.

CHAPTER 11

1 We understand that the F and E aspects or explanations of the framework may not translate into some other languages. Where this is the case, the framework should simply be referred to by its name, 7FE Framework.

CHAPTER 13

1 PRINCE2™ or Projects IN Controlled Environments 2, is a project management methodology that was developed by a UK government agency and is used extensively within the UK government as the de facto project management standard for public projects. It is widely recognized throughout the world as a robust project management methodology.

2   PMBOK™ stands for the Project Management Body Of Knowledge and is a project management methodology. The latest methodology is the fifth edition (2013) and is described in the book *A Guide to the Project Management Body of Knowledge.*

3   The definition of level 1 here is the first level of dissection of the organization's processes. This means the process levels are numbered from 1 to 5 and not level 0 to 4. Refer to Chapter 14 step 1 for a more detailed explanation.

4   The project director did not understand that technology systems alone do not execute business processes in the finance area. Finance processes, like most business processes, require people to be involved. Unless the people aspects of processes are addressed, then do not be surprised when the new processes either do not work or are suboptimal.

CHAPTER 14

1   http://www.gartner.com/it-glossary/enterprise-architecture-ea/

2   http://searchcio.techtarget.com/definition/enterprise-architecture

3   Process owners will be discussed later in this chapter.

4   A detailed description of each of these roles and its responsibilities is provided in Jeston and Nelis, 2008, ch. 5.

5   http://chrguibert.free.fr/cmmi12/cmmi-acq/text/pa-opd.php

6   An asset is defined as: "a resource with economic value that an individual, corporation or country owns or controls with the expectation that it will provide future benefit." Source: http://www.investopedia.com/terms/a/asset.asp#axzz1zuXkEvqy

7   The framework is available at: http://www.apqc.org/process-classification-framework in either PDF or Microsoft Excel format.

8   Specific industries include: Aerospace and Defence, Automotive, Banking, Broadcasting, Consumer Products, Education, Electric Utilities, Petroleum—Downstream and Upstream, Pharmaceutical and Telecommunications.

9   A *disbenefit* is defined as "an outcome perceived as negative by one or more stakeholders" (OGC, *Managing Successful Programs (MSP™) training manual,* 5th edition).

10   For a detailed analysis of the benefits, advantages and the potential options available refer to Jeston and Nelis, 2008, ch. 8.

11   http://te.thinkexist.com/Stephen R.Covey22, accessed July 22 2008.

CHAPTER 15

1   Small in this context refers to say a BPM activity for a $10m cost center with 120–140 people and 20–25 major processes.

CHAPTER 16

1   http://www.isixsigma.com/dictionary/voice-of-the-customer-voc/ (accessed 16 January 2013).

CHAPTER 17

1   There are many ways of achieving process redesign in a workshop. PostIt Notes, drawing on a whiteboard or piece of paper, etc. The issue is to ensure that the process can be seen and visualized by participants.

CHAPTER 18

1   www.valuebasedmanagement.net/methods_raci.html (accessed July 2005).

CHAPTER 19

1   www.dsdm.org
2   International Organization for Standardization, www.iso.org

CHAPTER 24

1   There are many other project management methodologies as well as these two.
2   www.spinroot.com/spin/Doc/course/Standish_survey.htm (accessed October 2012).
3   This typically occurs during the Launch pad phase.
4   This typically occurs during the Launch pad phase.
5   This typically occurs during the Launch pad phase and needs to be revisited during the Innovate phase.
6   This typically occurs during the Launch pad phase and needs to be revisited during the Innovate phase.
7   This typically occurs during the Launch pad phase and needs to be revisited during the Innovate and Develop phases.

CHAPTER 25

1   It is important to note that employees also include partners, such as key suppliers, distributors, contractors or other stakeholders. In the current network economy it is also essential that we adopt a broader view than just the traditional permanent employees of an organization.

2   Professor Mike West (Aston Business School, UK) referenced in Henderson and Thompson, *Values at Work: The Invisible Threads Between People, Performance and Profit*, 2004, Harper Collins.

3   Tenured Professor in Business at Harvard Business School, where she holds the Ernest L. Arbuckle Professorship.

4   People have a preferred learning style or way of taking information in. The three main forms of communications and learning are: visual, auditory and kinesthetic. While we use all three, we often have a preference. Visual communicators tend to see things in their minds and use images. Use words like: "see," "I see that." Auditory communicators tend to listen and talk. They prefer lectures and talks. Use words like: "hear," "it sounds right." Kinesthetic communicators tend to use movement and action. They prefer to learn by writing, acting out, pacing and gesture. Use words like: "touch," "I feel that is the case."

5   "Somehow this little chemical (oxytocin) is not only telling us what's good for society, be cooperative, trust other people, allowing us to live in big cities, it also tells you what's good for you as an individual" (Zak, 2005).

6   *Background:* http://www.mt-online.com/component/content/article/77-february2007/228-building-strength-based-organizations.html

7   http://en.wikipedia.org/wiki/Appreciative_inquiry

CHAPTER 26

1   Situational leadership as outlined in Hersey, 1997.

2   Keen, 1997; © Harvard Business School Publishing, reprinted here with permission.

CHAPTER 28

1   ARIS is a software tool that among other functionality allows the creating and maintenance of a process asset. Refer to www.softwareag.com

GLOSSARY

7FE Framework   A framework that needs to be adjusted and adopted by experienced BPM practitioners to suit the BPM activity circumstances. It is not a stringent "paint by number" methodology, as this approach will not address the specific needs and circumstances of individual BPM activities. Where the four "Fs" relate to the grouping of our ten phases (Foundation, Findings and Solutions, Fulfillment and Future) and the three "Es" relates to the three Essentials (Leadership, BPM Project Management and People Change Management).

Agile   An iterative way of software development. The budget and times are specified upfront and the required functionality is delivered in multiple releases (delivered through sprints), where the high-value release is developed first.

Benchmarking   The process of comparing one's business processes and performance metrics to industry bests or best practices from other industries.[1]

Bottom-up   Typically there is one or more passionate person(s) within the organization who believes that BPM can make a significant difference to the organization. They "sell" the idea to a manager who is able to provide all the resources for a pilot project to prove the concept and the organization's ability to implement it. The hope is then that success of BPM will spread throughout an organization.

BPaaS   Combines Business Process Outsourcing (BPO) and Software as a Service (SaaS). This provides an alternate model where existing offerings can be leveraged and various payment types can be offered, including pay as you go.

BPM activity width   Degree to which a BPM activity will change the processes and an organization. A small width relates to small improvements and a large width relates to disrupting the value chain of the organization.

BPM Enablement   The provision of the key architectures and detailed elements that must be provided to support and enable business capabilities to enhance the successful delivery of all components of the BPM strategy.

BPM Foundations   An agreed set of driving and guiding business foundation principles to manage business processes within an organization.

BPM House   A metaphor of a house has been used in this book to describe BPM.

Business Process Execution Language or BPEL More formally defined as WS-BPEL, it creates executable processes using the underlying building block of a Web Service (WS).

Business Process Management A management discipline focused on using business processes as a significant contributor to achieving an organization's objectives through the improvement, ongoing performance management and governance of essential business processes.

Business Process Management System BPM system comprises three broad areas and nine components as shown in Figure 7.1.

Business Rules A business rule is a statement that "defines or constrains some aspect of the business";[2] a business rule is intended to assert business structure or to control or influence the business's behavior.

Dis-benefit "An outcome perceived as negative by one or more stakeholder," *Managing Successful Programs (MSP(tm)) training manual,* 5th edition, OGC.

Driver A business reason or motivator that causes the organization to initiate action to achieve a business objective. For example an organization wants to expand its international markets, increase its revenue and achieve better economies of scale.

Embedding Embedding BPM in the organization is about being in a position where process improvement and process execution (business-as-usual) provide the most sustainable value to an organization.

End-to-end Considering a process from beginning (e.g., a customer requesting a service) to the end (e.g., customer receiving a service and paying for it).

Enterprise Architecture Gartner have defined enterprise architecture as: "the process of translating business vision and strategy into effective enterprise change by creating, communicating and improving the key requirements, principles and models that describe the enterprise's future state and enable its evolution."[3]

Others have suggested: "Enterprise architecture (EA) is a conceptual blueprint that defines the structure and operation of an organization. The intent of enterprise architecture is to determine how an organization can most effectively achieve its current and future objectives."[4]

Essential Not every process in an organization contributes towards the achievement of the organization's strategic objectives. Essential processes are the ones that do.

Governance The roles that individuals or committees undertake to manage accountability for decisions made (enabling success); manage business risk; and ensuring performance management expectations are achieved.

Governance of processes BPM is about managing your end-to-end business processes both now and into the future to ensure they are always relevant to the business. An essential component of governance is to have the ability to measure correctly. If you cannot measure something, you cannot continually improve and manage it. Process governance is also essential to ensure that compliance and regulations are adhered to.

Iceberg Syndrome An organization's *perception* of a BPM program often only relates to what is above the water line at a project level, but the *reality* is that most of the implementation effort is below the water—"out of sight." BPM is not just about projects; it is about the vital contribution that processes make in achieving the objectives of the organization, provided that a process focus permeates every manager and person in the organization.

Improvement   Is about making the business processes more efficient and effective or indeed turning an organization or industry value chain upside down or inside out. An example of this is a business transformation approach to BPM.

Key Performance Indicator (KPI)   A metric used to help manage a process, service or activity. Many metrics may be measured, but only the most important of these are defined as KPIs, and are used to actively manage and report on the process, service or activity (Kureemun and Fantina, 2011: 124).

Leadership   "The yardstick to measure good leadership is the culture of enduring excellence which a leader leaves behind after he is gone from the scene" (Chibber, undated).

Management of Process   There are two aspects to operational management of business processes: (1) management of business processes as an integral part of "management"; (2) management of business process improvement.

Maturity (BPM Maturity)   A model to assess and/or to guide best practice improvements in organizational maturity and process capability, expressed in lifecycle levels, by taking into account an evolutionary roadmap regarding: (1) process modeling, (2) process deployment, (3) process optimization, (4) process management, (5) the organizational culture, and/or (6) the organizational structure.

Metrics   "A standard measure to assess your performance in a particular area" (Kureemun and Fantina, 2011: 124).

Organizational Culture   Collective behavior of each person in an organization creates the organization's culture.

Outsourcing   Is the contracting out of a business process, which an organization may have previously performed internally or has a new need for, to an independent organization from which the process is purchased back as a service.

Performance Management   Refers to process and people performance measurement and management. It is about organizing all the essential components and subcomponents for your processes. By this we mean arranging the people, their skills, motivation, performance measures, rewards, the processes themselves and the structure and systems necessary to support a process.

PMBOK   *A Guide to the Project Management Body of Knowledge* (PMBOK Guide) is a book which presents a set of standard terminology and guidelines for project management.[5]

PRINCE2   An acronym for **PR**ojects **IN** **C**ontrolled **E**nvironments, version 2, is a project management methodology. It was developed by a UK government agency and is used extensively within the UK government as the de facto project management standard for its public projects. The methodology encompasses the management, control and organization of a project.[6]

Process   There are as many definitions of process as there are processes. However perhaps taking a simple view is best, "it is the way things get done around here."

Process Asset   A central repository of all the information the business needs to capture and use regarding its business processes. Business processes are documented using process models which are a visual representation of the steps and activities in a business process as well as the high-level links between processes.

Process gap analysis   Provides a comparison between the new and the old processes for the business, IT department and developers of the training material.

Process Model   Visual representation of the process and its steps.

Process Worth Matrix   This matrix provides a useful way of determining what business processes to invest in.

Quick win   An improvement early on in the BPM initiative, especially aimed at achieving belief and momentum.

Red Wine Test   Is a neurolinguistic technique enabling people to describe the future.

Root-cause analysis   A technique for determining the deeper and ultimate reason for the non-performance or problem with a business process.

Subject Matter Experts   People who provide insight and are experts for a process or activity.

Target Operating Model   A high level view of the future state of an organization's business-as-usual operating model. It represents the optimal method by which an organization's processes operate across the TOM components in order to align with and assist in the delivery of an organization's strategy.

Top-down   The approach is often characterized by an organization with senior executives who understand the benefits that a process focus will bring to the organization (and therefore BPM maturity is much higher to start with) and who drive it throughout the organization.

Trigger   An event or occurrence that causes an organization to initiate action to overcome or solve an individual issue or problem that is usually of an immediate nature (e.g., fraud) or imposed by an external force (e.g., legislative changes resulting in compliance changes).

Touch point   A business term for any encounter where customers and business engage to exchange information, provide service, or handle transactions.[7]

Value Chain   A chain of activities that an organization, operating within a specific industry, performs to deliver value to its customers for its products or services. This term was popularized by Michael Porter in 1985 in his book, *Competitive Advantage: Creating and Sustaining Superior Performance*.

Voice of Customer   A process used to capture the stated and unstated requirements/feedback from the customer (internal or external) to provide the customers with the best in class service/product quality. This process is all about being proactive and constantly innovative to capture the changing requirements of the customers.[8]

Waterfall   The traditional way of development. The scope is specified upfront and the development time and budget is subsequently specified. Typically, there is one main release of the developed software; however, there could be several releases.

Web Services   The W3C (the body that manages the Web Services specification) defines a "Web service" as "a software system designed to support interoperable machine-to-machine interaction over a network."

REFERENCES AND BIBLIOGRAPHY

Ahern, D. M., Clouse, A. and Turner, R. (2004). *CMMI Distilled: A Practical Introduction to Integrated Process Improvement*, 2nd edn. Addison-Wesley.

Arcball http://arcball.com/2010/05/forms-of-innovation/ (accessed 28 August 2012).

Blatter, P. (2005). Learning from manufacturers and industrialization. Presented at the IQPC BPM Conference, Sydney, April.

Bloem, J. and van Doorn, M. (2004). *Realisten aan het roer, naar een prestatiegerichte Governance van IT*. Sogeti Nederland.

Blount, F. (1999). Changing places: Blount and Joss. *Human Resources Monthly*, December.

Bossidy, L., Charan, R. and Burck, C. (2002). *Execution: The Discipline of Getting Things Done*. Crown Publishing.

Boswell, W. R., Bingham, J. B. and Colvin, A. J. (2006). Aligning employees through "line of sight." *Business Horizons*, 49, 499–509.

BPM Focus (2006). www.bpmfocus.com

Burke, W. W. and Litwin, G. H. (1992). A causal model of organizational performance and change. *Journal of Management*, 18(3), 523–545.

Burlton, R. T. (2001). *Business Process Management*. Sams Publishing.

Business Process Management Common Body of Knowledge—Business Rules Group . Developed and published by the Association of Business Process Management Professionals, Version 2.0, Second Release.

Cavanagh, J. (1999). Australia's most admired. *Business Review Weekly*, 15 October.

Chaffey, D. and Smith, P. R. (2008) *eMarketing eXcellence*, 3rd edn. Butterworth-Heinemann.

Chibber, M. L. (undated). *Leadership*. Sri Sathya Sai Books and Publications Trust.

Collins, J. (2001). *Good to Great*. Random House.

Cope, M. (2003). *The Seven Cs of Consulting: The Definitive Guide to the Consulting Process*. FT Prentice-Hall.

Covey, S. (1989). *The Seven Habits of Highly Effective People*. Simon & Schuster.

Covey, S. (2004). *The Seven Habits of Highly Effective People*, 15th anniversary edn. Simon & Schuster.

Curtis, B., Alden, J. and Weber, C. V. (2004). *The Use of Process Maturity Models in Business Process Management*. White Paper. Borland Software Corporation.

Davenport, Th. H. (2005). The coming commoditization of processes. *Harvard Business Review*, June, 83(6), 100–108.

Davenport, Th. H. and Harris, J. G. (2007). *Competing on Analytics: The New Science of Winning*, Harvard Business Press.

Davenport, Th. H. and Short, J. E. (1990). The industrial engineering information technology and business process redesign. *Sloan Management Review*, Summer.

Davis, R. (2001). *Business Process Modelling with ARIS, A Practical Guide.* Springer.

de Bruin, T. and Rosemann, M. (2007). Using the Delphi technique to identify BPM capability areas. Paper presented at the 18th Australasian Conference on IS, Toowoomba.

DeToro, I. and McCabe, T. (1997). How to stay flexible and elude fads. *Quality Progress,* 30(3), 55–60.

Drucker, P. (1991). The new productivity challenge. *Harvard Business Review,* November–December.

Drucker, P. F. (1999). *Management Challenges for the 21st Century.* HarperCollins.

Fisher, D. M. (2004). *The Business Process Maturity Model. A Practical Approach for Identifying Opportunities for Optimization.* Available online at: http://www. bptrends.com/resources_publications.cfm (accessed 17 March 2005).

Forrester Research (2003). Linking IT to Business Performance: It is Implementation that Matters. George Lawrie, launch of Regatta® book on implementation by Sogeti Nederland, Amstelveen, The Netherlands, 21 May.

Forrester Research (2011). *Dynamic Case Management: Definitely Not Your Dad's Old-School Workflow/Imaging System.* Report by le Clair, C. and Miers, D., 28 September.

Gartner (2005). *Delivering IT's Contribution: The 2005 CIO Agenda.* EXPPremier Report, January.

Gerstner, L. V. Jr. (2002). *Who Says Elephants Can't Dance?* Harper Business.

Gillot, J.-N. (2008). *The Complete Guide to Business Process Management.* Booksurge Publishing.

Glenn, Marie. (2008). *Organizational agility: how business can survive and thrive in turbulent times.* Economist Intelligence Unit, March.

Goldratt, Eliyahu M. (1999). *Theory of Constraints,* North River Pr.

Goldsmith, J. (1995). *Fortune,* 12 April.

Gray, B. (1989). *Collaborating: Finding Common Ground for Multiparty Problems.* Jossey-Bass Publishers.

Gulledge, Jr. T. R. and Sommer, R. A. (2002). Business process management: public sector implications. *Business Process Management Journal,* 8(4), 364–376.

Hakes, C. (1996). *The Corporate Self-Assessment Handbook,* 3rd edn. Chapman and Hall.

Hamel, G., with Breen, Bill (2008). *The Future of Management.* Harvard Business School Press.

Hamel, G. and Prahalad, C. K. (1994). *Competing for the Future.* Harvard Business School Press.

Hammer, M. (1993). *Fortune,* 4 October.

Hammer, M. (1994). *Fortune,* 22 August.

Hammer, M. (1995). *Fortune,* 12 April.

Hammer, M. and Champy, J. (1990). Reengineering work: don't automate, obliterate. *Harvard Business Review,* July.

Hammer, M. and Champy, J. (1993). *Reegineering the Corporation: A Manifesto for Business Revolution.* Harper Collins.

Harmon, P. (2003). *Business Process Change.* Morgan Kaufmann.

Harmon, P. (2004). *Evaluating an Organisation's Business Process Maturity.* Available online at: http://www.bptrends.com/resources_publications.cfm (accessed 17 March 2005).

Harmon, P. (2005a). Service orientated architectures and BPM. *Business Process Trends,* 22 February.

Harmon, P. (2005b). BPM governance. *Business Process Trends,* 8 February.

Harper, P. (2002). *Preventing Strategic Gridlock: Leading Over, Under and Around Organizational Jams to Achieve High Performance Results.* CAMEO Publications.

Harrington, H. J. (2006). *Process Management Excellence.* Paton Press.

Hawley, J. (1993). *Reawakening the Spirit in Work.* Berrett-Koehler.

Henderson, M. and Thompson, D. (2004). *Values at Work: The Invisible Threads Between People, Performance and Profit.* Harper Collins.

Hersey, P. (1997). *The Situational Leader.* Center for Leadership Studies.

Hindo, Brian (2007). At 3M, a struggle between efficiency and creativity. *Business Week,* 6 June.

Hriegel, R. and Brandt, D. (1996). *Sacred Cows Make the Best Burgers*. Harper Business.

Holloway, Mandy (2011). *Inspiring Courageous Leaders*. Messenger Group.

Indulska, Marta, Recker, Jan C., Rosemann, Michael and Green, Peter (2009). Business process modeling: current issues and future challenges. In *The 21st International Conference on Advanced Information Systems*, Amsterdam, The Netherlands, 8–12 June.

Jarrar, Y. and Neely, A. (n.d.) Six Sigma—friend or foe? Centre for Business Performance, Cranfield School of Management. Available online at: http://www.som.cranfield.ac.uk/som/dinamic-content/research/cbp/CBPupdate1-SixSigmaFriendorFoe.pdf (retrieved 10 February 2012).

Jeston, J. (2009). *Beyond Business Process Improvement, on to Business Transformation—A Manager's Guide*. Meghan-Kiffer Press.

Jeston, J. and Nelis, J. (2006–2007). Various articles in BP Trends (www. bptrends.com).

Jeston, J. and Nelis, J. (2006–2007). Various articles (www.management byprocess.com).

Jeston, J. and Nelis, J. (2008). *Management by Process: A Roadmap to Sustainable Business Process Management*. Routledge.

Kanter, Rosabeth Moss (2009). *SuperCorp: How Vanguard Companies Create Innovation, Profits, Growth, and Social Good*, Crown Business.

Kaplan, R. and Norton, D. (1996). *The Balanced Score Card, Translating Strategy into Action*. Harvard Business School Press.

Kaplan, R. and Norton, D. (2000). *The Strategy-Focused Organization: How Balanced Scorecard Companies Thrive in the New Business Environment*. Harvard Business School Press.

Kaplan, R. and Norton, D. (2004). *Strategy Maps: Converting Intangible Assets into Tangible Outcomes*. Harvard Business School Press.

Kaplan, R. and Norton, D. (2008). *Harvard Business Review*, January.

Keen, P. (1997). *The Process Edge*. Harvard Business School Press.

Kegan, R. and Leahy, L. (2009). *Immunity to Change, How to Overcome It and Unlock the Potential in Yourself and Your Organization*. Harvard Business School Press.

Kim, Chan and Mauborgne, Renée (2005). Blue ocean strategy. *Harvard Business Review*, October.

Koop, R., Rooimans, R. and de Theye, M. (2003). *Regatta, ICT implementaties als uitdaging voor een vier-met-stuurman*. ten Hagen Stam.

Kotter, J. P. (1995). Leading change: why transformation efforts fail. *Harvard Business Review*, 73(2), 59–67.

Kotter, John, (2012). *Leading Change*. Harvard Business School Press.

Kureemun, Baboo and Fantina, Robert (2011). *Your Customers' Perception of Quality: What It Means to Your Bottom Line and How to Control It*. Productivity Press.

Lewin, K. (undated). Frontiers in group dynamics. *Human Relations Journal*, 1.

Lewin, K. (1936). *Principles of Topological Psychology*. McGraw-Hill.

Lewis, L. (1993). Tandy Users Group Speech 1993 Convention, Orlando, Florida.

Luftman, J. N. (2003). Assessing strategic alignment maturity. In *Competing in the Information Age: Align in the Sand* (J. N. Luftman, ed.), 2nd edn. Oxford University Press.

McCormack, K. P. (1999). The development of a measure of business process orientation. Presented at the European Institute for Advance Studies in Management: Workshop on Organizational Design. Brussels, Belgium, March.

McCormack, K. and Johnson, W. C. (2001). *Business Process Orientation: Gaining the e-Business Competitive Advantage*. St. Lucie Press.

McKinsey (2002). Helping employees embrace change. LaClair, J. and Rao, R., *McKinsey Quarterly*, 4: 4.

Magretta, Joan (2011) Strategy essentials you ignore at your peril. *Harvard Business Review, HBR Blog Network,* December 22. http://blogs.hbr.org/cs/2011/12/strategy_essentials_you_ignore.html

Masaaki Imai (1986). *Kaizen: The Key to Japan's Competitive Success*. McGraw-Hill/Irwin.

Masaaki Imai (1998). *Kaizen*. McGraw-Hill Professional Book Group.

Maull, R. S., Tranfield, D. R. and Maull, W. (2003). Factors characterising the maturity of BPR programmes. *International Journal of Operations & Production Management*, 23(6), 596–624.

Miers, D. (2005). BPM: driving business performance. *BP Trends*, 5(1).

Murray, Alan, (2010). *The Wall Street Journal Essential Guide to Management*. Harper Business.

Mutafelija, B. and Stromberg, H. (2003). *Systematic Process Improvement using ISO 9001:2000 and CMMI*. Artech House.

Neely, A., Adams, C. and Kennerly, M. (2002). *Performance Prism: The Score Card for Measuring and Managing Business Services*. FT Prentice Hall.

Nelis, J. and Jeston, J. (2006–2007). Various articles (www.management byprocess.com).

Nelis, J. and Oosterhout, M. (2003). Rendement uit processen. *Informatie*, May (available online at www.informatie.nl).

Nelson, M. (2003). *Enterprise Architecture Modernization Using the Adaptive Enterprise Framework*. Mercator Group.

Newsletter for Organizational Psychologists, 1995.

Nixon, Bruce (2004). Creating a cultural revolution in your workplace to meet the challenges of the 21st century. *Training Journal*, October.

Nohria, N., Joyce, W. and Roberson, B. (2003). What really works. *Harvard Business Review*, July.

OGC *Managing Successful Programs (MSP(tm)) training manual*, 5th edition. OGC.

OMG (2008). Business process maturity model (BPMM)—Version 1.0. Retrieved 2 December, 2009, from: http://www.omg.org/

Paulk, M. C., Curtis, B., Chrissis, M. B. and Weber, C. V. (1993). *The Capability Maturity Model for Software, Version 1.1* (No. CMU/SEI-93-TR-24). Software Engineering Institute.

PMBOK (2013). *A Guide to the Project Management Body of Knowledge,* 5th edn. Project Management Institute.

Pol, M., Teunissen, R. and van Veenendaal, E. (2002). *Software Testing, A Guide to the TMap*®. Pearson Education.

Porter, M. (1980). *Competitive Strategy: Techniques for Analyzing Industries and Competitors*. Free Press.

Porter, M. (1985). *Competitive A1dvantage: Creating and Sustaining Superior Performance*. Free Press.

Porter, M. (1996). What is strategy? *Harvard Business Review*, 1 November.

Pritchard, J.-P. and Armistead, C. (1999). Business process management—lessons from European business. *Business Process Management Journal*, 5(1), 10–32.

Prosci (2011). Best practices in change management. Longitudinal benchmarking report. Prosci.

Reijers, H. A. and Peeters, R. (2010). Process owners in the wild: findings from a multi-method descriptive study. In Mutschler, B., Recker, J. and Wieringa, R. (eds) *Proceedings of the 1st International Workshop on Empirical Research in Process-Oriented Information Systems (ER-POIS 2010)*, CEUR Workshop Proceedings 603, 1–12. CEUR, Aachen.

Rogers, E. (1962). *Diffusion of Innovation*. Glencoe Free Press.

Rosemann, M. (2005; unpublished). *22 Potential Pitfalls of Process Management*.

Rosemann, M. and de Bruin, T. (2004). Application of a holistic model for determining BPM maturity. In *Proceedings of the AIM Pre-ICIS Workshop on Process Management and Information Systems (Actes du 3e colloque Pre-ICIS de l'AIM), Washington, DC, 12 December 2004* (J. Akoka, I. Comyn-Wattiau and M. Favier, eds). AIM.

Rosemann, M. and de Bruin, T. (2005). Towards a business process management maturity model. *Proceedings of the 13th European Conference on Information Systems (ECIS 2005), Regensburg, 26–28 May 2005*. ECIS.

Ross, Jeanne W., Weill, Peter and Robertson, David (2006). *Enterprise Architecture As Strategy: Creating a Foundation for Business*. Harvard Business School Press.

Rummler, G. A. (2004). *Serious Performance Consulting*. International Society for Performance Improvement and ASTD.

Rummler, G. A. and Brache, A. P. (1995). *Improving Performance*. Jossey-Bass.

Scheer, A.-G., Abolhassan, F., Jost, W. and Kirchmer, M. (2003). *Business Process Change Management*. Springer.

SEI (2009). CMMI for services, Version 1.2. Retrieved February 11, 2010, from: http://www.sei.cmu.edu/

Smith, A. (1909–1914). *Wealth of Nations*. The Harvard Classics.

Smith, H. and Fingar, P. (2002). *Business Process Management—The Third Wave*. Meghan-Kiffer Press.

Smith, H. and Fingar, P. (2004). *Process Management Maturity Models*. Available online at: http://www.bptrends.com/resources_publications.cfm (accessed 23 July 2005).

Spanyi, A. (2004). *Business Process Management is a Team Sport: Play it to Win!* Meghan Kiffer Press.

Stace, D. and Dunphy, D. (1996). *Beyond the Boundaries*. McGraw-Hill.

The Standish Group, Chaos report—data for 2004, 2006 and 2009.

Takeuchi, H., Osono, E. and Shimizu, N. (2008). The contradictions that drive Toyota's success. *Harvard Business Review*, June, 104.

Taylor, F. W. (1998). *The Principles of Scientific Management*. Dover Publications (reprint of 1911 original).

Time Magazine (2005). The science of happiness (cover story and special issue) 17 January, http://www.authentichappiness.sas.upenn.edu/images/TimeMagazine/Time-Happiness.pdf

Treacy, M. and Wiersma, F. (1997). *The Discipline of Market Leaders*. Perseus Books.

Van de Berg, H. and Franken, H. (2003). *Handbook Business Process Engineering*. BizzDesign B.V.

van den Berg, M. and van Steenbergen, M. (2002). *DYA(c): Speed and Alignment of Business and ICT Architecture*. Sogeti Nederland.

Van der Marck, P. (2005). Scoren met uw Waardecreatie (Scoring with your value proposition), at: www.managementsite.nl/content/articles/298/298.asp.

Van Looy, A., De Backer, M., Poels, G. and Snoeck, M. (2013). Choosing the right business process maturity model. *Information & Management*, 50(7), 466–488.

Van Looy, A., De Backer, M. and Poels, G. (2011). Defining business process maturity. A journey towards excellence. *Total Quality Management and Business Excellence*, 22(11), 1119–1137.

Van Looy, A., De Backer, M. and Poels, G. (2012). A conceptual framework and classification of capability areas for business process maturity. *Enterprise Information Systems*.

Vo Oech, R. (1990). *A Whack in the Side of the Head*. Thorsons.

Wagter, R., van den Berg, M., Luijpers, J. and van Steenbergen, M. (2002). *DYA(c): Dynamic Enterprise Architecture: How to Make it Work*. Sogeti Nederland.

Walton, M. (1986). *The Deming Management Methods*. Berkley Publishing Group.

Ward, J. and Peppard, J. (2002). *Strategic Planning for Information Systems*. John Wiley.

Waterman, J. R., Peters, T. J. and Phillips, J. R. (1980). Structure is not organization. *Business Horizons*, 23(3), 14–26.

Weisbord, M. (1992). *Discovering Common Ground: How Future Search Conferences Bring People Together to Achieve Breakthrough Innovation. Empowerment, Shared Vision, and Collaborative Action*. Berrett-Koehler.

Wertheim, E., Love, A., Peck, C. and Littlefield, L. (1998). *Skills for Resolving Conflict*. Eruditions Publishing.

Weske, M. (2010). *Business Process Management: Concepts, Languages and Architectures*. Springer.

Wheatley, M. J. (1994). *Leadership and the New Science*. Berrett-Koehler.

Whitney, D. and Trosten-Bloom, A. (2003). *The Power of Appreciative Inquiry*. Berrett-Koehler.

Zachman, J. A. (1987). A framework for information system architecture. *IBM Systems Journal*, 26(3).

Zak, Paul. J. (2005). Interview, in Horstman, M. Catalyst: Trust, ABC TV Science, ABC Online: http://www.abc.net.au/catalyst/stories/s 1481749.htm

Zak, Paul. J. (2008). The neurobiology of trust. *Scientific American*, June.

WEBSITES

BP Trends: www.bptrends.com

BPM Focus: www.bpmfocus.com

Dynamic Systems Development Method: www.dsdm.org

International Organization for Standardization: www.iso.org

Management by Process: www.managementbyprocess.com

INDEX